White Walls, Designer Dresses

The MIT Press
Cambridge, Massachusetts
London, England

Mark Wigley

White Walls, Designer Dresses

The Fashioning of Modern Architecture

This book was set in Sabon and Gill Sans by Graphic Composition, Inc. and was printed and bound in the United
States of America.

Library of Congress Cataloging-in-Publication Data

Wigley, Mark.
    White walls, designer dresses : the fashioning of mod-
ern architecture / Mark Wigley.
        p. cm.
    Includes bibliographical references and index.
    ISBN 0-262-23185-9 (hc : alk. paper)
    1. White in architecture. 2. Architecture, Modern—
20th century.
I. Title.
NA3485.W54   1995
729—dc20   95-33938
                                     CIP

For David

TAKE

Contents

Acknowledgments

x

I am publishing this text in the naive hope that it will relieve me of a fixation. The project gained momentum in the summer of 1989 at Sullivan and Wright's elegant Charnley House. As a research fellow in residence at the Chicago Institute for Architecture and Urbanism, I was fortunate enough to occupy an upstairs room that opens onto the wooden balcony jutting out over the entrance. Behind the small windows that symmetrically puncture the building's smooth masonry form, it was surprisingly cool. Each day a refreshing breeze from the lake made its way down the street and through the doorway. Thinking was easy. Some of the preliminary findings from those pleasant but intense days were published a year later in the *Journal of Philosophy and the Visual Arts*. By then, the fixation had locked on. I took any chance to study the white wall. The argument about clothing that was made by the original essay, with which this book begins, continued to grow and elaborate itself in a series of takes on the same question. Ten takes and I have called it a day, still feeling that so much has been left unsaid.

The book is indebted to the staff of the various institutions in which I carried out the research, particularly the Chicago Institute for Architecture and Urbanism, the Getty Center for the Study of the History of Art and the Humanities Special Collections in Los Angeles, the Courtauld Institute Library in London, The Netherlands Architecture Institute in Rotterdam, the UCLA Research Library Special Collections Department, the National Art Library at the Victoria and Albert Museum in London, the Museum of Modern Art Library, the RIBA Library in London, the Avery Library Classics Collection at Columbia University, and the Busch-Reisinger Museum at Harvard University. I would like to thank Evelyne Tréhin of the Fondation Le Corbusier and the research staff of the Öffentliche Bibliothek der Universität in Basel for providing some key documents. As always, Frances Chen and her staff at the architecture library at Princeton were especially helpful throughout. Different phases of the study were supported by a research fellowship at the Chicago Institute for Architcture and Urbanism, a Getty Center for the Study of the History of Art and the Humanities research support grant, and two grants from the Princeton University Committee on Research in the Humanities and Social Sciences. I am very grateful for that support. I would also like to thank Sarah Ogger and Debarati Sunyal for their assistance. Earlier versions of parts of the book were published in the *Journal of Philosophy and the Visual Arts* no. 2, 1990; *Assemblage* 22, 1993; and the collection *Architecture: In Fashion,* 1994. My thanks to the respective editors. At The MIT Press, I am grateful to Roger Conover for his ongoing encouragement, Melissa Vaughn for her editing, and Jeannet Leendertse for the design. My colleagues and students at Princeton have, as always, been a delight.

Above all, I am indebted to Beatriz Colomina for her tolerance of the fixation and her advice, without which this project would have remained but a pleasant summer memory.

The book is dedicated to my brother David, long lost but ever present.

Introduction

Why white? Why do we surround ourselves with white walls? What is it about their smooth surface that is so captivating? Where did we get them from? When?

The identity of modern architecture seems inseparable from the whiteness of its surfaces. The very idea that there is such a thing as "modern architecture," a set of principles or practices that unite an otherwise heterogeneous group of architects and buildings, seems to turn on the white walls they share. Yet these walls are rarely discussed. On the contrary, the fact that they are everywhere seems to render them strangely invisible. At the very moment that modern architecture is perceived as such, the whiteness that made such a perception possible becomes inconspicuous. The white wall is taken for granted. At most, generations of commentators have referred to it in passing as "neutral," "pure," "silent," "plain," "blank," "ground," "essential," "stark," and so on—a generic rhetoric that has circulated uncritically through the discourse until these qualities have been tacitly associated with the basic agenda of modern architecture without being explored, let alone challenged. But clearly the white wall is far from neutral or silent. For the modern architect, it speaks volumes. Indeed, nothing is louder. The white wall is precisely not blank. Its apparent passivity is but the curious effect of a whole set of coordinated actions by the discourse, a concerted campaign that began as soon as the majority of architects started to reach for cans of white paint. In a strange twist, the white wall was carefully silenced in the very moment of its success.

The remarkable pathology underlying this twist only becomes evident when the elaborate negotiations that made the white wall successful in the first place are carefully tracked. These negotiations started toward the end of the nineteenth century and took around forty years to reach some kind of accord between all the different trajectories that constituted the emerging avant-garde. It was not until 1927 that the protagonists were able to collaborate on a unified image of modern architecture on the side of a hill overlooking Stuttgart. In the infamous Weissenhofsiedlung, which received over half a million visitors and unprecedented coverage in the professional and popular press, sixteen of the most accomplished architects presented a unified front by contributing to a small estate of exhibition houses. The only restriction was that they use flat roofs and white exterior walls. Photographs of the idyllic collection seemed to capture the look of an immanent future, a coherent environment defined by white walls. The idea that modern architecture is white was successfully disseminated to an international audience. The identity of that architecture had finally been located in its white surfaces, surfaces that assumed an unparalleled force, so much so that they continue to define modern architecture long after architects started to remove the layer of paint in favor of the look of exposed concrete or metal. While the number of white surfaces may have been dramatically reduced, their definitive role remains. If anything, it becomes more decisive. Each such surface is ever more intensely charged. So intensely, it would seem, that the discourse cannot face them.

Even then, this seemingly innocent image of white architecture required the highly selective eye of contemporary critics, the polemical simplifications of black and white photography, and a sustained labor by an emerging historiography to ignore the diversity of colored surfaces presented at Weissenhof and by most "modern" buildings. Modern architecture was never simply white. The image of white walls is a very particular fantasy. It is the mark of a certain desire, the seemingly innocuous calling card of an unspoken obsession. Although the image is extremely powerful, it is also extremely fragile. It is vulnerable and yet is carefully protected and preserved by multiple institutional practices. It is almost always looked at in passing, lightly, obliquely, held in the periphery of the discourse, if not the blind spots that occupy its center. To confront this image here will be to explore the way that it has been constructed by patiently unpicking the delicate and twisted threads out of which it was woven, many of which were drawn out of mid-nineteenth-century discourse and yet continue to structure contemporary debates. Throughout the years in which the white wall was slowly invested with an extraordinary charge, very particular theories about whiteness were deployed, theories with idiosyncratic agendas and effects that need to be explored in some detail.

This does not involve rewriting the history of modern architecture. Rather, it involves looking into some of the blind spots, interrogating the historiography for what is routinely left out of the picture. Or, more precisely, what is left out in order that there can even be a picture in the first place. Only by looking at what is just outside the traditional frame is it possible to think about the white surfaces that quietly slide right through the middle of it. Rather than construct a new history, it is a matter of studying the unique structure of a key subtext that constantly works its way across the discussion of modern architecture, orchestrating much of that discourse while rarely becoming evident within it. Rather than bring new archival material to the surface, it is a matter of looking at the evidence lodged in the public record, sitting right there in front of us, nestled between the lines of the all too familiar literature, hidden only because it is so close to our eyes. To see it simply involves letting the texts speak for themselves. We do not have to dig so deep. After all, to explore the white wall is precisely to explore the surface itself. But the surface is far from superficial. Details matter. Textures are telling. To tell the story of the white wall here is to dwell on nuances, to dwell on and in the very thinness of the surface. Indeed, it is to follow those architects who have argued that the surface is the only place to dwell.

Observing the Dress Code

This exploration will use the work of the most famous, if not the most influential, of the modern architects, Le Corbusier, as a springboard. His *L'art décoratif d'aujourd'hui* (The decorative art of today) of 1925 digested much of the preceding debate to present one of the most definitive and revealing theories of the white wall. It argues that modern architecture can only be modern inasmuch as it is white and insists that this is not simply an aesthetic issue. The whole moral, ethical, functional, and even technical superiority of architecture is seen to hang on the whiteness of its surfaces. The book even goes as far as proposing that this whiteness could reorganize the moral fabric of the entire city by being imposed through some kind of police action: "Whitewash is extremely moral. Suppose there were a decree requiring all rooms in Paris to be given a coat of whitewash. I maintain that that would be a police task of real stature and a manifestation of high morality, the sign of a great people."[1] The mark of purity and integrity is the unmarked wall.

Le Corbusier was crazy about white. But while images of his famous houses of the 1920s played a crucial role in sustaining the tacit association between modern architecture and whiteness, even the most exhaustive accounts of those houses overlook their white skin. The whitewash is so taken for granted that it usually only comes up by way of negation. Critics discuss the way in which the architect eventually left behind "the image of the white, machine-age box"[2] of his early work. Or they talk of the resistance to thinking of him outside the machine aesthetic of "the white modern architecture of the first half of the twentieth century."[3] It is only when white goes away that it is talked about. It is symptomatic, for example, that Nikolaus Pevsner does not address the white wall in his 1936 canonic history of modern architecture but does so in a 1959 article that publishes a set of images contrasting Le Corbusier's buildings in their original state with their current state of disrepair:

Le Corbusier's houses can't please in decay. Concrete structures with walls designed to be rendered white make bad ruins. . . . Le Corbusier's style from 1920 into the 1930's has as its hallmark the smooth white surfaces of walls with metal windows cut into them without any intermediate moldings and with an uncompromising sharp horizontal line to set them off from the sky. These white surfaces must be white, these metal window frames free from rust.[4]

The white wall only becomes visible when it is removed or starts to degenerate. Those who refer to the whiteness do so in passing, employing the usual rhetoric of the neutral surface while making other points. The most that can be expected is a passing identification of the whiteness with machine age precision or the Mediterranean vernacular. But no details are elaborated. No analysis of the specific role or effect of the white wall is offered. The white surface is virtually effaced. It is usually only in texts that are not aimed at a specialized architectural audience that the whiteness of modern architecture and the theories behind it are pointed to, let alone discussed. In a series intended for readers outside architecture, Stephen Gardiner, for example, argues that Le Corbusier's white walls were as important as any other factor in making him the "leader" of modern architecture. Having quoted *L'art décoratif d'aujourd'hui* on the presence of whitewash in all mature vernacular cultures, he compares the way white links the buildings in a Mediterranean village to the way it links the buildings of modern architecture:

Whitewash was also a visual bond between the buildings of the island villages; like the bare essentials that hold people together, whitewash was a bond that held aesthetics together. . . . Thus white became the bond between Le Corbusier's early buildings. In consequence, it became the bond between all the European architectural modern movements of the 1920s and 1930s, white was the theme that held the total picture together.[5]

It would seem that it is all too easy to talk about white. Avoiding it requires effort. If it does indeed hold the "total picture" together, but is rarely being discussed by the dominant literature, something serious and problematic must be at stake here, something that only starts to come to the surface in the secondary literature. Take, for example, Lionel Brett's 1947 contribution on houses to the book series entitled *The Things We See*, which aims "to encourage us to look at the objects of everyday life with fresh and critical eyes," so that we can "buy with discrimination."[6] Its attempt to cultivate a discriminating appreciation of architecture accompanies an image of some generically white houses with the following explanation:

The skeleton thus poised upon the ground must next be clothed, and the purpose of this clothing, like any other, is partly protective, partly decorative. . . . But by the twentieth century the traditional ways of dressing-up a building had become stale; every possible way had been disinterred and reinterred. . . . Ornament was banished. . . . Houses, like their occupants, flaunted their anatomy, and while some had beautiful bodies that (while they remained young) delighted the passer-by, others had not. Any kind of clothing for the bare concrete seemed dishonest. Pure white was *de rigueur,* partly because of its exciting novelty, partly because it emphasized the smoothly mechanical texture, and pointed the contrast between it and surrounding nature.[7]

Supposedly, modern architecture strips off the old clothing of the nineteenth century to show off its new body, a fit body made available by the new culture of mechanization. The modern building is naked and the white wall accentuates that nakedness by highlighting its machine-like smoothness. The white paint is meant to be the skin of the body rather than a dissimulating layer of clothing. Although this association between whiteness and nakedness tacitly underwrites most discourse about modern architecture, Brett immediately calls the white surface into question, showing an image of a pristine modern house upon its completion alongside one on which the white paint is peeling off after a few years. The white wall is seen to have "presented a surface which could neither be cleaned nor happily left to weather. The modern house arrived in a blaze of glory and after a brief summer of astonishing beauty faded like a flower in the frost."[8] It is precisely this fragility that mainstream architectural discourse attempts to avoid by systematically avoiding the white wall when it is intact and, like Pevsner, calling for its faithful restoration when it falls into disrepair—not simply to protect the white surface from further abrasion or to keep the structure beneath it hidden, but rather to protect certain institutionalized assumptions about the relationship between them. The delicate layer of paint holds together a vulnerable conceptual structure that starts to be exposed when the layer cracks or flakes.

What has to be concealed is the fact that the white is a layer. After all, the stripping off of old clothes, advertised by the original promoters of modern architecture and by its contemporary dealers, is not simply a stripping of all clothing. Although everyone seems to be everywhere concerned with the beauty and purity of the naked body of industrialized structures, modern architecture is not naked. From the beginning, it is painted white. And this white layer that proclaims that the architecture it covers is naked has a very ambiguous role. Supposedly, it is inserted into the space once occupied by clothing, without being clothing as such. But the enigmatic nature of that insertion cannot be addressed so the white surface is almost completely ignored. The highly professionalized and regulated discourse is blind to it, or blinded by it. What cannot be seen is the obvious. No matter how thin the coat of paint is, it is still a coat. It is not simply inserted into the space vacated by clothing. It is itself a very particular form of clothing. And by sustaining a logic of clothing, modern architecture participates in many of the economies from which it so loudly announces its detachment.

It is not by chance that the literature directed away from architects, which does not hesitate to address or even criticize the white wall, also chooses to associate the logic of modern architecture with that of clothing. Take *An Introduction to Modern Architecture*, published in 1940 by the then assistant editor of *The Architectural Review*, J. M. Richards, for Pelican Books—a series aimed at the "common reader," the "layman who, aware of his own expanding role as man and citizen, will welcome the chance." Like Brett's later book, it describes just how "unsatisfactory" the white wall can be:

The cleanness and glitter of white walls are satisfying to the modern architect's eye, but in the English climate few white surfaces will survive. They soon become dingy. White walls are not foreign to this country, we have the successful precedent of Regency stucco buildings, which still look smart. But their smartness depends on regular re-painting with expensive oil paint, and in these days of financial instability we cannot afford to build in a way that commits us to so much future expenditure on upkeep. Modern architects have made many sad mistakes in using white surfaces that have not lasted.[9]

This criticism is grounded in a logic of clothing. The book repeatedly uses the analogy of dress and opposes modern architecture to the supposedly erratic fluctuations of fashion. Indeed, its introductory chapter argues that the book was written to enable the "man in the street to understand a little more what modern architecture is all about," because that architecture has been accompanied by fashionable imitations. The lay reader is to be trained to detect the "bogus modernism" that is the result "of the commercial exploitation of novelty or merely the wish to be in the fashion."[10] Although modern architecture is a style, it must resist degeneration into just another fashionable outfit. The next chapter begins by explaining the need for a "modern" style in terms of clothing. The word "style" has supposedly been contaminated by the nineteenth-century sense "of fancy costumes in which buildings may be clothed according to the whim of their designer." Architecture can only become truly modern by recovering the earlier sense of style as "more than a costume into which the carcass of a building had to be forced . . . a set of conventions corresponding more closely to the accepted conventions of dress than to the assumption of fancy costume."[11] It seeks the degree of order and consistency that can be found in the uniform standards of conventional dress, a generic style within which there is sufficient room for individual variations. Modern architecture is a coordinated ensemble, like that of the eighteenth century, when the ornamentation of houses, "the ribbons and ruffles, as it were, of its dress," were a harmonious part of the outfit. In the nineteenth century, the rapid transformation forced by the industrialization of everyday life dissolved the conventional dress of architecture, which ended up with "no habits more deeply rooted than those of fashion to keep it related to real life."[12] In the twentieth century, the standardized outfit to be worn by a mechanized culture has been identified. Modern architecture is ready to be worn. Yet the visible aging of the white wall calls into question that architecture's ability to transcend the turnover of fashionable styles. Superficial flaws become deep threats.

The same arguments can already be found in F. R. S. Yorke's *The Modern House* of 1934, which likewise promotes the modernization and standardization of architecture in terms of dress. The everyday attitude toward clothing is presented as the appropriate attitude toward buildings. Architecture should be as modern as one's dress:

Even in so personal a manner as dress man is content to conform to a standard, which has minor variations, but from which there is little departure. The owner of the pseudo-Tudor villa is quite aware of the ridiculous figure he would cut were he perchance to find himself at his office in doublet and hose, yet he does not realize that his olde worlde home is as absurd, and hampers movement just as much as obsolete clothing.

Whilst he is willing enough to conform to this standard, and finds there is still little scope for indulgence of personal taste, he fears a standard in architecture and likes his house in fancy dress.... The men who cultivate the perfect trouser-crease abhor straight unbroken lines in building, and those who detest the vulgarity of a personal display of jewelry are inclined to judge architecture by its wealth of ornament.[13]

Once again, the audience is not architects. Yorke, a founding member and secretary of the MARS group who would go into private practice with Marcel Breuer a year later, was commissioned by the *Architectural Review* to produce a promotional book for an audience unfamiliar with the modern architecture that the magazine was earnestly promoting to its professional readership. Clothing appears to be the easiest way to communicate the principles and virtues of this new architecture. The familiar logic of clothing is projected onto an unfamiliar kind of building. And yet the very ease of this association raises some doubts. The well-known enigmas of clothing get displaced onto architecture and prove extremely difficult to remove. The clothing analogy seems to invite in the world of fashion that it is designed to keep out. Yorke's text soon returns to the analogy of dress to explain how a period of "purification" of architecture from the nineteenth-century "building of fashion rather than of style" has occurred, "largely" under the influence of Le Corbusier. While modern architecture is like modern clothing, it must resist the pull of fashion. It may be a style, but that style emerges spontaneously from a rigorous concern with function, as has modern women's clothing:

The new work was not based on attempts to discover a new style or new shapes; the architects found a new expression through the new materials they employed in the construction of buildings to accommodate those who had found a new and more enlightened mode of living. Just as the clothing of women changed in appearance as it became more practical and healthy, cut on lines permitting greater freedom of movement, so the face of the building changes with freedom in planning and the employment of flexible materials.[14]

In the end, this argument turns on the status of the surface, the fabric of the garment rather than its cut. Yorke publishes side-by-side images of a sleek house by Luckhardt and Antor just before its white coat is added and just after, arguing that the modern architect searches for a "wall surface" that is "regarded, aesthetically, as a continuous plane; as a skin enveloping and expressing the surface of a volume."[15] While this seamless skin may be compared to that of a modern outfit, it also needs to be carefully detached from the economy of fashion typically associated with the realm of dress. Inasmuch as the smooth stuccoed surface (one that Yorke hastens to point out is subject to "cracking and discoloration") is a form of clothing, it raises the specter of fashion that would undo most of modern architecture's claims. A year later, Yorke's new partner Breuer uses the pages of *Architectural Review* to call for a "flat white wall," but insists that architecture has to resist the regressive forces of fashion that are exemplified by women's clothing.

More than just the trait that holds modern architecture together, the white wall is therefore the point of vulnerability by which that architecture can be unpicked. Ignoring it is one way of ignoring the internal contradictions that are at once the source of the strength of the architecture and the point of its greatest weakness. The nonprofessional literature that dares to address the white wall exposes the greatest fears of the professional discourse. In appealing to the image of clothing to communicate the advantages of modern architecture, it actually touches the very basis of the thinking from which that architecture emerged. By paying close attention to the precise formulations used, it can be demonstrated that the arguments about whitewash put forward by Le Corbusier and his colleagues drew extensively on nineteenth-century arguments about the relationship between architecture and clothing. To follow the twists and turns of the threads that tie these two seemingly irreconcilable sets of arguments together has something to offer contemporary discourse. It opens up the relationship between architecture and fashion that continues to haunt so many discussions. The blindness to the white wall turns out to be a blindness to the subterranean operations of fashion in the very polemics that emphatically reject fashion. The white wall turns out to be the lid on a can of very slippery worms, one that has understandably been left unopened for so long.

While some clues about this slippery content can be found in the popularizing literature, traces of the tell-tale association between the white wall and clothing can also be found within the dominant historiography. When Le Corbusier died, and a stream of obituaries began the process of turning him into a saint, Reyner Banham published an article in the *Architectural Review* asserting that, for all his less than saintly qualities, the architect should indeed be honored but as "the fashion-master of his age," the couturier with a keen sense of the right form whose every move was immediately picked up by his followers, or should we say clientele.[16] The ubiquitous white wall was clearly one such move, if not the most decisive. Yet four years earlier, in his *Age of the Masters: A Personal View of Modern Architecture*, Banham had noted that Le Corbusier's followers failed to change out of modern architecture's "teenage uniform of white walls" when their master had long discarded it:

Poised for world conquest, the new architecture discovered that it had a uniform by which friend could be distinguished from foe, a uniform whose adoption indicated that its wearer wanted to be considered as one of the gang. For twenty years—thirty in the case of some critics—the defence of modern architecture was the defence of that uniform quite as much as the defence of Functionalism, and there are still people today who cannot accept a building as functional unless it wears the uniform gear. But already in the early thirties, Le Corbusier was adjusting his dress, and incorporating sporty or tweedy elements not accepted by the rest of the gang. At Mathés, on the Biscay coast, he built a little holiday house with pitched roofs and random masonry walls and rough carpenter's woodwork.[17]

Ironically, the disciples continued to wear the white clothes designed by the fashion master precisely because they symbolized a refusal of fashion in favor of the rigors of function. After all, the one look that is hard to take off is the antifashion look. To take it off is to reveal that it is just one look among others. It is supposed to be the look that terminates the obsessive turnover of looks, acting as the stable surface behind the parade of ephemeral fashions, the neutral, or neutralizing, ground with which a building can test itself and other buildings for unwanted fashion infections by making them appear as ornamental "stains," as Le Corbusier put it, that stand out against its clean surface. Once exposed, these degenerate elements have to be isolated and either removed or framed off to prevent them from infecting the rest of the surface and thereby suffocating the structure that lies beneath it, or, even worse, penetrating the surface to infect the structure. More precisely, these interruptions of the silky smooth and surgically clean surface have to be framed in a way that makes it clear that they are the product of the external forces of fashion, rather than the erupting to the surface of some fundamental and untreatable infection of the structure that has always been there. Likewise, if what the white surface reveals is that some aspect of the daily practices and objects of the people that live within or around it is ornamental, whether it be their breakfast cereal or the building across the street, then these, too, must be treated as symptoms of fashion. The white surface is the antifashion look, both in the sense of the "look" of the tabula rasa, with every excess cleared away, and in the sense of an active look, a surveillance device scanning the very spaces that it has defined for the intrusions of fashion. The white wall is at once a camera and a monitor, a sensitive surface, a sensor.

This look to end all looks was hard for the modern architect to give up and even harder for the critic, whose work, after all, consists of nothing but surveillance. Even Le Corbusier did not simply abandon it. Rather, he started to install it like a security system within his projects, controlling each space by covering certain strategically located surfaces with white in a pattern that needs to be studied in some detail. The fashion master continued to market the antifashion look, but in a smaller, more efficient, model.

Now antifashion is, of course, a major part of the history of fashion. It is not just that every fashion has its critics, or even that fashion itself always has its critics. More fundamentally, a crucial part of fashion is the turning of antifashion statements into fashion. Fashions are, as it were, propelled forward by their criticism. The phenomenon is unthinkable outside the resistance to it. But was the antifashion statement of the white wall turned into a fashion statement? Or was it, from the beginning, a part of what it was critiquing, even a vital part? Is it the fashion industry itself that is stabilized by the white surface? What exactly is the strategic role of this surface? What does its very emptiness fill up? What cracks does it cover over? For whom? When? If it is a security system, what is secured, pinned down, locked up, hidden away? What violence necessarily accompanies, and even constructs, the seemingly innocent look? What are its guilty secrets?

To begin to answer this overflowing nest of questions requires a close examination of the way in which the white surface emerged out of architectural discourse's long-term, but largely suppressed, engagement with the antifashion movement in clothing design. It is a matter of patiently tracking this critical subtext of the discourse of modern architecture, one that is, in the end, so obvious that the historiographical tradition has had to work very hard to ignore it. Indeed, the reasons for this prolonged, if not institutionalized, diversion need to be established. Not to set the historical record straight but to show the particular ways in which its twists have been straightened out to produce a certain orthodoxy that still restrains the actions of writers and designers.

The dominant historiographical institutions do more than suppress the role of fashion in modern architecture. They also suppress the role of fashion in their own operations. Too often and too loudly do they certify that they and the avant-garde they describe are fashion-free. Indeed, one of the reasons that the strategic role of fashion is suppressed is that it reveals unpublicized aspects of the overdetermined identification that so many contemporary historiographic practices make with the historical avant-garde. To say the least, these practices are clearly directed at maintaining a certain conceptual and political order. This is not only the seemingly internal order of the discipline of architecture (which binds certain ideas and ways of dealing with ideas to clearly established social structures), but also the complex networks of contractual relationships that architectural discourse maintains with other disciplines and with many of the diverse practices of so-called everyday cultural life. Only by unearthing what the historiography is constantly attempting to bury can some of the highly suspect aspects of this institutional order be dislodged and the possibilities for different forms of action that are embedded within it be mobilized.

The white wall is a key site for exhuming such possibilities. Although rarely addressed as such, it is tacitly established as the very figure of the rejection of fashion by being positioned at the climax of a generic story, a cartoon that is endlessly repeated in different degrees of detail and with many different variations but that attains its force precisely because it is a cartoon—its extreme simplifications being the source of its considerable influence. This all-too-familiar story describes modern architecture as emerging out of the new space made available by the rejection of Art Nouveau. Supposedly, this artistic movement had finally disposed of the endless cycles of fashion sustained by the nineteenth century's eclectic turnover of styles, but was itself a fashion that had to be removed. It was the last fashion, a movement that sacrificed itself to what it destroyed, making possible a set of avant-garde practices free from the rule of fashion that had nervously covered over the shockingly different conditions of modern life installed by the new technologies of production, or, more precisely, reproduction. To rethink the white wall will be to rethink this story by returning to those who first wrote it.

This does not mean simply revisiting those canonic writers, like Nikolaus Pevsner and Sigfried Giedion, who helped to make a group of architects extraordinarily influential by giving them an official history. Rather, it is a matter of returning to those whose writings made such a group, and even the idea of a group, let alone a movement, possible. The story that the historians eventually told about modern architecture was actually written before it, by curious figures like Hermann Muthesius, whose opinions on most things made their way into the historiography and have been handed down by successive generations, usually without being acknowledged as such. Even today, his interpretations are simply presented as historical facts. Muthesius is, as it were, one of the main ghostwriters of the historiography. Indeed, it is easy to show that he assembled the basic material that was exploited much later by the canonic histories of modern architecture, regardless of their fundamental differences (whether, to take the two biggest examples, it be Giedion's monumental cataloging of glass-and-steel engineering constructions—in which Muthesius never even appears—or Pevsner's record of the Arts and Crafts tradition—in which Muthesius only appears at one key point). By rereading his texts, other aspects of the story come to light, aspects that disturb the very historiography that quietly bases itself on these texts, aspects not simply overlooked but suf-ficiently unsettling that these texts are rarely addressed in any detail.

One of the many such disavowed, as distinct from omitted, details is modern architecture's obsessive engagement with the realm of dress and the very econ-omies of fashion that it so loudly denounces. It is no coincidence that Ban-ham, who never gave up his original attempt to demystify the canonic histories of Pevsner and Giedion, pays closer attention to Muthesius and ends up employing the metaphor of dress to describe modern architecture and begins to point to the role of fashion within it. This lead has to be pur-sued much further here. More of the ghostwriters' texts have to be read in greater detail. The surface of the white wall has to be keenly scrutinized for traces of the very world of fashionable dress the rejection of which it suppos-edly exemplifies. The sensor must itself be placed under surveillance.

After all, even Banham does not go into the white wall as such. Although his innovative *Theories and Design in the First Machine Age* of 1960 does cite some of the key passages on white walls that eventually appeared in *L'art décoratif d'aujourd'hui*, it does so to explain the architect's respect for the in-dustrial vernacular rather than the specific role of whitewash, and later dis-misses the book as "a polemical work of only local interest."[18] The question of white is raised and then quickly withdrawn. While it is raised, the hint is dropped that Le Corbusier's admiration for whitewash derives from his "theo-ries about the beauty of banality" but it remains no more than a passing com-ment. It is necessary to go back to *L'art décoratif d'aujourd'hui* and explore it in much more detail. We need to return to the white wall and excavate its thin layer, looking for the traces of hidden closets within the very smoothness of its surface. By going further into the discourse about white, a whole other economy of dress can be brought back to the surface, an intriguing economy that dislodges traditional narratives.

In the end, it is not simply the actual dresses to be found in the closets of modern architecture and its discourse that embarrass traditional historiogra-phy. Rather, it is the dresslike quality of this architecture. The dresses them-selves would pose no problem inasmuch as they could be securely ghettoized in the supposedly inferior, as "feminine," domains of "ornament," "accessor-ies," "interior decoration," "Art Nouveau," "architect's partner," "homosex-ual," "woman," and so on. But they are almost always effaced rather than subordinated because they cannot be restricted to these domains and the very attempt to do so reveals that these domains are not so secure after all. What must be concealed is not the dresses as such but the fact that modern architecture—and, likewise, its historiography—cannot detach itself from what it emphatically defines as its degenerate other. The white wall at once suppresses and preserves the nightmares of the discourse. Its banality is deceptive, to say the least.

Oh, those Greeks! They knew how to live. What is required for that is to stop courageously at the surface, the fold, the skin, to adore appearance, to believe in forms, tones, words, the whole Olympus of appearance. Those Greeks were superficial—out of profundity.

—Friedrich Nietzsche, preface to the second edition of *Die fröhliche Wissenschaft* (*The Gay Science*), 1886.

The Emperor's New Paint

In 1959 Le Corbusier added a preface to his lesser-known *L'art décoratif d'aujourd'hui* of 1925, in which he had introduced his theory of the white wall. It describes the book as the result of an extended inquiry that began at the very beginning of his career with the deceptively simple question "*Where is architecture?*"[1] Whatever the white wall is, it plays some kind of role in determining the place of architecture itself, how it is placed before it places, how it inhabits culture before culture inhabits it, how it is itself housed. Far from a new finish on an old structure, the white wall is presented as a rethinking of the very identity of architecture. *L'art décoratif d'aujourd'hui* has to be understood in terms of the long institutional history that prescribes where architecture can be seen, what kind of vision is required, and who sees. This tradition presupposes that the fundamental experience of architecture is visual, that architecture is a "visual art." It locates architecture in the visual field before locating it in any particular site. Le Corbusier's text engages with this tradition and revises some of its fundamental assumptions. Architecture is no longer simply a visual object with certain properties. It is actually involved in the construction of the visual before it is placed within the visual. Indeed, vision itself becomes an architectural phenomenon. The place of architecture becomes much more complicated. A building can no longer be separated from the gaze that appears to be directed at it. Before having a certain look, the building is a certain way of looking. The white wall is intended to radically transform the status of building by transforming the condition of visuality itself. The seemingly simple idea that modern architecture should be white answers the question "where is architecture" in a way that reconfigures the limits and operations of architectural discourse. Le Corbusier's small book has a big role.

L'art décoratif d'aujourd'hui examines the objects of contemporary everyday life, condemning those that have ornate decoration and praising those without it. The lie of decoration is that it is added to objects as a kind of mask. It is a form of "disguise," a representational layer inserted between the new reality of the modern object that results from modern techniques of production and the new reality of modern life that those techniques make possible. Misrepresenting both, it produces historical and spatial alienation by sustaining a nostalgic fantasy in the face of modernity. Like so many everyday objects, architecture has to discard the representational debris that clutters the surface of its structures and distracts the eye from modernity.

This erasure of decoration is portrayed as the necessary gesture of a civilized society. Indeed, civilization is defined as the elimination of the "superfluous" in favor of the "essential" and the paradigm of inessential surplus is decoration. Its removal liberates a new visual order. Echoing an argument at least as old as Western philosophy, Le Corbusier describes civilization as a gradual passage from the sensual to the intellectual, from the tactile to the visual. Decoration's "caresses of the senses" are progressively abandoned in favor of the visual harmony of proportion. The materiality of representation appears to be abandoned in favor of the immateriality of clear vision. The eye finally transcends the body that props it up. Sensuality is conquered by reason. Or so it seems.

Upon closer reading, Le Corbusier's text is far from straightforward. It cannily subverts the very tradition it appears to be echoing and, in so doing, disturbs the place of architecture.

The Look of Modernity

The rejection of decoration in favor of the cultivated eye is explicitly understood as a form of purification. The argument culminates with the chapter entitled "A Coat of Whitewash: The Law of Ripolin," which advocates replacing the degenerate layer of decoration that lines buildings with a coat of whitewash. Whitewash liberates visuality. It is a form of architectural hygiene to be carried out in the name of visible truth: "His *home* is made clean. There are no more dirty, dark corners. *Everything is shown as it is.*"[2] The true status of the object is exposed. Cleansed of its representational masks, it is simply present in its pure state, transparent to the viewer: "Law of Ripolin, Coat of Whitewash: elimination of the equivocal. Concentration of intention on its proper object. Attention concentrated on the object. An object is held to be made only out of necessity, for a specific purpose, and to be made with perfection."[3] The look of modernity is that of utility perfected, function without excess, the smooth object cleansed of all representational texture.

The apparent consequence of this argument is tacitly rehearsed within the traditional interpretation of Le Corbusier's early work. His villas are read repeatedly in terms of a visual logic of transparency to structure and function, an abstract architecture that engages with the age of the machine. But, surprisingly, the polemical whiteness of the villas is not examined as such. It is taken for granted. The buildings are understood as objects, machines to be looked at, inhabited by a viewer who is detached from them, inhabited precisely by being looked at, whether it be by the user, visitor, neighbor, critic, or reader of architectural publications. The whitewash is tacitly understood as part of the look but so fundamental a part that it does not even have to be pointed out. Le Corbusier's elaborate arguments about the relationship between the white surface and the very act of looking, arguments that allow him to speculate about the unique status of architecture in industrialized society, are not examined.[4] The capacity for whitewash to rethink the fundamental definition of architecture is ignored. To say the least, the obvious tension between the opaqueness of the white surface and the supposed transparency of modern architecture is not problematized. Precisely by being made part of a look, the white wall is looked through. This privileging of the look seems to be supported by Le Corbusier's writing, which everywhere appears to privilege the visual. But the nature of that look and that privilege is not examined. The theory of the white surface is rendered as transparent to the critics as they imagine the surface to be. The critics have Le Corbusier's famous "eyes that do not see." But why is it necessary for the whiteness to be ignored by the manufacturers of the canon? What is preserved by this strategic blindness?

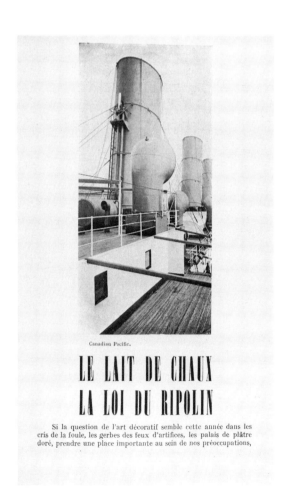

1.1
*"A Coat of Whitewash:
The Law of Ripolin."
Page from* L'art décoratif
d'aujourd'hui, *1925.*

Clearly, Le Corbusier's argument has to be understood in terms of the central role of whiteness in the extended history of the concept of cleanliness. Modern architecture joins the doctor's white coat, the white tiles of the bathroom, the white walls of the hospital, and so on. Yet the argument is not about hygiene per se. It is about a certain look of cleanliness. Or, more precisely, a cleansing of the look, a hygiene of vision itself. Whitewash purifies the eye rather than the building. Indeed, it reveals the central role of vision in hygiene. After all, the "clean" white surface is not such a simple thing.

The white surfaces that traditionally mark cleanliness do just that, they mark rather than effect it. The whiteness of supposedly hygienic spaces originated with the garments and cosmetic powders that were periodically changed in order to take the sweat of the body out of sight but not to remove it. Putting on a new white shirt was equivalent to taking a bath. As Georges Vigarello argues: "it was the treatment of clothes which, from the sixteenth century, created a new physical space for cleanliness . . . the whiteness and renewal of linen took the place of cleaning the skin."[5] The linen garments that were once hidden beneath layers of clothing slowly came to the surface to represent the condition of the body that they no longer even touch. The ideal of cleanliness that Le Corbusier appeals to originated as a style of clothing and a certain attitude toward clothing in general. It established a social order rather than a physical one. Even when laws were passed that controlled the amount of ornamentation on clothing, the white fabric was able to articulate levels of social distinction. Cleanliness was the visual effect that marked one's membership of a social class rather than the state of one's body. The book of hygiene was a kind of label that classifies the person who wears it.[6]

Eventually, the cleaning of clothes would be supplemented by the cleaning of the body. Toward the end of the eighteenth century, a concern developed for what was "behind appearance which could call into question the long relationship between cleanliness and dress, imposing on clothes other criteria than simply those of show. Surfaces and perfumes could no longer stand alone."[7] The mere look of white was no longer the guarantee of hygiene. Bathing became the rule, a social statement. But still, the whole economy of hygiene remains fundamentally visual rather than sensual. More precisely, it is all about bracketing the sensual out in favor of the visual. When white fabrics came to the surface of the outfit, they challenged the logic of the visible, complicating the traditional economy of vision by carving out a new kind of space.[8] The white surface "erects a screen" between the body and the onlooker, interrupting the eye's attempt to grasp the body. It brackets the body out. But, at the same time, it forces the body into the imaginary by advertis-

1.2
Ripolin Poster, Eugene
Vavasseur, 1898.

ing an inaccessible domain. The idea of the body is sustained without any sensory information being provided about the particular body being imagined. What distinguishes the white fabric from the forms of clothing that it displaced is the way it raises the question of the body that it conceals, hovering somewhere between revealing and concealing. The sensuousness of the surface has been reduced to a minimum in order for the general condition of the sensual world to be tested. In other words, it plays a crucial part in the very constitution of the category of the sensual that it appears to bracket out. The thin white garment produces the image of a physical body behind it, but it is a body that did not exist as such before.[9] Previously, the surfaces of a person's clothing had the role of their body. The white shirt opened up a gap between the body and its clothes. Despite being nothing more than a certain kind of image, its surface raises the question of a physical domain beyond images and, in so doing, defines a new kind of space. Indeed, it starts to redefine the very condition of space. As Vigarello puts it, the history of the concept of cleanliness "consists, in the last analysis, of one dominant theme: the establishment, in western society, of a self-sufficient physical sphere, its enlargement, and the reinforcement of its frontiers, to the point of excluding the gaze of others."[10] Whiteness plays a key role in the constitution of space, understood in terms of such an institutionally loaded economy of vision.

Likewise, Le Corbusier's arguments about whitewash are arguments about visuality that reconfigure traditional assumptions about sensuality and space. In appealing to the look of hygiene, he appeals to the enigmatic operations of the white shirt. The white wall, like the white shirt, institutes the very distinction it appears to merely demarcate, carving out a space that was not there before. The white surface does not simply clean a space, or even give the impression of clean space. Rather, it constructs a new kind of space. Or, at least, it restores the kind of space that was supposedly erased by the overly sensual decorative interiors and facades of nineteenth-century architecture. Such ornamental schemes block the fantasy of a body behind them and even the sense of a discrete body in front of them. The body of the building and the body of the observer disappear into the sensuous excesses of decoration. To look at decoration is to be absorbed by it. Vision itself is swallowed by the sensuous surface. The white surface liberates the eye by reconstituting the idea of a body hidden behind it, recovering a sense of space that has been lost. For Le Corbusier, the look of whitewash is not simply the look of modernity. Although he repeatedly employs the white walls of a transatlantic liner as a model for architecture, whitewash is not the mark of the industrialized twentieth century but of civilization as such:

Whitewash exists wherever people have preserved intact the balanced structure of a harmonious culture. Once an extraneous element opposed to the harmony of the system has been introduced, whitewash disappears. . . . Whitewash has been associated with human habitation since the birth of mankind. Stones are burnt, crushed and thinned with water—and the walls take on the purest white, an extraordinarily beautiful white.[11]

The collapse of authentic folk culture caused by the intrusion of foreign practices is marked by the loss of whitewash. It is the global dissemination of inauthentic forms through the new channels of communication (trains, planes, movies, magazines, and so on) that has peeled off all the white surfaces and fostered a degeneration into the sensuous excesses of decoration. But the white walls of the ocean liner mark the maturing of the very industrial culture that was once responsible for "brutally driving out" vernacular whitewash. It is the status of the object in the twentieth century that is new, not its coating with whitewash. Modernity is able to recover the purity of the ancient cultures it has desecrated, restoring the white surfaces it has graffitied. The neutrality of whitewash is more historical than formal.

Even then, it is not a passive neutrality. The whitewash is not simply what is left behind after the removal of decoration. It is the active mechanism of erasure. Rather than a clean surface, it is a cleaning agent, cleaning the image of the body in order to liberate the eye. The whitewash makes the objects of everyday life visible as any impurity, any decorative excess, would leave a "stain" on its surface: "On white ripolin walls these accretions of dead things from the past would be intolerable: they would leave a stain. Whereas the stains do not show on the medley of our damasks and patterned wallpapers. . . . If the house is all white, the outline of things stands out from it without any possibility of transgression; their volume shows clearly; their color is distinct."[12] More than just the appropriate setting for the look (a "neutral" background, like a gallery wall), and even more than the active removal of distractions from the eye, the whitewash is itself an eye: "Put on it anything dishonest or in bad taste—it hits you in the eye. It is rather like an X-ray of beauty. It is a court of assize in permanent session. It is the eye of truth."[13] It is not simply the look of cleanliness but a cleaning of the look, a focusing of the eye. Not a machine for looking at but a machine for looking.

But does this viewing mechanism only focus on the supplements of building: objects and people located inside, outside, or on its surfaces? What happens when it catches the building itself in its own look? What does it see in architecture? Exactly what qualities of architecture does it expose? Can all the stains be removed without destroying the fabric?

Le Corbusier's privileging of white clearly draws from his own experience of vernacular whitewash. At the end of the long tour through the East that he began at the end of 1910, he describes his new found love of white in a letter to his friend William Ritter: "In their crazy course, red, blue and yellow have become white. I am crazy about the color white, the cube, the sphere, the cylinder and the pyramid and the disc all united and the great empty expanse." [14] Not by chance does the preface of *L'art décoratif d'aujourd'hui*, whose examples are so often taken from this tour, refer to it as the critical moment in which he finally "discovered architecture" in response to his "unceasingly" asked question "*Where is architecture?*" [15] When he "succumbed to the irresistible attraction of the Mediterranean," [16] as he puts it, this attraction had everything to do with all the white walls whose "brilliant," "delicious," "dazzle" he repeatedly describes. This formative encounter with the white wall was clearly reinforced when his first Purist paintings eight years later were abstractions of whitewashed houses in the French countryside. The architect's appeal to the universal status of white seems to be founded on a highly specific and idiosyncratic set of personal experiences and fantasies.

At the same time, the description of these intense encounters is itself part of a very particular cultural discourse about whitewash that had been ongoing for a long time. This discourse clearly shaped Le Corbusier's accounts of his personal experiences. Indeed, it seems to have initiated and organized those very experiences. The architect's love affair with the whitewashed house is not so much an intimate experience as a social construction with its own history and specific agenda. The generic mythology of the architect as artist-genius tends to transform whitewash from an artifact produced and interpreted by elaborate collective discourses into a primal phenomenon that exceeds all discourse and is experienced personally by a uniquely sensitive individual. This transformation effectively buries the particular investments that are being made in the white wall, whether they be collective or personal. The strategic role of the wall all but disappears in favor of a brief flash of a single image of modern architecture as a simple echo of the supposed purity of the Mediterranean vernacular. Still, we can begin to uncover this role by scrutinizing the sources of Le Corbusier's argument.

The account of civilization as progress from the sensuality of decoration to the abstraction of form through the progressive removal of ornament is, of course, taken from the Viennese architect Adolf Loos's notorious criminalization of ornament: "The lower the culture, the more apparent the ornament. Ornament is something that must be overcome. The Papuan and the criminal

ornament their skin. . . . But the bicycle and the steam engine are free of ornament. The march of civilization systematically liberates object after object
from ornamentation."[17] Le Corbusier's text appropriates those of Loos much
more than its two brief references to Loos indicate.[18] In fact, it is everywhere
indebted to Loos.[19] In Loos's canonic essay "Ornament und Verbrechen" (Ornament and crime) of 1908, which Le Corbusier republished in the second issue of *L'Esprit Nouveau* in 1920, the removal of ornament is a process of
purification that ends up with the whitewash: "*The evolution of culture is
synonymous with the removal of ornament from objects of daily use.* . . . We
have outgrown ornament. . . . Soon the streets of the cities will glow like
white walls!"[20] This concern with whitewash can be traced throughout
Loos's writing. The degeneration of contemporary architecture is repeatedly
opposed to the construction of the vernacular house, which, as he puts it in
his "Architektur" essay of 1910, concludes when the peasant "makes a large
tub of distemper and paints the house a beautiful white."[21] The aesthetic purity of this traditional gesture is now guaranteed by principles of modern hygiene. As with Le Corbusier, the whitewash is seen as at once the mark of
modernity and tradition. Indeed, as Stanislaus von Moos points out, Le Corbusier was already extensively quoting from this very essay in 1913 without
acknowledging the source, and *L'Esprit Nouveau* advertised that it would
publish it although it never did.[22] Consequently, Le Corbusier's "Law of Ripolin" needs to be understood in a conceptual context that undermines the
assumptions that organize the architectural discourse that neglects it.

In my view, the "Law of Ripolin" of 1925 is a specific reference to the "Law
of Dressing" [*Gesetz der Bekleidung*] that Adolf Loos formulates in 1898. In
so doing, Loos legislates against any "confusion" between a material and its
dressing. Dressings must not simulate the materials they cover. They must
only "reveal clearly their own meaning as dressing for the wall surface,"[23]
identifying their detachment from a structure without identifying that structure. The outer layer of a building must be understood as an accessory without revealing that which it accessorizes. Loos does not simply advocate the
removal of decoration in order to reveal the material condition of the building as an object. What is revealed is precisely the accessory as such, neither
structure nor decoration. The perception of a building becomes the perception of its accessories, its layer of cladding.

The privilege of the whitewash is bound to this idea that the perception of
architecture is the perception of a layer of dressing that dissimulates the structure it is added to, a layer that can be as thin as a coat of paint. Indeed, for
Loos, the coat of paint is the paradigm. The "Law of Dressing" emerges
alongside a reading of the traditional whitewashed wall. The argument turns

Illustration of knot from Gottfried Semper, Der Stil in der technischen und tektonischen Künsten oder praktische Aesthetik, *1860–63.*

on an anecdote about the perception of the difference between a window frame that has been stained and one that is painted white. The twentieth-century invention of wood staining is opposed to the peasant tradition in which pure colors are set against the "freshly whitewashed wall." The transparency of the stain is dismissed in favor of the opaque mask of white paint: "wood may be painted any color except one—the color of wood."[24] Le Corbusier's argument has to be rethought in terms of a nineteenth-century logic of veiling rather than one of transparency.

Furthermore, Loos's "Law of Dressing" is, in turn, a specific reference to the "Principle of Dressing" [*Prinzip der Bekleidung*] formulated in the mid-nineteenth century by the German architect Gottfried Semper. Semper defines the essence of architecture as its covering layer rather than its material structure. This definition involves a fundamental transformation of the account of the origin of architecture on which so much of traditional architectural discourse tacitly or explicitly bases itself. Architecture is no longer seen to originate in the construction of material protection, a simple wooden shelter that is later supplemented and represented by successive ornamental traditions—such that ornament is always representative of, and subordinate to, the original structure. The story of architecture is no longer one of naked structures gradually dressed with ornament; "rather, it was with all the simplicity of its basic forms highly decorated and glittering from the start, since its childhood."[25] Architecture begins with ornament. It is not just that the architecture of a building is to be found in the decoration of its structure. Strictly speaking, it is only the decoration that is structural. There is no building without decoration. It is decoration that builds.

For Semper, building originated with the use of woven fabrics to define social space, specifically, the space of domesticity. But the textiles were not simply placed within space to define a certain interiority. They were not simply arranged on the landscape to divide off a small space that could be occupied by a particular family. Rather, they are the production of space itself, launching the very idea of occupation. Weaving was used "as a means to make the 'home', the *inner life* separated from the *outer life,* and as the formal creation of the idea of space."[26] Housing is an effect of decoration then. It is not that the fabrics are arranged in a way that provides physical shelter. Rather, their texture, their sensuous play, their textuality, like that of the languages that Semper studied, opens up a space of exchange. The decorative weave produces the very idea of a family that might occupy it, in the same way that a language produces the idea of a group that might speak it. Space, house, and social structure arrive with ornament. The interior is not defined by a continuous enclosure of walls but by the folds, twists, and turns in an often discontinuous ornamental surface.

The Emperor's New Paint

This primordial definition of inside and, therefore, for the first time, outside, with textiles not only precedes the construction of solid walls but continues to organize the building when such construction begins. Solid structure follows, and is subordinate to, what appear to be merely its accessories:

Hanging carpets remained the true walls, the visible boundaries of space. The often solid walls behind them were necessary for reasons that had nothing to do with the creation of space; they were needed for security, for supporting a load, for their permanence and so on. Wherever the need for these secondary functions did not arise, the carpets remained the original means of separating space. Even where building solid walls became necessary, the latter were only the inner, invisible structure hidden behind the true and legitimate representatives of the wall, the colorful woven carpets.[27]

The textile is a mask that dissimulates rather than represents the structure. The material wall is no more than a prop, a contingent piece of "scaffolding" that is "foreign" to the production of the building, merely a supporting player, playing the role of support, supporting precisely because it does not play. Architecture is located within the play of signs. Space is produced within the sensuality of language. As its origin is dissimulation, its essence is no longer construction but the masking of construction. Just as the institution of the family is made possible through the production of domestic space with a woven mask, the larger community is made possible through the production of public space through masquerade. Public buildings, in the form of monumental architecture, are seen to derive from the fixing in one place of the once mobile "improvised scaffolding" on which hung the patterned fabrics and decorations of the festivals that defined social life. The space of the public is that of those signs. Architecture literally clothes the body politic. Buildings are worn rather than simply occupied.

Semper identifies the textile essence of architecture, the dissimulating fabric, the fabrication of architecture, with the clothing of the body. His monumental treatise *Der Stil in den technischen und tektonischen Künsten, oder praktische Aesthetik* (Style in the technical and tectonic arts or practical aesthetics) of 1860 draws on the identity between the German words for wall [*Wand*] and dress [*Gewand*] to establish the "Principle of Dressing" as the "true essence" of architecture. The chapter entitled "Correlation of Costume with Architecture" explains the "intimate" relationship between clothing and the arts and demonstrates the "direct influence" of developments in clothing on developments in the arts. But architecture does not follow or resemble clothing. On the contrary, clothing follows architecture. The definition of domestic interiority precedes the definition of the interiority of the body.[28] The clothing of the individual follows the clothing of the family. The body is only defined by being covered in the face of language, the surrogate skin of the building. The evolution of skin, the surface with which spatiality is produced, is the evolution of the social. The social subject, like the body with which it is associated, is a product of decorative surfaces. The idea of the individual can only emerge within language. Interiority is not simply physical. It is a social effect marked on the newly constituted body of the individual. Culture does not precede its masks. It is no more than masking. In a footnote to his treatise, Semper argues that the highest art form is not that which detaches itself from the primitive use of decorative masks but that which most successfully develops that practice by dissimulating even the mechanisms of dissimulation:

I think that the *dressing* and the *mask* are as old as human civilization. . . . The denial of reality, of the material, is necessary if form is to emerge as a meaningful symbol, as an autonomous creation of man. Let us make forgotten the means that need be used for the desired artistic effect and not proclaim them loudly, thus missing our part miserably. The untainted feeling led primitive man to the denial of reality in all early artistic endeavors; the great, true masters of art in every field returned to it—only these men in times of high artistic development also *masked the material of the mask*.[29]

The subordination and dissimulation of material does not imply ignorance or disregard of material.[30] On the contrary, it is the "mastery" of material. Materiality is hidden by being mastered. Only through a detailed understanding of the construction can it be effaced—reduced to an invisible prop. The most sophisticated technical control is required in order that the technical world can give way to the weave of ornament.[31]

Repeatedly identifying architecture with clothing, Loos follows Semper's arguments closely.[32] This is nowhere more explicit than when he formulates the "Law of Dressing" in his 1898 essay "Das Prinzip der Bekleidung" (The principle of dressing) in which architecture emerges from textiles and structure is but the scaffolding added to hold them up:

The architect's general task is to provide a warm and livable space. Carpets are warm and livable. He decides for this reason to spread out one carpet on the floor and to hang up four to form the four walls. But you cannot build a house out of carpets. Both the carpet on the floor and the tapestry on the wall require a structural frame to hold them in the correct place. To invent this frame is the architect's second task.

This is the correct and logical path to be followed in architecture. It was in this sequence that mankind learned how to build. In the beginning was dressing.[33]

The textile masks the structure but does not misrepresent it. It hides the building but does not disguise it. Following Semper, Loos is against lying. The dressing dissimulates in the name of truth. It must register its independence without identifying that from which it is independent. Materials organize forms but the material of the dressing is different from that of construction, and the form of a building is only produced by its cladding. The structural prop is not revealed, even as prop.

In paying attention to the layer of paint, Loos continues to follow Semper, whose whole argument turns on the status of a coat of paint. Semper produces a history of paint within which the addition of a coat of paint to the surface of building is the way in which the original textile tradition was maintained in the age of solid construction. In this way, architecture, the "mother art," gives birth to the art of painting. This simulated textile, the painted text, becomes at once the new social language, the contemporary system of communication, and the new means by which space is constructed. Architecture is literally in the layer of paint that sustains the masquerade in the face of the new solidity because it is "the subtlest, most bodiless coating. It was the most perfect means to do away with reality, for while it dressed the material, it was itself immaterial."[34] Semper explicitly opposes the hegemonic tradition of the white surface, whether it be the practice of white buildings that he argues was instigated by Brunelleschi (in whose work "we find for the first time an unpainted, naked architecture"[35]) or in art history's adoration of the white surface, which he identifies with Winckelmann's influential writing. For him, everything has to do with color. It is the color of the paint that keeps the weave of the carpet alive, substituting the painting of walls for the dyeing of fabrics.

Semper's argument was based on the emerging archeological evidence that the ancient buildings of antiquity only appeared to be "naked" white stone because their layers of colored paint had been weathered off, including his own findings at the Parthenon. He interpreted this in a way that undermined the status of the building's structure to that of a mere prop for the layer of paint, arguing that white marble was only used by the Greeks precisely because it was a better "base material" for painting on. The marble is transformed from the traditional paradigm of authenticity into a "natural stucco," a smooth surface on which to paint. Its smoothness is no longer identified with the purity of its forms, but as the possibility for a certain texture. Architecture is no longer the decoration of a naked structure. The sense of the naked is only produced within the supplementary layer itself. The body of the building never becomes visible, even where it coincides with the decorative layer. The places "where the monument was supposed to appear white were by no means left bare, but were covered with a white paint."[36] All differences are literally inscribed in the surface.

Loos develops the "Principle of Dressing" into the "Law of Dressing" by prohibiting any coincidence between the structure and its cladding. While this has the specific consequence of disassociating whiteness and structure, the general purpose of Loos's law is to keep the naked-clothed distinction within the textual economy sustained by the layer of paint rather than between the layer and its prop. It is this agenda that organizes most of his arguments. While his demands for the removal of ornament and the purification of the sensual in the name of whitewash appear to be a rejection of Semper's privileging of ornament, they are in fact the maintenance of it. The whitewash is the extreme condition, the test case, of Semper's argument. Loos is not simply arguing for the abolition of ornament but for collapsing the distinction between structure and ornament into the layer of cladding, a layer between structure and ornament within which all distinctions are produced by being inscribed into the surface.

Prosthetic Fabrications

But what of the suggestion that Le Corbusier transforms the "Law of Dressing" into the "Law of Ripolin," in which there is no explicit rehearsal of Semper's argument? Indeed, it appears to be set up in direct opposition to Semper. Le Corbusier's whitewash removes precisely those accessories that Semper identifies as the essence of architecture: "Imagine the results of the Law of Ripolin. Every citizen is required to replace his hangings, his damasks, his wall-papers, his stencils, with a plain coat of white ripolin."[37] The textile tradition seems to be abandoned. Surface texture is erased. Indeed, decoration has to be removed precisely because it "clothes" the smooth modern object. Decoration is repeatedly described as clothing to be discarded in the name of the naked truth. While Semper locates architecture in the supplementary layer, whitewash supposedly purifies architecture by eliminating the "superfluous" in favor of the "essential." Le Corbusier's infamous *Vers une architecture* (Towards an architecture) of 1923 had already argued that the culture it promotes is one of "rejection, pruning, cleansing; the clear and naked emergence of the Essential."[38] For civilization to progress from the sensual to the visual, the sensuality of clothes has to be removed to reveal the formal outline, the visual proportion, of the functional body.

But the body cannot be completely naked as that would be to return to the very realm of the sensual that has been abandoned. There is a need for some kind of screen that remodels the body as formal proportion rather than sensual animal, a veil with neither the sensuality of decoration nor the sensuality

1.4

Illustration of
unacceptable fabrics from
L'art décoratif
d'aujourd'hui.

of the body. The whitewash is inserted between two threats in order to transform body into form. Folklore begins with "man naked, dressing himself."[39] The modern savage is not naked. On the contrary, purification results in the "well-cut suit":

Decoration is of a sensorial and elementary order, as is color, and is suited to simple races, peasants and savages.... The peasant loves ornament and decorates his walls. The civilized man wears a well-cut suit and is the owner of easel pictures and books.

Decoration is the essential surplus, the quantum of the peasant; and proportion is the essential surplus, the quantum of the cultivated man.[40]

Le Corbusier identifies modernity with modern clothes. His lists of exemplary modern objects that have been purified of decorative excesses always include clothes. It is not just that the garments form part of such lists. The very act of purification is explained in terms of the cut of a suit. *L'art décoratif d'aujourd'hui* begins by contrasting Louis XIV's "coiffure of ostrich feathers, in red, canary, and pale blue; ermine, silk, brocade and lace; a cane of gold, ebony, ivory, and diamonds" and Lenin's "bowler hat and a smooth white collar."[41] A photograph of the President of the Republic in a modern suit is symptomatically substituted for one of Lenin. The lists of modern objects almost always begin with clothes.[42] The first item in the museum "that contained everything," the archive of the twentieth century, is "a plain jacket, a bowler hat, a well-made shoe."[43] It is not by chance that the first thing we know of modern man, the first piece of evidence for his elevation from the degenerate realm of the senses into the realm of the visual, is his clothing. Indeed, Le Corbusier seems to suggest that clothes were the first objects of everyday life to lose their decoration: "But at the same time [that household objects were decorated] the railway engines, commerce, calculation, the struggle for precision, put his frills in question, and his clothing tended to become a plain black, or mottled; the bowler hat appeared on the horizon."[44] Clothing leads the way, acting as the link between the modernization of industrial culture that has already occurred and the modernization of architectural culture that is about to occur.

The clothing being praised here is unambiguously that of a man. The textureless white wall is associated with the generic man's suit organized around the "smooth white" shirt. Its austerity is tacitly opposed to the seductions of women's dress. On one double-page spread, Le Corbusier contrasts an image of the ornamented white dress of a famous ballerina to the sheer white walls in an image of an ocean liner from the same year. Her outfit is associated with the ornate interior of the ship. The sinuous motif of the backdrop in the theater is repeated in the ship, rendering its interior as theatrical and suspect as a woman's dress. On the following spread, the dress of the legendary singer Mistinguette (whose multitude of plumes, like those of Louis XIV, seems to have been plucked from the ostrich pictured in the book's very first

1.5
Louis XIV. Illustration from L'art décoratif d'aujourd'hui.

1.6
M. Gaston Doumergue, President of the French Republic. Illustration from L'art décoratif d'aujourd'hui.

1.7
Mlle. Mistinguette.
Illustration from L'art
décoratif d'aujourd'hui.

1.8
The Barrel of Diogenes.
Illustration from
Gottfried Semper, Der Stil
in der technischen und
tektonischen Künsten
oder praktische
Aesthetik, *1860–63.*

image) is associated with Art Nouveau architecture. Not by chance does the text identify Art Nouveau with femininity. At one point, it notes that through the dissemination of that architecture in magazines "young ladies became crazy about decorative art," speculating that this craze would have been enough to kill off the style had it remained the craze of women alone.[45] Indeed, it is precisely after noting that men have also succumbed to the craze of Art Nouveau ornament that the book makes its first call for a "crusade for whitewash." The white wall emulates the austere men's suit that holds the seductions of women's dress at bay and already participates in the modern world that architecture has yet to join.

In fact, clothing is much more than a historical precedent. Le Corbusier's whole thinking of the modern object is organized in terms of clothes. Objects are understood as "auxiliary limbs," "artificial limbs," prosthetic additions "supplementing" the fixed structure of the body. It is symptomatic that Le Corbusier draws on the story of Diogenes, who abandoned all his excesses, his clothing and possessions, and lived in a barrel that he walked around with. The clothing of the naked body with a barrel is cited as "the primordial cell of the house." [46] It is a model of purification and the fundamental identity between clothing and housing. The rejection of decoration is not a rejection of clothing. On the contrary, architecture is clothing. Modern architecture, like all the many sciences of artificial limbs, is a form of tailoring. The role of the artist is transformed: "He chucks up cornices and baldacchinos and makes himself more useful as a cutter in a tailor's shop, with a man standing in front of him and he, metre in hand, taking measurements. . . . Decorative art becomes orthopaedic, an activity that appeals to the imagination, to invention, to skill, but a craft analogous to the tailor: the client is a man, familiar to us all and precisely defined." [47] Decorative art is the prosthetic "art" of the tailor, an art centered on man, but no humanism. It is a science of the artificial, centered on the imperfect body, the "inadequate," "insufficient" body in need of protection by "supporting limbs."

It is the prosthetic supplements that support the body, not the body that supports the supplements. For Le Corbusier, all useful objects are clothes. The story of whitewash, as the endgame of the story of the modern object, is a story of clothing. The coat of paint is, after all, just that, a coat. It is still a form of dressing, albeit the most simple dress. Semper's argument has not been abandoned. Even without a visible texture, the smooth white surface remains a fabric. We are still in the domain of the textile. Le Corbusier makes a twentieth-century reading of clothes, a displacement of what constitutes clothes rather than a displacement of clothing as such. Hence the central paradox of the text: "*Modern decorative art is not decorated.*" Having been stripped of decoration, the white surface itself takes over the space-defining role of decorative art.

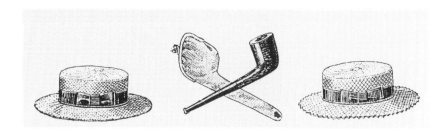

It is symptomatic that commentators omit clothing from the list of everyday objects used as models of the "Purist" sensibility that informed Le Corbusier's canonic white villas of the early 1920s. Unlike the other objects, clothes can only be understood as supplements. They make explicit the Purist concern with the perfected supplement that is at odds with the ideal of the authentic, irreducible object transparent to the gaze that is sustained by traditional criticism as a model of modern architecture and sound historiography. The removal of clothes from the picture makes a certain architectural theory possible, a theory that draws on and sustains a millennial tradition of assumptions that orchestrate a whole regime of cultural biases. This regime, which is codified in the philosophical tradition but drives so much of everyday cultural practice, routinely subordinates clothing as a suspect realm of dissimulation. And yet, for Le Corbusier, it is precisely such a supplement, the simple fabric, that is the possibility of thought itself: "The naked man does not wear an embroidered waistcoat; so the saying goes! . . . The naked man, once he is fed and housed . . . and clothed, sets his mind to work. . . . The naked man does not wear an embroidered waistcoat; he wishes to think."[48] Likewise in modernity, his original clothing, the house, is not embroidered. Its woven surface occupies the space between the new savage body of modern structure and the old seductive body of decoration. The thin opaque layer of whitewash masters the body in order to liberate the mind. The discretely clothed object makes pure thought possible by bracketing materiality away.

Le Corbusier systematically inverts his ironic taunt that "for the present we are most certainly not in the agora of the philosophers: we are only dealing with decorative art."[49] Architecture is more than simply an agent of any particular theory. It is theory's condition of possibility. It is not that a rational theory's ability to detach the superfluous from the essential leaves modernity with simple clothes, the "essential surplus." Rather, the very distinction between superfluous and essential is made possible by those clothes. Indeed, the distinction emerges in the text from a discussion of the simplicity of Diogenes' outfit. Philosophy emerges from the clothing of the philosopher. High theory is made possible by the low art of clothing. It is privately exceeded by that which it publically subordinates. The look of the whitewash is not simply that of traditional metaphysics, where the immaterial eye of reason precedes, scrutinizes, and subordinates the physical world, even though whitewash makes the effect of such a subordination possible. Like the white shirt, the white wall subverts the traditional logic by being neither strictly visual nor strictly sensual, while making that very distinction possible, facilitating the apparent domination of reason over the physical world that it cannily eludes. Rational thought emerges out of the very thinness of the surface.

It is important to note that although Le Corbusier appeals to reason and the modern techniques for rationalizing the built environment, he does not simply advocate a rational architecture. Indeed, he opposed such an architecture throughout the various shifts in his practice. Reason follows the clothing that is architecture but is not its endpoint. Architecture does not simply subordinate itself to the theoretical order it makes possible. While the whitewash is responsible for the emergence of the reason that may then be applied to the structure it covers, it does not exhibit the rationality of that structure, nor is it the result of that rationality. The truth made visible by the whitewash is not that of structural materials or construction technology but the truth of modern life. The layer of white paint exposes the "structure" of the "edifice" of modern culture rather than the structure of the edifice it is added to.[50] Le Corbusier is concerned with the relationship between clothes and everyday life rather than that between clothes and the body. He opposes the masking of cultural life but not the masking of the body. Structural conditions are never simply equated with those of everyday life. It is the prosthetic additions to

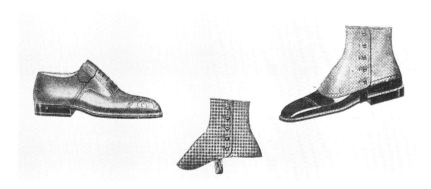

the body that are the possibility of everyday life, not the body itself. The supplementary decorative screen of folk-culture is "the perfect mirror of its people," as he puts it, because it exposes what is in front of it rather than what is propping it up. It reflects the truth of culture rather than that of physical material. Modern man can only exist in harmony with the realities of modern physical life by being isolated from them. The whitewash is a form of defense. It is not an extraordinary addition to everyday life but the representation of the ordinary to a subject increasingly anxious in the face of modernity, dissimulating structure in order that people can feel.

Decoration is not removed in favor of pure structure. The expression of construction is described as but a temporary "fashion" that followed the nineteenth-century separation of decoration from structure and is succeeded by the truly modern concern for straightforward, simple working clothes. For Le Corbusier, construction is mere reason, the rational tool by which man is set free. It is not a thing of interest in itself.[51] Indeed, it must be masked with a coat of paint.

This masking is often criticized as a departure from the rigorous theory of modern architecture that violates the critical ideal of transparency to the essential status of a rationalized object. One writer, for example, describes the way Le Corbusier's early villas "masqueraded as white, homogenous, machine-made forms, whereas they were in fact built of concrete block-work held in place by a reinforced concrete frame,"[52] while another argues that in the "white stucco box tradition" of the early work "the feel of the machine-made was more image than reality . . . all stuccoed and painted to try to give it the precision of machine products . . . traditional buildings decorated to look machine-made . . . the machine-age image."[53] Yet inasmuch as the "Law of Ripolin" translates Semper's "Principle of Dressing," the role of the whitewash is precisely that—masquerade—and the reality of the machine age is precisely the reality of the image. For Le Corbusier, structure can only begin to be exposed when it has been rationalized to the minimum, so reduced that it can only be seen as a subordinate prop. His central principles of the "free plan" and the "free facade" are no more than the attempt to free the building from being "the slave of the structural walls." His buildings are multiple layers of screens suspended in the air. Even where the structure seems to be exposed, it is actually clothed in a layer of paint, purified. Even the bones have skin, a self-effacing skin. Following Loos, the object is, like all modern slaves, a "self-effacing" prosthesis, with an "unassertive presence," marked only by the absence of decoration.[54] But this is not to say that the object is silent. Again, it is clear that the white is not neutral. The "aesthetic of purity" speaks loudly about silence. Purist rather than pure, the building exhibits the look of the naked, the clothing of nakedness, the clothes that say "naked." Nakedness is added and worn as a mask.

In such an account of architecture, construction technology does not simply produce new forms but lighter props for form. Technological progress is the increasing reduction of construction. Structure is but a frame for a skin, a cloth, the clothing of modernity. The house may be a machine but inasmuch as it is architecture, it does not look like one: "Art has no business resembling a machine (the error of *Constructivism*). But the means of art are set free. Illuminated with clarity." [55] The look of the machine is transformed into the look at art, a new look made possible by the machine. The white coat is a "channelling of our attention only to those things worthy of it." [56] It is actually a way of looking away from the structure toward art: "In this mechanical, discreet, silent, attentive comfort, there is a very fine painting on the wall." [57] Suspended in the void between structure and decoration, the whitewash is a new, strange ground, a floating "platform," as Le Corbusier puts it, on which objects "stand out" as either artistic or utilitarian. The look of the whitewash splits the incoming gaze into the utilitarian look of rational theory and the seemingly disinterested aesthetic gaze. It organizes the eye, classifying objects and presenting them to the appropriate view. The inhabitant of white architecture becomes a discriminating viewer, exercising a newly found sense of judgment. If, following Semper, to occupy a building is to wear it, then to wear a modern building is to wear a new set of eyes.

Le Corbusier repeatedly separates utility from aesthetics and prohibits any "confusion" by placing them in a vertical hierarchy in which art subordinates rational utility. Utilitarian objects are the "platform of art" and reason is the "support" of aesthetics, but support in the Semperian sense, a supplementary prop that comes after, and is subordinate to, that which it holds up: "Even before the formulation of a theory, the emotion leading to action can be felt: theory later gives support to sentiment in a variety of seemingly incontrovertible ways." [58] Rational theory is organized by and for the emotional realm of art. The whitewash does not bracket materiality in order to simply construct a space of pure rationalization. It screens off the object in order to make a space for art, which necessarily employs theory as a prop. It literally frees an eye for art.

But what is the status of this look that precedes that of rational theory? Is the "detachment," "disinterest," and "distance" from materiality that the whitewash produces simply that of the traditional aesthete? Exactly what is it to look at the white wall?

It must recalled that Semper's argument is explicitly set up in opposition to the account of architecture sustained by the philosophy of art. Aesthetics is seen to subordinate art by isolating it in a discrete field. For Semper, art and philosophy belonged together in antiquity. Indeed "philosophy was, as it were, an artist itself."[59] But it detaches itself from art by subjecting artistic practices to a regime of alien categories that all follow from an original split of the art-object from its accessories.[60] The isolation of accessories leads to the isolation of all the arts from the rest of culture and from each other. Theory presents itself as the adjudicator of what is essential and what is accessory. Art is rendered into an accessory, then that accessory is itself divided into essential and accessory arts, then each of those is divided into essential and accessory elements, and so on. Semper argues that this suspect regime of endlessly spiraling judgments was actually put in place by an original division of architecture into fundamental material structure and merely contingent accessories, a division that entraps it: "In ancient and modern times the store of architectural forms has often been portrayed as mainly conditioned by and arising from the material, yet by regarding construction as the essence of architecture we, while believing to liberate it from false accessories, have thus placed it in fetters."[61] Ironically, the structure of a building acts as the model for the subordination of accessories, but within the newly subordinated domain of art the accessories that were detached from that structure (like the wall paintings that took over the original space-defining role of the wall hangings but were then detached from the wall to become framed paintings) are elevated into "high" arts. Hence architecture's "organizing and at the same time subordinate role" in the "household of the arts."[62] The philosophical regime is based on the control of architecture. Theory is liberated by confining architecture to a single place.

Throughout his writings, Semper opposes the attempt to locate architecture in a particular place that is made possible by the original distinction between structure and decoration. His strategy is to invert the distinction between high art and low art that follows from it.[63] The treatise opposes "the perversity of modern artistic conditions, according to which a wide gap, unknown to the Greeks, separates the so-called small arts from the so-called high arts."[64] While the philosophical tradition employs the architectonic image of a decorated structure to subordinate craft as merely "applied," Semper counters that craft is not applied art. It is neither applied to something nor has it been detached from something else. Craft begins with weaving that simply originates as building.[65] It precedes the structure on which it might be propped, and all the other crafts emerge out of it. Semper bases his theory of architecture on these "low" decorative arts rather than the monumental "high" arts. In so doing, he inverts the traditional architectonic, subordinating structure to decoration by demonstrating that the "false" accessories are actually the "true" essence of architecture.

This inversion necessarily distorts the traditional economy of vision based upon a carefully preserved image of architecture in which that which is seen on the outside supposedly articulates, and is subordinate to, some inner truth: "Even where solid walls become necessary they remain only the inner and unseen structure for the true and legitimate representatives of the spatial idea: namely, the more or less artificially woven and seamed-together, textile walls . . . the *visible* spatial enclosure." [66] The truth of architecture is now located in its visible outside rather than its hidden interior. The Roman substitution of unpainted colored materials for the Greek use of colored paint, which lets the material "speak for itself," is condemned as a loss of the Greek "conviction . . . that inner content should conform to outer beauty," [67] rather than the other way around. The inside submits to the authority of the outside. Indeed, the inside is at most an extension or effect of the exterior surface. The "true" wall is its visible "artificial" surface. The "invisible" structure is secondary. Everything is reversed to the extent that "naked architecture," the absence of a coat of paint, is described as a "disguise." Everything is in the surface. Architecture turns out to be nothing more than texture. To wear a building, by entering it, is to feel its weave. More precisely, to feel the surface is to enter. Occupying a space does not involve passing through some kind of opening in the surface, like a door, to find an interior. To occupy is to wrap yourself in the sensuous surface.

Architecture is to be found in the sensuous play of surfaces rather than the lines that seem to mark the limits of those surfaces. While traditional discourse subordinates ornament and then, within ornament itself, subordinates color to form, Semper privileges color over form, insisting that it came first before radically complicating the distinction between them and thereby promoting a completely different sense of visuality. [68] In countering aestheticians who argue that applied color "must confuse the forms and pamper the eye," he argues that the immediately visible condition of the wall "brings the eye back again to the natural way of seeing, which it lost under the sway of that mode of abstraction that knows precisely how to separate the visible and inseparable qualities of bodies, the color from the form." [69] Once form cannot be separated from color, the institutionally preserved figure of architecture is radically displaced. The seductions of the surface displace the formal proportion worshipped by the institutions of high art, producing a visuality so entangled with a sensuality that cladding materials are analyzed in terms of their feel, their tactility, and smell becomes part of the essence of a building. [70]

The "visible spatial enclosure," the surface texture that constitutes the architecture of the mask, is produced by this convolution of vision and sensuality.[71] Architecture no longer simply occupies the visual. Its sensuality is not screened off by the white surface in the name of an uncontaminated eye. Visuality becomes a construction of necessarily sensuous social transactions and the eye is unable to detach itself from what it sees. For Semper, the social is sensual. The eye feels the colored paint just as the body feels the weave of clothing. Indeed, it is the eye that holds the larger set of clothes that the building is against the body. Far from a disembodied form of perception, the eye anchors the body in space.

It is in the context of this particular displacement of the visual that Le Corbusier's appropriation of "low" cultural objects like an industrial warehouse, a man's suit, or a filing cabinet has to be rethought. His convolution of the relationship between the everyday object and the art object disturbs the place of architecture and therefore the visuality it constructs. In the middle of *L'art décoratif d'aujourd'hui*, engineering, which is supposedly the realm of pure structure, is identified as the new decorative art and the book's original question "where is architecture?" is reformulated: "Can one then speak of the architecture of decorative art, and consider it of permanent value?" Le Corbusier attempts to clarify the question by separating art from decorative art and placing them in a hierarchy.

The Permanent value of decorative art? Let us say more exactly, of the *objects* that surround us. This is where we exercise our judgement: first of all the Sistine Chapel, afterwards chairs and filing cabinets; without doubt this is a question of the secondary level, just as the cut of a man's suit is of secondary importance in his life. Hierarchy. First of all the Sistine Chapel, that is to say works truly etched with passion. Afterwards machines for sitting in, for filing, for lighting, type-machines, the problem of purification, of cleanliness, of precision, before the problem of poetry.[72]

The generic type-form of standardized objects is subordinated to the individual artwork. While the prosthetic type-form is universal, and makes available a new way of life by extending the body in new ways, it can be outdated by a new type, thrown away in favor of ever greater extensions. But the artwork made possible by a particular set of type objects in a particular time and place is permanent.

As in the aesthetic tradition, art is supported on the utilitarian objects that come "before" it but remain secondary to the disinterested eye. Art is the supplement of the supplement. It decorates the type-objects that decorate the body. The tension between art and decorative art is actually between two kinds of decoration, two kinds of clothing—or, more precisely, between two layers of clothing. While the model of decorative art is yet again "the cut of a man's jacket," the model for art, the Sistine Chapel, is precisely the paradigm of the painted surface, Semper's clothing of space. In fact, the difference between them is social. It is a choice between the collective "mirror" of decorative art and the individual "mirror" of art, the suit worn by everyman and the seamless frescoes worn by one space.[73] What is so intriguing about Le Corbusier's argument is that architecture cannot simply be placed in either domain. He always identifies architecture with both: "Architecture is there, concerned with our home, our comfort, and our heart. Comfort and proportion. Reason and aesthetics. Machine and plastic form. Calm and beauty."[74] Architecture is neither one nor the other. It is produced in the play between the two, the complex exchanges that occur between the generic type suit and the one-off designer outfit. The question of architecture's place is symptomatically not answered. The text is unable to simply place architecture within its own categories.

The same enigma can be found throughout Le Corbusier's writing. The opening of his most famous text: *Vers une architecture*, for example, attempts to place architecture by splitting it from engineering as one might split art from utility. But the division is immediately confused. On the one hand, architecture exceeds engineering: "ARCHITECTURE is a thing of art, a phenomenon of the emotions lying outside questions of construction and beyond them"[75] but, on the other hand, "engineers produce architecture." The generic industrial structures produced by engineers are more poetic than the work of any architect. Ironically, art is produced by a certain disregard for artistic value. An obsession with standard solutions produces the unique event. Yet it is precisely in the face of this displacement of the institutional practices of architectural discourse by engineering that the possibility of architecture, the "essential surplus," is announced:

Nevertheless, there does exist this thing called ARCHITECTURE. Admirable thing, the most beautiful. The product of happy peoples and that which produces happy peoples.

Happy cities have architecture.

Architecture is in the telephone and in the Parthenon. How easily it could be at home in our houses![76]

These easily overlooked sentences from the beginning of the first chapter of probably the most influential text in twentieth-century architectural discourse at once raise and complicate the question of the place of architecture. Architecture is itself housed. It has a home. But more than that, it houses itself. The new architecture of the telephone inhabits the old architecture of the house. The sentences involve more than just a juxtaposition of high and low art. It is not that the telephone is now to be thought of as a beautiful object available for appropriation by the detached eye. Rather, the Parthenon has to be thought of as a system of communication like the telephone. And the telephone has to be thought of as a means of production of space like the Parthenon. The telephone, like all systems of communication, defines a new spatiality and can be inhabited. It is the modern equivalent of Semper's weaving. Not by chance does Le Corbusier's archive of visual material for *L'Esprit Nouveau,* within which the essays making up *Vers une architecture* were first published, contain a diagram showing the weavelike structure of the international telephone network. Indeed, telephone companies had from the beginning portrayed the telephone operator as a weaver of telephone lines. Like the coat of paint, the telephone is a form of clothing that can be occupied, but not by some preexisting culture. It is a new language that produces rather than represents modern culture. The telephone institutes a new community in the same way as the woven carpet instituted the family. *L'art décoratif d'aujourd'hui* makes this transformation from one technology of communication to another explicit: "Here, in widespread use in books, schools, newspapers, and at the cinema, is the language of our emotions that was in use *in the arts* for thousands of years before the twentieth century. We are at the dawn of the machine age. A new consciousness disposes us to look for a different aesthetic satisfaction from that afforded by the bud carved on the capitals in churches."[77]

Denna härva är blott skenbar — vid närmare påseende ger den en översikt över det europeiska telefonnätets förbindelser.

1.11
*International telephone
network. From the file
cabinet collection of
material for illustrations
in* L'Esprit nouveau.
Fondation Le Corbusier.

1.12
*"Weavers of Speech."
National magazine
advertisement for Bell
System, 1915.*

In Semper's model, the idea of the individual can only emerge within the institution of domesticity. Even the interior of the body is produced for the first
time when its surface is marked with tattoos then clothes in response to the
definition of the interiority that is the family, which is itself constituted by the
construction of the textured surface that is the house. The idea of an individual speaker with an interior life only emerges within language. Interiority is
not simply physical. It is a social effect marked on the newly constituted body
of the individual. Just as the language of the carpet produces the speaking
subject in need of representation through clothing, the new means of communication produce a new individual in need of self-definition through art. Art,
for Le Corbusier, is the mark of the individual. It is the systems of representation detached from the physical definition of interior that actually constitute
shelter and make possible the "inner life" that he repeatedly identifies as the
goal of architecture: "The human spirit is more at home behind our fore-
heads than beneath gilt and carved baldacchinos."[78] Home is an effect of the
appropriate decorative art, the art that is, by definition, "something that
touches only the surface."[79] Enclosure is a surface effect. While architecture is
housing—the production of shelter—this is, for Le Corbusier, as it was for
Semper and would later be for Heidegger, primarily a question of representation. As he puts it in *Quand les cathédrales étaient blanches* (When the cathedrals were white): "The terminology employed today is no longer exact. The
word 'architecture' is today more understandable as an idea than as a material fact; 'architecture': *to order, to put in order.*"[80] Architecture constructs
through classification. The lines it draws are not simply material. Rather, they

are the framing, the "look" of different systems of representation. The white-wash is but one such system. It cannot simply be placed in either equipment or art because it is the mechanism for making the distinction between them. It is a system of classification defined in its intersection with other systems, each of which reframes the others. The traditional look of the whitewash, the limit condition of the painted wall, is transformed by its interaction with new systems of communication, new surfaces in which people wrap themselves.

In *Le voyage d'Orient,* Le Corbusier's record of the original tour in which he fell in love with white walls, he describes how cinema, radio, photography, trains, and gramophone records have violently driven out vernacular white-wash, exporting the taste for decorative bric-a-brac to an international audience that promptly covers and colors the once purified walls of its old buildings.[81] It is only "far from the major lines of communication" that "the walls are white" and "each spring, the house that one loves receives its new coat: sparkling white, it smiles the whole summer through foliage and flowers that owe to it their dazzle."[82] *L'art décoratif d'aujourd'hui* simply elaborates this observation to formulate the "Law of Ripolin":

In the course of my travels I found whitewash wherever the twentieth century had not yet arrived. But all these countries were in the course of acquiring, one after the other, the culture of cities, and the whitewash, which was still traditional, was sure to be driven out in a few years by wall-paper, gilt porcelain, tin 'brassware', cast-iron decoration—driven out by Pathé-Ciné and Pathé-Phono, brutally driven out by industry, which brought complete confusion to their calm souls.

Once factory-made brassware arrives, or porcelain decorated with gilt seashells, whitewash cannot last. It is replaced with wall-paper, which is in the spirit of the new arrivals. Or, as long as whitewash lasts, it means that the brassware has not yet arrived, because the white-wash would show it up. Pathé-Ciné or Phono, which are the mark of the times, are not hateful—far from it—but Pathé incarnates, in these countries living on the morality of centuries of tradition, the dissolving virus which in a matter of years will break everything down.[83]

But now the same systems of communication can be used to restore the lost whitewash. Having been destroyed by them, the whitewash returns so that the architecture implicit in those systems of communication can emerge. Far from covering old forms, the whitewash facilitates the development of new forms, understood as new ways of looking at the world.

The whitewash is able to effect this transformation by being inserted into the gap between structure and decoration in a way that constructs a space for architecture that is neither simply bodily or abstract. It occupies the gap in the cartoon-like image of architecture that organizes traditional accounts of vision. An almost immaterial fabric that traces the convoluted lines stitching the tactile and the visual, its visuality is not that of traditional aesthetics. Like the polychrome wall dressing that Semper describes, the whitewash is produced where the visual cannot be simply detached from the sensual and each is transformed. As Le Corbusier puts it: "Our hand reaches out to it [the modern object] and our sense of touch *looks* in its own way as out fingers close around it."[84] Architecture is compacted into the thickness of the mask that makes this sensuous vision possible.

The eye of the whitewash, like the decorative art of the past, is first and foremost a system of representation. Such systems change as technologies are transformed. Modernity is the production of new ways of looking before it is the production of new forms. Le Corbusier finds what he calls a "new vision" in industrialized buildings and clothing styles that architecture, as a high art, a "visual" art in the traditional sense, actively resists. This reconfiguration of vision is sustained by the thickness of paint into which architecture is collapsed, Semper's "nonbodily surface" between inside and outside. Flattened, it is pure image, a two-dimensional projection of modern life. The white wall is a screen on which culture is projected: "The white of whitewash is absolute: everything stands out from it and is recorded absolutely, black on white; it is honest and dependable."[85] It is a recording device on which other textualities are registered, and with which they are accommodated.

Architecture is to be found in these new textiles. It responds to transformations in the systems of communication—railway, automobile, aeroplane, gramophone, radio, camera, cinema, and telephone—before it responds to the isolated objects of industrialized everyday life.[86] Le Corbusier reinterprets the whitewash of vernacular culture in terms of these contemporary mechanisms, new languages that appear to operate increasingly independently of buildings. He places architecture within systems that do not require a structural prop. The whitewash dematerializes building in order to make a space for these systems, a space for new spacings, new sensualities. It is a double gesture. Architecture accommodates the new systems and is, at the same time, accommodated within them. The seemingly straightforward and clearly articulated white wall participates in a radically convoluted geometry that eludes conventional analysis of visual form. It is folded into other less visible fabrics in intriguing knots whose twists echo those that Semper studied so closely.

In the end, the whitewash promoted in *L'art décoratif d'aujourd'hui* answers the leading question of Le Corbusier's youth—"Where is architecture?"—by locating architecture in the seemingly elusive space of communication, a space that is only partially visible as such. In the same year, he reopens the question in an essay literally entitled "Où en est l'architecture?" that confronts his earlier definition of the house as a "machine for dwelling," seeing such a mechanism as being but one stop on the way toward architecture and concluding: "Where is Architecture? It is beyond the machine."[87] The question does not go away. Indeed, it is opened further by every attempt to close it. *Croisade, ou le crépuscule des académies* (Crusade, or the twilight of the academies) of 1933 again asks "What is architecture? Where is architecture?" and answers that architecture is in the ordering of the material world, as exemplified in the order of nature, rather than in the highly decorated monumental buildings promoted by the academies.[88] The smooth metal surfaces of modern engineering structures are architectural inasmuch as they establish a unique order and thereby make available a new world and a new way of engaging with that world. In a polemical illustration, the static view of the ornate surfaces of a palace is literally displaced by the mobile view from the front of a train, one that reframes both the old buildings of the city and the new engineering structures that now inhabit that city. For Le Corbusier, the new architecture is not so much to be found in the smooth metal surfaces of the train but the view that those surfaces make available. One system of communication is displaced by another. Architecture is a way of looking, a way of asking questions rather than a phenomenon to be found in a certain place.

1.13
Illustration from Le Corbusier, Croisade, ou le crépuscule des académies, *1933.*

Twenty-five years after Le Corbusier "discovered" architecture in the white walls of the Mediterranean vernacular, his last extended discourse on the unique status of white walls, *Quand les cathédrales étaient blanches* of 1937, returns to the same question. Because it is the gesture of placing, architecture has no intrinsic place: "Where does architecture belong? In everything!"[89] It can only be placed by a specific architecture, an ensemble of representational techniques which preserves specific institutional agendas. Le Corbusier's arguments about whitewash disturb such agendas and mobilize new techniques. They translate Semper's argument in the face of the emerging twentieth-century systems of representation, subverting the account of architecture with which traditional discourse has tacitly organized its sense of visuality long before it explicitly attempts to place architecture within the visual. The architect sketches not so much a new kind of object with a particular look, but an architecture by which the institution of architectural discourse can occupy the decorative art of today, the sensuous space of communication—an architecture that is all but invisible to the art-historical servants of philosophy. It is not just the white coat that is so routinely overlooked by the discourse but also these less obvious garments that the modern architect would have us wear. To even begin to grasp their architectural function, and thereby address the question "where is architecture" that has become even more urgent in an electronic age, it is necessary to return to the old logic of clothing that underpins the white wall. The white layer needs to be explored much more slowly and in much more detail. It is a matter of going even deeper into the surface.

The fashion has somewhat worn itself out, but to white the word fashion never can apply. White always has been used and probably always will be in some form or other, in every dwelling.

    —C. H. Eaton et al., *Paint and its Part in Architecture*, 1930.

2

The Fashion Police

When Le Corbusier reactivates the white wall, he attempts to mobilize it to the most modern of agendas while crediting it with some kind of trans-historical status. The white garment is meant to be at once up-to-date and timeless. The architect enters the fickle world of clothing to extract the seeming stable order of the man's suit. While all such type-forms are meant to be changed, the changes have to last much longer than a season. The white wall is meant to precede fashions rather than participate in them. At the end of *L'art décoratif d'aujourd'hui,* Le Corbusier argues that the "decisive" phase of his formative years began when he rejected the architectural fashions of the metropolis and headed off in search of the world as yet "unspoiled" by such suspect trends:

This [phase] again finds me travelling abroad in quest of the lesson that will clarify my mind, and in an attempt to capture the source of art, the reason for art, the role of art. I acquainted myself with the fashions of Paris, Vienna, Berlin, Munich. Everything about all these fashions seemed to be dubious. . . . I embarked on a great journey, which was to be decisive, through the countryside and cities of countries still considered unspoiled. . . . After such a voyage my respect for decoration was finally shattered.[1]

The discovery of white walls in the Mediterranean, the buildings "clothed in a majestic coat of whitewash," as *Le voyage d'Orient* puts it,[2] is the discovery of the clothing that precedes fashion, the garment that enables the fashionable condition of all other garments to be exposed and removed. The garment that, if you put it on, allows you to appear undressed. Still, like Semper, Le Corbusier has to guard against the ever-present dangers of fashion that his understanding of architecture as clothing raises. If the decorative styles he wants to strip off are "no more than an accidental surface modality, super-added to facilitate composition, stuck on to disguise faults, or duplicated for the sake of display,"[3] the whitewash that displaces them is just as much a surface modality that exposes architecture to all of the same risks. By removing the authority of the structure and investing everything in the surface, the architect exposes architecture to the degenerate potential of the surface that modern architecture is meant to stand against. Drifting somewhere between the fickle world of fashion and the permanence of art, architecture needs to be disciplined against the dangers posed by its very means of operation. Because this discipline cannot be provided by the structure, the only role of which is to prop the garments up, a whole new regime of control has to be instituted to regulate the surface.

Modern architecture was explicitly launched against fashion, and its white surfaces played a key role in that attack. Its very modernity was repeatedly identified with the rejection of architecture's nineteenth-century immersion in the world of fashion. As the architecture's most influential manifesto—*Vers une architecture*—puts it, the "styles" of nineteenth-century architecture are but "the old clothes of a past age," clothes that "are to architecture what a feather is on a woman's head; it is sometimes pretty, though not always, and never anything more."[4] For Le Corbusier, it is not just that this feminine clothing is a superfluous accessory added to the body of architecture, a decorative mask irresponsibly changed according to the dictates of the latest fashion. Even the organization of the building's structure that such fashions mask has been subjected to the seasonal mentality of fashion, because "architects work in 'styles' or discuss questions of structure in and out of season."[5] But with the relentless emergence of new technologies that both mark and instigate modernity, the old clothes no longer even fit the body: "construction has undergone innovations so great that the old 'styles,' which still obsess us, can no longer clothe it; the materials employed evade the attentions of the decorative artist."[6] It would seem that modern architecture literally begins with the removal of the florid fashionable clothing of the nineteenth century. The first act of modernization strips architecture and the second disciplines the structure that has been exposed. Both are explicitly understood as acts against the suspect forces of fashion. Modern architecture disciplines itself against fashion from the beginning.

Each of Le Corbusier's polemics is framed by such a rejection of fashion. His original manifesto for Purism, written with Amédée Ozenfant in 1920, concludes by saying: "One could make an art of allusions, an art of fashion, based upon surprise and the conventions of the initiated. Purism strives for an art free of conventions which will utilize plastic constants and address itself above all to the universal properties of the senses and the mind."[7] The seminal "Fünf Punkte zu einer neuen Architektur" (Five points of a new architecture), written with Pierre Jeanneret in 1927 to describe the thinking behind their houses for the Weissenhofsiedlung, begins by asserting: "Theory requires precise formulation. We are totally uninterested in aesthetic fantasies or attempts at fashionable gimmicks. We are dealing here with architectural facts which point to an absolutely new kind of building."[8] Likewise, Le Corbusier's account of the overall trajectory of his work in the 1929 introduction to the first volume of the *Oeuvre Complète* symptomatically begins by opposing fashion:

As I believe profoundly in our age, I continue to analyze the elements which are determining its character, and do not confine myself to trying to make its exterior manifestations comprehensible. What I seek to fathom is its deeper, its constructive sense. Is not this the essence, the very purpose of architecture? Differences of style, the trivialities [*frivolités*] of passing fashion, which are only illusions or masquerades, do not concern me.[9]

The text then literally applies this generic image of fashion—as the exterior mask of an age that contradicts or dissimulates its inner structure—to buildings. The inner truth of modern construction is opposed to the exterior lie of the decorative masquerade that conceals it. The mask worn by a building veils its construction by literally covering it and by misrepresenting it. But it is not simply the disorderly surfaces of ornament that pose a serious threat. Rather, it is their concealment of an internal disorder. Le Corbusier goes on to cite his mentor Auguste Perret's claim that ornament "always hides some fault of construction." Indeed, it is not that the superficial ornament is necessarily disorderly. On the contrary, it is precisely by representing a nonexistent order that the ornament can most threaten order. As such representations are rapidly changed according to the whims of fashion and independently of the structures they appear to articulate, this threat is greatly intensified.

Fashion is therefore the greatest danger of ornament, the extreme case of the ever-present risk of "mere" decoration against which architecture must be constantly disciplined. Le Corbusier predictably describes his own work as proceeding while "the architects of all countries were still busy *decorating*" but adds in parentheses: "whether with or without the direct application of ornament."[10] The crime of the architect-as-decorator is not simply decorating architecture by adding gratuitous ornament to it, but rendering architecture decorative by making it subservient to the fickle sensibility of fashion rather than fixed standards like those offered by the new means of industrialized production. The risk of decoration is nothing more than a certain mobility of representation, an instability of the surface that effaces the ancient sense of order that the latest technologies unconsciously revive. The modern is advertised as the return of the transcultural and transhistorical truth that Le Corbusier repeatedly associates with the architecture of ancient Greece.

Regardless of its particular relationship to ornament, the change to a "modern" architecture has to be disassociated from a change of fashion in every detail. It must be presented as a change of an entirely different order—a difficult claim to make and one that must constantly be reasserted because it is so vulnerable to the counter-charge that nothing could be more fashionable, more a la mode, than "the modern." Furthermore, once architecture has changed, there cannot be very much additional mobility. Each subsequent change, no matter how minor, has to be differentiated from fashion by being tied to the logic of a fundamental break necessitated by new materials and the technologies by which they are assembled. Construction and function must be seen to immobilize and thereby subordinate all the surfaces of architecture.

Indeed, the building must somehow exhibit this subordination. Or, more precisely, its surfaces must exhibit their subordination to something either hidden within them or displayed in front of them that is of a higher order. The inevitably time-bound surface must somehow exhibit timeless values. In the very name of modernity, time must be brought to a standstill. In the end, it is this exhibition of the subordinated surface, rather than an exhibition of the new means of production, that renders architecture modern. In a strange way, architecture can become modern before it fully engages with the forces of modernization. Its surfaces are not simply cleansed of ornament, the structure stripped of clothing, the layers of representation scraped off to expose the abstract forms of modern life, and so on. Rather, the surfaces are trained to represent the very process of cleansing, stripping, and scraping. The resistance to fashion is not so much achieved as constantly staged. Modern architecture is a kind of performance, both in terms of the specific details of buildings and the discourse that frames them. The white surface obviously plays a key role in this performance by announcing that the building is naked.

Much of the discourse around modern architecture can therefore be understood as an ongoing preemptive defense against the charge that it is itself a fashion. Fashion is portrayed as an insidious phenomenon that will inevitably return to contaminate the pure logic of architecture unless it is consciously held in check. To resist it requires a special vigilance. Most of the discourse of modern architecture is written by self-appointed watchdogs through which it constantly monitors itself, publicly censoring certain architects, building types, compositions, materials, and details as "decorative." The surfaces of both buildings and the texts that describe them are religiously scrutinized for signs of such "degeneration," "deviance," "contamination" and so on; each such term being explicitly mobilized in reference to suspect stereotypes of race, class, gender, and sexual orientation. But it is the word "fashion" that usually marks the ultimate moment of excommunication. To be branded as "merely" fashionable is to be ostracized.

This watchdog mentality is exemplified in the writings of Sigfried Giedion, the leading promoter of the movement and the very active secretary of C.I.A.M. (Congrès Internationaux d'Architecture Moderne), its at once promotional and defensive—if not disciplinary—body. He describes modern architecture as the effect of an ethical refusal of the seductions of fashionable

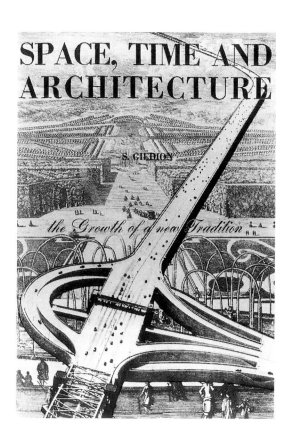

SPACE, TIME AND ARCHITECTURE

S. GIEDION

the Growth of a new Tradition

2.1
Cover of Sigfried Giedion, Space, Time and Architecture, *1941.*

2.2
Cover of Sigfried Giedion, Bauen in Frankreich. Eisen. Eisenbeton., 1928. Design by Lászlo Moholy-Nagy.

clothing in *Space, Time and Architecture: The Growth of a New Tradition,* a heavy book based on a series of lectures delivered at Harvard University between 1938 and 1939 at the invitation of Walter Gropius. The book was published in 1941 and immediately became the standard textbook on modern architecture for generations of architects and was regularly updated until a revised and enlarged version of the fifth edition came out 1969, a year after his death. Like Le Corbusier, Giedion identifies the styles of nineteenth-century architecture as fashion-conscious clothing, describing them as "the Harlequin dress of architecture." In so doing, he picks up the expression used by nineteenth-century critics to condemn stylistic eclecticism but argues that it refers to "a disease which is still malignant in our day," before adding, "nevertheless, beneath all the masquerade, tendencies of lasting importance lay hidden and were slowly gathering strength."[11] Underneath the dissimulating and distracting layers of fashion that cover architecture, new technologies of construction were supposedly developing. The removal of fashion is again literally identified with the removal of ornamental clothing. Without fashion, there is "no disguise of structure." Relieved of the burden of carrying a mask, structure is able to develop freely and a new architecture emerges that embodies truths of material construction and functional utility independent of the vagaries of fashion.

This argument had already been put in place by Giedion's *Bauen in Frankreich. Eisen. Eisenbeton.* (Building in France. Iron. Concrete.) of 1928, which, in turn, was based on a series of articles he had published in the Berlin art journal *Der Cicerone* over the two previous years. Again, nineteenth-century architecture is seen to wear a "historical mask," which veils the emerging forms of construction that are fundamentally changing a building's mode of operation: "the new system was shrouded in the old formal decorations."[12] The endless search for style is dismissed as but "wrinkles on the surface," "academic encrustations," the "haut-goût" of "architectural appendages" that "suffocate the building spirit." The book attempts to "peel off an outer layer from the century" in order to expose the modernity trapped underneath this suffocating mask. It does so by looking at the various transformations of buildings that occurred before architects got a chance to wrap them up in fashionable clothes and those parts of buildings that architects did not bother to clothe because they thought no one was looking, the adventurous developments hidden, as Giedion puts it, "behind the scenes" of architecture. To go around and behind the architects, he examines everyday, anonymous, and temporary constructions that had been put in the

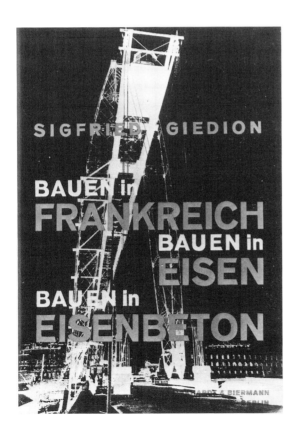

hands of engineers. The architects are then measured against the engineers. Their role is simply to transfer the new engineering realities to the sphere of "living space" by subordinating all surface play to the rigors of structural work, smoothing out the prematurely wrinkled skin of the building's young body, then putting that attractive body to work on new tasks.

The book is highly selective of the architects, buildings, and details with which it makes its case; praising those who, like Henri Labrouste, "saw the construction as the intimate side of architecture—the outside of buildings being mere wrapping (envelope) or skin" and slighting those like the "elegant," "formalist" Rob Mallet-Stevens, who apparently concern themselves only with the skin and thereby assist architecture's regression into the decorative folly of fashion.[13] The book everywhere discriminates between progressive and regressive developments, monitoring architectural discourse like some kind of surveillance device looking for small flaws, traces of decorative play that act as telltale signs of a recurrence of fashion. *Space, Time and Architecture* resumes this surveillance operation, but on a much larger scale, broadening the field of inquiry and adding more and more territory with each successive edition, while remaining just as selective, if not more so. Those modernists who were previously identified with fashion, like Mallet-Stevens, are no longer even mentioned, a gesture that, as Richard Becherer has argued, was faithfully repeated by subsequent historians.[14] As the years pass, the book maintains its alert stance against any possible contamination of the cause by fashion.

It is crucial to note that this sense of fashion—operative, if not an organizing force, in so much of the discourse around modern architecture—is explicitly associated with a psychology. *Bauen in Frankreich* identifies the new reality hidden behind the dissimulating layers of ornament, which have been mobilized by fashion's obsessive logic of compulsory change, with the "unconscious" of architecture: "In the 19th century, the construction only played a subconscious role. On the outside the old-fashioned pathos reigned ostentatiously. Underneath, hidden behind the facade, the foundations of all our present being took shape."[15] The story of modern architecture is the story of how this unconscious constructive reality came to the surface and "leaked out." This quasi-therapeutic narrative is continued in *Space, Time and Architecture,* which again describes modern construction technologies as "the unconscious," and elaborates the point by tacitly associating the role of the historian with that of the psychoanalyst who patiently reads the surfaces, looking at the marginal traces of everyday life for the small and easily overlooked gaps, slips, and displacements that mark the relentless operation of a repressed system.[16] The book attempts to trace the way these unconscious tendencies gave rise to a new architecture by eventually forcing their way to the surface.[17]

It is only in the less obvious, usually overlooked, domain of anonymous industrial buildings, or the backs and hidden details of public buildings, that these developments occur. They necessarily take place out of sight, away from the eyes that would find them shocking and demand that they be covered with clothes. As Giedion puts it, "the moment the nineteenth century feels itself unobserved and has no longer to make a show, then it is truly bold."[18] Unrestricted by ill-fitting clothes designed only to please a nervous external eye, construction is finally able to emerge and transform itself. As the new forms of construction gain confidence, they are able to gradually move from the back stage to the foreground, such that "the undisguised shapes . . . that mark the rear and unobserved portions of railroad stations and factories begin to make themselves felt in the front walls of buildings," particularly in temporary constructions like Paxton's Crystal Palace, which, symptomatically, "aroused feelings that seemed to belong only to the world of dreams."[19] The dreamworld of architecture starts to become visible. Eventually, architects are able to take responsibility for this dreamworld in permanent buildings in a gradual process that begins with Peter Behrens's engagement with factory design in 1909 and slowly develops, until finally, when the sheer glass curtain wall of Walter Gropius's 1925–1956 Bauhaus building in Dessau wraps itself around the corner, the unconscious of architecture has become

2.3
Walter Gropius, Bauhaus Building, Dessau, 1926. Illustration from Sigfried Giedion, Bauen in Frankreich.

the consciousness of the enlightened architect. Modern architecture arrives as such when the details of Gropius's design are understood "not as unconscious outgrowths of advances in engineering but as the conscious realization of an artist's intent."[20] It is not that the unconscious of architecture has finally been liberated, or even absorbed into the architect's consciousness. Rather, it has been relocated, accommodated, and disciplined.

This discipline is required because, for Giedion, the suspect desire to adorn architecture with fashionable clothing is not produced by a love of clothing but by an anxiety about what that clothing will cover. The historicist clothes are not simply old garments that are no longer necessary or fit the new body of architecture badly. Rather, they have only recently been put on to deny that there is a new body. *Bauen in Frankreich* specifically identifies the use of historical clothes as a mask that is worn to cover new anxieties about industrialization: "The nineteenth century disguised its new creations with a historical mask, indifferently in all fields. This is just as true for architecture as it is for industry or society. New building methods were invented, but they created a climate of fear which suffocated them with an uncertainty, relegating them to behind the scenes of stone."[21] The apparently gratuitous changes of fashion are actually a form of nervous resistance to the real changes going on. Hidden by the apparently playful surfaces of eclectic decoration is the serious fear of mechanization. As a result, "all the century's buildings were put up with a guilty conscience or with insecurity, so to speak."[22] Ironically, inasmuch as fashion is a symptom of the repression of modernity, it becomes, for Giedion, an inadvertent symptom of modernity. The more frenetic the changes in clothing, the more insecurity must have been produced by modern techniques, encouraging the historian to uncover their hidden operations. For the psychohistorian, the dissimulating movements of fashion end up pointing to the very reality they attempt to conceal.

This association between fashion and insecurity is elaborated in the article "Mode oder Zeiteinstellung" (Fashion or the condition of the times) that Giedion published in a 1932 issue of *Information,* the anti-fascist magazine he edited. It warns against again being "suffocated," as in the nineteenth century, by "complexes about the past" that cover up the nightmares of the present: "Insecurity and the need to come out in favor of second-hand issues only reigns everywhere. Fashion reigns everywhere in place of seriously taking sides on the issues of the age."[23] People use fashion to "shield themselves on two sides." But this defensive layer of "surface appearance" is not simply made up of old styles laid over new structures. It is also made up of new styles laid over old structures. Objects are chosen that look modern: "That is, the external formula of new products that really stem from their own time

2.4
Frontispiece of
Information *(Zurich),*
June 1932.

are borrowed and applied to the old body or the old mentality, just as one glues on ornament."[24] Consequently, most contemporary objects are neither old nor new. They neither promote nor resist the modern age. Rather, they replace the "condition of the times" with a persistent code of "fashionable conduct" that affects all objects, including architecture and urban design. This "intrusion of second-hand fashion in all areas of design" produces and is produced by a profound psychological insecurity in which "we are internally divided." More precisely, "self-certainty has dwindled" and "everyone feels it in their own person."[25] Giedion actually proposes that history is the only agent of recovery from this malaise because it can provide "an overview of our ego" that tracks the way in which modern developments have already, albeit slowly, "penetrated the general consciousness" despite fashion's concerted attempt to stall them.[26] History is literally prescribed as the appropriate therapy for the neurotic addiction to fashion. By systematically uncovering the fundamental condition of modern life that lies beneath the dissimulating layers of fashion, the historian can facilitate the emergence of the "new order" without anxiety. Writing history is a form of construction rather than a commentary on it. As Giedion concludes: "Today categorizing is more important than inventing."[27] New forms are produced by reclassifying old ones.

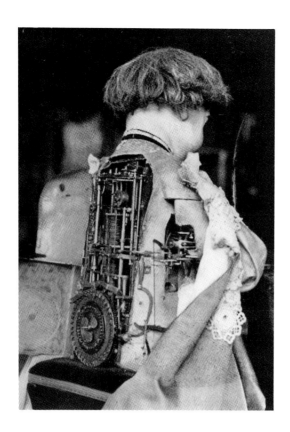

2.5
*"Automaton: writing
doll, made by Pierre
Jaquet-Droz, Neuchâtel,
about 1770." Illustration
from Sigfried Giedion,*
Space, Time and
Architecture.

It is not surprising, then, that such a bond between fashion and the insecurity of the modern underwrites *Space, Time and Architecture,* Giedion's explicit attempt at such a therapeutic history. The text guards itself against the darker side of industrialization as much as it guards itself against fashion: "the destruction of man's inner quiet and security has remained the most conspicuous effect of the industrial revolution. The individual goes under before the march of production; he is devoured by it."[28] Indeed, for Giedion, the threat to humanity is made emblematic by the figure of the *automaton,* the mechanized human, the unfeeling robot. Industrialization is seen to have produced a fatal split between feeling and thought, a split that would become the major theme of his extraordinary *Mechanization Takes Command* of 1948. The staccato attacks on fashion that punctuated Giedion's early essays were gradually propped up by a detailed analysis of the conditions that are seen to have forced the adoption of fashion as a kind of psychological defense.

This analysis was continued in Giedion's Mellon lectures, delivered in 1957 at the National Gallery of Art in Washington, D.C. He looked at the origins of the arts in order to find some prehistoric condition that could be found within contemporary artistic practices, grounding their radical explosion of space and time in some fundamental condition of the human psyche. The lectures attempt to find a fixed structure that underpins current changes and distinguishes them from changes in fashion. For some years, the lectures were elaborated into manuscript form and then summarized in the inaugural Gropius lecture at Harvard in 1961 under the title "Constancy and Change in Architecture" before being published in two large volumes: *The Eternal Present: The Beginnings of Art,* which came out one year later, and *The Eternal Present: The Beginnings of Architecture,* which was published in 1964. The first volume begins by repeating the quasi-psychoanalytic claim that a history "of what has been suppressed and driven back into the unconscious," is needed to counter the "incessant demand for change for change's sake."[29] The relentless and psychologically damaging logic of fashion can only be blocked by "restoring" these buried conditions. Giedion argues that while the historical avant-garde produced radically new work, effecting an "optical revolution" that launches a "new tradition," its very newness involves the recovery of transhistorical constants, such that by the sixties "a painting of 1910 does not hurt the eye as something 'out of fashion', something alien to the present day."[30] Furthermore, such work is understood as a weapon against fashion to be deployed in the everyday battle for psychological security. The same argument underwrites the second volume, which attempts to isolate modern architecture from fashion by grounding it in prehistory, producing a history of three "space conceptions" through the millennia in which the third one, still being produced, is seen to recover much of the first one that "develops instinctively, usually remaining in the unconscious."[31] No matter how high-tech it is, an architecture is only modern inasmuch as it reconnects anxious people to their pretechnological roots.

Giedion would go on to elaborate this history in his last book *Architecture and the Phenomenon of Transition,* the final manuscript of which he delivered the day before his death in April 1968. His lifelong attempt to find a solid ground from which the restless movements of fashion could be distinguished from the necessary evolution of a new order had mobilized massive historiographic resources and produced a succession of monumental volumes that monitored a millennial field with a series of simple but globalizing arguments.[32] The surveillance operation that began on the pages of *Der Cicerone* had covered an ever-increasing territory with a methodical sweep whose encyclopedic quality was already established with Giedion's barrage of articles for *Cahiers d'Art* between 1928 and 1934 that systematically surveyed the production of modern architecture in each country of the world before being literalized when he was asked to do the architectural entries for *Encyclopedia Britannica* in 1957.

But, as this sheer weight of material might indicate, Giedion had long been on the defense. It is not by chance that he was reaching back as far as the ancient Egyptians for security at the very moment that he was adding a new introduction to the final edition of *Space, Time and Architecture* that portrays contemporary architecture as having to purge itself of fashion in the same way as it had at the turn of the century. Modern architecture is seen to have regressed into a form of stylistic eclecticism resembling that of the nineteenth century it had worked so hard to displace. He condemns the new "fashions" of the architecture of the 1960s that, after the International Style "had worn thin," exhibit a "tendency to degrade the wall with new decorative elements."[33] The purity of modern architecture has not merely given way to the immoral excesses of the 1960s that disfigure the smooth white wall. Rather, modern architecture has itself been appropriated as a fashionable style of "en vogue" superficialities. Insisting that modern architecture is "not a sudden, quickly devalued, fashion,"[34] Giedion defends the original polemic of his own textbook from appropriation as a set of fashion tips.

In so doing, he echoes his original defense of the first polemic on the subject—Otto Wagner's 1896 manifesto *Moderne Architektur,* which, like *Space, Time and Architecture,* was, as Giedion puts it, "soon translated into many languages" and "became the textbook of the new movement." Just as he had defended that manifesto against the critics who claimed when it was first pub-

2.6
*Sigfried Giedion (sitting)
with Walter Gropius at
CIAM 6, Bridgewater,
1947.*

lished that Wagner was "a sensation-monger, a train-bearer of fashion,"[35] Giedion resists the possibility that his own attempt to detach fashion from architecture is nothing more than the preparation for a new fashion. In fact, he had already defended modern architecture against the threat of dismissal as a new fashion in a newspaper article of 1927 entitled "Ist das neue Bauen eine Mode?" (The new building, is it a fashion?)[36] The argument about fashion written into all of his work is, from the beginning, at once an attack and a defense.

The double-sided quality of Giedion's engagement with the question of fashion is exemplary of the whole discourse. The same identification of fashion with a generalized psychopathology of insecurity in the face of modernity can be found throughout the promotion of modern architecture. And it is not that this generic argument is simply applied to the ready-made forms of that architecture, or even used to supervise their construction. Rather, modern architecture is constituted as such by that very argument. The argument produces what it appears to merely describe. Giedion, for example, does not pretend that his writing simply offers a commentary on an existing tendency, acknowledging, with his very first lines, that he actively constructs that tendency as such because the historian inevitably rearranges the past in the light of present conceptions and "the backward look transforms its object."[37] In an extraordinary gesture, the reader of *Space, Time and Architecture* is first taken through a lengthy chapter on the active role of history in everyday life and in the production of architecture. But perhaps only the acknowledgment that this is the case is unique. The wider discourse about modern architecture and the events that it addresses, including the specific details of architectural designs, are likewise structured by particular arguments about fashion. In fact, the antifashion argument has a unique privilege, a special hold on the protagonists, a vicelike grip on the discourse that appears to employ it only occasionally, if not tacitly.

The grip has yet to be eased. Contemporary discourse about architecture continues to be organized around nervous but sustained attacks on fashion. If anything, the campaign has been stepped up. All forms of debate are punctuated by sermons on the complicity between architecture and fashion, the symptoms of which can seemingly be found everywhere. In addition to the traditional sense of architectural styles as fashions, there are the obvious symptoms like architects appearing in advertisements for clothing designers and stores, the featuring of architects and buildings in fashion magazines, fashion supplements in architectural magazines, fashion designers branching out into architectural design, architects branching out into designing clothes and other fashionable objects, the signature architecture of fashion stores, the emergence of fashion magazines specializing in promoting architecture, and so on. But there are also the less obvious symptoms: the strategic role of architecture in fashion images, the architecture of the fashion show, the actual "look" of architects, the architectonics of clothing, the ongoing transformations in the language used by architects and critics, the oblique but critical role of architect-designed objects and spaces in establishing identity in the mass media, and so on. Indeed, a whole terrain of effects presents itself, if not imposes itself, and demands some kind of sustained reading.

The phenomenon is often referred to but its symptoms have rarely been examined in any detail. Rather, they are simplistically and repeatedly identified as unquestionable evidence of the commodification of architectural discourse that is by now routinely associated with "postmodernism." In the most developed of such arguments, architectural discourse is not understood as postmodern simply because of the concern some of its participants might have with eclectic practices of decoration. Rather, it is the way the discourse itself operates as a form of superstructural decoration in contemporary society—despite architecture's ostensibly structural relationship to the dominant economic forces, given the amount of resources it inevitably mobilizes. This decorative role is portrayed as a loss of political agency, or, more precisely, the loss of a critical political agency in favor of a relentlessly conservative maintenance of given power relations. The conservatism of the discipline is not identified with the static nature of its forms, its conservation of an aesthetic or technological tradition, but with its fluidity, its capacity to circulate and recirculate heterogeneous forms in response to the eccentric rhythms of a fickle market. Architecture's complicity with the most transient aspects of commodity culture is seen to parallel and support its apparently tangential cultural role—one whose very tangentiality masks a fundamental complicity, a passivity that actively preserves suspect socioeconomic structures. Its fashion-conscious concern for "the look" that can be sold to an empowered client assumes political force, sustaining the overt and covert mechanisms of that empowerment.

It is in these terms that the discipline of architecture is seen to participate in the general phenomenon of postmodernism, understood as a collapse of the millennial discourses organized around the unified subject, originality, authorship, identity, and so on. Each of these threatened values is identified with a sense of interior. The phenomenon is no more than a crisis of interiority in which a whole series of supposedly stable interior values are displaced onto seemingly ephemeral exterior surfaces. Indeed, it is often explicitly described as a fetishistic obsession with surface at the expense of (what was once understood as) a concern for material and economic structure. It should go without saying that this generic description becomes all too literally applied when architecture is described as postmodern inasmuch as it is dedicated to the production and reproduction of fashionable surfaces.[38] But it is important to note that this generic account is not simply applied to architecture. On the contrary, architecture is its paradigm. Since around 1984, almost all the influential writers on the question of the postmodern, whether for, against, or sideways, have addressed architecture in order to elaborate their position, arguing that not only is it the field in which the term first gained currency but also that it articulates the phenomenon more clearly than any other. Architecture has become the vehicle of both the celebration and condemnation of the so-called postmodern condition.

Indeed, it can be argued that the construction of the very category "postmodern" turns on a certain account of architecture, or, more precisely, a certain account of "modern" architecture. Contemporary trends in diverse fields, trends that threaten the very identity of those fields, are contrasted with the rejection of decorative surface by modern architects in favor of fundamental social structure. Images of white buildings by Le Corbusier are used surprisingly often to exemplify this social project. The rejection of nineteenth-century eclectic styles in favor of the clean-edged smooth white surface is used as a model for the contemporary critic's own rejection of postmodernism. In a quirky, but common, form of transference, the apparent rejection of particular forms by a particular historical avant-garde is tacitly extended into a model for the contemporary rejection of the means by which forms are reproduced, circulated, and consumed in the, by now, electronic marketplace. The white surface is deployed, as it were, against surface. It apparently neutralizes the seductions of surface exploited by postmodernism and thereby makes available the structural issues that the fashionable play with external effects is designed to cover.

These images of white walls are usually installed without discussion, as if they have a unique ability to exemplify the complex arguments they punctuate. Their pale, almost ghostly, surface haunts the discourse like a spectral guarantee of some unspoken order. The polemical struggle over the contemporary economy of fashion is somehow underwritten by these less than innocent images. And when that discourse, as it were, returns to architecture by addressing architecture's involvement in the postmodern economy, their already complicated role is, at the very least, further convoluted. Or, more precisely, some of the convolutions that already structure architectural discourse become evident. The strategic status of these images is transformed. Some of their already strange effects become even stranger, while others are normalized in institutionally crucial ways. Likewise, the argument about the general phenomenon of fashion that the images supposedly secure is displaced and other arguments emerge that, in turn, open up new readings of architecture.

To even begin to address the complex role that fashion plays in the contemporary commodification of architecture, we must return to the sense of modern architecture that is seen to precede it. In particular, we must return to the white wall and scratch its surface to see exactly what it is made of.

Closet Operatives

If modern architecture haunts contemporary debates then it is itself haunted by the specter of fashion. Fashion provides the basic frame of the discourse, its limit condition. Although the phenomenon is rarely, if ever, analyzed as such, and the term is only occasionally invoked to reestablish the limits, the space of modern architecture is defined by its exclusion of fashion. Furthermore, fashion is everywhere inscribed within the very system it delimits. It is never simply excluded. Or, more precisely, the very gesture of exclusion is so institutionalized that fashion ends up being a vital part of the system. Throughout Le Corbusier's canonic writings, for example, the rhetoric of "eternal truth," "spirit," "work," "order," "vigorous," "erect," "virginal," "rational," "standard," "essential," "honest," "life," "deep," "internal," and so on, is routinely opposed to that of "disorder," "chaos," "congestion," "intoxication," "play," "dishonesty," "illusion," "weakness," "sentimental," "trivial," "lies," "prostitution," "caprice," "arbitrary," "dishonesty," "death," "cosmetic," "seduction," "superficial," "veneer," "fake," "substitute," "superficiality," and so on. Each of the latter set of terms, which are always used to mark that which his work attempts to resist, are, in the end, and at symptomatic moments (whose specificity needs to be carefully analyzed in detail), identified with fashionable clothing styles. Fashion is the key.

Still, these isolated identifications offer only a preliminary map of the complex network of associations between clothing and architecture that underpin Le Corbusier's texts, organizing them—even if often against their apparent grain. The line of argument about fashion only occasionally becomes evident because it is twisted, folded over on itself in an eccentric geometry, a series of knots that, in their very convolution, tie together the discourse on modern architecture. It is not the overt argument about fashion that structures the texts but the complications of that argument, complications that rarely become visible as such. These complications, which not only bind Le Corbusier's texts together but also bind them to other texts in architecture and in other disciplines, profoundly disrupt traditional accounts of modern architecture. It is only by actively neglecting them that those accounts have been able to sustain certain suspect institutional structures. And it is only by reopening the question of fashion that these structures can begin to be interrogated.

Clearly, the enigmatic argument about fashion that underwrites modern architecture needs to be patiently tracked through its conceptual variations and historical specificity in much more detail to comprehend its considerable strategic effects. But how exactly should this be done? Fashion is never simply an object that can be scrutinized by a detached theory. The phenomenon, if that is what it is, can never be detached from the way it is read. Just as Le Corbusier passes seamlessly from describing himself as a kind of archaeologist of his own time, who recovers the inner logic of the age by going beyond the outer layers of fashion, to describing his work as being likewise stripped of fashionable ornament, Giedion's account of the modern architect is exactly the same as the account of the historian which precedes it. Supposedly, both the architect and the historian strip their objects of fashion. The opening chapter of *Space, Time, and Architecture* clarifies the therapeutic mission of history that had been prescribed in "Mode oder Zeiteinstellung?" by describing the task of the historian as clearing away the layers of fashion to discover the elemental truth they conceal and building a structure devoid of misleading superficial detail. The historian is an architect who must distinguish between the "transitory facts" and "constituent facts" that are usually "intermingled" in each site of investigation. Transitory facts are those with the seductive "dash and glitter" of fashions whose surface disorder must not be confused with the inner order of constituent facts, which, "when they are suppressed, inevitably reappear":

[the historian] can tell more or less short-lived novelties from genuinely new trends. . . . At first appearance they may have all the éclat and brilliance of a firework display, but they have no greater durability. Sometimes they are interlaced with every refinement of fashion. . . . These we shall call transitory facts. Transitory facts in their dash and glitter often succeed in taking over the center of the stage. This was the case with the experiments in historical styles that went on—with infinite changes in direction—throughout the whole nineteenth century.[39]

Giedion rehearses and elaborates the same point in *Mechanization Takes Command*. The historian's quasi-psychoanalytic reading is necessary because the surface play of fashion, the simulations of change with which each age nervously "drapes" itself, is actively involved in the suppression of the "fresh impulses," the constituent facts that have produced the nervousness because they are the possibility of real change. When these "repressed" impulses "come up again in man's consciousness," as they will inevitably do, they "form the solid ground for new departures," [40] the ground on which the architect/historian can construct a new way of life. The book attempts to foster such changes by directing attention to the various coming to terms with the unconscious that have already occurred. Consequently, its concern for the "symptoms" that are "at work beneath the surface" is a concern for the "influence of mechanization where it was not hampered by fashion." [41]

Here, as everywhere else, Giedion does not so much address fashion as invoke it. What is fashionable is, by definition, bad. The successive generations of historians of modern architecture have presupposed the same condemnation of fashion, sharing it with the historical figures they describe. It is in this way that they are, in the end, "operative" in Manfredo Tafuri's sense. In the very moment of asserting their neutrality under the guise of scholarly detachment, they insist on a particular ideological formation by projecting present values onto the past in order to project them into the future. [42] Even Tafuri, for whom Giedion is the very model of the operative critic, is operative by virtue of the way he positions fashion as an unproblematically pejorative term. Indeed, it can be argued that the very concept of operative criticism is itself operative inasmuch as the strategic abuse of history it refers to is aligned with fashion.

When Tafuri's influential *Teorie e storia dell'architettura* (Theories and histories of architecture) introduced the category of operative criticism in 1968 precisely to counter it, a footnote identifies its most degenerate forms as those organized by fashion: "One cannot sufficiently condemn the naive or snobbish attempt to read historical phenomena by 'present' yardsticks of those, who, for the sake of feeling 'alive' and up-to-date, reduce critical transvaluation to exhibitionism and fashion." [43] This opposition between history and fashion, which he symptomatically shares with the openly operative Giedion, [44] is exhibited in the opening lines, which identify the book's task as that of mapping the specific obstacles facing "historians who refuse the role of fashionable commentator, and who try to historicize their criticism." [45] These obstacles, in turn, are identified in the book's introduction with the unavoidable contradictions at work in the very idea of a history of the modern, given the ostensibly anti-historical stance of modern architects. When noting that contemporary architectural tendencies actually maintain this stance "behind the mask" of the new myths used to distance themselves from the historical avant-garde, Tafuri preserves the traditional opposition between a history that is critical in that it "digs deeper" and one "swallowed up by the daily mythologies," understood as fashionable masks: "The present moment, so totally bent on avoiding, through *new myths,* the commitment of understanding the present, cannot help turning even the researches that, with renewed vigor and rigor, try to plan a systematic and objective reading of the world, of things, of history and of human conventions into *fashion and myth*."[46] Tafuri actively resists the possibility, embedded within his own text, that what actually bonds contemporary practices to those of the historical avant-garde might not be what lies behind the fashionable mask but the fashionable mask itself.

This resistance is tested when the text later addresses the affinity between what seems to be a fashionably historicist use of "architectural images" by the Neo-Liberty school in Italy and the antihistorical stance of the modern movement it appears to emphatically reject. But the affinity is quickly described as being "underneath an immediately fashionable phenomenon"[47] rather than at the same level. The "garish" "farce" of Neo-Liberty that the text symptomatically identifies with Art Nouveau, the Baroque, and Fellini, and whose "equivocal quality" supposedly parallels the bourgeoisie's "own evasive costume," is seen to occur on the "fringe" of the modern project rather than contradicting or opposing it.[48] But it is seen to participate in that project because it only "flirts" with history and fails in its attempted "fetishism" of the architectural object, while leaving unquestioned the avant-garde's own fetishistic flirtations. Furthermore, what Neo-Liberty merely appears to reject is not the avant-garde itself but the consequence of its transformation into a fashionable form of eclecticism with the so-called International Style. In this way, modern architecture is doubly immunized against prosecution on the charge of fashion.[49]

Likewise, the book attempts to negotiate the specific terms of the same immunity for the historian, looking for the ways in which research can avoid becoming "another transient fashion under the flag of evasion,"[50] even if that involves a sustained silence.[51] The historical avant-garde acts here, as it does for so many contemporary writers, as the model of Tafuri's own practice. Consequently, it is exempted from certain interrogations that might threaten that practice, even in the middle of such a comprehensive and nuanced reading. Despite the book's constant call for a vigilantly self-critical stance like that supposedly assumed by the avant-garde, its analysis is, from the beginning, vulnerable to its own arguments about operative criticism. It is surprisingly reluctant to acknowledge the institutional practices it leaves intact, if not tacitly defends, most of which have survived the subsequent transformations in Tafuri's work. Despite the invaluable insights of his at times explicitly Nietzschean accounts of the ruses of history, his equally sophisticated accounts of the complex economies of the mask operating in different historical sites are never quite extended to his own practices as a historian, or even those of his practices that he later, emphatically, rejects.[52] While it can be demonstrated that his most Nietzschean account of history turns around, if not emerges out of, a certain account of fashion—to such an extent that it is illustrated with an image of a woman in a fashionable nineteenth-century dress which is polemically opposed to an image of a naked body which is in turn opposed to an image of a body without skin— Nietzsche's own refusal of a distinction between fashion and history is never mobilized.[53] On the contrary. Ten years after he distances himself from the final edition of *Teorie e storia dell'architettura,* Tafuri is still able to criticize the work of postmodern architects because "history has been reduced to fashion" and, like Giedion, he associates this with "anxiety" and "the sense of insecurity."[54] The term "fashion" retains its old disciplinary role in his argument, as it does throughout the economy of architectural theory that he is analyzing.

Indeed, later generations of "critical" writers have preserved this role for the term, deploying it at key points in their analysis without ever subjecting it to that analysis. The critical writer is understood to be, by definition, detached from fashion. Alternative modes of scholarship that are skeptical of the possibility of such a detached position are often dismissed as "fashionable," "chic," "modish," and so on by proponents of well-established modes of research who presuppose that fashion is inherently bad and have difficulty recognizing that their own adherence to one mode among others, let alone acknowledge the structural role of fashion in those sections of the archives that they privilege. As a disciplinary concept, fashion necessarily remains untheorized. It props up theory rather than subjects itself to theoretical analysis. To address the question of fashion and architecture here will inevitably be to address the curious role of theory in the constitution of architecture.

But can one suggest that any inquiry into fashion must reform or deflect the modes of inquiry, if not tease the limits of a discipline that constitutes itself by ostensibly rejecting fashion, whether that discipline be that of architecture or scholarly argument in general, without having that very suggestion either uncritically embraced by certain well defined groups of readers or uncritically censored by other groups as too fashionable? Probably not. And would not a rigorous interrogation of fashion, whatever that might mean, be rigorous only insofar as it confused the distinctions between such groups? Probably.

Anyway, it goes without saying that no discourse can simply isolate itself from fashion. At the very least, one is bound to ask here whether the question of fashion necessarily succumbs to what it addresses. To what extent does the very posing of the question commit us to a particular fashion regardless of our ostensible position on the subject? Either way, a more detailed (and fashion is, of course, always a question of details) account of fashion and its multiple and often conflicting relationships with architecture is needed. In the end, it is a question of the precise way that fashion is usually "intermingled," as Giedion says of the "dash and glitter" of transitory facts, with what seems to be its other. To scratch the white surface here will be to look for the ways in which it is constructed out of the very operations of fashion whose exclusion it supposedly confirms. To show, that is, that the supposedly neutral white surface glitters—dazzling its audience in a way that fosters a series of bizarre, but extremely influential, collective hallucinations.

2.7
Illustration from Manfredo Tafuri's "Il 'Progetto' Storico," Casabella, *1977.*

I met a whole swarm of architects who were seeking for the New, and sometimes found it.

—Paul Poiret, *En habillant l'epoque,* 1930.

13

Scratching the Surface

If modern architecture is nothing more than a particular form of clothing, then the sustained attack on fashion has to be carefully distinguished from an attack on clothing. It is necessary to explore the precise relationship between the white coat and the psychic and material economies of fashion by tracing the elusive role of Semper's identification of architecture and dress right up into the formulation of canonic modern architecture in the 1920s, following closely its seemingly relentless trajectory through the discourse as it affects, and even organizes, diverse and well-known formulations—many of which might appear, at first, to contradict it.

Building Modern Clothing

The first thing to take into account is the direct influence of Semper's argument. Take, for example, Louis Sullivan and Adolf Loos, the two so-called father figures of modern architecture who are repeatedly and simplistically identified with its two dominant advertising slogans: "form follows function" and "ornament is a crime." In each case, Semper's arguments are evident in the architect's writings and designs. Not only does Loos explicitly formulate his "Law of Dressing" as a slight modification of Semper's "Principle of Dressing" but he repeatedly identifies architecture with clothing design throughout his many essays, defending this association in the decisive "Architektur" essay of 1910, which praises the vernacular use of whitewash, by paraphrasing Semper's basic premise:

Many will have had doubts over my last remarks, doubts which are directed against the comparison which I have drawn between tailoring and architecture. After all, architecture is an art. Granted, it is for the time being. But have you never noticed the strange correspondence between the exterior dress of people and the exterior of buildings? Is the tasselled robe not appropriate to the Gothic Style and the wig to the Baroque? But do our contemporary houses correspond to our clothes?[1]

Likewise, Sullivan participated in the circle that studied, translated, and published Semper's theory in Chicago.[2] The effects of the theory on his writing—in its specific privileging of ornament—and his work—in its fabric-like weaving of ornamental surfaces—are obvious,[3] as it is in the work of his apprentices Frank Lloyd Wright and Walter Burley Griffin (when working in partnership with Wright's assistant Marion Mahony). It even becomes a kind of manifesto in Sullivan's use of "tapestry brick" arranged to give the building a finely textured surface like that, as he puts it, of an "oriental rug," and Wright and Griffin/Mahony's simultaneous development of "textile" construction systems. In each case, the decorative surface is literally woven into a structural frame for the building or, rather, the structure itself is woven into a decorative pattern. After all, Semper's argument does not simply privilege ornament. It equally involves the clarification of the structural frame.

Indeed, it can be argued that it is precisely the influence of Semper that leads to Loos and Sullivan's stereotypically modern call for a stripping of ornament. Loos visited Sullivan during the time that he was studying Semper, initiating a lifelong correspondence of mutual admiration, and later, as is often pointed out, based his infamous "Ornament and Crime" essay of 1908 on Sullivan's well-known "Ornament in Architecture" essay of 1892 that proposes a moratorium on ornament in favor of "nude" buildings.[4]

As "fathers," Loos and Sullivan are, of course, treated ambiguously by the historiographers of modern architecture. Giedion is clearly nervous about them. This nervousness is arguably produced by their debt to Semper, which commits them at once to ornament and to its reduction, making them exemplars of the modern project and historical figures who must be held apart from that project lest their ambiguity contaminate and irreducibly complicate the formulation of a marketable canon. Although this early isolation has been successively renegotiated as each respective figure—and the image of modern architecture with which they are both held in ambiguous tension—is repeatedly reconstructed, the nervousness remains. Although images of Loos's Villa Steiner and Sullivan's Schlesinger and Mayer (now Carson Pirie Scott) department store, for example, still populate most of the standard histories and

3.1
Louis Sullivan, Schlesinger and Mayer department store, 1899–1904, as published in Architectural Record, *July 1904.*

3.2

*Detail of Schlesinger and
Mayer department store.
Illustration from Sigfried
Giedion,* Space, Time and
Architecture *with the
caption: "Outstanding
for strength and purity of
expression even in the
work of Louis Sullivan."*

cement certain key transitions in the respective arguments, the images almost
always show the undecorated white orthogonal rear of the villa and privilege
the orthogonal frame faced with white terra cotta tiles of the department
store, rather than the curved front (let alone the more ornate interior) of the
former or the heavily ornamented ground floors and entrance of the latter.
Giedion goes as far as to insist that the curve of the entrance was imposed on
Sullivan by his client and publishes a second image that zooms in to exclude
all the ground-floor decoration and leave only the white surfaces above. The
successive readings of each figure have depended on holding these tendencies
apart, maintaining, as it were, the thin line between simple, abstract, white
surfaces and complex, sensuous, colored decoration, a line that seems to be
actually marked across the face of Sullivan's building.[5] But this task has
proved increasingly difficult. In the end, the line is not so straight or distinct.
If Giedion had zoomed in even further, his canonic image would have revealed that the white frame actually participates in an extraordinarily dense
ornamental scheme. Indeed, the icons carry a specific threat to the canon
they supposedly represent: the threat raised by Semper's argument that the
clean white abstract frame cannot in the end be separated from the very decorative play it appears to have decisively neutralized.

After all, Sullivan's call for a removal of ornament is not a call for the eradica-
tion of ornament. On the contrary, it is an attempt to rationalize the building
precisely to better clothe it with ornamentation that is more appropriate and
more carefully produced, such that "our strong, athletic and simple forms
will carry with natural ease the raiment of which we dream, and that our
buildings thus clad in a garment of poetic imagery, half hid as it were in
choice products of loom and mine, will appeal with redoubled power."[6] Sullivan goes on to say that, despite the "fashion" to consider ornament as something that can be either added or removed from a building, ornament can
never simply be separated from the structure it clothes, regardless of how decorative or plain the building is and the merely contingent fact that it might be

applied later in the process of construction. The woven ornamental surface, which he elsewhere calls "the fabric of a dream, a fabric of enduring reality," produces the spirit of the building rather than receiving it from the structure. Likewise, in 1924, Loos wrote "Ornament und Erziehung" (Ornament and education), a follow-up to "Ornament and Crime," to correct those who took the latter as advocating the banning of ornament.[7] Both architects closely follow Semper's own call for a tactical reduction of ornament that would in the end liberate it from the structure it is meant to cover and subordinate, allowing one to "devote oneself lovingly to the innocent needlepoint of decoration,"[8] a convoluted but decisive argument that at once organizes and deeply threatens the official discourse around modern architecture.

The, by now institutionalized, nervousness in the face of this threat points to the more oblique, and perhaps ultimately more decisive, undercurrent of Semper's "Principle of Dressing" in architectural discourse that passes through the complex filter of one of Loos's contemporaries, the Viennese art historian Alois Riegl, who at once promotes and counters Semper's thinking. Riegl had an extremely strong influence on the so-called pioneers of modern architecture. His 1893 treatise *Stilfragen* (Problems of style: foundations for a history of ornament) presents itself as an attempt to counter the "materialist interpretation of the origin of the art" promoted in the 1860s by writers who wrongly associated it with Semper. Arguing that Semper never privileged material technique and function over art,[9] the text attempts to restore the privilege of ornament over structure, acknowledging that it is merely echoing Semper's basic "proposition" when asserting: "It is the urge to decorate that

3.3
Detail of Schlesinger and Mayer department store fenestration.

is one of the most elementary of human drives, more elementary in fact than the need to protect the body,"[10] and footnoting the passages of Semper's *Der Stil* that argue that buildings were produced and elaborated before any clothes, the very passages upon which Semper based his central argument that architecture is nothing more than a form of clothing. Riegl does not counter this claim. On the contrary, it is precisely Semper's "theory of dressing as the origin of all monumental architecture" that persuades him that Semper was not simply a materialist as his followers had interpreted. Nevertheless, Riegl's relationship with that argument is ambivalent. In fact, he identifies the basic project of his book as playing down the importance of textiles and clothing by countering Semper's use of the production of clothing as a general theory of all art. Textiles and clothing are now to be understood as but a subset of the general category of "surface decoration."[11]

But while textiles and clothing do literally appear as mere subsections of the text, it is crucial to note that Riegl (who began his career as the keeper of the textile collection at the Museum of Art and Industry in Vienna and whose first two books were on textiles) is actually employing Semper's argument in the very act of criticizing it. It is Semper, after all, who argues that the basic role of clothing is not physical protection but surface decoration. For him, all decoration is clothing. Through a kind of transference, or, rather, countertransference, Riegl ends up taking over Semper's argument—and the whole logic of the internal elaboration of ornamental motifs that follows from it—in the guise of dismissing it. In reducing the importance of textiles, he clearly reduces the importance of the specific technology of decoration that Semper privileges as the origin of all decoration but he does not reduce the importance of clothing as such. The "law of *kunstwollen*" he formulates is not simply substituted for that of dressing. Rather, the conceptualization of dressing is suppressed only to resurface throughout his writing in a displaced form.

It is precisely through this kind of displacement that Semper's thinking, without being acknowledged as such, infiltrates much of the discourse around modern architecture—even organizing many of those texts that explicitly claim to counter his views. In its displaced form, the clothing argument is very elusive but all the more decisive in its effects. Ironically, it can be argued that Riegl became influential in architectural discourse precisely because his view, unlike Semper's, subordinates architecture and thereby sustains a tradition fundamental to that discourse. While Riegl accepts the idea that clothing is the origin of architecture, he rejects the idea that it is the origin of all the arts. Architecture, as an art of clothing, is a merely a subsection of art rather than, as Semper maintains, its mother. But, and this is the twist crucial to the institutional politics of the discipline, this subsection is then given unique exemplary power.[12] It is architecture that is seen to exemplify the condition of art. When Riegl repeats the argument about Semper in his *Die spätrömische Kunstindustrie nach den Funden Österreich-Ungarn* (The late Roman Art Industry according to the findings of Austria-Hungary) of 1901, he goes on to assert that the laws of *kunstwollen* are best revealed in architecture.[13] Following the strange dynamics, at once conceptual and institutional, that have always organized the architectural discipline, the clothing that is architecture becomes the paradigm of a general theory in which it is actually subordinated.

Not surprisingly, Riegl's ambivalence about Semper made its way into architectural discourse. In fact, the ambivalence assumed a specific strategic effect, a disciplinary function without which "modern architecture" could not be constituted as such. Despite the fact that he saw himself as waging a largely unsuccessful campaign against the materialist position, Riegl was extraordinarily influential on architectural discourse. This influence is particularly evident in the various institutions from which modern architecture is seen to emerge, like the Vienna Secession, the German Werkbund, the Bauhaus, and so on. His arguments are explicitly cited by figures as diverse as Otto Wagner, Henry van de Velde, Hermann Muthesius, Walter Gropius, Peter Behrens, Richard Neutra, and Ludwig Hilbesheimer, to name but a few. Typically, they deploy Riegl's rejection of materialism against the kind of extreme functionalism or structural rationalism that the canonic accounts of modern architecture promote as the very core of that architecture, even though those accounts are supposedly based on their work. In fact, it is precisely through their resistance to the cartoon accounts of the modern pushed by the successive generations of propagandists that the clothing argument is smuggled into the basic thinking of modern architecture. And it is only by systematically playing down this resistance, in order to avoid certain enigmas of functionalism, that the strategic role of the argument has been overlooked. After all, the unique capacity of architecture to exemplify the transcendence of material by art that Riegl refers to is, in the end, its Semperian capacity to mask that materiality, to clothe the body of the building with art, since architecture is, from the beginning, nothing more than an art of clothing, or, rather, the very art of clothing itself.

The rejection of "materialism" is most explicitly spelled out by Peter Behrens, who is routinely identified as one of the first architects to successfully apply the signature of the artist to previously anonymous industrial structures. In his 1910 lecture "Kunst und Technik" (Art and technology) he argues for a "battle" against the emerging credo of function, materiality, and technology, crediting it, and the associated call for the excessive reduction of decoration, to the influence of Semper's theories, citing Riegl's critique in order to claim the architect's superiority over the engineer.[14] In this complicated maneuver, the basics of Semper's argument are again transferred into Riegl's name and its misreadings are transferred to Semper's name.[15] By being, like Riegl, ambivalent about whether the fault lies with Semper or his disciples, Behrens is able to maintain a commitment to both technology and art's capacity to transcend the materiality of that technology. Riegl's argument is particularly attractive because it establishes a place for the architect in an industrialized world that threatens to make such a figure redundant.

And this position is not simply passed over with the formation of high modernism. On the contrary, it defines it. Gropius faithfully repeats the argument in his famous 1913 essay "Die Entwicklung moderner Industriebaukunst" (The development of modern industrial architecture), which singles out Behrens's factory design.[16] Then Giedion, who seems to privilege the engineer and the new modes of construction more than anyone else, applies the same argument to Gropius. When he identifies Gropius's Bauhaus building as the paradigmatic work of the newly conscious modern architect, it is not due to the dominance of function in it but to its domination of function. In this moment of enlightened self-consciousness, in which architecture finally becomes as modern as the society it is designed for, the realm of construction governed by the unconscious engineer is transcended by the sense of art unique to the architect: "In this building Gropius goes far beyond anything that might be regarded as an achievement in construction alone."[17] The decorative surfaces frenetically manipulated by fashion up to that point have not simply been abandoned in favor of the self-evident rigors of structure. Rather, the structural unconscious is mastered by the architect, disciplined by art. Function is no longer the source of art but something that must be tamed by it.

Giedion eventually credits Riegl with this argument. In 1962, his *The Eternal Present: The Beginnings of Art* identifies Semper as the source of the "materialist" argument summed up in the expression "form follows function," in which art history was "trapped" until Riegl identified its "crippling influence."[18] Two years later, this claim is elaborated further when *The Eternal Present: The Beginnings of Architecture,* which organizes itself around Riegl's analysis of space, argues that "few conceptions have been so fruitful for research in art history as his conception of the *Kunstwollen.* This was the battering-ram used against the materialist aesthetic of Gottfried Semper, which had held the stage for sixty years."[19] Giedion's analysis is everywhere indebted to Riegl. In fact, he repeatedly argues that all he is doing is updating Riegl's accurate history of two space conceptions by adding a third one that only started to emerge after Riegl's analysis was published. Throughout his writings, he echoes Riegl by insisting that architecture is the spiritual transcendence of material conditions.

Clearly, much of Le Corbusier's writing is devoted to establishing the same position (although its sources in German discourse—let alone art history—are of course concealed). The rhetoric of function and structure is invariably covered by an argument about art. The opening pages of *Vers une architecture*, for example, rehearse exactly the same argument about the engineer and the architect in the face of the architect's apparent redundancy in the modern world, concluding, in typically propagandist style:

Finally, it will be a delight to talk of ARCHITECTURE after so many grain-stores, workshops, machines and sky-scrapers. ARCHITECTURE is a thing of art, a phenomenon of the emotions, lying outside questions of construction and beyond them. The purpose of construction is TO MAKE THINGS HOLD TOGETHER; of architecture TO MOVE US.[20]

In these famous pages, the fundamental difference between the engineer and the architect has to do with the "look." It is by satisfying the eye that the materiality of buildings can be transcended. Although the engineer's calculations of the internal logic of structure necessarily involve a certain "taste," the architect must consider the external appearance of the forms and "reward the desire of the eyes." The machine is a model for architecture only insofar as it has already transformed the "outward appearance" of the world, a transformation that has been ignored by clients, who only ask for historical styles because they have "eyes which do not see." This concern with the look of transcended industrialization follows from Behrens's lecture, which is not so surprising given that Le Corbusier was working in Behrens's office during the same year that the lecture was delivered. And, as Behrens's argument is ultimately based on Semper's account of the bond between clothing and architecture, the clothing argument has not simply disappeared. It is precisely the ultimate privileging of the external "look" over the internal structure that renders the role of the modern architect one of choosing the correct clothing for the newly industrialized body of architecture.

The Architects' Dresses

The literal question of clothing does not fade away in favor of a disciplined, or, rather, disciplinary, "look." On the contrary, Behrens (like his wife Lilli) was actually designing dresses at the turn of the century. In so doing, he rigorously practiced the collapse of the traditional distinction between the high and low, fine and applied, arts, which Semper had repeatedly called for after his 1850 contact with the design circles in London, whose intense debate about the status of ornament initiated the thinking behind the Arts and Crafts movement. This thinking, which would eventually be associated with William Morris before being gradually exported to Germany, had, as Harry

Mallgrave argues, an enormous and immediate impact on Semper's position. It encouraged him to privilege the "Principle of Dressing" that he had only formulated the year before, completely reversing the traditional prioritizing of fine over applied art and placing new emphasis on "style" by giving ornament the central role in art.[21] Likewise, Morris repeatedly argued that clothing articulates social relations, and designed fabrics and dresses accordingly.

Indeed, his own work started when he joined the group of "Pre-Raphaelite" artists who were able to launch a new movement by painting women wearing particular dresses in particular interiors. Semper's and Morris's respective privileging of textiles was to have a major impact on subsequent discourse. As Giedion notes in *Mechanization Takes Command,* Semper remained the key figure for the Arts and Crafts movement up until 1910. This, of course, is the year that Behrens explicitly voiced Riegl's criticism of Semper's theory but tacitly maintained that very theory, moving it, as it were, underground, but in no way weakening its influence. And not by chance is it the year that Giedion's texts repeatedly chose to mark the end of the rule of fashion.[22] In the general commitment to applied art and the specific privilege of the arts of clothing, the Arts and Crafts movement was Semperian from the beginning. Having started as a painter and forming his own Arts and Crafts organization in 1898, Behrens's dress designs were an almost inevitable consequence of his commitment to a movement tacitly indebted to Semper's "Principle of Dressing."

This integration of architectural design with clothing design is even clearer in the work of another architect who was influenced by Riegl, Henry van de Velde, who faithfully imported the philosophy of Morris (publishing a book on him in 1898) and launched Art Nouveau in Belgium along with Victor Horta before distributing it in France and Germany. Like Frank Lloyd Wright, he faithfully sustained Morris's polemic by first designing many dresses for his wife Maria Sèthe to match his innovative design for their own house, and then designing dresses to go with the houses he did for the clients that the house attracted. Following the Arts and Crafts tradition, which, like its gurus Morris and Semper, gives ornament a structural rather than subordinate role, van de Velde elevated ornament into the major creative force of design, arguing that is the "heart's blood" of art and that the territory it needs to enrich includes all everyday objects, buildings, furniture, clothing, jewelry, books, utensils, wallpaper, textiles, light fittings, and so on. The revision of dress design is understood as a necessary part of a revision of the entire environment to produce the infamous *Gesamtkunstwerk* (total work of art). As Karl Ernst Osthaus—the industrialist and architectural patron whose wife wore gowns and jewelry designed by van de Velde to match the house they commissioned from him—said in 1906, a year before the house was com-

3.4
*Peter Behrens, house
dress, 1901.*

3.5
*Maria Sèthe and Henry
van de Velde in the first-
floor studio of their
house at Blomenwerf, ca.
1898. Dress made in a
William Morris fabric to
a design by Henry van de
Velde.*

pleted: "woe to the lady who would enter such a room in a dress that was not artistically suitable."[23] But such dresses did not simply complete an ornamental scheme. Rather, the privileging of ornament is linked, from the beginning, to a certain sensibility about clothes. Clothing is not understood as an accessory to an architectural space but as its very condition.

Is this concern with clothing a concern with fashion? Van de Velde's critics certainly thought so. His opponent in the famous fight at the 1914 meeting of the German Werkbund in Cologne was Hermann Muthesius, the architect who (following the lead of Robert Dohme's *Das englische Haus* of 1888) had introduced the Arts and Crafts philosophy to Germany in a long series of essays and books and who had long been an outspoken critic of fashion. In 1902, for example, his "Die moderne Umbildung unserer äesthetischen Anschauungen" (The modern reorganization of our aesthetic points of view) had condemned the relentless cycles of fashion, offering his own psychological explanation for its degenerate influence and arguing that "fashion is not limited to clothing; there are also fashions in art" which produce rapidly changing styles.[24] Repeatedly declaring Art Nouveau (and its German variation, Jugendstil) to be just such a fashionable style that had already "mummified" architecture with an excess of ornamentation, Muthesius called for a massive reduction in the amount of ornament. His promotion of the need to "discover the functional form without decoration, without ornament, without any trace of the activity of old decorative aesthetics,"[25] was based on the claim that excesses of ornamentation are always produced by fashion. Art Nouveau is seen to continue the subjection of architecture to fashion, restarting the very cycles of stylistic turnover that it had at first appeared to stop.[26] For Muthesius, as his "Weg und Ziel" (Means and goal) of 1905 argues, this subjection began with the "regurgitation" of old styles in the nineteenth century. The "basic principle" of the "demand for variety led by fashion" is to compromise utilitarian form by drowning it in ornament.[27] The removal of this regressive layer makes available the new art of the machine. Muthesius's "Kunst und Machine" (Art and Machine) essay of 1902 had already extended Morris's thinking by overturning his refusal of the machine, insisting that to not show how something is produced today is merely to produce a degenerate form of "dressing" [*verkleidung*].[28] It is not a question of showing the actual structure of the object. To accept the new condition of the object is simply to refuse to clothe it in a fashionably old-fashioned dress, a point that was emphatically restated in Muthesius's address on "Architektur und Publikum" (Architecture and the public) delivered to the 1907 International Congress of Architects in London:

If we were not so caught up in the prejudices of our time to the point of being unable to judge, the striving to dress modern tasks in historical forms would appear just as ridiculous as if a person possessed different masquerade costumes and undertook to appear today as a gothic knight tomorrow as a French courtesan the next day as an ancient Greek. Because these strivings for style are nothing other than artworks of dressing which come out of a certain characterlessness and groundlessness of architecture.[29]

Even the attempt to reject historical dress in favor of a modern style is to dress, and thereby suffocate, the object. In *Stilarchitektur und Baukunst* (Style-architecture and building-art) of 1902, Muthesius rejects the attempt "to arrange the outer stylistic dress of buildings in a manner that at the time looked modern."[30] The very search for a modern look is not modern. Modernity is not a look. The modern is an unconscious effect of new conditions rather than something produced by artists. Indeed, to seek it is necessarily to lose it, as he argues in a 1903 article on English country houses: "Herein lies the unconsciously modern. To want to be 'modern' on principle is unobjective and is therefore very unmodern. One is modern when one is as objective as possible and thinks of nothing other than the demands at hand. To look for the modern in external details is the erroneous way of the nineteenth century, to look at artistic things from the wrong side."[31] Inasmuch as Art Nouveau actively seeks a modern look, it is seen to be, like the historical eclecticism it rejected, a degenerate form of dress. More precisely, its decorative excesses are seen to be nothing more than those of fashion—excesses whose model is to be found in women's dresses.

In contrast to such architectural fashions, Muthesius insists on the need to standardize architectural practice by settling on certain generic type-forms. Indeed, it can be argued that while the ostensible theme of the 1914 debate in Cologne was the freedom of the individual artist versus the establishment of such shared standards, the tacit argument is about disciplining design against fashion. At a key point early in his speech, Muthesius touches the question of fashion. His central argument is that the obsessive application of the word "art" to all domains (including, symptomatically, the idea of "Art in Men's Suits," along with art in the house, the street, the shop-window, and so on) has lead to a proliferation of excessive ornament that destroys the aesthetic order produced by anonymous craftspeople. And it is preceded by the claim that purely commercial interests are already seeing the Werkbund's designs as "the new fashion" to be exploited.[32]

Without addressing, let alone defending, fashion, van de Velde responded in favor of the individual artist over the anonymous worker and was supported by the other older members of the Werkbund, and even the young turks like Walter Gropius and Bruno Taut. The rights of the individual artist were repeatedly aligned with a sense that modernity involved ongoing aesthetic change, changes of mode guided by the artist controlling everything in the environment. The signature designer was successfully defended against the anonymous, collective production of standards. But the debate is usually understood as a watershed in the formation of modern architecture because the proposed agenda that Muthesius reluctantly withdrew, with its extreme reduction of ornament and attempted standardization, ended up becoming the ostensible agenda of modern architecture. Consequently, historians tacitly, but routinely, identify Muthesius with the final rejection of fashion that supposedly allowed modern architecture to emerge. In fact, the extent to which they reproduce, but rarely cite, Muthesius's opinions is remarkable. In a sense, Muthesius is responsible for an entire historiographical tradition within which he only appears at one key point, if at all. Precisely because the whole project to discipline fashion turns around him, it overlooks him.

The rejection of fashion is, of course, equally explicit in the writings of another of van de Velde's critics, Adolf Loos. Like Muthesius, Loos rejects the very idea of architecture as a high art sealed by a designer's signature. While accepting and elaborating Semper's argument that architecture is a form of clothing, he condemns fashion in favor of the anonymous evolution of standards. Writing extensively about fashion, in successive articles about hats, shoes, underclothes, fabrics, men's and women's clothing, uniforms, and so on, his opinion is seemingly clear-cut and extreme:

Ladies' fashion! You disgraceful chapter in the history of civilization! You tell of mankind's secret desires. Whenever we peruse your pages, our souls shudder at the frightful aberrations and scandalous depravities. We hear the whimpering of abused children, the shrieks of maltreated wives, the dreadful outcry of tortured men, and the howls of those who have died at the stake. Whips crack, and the air takes on the burnt smell of scorched human flesh.[33]

Women's fashion is identified with ornamentation, which in turn is identified with sensuality, in particular man's "sickly sensuality," which the ornaments are intended to attract. For Loos, ornament is the mark of servitude. The woman uses ornament to make the man a slave to his own pathological sexuality precisely because she is herself a slave. After all, when ornament is identified with crime in the notorious essay, the crime is explicitly sexual, or, rather, is sexuality itself. The critique of the immoral seductions of fashionable clothing is extended into a critique of the immoral seductions of the clothing of buildings. Such dissimulating layers of clothing are repeatedly opposed whether they are draped over the inside or the outside of buildings. On the outside, Loos condemns the use of architectural styles, fashionable facades that are literally "nailed on" to the structure, as but "costume" in the sense of dead clothing, imitation clothes. Likewise, on the inside, he condemns the fashion-conscious search for a "stylish home" assisted by the new figure of the "decorator" who single-handedly, like the fashion designer, establishes a particular style for the inhabitant. This figure displaces the traditional selection of furnishing and clothes produced by different craftspeople whose anonymous work fits together because they are independently harmonious with their own time.[34] Inside and out, modernity is effaced by the very fashions that claim to express it.

While attacking the Arts and Crafts movements for attempting to impose their individual signatures on the whole environment, Loos repeatedly singles out van de Velde, as in his cutting line: "there will come a time when the furnishings of a prison cell designed by Professor Van de Velde will be considered a harshening of the punishment."[35] He constantly teases the designer, even parodying the designing of clothes to match architectural interiors by suggesting that one would have to change clothes when changing rooms.[36] But the problem is not simply the actual designing of such clothes by an architect. Loos sees all of van de Velde's architectural work as the design of women's dresses. When the infamous "Ornament und Verbrechen" (Ornament and crime) essay attacks van de Velde as a "modern producer of ornament" pathologically "disowning his own products after only three years," it counters this subordination of design to fashion with the principle that "the form of an object should be bearable for as long as the object lasts physically" and illustrates the point in terms of dress: "A suit will be changed more frequently than a valuable fur coat. A lady's evening dress, intended for one night only, will be changed more rapidly than a writing desk. Woe betide the writing desk that has to be changed as frequently as an evening dress, just because the style has become unbearable."[37] The problem with van de Velde is not simply that he designs dresses but that he confuses the specific demands of architecture with those of dresses.

Loos likewise attacks Josef Hoffmann, Josef Maria Olbrich, and the other Viennese Secessionists. Again, he criticizes their use of internal and external masquerade in architecture but does so by literally criticizing the clothes they wore as being a form of masquerade, accusing them of using imitation ties, an accusation taken so seriously that Hoffmann angrily denies it in print. It is not just that the error in their own clothes supposedly reflects the error of their whole project. The project literally involves the redesign of clothing. Hoffmann, like van de Velde, was designing dresses and even teaching fashion design within his class at the School of Arts and Crafts, an institution that, as Kenneth Frampton notes, had originally been founded to carry out Semper's educational program.[38] Although it was a special architecture class, it embraced the entire design, or, rather, designable, environment; architec-

ture and dress being seen to have the "same preconditions of creation" as his assistant of the time put it.[39]

Furthermore, in 1903 Hoffmann founded the Wiener Werkstätte with the painter Kolomon Moser that was modeled on the English workshop tradition initiated by Morris that Hoffmann had seen on a tour guided by Muthesius the year before. The new workshop, which was devoted to all the applied arts and had its first exhibition a year later in the Berlin "Shop for Art and Craft" run by van de Velde, was extremely influential in design circles throughout Europe, especially those of fashion design. Given that it assumed responsibility for the total environment (furniture, table settings, flower arrangements, garden layouts, wallpapers, utensils, book design, and so on, in addition to buildings), dress was necessarily a major concern. Moser, like Hoffmann, designed dresses in the same spirit as the decorations he painted for so many of Hoffmann's interiors. Although it did not have a fashion department with its own tailor's workshop until 1911, members of the Werkstätte designed dresses from the beginning and had them constructed at the Schwestern Flöge, a fashion salon run by the three Flöge sisters that catered to the progressive upper middle classes. Even the salon was designed by Hoffmann in 1904. When the Werkstätte's own fashion department opened, its director, Eduard Wimmer, set about "the creation of a modern 'Viennese fashion' appropriate for women living in Wiener Werkstätte designed dwellings."[40] But the Werkstätte dresses were to have a major impact on not only Viennese fashion circles but also those of Germany and even Paris.

In 1910, the Werkstätte opened its own fashion salon, selling fabrics, dresses, hats, shoes, leather goods, bags, and accessories.[41] By 1924, it employed 150 people and was growing into a chain of stores that eventually had branches in Karlsbad, Zurich, New York, and Berlin before the Werkstätte collapsed in 1931. Unlike the Schwestern Flöge, which had from the beginning participated in the emerging ready-to-wear trade (through Emilie Flöge's biannual appropriations of Paris fashions) and the sale of one-off art dresses designed by her and the Secessionist circle (some by Hoffmann but most by Wimmer and the notorious Gustav Klimt), the Werkstätte specialized in the later exclusive and expensive market.[42] In the face of the increasing mass production of fashions, its obsessive concern for handicraft was unable to hold a market. Nevertheless, it was the last department of the Werkstätte to close and its designs had greatly influenced the very ready-to-wear trade that made it redundant.

The relationship between the workshop and the evolving international fashion world was complex. From the beginning, all the Werkstätte dresses were widely published in Paris and the original salon had been regularly visited by

Paul Poiret, the leading French fashion designer who was Hoffmann's friend at the time and whose neo-empire line had clearly influenced the original Werkstätte designs. Poiret, who pioneered most of the modern apparatus of fashion publicity (like trained models), held a major fashion show in Vienna in 1911. He was, in turn, influenced by the dress designs he saw at the Werkstätte, organized a show of them in his Paris salon and had a huge quantity of their fabrics and accessories sent back to Paris for use in his own collections.

Furthermore, while describing Hoffmann's control of both the house and the dresses worn within it as a form of "slavery" that subordinates the inhabitant's personal taste,[43] Poiret was sufficiently affected by Hoffmann's interiors that he commissioned a house from him in 1912. Although the scheme was abandoned, it is no coincidence that the eventual architect for the house, Mallet-Stevens, who was greatly influenced by Hoffmann, designed fashion stores for shoes, clothing and jewelry. Mallet-Stevens's architecture was used in films as sets framing clothes designed by Poiret and was singled out by Giedion as the paradigm of the ever present danger that modern architecture might become nothing more than surface fashion design and then effaced from the historical canon. Poiret had even been inspired by all this to branch out into the field of interior design himself, opening a workshop based on the Wiener Werkstätte called Atelier Martin that, as Isabelle Anscombe puts it,

3.6
Josef Hoffmann, Summer dress. Published in Mode *(Vienna), 1911.*

3.7
Emilie Flöge and Gustav Klimt, c.1905. Österreichische Nationalbibliothek, Vienna.

"established the tradition in France of not only bringing fashion closer to the fine arts, but also allowing fashion to flow outwards into the decorative environment."[44] To do this, Poiret hired and trained a group of designers that produced very Hoffmann-like objects, fabrics, interiors, and buildings.

Such a blurring, if not effacement, of the line between architecture and fashion had been going on at the Werkstätte since at least 1903. Wimmer had been trained as an architect with Hoffmann at the *Kunstgewerbeschule* (School of Industrial Arts) before becoming the director of the fashion department. Indeed, he was repeatedly described in the press as the workshop's "architect of fashion." This blurring continued after Hoffmann's architectural office was separated off in 1912 (as a result of a legal suit over the division of fees). In the Primavesi country house of the following year, for example, the guests (who frequently included Hoffmann and Klimt), whether male or female, had to wear specially designed silk gowns made of Werkstätte fabric that matched the dense abstract patterns that dressed most surfaces of the building itself.[45] Klimt, who promoted his art dresses as an antibourgeois "symbol of independence and informality, as the epitome of fashionable freedom and one's unique individual style,"[46] had long advocated and designed such unisex gowns, and often wore them. A crucial part of this sense of freedom was the effacing of the distinction between fashionable dress and architecture. What was, for Loos, the new prison-house of fashion was, for the Secessionists, the long awaited release.

Dressing Down the Feminine

With the Secessionists' inclusion of the domestic domain that was traditionally associated with women within the space of high art, the production of designs for women, the opening of an institutional space for women designers (since 1913 the majority of Werkstätte designers were women), and the blurring of traditional markings of gender, in addition to the overall concern with the stereotypically feminine domain of ornamentation, it is not surprising that Loos, like Karl Kraus, attacks the Werkstätte as "feminine" in its contaminating use of fashion: "Whenever I abuse the object of daily use by ornamenting it, I shorten its life-span, because since it is then subject to fashion, it dies sooner. Only the whim and ambition of women can be responsible for this murder of material—and ornamentation at the service of woman will live forever."[47] In 1927, Loos went even further in a public lecture entitled "The Viennese Woe: Wiener Werkstätte," whose goal was, according to a newspaper report, to "finish the dying Wiener Werkstätte with the claw-stroke of his speech." It attacked the "feministic eclectic rubbish arts and crafts of the Wiener Werkstätte" in such vitriolic terms that it lead to a reply from Hoffmann, much debate in the newspapers, and a libel suit.[48] The workshop and its products were vilified as feminine: "To bring us first-rate work no architects are needed, no arts and crafts students and no painting, embroidering, potting, precious-material-wasting daughters of senior civil servants, or other *Frauleins*, who regard handicrafts as something whereby one may earn pin-money or while away one's spare time until one can walk up the aisle."[49]

Loos's attack exploits the millennial tradition in which ornament is identified as a feminine principle that needs to be disciplined, literally domesticated, restrained if not actually contained within the interior by a masculine structure. Despite his personal vendetta against Hoffmann, his argument is not so much idiosyncratic as it is institutional. Indeed, it faithfully echoes Germain Boffrand's mid-eighteenth-century attack on Rococo in the *Livre d'Architecture:*

Fashion, at various times (and especially in Italy) has taken pleasure in torturing all the parts of a building, and has often tried to destroy all the principles of architecture, whose noble simplicity should always be preserved. . . . Ornamentation has (in the work of Guarini and Borromini) passed from the interior decoration of houses, and from the carved woodwork for which delicate work is suitable, to exteriors, and to works in masonry, which require to be worked in a more vigorous and more masculine way.[50]

Likewise, the Secessionists are seen to have released ornament from the interior and allowed it to contaminate the very structure that is supposed to control it. The Arts and Crafts principle that decoration should become the structure is seen as a direct threat to masculine authority. This perception that Hoffmann and his circle had feminized architecture by concentrating on a "surface style" was not a passing sentiment in the literature framing modern architecture.[51] Loos's reaction is far from isolated. Rather, it acts as a structuring claim in the discourse that apparently must be repeated in order to be effective, even within Loos's own writing. When his 1908 essay "Kulturentartung" (Cultural degeneration) dismisses the aims of the newly established Deutscher Werkbund as laid out by Muthesius, for example, he argues that it is necessary to relaunch his earlier successful attack on both the clothes worn by the Secessionists and their attempt to "infect" the world of tailoring.[52] Likewise, the Wiener Werkstätte is often invoked by other writers as the model for the way fashion mobilizes the greatest dangers implicit in all ornament, the danger against which modern architecture must vigilantly guard by disciplining not only buildings but the people who produce them, those who live in them, and even, if not especially, those who write about them.

Even Giedion uses a 1950 essay on Richard Neutra to credit Loos with turning to England and America to find "a cure for the effeminate Viennese taste."[53] In fact, Giedion, who has little time, and even less space, for Loos, condemns the Wiener Werkstätte in the first of his periodic surveillance sweeps against fashion in architecture. His 1926 "Zur situation deutscher architektur" (The state of German architecture), which launched the series that became *Bauen in Frankreich*, attacks what he sees as the revived precedence of decoration over architecture, criticizing the Wiener Werkstätte in particular for its "playful and irrelevant quality," which he calls "the curves of a nervous feminism [*nervösen feminismus*]."[54] This association of fashion with the dangers of femininity occurs again when the essay later identifies the Arts and Crafts movement in general with an "over-cultivated feeling for the surface charm of materials linked up with *soigné* and somewhat effeminate [*verweichlichten*] feeling for plushy furnishings."[55] In contrast, he insists again that modern architecture is "inartistic, unfashionable." In France, it is supposedly easier for Le Corbusier to "fight . . . against the adjustment of taste, which is all the more dangerous," because the decorative arts were never so dominant there. But still, it is only by assuming an extreme functionalism that resists "external assimilation" by the style-mongers that "a movement stays almost safe from fashionable dilution [*modischen Verwässerungen*]."[56] The essay concludes by objecting to "this 'taste' which so easily lets architectural matters slip into dangerously fashionable realms [*modezone*]. Now is the time to attempt once again to break away from superficial attraction and to re-establish architecture as functional art."[57] It is not enough for architecture to be "almost safe." "Almost safe" is apparently unsafe. Fashion is lethal in even the smallest of doses.

In fact, Giedion implies that even the most extreme commitment to function cannot inoculate architecture against fashion. Inasmuch as it is an art, albeit a "functional art," it cannot leave the surface behind and so remains open to the very appropriations it tries to resist. Although the shape of modern architecture is actually produced by its ongoing attempt to resist the fashion market, it remains, for Giedion, all too attractive to that market. The threat of fashion, which is to say the feminine threat of "superficial attraction," is permanent, as must be the masculine resistance to it. After all, the threat is, as it was for Loos, that of sexuality. Throughout Giedion's texts, the psychological complex in which fashion necessarily participates is tacitly linked to questions of sexuality. The "schizophrenic" division between feeling and thought produced by the mechanization of everyday life and covered over, if not repressed, by fashionable decoration, is a form of sexual degeneration, as is the decorative cover. Ornaments are understood as sexual lures. *Space, Time and*

Architecture identifies the licentiousness of fashionable ornament when it literally speaks of the "erotic facade" which must be stripped off buildings and abandoned to produce the "impersonal, precise and objective spirit" of modern architecture.[58]

But this spirit, which is exemplified by the engineering triumph of the huge spans in the 1889 Galerie des Machines, is not desexualized because the structures are naked, or even clothed in a modestly plain dress. The sexuality is displaced rather than effaced. Alongside images of the Galerie's apparently naked steel frame, Giedion publishes a "popular" nude from the same year, arguing, in the caption, that "with its facile histrionics and its full share of erotic facade, it met all the demands of its day."[59] Symptomatically, the stripping off of this erotic facade is identified with the way a Degas painting of a clothed ballerina apparently locates "the nascent prostitute in the young dancer." Giedion sees the labor of the modern architect, and his own as a historian, as being, like Degas, that of taking sexuality away from the surface, relocating it in some interior rather than abandoning it. Like the psychoanalyst, they locate a cauldron of sexuality behind apparently innocent surfaces. If the modernists' "stripping" off of decorative clothes is a moral act, the morality is sexual. The disciplining of fashion is, in the end, an attempt to discipline, as distinct from reject, sexuality.

This puritanical logic becomes even more evident in the introduction added by Giedion in 1962 to the final edition, which calls for the disciplining of the contemporary architects who have apparently transformed modern architecture itself into a "fashion" by decorating it. The sacrilegious "tendency to degrade the wall with new decorative elements" that has "infected" the architects is symptomatically condemned because it "flirts with the past" and produces "playboy fashions" in a "romantic orgy."[60] The crime of decoration is always sexual and the historian-therapist must constantly guard against flirtations with the surface that succumb to the inherently feminine ruses of fashion. Indeed, in the very name of resisting sexuality, the historian must, as the text variously says, "penetrate," "drive boreholes into," "enter into," "probe into," the surface.

These are not passing metaphors. Sex is not even a metaphor here (if it ever is). The opposition between the Degas and the popular nude is a trace of the extensive research that Giedion was carrying out in 1936 into what he called "the ruling taste," which was interrupted when Gropius invited him to come to Harvard to give the Charles Eliot Norton Lectures that would be published as *Space, Time and Architecture*. In 1955, he published some of this early research, analyzing the "erotic mode" of popular paintings of the mid-nineteenth century by the Dutch artist Ary Scheffer, whose "sentimentally

120. International Exhibition, Paris, 1889. *Base of three-hinged arch.*

121. EDGAR DE-
GAS, "The Dancer."
Degas, the most dar-
ing experimentalist
among the painters of
the period and the ex-
act contemporary of
Eiffel, projects his
dancers stripped of
all erotic façade. He
shows their dis-
tended nostrils and
all the tenseness of
straining effort. Max
Liebermann remarks
(in "Pan," the most
"precious" of the Ger-
man avant-garde re-
views, p. 195) that
"he seems to disguise
his models and to see
the nearest prostitute
in the young dancer;
no other painter has
so completely subdued
the novelistic element."
This painting exhibits
in its field the imper-
sonal, precise, and ob-
jective spirit which
produced construc-
tions like the Galerie
des Machines

had been used to such an extent. The eye of the contemporary
onlooker was confused by these strange dimensions. Even
Anatole de Baudot, one of the first to open a path for contemporary architecture, declares that the proportions are a
failure, and the Belgian constructer Vierendeel complains that
" this lack of proportion produces a bad effect: the girder is
not balanced; it has no base . . . it starts too low. . . . The
eye is not reassured. . . . The supports of the Galerie des
Machines show another fault: they are too empty."

It is precisely the features that are criticized which pointed
to later developments. Here construction is unconsciously
moving toward aesthetic feelings which did not find
their equivalents in art and architecture until decades
later.

*Construction
moves uncon-
sciously toward
new aesthetic
feelings*

3.8
*Pages from Sigfried
Giedion,* Space, Time and
Architecture.

veiled lasciviousness" apparently "paralyzes the capacity for judgment."[61] Already, Giedion's 1944 call for a "new monumentality" had chosen the seemingly copulating figures in 1930s sculptures by Gustav Adolf Vigeland as the "acme" of the "pseudo-monumentality" that is blocking the emergence of an appropriate urban architecture that would bring to the surface the unconscious feelings buried by such popular fashions.[62] Even his 1962 book, *The Beginnings of Art,* begins by arguing that most art originates in symbols of procreation but that these figures ("with their heavy breasts, protuberant belly, and exaggerated buttocks") should not be interpreted, as they would be by a nineteenth-century mentality, "merely as lust," "eroticism," and "prehistoric pin-up girls."[63] Giedion identifies the innocence of certain apparently sexual images in the same way that he had earlier identified the sexuality of certain apparently innocent images. Furthermore, he argues that images of seduction and seductive images actually inhibit sexuality. His 1954 book on Gropius, for example, argues that the seductive images of the "ruling" taste, which "have become part of the dream world of the masses and their representatives," are used "impotently" to oppose "truly creative art, whose roots reach back into the ancient ages."[64] The ancient potency of modern art, with which the impotence of overtly sexual images is to be cured, is always sexual. It comes as no surprise, then, that the later books argue that the weapon against the all too seductive surface provided by modern art's recovery of these ancient origins is "spatial penetration." In an old, if not the oldest, story, seduction is to be countered with (phallic) control.

Giedion's sentiment, his argument, and even his methodology, is not unique. One by one, the historians of modern architecture, with their very different agendas, attempt to leave fashion behind by associating it with sexuality's (feminine) threat to (masculine) order and guarding against its return. They operate surgically on the available evidence, and change the terms of what constitutes evidence, within certain definite but unspecified limits. The most obvious symptom of this operation is that all the figures being addressed here—Behrens, van de Velde, Horta, Hoffmann, Loos, Sullivan, and so on—are routinely divided into those elements of their designs or writing consistent with a canonic, almost cartoon-like, image of modern architecture, and those that are not. Each is tacitly or explicitly split into two clear-cut and gendered sets of qualities and their work is portrayed as the struggle between the two, any blurring of the distinction being associated with the feminine qualities that must be overcome to produce a modern architecture. The much-advertised clarity of modern architecture is no more than the drawing of a line that genders, and the effacement of any blurring, twisting, or convolution of that line. It is not by chance that Giedion begins his final attempt to ground modern architecture in a transhistorical order by insisting that the pre-historic bisexual figures of procreation be disassociated from desire. The regulating lines of modern architecture turn out to be those that regulate desire. The modern erects itself as such by refusing the collapsing or weaving of these all too straight lines into a sensuous surface.

In this way, a prehistory is constructed and invested with a sense of momentum. Modern architecture is portrayed as the inevitable product of irreversible psychic forces long at work. The prehistory from which it emerges is explicitly and tacitly identified with fashion. No matter how blurred, multiple, and unevenly developed (if not invisible) the line between the canon and its prehistory, fashion is clearly left behind. In the end, the line cordoning off fashion may be the only one drawn with any regularity and confidence—no matter how tacitly. Indeed, it is precisely the tacit nature of the argument, the sense that it almost goes without saying, needing only the smallest punctuation to mark its presence, that confirms the extent to which it is seen to be beyond question. The generic sense that modern architecture is preceded by fashion is so strong precisely because it is seen to require only the lightest prop.

Much is made, for example, of the fact that the young Le Corbusier sought and received a job with Hoffmann, accepted it but asked for a short delay to make a trip from which he never returned. His Arts and Crafts background is carefully split off from his "pioneering" work, treated as a necessary but insufficient and ultimately inadequate space whose critique provides the crucial step forward. In this way, the paradigmatic sites of an explicit parallel between dress design, fashion, and architecture are seen as but crucial stepping-stones to a new form of practice within which the commitment to fashion and the dresses are literally left behind, rejected, and forgotten—even by the historians. The designing of dresses is thrown back into the prehistory of modern architecture and, even there, any mention of it is hard to find. Behrens's many dress designs are almost never referred to in supposedly comprehensive monographs on his work.[65] Even van de Velde's and Hoffmann's dress designs are almost completely effaced from architectural scholarship,[66] including that which condemns the designers for embracing fashion. Not only is the activity of dress designing (to say nothing of the specific properties of the designs) suppressed; it is deemed somehow too embarrassing to even pick up in order to discard. With the notable exception of Beatriz Colomina's persuasive analysis of Loos's arguments about fashion,[67] even the decisive question of clothing is withdrawn. It is as if to touch the question is somehow to already be contaminated by the danger of fashion it carries. A simplistic account of the "modern" attack on ornament is all that survives from the extremely complex and contradictory attempt to discipline clothing at the turn of the century in which architects played such an important role.

But clearly things are not so simple. It's not just that the historians, unlike Loos, do not analyze fashion or its relationship to architecture. It is precisely this absence that structures the discourse. When the line between modern architecture and fashion does become explicit and the rejection of fashion by that architecture is addressed, it is always in isolated moments (even with such antifashion zealots as Giedion) and almost always to clarify some point about the status of function. In fact, what usually happens is that the tacit argument about fashion is encouraged to slide into and over the argument about function. All we learn is that function is what fashion is not. Function ends up appearing more certain without having been opened up any further. On the contrary, some uncertainty about it has been covered up. In this sense, a map of the confident rejections of fashion in the historiography of modern architecture would actually be a map of its insecurity: a map of cracks in the apparently smooth surfaces of the cartoon image it constructs, cracks that harbor the very uncontrollable forces whose presence is being denied. The explicit rejections of fashion might actually be the most precise map of its enigmatic operations, operations that structure the discourse, but only appear within it at idiosyncratic moments.

I left Paris without a hat, wearing a grey suit. I took off my jacket in Miami. I went game-fishing on the Gulf Stream, and I had my shoes shined 4 times, my pants ironed 3 times. I spent 6 weeks in committees (3 languages), speaking with individual persons, vehicle: 3 languages, went by Iceland, Greenland, saw some icebergs, New York the Tropics the Equator. Not once did I brush the collar of my jacket.

—Le Corbusier, "Sketchbook D16," 1950.

4

Redressing Architecture

Modern architecture cannot be separated from dress design. On the one hand, the architects working as dress designers are completely modern in terms of the stereotypical image of modern architecture as the systematic reduction of ornament and dedication to function. On the other hand, the anti-ornamentalists are completely dedicated to clothing. And these gestures cannot simply be separated. The aspects that mark certain figures as precursors to the modern cannot be separated from those the modern means to leave behind. The much advertised line between fashion and modernity does not pass between modernity and dresses. Indeed, there is no such line. The long-standing and extremely agitated discussion about such a line serves only to mark its absence. The modern architect is first and foremost a creature of dress. The very dismissal of fashion is a fashion statement, worn to great effect.

Unsecuring the Line

Both sides of the stereotypical opposition between fashion and modern architecture frustrate the terms that are usually used to hold them apart. Although Hoffmann, for example, instituted a fashion department, his 1898 essay "Das individuelle Kleid," which first announced his commitment to dress design, defended individual clothing styles that express individual character against the uniform styles that have been imposed by the "tyranny of fashion."[1] Standardization is understood as an effect of fashion rather than a form of resistance to it. When Hoffmann later appears to consolidate his commitment to fashion by writing to a newspaper and proposing a "fashion bureau" for Vienna, he again sounds like all the outspoken critics of fashion in arguing for modern clothing styles that are consistent with the automobile and in opposing any form of masquerade.[2] Likewise, van de Velde rejects stylistic eclecticism as masquerade, as if "one had to end up by completely wearing out the tattered clothes of one's older brother."[3] After all, his primary influence was Morris, for whom the poverty of historicism, as Pevsner points out, was "masquerading in other people's clothes."[4] Indeed, when van de Velde opposes Muthesius's ideal of universal standards at the Cologne meeting of the Werkbund, he does so precisely because, in his view, any "universally valid form" would be but a "mask."[5] His whole project is governed by an obsessive rationalism directed against the dissimulations of clothing, as can be seen when his *Memoires* describe the logic with which he designed the dresses to match the interiors of his house as a pervasive rationalism understood as a moral code which excludes all "fantasy."[6] The house is not in-

87

tended as a fashion statement. On the contrary, giving ornament the privileged role does not mean the total subordination of construction and function. Rather, it involves blurring the difference between them. Van de Velde's argument is precisely that which is typically used to mark modern architecture's rejection of fashion: "its construction and exterior form must adapt themselves completely to the aim for which they were created . . . no ornament which does not insert itself organically can be considered as valid. Anything which lies outside this constructive vision is, in applied art, senseless, irrational and sterile." [7] His concern with ornament is a concern with the particular qualities of line, understood as that which fuses construction and ornament. The line of ornament has to be disciplined, restrained in a way that liberates the "line of construction" that "refuses to conceal its activity behind an unjustified excess of ornamentation." [8] From the beginning, van de Velde employs smooth surfaces with simple decoration, favors mass production, and finally, like Hoffmann, has no hesitation in placing his rationality in a historical trajectory with canonic modern architecture. [9] He explicitly opposes fashion, insisting that his own work was never a "vogue" and bitterly opposing the transformation of Art Nouveau into one. [10]

In his 1929 lecture "Le nouveau: pourquoi toujours du nouveau?" (The new: why always the new?) van de Velde opposes the "newness" of his architecture to the "novelty" of fashion. He argues that the individualist variations of the early Art Nouveau work were seized upon by manufacturers who appropriated only its most superficial elements and transformed them into a fashion with the eager backing of the magazines for the "new art" that emerged precisely in order to promote such trends. No matter how rigorously the artist strips away the degenerate layers of old fashions, it is always possible that "a 'false newness' under some clever disguise may come into vogue" through the "specter of ornamentation" that haunts all forms of production and "has not changed its methods of seduction since men first began to barter." [11] To resist such a seduction of artworks into a fashion, "we had to disabuse those who saw us only as 'purveyors of the new' of the idea that after *this* new style, we should bring them another" [12] by demanding an unchanging, essential order. The newness of contemporary architecture had to be seen as the product of logic rather than the dictates of fashion. Van de Velde's repeated call for rational principles that uncover "essential forms" by insisting on "the fatal determination of shape by function" is therefore explicitly directed against fashion. He symptomatically concludes that the constant "menace" of ornamentation can only be resisted by a rigid "submission to discipline" that transforms the early individualist experiments into a single unified style, a "*style of the machine,*" no less, that is protected from the rav-

Redressing Architecture

ages of fashion. Furthermore, the lecture's model for an architecture that "elevates itself above fashion," by "abstaining from ornament," is the "pursuit of pure forms and the pure line" in women's clothing. While Van de Velde is repeatedly condemned for transforming architecture into fashion by treating it like dress design, he turns to dresses to resist fashion.

Likewise, the Secessionists oppose the transformation of their work into a fashion, objecting to their own influence as "a loud fashion" precisely because that fashion is not faithful to the fundamental principle of construction that organizes both their buildings and dress designs.[13] Indeed, they see their commitment to dress design as being responsible for their principle of construction rather than a means to disregard it. Hoffmann's eloquent essay "Simple Furniture" for *Das Interieur* in 1901, argues that modern dress should be the model for an environment that would "give a fitting shape to our modern feeling and thinking" and asks: "How does it happen that people who make an effort to be dressed according to the latest pattern, act at home as if they were living in the 15th or 16th century?"[14] The text immediately goes on to condemn stylistic dress as pathological masquerade.[15] And if each such style is "a borrowed lying mask," it is not just an ill-fitting and untimely set of clothes for the building. It is also a kind of fashionable but uncomfortable clothing for the designer. As Hoffmann says of other designers: "most of them are intent on squeezing themselves into some trend."[16] Against this hopeless quest for the latest fashionable style, he promotes structural and functional "honesty," arguing that "I think we must above all consider the respective function and the material,"[17] a sentiment he repeatedly identifies with his teacher Otto Wagner. Indeed, as Le Corbusier will do much later, the essay criticizes museums for neglecting the modern, asking "have you ever seen a beautiful machine in a museum of arts and crafts?" and arguing that it is necessary for such institutions to "search out the traces of the 'Modern' in this and other infallible things."[18] This sensibility cannot so easily be separated from that which will reject it as mere fashion.

Furthermore, as Jane Kallir points out, despite the apparent obsession with handicraft, the workshops of the Wiener Werkstätte were not only highly mechanized, even making a number of significant innovations in the modern workplace; many of their designs were licensed to outside manufacturers and mass-produced in large numbers.[19] And Hoffmann ends up designing the provocative, but somewhat overlooked, prefabricated steel house in 1928 (which Bruno Taut had immediately published in *Modern Architecture* a year later, alongside one of his own house designs and Gropius's prefabricated house for the Weissenhofsiedlung of 1927). Its modernity (in terms of the canonic cartoon) cannot be as easily detached from his earlier work as might be imagined. Again, like van de Velde, Hoffmann does not simply fit the stereotype constructed for him. The line between fashion and modern architecture is, at the very least, insecure.

Even Mallet-Stevens, Giedion's paradigm of the architect-as-fashion-designer, repeatedly opposes the excesses of decoration and writes a piece called "La mode et le moderne," (fashion and the modern) that refuses to privilege fashion over function. On the contrary, it condemns the continued presence of old fashions that block the emergence of a modern—because functional— form appropriate for the "man of today." He uses the example of all the anachronistic features of contemporary clothing, but also argues against any superficially "modern" styling: "Aerodynamics in the automobile is not always essential, it is often merely a fashion. It is no longer the result of calculations, it is a "shape" like a hat. The history of dress is a long one of nonsense, of unreasoned extravagance. . . . If certain now useless fashions still survive, new ones arrive to impose themselves without reason."[20]

This complication of the line between fashion and modern architecture is not simply an example of the way that no historical event conforms to its description upon closer examination. Rather, these particular events are fundamentally enigmatic in their engagement with fashion. At the very least, it becomes clear that a figure's relationship to fashion can have almost nothing to do with what that figure says about fashion. Just because people design dresses does not mean that they will argue in favor of fashion. Likewise, those who attack fashion may actually be engaged with it. Both sides of the stereotype are irreducibly complicated. In the same way that the agenda of the dress designers is stereotypically modern in its attempt to discipline ornament, those who are ostensibly anti-ornamentalist are obsessed with clothes, a fixation that can never simply be separated from the very lure of fashion they claim to be staunchly resisting. Not only do their respective photographic portraits reveal a studious attention to the construction of a stylish ensemble; their respective polemics seem to find the question of clothing irresistible.

This is, of course, most evident in Loos, who appears to be the most outspoken opponent of fashion. Following Semper closely, he sees clothing not just as an analogy for architecture but as its very model, both as a general philosophical principle, as articulated in his "Law of Dressing," and as a literal exemplar, in contemporary clothing styles. In the "Architektur" essay of 1910, he argues that nineteenth-century fetishists of ornament, who covered buildings with eclectic styles in an always-frustrated attempt to find a modern style, did not realize that the tailor and other craftsmen had already quietly and anonymously produced the style of the twentieth century—a style that would probably have been blocked had the brand-name architects deigned to enter the world of clothing design:

In their arrogance, the warped people by-passed the reform of our clothes. For they were all serious men who considered it beyond their dignity to bother about such things. Thus our clothes were left alone to reflect the true style of our period. Only the invention of orna-ment was becoming to the serious, dignified man . . . what was true in the case of clothes was not the case for architecture. If architecture had only been left alone by those warped people, and if the clothes were reformed in terms of old theatrical junk or in the Secession-ist manner—there certainly were attempts in this direction—then the situation would have been the other way around.[21]

This anonymous transformation of clothing is exemplified in the gradual evo-lution of the man's suit in England. Loos emphatically privileges the relative standardization of men's clothes over the variation of women's. Male attire is supposedly detached from the many dangers of sensuality that are carried by the ornament that defines women's fashion. He does acknowledge a certain mobility in male fashion as "the masses" appropriate the clothing styles with which the aristocracy attempts to differentiate itself, but draws a distinction between this regular, almost logical, movement and the uncontrollable sexual forces driving women's fashions:

On the one hand, then, change in men's fashion is effected in such a way that the masses go rushing headlong in their desire to be elegant; in this way the originally elegant style is de-based in value, and those who are genuinely elegant—or better, those who are considered by the multitude to be elegant—must cast about for a new style in order to distinguish them-selves. On the other hand, the vicissitudes of women's fashion are dictated only by changes in sensuality. And sensuality changes constantly.[22]

For Loos, men's clothing is led by people of highest standing while women's is led by those of the lowest standing, or more precisely, those who confuse the system of standings. The greatest enemy is the *parvenu*, the pretender who acts the part by assuming the costume of another class. If men's fashions are led by the gentleman, women's fashions are led by the coquette who em-ploys her sexuality to bypass class distinctions. The sensuality of women's clothing upsets all forms of rationality, rendering insecure all distinctions, es-pecially those of class, which are, for Loos, all too rational. In opposing the rationality of male dress to the sensuality of female dress, he is able to iden-tify fashion at once with the dangers of women and with their subordination. As Elizabeth Wilson notes: "In the nineteenth century fashion had come to be associated almost entirely with women's clothing, while men's clothes have since been perceived (inaccurately) as unchanging. Fashion as a mania for change could therefore the more easily be interpreted either as evidence of women's inherent frivolity and flightiness; or—the other side of the coin—as evidence of women's subjection and oppression."[23] Loos explicitly identifies the designs of Hoffmann and the others with women's clothing, telling them just after the formation of the Wiener Werkstätte to give up architecture: "One cannot deny you a certain talent, but the area it covers is quite different from that which you imagine. You have the imagination of dressmakers [*damenschneiders*]; so make dresses [*damenkleider*]!"[24] The designers are condemned for feminizing architecture by treating it as women's clothing, subordinating it to the suspect dictates of art. In contrast, his own designs, which deliberately refuse the label of art, are identified with men's clothing. He extracts from his articles on underclothes, hats, shoes, monocles, socks, uniforms, and so on, the coherence of a gentlemen's wardrobe turning around the restrained business suit that had evolved in England.[25] This suit is privileged because of its functional comfort, which results from the way the style of everyday street clothes gradually absorbed the innovations in sports clothes required to handle their specific functional demands.

But, as Beatriz Colomina has argued, the comfort of the modern suit, like that of modern architecture, is not merely physical. The function of modern clothes for the man is also—if not primarily—psychological. More precisely, the look of function provides a newly required psychological advantage. Inasmuch as men's clothing is standardized, it is able to act as a mask behind which the individual is shielded from the increasingly threatening and seemingly uncontrollable forces of modern life (forces that were themselves understood as feminine). In the article "Die Herrenmode" (Men's fashion), Loos determines that the ideal of modern dress is "being dressed in *such a way that one stands out the least* . . . to be conspicuous is bad manners."[26] As Colomina observes, this effacement of the individual relates to fundamental transformations in metropolitan life. Having tracked Loos's crucial identification of architecture with clothing, she notes that his architectural clothing corresponds with Georg Simmel's account of fashion as a mask:

Loos writes about the exterior of the house in the same terms that he writes about fashion. . . . [He] seems to establish a radical difference between interior and exterior, which reflects the split between the intimate and the social life of the metropolitan being: outside, the realm of exchange, money, and masks; inside, the realm of the inalienable, the nonexchangeable, and the unspeakable. Moreover, this split between inside and outside, between senses and sight, is gender-loaded. The exterior of the house, Loos writes, should resemble a dinner jacket, a male mask; as the unified self, protected by a seamless facade, the exterior is masculine. The interior is the scene of sexuality and reproduction, all the things that would divide the subject in the outside world. However, this dogmatic division in Loos's writings between inside and outside is undermined by his architecture.[27]

The mask is a means of mental survival. The man cannot afford to wear his sensuality or any other part of his private life on the surface like a fashionable woman does. Masculinity is no more than the ability to keep a secret; and all secrets are, in the end, sexual. The disciplinary logic of standardization is, of course, psychological.

In promoting the standardized mask, Loos circulated the same intelligence reports as his fellow anglophile, and "cultural spy," Muthesius, whose introduction to *Das englische Haus* (The English house) of 1904–1905 associates the simplicity and comfort of English houses with the simplicity of English clothes: "The Englishman . . . even avoids attracting attention to his house by means of striking design or architectonic extravagance, just as he would be loth to appear personally eccentric by wearing a fantastic suit. In particular, the architectonic ostentation, the creation of 'architecture' and 'style' to which we in Germany are still so prone, is no longer to be found in England."[28] Both architects explicitly interpret standardization in terms of clothes.

Given Le Corbusier's profound, but largely unacknowledged, debt to Loos, it is not surprising that when *Vers une architecture* makes a Muthesian argument about standardization, it turns on the same distinction between men's and women's fashions. The illustration for the emphatic claim that "Architecture is governed by standards" carries the caption: "It is a simpler matter to form a judgement on the clothes of a well-dressed man than on those of a well-dressed woman, since masculine costume is standardized," and is preceded by the Loosian claim that "decoration is of a sensorial and elementary order, as is color, and is suited to simple races, peasants and savages. . . . The peasant loves ornament and decorates his walls. The civilized man wears a well-cut suit and is the owner of easel pictures and books."[29] The well-cut suit again acts as the model for a modern architecture, an architecture of its own time. Le Corbusier's sporadic attacks on fashion are matched by equally sporadic appeals to men's fashion, understood not as fashion but as standardization.

The gendering line the protagonists and their promoters wish to draw between fashion and modern architecture is clearly an extremely complicated and fragile one. Its contours need to be traced much more carefully in order to identify the structural role of these complications, some of which are generic to fashion while others arise in fashion's specific engagement with architecture.

The generic complication of fashion is that it is not possible to promote ephemeral fashions without making certain claims about truths beyond those fashions. Even the specific identification of a temporary style requires claims about systems of representation, effects of materiality, line, surface, structure, and so on. These claims are not stable reference points against which "the look" is made to appear, such that precise changes of look become visible over time; they are properties of the look itself. Far beyond the ironic necessity that the fashion industry has to construct itself as one of the most stable institutions in order to register the variations that it promotes, there are elements embedded within any fashion that are seen to exceed the precise time and mood that the fashion supposedly marks. Likewise, it is not possible to withdraw oneself from fashion without deploying certain arguments governed by fashion. Opponents of fashion inevitably fall victim to the very mobility of external surfaces that they condemn. As the conditions of fashion change, the specific arguments against it must necessarily change. Fashion is not so much a specific set of institutional practices as it is a specific set of paradoxes.

Important here is the structural role that this ultimate impossibility of drawing a clear-cut line between fashion and antifashion plays in architectural discourse and, more particularly, the role it plays in the discourse of modern architecture. Inasmuch as that discourse turns on certain claims about fashion, these complications assume an unacknowledged (perhaps unacknowledged because so extraordinary) force. In order to interrogate the strategic effect of these irreducible paradoxes of fashion in modern architecture, it is necessary to patiently scan the broad field of its discourse to accumulate enough of the dispersed traces of their operation that their idiosyncratic but insistent rhythm can begin to emerge.

Arresting the Fashion Police

The effects of the paradoxes of fashion can be seen in all the protagonists of modern architecture. Take Walter Gropius, the architect that Giedion, in his relentless crusade against fashion, singles out in 1941 as the paradigm of the modern architect, as does Nikolaus Pevsner in the rival history published five years earlier under the unambiguous title *Pioneers of the Modern Movement from William Morris to Walter Gropius.* When Pevsner concludes with a celebration of Gropius, he goes out of his way on the very last page to insist (as he will do in *Industrial Art in England* a year later)[30] that modern architecture is "a genuine style, not a passing fashion."[31] Gropius is promoted as the model of the rejection of fashion. And indeed he does constantly attack fashion, siding with van de Velde against Muthesius in 1914 and campaigning persistently (if unsuccessfully) for several years to oust him from the Werk-bund leadership, but eventually appropriating most of his arguments (claiming much later that the fight was really about Muthesius's "unpleasant" personality rather than about his ideas).[32] Gropius ends up as a leading exponent of the view that modern architecture is first and foremost the attempt to produce standard objects through "the elimination of the personal content of their designers."[33] Supposedly, by guarding against "arbitrary and aloof individualism," it is possible to produce standard types that exert a "settling and civilizing influence on men's minds" in the face of modernity, rather than perpetuating the neurotic cover-up achieved by putting on protective layers of fashion. It is on the basis of this quasi-utopian rejection of the economic and psychological imbalances of fashion that Gropius literally spends most of his career attempting to perfect a standardized system for the mass production of housing units. But his supposedly generic resistance to fashion is equally ex-plicit in the projects for which he was constructed as one of the "masters" of modern architecture: his hanging the first curtain wall on the Faguswerke building, his founding of the Bauhaus school, and his design of its new build-ing when it later moved to Dessau.

The campaign against fashion was aligned with the strategic use of white. More precisely, it was aligned with a renegotiation of the role that white had played in the earlier work that critics try to restrain within the categories of Arts and Crafts, Art Nouveau, Secessionist, and so on. Gropius and Meyer's 1913 design for worker's housing at Alfeld-Delligsen, which Gropius (like so many of the modern architects seeking to suppress their early work) will later dismiss along with his other projects of the time as "*solcher Dreck*" (such muck), is indebted to the tradition of the English country house promoted by

4.1

Walter Gropius and Adolf Meyer, perspective rendering of Bernburg Machine Factory Worker's Housing at Alfeld-Delligsen, 1913–1914.

4.2
*Walter Gropius and
Adolf Meyer, Factory and
Office Building for the
Werkbund Exhibition,
Cologne, 1914.*

Voysey with the abstract geometry of its pitched roofs and whitewashed plaster walls. In the renderings for the client even the doors are painted white, but when the building was built the wall coloring had two tones and the doors were dark. The architect's struggle to find modern forms involves a struggle to find the appropriate role for white. Although the sheer curtain wall of the Faguswerke was framed in unpainted brick, the famous staircase that it exposed was white. Indeed, the colored perspective rendering uses zinc white to show the brick turning white as it catches the light.

Likewise, the twin staircases of Gropius and Meyer's factory and office complex for the 1914 Werkbund exhibition in Cologne, with which Pevsner's relentless linear history finally terminates, are white. Pevsner's concluding claim that the staircases attain a "sublime" transcendence of materiality unmatched since the medieval cathedrals is dependent on the white behind the glass. Not by chance does he use this design to finally assert that the new architecture is not a "passing fashion." In fact, the building presents quite a complex argument about white. The white on the stairs is extruded into white walls that are suspended behind the glass as it passes around the sides of the building. On the ground floor, recessed lines in the brick side walls are lined up with the metal window frames to produce the effect of a continuous wrapper, as was originally proposed and does occur on the floor above. Where the structure behind those brick walls becomes visible at each end, it is painted white so that the brick floats as a decorative panel, sharing some of the lightness of the glass that it is lined up with. Within the panel, a square section of the brickwork floats because it has been painted white and a deep recess has been placed around it. Toward the top of the ten courses of brick that form

4.3
Walter Gropius. Bauhaus building, Dessau, 1925–1926. Photograph by Lucia Moholy Nagy. Getty Research Center, Resource Collections.

4.4
Walter Gropius, Dessau-Törten Estate, Kleinring. Built 1928. Photo: Musche, Dessau.

the slender base of this composition, one is made of the same pale yellow limestone as the rooftop pavilions to produce a thin line that passes around to the front of the building, where again a white figure is embedded in a floating field of bricks. The limestone facade is organized in a series of Hoffmann-like vertical stripes, and the unpainted brickwork around the entrance floats against this background as if it were a separate building. Within that figure, the sculptured curved side walls of the entrance are also white. But their whiteness is different from that of the plastered surfaces behind the glass, which is in turn different from that of the floating squares on the side walls. In addition to the elaborate play between white and reddish brown or pale yellow, the building offers a play between different whites.

By the time Gropius completed the Bauhaus building at Dessau, all the brick construction had been plastered over and painted a unified white as bright as that of the walls behind the glass. The curtain wall was now suspended between, and opens onto, smooth white surfaces. It at once framed and was framed by whiteness. If Giedion describes this building as modern architecture finally becoming conscious of itself, then that liberating moment was the one in which architects actively chose to use white, the point at which white was exhibited as such: when architects exhibited the exhibition value of white. To say the least, Gropius's architecture cannot be thought of outside its use of white. All the various technologies that he deployed were reconfigured with a white layer; whether it was the cinderblock walls of the Dessau housing units, the thin asbestos panels of the cement house for the Weissen-hofsiedlung, or the brick and boards of his own house in Lincoln, Massachusetts. More than a role model for the creative use of such technologies, Gropius stands for the tacit link between a politicized discourse against fashion and certain properties of white surfaces. Because this link is never addressed as such, its enigmas only become evident by patiently tracking the way in which his discourse is always underpinned by a specific argument about surface that is itself established by a generic narrative about clothing.

It must be recalled that the Bauhaus originally occupied the building that van de Velde designed for the Weimer Academy of Arts and Crafts he had founded in 1907, and which Gropius's new school literally replaced, along with the parallel Academy of Fine Arts, directed at the time by Fritz Mackensen. Given that van de Velde's school, like the Wiener Werkstätte, focused on the decorative arts it is not surprising that Gropius described its curriculum as too superficial; or that he viewed this superficiality in explicitly gendered terms. The first letter from Mackensen soliciting Gropius's involvement (but veiling van de Velde's own recommendation that Gropius should take the position) argues of van de Velde's curriculum: "In time it turned out that architecture, the important element, was neglected, and what remained received a somewhat feminine character."[34] The second letter argues that the school made "only trivial things . . . almost nothing that fits in the framework of architecture. The students were for the most part ladies."[35] Although the Bauhaus has often been described as the culmination of Semper's thinking in its polemical refusal of a distinction between fine and applied art, and despite its unacknowledged indebtedness to the training methodologies developed at both the Wiener Werkstätte and van de Velde's school, it is significant that not just dress design but clothing in general was eliminated from the program.

Only textile design remained, introduced as an autonomous workshop in order to meet the requirement of the Weimar Constitution that women students be admitted without restriction. Despite this official policy of equality, one publicly endorsed by Gropius when he took the position, all the women students were unofficially forced to take the textile workshop initially run by the painter Johannes Itten (although its looms, symptomatically, belonged to the crafts teacher, Helene Börner, who had previously taught weaving and embroidery in van de Velde's school) and were excluded from the other workshops, including the prestigious architecture department when it was finally introduced in 1926. In this way, the traditional split between high and low art supposedly undermined by the institution was actually maintained in traditionally gendered terms. After only a year of the school's operation, when women were already in the majority, Gropius, who wrote detailed articles on the way modern architecture actively facilitated the breakdown of the "patriarchal family" and the corresponding emancipation of women,[36] yet who would deny them access to his own workshops, even attempted to have the official policy changed by limiting the overall admission of women and legislating that they be confined to the textile workshop.[37]

Of the enormous production of fabrics by the workshop, many of which entered mass production under license with a Berlin textile company, most was intended for interior decoration. Although some of the later designs for curtains were also purchased by clothing manufacturers, the only clothing designs in the comprehensive inventory of student work that the Bauhaus had bought, up until the 1925 move to Dessau, were some caps and children's clothes.[38] Outside of Schlemmer's famous theater designs (proposed, significantly, as "trial balloons" for a new architecture, in which the actor appeared "not as the vehicle of individual expression, but standardized through costume and mask"),[39] one of the few traces of clothing design was that of the teachers' own clothes. According to one of their students, van Doesburg "favored a stiff black hat and fashionably-cut suits . . . sporting a monocle, black shirt and white tie (both to the amazement of the local residents)," while Itten designed special Bauhaus work clothes, "a monkish outfit" made at the school with "funnel-like trousers, wide at the top and narrow at the

4.5
Walter Gropius, ca.
1923.

bottom, and a high-necked jacket fastened by a belt of the same material," which only he and his most devoted students wore and that was emphatically rejected by Gropius as gratuitous "fancy dress."[40] Symptomatically, van Doesburg was not given a full-time position and Itten was eventually forced out and replaced by László Moholy-Nagy who, as Pevsner points out, is symbolically photographed at the school in overalls, the American workman's uniform that Loos had predicted will eventually take over from the suit in the world of everyday dress.[41] It is not by chance that Herbert Bayer goes out of his way to praise Gropius for dressing like a regular person in restrained clothes in order to sustain his polemical call for standards:

gropius wore black trousers, white shirt, slim black bow tie,

and a short natural-colored leather jacket

which squeaked with each movement.

his short mustache, trim figure, and swift movements

gave him the air of a soldier

(which in fact he had been until recently).

gropius' manner of dress was in contrast

to the generally fantastic individualistic appearances

around the Bauhaus.

it was a statement of his opinion

that the new artist need not oppose his society

by wearing dress that, to begin with,

would set him apart from the world he lives in,

that the step toward common understanding

would be acceptance of such standards

as would not infringe on a free spirit.[42]

The modern architect, like the modern city dweller and the modern building that Loos describes, is not meant to stand out. Although the first modern buildings may stand out from the dominant architecture left over from a previous time, the end point of the modern project is standardization: if not a uniform per se, a certain uniformity. The look of the architect has to participate in the economy of modern architecture.

Gropius's comprehensive detachment from fashion, and women's clothes in particular, is again linked to a rejection of "masquerade" in architectural design. When his "Die Entwicklung moderner Industriebaukunst" (The development of modern industrial architecture) of 1913 praises Behrens's factory designs, it is because they abandon the traditional use of a "sentimental mask" that covers the "naked form of utilitarian building," "distorting the true character of the building by allowing it to masquerade in borrowed garments from an earlier period . . . a period got up in fancy-dress."[43] But it is not a question of simply opposing the naked mechanized body to the fashionable clothes that disguise it. Like Behrens, Gropius follows Riegl in arguing against extreme functionalism understood as "materialism." Functionalism, like ornamentalism, is seen as the product of "superficial minds." Although it is necessary to achieve what his *The New Architecture of the Bauhaus* calls the "liberation of architecture from a welter of ornament,"[44] this liberation is seen as only one side of the modern project. The other is to employ art to counteract the horror of the mechanization of the material world, the tyranny of the machine, whose "misuse" is creating what he elsewhere calls a "soul-flattening mass mind."[45] This horror of the "new world order" of the machine is symbolized, as it would later be for his promoter Giedion, by the "sub-human, robot-like automaton."[46]

Mechanization is seen as a means of liberation and not an end in itself. On the contrary, it is a nightmare if undisciplined by art, which must engage with the very structures of modern life, modifying new buildings even while lightly clothing them. It is the clothing that must engage with, rather than dissimulate, the newly mechanized body. As Gropius would argue in his "Eight Steps to a Solid Architecture" of 1954, the insecurity produced by a new organization of building cannot be disguised by a "new look" generated by the architectural fashion industry:

The stark and frightening realities of our world will not be softened by dressing them up with the 'new look' and it will be equally futile to try to humanize our mechanized civilization by adding sentimental fripperies to our homes . . . architecture will reveal the emotional qualities of the designer in the very bones of the buildings, not in the trimmings only.[47]

For Gropius, a modern style would be just as evasive as the old styles, and ultimately just as much of a trap, sustaining the very nightmare it attempted to disguise. As he puts it: "it is just as easy to create a modern straightjacket as a tudor one."[48] The problems of the age cannot be solved by new clothes, no matter how modern they look. Gropius, like all his peers, is everywhere against fashion. His generic attack on style is an attack on "personal whims or fashionable styles," the "newest local fashions which disappear as fast as they appear."[49] This had already been made clear in his "Ornament and Modern Architecture" of 1938, which paraphrases Muthesius in arguing that "true ornament" is the product of the collective unconscious over a period of time rather than individual desires that can only produce "transitory fashions," which, like all fashions, are "doomed to failure." Opposing any form of "masquerade," the text emphatically concludes that: "Instead of wearing again and again the self-deceiving garment of former periods . . . let's face the future. *Forward* to tradition. The Ornament is dead! Long live the Ornament!"[50]

It must be emphasized again that this promotion of standards against fashion is not against clothing per se. On the contrary, clothing acts as the very model of standards. In a 1924 article called "Wohnhaus-Industrie" (Housing—industry) that promotes the industrialization of building, Gropius had argued that architecture should follow the modern standardization of clothes:

Is it a reflection of man's way of life that each individual's dwelling should differ entirely from that of every other individual? Is it not a sign of intellectual impoverishment and fallacious thinking to furnish a dwelling in rococo or Renaissance style while identical modern clothes are worn in all parts of the world? . . . *The majority of citizens of a specific country have similar dwelling and living requirements; it is therefore hard to understand why the dwellings we build should not show a similar unification as, say, our clothes, shoes or automobiles.* The danger of undesirable suppression of legitimate individual requirements should be no greater here than in the case of fashions.[51]

When discussing standard types two years later in an essay on "Principles of Bauhaus Production," Gropius returns to the exemplary quality of "modern" clothes: "Modern man, who no longer dresses in historical garments but

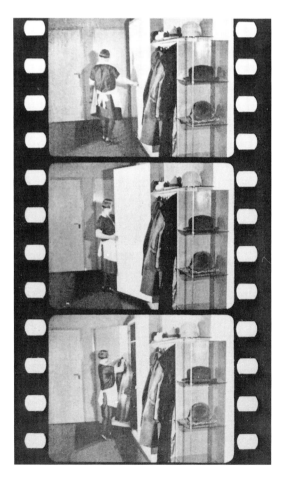

4.6
Illustration from Walter Gropius, Bauhausbauten Dessau, *1930, with the caption: "Apartments of the Bauhaus masters: built-in clothes closets in the vestibule of the Gropius detached house."*

4.7
Illustration of psychological effect of visual patterns, from Walter Gropius, "Design Topics," Magazine of Art, *1947.*

wears modern clothes, also needs a modern home appropriate to him and his time, equipped with all the modern devices of daily use."[52] It is not by chance that Gropius paid so much attention to the place of clothes in the modern house, using a 1930 Bauhaus book to publish cinematic sequences of coats, hats, shoes and shirts being stored away (symptomatically, the man's clothes are dealt with by a maid and the woman's are dealt with by herself).[53] The question of the house is first of all a question of clothing. Even when addressing Behrens in the 1913 essay, it was a question of dress. Behrens's architecture is modern because it "convey[s] the impression of coherent architecture which has at last discovered the right dress for the life style of the times and firmly rejects the romantic residue of past styles as cowardly and unreal."[54] And, as Gropius says of the enlightened industrial client: "a handsome outfit reflects on its wearer and the new design will encourage positive conclusions as to the character of the firm as a whole."[55] To dress oneself up in the right architecture is to modernize oneself. Likewise, a handsome surface reflects well on the building it clothes. Although a "new look" cannot in the end cover over the problems of mechanization, the solving of those problems is best exemplified by the correct choice of clothes.

In fact, the look is all important. Gropius ends up arguing that the experience of architecture is fundamentally optical. Equating the human eye with a camera, he argues that architecture is not a question of material or structural reality but of the effect of the particular surfaces it presents to the observer. At one point, his "Is There a Science of Design?" of 1947 goes as far as comparing the effect on the psychological perception of a building produced by the addition of particular patterns to the effect of the same patterns on a woman's swimsuit. In adding these patterns of parallel lines to the original photos, he elaborates a "fashion tip" that he found in a newspaper. The optical effect of such lines is apparently "an important fact to know for architecture and fashion design."[56] In going on to describe a number of such optical effects, Gropius offers his own set of fashion tips, suggesting that the "surfaces" of architecture can be deployed in a way that produces the much

needed "stimulation." These tips are presented as the "common denominator" of design, the basic "language" with which the designer can "organize the psychological effects of his creation at will." Modern architecture is understood as a kind of ongoing research into this language of sartorial effects.

Although such theories of perception are used to determine the correct choice of clothes for architecture, this choice is not meant to restrict the choices of its occupants. On the contrary, Gropius uses his 1924 article on industrialized housing to argue that standardized clothes act as a model of individual variations within the collective social body: "Adequate freedom remains for the individual or national character to express itself, exactly as in the case of our clothing, and yet all of it will bear the stamp of our era."[57] A year later, when he publishes the work of the Bauhaus workshops (which, of course, does not include clothes), he renegotiates the long-debated relationship between standard types and individual expression by appealing to the standardization of clothes in the face of fashion: "A violation of the individual by the production of types is to be feared as little as a full uniformization of clothing by the dictates of fashion. Despite the typical homogeneity of the separate parts, the individual reserves a free play of personal variation."[58] It is not surprising that two years later Gropius's "How Can We Build Cheaper, More Attractive Houses?" literally argues that the standard parts of an industrialized architecture should be purchased "off-the-peg," like shoes, and that their "recurrence in differently shaped buildings will have an orderly and soothing effect as does the uniformity of our clothes."[59] And by the time of *The New Architecture and the Bauhaus* of 1935, these isolated claims had been gathered together and reformulated as a concise argument:

The repetition of standardized parts, and the use of identical materials in different buildings, will have the same sort of coordinating and sobering effect on the aspect of our towns as uniformity of type in modern attire has in social life. But that will in no sense restrict the architect's freedom of design. For although every house and block of flats will bear the unmistakable imprint of our age, there will always remain, as in the clothes we wear, sufficient scope for the individual to find expression for his own personality.[60]

Indeed, Gropius's 1910 "Program for the Establishment of a Company for the Provision of Housing on Aesthetically Consistent Principles" had already credited this "civilizing" transnational uniformity of clothing types to fashion itself: "National costumes tend to disappear and fashion is becoming a common factor in all civilized countries. In the same way there is bound to be a common factor in all civilized countries."[61] But having dislodged regional characteristics, fashion must be disciplined, brought into line, a line it cannot twist. Because standardizing clothes in this way is not to impose a uniform, Gropius uses a late address of 1953 to literally criticize the West Point military uniforms shown in a photograph for their "deliberate rigid conformity; de-individualization of the wearer" in contrast to the variations evident within a photograph of the traditional dress of Japan and India that is captioned: "Unity of basic cut, but individual variation of patterns and accessories."[62] Standardized architecture, the architecture that resists fashion, is a basic wardrobe of garments that go together in different combinations. Gropius's industrialized housing projects were always conceived as kits of standard parts that could be purchased and assembled in different combinations, mix-and-match architecture that, with the judicious addition of patterns and accessories, supposedly enables endless variations without participating in the degenerate economy of fashion. And, of course, each part, each garment, was coated in white to signal its resistance to that economy. Not by chance does the colored rendering of the factory and office complex for the Werkbund exhibition of 1914 have two stylishly dressed women stepping into the foreground. The modern cut of the outfits is associated with the calibrated play of glass and white surfaces behind them. As Gropius's search for industrialized form discarded most of the references to Wright and the Secessionists that are so evident in this building, the outfits were also modernized; the equivalent woman in the foreground of the colored rendering of the curved glass walls of the 1927 project for a "total theater" is only marked by the extremely simple lines of her outfit. Building and dress are progressively perfected.

But this rejection of fashion in favor of standardized clothes, like all such attacks, threatens to turn against the person who makes it. From the beginning,

4.8

Walter Gropius and Adolf Meyer, rendered perspective of Factory and Office Building for the Werkbund Exhibition, Cologne, 1914.

Gropius preemptively defends himself against this threat by denying that the Bauhaus itself is concerned with producing a house style, a new fashion, a "vogue" of "bauhaus garb."[63] The constant threat is that the removal of ornament might itself be perceived as a fashionable move. Indeed, he must immediately defend himself against repeated claims that the role of the school was precisely to produce an easily marketed fashion line. *The New Architecture and the Bauhaus* notes that "We had also to hold our own in another direction: against detractors who sought to identify every building and object in which ornament seemed to be discarded as examples of an imaginary 'Bauhaus Style'; and imitators who prostituted our fundamental precepts into modish trivialities."[64] The book attempts to defend the whole project of modern architecture from such accusations and appropriations:

Although the outward forms of the New Architecture differ fundamentally in an organic sense from those of the old, they are not the personal whims of a handful of architects avid for innovation at all cost, but simply the inevitable logical product of the intellectual, social and technical conditions of our age. . . . But the development of the New Architecture encountered serious obstacles at a very early stage of its development. . . . Worst of all, 'modern' architecture became fashionable; with the result that formalistic imitation and snobbery distorted the fundamental truth and simplicity on which this renaissance was based. That is why the movement must be purged from within if its original aims are to be saved from the straight-jacket of materialism and false slogans inspired by plagiarism or misconception.[65]

From the beginning, the protagonists of modern architecture attempted to discipline not only the material building but also their colleagues. In a sense, Giedion attempted to carry out the "purge" Gropius called for, relentlessly negotiating between the danger of the straight-jacket on the one hand and that of fashionable clothes on the other, the encyclopedic scale of his work veiling the specific exclusions and censorships necessary to disassociate modern architecture from fashion. In the end, he failed to save his favorite architect. Gropius's defense eventually collapsed; by the mid–1960s he was routinely condemned as a fashion-monger. The critics even dismiss his first curtain wall, hung at the Fagus factory in 1911, around which Giedion and Pevsner's extraordinarily influential narratives were organized, such that the building, as Banham puts it, "is frequently taken to be the first building of the Modern Movement properly so-called."[66] It ends up being identified as but a decorative front added to give a modern "look" to a traditional structure whose internal layout and details (except for a very Hoffmann-esque lobby) had in fact already been designed by another architect. The client literally commissioned Gropius to "see what you can do with the facade," providing the *künstlerische* ("artistic") design for the project "in order to give the whole plant a *geschmacksvoll* (tasteful, even "fashionable") appearance."[67] The famous floating glass wall that supposedly unmasks architectural space

4.10
Faguswerke, 2nd floor of the main building staircase. Building completed 1913/14. All interior fittings 1922/23. Photo: Edmund Lill, Hannover, 1923.

turns out to be but a fashionable mask of transparency disguising what it apparently reveals. And this masquerade is treated as exemplary of Gropius's life work rather than its necessarily limited beginnings, let alone as a clue to the operations of all modern architecture. He ends up being vilified in surprisingly dismissive terms by influential writers of the following generation, like Colin Rowe, and their followers. While marketing their own form of analysis that is itself extremely vulnerable to the very same critique, they argue that he is an inadequate architect who produced a marketable style for easy consumption, even crediting his emphasis on a "camouflage of retinal excitement" that supposedly reinforces a logic of the "false front" with the emergence of postmodernism.[68] The anti-fashion argument has turned on its most dedicated promoter and devoured him.

Why is it that the other "masters," his fellow apprentices in Behrens office, Le Corbusier and Mies van de Rohe, and all their colleagues, are not brought before the inquisition even though so many of them seem more vulnerable to the charge? Indeed, Gropius's collapse into fashion is often opposed to Le Corbusier's resistance to it.[69] He is, as it were, the master who had to be sacrificed in order to maintain the good name of modern architecture, removing the taint of fashion without threatening the movement. But the convolutions of fashion are clearly not unique to Gropius. They can easily be found in all his contemporaries who, although never dismissed, let alone with such brutality, employ exactly the same arguments against fashion in favor of standardized clothing but, in so doing, likewise organize modern architecture around the necessity for a certain "look" inextricably linked to the world of fashion. Gropius is not even an especially good example of the fashion trap. Indeed, he may well have been singled out for excommunication precisely because of his lifelong commitment to industrialized housing (where the aesthetic choices are supposedly made by the client rather than the name designer) and his parallel commitment to collaboration. Both gestures blur the artist's signature and thereby threaten the very idea of mastery. In the end, Gropius effaces the ostensible gap between high signature design and the marketplace, a move that had already been formulated in the Bauhaus ideal of the "anonymous designer" and was maintained by his refusal to disguise the "commercial" basis of his late work. It is one of the intricacies of the fashion trap that those who are dismissed as fashionable are usually dismissed because something in their practice exposes the duplicity of the antifashion argument. Precisely by being more rigorous in certain dimensions of his opposition to fashion and thereby redefining certain institutional practices, Gropius is dismissed by those who wish to preserve those practices. After all, the attempt to discipline figures like Gropius is no more than an attempt to preserve the discipline.

Disciplining the Surface

In fact, Gropius's use of the standardization of modern clothing as the model for modern architecture and the corresponding promotion of the calculated "look" of modernity is written into the entire discourse around that architecture. Take his colleague in the Deutscher Werkbund, Bruno Taut, for example. His *Modern Architecture* of 1929 opens with the generic contrast between the "old-fashionedness" of the contemporary house and the style of modern clothes, asking how it would look if the "be-wigged, long coated gentlemen and ladies in hoops" that belong to that architecture were to ride in the latest car.[70] Taut concludes that "tailors and dressmakers," like the engineers and constructors of modern technical equipment, "have merely accomplished what we architects now consider necessary to accomplish in our own profession."[71] This general claim resonates throughout the specific details of the text, as when it criticizes the use of architectural styles to mask the new reality of engineering construction, which is so prevalent that the architectural term "facade" has become the general term for "mask" and a pervasive logic of fashion has taken over: "As in the face of an incontrovertible law of nature, we must bow to the fact that in architecture there will always be some who, like wholesale outfitters and costumers, will have saleable models and 'designs' in stock, people who are ever on the look out for the newest patterns and 'dernier cri,' which, accordingly, they are able to turn into cash."[72] Against such fashion retailers with their ready-to-wear architectural fashions, Taut later defends the standardized business suit as a model for architecture, arguing that neither modern business leaders nor their buildings need old-fashioned "costume" or "fancy-dress" to signify their prestige. Just as the business leader "might miss the ease of his tailored suit" if he were "attired in the trappings" of old wealth, "so would the fulfillment of purpose suffer under the stress of an architectural 'costume'."[73] Nevertheless, almost all state buildings are seen to employ such an "absurd masquerade"; the new League of Nations building exemplifies it by adopting a "masquerading attitude" that establishes a "disguise covering the clean-cut reality of the building's purpose."[74] Not surprisingly, Le Corbusier's rejected scheme is offered as the model of a well-tailored building. Later in the text, the social consequences of removing the clothing of architectural styles are drawn out by comparing the way the building has traditionally been forced to labor "under the disguise and shrouding of the purpose itself" to the way the "workman" has traditionally been forced to "wear a special costume, just as waiters today still wear their dress-suits" when working in the presence of the ruling class.[75] While opposed to the whims of fashion, modern architecture is, from the beginning, an art of tailoring.

Similar arguments can be found in the influential essays of Theo van Doesburg of the same time. His May 1925 article for *Het Bouwbedrijf,* for example, explicitly argues that the new goal throughout European architecture is a form of tailoring that privileges form over decoration: "The architecture of the past, which over-indulged in decorative ostentation, was stripped of its earrings, necklaces and lace frills. What counted most was 'tailoring'. Everything that did not belong to the essence of the architectural *form* was eliminated."[76] Significantly, it is German architects, like Behrens, Gropius, Otto Wagner, and Adolf Loos, who have been "reared with excellent theories (for instance Semper's *Der Stil*),"[77] that are seen to have effected this move toward a more functional dress for architecture—as distinct from an architecture in which all dress has been removed. Likewise, van Doesburg's May 1926 article for *Het Bouwbedrijf* argues: "As during the course of time the tailoring of our clothing, the shapes of transportation vehicles, our hairdos, handwriting etc. have changed, so has the 'tailoring' of architecture changed—and because of the same reasons."[78] The specific role of this tailoring is identified in another essay of the same year that addresses the industrialization of architecture along assembly line principles. Symptomatically, this is illustrated with a photo of a "Ladies' Fashion Boutique" called "Femina" that was designed in 1923, described as "facade-architecture with reminiscences of the Wiener Werkstätte."[79] Such individual fashions are opposed to the sense of standardized tailoring that had been promoted by Loos:

It is always a sign of a kind of narrow-mindedness when a person dresses very individualistically, according to his or her own design and own tailoring. "The modern, intelligent person must present a mask to other people," says Loos. This mask is the general life form, originating from necessity and culture, a person's life habits, his clothing and physiognomy, all crystallized together in his dwelling. His dwelling is his mask.[80]

The removal of the decorative mask of fashion is clearly not the removal of all masks. If for Loos, as Colomina argues, the exterior of the house should discretely mask its interior in the same way that the nervous individual is securely walled in by a business suit or dinner jacket within the crowded metropolis, then ornament is to be disciplined rather than removed. After all, the structure it covers is not so secure. On the contrary, it is the source of all insecurity, including that experienced by the discipline of architecture. Like the building, the architect has to blend in with the crowd. As Margaret Olin puts it when describing Loos's use of Semper:

[While Loos] cleansed his surfaces of ornament to reveal underlying structures, the same goal led the nineteenth-century architect to cover surfaces with ornament, revealing structure through clarification and punctuation. . . . The covertly symbolic nature of self-representation in modernism is more obvious in human self-representation as expressed in clothing. Modernist architects were in agreement that such representation should be forthright, and done without ornament. Yet the modernist demonstrated his lack of ornament only by cladding himself in the symbols, such as the "correct hat," that demonstrate one's membership in society.[81]

The logic of the well-cut suit is that of the disciplined surface, the set of clothes whose smooth surface maintains certain distinctions (notably, masculine versus feminine, upper versus lower, and so on) yet gives nothing away. Everywhere, the discourse of modern architecture turns on the privileged status of the smooth surface. For van Doesburg, for example, the search for well-tailored architecture corresponds to the search for forms with *an inner purity and with an outer surface of equal merit.*[82] Despite his rejection of the dangerously fashionable manipulation of surface, the end point is always the surface. In a Semperian sense, structure has to be disciplined in order to make the right surface possible. The final goal is the surface, not the construction that supports it. Architecture is no more than an effect of surfaces, an effect that is facilitated by the structure that props the surfaces up, but one that is, in the end, independent of that structure. Van Doesburg's review of the

1927 Weissenhofsiedlung makes it clear that for him as for Gropius, even while he criticizes Le Corbusier's excessively painterly concern with "surprising visual effects," it is the look of the surfaces presented to its occupants, understood as the look of its clothing, that determines the effect of architecture:

It is my utter conviction . . . that only the *ultimate surface* is decisive in architecture . . . the ultimate surface is in itself the result of the construction. The latter expresses itself in the ultimate surface. Bad construction leads to a bad surface . . . the finishing touch is in the finish of the surface . . . the development of the ultimate surface is essential . . . only the surface is of importance to people. Man does not live within the construction, within the architectural skeleton, but only touches architecture essentially through its ultimate surface (externally as the city scape, internally as the interior). The functional element becomes automatic, only the summarizing surface is of importance, for sensory perception as well as for psychological well-being. It has an impact on the morale of the inhabitant. . . . Houses are like people. Their features, posture, gait, clothing, in short: their surface, is a reflection of their thinking, their inner life.[83]

This physiognomic privileging of the surface, and the smooth surface in particular, understood as a form of clothing, is especially evident in Giedion's writing. It is even written into his historiographical method which involves interrogating the multiple surfaces of everyday cultural life. He always describes history in terms of surface. The forward to *The Beginnings of Art,* for example, refers to "our attitude towards the past, that measureless container of human experience, only fragments of which come up to the surface, most of it lying dominant in unfathomable depths," before going on to argue that "both above and below the surface of our present age there is a new demand for continuity."[84] Giedion inherited this approach from his teacher, Heinrich Wöfflin, whose "psychology of art" involves scrutinizing all the surfaces of society, especially its clothes. Indeed, Wölfflin (an earnest supporter of clothing reform)[85] literally equates the surfaces of architecture with those of clothes, as is already made clear by the way he begins the conclusion of his doctoral dissertation *Prolegomena to a Psychology of Architecture* of 1886 under the influence of Semper: "We have seen how the general human condition sets the standard for architecture. This principle may be extended still further: any architectural style reflects the *attitude and movement of people* in the period concerned. How people like to move and carry themselves is expressed above all in their costume, and it is not difficult to show that architecture corresponds to the costume of its period."[86] In order to show how "a psychological feeling is directly transformed into bodily form," Wölfflin goes on to compare Gothic architecture to the shoes and hats worn by its inhabitants. He does so in a way that makes it clear that the material structure is completely subordinated to the look of the dressing. The psyche is invested in the surface: "The human foot points forward but does that show in the blunt outline in which it terminates? No. The Gothic age was troubled by this lack of the precise expression of a will, and so it devised a shoe with a long pointed toe. . . . The width of the sole is a result of the body's weight. But the body has no rights; it is material, and no concessions are to be made to senseless matter. The will must penetrate every part." [87]

Likewise, Giedion's approach remains Semperian (despite its overt rejection of Semper in the name of Riegl), inasmuch as it too focuses on smaller-scale anonymous forms of production. [88] The qualities he seeks in *Space, Time and Architecture,* while everywhere opposing fashion, are "flat unmodulated surfaces . . . naked wall . . . flat surface . . . no restlessness or turbulence." Until "the pure flat surface" of modern architecture, the wall had been "either chaotically dismembered or deception." Indeed, modern architecture is seen to modern only insofar as it transforms the status of the surface: "Surface, which was formerly held to possess no intrinsic capacity for expression, and so at best could only find decorative utilization, has now become the basis of composition . . . surface acquired a significance it had never known before." [89] This new status is explicitly opposed to the superficial qualities of fashion. The flat wall, the plane surface, is "not simply another transitory fashion but an inner affinity," [90] a moral identification with inner human needs that, as he says later, "were just coming to the surface." Because these fundamental needs transcend history, the place to find them is in prehistory. Giedion's last books, the two on *The Eternal Present,* go to a lot of trouble to demonstrate that art originates with the "smooth, shadowless plane surface." [91] Modern art is thus seen as therapeutic inasmuch as it recovers this primordial surface in the face of all the decorative excesses that actively suppress it. What comes to the surface, then, is the smooth surface. All Giedion's talk about the need to penetrate the surface in order to avoid its seductions does not lead to its rejection. On the contrary, it is all about the preservation of a particular kind of surface, one that can discipline the ornamentation that might be embroidered upon it. All the scholarly rhetoric about the need for depth gives way to a formidable regime of the smooth surface.

In fact, Giedion's grand narrative about the three space conceptions that have orchestrated the millennia is nothing more than a history of the status of surface. It follows Riegl in beginning with the Egyptian and Greek conception in which the prehistoric play of "endlessly changing surfaces" is reassembled to create a "smooth unbroken plane," a sensuous surface without any sense of space. [92] This in turn gives way in the middle of the Roman period to a conscious search for space, understood as the depth of an interior. When modern art begins to produce the third conception, this is framed as a return to the first conception, if not its prehistoric origins, inasmuch as there is no longer a clear-cut distinction between inside and outside; rather, there is a collage of suspended and mobile surfaces in which, in its definitive form, "solid and void, inside and outside, flow continuously into one another."[93] Naturally, Giedion sees modern architecture, and Le Corbusier's work in particular, as exemplifying this "rediscovery of the surface plane."[94] Indeed, Giedion's loyalty swings from Gropius to Le Corbusier in order to preserve this analysis; the new introduction to the last edition of *Space, Time and Architecture* insists that "Le Corbusier was more closely connected than others to that Eternal Present which lives in the creative artifacts of all periods."[95]

Clearly Le Corbusier, like Giedion, presents the smooth wall as a moral code rather than a fashion statement. The emphatic privileging of the surface is equally explicit in his writing. When he insists that architecture should be stripped of its outmoded fashions, he maintains that its body is still "clothed" by a surface—a surface that, no matter how thin, still has the capacity to threaten the mass it covers. That it must, therefore, be disciplined, is apparent in the second (and almost always omitted) part of what is probably Le Corbusier's most often cited statement: "Architecture being the masterly, correct and magnificent play of masses brought together in light, the task of the architect is to vitalize the surfaces which clothe these masses, but in such a way that these surfaces do not become parasitical, eating up the mass and absorbing it to their own advantage."[96] It is no surprise that Giedion is one of the few writers to cite this passage in full, which he does at the conclusion of *The Beginnings of Architecture.*[97] His claim that Le Corbusier leads the way in the modern "revitalization" of the surface comes directly from Le Corbusier's writings, which present a comprehensive theory of the disciplined surface. Much more of *Vers une architecture,* for example, is devoted to the question of surface than the section literally entitled "Surface." With the removal of the dead clothes, the surface fabric must be "appropriated" again by the internal logic of the building, "revitalized from within," such that forms "display their own surfaces."[98] This requires a new kind of surface, a new kind of cloth that is neither completely opaque or completely transparent to the forms it covers. The thick "old clothes" produced by the "surface decoration of facades and of drawing-rooms" are to be supplanted by the recovery of the architecture of the "great periods" when "facades were smooth" and "walls were as thin as they dare make them."[99] The surface is not simply recovered by utility. Rather, it assumes its own utility, its function becoming more important than that of the building it clothes. Rather than lining an architectural space that facilitates certain functions, the surface produces the effect of space in the first place. For Le Corbusier, the specific dilemma is how to rupture this surface for functional reasons while maintaining the strategic effects of space and mass it produces.

Furthermore, this exemplary surface that actively resists the immoralities of fashion, and around which the discourse of modern architecture organizes itself, is not simply smooth. It is white. The disciplined surface is exemplified by the white wall. In the face of the wild colors of the old clothes embraced by the "sensualists," Le Corbusier counters: "There is only one color, white; always powerful since it is positive."[100] This stark opposition between fashion and the white wall becomes even more clear in *L'art décoratif d'aujourd'hui:*

What shimmering silks, what fancy, glittering marbles, what opulent bronzes and golds!

What fashionable blacks, what striking vermilions, what silver lamés from Byzantium and the Orient! Enough.

Such stuff founders in a narcotic haze. Let's have done with it.

We will soon have had more than enough.

It is time to crusade for whitewash and Diogenes.[101]

It must be remembered that Diogenes is a key figure for all the writers that Le Corbusier appropriates extensively: Behrens, Loos, Muthesius, and Morris. Like the other "ornamentalist," Semper (and his disciples Sullivan and Loos), Morris uses Diogenes's polemical refusal of excess (including the distinction between clothes and house) as a model for the reduction of ornamentation in favor of essentials that allows ornament to then be liberated without degenerating into gratuitous style. Symptomatically, Morris approves of Diogenes's minimalist house at the beginning of an essay that ends by arguing that the way the "simplicity" of contemporary women's dress design has resisted the "extravagances of fashion" is the appropriate model for reform in the other arts.[102] Le Corbusier's reference to Diogenes is therefore charged in a very particular way. His text, as always, is organized around its sporadic jabs against fashion. It attacks the Sun King's "coiffure of ostrich feathers, in red, canary, and pale blue; ermine, silk, brocade, and lace" as an "intoxication."[103] Elsewhere, it lampoons a book entitled *Fashionable Architecture* and a journal subtitled *Literature, Art, Fashion.* The historical styles, which are described as random surface "modalities," "narcotic fetishes," are yet again linked to misplaced sexuality. But still, this "quasi-orgiastic decoration" must be replaced rather than simply removed. Even the idea of "expressing the construction" is dismissed, as it had been by Sullivan, as being no more than a "fashion."[104] The body is not to be exposed. It is not a question of wearing clothing which represents the structure it covers, but of wearing minimal clothing, a decent cover. The surfaces that clothe architecture must remain a discrete mask.

Again, it is crucial to understand that for Le Corbusier these surfaces produce space as such rather than appear "in" it. The house, for example, is defined by surfaces. It is nothing but a set of surfaces. As can be seen *La Ville*

Radieuse (The radiant city) of 1935, Le Corbusier's understanding of housing is literally that of the "habitable surface," which is to say, the surface that caters to all the body's needs and thereby frees the mind. It is in this sense that he associates surface, cleanliness, order, morality, and tailoring: "To walk over a clean surface, to look at an orderly scene. Live *decently*. Only the tailor, the shoemaker and the laundryman help us to hold on to the right to remain the intellects of the universe."[105] Le Corbusier's architecture is indeed a tailored architecture. Although the body of the building has been exercised, becoming leaner and fitter, like those that promenade within it, the design of its outfit is a separate problem. A thin mask is required but a mask nonetheless—one that transforms the psychological effect of the structure it veils.

This layer becomes visible as such when Giedion publishes before and after images of Villa la Roche in a 1927 issue of *Der Cicerone* (and later in *Bauen in Frankreich*) that demonstrate the extent to which the machine age finish of white-painted stucco is but a "look" that veils the basically handcrafted structure beneath, just as Badovici's publication of before and after images of Villa Savoye will do in a 1931 issue of *L'Architecture vivante*. While Le Corbusier himself never publishes such revealing images (and Giedion leaves them out of *Space, Time and Architecture*), it is clear that he actually perfects the mask before perfecting the construction underneath, mastering the image of modern functionality before functionality itself. He ultimately gives up on the white exterior surface only because he lacks the technical control to avoid cracks—cracks that completely subvert the status of the surface by revealing that it is but a coat. The central issue is always the technology of the surface itself rather than the technology of what it covers.

Abb. 22, 23. Le Corbusier: Haus Laroche in Auteuil. Architektonische Durchblutung der Skizze Abb. 19
Links: die Struktur
Rechts: der ausgeführte Bau

4.11
Le Corbusier and Pierre Jeanneret, Villa La Roche (1923), as published by Sigfried Giedion in Der Cicerone, *1927.*

4.12
Le Corbusier and Pierre Jeanneret, Villa Savoye, Poissy (1928–1930), as published in L'Architecture vivante, *1931.*

LC ET P. J.

LA MAISON SAVOYE A POISSY. 1928-30

L'ARCHITECTURE VIVANTE

ÉTÉ MCMXXXI

ÉDITIONS ALBERT MORANCÉ

2

The white wall has to be understood in terms of the specific argument about clothing and architecture that Le Corbusier imported, stripped of its signature, and redistributed (along with so much of the German discourse). This argument ties the "Law of Ripolin" back to Semper's "Principle of Dressing" through the intermediary of Loos's "Law of Dressing." The initially surprising connection is far from arbitrary. Not only was Le Corbusier drawing on a German discourse multiply indebted to Semper's arguments, but his particular translation of that discourse required at least a minimal staging of those very arguments. It is not by chance that the very first essay that Le Corbusier, Ozenfant, and Dermée published in the first issue of *L'Esprit Nouveau*, written by Victor Basch, turns on Semper's account of the industrial arts, or that the second part of the essay begins the second issue in which Adolf Loos's "Ornament and Crime" is republished. Semper is, as it were, put in place to prop up the new discourse and then the prop is quickly thrown away.

Likewise, when Giedion produces an extreme version of Le Corbusier's argument, by elaborating on the transhistorical integrity of the smooth surface, it is not simply to establish a clear-cut opposition between the dissimulating texture of ornament and Art, which is seen to begin with such a surface. Giedion overtly follows Riegl (who is covertly following Semper) in arguing that art does not simply begin with the plane surface but with everything that might go on upon that surface, including and especially ornamentation. The plane surface is, then, no more than the mechanism for establishing that whatever goes "on" is ornamentation. The smooth surface is that which makes ornament visible. It is the very possibility of ornament as such, and therefore the possibility for a history of ornament as a history of culture's impressions upon it. But it cannot simply be separated from the ornament it makes visible as such. Giedion ends up, immediately after dismissing "the materialist approach of Gottfried Semper and his followers," [106] by approving of Riegl's close echo of Semper that "sees ornamentation as the purest and most lucid expression of artistic volition." [107] In its very smoothness, the primordial surface participates fully in the ornamental economy of surface effects that it supposedly disciplines. Likewise, its whiteness participates fully in the economy of clothing whose excesses it supposedly restrains.

At first glance, it is clear that if women's fashion is almost invariably constructed as the limit of the discourse of modern architecture, the mark of its supposedly personal and feminine outside, then the mark of the inside, of the standard, of impersonal masculine detachment, is the white wall. Consequently, when fashion does become explicit, it is likely that the white wall, whose effects are usually mobilized without being marked, becomes explicit, and vice versa. When Marcel Breuer's essay in the March 1935 issue of *Architectural Review* entitled "Where do we Stand?" opposes the dangers of the "purely transient vogue" to the integrity of "winning color, plasticity, and animation from a flat white wall," for example, it is not surprising that it follows an explicit attack on women's fashions:

The 'new' in the Modern Movement must be considered simply a means to an end, not an end in itself as in women's fashions. What we aim at and believe to be possible is that the solutions embodied in the forms of the New Architecture should endure for 10, 20 or 100 years as circumstances may demand—a thing unthinkable in the world of fashion as long as modes are modes. It follows that, though we have no fear of what is new, novelty is not our aim. We seek what is definite and real, whether old or new . . . we have tired of everything in architecture which is a matter of fashion; we find all intentionally new forms wearisome, and all those based on personal predilections or tendencies equally pointless. To which can be added the simple consideration that we cannot hope to change our buildings or furniture as often as we change, for example, our ties.[108]

For Breuer, as for all his colleagues, the Modern movement is the architectural equivalent of the masculine resistance to fashion. The white wall is an item of clothing, authorized at once by modernity and the classical tradition, a recovery of the spartan puritan dress that befits the controlled nobility required in the face of mechanized life. It is a kind of athletic dress. After all, Loos had argued that the rationalization of men's clothing derives from its adoption of the transformations in sports dress. The white wall is the sports outfit of architecture, a thin coat over the newly pumped-up body of the building, an exercise outfit like those that can be found in so many images of modern architecture that show its occupants working out, as in Breuer's own 1930 interior "for a lady gymnastics teacher." And it is not by chance that the figure is that of a woman: Loos had gone as far as to claim that the adoption of sports dress by women would not just symbolize but actually effect their emancipation in its resistance to the immoral economy of fashion.[109] The body that needs to be tamed, disciplined by the emerging and regular rhythms of anonymous production, was understood to be feminine. The horror of mechanization is precisely its potential to release the very femininity it is supposed to control—the possibility that it might itself, in disordering the surfaces of everyday life, be feminine.

The figure of the woman in the white sports outfit can be found throughout the promotion of modern architecture. It is even used to establish the fundamental relationship between architecture and dress, as can be seen in a series of articles that were published alongside Breuer's call for the flat white wall that resists fashion. In the previous issue of *Architectural Review*, Geoffrey

Boumphrey collages an image of a woman in an old-fashioned dress into a room with Louis XV decoration, noting the harmony between them before relocating the woman into a modern gymnasium and asking "WHY is our eye so offended by the juxtaposition of fancy dress and gymnasium? . . . Miss Mildew's dress is suggesting one thing, her gymnasium is suggesting another. And what do they suggest? The gym, function—the dress, facade." An image of a woman in a trim white sports outfit is then collaged into the same space alongside the declaration "star, costume and setting are all of a piece—and a very nice piece too! But we must tear our eyes reluctantly away and get back to Miss Mildew." After criticizing any dissonance between clothing and space, Boumphrey is able to conclude that "clothes are part of the decoration . . . but fancy dress cannot be allowed. . . Modern decoration should suit modern dress—and modern dress suit modern life." [110] The attraction of the stripped-down white walls of modern architecture is unambiguously aligned with an erotically charged image of a woman flexing her body in a minimalist white outfit.

Perhaps the paradigm of modern architecture, in its simultaneous engagement with and resistance to mechanization, is the white tennis outfit at the

4.13
"The new practical tennis costume, whose general introduction in America is striven for." Illustration from Sigfried Giedion, Befreites Wohnen *(1929), originally taken from* Illustrietes Blatt *(1929).*

4.14
Traffic policeman in Milan. Illustration from Sigfried Giedion, "Situation de l'architecture contemporani en Italie," Cahiers d'art, *1931.*

end of Giedion's 1929 *Befreites Wohnen* (opposite an image of André Lurçat's white rooftop gymnasium) that is worn by a woman that smiles coyly at the reader across the net—rather than the white uniform of the traffic policeman that Giedion smuggles into a 1931 survey of Italian architecture as if it is a kind of self-portrait of the historian directing the flow of architectural movements. But why is Giedion's tennis outfit exhibited by a fashion model? Why has the image been taken from the fashion pages of an illustrated magazine? And why does the frontispiece of the book display a quote from Henry Ford—the very figure of mass-production and standardization—that appears to embrace the rapid turnover of clothing styles: "The form of housing will be transformed with the same speed that changes occur in the style of clothes and even the domestic situation will undergo alterations. Until now it took a lot of time, but from now on progress will set a very fast pace."[111] The logic of standardization seems to stand here for the accelerated circulation of fashions rather than the reverse. This raises the possibility that the white wall, supposedly marking the loss of fashion, may itself be nothing more than a fashion statement, ready to be changed in the next season. All the elaborate attempts to isolate the white wall from fashion, locating it within a millennial tradition passing from ancient Egypt through the Mediterranean vernacular, may, in the end, be insufficient to block the obvi-

4.15
*Illustration from
Geoffrey Boumphrey's
"Facade and Function,"*
Architectural Review,
1935.

ous thought that it is just a look. But not just any look: It is the look of a resistance to fashion, the antifashion look.

The unique complications of this architectural fashion that so loudly proclaims its detachment from fashion need to be patiently traced and its historical specificities need to be carefully established in order to understand modern architecture's precise strategic role. Only after such an analysis would the nuances of the contemporary commodification of architectural discourse start to become visible. Clearly, the twisted but dominant (indeed, dominant because twisted) pathology of the antifashion look does not go away when white architecture is no longer in vogue. "White" architecture is not so white anyway. Most of the canonic walls were off-white (which necessitates an interrogation of the strategic role of a surface just short or long of white) and some of the most famous were actually lightly colored and only appear white in photographs, while the rest played a key role in organizing a whole system of polychromy. It is the "idea" of the white surface that plays a key role in holding together a specific conceptual economy, giving architecture a certain cultural status by maintaining certain assumptions about surface in general, rather than engaging with particular surfaces. The white surface marks the disavowal of the structural role of surface. The existence of one surface that denies surface—whether it be in one part of a building, or one part of a theory, or one historical moment—sustains an economy in which surface is everywhere subordinated. But this subordination is itself only ever a surface effect. It is the self-subordination of a surface that is more controlling than controlled. Modern architecture is never more than a surface effect. This is in no way to call into question its force. On the contrary, it derives its force from the surface, concentrating its energies on the outer layer made available to the viewer, who is understood in Gropius's terms as a camera passing through the building. One photograph, that of the white wall, is seen to exemplify the whole process. It is the exposure of the exposure, the exposure of the surface that exposes everything.

To look closely at this white surface is to begin to call into question a cultural regime with wide-ranging effects, of which the blind-spots of the dominant architectural historiography is but one symptom. A key symptom nevertheless, because that regime can only operate as a disciplinary mechanism by appealing to a certain image of architecture. It is not by chance that would-be cultural critics within and outside architectural discourse actually consolidate the very economy they claim to critique by employing this image. They appeal to, and protect, a generic image of modern architecture, the image of the subordinated surface. To see that this subordination is but a surface effect is not just to rethink modern architecture. It is also to displace the terms of political critique. To say the least, it becomes difficult to detach the so-called postmodern fashion industry from the so-called modern avant-garde.

Of course, these phenomena are very different and should never be confused. But neither can they simply be separated, let alone opposed, on the grounds that one accepts fashion and the other rejects it. Indeed, fashion is one of the things that bind them together in ways that the apologists for both forms of practice might find disconcerting. If the historical avant-garde still serves as the model for theorists who oppose fashion, it must be remembered that it is also the model for the very theorists and practitioners that they condemn. A more nuanced understanding of the way architecture participates in the contemporary economies of fashion would result from investigating the specific engagements with fashion that underpin critical practices rather than attempting to isolate architecture from fashion or mourning the loss of some mythical isolation in the near or distant past.

124

Because the extraordinarily overdetermined surface of the white wall is one of the strongest threads that stitch together the current marketplace of architectural discourse and that of the historical avant-garde, in ways that produce discomfort for the promoters of both, such an investigation might well begin by returning to the white surface to scratch the seemingly interminable itch produced by such an antifashion fashion.

After all, when Giedion tries to hold the line between the white surfaces of Sullivan's department store and the ornamental scheme of its ground floors, it is not by chance that the role of that ornamentation is literally to frame fashion displays in the store windows. Giedion, who always associates fashion with ornament, and collected fashion plates of the period, was clearly aware of this. His text had already noted that American department stores emerged from "ready-to-wear clothing concerns" and even reproduced one of their earliest advertisements.[112] To exclude the ground floors was no more than the attempt to hold the line between modern architecture and fashion. To note that the fashions displayed in the windows were actually to be found above the line in the third and fourth floors (with "dress accessories" and "fabrics" on the lower floors) and, likewise, that Sullivan's ornament cannot be contained to the ground floor—that it passes up through the building's very struc-

4.16
White shirts framed by Louis Sullivan's Schlesinger and Mayer department store (1899–1904), as published in Architectural Record, *July 1904.*

ture, such that the white surface emerges from it, rather than exposes and excludes it—is only to say that the line between architecture and fashion is endlessly convoluted. Not only can fashion never be cut off from modern architecture, modern architecture emerges from the very economy of fashion that it so loudly condemns. Indeed, its very rejection of fashion is a product of that economy. The antifashion fashion holds a unique grip on architectural discourse. To return yet again to the white surface will be to explore the complications of this simple, if not obvious, thought.

All through, as we discuss fashion in the house's face and form and clothing, it will do no harm to realize that we are skating the surface of a lake of unknown depth.

—Lionel Brett, *The Things We See: Houses*, 1947.

The Antifashion Fashion

As is well known, the institutions of fashion were subjected to a sustained assault throughout the second half of the nineteenth century by the dress-reform movement, an assault that came to transform the condition of dominant clothing designs. The movement was a unique blend of medical, socialist, feminist, and artistic rejections of fashion.[1] From the 1830s on, the medical profession lobbied for "healthier" dress, opposing the forces of fashion that literally constrained the body with tightlacing and heavy fabrics. Their call for lighter fabrics and a "free play between the dress and skin" was later aligned with the crucial association between a resistance to "the tyranny and vagaries of fashion" and emancipation. While doctors promoted the activities of tennis, cycling, sailing, ice skating, mountaineering, trekking, riding, and so on, as vital sources of health, feminists identified them as key sites of women's newly achieved mobility. Eventually, the specific changes in cut and fabric that these activities required were hailed as the appropriate transformations of everyday dress for both men and women. To be modern was to be mobile and to have this mobility registered in one's dress.

This gradual transformation received its major boost in 1884 when the International Health Exhibition in London included an important section on hygienic dress that was highly promoted and theorized. By then, the at once political and medical agenda of dress reform had been reinforced by an increasingly common, and eventually generic, association between hygiene and beauty. The artistic tradition launched by the so-called Pre-Raphaelite circle turning around Gabriel Rossetti, out of which the Arts and Crafts organizations emerged in the 1860s, produced images of women in flowing dresses that were intended as utopian images of an enlightened, because socialist, society.[2] Their insistent equation of utility and beauty merged completely with the parallel discourses of health and emancipation and assumed considerable force. In the end, the distinction between their "art dresses" and "health dresses" became blurred in a way that allowed for the radical transformation of the dominant clothing styles.

Yet this influential alliance of clothing reformers did not merely transform modern dress. It produced the very sense that dress could be modern, as in timely, a form of its time, one consistent with the realities of a new epoch instead of a means of covering up these realities: the sense, that is, that one could, and should, move from "mode" to "modern." For all its ostensible functionalism, reform dress produced foremost an *image* of modernity that was actually understood as the very possibility of a modern life, rather than an adjustment to it or representation of it. A functional image, then, but an image nonetheless. An image that, like all images, could be lived in. And architectural discourse engaged with this image over an extended period of time. But, eventually, it began to disavow that it had done so and the disavowal was, as it were, monumentualized by the historiography. In fact, the disavowal became complete in the very moment that the engagement with dress reform produced its most spectacular results with the canonic projects of modern architecture in the 1920s. The projects could only be canonized by the historiography inasmuch as its story, and the institutional practices with which it is manufactured, maintained, and distributed, faithfully reproduced the disavowal of the projects' indebtedness to, and participation in, the world of dress.

The Architecture of Antifashion Dress

In fact, otherwise bitter opponents in architectural discourse, even, if not especially, opponents on the very question of fashion, were united in their commitment to clothing reform. Adolf Loos's famous attack on fashion and support for the transformation of clothing brought about by the new sports activities (along with his seemingly disingenuous support for the emancipation of women such a transformation would effect), arguments that he systematically applied to architecture, were, of course, taken directly from the clothing reformers, as were his sermons on the glories of wool, riding breeches, certain kinds of socks, boots, and so on. But so, too, were the arguments of Henry van de Velde, who Loos routinely attacked for launching the architectural fashion of Art Nouveau and thereby disseminating a personal fetish for decoration under the name of "art." The very intensity of their well-known disagreement about fashion in architecture (which parallels the even more hostile one between Loos and Hoffmann) derives from the less well known fact that both supported the rationalization of dress, and even

5.1
*Adolf and Elsie Loos and
the Verdiers, ca. 1920.*

shared the same taste for English clothes.[3] Their struggle was precisely over what such an antifashion approach would mean in architecture.

Architects were not just influenced by the debate about clothing reform. They played a major role in it. Van de Velde, for example, not only designed reform dresses but was, in fact, the leading figure of the movement in Germany, along with his fellow painter Alfred Mohrbutter. In 1900 he published a book entitled *Die künstlerische Hebung der Frauentracht* (The artistic improvement of women's dress) that aligned his philosophy of clothing with that of architecture, presenting clothing as the final frontier for artistic reform. The book leaves the reader in no doubt as to the main obstacle to this reform: "Fashion is the vigilant watcher of its own imagined world. It is the great enemy, who is also the cause of the ruination of all ornamental and industrial arts, and even led so-called high art to degeneracy."[4] Rather than defend the specific details of his own designs, van de Velde offers a long essay on the ways in which clothing designers, like all the other industrial artists, can successfully resist the degenerate forces of fashion. The text begins by declaring that the only defense against fashion is art: "The artists have been the opponents of fashion since time immemorial. But their opposition was not a planned one; it didn't bring anything new and formulated no ideal which could have been placed in opposition to fashion. It would have remained

5.2

Henry van de Velde, tea gown, 1900, as published by Maria van de Velde in Album moderner, nach Künstlerentwürfen ausgeführter Damenkleider, *1900, and* Dekorative Kunst, *1901.*

quite fruitless if it had not maintained and disseminated the feeling of outrage."[5] The book then attempts to plan such an assault on the institutions of fashion by laying out the tactics that could focus and deploy the outrage against fashion experienced by artists and by the growing number of women who, like most men who supposedly prefer ongoing "comfort" to the fluctuations of styles, are no longer willing to subject themselves to it.

For van de Velde, the institutions of fashion, like the clothes that will overturn them, are "modern." In other words, one modern practice that misrepresents the fundamental conditions of modernity will have to be dislodged by another that exposes this condition. Fashion is not older than the reform movement that attacks it. They run in parallel, each defining the other. The book argues that modern fashion is specific to the second half of the nineteenth century. Supposedly, until around 1840 each change in clothing had its own logic and lasted for an entire epoch. With the collapse of this logical progression (which, following the theory of Charles Darwin's son George, van de Velde describes as an incremental process of evolution in response to changing functional demands), a frenetic pathology of illogical changes for change's sake has taken over, one that "despite its dependency on the creation of the new, does not move forward at all."[6] In this imposed rule of the irrational, a "complete derangement grasped hold of the personality and destroyed the last remanent of its will power."[7] A spirit of submissiveness that turns everyone into "slaves of fashion" infects the people, instituting a degenerate rule of fashion that can only be countered by restoring a logic as rational and permanent as the one that preceded it.

The book came out a couple of months after an exhibition of dress designs at Krefeld, the center of the German textile industry, that was organized by Mohrbutter. Entitled *Damenkleider nach Künstlerentwürfen* (Women's dresses designed by artists), it attempted to "storm the barricades of the reigning fashion, which until that moment had appeared invulnerable."[8] If van de Velde's book provided the theoretical polemic of the exhibition, the dresses themselves, of which his own designs played a prominent part, were at the same time published by his wife, Maria van de Velde (Maria Sèthe).[9] During the exhibition, he lectured on the specifics of his designs and elaborated further the general agenda of dress reform that was mapped out in his book. The lectures make it clear that van de Velde did not design his dresses to match his architecture but, rather, saw them as exemplifying the very same principles. Indeed, these principles are presented as architectural principles.

This is not so surprising given that van de Velde's other texts of the time, like his "Was Ich will" (What I seek) of 1901, identify the "sole principle" of art, which passes from architecture to clothing, as being "that of construction":

5.3
*Alfred Mohrbutter, street
dress, 1902, as published
by Anna Muthesius in*
Deutsche Kunst und
Dekoration, *1904.*

"And I extend this structural principle just as far as I possibly can—to archi-tecture as well as to household utensils, to clothing and to jewelry."[10] Simply put, clothing is to be rethought in structural terms. As his book on dress ar-gues, the rule of logic that preceded the rule of fashion in all the arts, and that should be restored, is "the beauty of the skeleton [*Gerüst*]" that "is these days so hidden, so covered over with wandering, unfitting, and fantastic decorations, that it is truly a labor to detect it."[11] This skeleton is always un-derstood as that of a building. Fashion, then, is no more than the complete burial of the underlying skeleton by an irrational facade: "highly illogical con-structions that, without a visible skeleton [*skelett*], allow a cloud of bows, puffs, flounces, and pleats to run amuck over all the contours of the body, and reconfigure it to an unformed mass of flesh, which doesn't permit the least inkling of the proportions of limbs and joints, and in which the beauty of the human figure has been completely lost."[12] The surface is agitated to efface the structure.

Fashion even dictates that the traces of the construction of the drapery that conceals the skeleton must be effaced. Van de Velde counters that a dress should be thought of as a building whose basic structure should remain visible and be articulated by the ornamental surfaces added to it, whose own construction should also remain visible. The book, symptomatically, returns to the equivalence of architecture and clothing to argue that although different costumes must be designed for all the new activities that define the unique "atmosphere of modern life"—such as the car, the bicycle, and the machine room—the same basic principles are at work:

It could very well happen that in our efforts to invent such costumes for the special purposes of the present, we discover the correct general construction principle of clothing that then could be applied to a street dress or to a work or travel suit. The principles of construction for a farm house and for a cathedral are the same. We must also subject clothing to tectonic principles. Our creations in this area must show in their appearance a consistent construction, which makes the determining purposes and the applied construction technique apparent.[13]

Rather than simply submit architecture to fashion, as his outspoken critics like Loos and Muthesius repeatedly asserted, van de Velde employs architectural principles to actively resist fashion. In fact, throughout the nineteenth century, clothing reformers had always associated dress with architecture. In the pamphlet accompanying the display of hygienic dress at the 1884 International Health Exhibition, for example, E. W. Godwin states: "As architecture is the art and science of building, so dress is the art and science of clothing. To construct and decorate a covering for the human body that shall be beautiful and healthy is as important as to build a shelter for it when so covered that shall be beautiful and healthy."[14] The dress reformer is a kind of architect. Modern dress is, by definition, modern architecture. Van de Velde's analysis of dress in architectural terms simply exploits an opening that had been made a long time before, an opening that was crucial to the development of both domains.

Van de Velde makes the same architectural analysis of clothing two years later in an article entitled "Die neue Kunst-Prinzip in der modern Frauen-Kleidung" (The new art principle in women's clothing), for the widely read *Deutsche Kunst und Dekoration*, which emphatically opposes fashion to the modern principle of function, describing the degenerate "psychology" of fashion that must be overcome and citing his earlier book and the parallel book by his wife.[15] By then, these arguments had already had a major impact. As the article notes, similar exhibitions of art dresses had been held in Dresden, Leipzig, Berlin, and Wiesbaden over the previous two years, under such titles as "The New Female Fashion." They probably influenced Josef Hoffmann's sudden, but profound and long-term commitment to dress design in 1903. The dresses he designed and those enormously successful ones produced in the Wiener Werkstätte he founded with Koloman Moser were all "rational" reform designs. More precisely, they employed the famous empire waist of Paul Poiret in a tactical compromise between reformist antifashion functionality and a fashionable line, the stripped-down look of function and the desirable curve—the very compromise that van de Velde had argued was the only strategy that could radically displace fashion from its throne.

That van de Velde's and Hoffmann's dresses were reformist was inevitable given that the workshop movement that they imported and promoted maintained the Arts and Crafts logic initiated by William Morris and Gottfried Semper. Both of their mentors, in identifying architecture with clothing, argued that ornament is everything and yet refused to subject it to fashion; they insisted that it be carefully rationalized, disciplined against the forces of fashion that constantly threaten to appropriate it. Just as Semper consistently opposed what he called "the inane influence of fashion,"[16] Morris repeatedly

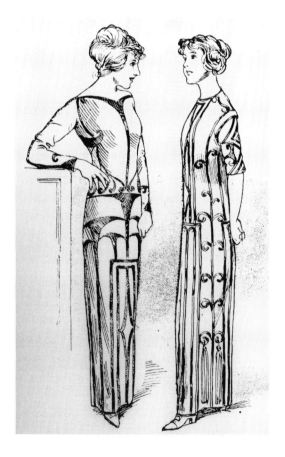

5.4
Josef Hoffmann, fashion designs, ca. 1910.

condemned fashion and called for a reformation of clothing. In his very first lecture, "The Lesser Arts of Life," given at the end of 1877 in support of the newly formed Society for the Protection of Ancient Buildings, he concludes by describing the contemporary freedom of "the rational and beautiful costume" that has resulted from women resisting fashion: "Extravagances of fashion have not been lacking to us, but no one has been compelled to adopt them; every one might dress herself in the way which her own good sense told her suited her best." [17] And this good sense turns out to be that of the animated, but not dissimulating, surface:

Garments should veil the human form, and neither caricature it, nor obliterate its lines: the body should be draped, and neither sewn up in a sack, nor stuck in the middle of a box: drapery, properly managed, is not a dead thing, but a living one, expressive of the endless beauty of motion. . . . You must specifically bear this in mind, because the fashionable milliner has chiefly one end in view, how to hide and degrade the human body in the most expensive manner. She or he would see no beauty in the Venus of Milo; she or he looks upon you as scaffolds on which to hang a bundle of cheap rags, which can be sold dear under the name of a dress. [18]

The dresses that Morris so carefully matched with certain interiors to produce images of a utopian reformed society, like the reform dresses worn by his wife, Jane Morris (who was, of course, Rossetti's most important model for the new Pre-Raphaelite look), were based on flowing medieval fabrics uninterrupted by the prosthetic line of the corset and were framed by abstractly decorated rooms. The much-advertised need to reform the objects of daily use was but a part of the need to reform all the spaces that enclose the body, whether those of the building or of clothes, understood as social institutions, institutions ever vulnerable to fashion. [19] All the subsequent Arts and Crafts organizations that Morris's work spawned maintained close ties with the clothing reform circles and played a major role in the formation of the Rational Dress Society in 1881 and the Healthy and Artistic Dress Union in 1890. In a sense, the short-lived journals of these organizations were Arts and Crafts publications devoted to the question of dress.

Hoffmann carried this sensibility into the Deutsche Werkbund when he became one of its twelve founding artists and the Wiener Werkstätte became one of the twelve founding manufacturers. Indeed, the association included a number of dress reformers. Bernhard Pankok, Richard Riemerschmid, and Paul Schultze-Naumburg were among the original dress designers in the 1900 exhibition; Peter Behrens joined them in the follow-up exhibition in Leipzig a year later. In fact, as a group, the Werkbund architects were all dress designers. In 1903 Schultze-Naumburg published an influential book, *Die Kultur des weiblichen Körpers als Grundlage der Frauenkleidung* (Culture of the fem-

inine body as the foundation of women's dress), in which he applies his general argument that social reform depends on clothing reform specifically to the removal of all the constrictions on the "natural" body imposed by tight clothing to produce a fashionable shape.[20] He then illustrates the contrast between the natural body and the fashionable body in an endless succession of images of naked women and pubescent girls, culminating in a pseudoscientific display of deformed feet. The extreme nationalism, if not psychosexual obsession, of his supposedly aesthetic, medical, and ethical argument—which would become explicit in 1904 when he founded the Bund für Heimatschutz organization and would culminate in his role as a leading Nazi ideologue with a "biological" theory of the history of art—was actually launched by an attack on fashion.[21] Fashion is always the site of discourses of both liberation and control, discourses that are, in the end, completely entangled. The specific politics of each of the Werkbund architects can be traced through the subtle modifications of their relationship to the question of fashion, beginning in each case with their polemical commitment to the design of reform dress.

5.5
Jane Morris posed by Dante Gabriel Rossetti, 1865.

5.6
Peter Behrens, society dress, 1902, as published in Deutsche Kunst und Dekoration, *1902.*

Even Hermann Muthesius, who initially supported the Heimatschutz but then cautioned against its extreme possibilities,[22] and who was, along with van de Velde, the main initiator of the Werkbund idea, was closely linked to the dress-reform movement. While living around the corner from Morris in London between 1896 and 1903, studying the Arts and Crafts movement for the Prussian government and preparing his enormously influential *Das englische Haus* (published in three parts between 1904 and 1905), he was accompanied by his wife Anna Muthesius, who designed dresses and was herself preparing a book on dress reform to be called *Das Eigenkleid der Frau* (The individual-dress of the woman).[23] In 1904, a year after her book was published, she repeated its argument in a review of an exhibition of art dresses by Else Oppler. Oppler had been a student of van de Velde's and then a master's student of Peter Behrens's in 1901, but within a year her dresses were exhibited alongside his, as well as those designed by his wife, Lilli Behrens, at Leipzig and she was proclaimed the hit of the exhibition.[24] In 1904

5.7
Comparison of the "natural" and the "fashion" body. Illustration from Paul Shultze-Naumburg. Die Kultur des wekblichen Körpers als Grundlage der Frauenkleidung, *1903.*

5.8
Cover design by Francis MacNair for Anna Muthesius, Das Eigenkleid der Frau, *1903.*

5.9
*Else Oppler, summer
street dress, 1903, as
published by Anna
Muthesius in* Deutsche
Kunst und Dekoration,
1904.

5.10
*Anna Muthesius, house
dress, as published by
Alfred Mohrbutter in* Das
Kleid der Frau, *1904.*

she took over the new ready-to-wear department of a Berlin department store where she gave one last exhibition of art dresses. In reviewing this exhibition, Anna Muthesius condemns Paris fashions in favor of "antifashion dress" [*Anti-Modekleide*], asserting that while the dress-reform movement has yet to have a major impact, outside of the "high hedge that encloses the small cultural world" of artists and enlightened women, the production and display of such clothes in department stores will have the desired effect of popularizing the designs. Furthermore, she argues that what she sees as the excessive ornamentation of the early art dresses at the Krefeld exhibition has already been eliminated in favor of a concern for the construction [*Aufbau*], material, color, and fit of the garment.[25] And it is in this systematic movement from the seductions of ornamentation to the rigors of structure that the "modern art character" of contemporary designs is produced. The modern dress that can be successfully launched against fashion is modern because it is not decorated. Muthesius exemplified this in her own dress designs, which were featured in Mohrbutter's definitive book of the same year, *Das Kleid der Frau.* While the book is dominated by Mohrbutter's designs (in photographs, sketches, and hand-colored drawings), the second image illustrating its opening discussion of the principles of dress reform is a photograph of what appears to be Anna Muthesius modeling one of her house dresses. In the gallery of designs that follows, the same dress appears in a different pose. Mohrbutter actually uses a drawing based on this second version as the cover image for the book. Muthesius played a significant role in the debate.

Given that Hermann Muthesius always consulted with Anna Muthesius on all the interiors, colors, and furnishings of his architectural designs,[26] it is unsurprising that her argument can be found embedded throughout his writing. In an essay of 1901 he points to Rossetti's reform of artistic dress, through paintings of "fantastic women's costumes," when crediting Rossetti with the entire reformation of all the industrial arts that would be carried out by Morris.[27] Many of his essays maintain this link, repeatedly identifying architectural style as fashionable dress that needs to be reformed. Muthesius wages his long and influential campaign against fashion in architecture through this

5.11
*Hermann Muthesius
before being sent to
England in 1896.*

identification of architecture with clothing. It is not by chance that when his
"Kultur und Kunst" (Culture and art) of 1904 attacks the ornamentalism of
the "fashion" for van de Velde's Art Nouveau he associates ornament with
clothing: "Here the classic error was made of mistaking ornament for art. In
reality, the former does not make the latter, just as a priest's cassock does not
make the concept of religion."[28] This is understood to be more than just a
convenient metaphor for architectural discourse. Rather, it is a literal model
for design practice. Architecture must reform itself in the same way as clothing, stripping off the excess layers of decoration to liberate and mobilize the
underlying structure. Although these excesses are seen as excesses of clothing, the problem is not clothing per se, but fashion. If ornament is clothing,
excesses of ornamentation are always produced by fashion. The model for architectural reform is the resistance to fashion that can be found within contemporary clothing design. Symptomatically, Muthesius organizes an essay of
1902, *Die moderne Umbildung unserer äesthetischen Anschauungen* (The
modern reorganization of our aesthetic point of view), around the evolution
of the man's suit:

We are not thinking about the current revolution in industrial arts about which it cannot yet be said what about it is fashion and what is lasting development. It has to do with the much larger section of time in which modern life has seen its development, the time since the eighteenth century. Whoever wishes to become aware of the drastic change that our aesthetic way of looking has gone through in a certain area during this time should observe the men's clothing of the eighteenth century and that of the nineteenth century. Back then, the silken skirt with precious embroidery, the powdered wig, and the ruffled shirt, were customary; today, the simple black frock coat with the unadorned white cravate over the plain white ironed shirt is the norm, even the official dress. What man today would feel at ease in the suit of the eighteenth century? If we look at the items of use surrounding us we will find the same change.[29]

Muthesius often points to the standardization of the man's suit as a model for architecture, arguing that it is not only stable over time, but crosses, if not effaces, all social distinctions. The resistance to fashion achieved by discarding ornament is symbolized by the plain white shirt on which the suit is based. Such a removal of ornament in favor of utility, seen as the "sign of the time" and exemplified in clothing, can be found "almost as unmistakably" in other anonymous productions, such as ships, automobiles, engineering constructions, and machines. The famous paradigms of modern architecture are presented as good examples of the relentless process of modernization, but not as good as clothing design. Indeed, Muthesius goes as far as to argue that "only one thing has come over to our time unfalsified: our modern suit." The ideal for architecture, which is still "cloaked" with decorative layers "pasted on" like a "masquerade," is to be "tailor-made," like the simple suit, and to reject the artist-designed outfit. Indeed, the suit is itself a form of resistance to art because it has maintained its simplicity and "cannot be again 'beautified' in the sense of an ornament—or style—art."[30]

In 1903 one of Muthesius's most influential essays, "Stilarchitektur und Baukunst" includes a section entitled "Dress and Dwelling" that repeats his praise for the "continuous simplification" of the man's suit that transcends class distinctions, but adds that "Even with women's dress, which still takes artistic considerations into account to the highest degree, there are already transformations toward simplicity and unconditional functionality—changes which, stemming primarily from England, we express by the concept 'tailor-made.'"[31] One year later, in "Kultur und Kunst," Muthesius again attempts to describe "that which is unharmonic in our present culture" by contrasting the "thoroughly different attitudes" toward clothing and architecture:

In our clothing, we have pretty much clear concepts about the practical use, about respectability and worth. In our dwellings we have not the slightest idea. In our clothing, we avoid that which is rawly striking and would refuse to wear a mask, yet in our dwelling, market-fair junk and the masquerade predominate. There unity—at least in the men's suit—and tradition rules, here gay colors and pointlessness; there we meet with a sense for purity, here a total blindness to the unreliability of current furnishings. And yet more: there we are prepared to be victims, here this is not the case. If one only considers how our ladies insist that the details of their outfit match together, how easily they pay a considerable sum for a coat, an adornment of fur, in order to give a unified configuration to their outfit! But in the dwelling, reds, greens, and yellows are placed next to each other as if here there were no principles of taste and the expenditure of five hundred marks for the tasteful improvement of the basics of a room seems, even to the rich, to be unheard of.[32]

This argument is not an isolated and incidental gesture in Muthesius's writing. It was repeated in 1911 in his key address to the Werkbund congress, entitled "Wo stehen Wir?"(Where do we stand?), which, as Banham argues, gave the sought-after aesthetic direction to the otherwise dispersed tendencies of the association by launching the idea of standardization, which is to say, the virtues of efficient type-forms versus the excesses of individual artistic fantasies.[33] The speech associates architecture with clean clothing but disassociates it from fashion, despairing that it has lost the dominance over the other arts that Semper rightly accorded it and in a rigorously Semperian manner rejecting the idea that function, material, and technology are more important than form. Although an educated people should "experience as urgent a need for form as for clean clothes," even the "man who goes to the best tailors" in Germany, unlike his English equivalent, still does not bother to go to an architect when building a house.[34] For Muthesius, the nation will attain the required level of good taste "only when every member of the population instinctively clothes his basic needs with the best forms available,"[35] but this clothing must not be fashionable. On the contrary, the architect and the client have to be "unconcerned about passing trends" that are manufactured for "fashionable society, as fickle as ever and incapable of recognizing permanent values," because "the ephemeral is incompatible with architecture" and architecture is the true mark of culture.[36] The dignity of Germany depends on the reformation of its architectural clothes rather than on their stylish cut.

Muthesius's whole attack on fashion, an attack that was not only absorbed and reproduced by the subsequent generation of architects who launched modern architecture, but was also absorbed uncritically by the historiography of this movement, is aligned with a certain unacknowledged acceptance of Semper's argument that architecture is clothing. For Muthesius, dress is more than a model or metaphor for architecture. Dress is architecture and architecture is dress. Just as in one of his essays he says that "the dwelling is, however, only the wider dress that surrounds us," in another he talks of "our clothing, the narrower dwelling that surrounds us."[37]

In fact, Muthesius's lifelong campaign for the reduction of the free play of ornament in favor of standard type-forms, the development of a comprehensive workshop tradition, the privileging of the English precedents, and so on, is completely based on Semper's well-known argument in his 1852 essay *Wissenschaft, Industrie und Kunst* (Science, industry and art) that the preservation of "standard types" would allow gradual change in forms, whereby "the new becomes engrafted onto the old without being a copy and is freed from a dependence on the inane influence of fashion."[38] Before going on to specify the kind of workshops required, Semper insists that the designer must avoid being a "slave" to "the latest fashion" dictated by the market. This does not mean abandoning the market. On the contrary, he calls for architecture to "step down from its throne and go into the marketplace, there to teach—and to learn."[39] The designer should dictate to fashion rather than be dictated by it. The role models are those who have already "abolished the principle of serving fashion and proceeded to mark out a path for fashion to follow."[40] In the future, Semper argues, everything will be "tailored to the marketplace" as it is in America's industrialized housing industry, which mass produces standard parts that can be ordered by catalogue and assembled anywhere.[41] If architecture is clothing and clothing is architecture, then the designer is a tailor who crafts standardized clothes for a machine age, rather than a specialist in haute couture. Semper illustrates his argument about such standard types by showing the continuity by which the original production of fabrics to define space has been maintained throughout the millennia, despite the successive and radical changes in the technologies that have had to play the role of these fabrics. It is significant that when he repeats and elaborates the argument in his treatise *Der Stil*, in order to establish the "Principle of Dressing" as the central principle of art and culture, he again condemns those who would operate as "embellishers of form," inasmuch as they only "serve the *fashion of the day*" instead of organizing it.[42] The identification of architecture with clothing is inseparable from the attack on fashion.

The entire platform of Muthesius's campaign had thus been laid out by Semper. But, in a pattern that would be endlessly reproduced, when Muthesius repeatedly argues, like Semper, that material structure and utility is an insufficient basis for architecture, he echoes Alois Riegl's inaccurate but influential claim that it is precisely Semper who is responsible for this privileging of the physical structure. Semper's radical privileging of the ornamental clothing over the structural prop it covers is effaced. His understanding of architecture as dress is suppressed in the very moment it assumes its greatest force. In this way, the more radical consequences of this understanding are at once mobilized and disavowed.

Under the cover of Riegl's "criticism," Semper's argument remains tacit but operative throughout the discourse of modern architecture that is so indebted to Muthesius. When Walter Gropius, for example, gained authority within the Werkbund and appropriated the very call for standardization that he had originally and persistently criticized Muthesius for making, going on to pursue the ideal of industrialized housing, he was clearly doing no more than to echo Semper's program—even though it is precisely at this moment that he, too, began to rehearse Riegl's ostensible criticism of Semper. Symptomatically, he also kept using apparently incidental clothing analogies to describe his work, as did all his colleagues. And, like Gropius, Muthesius and the others remained vulnerable to the very antifashion argument that they were so earnestly promoting. At any moment, their attacks on fashion could be turned on their own work. Indeed, not by chance was Gropius so publicly and so brutally denounced as a fashionmonger, stripped of his master's title so late in his career, at the very moment that Banham had so persuasively demystified the saintly purity and integrity of the movement. If Gropius was sacrificed to preserve the good name of the movement, he was sacrificed because that name was already in question. The multiple evils of fashion were displaced onto one figure who was then ceremonially excommunicated to deflect attention from the elusive but pervasive engagement with fashion that permeates all the operations of modern architecture.

From Mode to Modern and Back

From its original foundation, the Deutsche Werkbund had been opposed to certain dangers of fashion and yet engaged with it. The idea for such an association had been promoted by Muthesius for some years but was only enacted in the middle of the storm of protest against his inaugural lecture at the Berlin Commercial University in the spring of 1907, which condemned German applied arts for being a degenerate fashion industry and outlined a new program for the Arts and Crafts. The speech opposes the "swiftly changing fashions" of the late nineteenth century, with its mass production of "ornamental aberrations" that obliterate national character, to the work of the new movement, exemplified by that recently exhibited by the Dresden Werkstätte, whose reform of the small-scale object could act as a model for the reform of architecture. The terms of this speech became the basic terms of the Werkbund program. The original memorandum on how the Werkbund would operate, drafted by the executive committee immediately after the very first meeting of the association, identifies its central goal as "quality" and opposes this to fashion: "Work from the Werkbund, however, means in every case overcoming a fashion through quality."[43] From the beginning, the association identified itself as the promotion of reform against the forces of fashion that efface national identity. The dominance of the French in fashion and design had to be replaced by a more sober German taste that could be exported to an international market without succumbing to the dangers of gratuitous decoration that the market encouraged. But, as Joan Campbell notes, there was a constant struggle within the association over the issue, such that by 1931 many of its younger members felt that the very attempt to produce the appropriate unified style for the time could not help but end up producing "ephemeral fashions."[44] In fact, this conflict is already embedded within Muthesius's speech of 1907: he argues there that although the Arts and Crafts movement is necessarily concerned to produce "a new style of living," it must have nothing to with "the so-called 'modern style'" derived from Art Nouveau and Secessionist designs because these were merely fashions and "the ideas inherent in our movement are too serious for us to indulge in frivolous dalliance with changing fashions."[45] He asserts that the excessive artistic individualism at Dresden had already blocked the emerging functionalism of the objects. This defensive line between honorable style and unacceptable fashion was always a difficult one to draw and it tended to move, however vigilantly it was monitored.

Muthesius's pivotal and infamous debate with van de Velde at Cologne in 1914 was merely the continuation of this foundational conflict. Although Muthesius argued for the artistic value of function and van de Velde symmetrically insisted on the functionalism of art, both sides were supporters of reform dress and both were opposed to fashion. Their actual positions had always been much closer than the histrionics of the debate between them, and those of the successive historians who have monumentalized the debate, would indicate. Although Muthesius's much-read *Stilarchitektur und Baukunst* of 1902 had attacked Art Nouveau for being a fashion, the second edition of the following year was careful to note that it only became a fashion when the curving lines of van de Velde's work were appropriated and abused by commercial interests.[46] Indeed, the essay appears to have taken its argument that the designs of the dress-reform movement were inadequate, because they only satisfied the dictates of function and neglected those of aesthetics, directly from van de Velde's book on dress.[47] Van de Velde is portrayed as an unwitting and unwilling accomplice of fashion. On the other hand, van de Velde had not simply promoted individual styles. He argues in his book that although clothing worn inside the house might reflect personal taste, that worn outside it should be standardized, even concluding an extended discussion of the way in which clothing can actually sustain the apparently contradictory impulses toward individuality and commonality by saying

5.12
*Display of Wiener
Werkstätte fashions,
Deutsche Werkbund
exhibition, Cologne,
1914.*

that he is "not far" from supporting a completely standardized dress and noting this as one aspect of the fashion industry that should be preserved.[48]

What was really at stake underneath the exaggerated policy statements of the 1914 debate was the precise compromise between reform dress and art dress that should be adopted. It has to be remembered that Wiener Werkstätte fashions were prominently exhibited at Cologne in a room within Hoffmann's Austrian pavilion designed by Eduard Wimmer (yet another architect-cum-fashion-designer) that apparently attracted the greatest attention at the exhibition. A lattice of fashion plates was used as a kind of wallpaper, wrapping and defining the space, while individual dresses stood up over layers of fabrics in glass cabinets. The question of fashion, then, was very much in the air as Muthesius and van de Velde debated. The struggle between them was not simply between artist-designed and standardized clothes, the mass production of a number of unique lines carrying a signature that would change with changes in artistic sensibility and the mass production of anonymous ready-to-wear types that would only be modified gradually over time. It was an attempt to specify the appropriate compromise.

After all, the Werkbund was no more than the endeavor to bind artists to manufacturers of a larger scale than the small handcraft-based workshops that the Prussian government acting on Muthesius's recommendation had already added to the different schools of applied art. The association was more nationalistic than antifashion. In 1915 it even held a fashion show in Berlin organized by Lilly Reich, who had studied textile and fashion design with Hoffmann at the Wiener Werkstätte between 1908 and 1911, under the aegis of the newly formed Office of the German Werkbund for the Fashion Industry. The show was an attempt to mobilize wartime xenophobia to transform the entire German clothing industry. Defending their commitment to all aspects of German design "from granite and concrete structures to female clothing, from city planning and housing to office design, from the theater to the cemetery," the association promoted the idea of a German fashion industry independent of foreign influence that would parallel a military empire.[49] Such sentiments had been thoroughly established ever since Paul Poiret's 1911 exhibitions in Germany had acted as the final catalyst for the long-brewing resentment of local clothing manufacturers to foreign domination, embroidered by conservative cultural critics into the claim that modern fashion posed a direct threat to aristocratic as well as national identity. But while the Werkbund sponsored several promotional pamphlets and received a lot of press, its members disagreed internally on the particular choice of style to be promoted and were ultimately distrustful of the major clothing manufacturers' commitment to quality design. After a compromise promoting smaller scale collaborations

5.13
Cover of Die Form
special issue on fashion,
1930.

5.14
Shoe design from Die
Form, *1930.*

between individual artists and fashion boutiques, the project was abandoned within a year.

This unsuccessful project was merely the continuation of the ideals of clothing reform that were in place before the Werkbund began and that, arguably, were pursued again after the war with the association's escalating commitment to modern architecture with the rise of Gropius, Bruno Taut, and Mies van der Rohe. Alongside its promotion of modern architecture, the Werkbund magazine *Die Form* periodically published essays on fashion design and devoted special issues to fashion in 1926 and 1930 that included extensive historical, philosophical, and ethical essays in addition to the display of recent trends in all aspects of clothing, styles, fabrics, and accessories. These texts continue to be organized around the original debates and the question of architecture is written into them. The 1930 special issue, for example, includes an article that explicitly addressed the Muthesian question of "type" clothes versus "individual" clothes and another entitled "Comments of an Architect on Fashion" that insists on the analogy between architecture and fashion.[50]

Lilly Reich had collaborated with Anna Muthesius on a couple of crucial projects (having met and befriended her when they were both designing window displays for department stores), assembling parts of the Haus der Frau directed by Anna Muthesius and Else Oppler at the 1914 Werkbund exhibition in Cologne. In 1922 she published a key article on fashion in *Die Form* entitled "Modefragen" (Questions of fashion) that interrogates the "image" produced by the fashion industry, posing the question of "how, and if, our time is mirrored in it and has found a form." She argues that the frenetic pace of the industry "constricts any stability and any calm, organic development" and instead produces seductive, but empty, decorative fantasies:

The organic unity of the cut is misunderstood and a resolution of construction is faked, and only with buttons and tacks is the drapery held upright. The impression is continually disconcerting. Just the costliness and beauty of the material is seductive. The aesthete is satisfied, the snob even more but nothing remains but a vain exterior skin. . . . By tomorrow, the good idea of a fabric from yesterday or today is available in one hundred variations. Not only clothing, nay, one's whole appearance is schematized and imitated. Every third woman is a plagiarist of the first and this first is a copy. . . . The Procrustean bed of fashion shortens or lengthens the woman's body within just a few months, not, as it used to be, within several years or decades.[51]

Two years later, Reich opened a studio for "Interior Design, Decorative Art and Fashion" in Berlin and another for "Exhibition Design and Fashion" in Frankfurt. In 1932 she took over the Weaving Workshop and Interior Design Department of the Bauhaus, having collaborated with its new director, Mies van der Rohe, for many years. Reich worked on most of his projects, not only on all the famous interiors, including the canonized Barcelona Pavilion, and the many exhibition designs, but also on the furniture designs and a series of textile designs produced for Krefeld manufacturers. These textiles were exhibited in Barcelona but the commitment to fabrics had already begun with the Silk and Velvet Café they prepared in 1927 for the symptomatically entitled Exposition de la Mode in Berlin, whose spaces, as in many of their later houses, were entirely defined with suspended fabrics of many colors.

Much of this collaboration—as is the case with almost all of the many such relationships in modern architecture that confuse the overdetermined opposition between the "masculine" domain of structure and the "feminine" domain of ornament—has been stricken from the apparently exhaustive accounts of the "master" (including, remarkably, those on his "interior design"), which have difficulty accommodating even his commitment to textiles.[52] The mastery of modern architecture is once again threatened by the supposedly feminine wiles of the decorated surface. Indeed, interior design itself poses a significant threat. But Reich's work cannot be surgically removed from architecture, let alone Mies's, and discarded. It is not just that her sensitivity to interior design "amplified" the "architectural fundamentals" rather than merely supplementing them, as Franz Schultz points out.[53] The work was never simply interior design, as if interior design is ever simple. Already, the famous "The Dwelling of Today" exhibit at the German Building exhibition of 1931, which was completely surrounded by a "materials" exhibit she prepared, included one of Reich's house designs built alongside that by Mies and the model apartments by Gropius, Breuer, Hilberseimer, and so on. In 1945, two years before her death, the title of her new studio in Berlin was emphatically changed to "Architecture, Design, Textiles, and Fashion" to reflect this lifelong shift. Like most of the major figures of the movement, Reich moved from so-called interior decoration to architecture. Unlike them, she did not leave the label "fashion" behind. On the contrary, her attitude to architecture is explicitly organized by her specific arguments for the reform of fashion.

To think about fashion and architecture is not simply a matter of recovering such strategically neglected figures and studying their work. It is also a question of studying the extent to which the very commitment to fashion for which they have been neglected (usually by associating it with their gender or sexual orientation) actually organizes the work of those who have been promoted in order to produce a specific image of modern architecture, an image the specificity of which is completely determined by, if not determining of, the contemporary agendas of the historians who actively construct and maintain it.

Likewise, it is necessary to investigate the way in which the specific critiques of the fashion industry offered by those figures who are neglected precisely because they embrace fashion disturbs this image and calls into question its institutionalized reproduction. Reich, for example, is not just a figure of the repression of fashion. She is also a figure of the repression of something within fashion, the drive for essentials and order within its very domain of flux, marked by her attempt to maintain a distinction between fashion and style: "Today's fashion has no style, it is only ever fashionable. The schema that is culled out and becomes a mania in faster and faster repetition is a purely decorative one. . . . The culture of its wearers sits only on their own bodily surfaces."[54] Style is seen to be that moment within fashion that transcends fashion and yet cannot be produced outside of fashion. To produce it, fashion has to be "disciplined" by reducing decoration. Like the modern architect, the fashion designer, concerned only with the outer layer, places this surface under surveillance, even attempting to turn it into a surveillance device that exposes the conditions of life in the age of the machine. Reich argues, like Loos, that "clothes are articles of use, not works of art," even insisting that they must be subjected to "typification," as in the standard type-forms of "outdoor dress" and "athletic clothing." So not only do those designers, like van de Velde, who are discredited as "fashionable" actually articulate the antifashion arguments that will ultimately be seen as canonic of "Modern Architecture"; in addition, those who nominate their concern as fashion per se, like Reich, deploy the very same arguments.

Once again, it must be emphasized that fashion cannot be separated from resistance to it. They are tangled together in a complex knot that is responsible for so much cultural discourse and the diverse institutions within which it occurs. Just as the apparent sites of fashion are inhabited by resistance to it, the apparent sites of such resistance are inhabited by fashion. The struggle between them is internal, then. In fact, it is less a struggle between opposing forces than a structural condition with particular effects, of which modern architecture is but one. The presence of fashion designers within modern architecture is one thing. That these designers espouse the theory of modern architecture, let alone make the flux of fashion into one of its preconditions, is another. To say the least, it breaks down the division between fashion and modern architecture even further. The modern architect's weakness for fashion is matched and intensified by the fashion designer's weakness for modern architecture. Modern architecture ends up being stitched ever more tightly to the realm of dress.

Fashion is found in the obscurity of the lived instant but the collective lived instant—fashion and architecture (in the nineteenth century) emerge from the dreams of collective consciousness.

—Walter Benjamin, *Passagen-Werk*.

White Lies

The more that the role of dress design is tracked through the formative years of modern architecture, the less it appears to be just another of the subtexts of the discourse. Indeed, it is worth considering to what extent the whole logic of modern architecture is that of dress reform. When so many popularizing texts casually employ the analogy of dress to communicate the principles of modern architecture to nonarchitectural audiences they may unwittingly be touching the fundamental logic of that thinking. Perhaps it was only by thinking of architecture as a form of dress design, and subjecting it to the increasingly dominant regimes of clothing reform, that it could even be portrayed as modern. The modern building is only modern because it is like a modern outfit.

The Fashion for Reform

Architects like Hoffmann, van de Velde, Loos, and Behrens did more than apply architectural arguments to dress design; they extended the arguments of dress reform to architecture. Although van de Velde, for example, everywhere insists that he thinks of clothing in architectural terms and even identifies clothing as the "last" frontier for a systematic resistance to fashion that "first" began with architecture, just as the very first clothes came after the first buildings,[1] his arguments are actually drawn from the dress reformers rather than from the architects. At one point in his book on dress he admits that before the transformation of architecture and the other industrial arts, fashion "already suffered a first proper attack several years ago" with the organized assault by the "fighters" for "reform-clothing." The only reason that "fashion successfully resisted" this assault and "rules today as absolutely as before" is that the reformers naively privileged function and neglected art. Their clothing "has something puritanical about it, something dry and plain, which is repellant" and cannot be accepted by the people even though it achieved the crucial victory of getting rid of the corset, the abominable "instrument of torture" with which fashion abused the woman's body.[2] His follow-up essay on dress for *Deutsche Kunst und Dekoration* cites this passage again and argues that "the clothing-reform movement, which is running parallel with our own, but took on a particular configuration *before* our own, can in certain points (for example, in respect to hygiene) meld together with it."[3] Indeed, van de Velde's book on dress was, in essence, the attempt to achieve this melting together of utilitarian purism and aesthetic beauty. And his specific agenda for a modern architecture emerges from this attempt rather than organizes it.

Likewise, it is not by chance that van de Velde's tireless critic, Loos (whose wife, Lina, naturally wore reform dresses), frames his arguments about ornament in terms of clothing reform. In fact, his famous essay on women's fashion was republished in 1902 in a special issue of the woman's magazine *Documente der Frauen* that was dedicated to clothing reform before he used such reforms as a model for architecture. Given his explicit and enthusiastic embrace of Semper's "Principle of Dressing" as the appropriate theory of architecture, it is unsurprising that the movement from clothing reform to architecture can be traced throughout his work.

Each architect tests his work against the model of the rationalization of dress. The discourse of modern architecture thus literally occurs within that of clothing reform. All the standard arguments on behalf of modern architecture had already been made in the realm of dress design. The reformists had long argued for the simple cut, the pure line, and the reduction of ornament as part of the general argument about function (and the related discourse on hygiene and exercise) that formed the basis of their position. The virtues of the clean white surface had, of course, first been elaborated in the realm of dress. From the beginning, the clothing reformers had presented their arguments as arguments for social reform in precisely the same way that the "modern" architects eventually would. Even the moral argument that would become embedded in the polemics of these architects is explicitly and repeatedly laid out in the earlier debate about clothing. If, more than anything, the logic of clothing reform is the logic of the "good fit," both physically and socially, it is significant that its rhetorical traces can be found throughout the discourse of modern architecture. So much of the critical debate about architecture is devoted to the question of "fit." Richard Neutra, who carefully sketched the clothes worn in every country that he visited throughout his life, for instance, extends the arguments of his teacher Loos by arguing that the logic of the good fit exemplified by sports clothes, but also operative in the "suit of clothes that we order from the tailor to fit our requirements and measurements exactly," is primarily that of attaining "nervous comfort."[4] And the very argument against fashion that is Neutra's strongest memory of Loos, and that all the other modernists insist on so often, too often to not arouse a certain skepticism, derives from dress reform.[5]

So when polemicists and propagandists such as Muthesius, Loos, Gropius, Taut, and van Doesburg refer to the modernity of clothing styles to describe the qualities of a modern architecture, they are not simply employing a convenient metaphor, or even a model. Dress reform is the very source of their argument. But this source is, of course, played down. Architecture cannot subordinate itself to the effeminate domain of clothing design and maintain its macho logic of "mastery," "order," and so on. After all, it takes a real man

London, S. Paul, Bank Holyday Aug 4

to tame the feminine ruses of ornament. This suppression is clumsily effected by writers like Giedion who overprivilege the supposedly hypermasculine domain of engineering construction as the real source of modern architecture, but it is no less evident in those who try to produce a more nuanced account. It is not surprising that Loos, in whose writing the clothing argument is most conspicuous, reappears in the historiography of modern architecture in 1936 with Pevsner's claim, in the polemically entitled *Pioneers of the Modern Movement from William Morris to Walter Gropius,* that the Arts and Crafts movement constitutes the dominant "source" of modern architecture. But Pevsner, too, stays away from the question of clothing, linking modern architecture to all the decorative arts except that of dressing.

The impact of the clothing argument can, nevertheless, be traced throughout Pevsner's text and in each of its subsequent revisions. Indeed, the sense of clothing reform even surfaces within Giedion's texts, especially in those moments when he somewhat reluctantly acknowledges the contribution of Art Nouveau to the gradual emergence of modern architecture. Symptomatically, it is when he argues that Victor Horta's famous house pioneers certain conditions of modern space, by introducing the "free plan" that Le Corbusier would later exploit, that the rhetoric of the "good fit" surfaces. By using iron constructions "stripped of their Gothic or Renaissance clothing," the house is supposedly "the first of these famously modern dwellings which fit their owners like faultlessly cut coats."[6] But the sense that clothing is anything more than a metaphor in such passages is, however, covered over by Giedion's punctual attacks on fashion.

Giedion's knowledge of the history of clothing reform does become explicit in *Mechanization Takes Command* but again it is seemingly kept apart from architecture. At one point, for example, the book contrasts an image of a woman in a corset to an image of a man wearing the late nineteenth-century health garments of Dr. Arnold Rikli. The clothes illustrate an extended argument about hygiene. But after spending some pages detailing Rikli's "atmospheric bath" cure, the text points out that although the clothes he prescribed were "quite out of question in the time of parasols, high-collared and corset-like clothes," and worn only by eccentrics in the sanitorium, fifty years later "replicas" of the outfit "await the man in the street at every clothing store." Like the plain unornamented glasses designed by the architect Philip Webb in 1859, which were identical to those mass-produced half a century later, "their functional simplicity already embodied the inherent trend of the period."[7] The health clothes reveal the unconscious tendency hidden behind the play of fashion that will eventually surface to define a new age. Yet again, Giedion's enemy is fashion. The corset is identified with the oversexed "ruling taste" governed by fashion while the reform clothes exemplify its demise. Even before it launched its discussion of hygiene, the book had illustrated the "apparel of the ruling taste" with an image of a woman in "The New Ideal Bustle" of the 1880s, which is placed alongside a supposedly degenerate nude of the same period.[8] The unornamented white enamel bathroom fittings that emerge in parallel with the smooth surfaces of modern architecture are clean because they have been cleaned of fashion.

6.3
Dr. Arnold Rikli's garments for the atmospheric cure, ca. 1870. Illustration from Sigfried Giedion, Mechanization Takes Command, *1948.*

But if modern architecture is truly a form of clothing reform, it cannot so easily resist fashion. Reforms tend to become fashions. For example, within two years of the groundbreaking 1900 exhibition of reform dresses by van de Velde and the other architects who would later found the Werkbund, the same designs had already appeared in mainstream fashion magazines as the work of the leading fashion salons.[9] Far from countering the institutions of fashion, most earnest attempts to create styles against fashion are uniquely attractive to the very fashion industry they seek to foil. As Anne Hollander argues, "Whenever antifashion clothing has made itself noticeable, either by ostentatiously going against the mode or by becoming the uniform of an ideological movement, the impulse within fashion to make capital of what is new and disturbing converts it speedily into fashion."[10] Already by the 1890s, many features of reform dress had made their way into high fashions. The designs of Poiret, the very figure of haute couture, were but the most notable expression of this heavy influence. Women's fashions were so much affected by reform that by the 1920s they looked more rational than the men's, a fact that took architectural theorists, like Le Corbusier, some years to acknowledge. In this way, reform designs moved from being a project for social reform to being a way of resolving the difficulty of maintaining social identity in the metropolis. Likewise, it can be argued that the architectural practices based on these clothing reforms moved from critical practices into ways in which architects could maintain social identity by adopting the right look.

Of course, this is consistent with Tafuri's by now classic argument that any critical practice in architecture will inevitably be neutralized by the forces of fashion that it attempts to critique. But what such an account of the commodification of critical practices symptomatically neglects is just how complex is the construction of identity effected by the strategic adoption of fashions. This complexity has been the subject of much contemporary research that has evolved a long way from the classic analyses at the turn of the century and constitutes a significant resource for contemporary architectural discourse.

To say the least, fashion is clearly not by definition an acritical conformism. It is just as able to mobilize a critical potential as neutralize it. Furthermore, it is not simply that the good intentions of reformists are always appropriated, confused, and countered by the fashion world. The arguments for dress reform on which the discourse of modern architecture was based, for example, cannot be detached from fashion at their very origin. For a start, as Elizabeth Wilson argues, not all reformers were completely antifashion.[11] And, in the end, and more importantly, any antifashion that attempts to establish a timeless style is always itself a fashion statement, no matter how much its promoters insist on their opposition to fashion. Moreover, it is the very intensity of their opposition that traps them within it. As Anne Hollander puts it:

To counteract evil fashion, the ideal of establishing an absolute and unchanging beauty and practicality in the design of dress has repeatedly been conceived. It has also proved consistently elusive, never itself exempt from the fashion in beauty and practicality current at the date of its proposal. . . . People still like to speak against the phenomenon of fashion while enjoying it at a distance, although the same people are usually participating in it while looking the other way.[12]

Indeed, the whole discourse against fashion is organized by a certain covert participation in the very economy being condemned. The designs proposed as the much-needed reform of a degenerate economy of fashion are invariably derived from tendencies already marked within this economy. The promoters of antifashion, who necessarily employ the same marketing devices as those they oppose, "are likely to propose a way for clothes to look that is not really revolutionary but evolutionary and likely to emerge anyway in the normal course of fashion before long."[13] After all, nothing could be more in the spirit of fashion than selecting certain marginal elements of design and making them the model. The distinction between "model" and "mode," let alone "modernist," is always fragile. The very idea of being modern cannot be detached from fashion. What could be more fashionable than the desire to be modern?

In other words, to think about architecture and fashion is not just to think of modern architecture's dependence on reform fashion but also to think about the fashion for reform. If, in 1930, Le Corbusier reveals the basic source of the discourse of modern architecture by praising the women's "reform" of their clothing as a liberating refusal to "follow fashion" and arguing that "the spirit of reform has only just appeared,"[14] what about the generic sign of the reform of architecture—the white wall that was routinely associated with the reform ideal of "good fit" in the 1920s and that still haunts the discourse today?[15] Can the disciplined surface exemplified by the white wall, the lightweight sports clothes for the newly athletic body of architecture, which seems so different from the radically colored, patterned, and textured surfaces of even the most austere reform dresses, be detached from fashion?

Putting on the White Coat

Perhaps the best way to begin to answer this question is to pay closer attention to the work of Otto Wagner, the father of the sibling rivals Hoffmann and Loos, who is so often identified as the pioneer of both the theory of modern architecture and the corresponding practice of the white wall. One of the

6.4
Otto Wagner, Post Office Savings Bank, Vienna, 1904–6. As illustrated in Nikolaus Pevsner, Pioneers of the Modern Movement from Morris to Gropius, *1936.*

few things shared by the diverse histories of modern architecture is that they tend to link Wagner's Post Office Savings Bank of 1904–1906 with Hoffmann's Stoclet Palace of 1905–1910 and Loos's Villa Steiner of 1910. Whether the histories are organized by a Giedionesque emphasis on structural engineering or a Pevsnerian emphasis on decorative art, or an exotic cocktail of the two, these three buildings (or, more precisely, particular images of them) are brought together. The intersection of Wagner's "white hall" (Giedion), Hoffmann's "flat surfaces . . . made up of white marble slabs" (Giedion), and Loos's "white unadorned prism" (Frampton) acts as a relatively stable pivot point for all the different historiographic trajectories. These white buildings are routinely gathered together to mark the final achievement of some kind of critical mass, one with a particular quality.[16] As might be expected, the buildings are seen to prefigure the canonic form of modern architecture. When addressing Loos's house, for example, Pevsner asks, "who, without being informed, would not date this house about 1924–25, or even later?"[17] And in later versions of his argument, he progressively moves the date to 1930.[18] But it is more than just a prefiguration since "Loos achieved the new style completely and without any limitation."[19] Pevsner argues that

the three white buildings by the three architects actually enact the thinking usually associated with the late 1920s rather than simply announce its trajectory.[20] Throughout the historiography, their premature modernity is repeatedly described as a strange, if not uncanny, effect.

To give them this unique status, each of these buildings, like all the others that are assembled to construct a prehistory of the modern, has to be split, but, unlike those others, the traces of this split have to be effaced. Their respective ornaments are left behind in modern architecture's prehistory of decoration, clothing, and fashion, while the white surfaces are, as it were, peeled off and deposited in the twentieth century. The feminine curves that Art Nouveau had released are finally returned to the closet so that the "taut and hard," "stable and dignified" forms of the new architecture can assume authority—and one can clearly sense the historians' relief.[21] It is this critical maneuver that constructs the identity of modern architecture as such. The character of all the canonic buildings of the "movement," the character whose existence makes possible the very idea of a movement, an idea that can only be imposed on the historical archives with considerable violence, but a violence already enacted by the designated protagonists in these archives, is established by a particular reading of a specific trio of buildings that preceded them.

What this critical maneuver must efface is that the white skin of these buildings participates fully in the economy of clothing that is said to be left be-

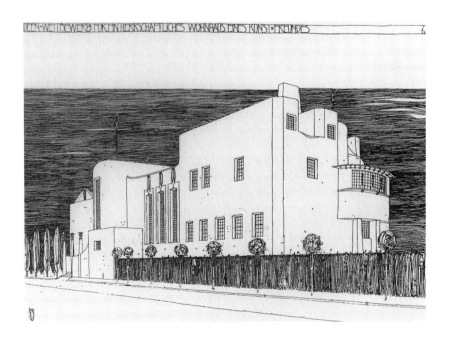

6.7
Charles Rennie Mackintosh and Margaret McDonald, Haus eines Kunstfreundes *competition entry, 1901. As published in* Meister der innen Kunst, Charles Rennie Mackintosh Glasgow, *1901.*

hind. In fact, it can only be peeled off by the historiography and mobilized to particular ends because it is a layer of clothing. To suppress this fact, the whiteness is almost never addressed as such, other than by noting that Wagner's and Hoffmann's surfaces are constructed out of thin sheets of white marble and by crediting Charles Rennie Mackintosh's equally white "House for an Art Lover," which had been submitted to the 1901 Darmstadt competition of the same name, as the obvious influence on all three designs. It is not by chance that the source of the abstract white surface that supposedly leaves behind Art Nouveau's sensuality is actually an Art Nouveau house. Mackintosh's work, and its whiteness in particular, was heavily promoted by Muthesius. While arguing that its transformation of the interior into a work of art went too far for everyday use, such that "the man or woman of today—especially the man in his unadorned working attire—treads like a stranger," he identifies the "austerity" of its white vocabulary as the model for the future.[22] Nor is it a coincidence that on this design, as with all his work, Mackintosh collaborated with his wife, Margaret McDonald, who produced the art dresses that Anna Muthesius would write about in 1903. The year before, they had, as equals, exhibited in the Scottish section of the Viennese Secession. Their work had a major impact on Wagner and his two followers, who immediately picked up the language of plain white exteriors and isolated ornamental motifs incorporated into the equally white interiors, since all three already thought about architecture in terms of clothing. Loos, as always, clarifies the point. The white surface is unashamedly prefashionable clothing:

White plaster is a skin. Stone is structure. Despite the similarities in their chemical composition, there is a great difference in the way the two materials are used. . . . When plaster shows itself candidly as a covering for a brick wall, it has as little to be ashamed of in its humble origin as a Tyrolese with his leather trousers in the Hofburg.[23]

A specific use of the white wall became the accepted application of Semper's "Principle of Dressing." Suddenly, it became clear that modern dress was white, and the three architects did not hesitate to put it on. After all, Semper's principle had originally been formulated to explain why ancient buildings employed a coat of white paint on top of their white marble wherever the pattern of their decorative clothing was meant to be white. And what was so striking about Mackintosh and McDonald's work at the time was that its white surfaces cannot be separated from its ornament. The ornamentation is itself white and seems to grow out of the white surfaces that might, at first, seem to merely frame it. Thus the stable point in the historiography of modern architecture turns out to be a specific, but repressed, reading of Semper that charges the white wall with maintaining the very responsibility for clothing the building that it seems to abandon.

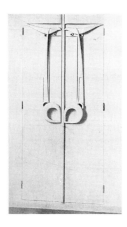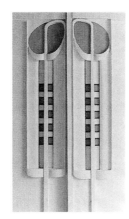

Wagner's Post Office Savings Bank seems to facilitate the effacement of these generic historiographic maneuvers, and is therefore usually deployed the most decisively. It is not by chance that all of the arguments about clothes whose trajectory and complications we have been patiently tracing here are already in place in Wagner's manifesto of 1896, *Moderne Architektur*. And the enigmas of fashion that surface sporadically throughout the discourse, but whose structural role remains unclear, are more clearly articulated in this text than in any other.

The manifesto, which Wagner presented to defend his proposed curriculum for the Academy of Fine Arts, opposes architectural fashions, understood as forms of clothing. In his inaugural lecture on accepting the post in 1894, he dismisses eclectic styles as fashions in the usual manner: "The matter has even gone so far that architectural styles almost change like fashions."[24] In the subsequent manifesto, he elaborates the point by identifying these fashions with theatrical costumes, decorative additions that "cannot but make an impression similar to that of someone attending a modern ball in the costume of a past century," appending, in the second edition of 1898, "even rented for the occasion from a masquerade shop."[25] In contrast to this masquerade, modern sports and business clothes become the model for architecture: "A man in a modern traveling suit, for example, fits in very well with the waiting room of a train station, with sleeping cars, with all our vehicles; yet would we not stare if we were to see someone dressed in clothing from the Louis XV period using such things."[26] In the third edition of 1902, Wagner adds the complementary argument: "It is simply an artistic absurdity than men in evening attire, in lawn tennis or bicycling outfits, in uniform or checkered breeches should spend their life in interiors executed in the styles of past centuries."[27] Throughout the book, architecture is repeatedly identified with clothing in a thoroughly Semperian manner:

■ Even a slight gift of observation must awaken in us the conviction that outward appearance—man's clothing in its form, color, and accessories—is fully consistent with each period's artistic viewpoints and creations and cannot even be imagined otherwise.

■ No epoch, no style has been an exception to this. This fact is vividly seen in comparing costume designs with contemporary works of architecture.[28]

Likewise, Wagner's architectural practice is also an architecture of clothing. Wagner clips the smooth white surface onto the interior and exterior in discrete panels that are pinned together by aluminum bolts whose heads are left visible to mark unambiguously the cladding's autonomy from the structure it covers without revealing this structure. It is hard to think of a more polemical articulation of Semper's theory of dressing. While being a possible candidate for Riegl's critique of the "materialism" of Semper's followers because of his pioneering work on public engineering systems and outspoken defense of function and materials, Wagner actually adopts and transforms Riegl's argument in his manifesto and, in so doing, like Riegl, confuses Semper's argument. But his architectural projects faithfully restore this argument. Even the extraordinary sophistication of the engineering construction in both his public works and individual buildings is consistent with Semper's claim that the all-important surface fabric depends on the precision with which the always secondary structural prop is constructed. The rationalization of structure reestablishes, rather than threatens, the importance of the surface.

While Wagner's architecture is dressed up, it would seem that it is not intended to be fashionable. Indeed, in 1914, as Harry Mallgrave points out, the title of the fourth edition of the manifesto was changed to *Die Baukunst unserer Zeit* (The building art of our time) in response to Muthesius's condemnation of the German words *Moderne* for its links with *Mode* and *Architektur* for its association with the styles, in favor of *Baukunst* (The art of building).[29] Yet things are not so simple. Wagner is not against fashion. On the contrary, he embraces it, including "fashion," along with "styles of living" and "etiquette," in his list of the important influences on form, just as he did later in his work on the city.[30] His problem with eclecticism is not fashion per se but the "discord between fashion and style," and the fault is not on the side of fashion but that of art. Fashion is a precise measure of modernity while art is fickle and untrustworthy:

■ Modern man has surely not lost his taste; today he notices more than ever the smallest error of fashion, and certainly fashion is more difficult today than ever before.

■ Our clothing, our fashion, is dictated and deemed proper by the public at large, and this precludes even any hint of error. Since the discord is not to be sought in that, naturally it must lie in today's works of art.[31]

168

The public's "extraordinary sensitivity" to fashion and indifference to art is only partly blamed on the implicit rigidity of artistic taste. Mainly, it is the fault of an artistic practice that is simply not modern: "no work of our time." This argument is reinforced in the third edition when Wagner adds a long section on the relationship between art and everyday life. Despite the "parasitic" vulgarization of the Secessionist designs, he approves of the public's acceptance of the need for the appearance of rooms to "harmonize" with the appearance and occupation of its inhabitants.[32] He goes on, very much in the manner of Semper and Morris, to suggest that artistic reform can only follow the transformation of fashions effected by the very women that construct and wear them:

■ Human clothing is located at the outer limits of the concept "art in industry" and surely no words would need be spent on this subject if artists were not repeatedly making attempts to conquer this field too, as it were, for art.

■ Since the principles repeatedly expressed hold true with regard to men's clothing and all assaults against them have been completely ineffective, we can really only discuss women's clothing. From the artist's point of view, women's clothing is considered to be decidedly more beautiful than men's. An essential change in both is possible only when art filters down and has a formative effect on the public. It is always reserved for social conditions, however, to play the leading role.

6.10
Wagner, Post Office Savings Bank, sectional perspective, as published in Einige Skizzen. Projekte und Ausgeführte Bauwerke von Otto Wagner: Band III, *1906.*

6.11
Wagner, Post Office Savings Bank, cladding detail, as published in Der Architekt *(Vienna), 1906.*

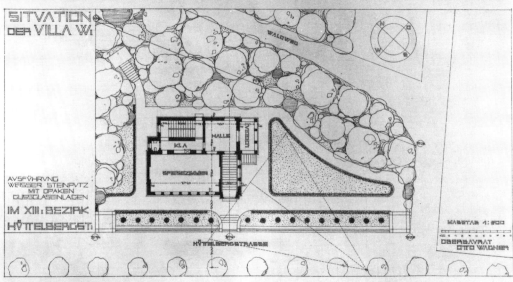

■ Thus fashion or style in clothing can only derive from the public. Since women in this case are the major participants, it could almost be said that, because of their artistic tutelage, the artistic contribution of half of mankind is frustrated—achieving a result that is no doubt unsatisfactory.[33]

This identification between fashion and modern architecture is even evident in Wagner's drawing technique, which often juxtaposes the cladding of smooth white marble panels with stylish figures wearing the latest fashions (a technique whose strategic role and evolution through the present needs to be studied in detail). The white surface does not simply frame the fashions as a kind of backdrop. It is itself a fashion statement. The building is being looked at by the figures, or, more precisely, by the look they are wearing. In fact, Wagner's manifesto elaborates a detailed theory of the look, specifying the position from which buildings should be seen and how their design should be modified to produce the right "effect" from that position. The user of the building is described as "the viewer" whose desire for a modern "image" is to be satisfied by the architect. Gropius's public announcement that architecture is a surface effect, for which he was excommunicated, had already been made in Wagner's text.

Indeed, Wagner's simultaneous opposition to fashion and commitment to it marks all the subsequent discourse, including that of the pious watchdogs. Although he was heavily criticized at the time for embracing fashion, his position underwrites much of the debate that extended right through the historical avant-gardes and even continues today.

6.12
Otto Wagner, the second Villa Wagner, 1912, perspective and plan.

Just Looking, Thanks

While Loos accepts that "fashion is just a tyrant,"[34] he repeatedly goes out of his way to exempt Wagner from the criticism that he directs at the rest of the Viennese Secession and, in the end, even he is not simply against fashion as such. In a 1919 essay called "Antworten auf Fragen aus dem Publikum" (Answers to questions from the public), which gives advice on many aspects of clothing (riding breeches, monocles, sportswear, overalls, and so on), he warns against those who dismiss whatever they do not like as being a fashion, arguing that the particular fashions of a time are always eventually recognized as its style, whether they be clothing or architectural fashions:

The 'worker's newspaper' errs when it intends to apply the word fashion only for dressing [*Bekleidung*], that is to say, the work of tailors, hatmakers and shoemakers. That is wrong. Fashion is the style of the present. About everything which displeases one, be it now a symphony, a drama, a building, everyone believes to have passed an annihilating judgement by calling out in exasperation: That is not a style, that is a fashion! Quite right, but in a hundred years one calls the fashion of the time its style, whether it has to do with ladies' hats or cathedrals. (Frau X appears at the masked ball in the style of the fourteenth century, that might still be acceptable, but it's already more dubious when chapels are built according medieval fashion). Or does one want to make articles of clothing despicable with the observation that they are subject to change? Then one would have to apply the same standard to artworks.[35]

> Having linked clothing and architecture in this way, Loos goes on to say that the progress toward rational simplification that has been made in the apparently decorative and fickle world of clothing fashion far exceeds that of architecture:

Now it is indeed true that with respect to these that much superfluous work is wasted. But not more than with respect to other industries. On the contrary: our clothing has, compared to other centuries, become far simpler, which one cannot claim about our house facades. Just compare the serene, noble old Vienna houses with the riotous ornamentation which gives the key to the new houses of today.... Our tailors, our shoemakers, our hatmakers, have progressed the most in ornamentlessness: may the other industries soon fall in line![36]

> In fact, for Loos, fashion is the only means of maintaining identity in a changing world. It is a figure for stability. While he clearly inverts Wagner's privileging of women's fashions over men's, the "feminine" pleasure of fashion is not abandoned, but rather, like all things feminine, disciplined. In the end, all of Loos's writing can be understood as nothing more than the attempt to discipline fashion.

> The gradual purification of man's dress that Loos promotes as the model for a modern architecture is not simply a craft production outside the economy of fashion. Nor is it strictly anonymous. Loos nominates his favorite tailors in Vienna and London, craftsmen who are privileged precisely for their sensitivity to the fashion world, their ability to keep a fashion secret and thereby give the aristocratic gentleman some time before his stylish look is swallowed up by the ever-present market of imitators. When Loos writes that modern clothes are those that stand out the least (an argument that has been analyzed in detail by Beatriz Colomina),[37] fashion is clearly dictated by the environment within which it appears, and this is not only a gender but also a class environment. The imaginary client is always a "gentleman." Although the well-dressed gentleman is the one who does not stand out, gentlemen must, in the end, stand out. The best tailor offers a cut that satisfies the always double function of fashion—mask and marker—by which the surface layer at once bonds the individual to a group and detaches this group from others. This duplicity intensifies as the shared surface that sustains each such

collective identity on the outside at the same time maintains individual identities as it "allows the interior to be *intimate*," as Colomina puts it when describing Loos's sense of fashion.[38] The surface is an elaborate mechanism for concealing and preserving, if not constructing, identity. Everywhere in Loos's texts, fashion is that which maintains aristocratic privilege in the absence of the dress regulations that once imposed this differentiation. This is why his article on men's fashion clarifies his formula "an article of clothing is modern when the wearer stands out as little as possible," by adding "at the center of culture, on a specific occasion, in the best society."[39] Since the upper classes must find a new fashion as soon as they are imitated by those "below" them, modern fashion, for Loos, is not what is exhibited in the streets but a secret kept by the best tailors, tailors who are the best precisely because they can keep such secrets. Rather than escape fashion, the idea is to be at the source of the vertical economy of fashion, one of the select few confided in by the master tailor. Loos describes how difficult it is to find and be accepted by such a tailor, even complaining bitterly that Hoffmann stole his tailor after he criticized his clothes. He incriminates Hoffmann by identifying him with all the counterfigures—the parvenu, the dandy, and the coquette—who disrupt the slow-moving cycles of fashion that faithfully preserve social distinctions. Everywhere, Loos condemns those, like the Secessionists and the Werkbund members, who attempt to push fashion along.

The problem with women's fashion is not that it is fashion but that it changes so quickly. Loos identifies modernity with a certain resistance to change, a slowing of fashion, rather than its rejection. The most modern person or object is the one that changes but changes the slowest, as becomes evident in his article of 1898 on hats, the hats, of course, of a gentleman: "Fashion advances slowly, more slowly than one usually assumes. Objects that are really modern stay so for a long time. But if one hears of an article of clothing that has already become old-fashioned by the following season—that has become, in other words, unpleasantly obvious—then one can assume that it was never modern, but was trying falsely to pass itself off as modern."[40] To endlessly modernize everything is to resist the modern. Symptomatically, Hoffmann is just as much a critic of the fashion hungry parvenu as Loos. Even his original "Work Program" for the Wiener Werkstätte, written in the same year as he started designing dresses, explicitly opposes such a dissimulating figure.[41] What they really disagree about is not the importance or correctness of fashion but the correct time frame for architectural fashions, the distance between the architectural seasons. As Sekler argues,

Hoffmann completely disregarded the different temporal rhythm appropriate and possible for each art form: on the one hand, shortlived fashion, and on the other, architecture built to last. The danger of taking the analogy of fashion design and architectural design too seriously could become especially great for an artist like Hoffmann, whose abundant inventions of form always pushed in the direction of change and innovation.[42]

The question of fashion is really a question of time.[43] The struggle between Loos and Hoffmann was over correct cycles. Loos's position is faithfully echoed by Neutra: "Ladies' apparel may be designed to last only for a season. It would be a sorry mistake to be similarly carefree or arbitrary in designing a house."[44] In fact, Loos does not criticize ornament because it so easily succumbs to fashion. Rather, ornament is, by definition, fashion itself. While the note to his 1924 revision of the "Ornament and Crime" essay maintains his standard attack on organizations like the Wiener Werkstätte and the Deutsche Werkbund, for claiming to oppose the "tyranny of fashion" and yet having actually been set up "in order to create a German fashion," the corresponding text it is attached to argues that:

Twenty-six years ago I claimed that ornament in objects of daily use disappeared with the development of humanity. . . . I have never meant by that, which purists have urged ad absurdum, that ornament should be systematically and consistently abolished; but where ornament has vanished, due to the necessities of time, it cannot be installed again, just as man will never go back to tattooing his face. The object of daily use lives as long as its material lasts, and its modern value resides in its solidity. Whenever I abuse the object of daily use by ornamenting it, I shorten its life-span because, since it is then subject to fashion, it dies soon. Only the caprice and ambition of women can be responsible for this murder of material— and ornamentation at the service of woman will live forever. A useful object, such as fabrics or wallpapers, whose durability is limited, remains at the service of fashion and is therefore ornamented.[45]

Ornament is aligned with time rather than against structure. To produce a modern architecture is not to strip the ornament off a building, but to preserve the building from the fast-moving time of the fashion world that would render it ornamental, whether the particular look is highly decorative or not. To be a modern architect is to act in a way that does not accelerate architecture's inevitable participation in the evolution of fashions. In the end, the struggle with Hoffmann is about whether the architect should lead or follow fashion.

There is plenty of evidence that Loos is not simply opposed to Hoffmann, before, after, or during their bitter fight. Loos praises Hoffmann before, Hoffmann insists his students listen to Loos during, and Loos praises Hoffmann immediately after their most violent episode, with Hoffmann returning the favor. Perhaps the very extremity of Loos's contempt for Hoffmann results from what is really contempt for himself, overattacking an outside in order to preempt the very same charge being leveled against his own interior. Perhaps

Hoffmann acts as a figure for Loos's own production of "feminine" sensuous surfaces (fur, finely grained marble, water), if not his own femininity. Not by chance does Loos attempt to condemn Hoffmann's clothes and Hoffmann angrily deny his charge. Both were obsessed with wearing the right clothes, but, moreover, they ended up wearing the same ones, and this obsession explicitly organizes their position on architecture. Just as they shared a concern with the line of men's clothing in opposition to the color and pattern of women's clothing, both, as it were, defensively framed themselves with colorfully dressed women to maintain certain sexual secrets and had a preference for buildings with cool exteriors and hot interiors. Indeed, Loos's famous "Architektur" essay of 1910, which praises the whitewashed vernacular in an isolated countryside that would be violated by the arrival of architecture, seems to echo Hoffmann's early essay of 1897 on the very same kind of scene with its "brilliantly white walls," which insists that if architecture arrives there it should be limited to the interior.[46] They both reject the masquerade of clip-on architectural styles as an absurd and neurotic costume drama but preserve the idea of dress, whether of the person or the building, as a mask appropriate for nerve-wracking times. Likewise, they disassociate the white surface from fashion but choose the white coat precisely because, in the end, both are committed to fashion.

Although Loos identifies Hoffmann with the ornamentation that marks women's fashions, the debate between them concerns more than the degree of ornamentation. It is not that the less the ornament, the less the involvement in the economy of fashion. The reverse is often the case. As early as 1898, Loos's "Die Intérieurs in der Rotunde" (Interiors in the rotunda) actually argues not only that simplicity itself can be a fashion but even that it feeds fashion's relentless cycles.[47] The simplicity of the modern white surface does not place it outside of fashion. On the contrary, it is enveloped, from the beginning, in fashion. The white wall is, first and foremost, a fashion statement, even if it need not be, as it were, designed, but simply appropriated from the vernacular or antiquity as a ready-made. Just as the logic of clothing reform cannot be detached from that of fashion, because reform inevitably becomes fashion and is, anyway, always a fashion move from the beginning, modern architecture is at once trapped within and actively producing a fashion economy. The very thing to become fashionable was, of course, the white wall that was meant to symbolize the stripping away of fashion.

Even the other mentor of the antifashion argument, Muthesius, who similarly praises the white surface, whether that of the modern shirt or that of a building, does not simply detach this surface from fashion. In fact, despite his notorious attacks on specific fashions (attacks that literally structured the discourse of modern architecture) he is not against fashion as such. Like van de Velde's argument that the original clothing reformers failed in their attack on fashion precisely because they did not offer a new fashion to replace it and thereby turn fashion against itself,[48] Muthesius's infamous speech of 1914 asserts that the Werkbund is being exploited by commercial interests looking to market a new fashion, but immediately goes on to say: "However, it would be a mistake on behalf of the Werkbund to be outraged by this. Let's be clever and recognize that we have a new factor of power at hand, that our area of influence has extended enormously through this sudden popularization. It is up to us to put this power to good use."[49] In fact, a year later Muthesius insists on the "politicoeconomic importance" of fashion in "Der Krieg und der deutsche Modeindustrie" (War and the German fashion industry), an essay published in the popular magazine *Die Woche*. Between the magazine's call for financial contributions to the war effort and its detailed description of troop movements, Muthesius rejects the idea of a characteristically German fashion, because fashion "overcomes the boundaries of individual countries," but argues that an independent fashion industry is vital to Germany's assumption of superiority in all the arts and that the war will greatly assist this cause. He aligns fashion with architecture and the other industrial arts, arguing that the Werkbund originally involved itself with reform clothing to foster a debate within the fashion industry that would raise its standards. He suggests, however, that it is the strength of the fashion industry that counts rather than the reform aesthetic and asserts that architects and designers should no longer design dresses because it is not their life's work.[50]

Muthesius is not completely against the look. Indeed, as we have seen, he repeatedly argues that considerations of purpose, construction, and material alone are inadequate descriptions for all the arts. When he praises the modern suit, for example, he is not boasting that its removal of ornament has led to a pure utilitarian form. Utility per se is insufficient. Rather, he views the surfaces of the suit as mechanisms for displaying the look of utility, the aesthetic of the machine. The white surface of the modern shirt, which exemplifies the active refusal of superficial dissimulations, is itself nothing more than the maintenance of this machine look. Instead of abandoning exterior appearance in favor of inner mechanism, the modern surface maintains the outward appearance that nothing external has been added. This is made clear in *Stilarchitektur und Baukunst*:

Today's simple clothing also in no way consists strictly of utilitarian elements. Our elegantly dressed gentleman still wears a top hat, patent leather shoes, and silk lapels—elements that might also be compared with certain polished and nickel-plated parts of a machine. In both cases they seem to have been brought into being by a specific requirement for cleanliness—a demand that aims not only to hinder undesired accumulations of dirt but also wants always to demonstrate symbolically that it is not present, that everything is neat and in the best of order. In this demand our starched white linens also find their justification.[51]

Likewise, the white surfaces of modern buildings that model themselves on modern clothing maintain a certain look. Indeed, one of the very last articles, if not the last, that Muthesius wrote, (it was published to commemorate his death in 1927), turns the tables on modern architecture at the very moment that it thinks it has broken away from fashion. The essay, called "Kunst und Modeströmungen" (Trends in art and fashion), opens by announcing that "there is nothing constant in this world except change," and then argues that while the "swings" of fashion are most evident in the world of clothing, they are also evident in the world of visual art and even in the "supposedly strict and unbending" world of science, in addition to those of religion, ethics, morals, and social values. The ubiquitous phenomenon of fashion does not contaminate these areas of modern life. On the contrary, Muthesius argues that fashion provides a "mirror-image of the perceptions of the age." While fashions in art, like all the other kinds of fashion, begin with the basic human need for perceptual variation but, in the end, are driven by purely commercial instincts and backed up by publicity campaigns that disseminate labels and slogans in the newspapers, such a fashion industry can never impose certain forms on the market. Rather, "there is an inner relation between the swaying values of taste—which no one can control, but can be comprehended prophetically—and that which is launched, which is how a fashion is brought into being."[52] It is not that certain forms satisfy modern needs; the modern need is for a certain mobility of form. Like Wagner, Muthesius sees the very mobility of fashions as matching the basic condition of the modern subject. And thus the structural role of fashion should be acknowledged rather than dismissed or censored.[53]

Given that Muthesius was the figure responsible for promoting the very concept of *Sachlichkeit* in his early essays, it is significant that he finally argues that the so-called *Neue Sachlichkeit* architecture, which is so indebted to his writings, with its "flat roofs," "cantilevered slabs," and "great glass surfaces" with "every window continuing around the corner," is just such a fashion, the only difference being that it promotes itself as being founded on a platform that supposedly exceeds fashion: function, economy, construction, health, and applicability. For Muthesius, this platform is but the cover for the "purely aesthetic" concerns that actually organize the form of modern architecture. Once again, he rehearses Riegl's argument that the real generator of style is an external "will-to-form" rather than the internal realities of material and construction that Semper supposedly supported. In fact, he argues that it is precisely the privileging of construction that leads to an architecture of "pure externalities" that is as much an "excess" as the fashion for Art Nouveau that it displaced. While modern architecture is taken to be "engineer like" and therefore "rationalist," as, he notes, van de Velde's work was, "in truth, it moves according to fashionable externalities" and will itself be displaced in due course. He makes the point, of course, through the "immediately pressing" comparison between modern architecture and the "ever-changing clothing fashion":

In clothing, our women know exactly that usefulness stands behind good appearances. The circumstance that the former health-reform clothes disappeared very quickly again from the screen best shows how little usefulness means in clothing. Indeed, women gladly take upon themselves every inconvenience, yes, even absurdity, if they can only achieve a good appearance. Even with men, the standpoint of good form takes the front seat. Why precisely in architecture does one refuse to see that everything depends on beauty and the form is primary?[54]

Unlike clothing designers, architects are unable to acknowledge that modern architecture is but a passing fashion, one linked to clothing. Muthesius made the same point in "Die neue Bauweise" (The new way of building), in which he reviewed the Weissenhofsiedlung exhibition of white buildings of 1927. Maintaining that "the new form has such a tyrannical effect on its promoters" that they "suppress" other tendencies in favor of questionable motifs like the flat roof, he concludes: "That fashion deals with novelty in form is well known among the representatives of the dress art, while the representatives of the so-called new architecture reject with outrage any hint of what can change in the forms they promote and see those forms as wisdom's final conclusion. But the memory of the fast end of the Jugendstil, which had been defended with so much enthusiasm, is still fresh."[55] The new style is just that, a style destined to be abandoned for a new outfit that will also be discarded in time.

Giedion, on the other hand, reviewed the same exhibition for a Swiss newspaper in an article entitled "Ist das neue Bauen eine Mode?" (Is the new architecture a fashion?), which concludes the answer to its question by asserting that the new architecture is "a legitimate movement that may not be disregarded," as distinct from a fashionable celebration of "mere antics with form."[56] This claim would be repeated throughout Giedion's writings and become inscribed within his monumental history of modern architecture. But not simply inscribed. The defense of modern architecture from the accusation that it is merely a fashion actually produces the history within which it appears to be but one claim among many. This was already made clear in the 1932 article "Mode oder Zeiteinstellung?" (Fashion or the attitude of the times?), where Giedion insisted that history is the appropriate weapon with which to attack fashion. He begins by condemning the rule of fashion that "demands 'individual pieces' that are tailored while on the body, or at least look that way," such that, "from the garter to architecture, nuance reigns" and the "general" functional principles of modern life are lost behind an ever-changing display of "surface appearances."[57] He concludes by arguing that the recovery of these new principles requires a history that identifies the basic "attitude of our times," the "sameness" behind the constantly changing and apparently diverse surfaces that surround and wrap the individual, the new order of modern life that fashion works so hard to conceal.[58]

Space, Time and Architecture is, of course, the result of Giedion's attempt to produce such a history. The text is literally launched against fashion. The endeavor to isolate modern architecture from fashion that only surfaces within it every now and then is actually its overriding agenda. In fact, rather than describe the architect's rejection of fashion, the text effects it. Supposedly, history itself peels away the degenerate layers of fashion to make possible a certain architecture, an architecture true to its time. Instead of simply analyzing a historical phenomenon, Giedion attempts to make a space for modern architecture, a site on which architects can then build. He presents himself as a kind of building contractor, if not an architect. Indeed, the modern architects his text describes are understood to be modern only inasmuch as they themselves have acted as historians of their own time.

Given that Muthesius ended up aligning modern architecture with fashion, it is no surprise that he fails to appear within Giedion's history. His key role in establishing the conceptual framework of this architecture (including, ironically, its polemical opposition to fashion) and the institutional structures through which it, and even its history, could emerge is effaced. He is banished from the scene for having dismissed the very architecture he made possible and his name is quietly removed from the many things he left behind. But because he sees fashion as articulating modern culture's fundamental condition within its apparently casual surface play, Muthesius does not simply dismiss modern architecture. Its engagement with fashion does not mean it is alienated from the fundamental condition of its time. Quite the contrary. Having identified modern architecture with fashion, Muthesius argues in "Kunst und Modeströmungen" that what will remain when modern architecture is itself replaced by another style (one that will also emphatically proclaim itself to have finally conquered fashion), the cultural reality embedded within its superficial fantasy, is the general "tendency toward simplification" that has governed cultural production for some time, in the same way that the passing women's fashions have maintained the utilitarian transformations initiated by the sports clothes embraced by the women's movement. It is not just that architectural reform, like clothing reform, cannot resist, let alone replace, fashion. Reform is actually carried out by fashion. Modern architecture makes its contribution to cultural development by virtue of being a transitory fashion rather than by resisting it.

Purifying Fashion

Again, it must be emphasized that modern architecture did not simply become fashionable. Rather, it was, from the beginning, organized by the operations of fashion that underpinned its very attacks on fashion. The enigmas of fashion that Wagner's appropriation of Semper's clothing argument makes explicit, and that work their way through all the protagonists in the uneven formation of modern architecture, are eventually inherited by Le Corbusier. As always, these enigmas do not just disturb, interrupt, or transform his work, but structure it.

After all, as Nancy Troy so persuasively argues, Le Corbusier's original role as a decorative artist and his subsequent work as an interior decorator (between 1912 and 1917) cannot be separated from his later role as an architect, despite his changing his name from Charles-Edouard Jeanneret to preserve such a distinction.[59] His canonic work remains embedded within the thinking of the German Arts and Crafts movement that he studied while working for Behrens and that he systematically, but polemically, summarized in his first, and surprisingly influential, book, *Étude sur le mouvement d'art décoratif en Allemagne* of 1912. On his return from Germany, Le Corbusier accommodated, publicized, and applied this thinking rather than leave it behind and, in so doing, internalized the unresolvable conflict over fashion that structured the German discourse.

At one point in the *Étude*, having earlier noted, in passing, the Deutsche Werkbund lecture series that contrasted "Fashion and Taste" as part of the association's highly successful program of courses for fabric designers, the textile industry, and merchant organizations (a program that, significantly, included the closely related series on "The Ornamentation of the Surface" and "The Question of Truth or the Question of Appearance"), Le Corbusier addresses the Werkbund's stance on public buildings in a way that already makes the generic association between fashion and decoration that will punctuate all his later texts: "The artistic impression of the building does not lie only in the display of exterior decorations that, after all, are only a matter of fashion, but before anything else in the expression of the grand forms born of the program and technical necessities and dependent on the complete satisfaction of the needs of the epoch."[60]

But Le Corbusier did not simply abandon fashion by abandoning decoration. In fact, he did not abandon decoration. Not only did his later texts rehearse the arguments of Behrens, Loos, and Muthesius with very little modification, but he remained indebted to the very figures that they criticized for producing "decorative fashions," like van de Velde and Hoffmann, whose workshops and teaching his 1912 text had described in detail. Troy revises the traditional reading by pointing out that Le Corbusier did not turn away from the decorative arts in turning down Hoffmann's offer of a job in favor of one with Auguste Perret, but actually sought work with the equivalent decorative artists in Paris and actively participated in their discourse and projects: "The work to which Jeanneret was most attracted in late 1913 was the product of a closely knit group of fashionable and controversial artists who occupied a well-defined position on the Parisian decorative arts scene."[61] Indeed, it could be added that, like Loos, his thought remains much closer to Hoffmann than has been acknowledged. While he opposes Hoffmann as "decoration" and Perret as "construction" in the introduction to his *Oeuvre complète*, for example, Le Corbusier remains supportive of Hoffmann throughout his life, just as Hoffmann remains supportive of him. And inasmuch as he repeatedly identifies Hoffmann as the "pioneer" of modern architecture, it would seem that modern architecture emerges from rather than discards decoration.[62]

It was not by chance that Le Corbusier, like Hoffmann, would marry a fashion model; nor that he would design a house for Paul Poiret, a project that was taken over by the much-maligned, because supposedly fashion-conscious, Mallet-Stevens, who also designed a house for the couturier Pierre Patout. After all, Le Corbusier apparently first met Poiret at a Berlin salon in 1910, when Poiret was studying the very same buildings and "modern interiors" and speaking with the very same figures (including Hoffmann, Muthesius, Behrens, and Osthaus) as Le Corbusier and dreaming, as Poiret later put it, "of creating in France a movement of ideas that should be capable of propagating a new fashion in decoration and furnishing."[63] Le Corbusier became entangled with this movement as he literally moved in Poiret's circles, frequenting the same salon, one run by Natalie Barney in his neighborhood in Paris. The fashion world was very much part of his milieu, as it was for most of the avant-garde. The overt dismissal of fashion that punctuates Le Corbusier's writing must therefore be analyzed in terms of his ongoing engagement with it.

Such an analysis would have to return to where we began: the polemical rejection of fashion in the Purist manifesto that Le Corbusier wrote in 1920 with

Amédée Ozenfant. It is a matter of rethinking the way Le Corbusier began his reformation of architectural practice by ostensibly discarding both its and his own decorative past: "One could make an art of allusions, an art of fashion, based upon surprise and the conventions of the initiated. Purism strives for an art free of conventions which will utilize plastic constants and address itself above all to the universal properties of the senses and the mind."[64] At the very least, this apparently unambiguous claim has to be rethought in terms of the fact that Ozenfant was actually in the fashion business with Poiret's sister, the dress designer Germaine Bongard, when Le Corbusier first met him and returned to it when their collaboration broke down, opening a ready-to-wear boutique called *Amédée* in 1926 that was run by his second wife, also a fashion designer, while angrily accusing Le Corbusier of appropriating all his ideas and techniques. The purist project was never a departure from fashion design, a brief interlude in an entirely different, if not opposed, practice, a practice that ultimately forced the separation. On the contrary, Ozenfant had already criticized the separation of fashion and fine art in his own journal *L'Elan* and the first purist exhibition of paintings by him and Le Corbusier in 1918 was held in Bongard's fashion salon, which had been transformed into an art gallery during the war but continued to exhibit her fash-

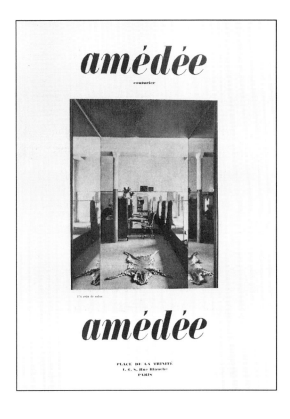

6.13
Full page advertisement for Ozenfant's fashion house, published in Cahiers d'art, *1926.*

6.14
Full page advertisement for Germaine Bongard's fashion house, published in L'Esprit Nouveau *nos. 11–16, 1921–1922.*

Dessin de MARIE LAURENCIN

une robe de **Jove** couturier

5, RUE DE PENTHIÈVRE   PARIS

ions along with the most influential exhibitions of the avant-garde at that time. Indeed, Ozenfant describes purism as an outgrowth of his work on fashion: "1918. . . . I went to Bordeaux to earn my living associated with the sister of Poiret designing dresses. . . . In this atmosphere of purity and calm, I developed my program—*the search for constants*."[65] While he later identifies the origin of purism with the very whitewash of the vernacular buildings that he painted there ("purified images of the little farms, themselves so pure: painted and repainted each spring with virtuously virginal whitewash," "so pure, so white, so purist"), in fact, Ozenfant identifies the search for constants with the fickle world of fashion.[66] The purist rejection of decorative excess emerges from the very world of fashion it appears to reject:

Madame Bongard transformed her *maison de couture* into JOVE. Painter and poet of class, she knew that the true haute couture is not submitting to the seasonal decrees of the *petit* commercial fashions, but to the same permanent laws that have always ruled all the plastic arts. The dresses that she created were never out of fashion because they were not *a la mode* of the instant: they were simply beautiful.

The practice of couture taught me the enormous difference between fashion and couture, between the couturier that conceives and constructs dresses and those that do it through the trial and error of chance. I thus understood that there is not a *very beautiful* dress of to-day that could not have been in ancient Egypt, China or Greece. It will not have been in the latest fashion, that's all. There are not beautiful fashions, there are only bad ones—like that of the crinolines, which had been ugly and ridiculed throughout their time. In the end, if a work of art goes out of fashion, it is because it is only at the level of fashion; even if tartan came back in fashion, it is always above fashion.

Fashion, and this is quite curious, helps me to understand why certain forms and colors survive centuries when the majority perish as soon as they are born. This experience encouraged my research into the visual constants and psychological universals that was to be called Purism.[67]

Once again, that which exceeds fashion emerges out of, and only out of, fashion. But now we are on the very threshold of "modern architecture." The essential condition it seeks is to be found within the very domain of fashion that seems to mark its loss, disregard, degeneration, or abuse—a possibility that even Morris had significantly kept open in the exact moment of condemning fashion designers in his 1877 lecture: "But one good thing breeds

6.15
"Fashion has changed, but the bicycle-type is already established." Illustration from Amédée Ozenfant, Art, *1928.*

another, and most assuredly a steadiness in fashion, when a good fashion has been attained, and a love of beautiful things for their own sakes and not because they are novelties, is both human, reasonable, and civilized."[68] And inasmuch as purism, the very doctrine of the modernist attempt to discard anything inessential in favor of the naked type-form, is in some way bound to the economy of fashion, so, too, is the white wall that serves as the very figure of this project. The specific operations of this wall will need to be traced more precisely. In particular, it is necessary to investigate its strategic role in Le Corbusier's work. The white wall must be subjected to a far more thorough interrogation in relationship to the specific ways that the association between dress and architecture operates in his work, not only orchestrating his critical system of polychromy but also structuring his urban theories, until, finally, he ends up designing not just textiles and wall hangings but even dresses.

From the moment that Le Corbusier accepted the basic association between architecture and clothing, as Troy notes, in a report on drawing education dated December 1914 (but not published until four years later),[69] he had already inherited the enigmas of fashion that have accompanied the argument ever since it was formulated by Wagner under the influence of Semper. Those enigmas organized all his work and his astonishingly skillful publicity campaign exported them to an international market (with a little help from his friends). They are now resurfacing with the frenetic pathology of the so-called postmodern economy of design. Much of this economy is but a legacy of the historical avant-garde. Le Corbusier's work emerged out of, as distinct from being subjected to, the convoluted operations of fashion that have become all too visible today. Inevitably, we will have to go back and reflect on how the traces of these operations are literally marked on the surface of each of his projects.

Such a reflection might dwell on the fact that when the little-known 1914 report in which Le Corbusier associates modern architecture and clothing (by announcing that "we find the true witnesses of a modern style, still incomplete it is true and sometimes also made-up [*maquillé*], in modern dress, in the engines of war and transport, and in the machine-made"), it immediately follows an approving rehearsal of the Loosian critique of ornament that lays out much of the theoretical position he would later promote. It already cites, for example, the line from Loos that would later organize his key book *L'art décoratif d'aujourd'hui*—"the measure of the development of a culture is the disappearance of ornament from the objects of use"—and makes a Muthesiusian call for the examination of *formes-types*.[70] Given that, as Troy demonstrates, the text eventually played a critical role in the launching and trajectory of Le Corbusier's career, and marks the always ambiguous relationship between modern architecture and decorative art, it is crucial to note that here the new figure of the "modern architect" is to improve on the all-too-fast and therefore "superficial" attempts of such a figure to assume responsibility for the whole environment, under the guidance of the German Arts and Crafts movements, by taking over all the traditional applied arts and gathering the requisite skills and "even penetrating as far as the modeling salon of the fashion designer."[71] It was no coincidence that Le Corbusier had visited and sketched the fashion salon of the Wiener Werkstätte shortly after it opened in 1911.[72] Yet again, "modern" emerges from "mode." Nor was it coincidental that the text was written at the end of the year in which Le Corbusier had first proposed the infamous Dom-ino system, around which the "Five Points for a New Architecture," with its generic attack on "fashionable gimmicks," would later be organized.[73] The need to study fashion once again intersects with the need to reject it.

Dom-ino, which so obviously responds to Muthesius's call for standardization in the face of fashion, is repeatedly identified as the most important formal principle of Le Corbusier's work, "the real starting point" of his career, as Giedion puts it. But its simple diagram, probably the most reproduced of all of his drawings, actually enacts the little-known clothing argument. The building system, which rationalizes structure in such a way that all walls become at most light screens, if not curtains, drawn, more or less, across the openings, is a fundamentally Semperian system in which structure is merely the technologically refined but secondary prop, a scaffolding for thin surfaces hung like textiles to define social space. And the social space is also the material space. The structure is not even functional. The fabrics do all the work. In the end, there is no body, no flesh to be either exposed or clothed. Just "a bone structure," as Le Corbusier puts it, a skeleton, that is "completely inde-

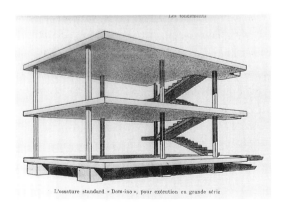

L'ossature standard « Dom-ino », pour exécution en grande série

6.16
Le Corbusier, axonometric diagram of Dom-ino system, 1914, as published in the first volume of the Oeuvre complète *in 1929.*

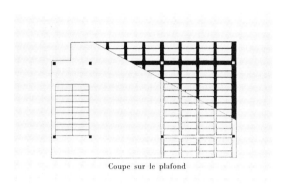

Coupe sur le plafond

6.17

Le Corbusier, suspended "platform" of Dom-ino, as published in the first volume of the Oeuvre complète *in 1929.*

pendent of the functional demands."[74] Perhaps it is not even a skeleton. Perhaps it is really a surrogate body, an empty mannequin on which to hang clothes, decorative surfaces that, like all clothes, project the image of a certain body rather than cover a ready-made one.

After all, what must never be overlooked, as its significance cannot be overestimated, is that the structure as such never appears, however light the fabrics it holds. It never appears in Le Corbusier's buildings as an object the way it does in the famous drawing, nor even as a few protrusions of such an object. Indeed, it does not appear as such even in the drawing. The lesser-known drawing that accompanies the canonic image shows how the internal structure of the suspended "platforms," the matrix of reinforcing bars, the skeleton of the skeleton, is covered over by the smooth surface of the concrete it reinforces. Le Corbusier draws this surface as if it were a skin being discretely pulled over the exposed innards of the structure. Furthermore, even this protective skin is not seen within the building. When the structural frame, the subordinate prop, seems to become visible, as when the columns float within the flowing space defined by the suspended fabrics or when the underside of the platforms are exposed as a ceiling, the prop itself is coated with white, clothed in a thin white coat, a coat worn by those who claim to detach themselves from fashion, but a fashionable coat nonetheless. Perhaps, in the end, Le Corbusier is indeed like the "fashionable milliner" that William Morris describes. Perhaps, in the end, the core of modern architecture is but a "scaffold on which to hang a bundle of cheap rags, which can be sold dear under the name of a dress."

Our temples are no longer painted blue, red, green and white like the Parthenon. No, we have learnt to feel the beauty of naked stone.

—Adolf Loos, "Architektur," 1910.

Deep Skin

Le Corbusier's insistent promotion of the white garment is explicitly based on an attack on the excesses of color. *L'art décoratif d'aujourd'hui* launches his impassioned campaign for whitewash precisely at the moment that it criticizes the fashionable use of color. The book slowly gathers momentum until its tenth chapter announces that "the hour of architecture" has arrived. Designers are finally ready to give birth to modern architecture by embracing the already century–old age of the machine and liberating useful forms from the ornamentation that constricts them. Even decorative artists sense that the days of decoration are over. But in this potentially cathartic moment, a degenerate orgy of color has quickly taken the place of the decoration that has been stripped off. The naked body has been clothed with color in the very moment of its exposure. The decorative artist's intricate folding and marking of the surface has simply given way to an equally suspect play of colored surfaces. It is in the face of this "narcotic haze" of coloration that Le Corbusier makes his first call for a regime of white:

However, as a by-product of the new-born architecture, a taste for polychromy is joyfully running riot. Color for its own sake has really caught the imagination.

Symphony of colors, triumph of the decorative ensemble. Colors and materials. Color used for display. Now that one is involved in it, one might as well do it well. Some fine mixtures have been cooked up. Colors, materials.

What shimmering silks, what fancy, glittering marbles, what opulent bronzes and golds! What fashionable blacks, what striking vermillions, what silver lamés from Byzantium and the Orient! Enough.

Such stuff founders in a narcotic haze. Let's have done with it.
We will soon have had more than enough.
It is time to crusade for whitewash and Diogenes.[1]

The book's final chapter then elaborates the economy of whitewash that must be installed in this historical moment of coloration to transcend both color and history, or, more precisely, to transcend history by suppressing color. Throughout the book, color has been associated with femininity, sexuality, intoxication, addiction, and savagery—the very qualities a modern architecture must suppress in order to constitute itself and then vigilantly monitor its own surfaces to guard against their return. Indeed, one of the key roles of the whitewash is to expose and "record" the color of all the objects placed in front of it: "If the house is all white, the outline of things stands out from it without any possibility of mistake; their volume shows clearly; their color is distinct."[2] The white surface exposes color, presents it for disciplining. It keeps an eye on all the objects it frames. But before that, it keeps an eye on itself, watching its freshly laundered and neatly folded fabric for the stain of color.

The twist is that such obsessive self-surveillance is needed precisely because color is not foreign to the very mechanism of surveillance. The white wall cannot so easily detach itself from the colors that it turns over to the authorities. Indeed, its very whiteness is made out of them. It is white only inasmuch as it can hold all color within itself. Furthermore, while the old dissimulating texture of ornament might live on in dramatic color schemes, those schemes are not old. They are, as Le Corbusier puts it, a "by-product" of the search for the new. The puritanical gesture of cleansing somehow releases the very desires it is attempting to control. The modernization of architecture is held up by one of its own side effects. Modern architecture threatens itself from within. Color cannot simply be banned. It can only be controlled, held inside the white surface for as long as possible and then highly regulated whenever it escapes.

The threat that Le Corbusier faces is therefore internal to his own work. Indeed, while legislating the use of white and even calling for a police action to enforce it in the face of an unruly riot of color, he actually employs color throughout his work, a critical move that is largely effaced by the black and white reproduction of his work and the generations of black and white criticism that disseminated it. That criticism, which managed to survive the color reproduction of the work, only serves to make the intense coloration of the projects even more striking and intriguing. Given the relative consistency of the palette that Le Corbusier used over the years, his work is simply unthinkable outside of its color scheme. To strip off the outer layer of colored paint by ignoring it, as most of the commentators do, is to fundamentally redesign each project, to actively transform the architecture being discussed.

Clearly, Le Corbusier did not so much turn to color as return to the privilege of color within the decorative arts tradition of his early training under Charles L'Eplattenier, which is evident in his systematic documentation of colors in his studies and the detailed color schemes of the early projects he completed before the canonic buildings of the 1920s. Although some of the early surfaces are white, most are covered with color and intricate patterns that are indebted to the theory of polychrome ornament presented in Owen Jones's *Grammar of Ornament*.[3] Of course, it is precisely this tradition of decorative art that appears to be emphatically swept away by *L'art décoratif d'aujourd'hui*. But if, as has been argued here, the role of this text is to translate and absorb the decorative arts into new technologies rather than simply abandon them, his eventual return to color is not so surprising. If the white surface maintains the decorative tradition whose absence it appears to mark, the appearance of color is the return of something that was absorbed into the white surface rather than simply excluded by it. But what precisely is it a return of?

Blinding Color

It is not that Le Corbusier called for a totalizing regime of white and then modified his stance by admitting color. Even the infamous L'Esprit Nouveau pavilion of 1925, whose exhibition the publication of *L'art décoratif d'aujour-d'hui* was timed to coincide with, had a striking color scheme. Far from the white box that appears in photographs, it was covered with white, black, light gray, dark gray, yellow ochre, pale yellow ochre, burnt sienna, dark burnt sienna, and light blue. The proclamation of the "Law of Ripolin" is strangely paralleled by the very application of colored surfaces that it bans. In fact, the practical use of color preceded its theoretical rejection in favor of white. The first projects with which Le Corbusier appeared to abandon his commitment to the decorative arts were indeed white. Through all the speculative variations of the Dom-ino concept in sketches, renderings, and models, the colors that had been applied to the early houses and interiors were seemingly to be displaced by whitewash. But this displacement was shortlived.

7.1
Le Corbusier and Pierre Jeanneret, L'Esprit Nouveau pavillion, 1925. As published in Oesterreichs Bau- und Werkunst, *1925/6.*

7.2
Le Corbusier and Pierre Jeanneret, Villa Besnus at Vaucresson, elevation, 1922. Fondation Le Corbusier.

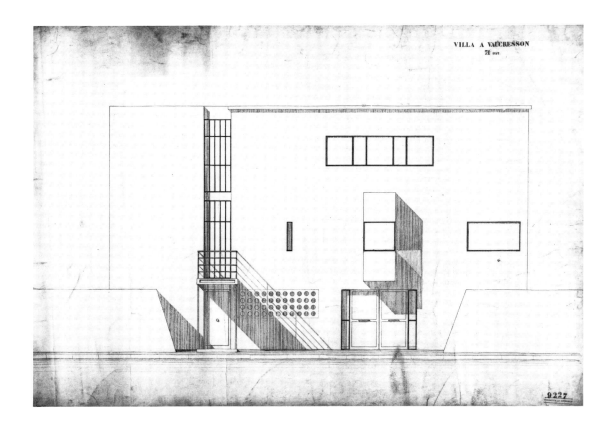

The first of the canonic buildings, the Villa Besnus at Vaucresson, which Le Corbusier started to design with his cousin Pierre Jeanneret at the end of 1922 and was constructed by the end of 1923, was polemically white. The garage doors were painted white to match the wall that they swing out from, as is the metalwork over the entrance. Even the window glass is rendered white in the original drawing of the street elevation. The effect is that of a continuous white surface that is lightly punctuated by the thin lines of the dark window frames and mullions (which are actually painted white on the interior). This effect was carefully produced and disseminated. In 1923 the project was published in an issue of *L'architecture vivante* (along with a white house by Loos). The elevation, plans, and sections were reproduced alongside two photographs of a white model of the building in which the windows are made of the same material as the walls to produce the sense of an unpunctured surface (like the model of the Maison Citrohan whose exhibition at the Salon d'Automne in 1922 was responsible for attracting the client at Vaucresson). The model, which was also exhibited at the Salon d'Automne in 1923, carefully sustains, if not enhances, the polemical effect of the elevation. When the building was completed, the standard photographs were (like many of the famous photographs of Le Corbusier's work) taken with the curtains drawn so that the surface of the glass becomes white, like that of the opaque glass that screens the stairway next to the entrance. Furthermore, these photographs have been extensively retouched to intensify this whiteness and isolate the building from its less utopian surroundings. The building is made to conform to the idealistic model that had in turn been made to conform to the original elevation. When these photographs immediately made their way into influential books like Gropius's *Internationale Architektur* of 1925 and J.P.P. Oud's *Holländische Architektur* of 1926, they made a significant contribution to the white image of modern architecture. It is not by chance that when Le Corbusier publishes the white exterior and interior of the villa in the first volume of the *Oeuvre complète* in 1929 he also presents a new rendering of the original elevation, a watercolor wash that intensifies the sheer white surface. The building is an essay on whiteness.

The first volume of the *Oeuvre complète* presents the Villa Besnus as the first attempt to find a constructed form for Le Corbusier's earlier theories and sketches. Indeed, it was in this design that "the 'free plan' was discovered (placing the bathroom at the center of the floor plan). Both the window form and its module were defined."[4] Likewise, Le Corbusier's last book, *L'atelier de la recherche patiente* (Studio of the patient search) of 1960, makes the seemingly unambiguous statement: "1922. This house at Vaucresson really

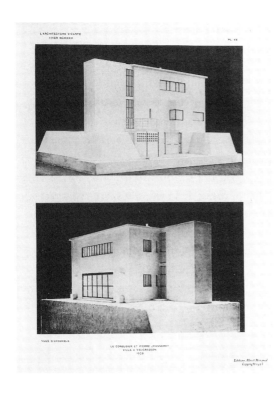

7.3
Marquette of Villa Besnus, 1922 as published in L'architecture vivante, *1923.*

7.4
Street facade of Villa Besnus, as published in the first volume of the Oeuvre complète *in 1929.*

marked the beginning of Le Corbusier's architectural research. Until then he had no creative ambitions of any kind. He was thirty-one when he embarked upon a career which inspired a new approach to architecture."[5] During an interview made a month before his death (which was posthumously distributed on a phonograph record), he described it as his "first commission" and "first construction," claiming that "it gave me an incredibly hard time" because it was "terribly difficult to deliver the modern architectural aesthetic."[6] The all-white building is presented as the first building in a carefully reconstructed image of his career.

All the earlier houses, with their pitched roofs, decoration, and coloration, are suppressed so that the history of Le Corbusier's work can begin with a clean white slate at Vaucresson. They are left behind along with his original name, Charles-Edouard Jeanneret. Although the Villa Schwob of 1916 did appear in *Vers une architecture* of 1923 and is included in the posthumously published *Le Corbusier 1910–1965* (the more compact compendium of his work, which he hoped would be more affordable to students), the first volume of the massive *Oeuvre complète*, which was published in 1929, did not even include the house. It would seem that color (along with the architectural practices associated with it) has to give way to white. But, curiously, the Villa Besnus is not included in *Vers une architecture*'s extensive survey of projects, which was updated in the second edition of 1925. Indeed, it is the only project produced between 1915 and 1925 to be excluded. Nor does it appear in *L'art décoratif d'aujourd'hui* of the same year, in which the call for a regime of white was made. The photographs only appear a year later in the *Almanach d'architecture moderne* and even then it is shown after buildings that actually followed it. In Le Corbusier's subsequent surveys of his career, its

position wanders. Sometimes it comes after the later buildings, sometimes before them. Many times, it simply disappears. To say the least, it is treated ambiguously and this ambiguity made its way into the historiography that has worked so hard to maintain a white image.[7]

What makes this ambiguous status so striking, if not paradoxical, is that the Villa Besnus seems to be Le Corbusier's only all-white building.[8] The only building that cannot be easily placed in the white story is the white one. In the summer of 1924, before any other buildings were completed, color suddenly returned. In the late stages of the construction of the Ozenfant atelier in Paris, the architect sent the builder a color scheme for the interior walls. It specified that the exterior would remain white but the ground-floor kitchen would be green and burnt sienna and the gatekeepers' room and toilet in light pink. On the second floor, the main entrance in ultramarine, the kitchen in green and burnt sienna, the museum in terra umbra, the bedroom and dressing room in red panelling, and the gallery in green and terra umbra. On the top floor, the library in terra umbra.[9] At the same time, the surfaces of the housing scheme at Pessac and the Villa La Roche-Jeanneret were systematically colored. In the first volume of the *Oeuvre complète,* Le Corbusier describes the Villa as the "first test of polychrome,"[10] a built manifesto for a new way of defining space.

Constructed shortly afterward, the L'Esprit Nouveau pavilion merely continued this polemical experiment with the same set of colors. Yet that use of
color is not accounted for in the set of four books (*Vers une architecture*
[1923], *La Peinture moderne* [1925], *Urbanisme* [1925], and *L'art décoratif
d'aujourd'hui* [1925]) that, as Le Corbusier put it, "comprised the theory of
which the Pavilion was intended to be the realization."[11] While *La Peinture
moderne* describes the "scientifically" precise use of the same set of colors in
"purist" paintings, the other books distance themselves from color. The logic
of color in painting is seemingly held apart from that of architecture. Color
in architecture is not theorized as such. On the contrary, it seems to be prohibited by the "Law of Ripolin." For a time, Le Corbusier appears to operate
outside his own law. It is not until the following year that he starts to account
for the color scheme of the pavilion in *Almanach d'architecture moderne,* the
very book that publicized the all-white Villa Besnus but also illustrates the
first three projects with which he started to redeploy color without referring
to their coloration. The captions to the images of the pavilion describe the
color of each surface while the text briefly describes the thinking behind the
choice of colors before announcing some kind of distance from the totalizing
theory of white that had been presented the year before: "Entirely white, the
house is like a cream jug."[12] Despite *L'art décoratif d'aujourd'hui*'s call for an
architecture of prosthetic type-objects, it would seem that the modern building must be more than an everyday object extracted from a purist painting,
more than the white geometric figure that seems to haunt every such painting
as some kind of vestigial trace of the white buildings that were the subject of
the very first of these paintings. While Purism evolved from studies of the elemental figures of whitewashed houses into studies of everyday objects like
jugs, bottles, and glasses, the architecture based on the condition of those objects is no longer simply white. Le Corbusier finally begins to account for his
colored paint two years after he started applying it. Even then, he does not
offer a theory of colored architecture, just a set of hints about how such a
theory might be elaborated and a rejection of the all-white building. An old
theory appears to be abandoned without a new one being adopted as such.

What is even more intriguing is Le Corbusier's use of the "Law of Ripolin" to
prohibit color a year after he has started to deploy color. At the very least, it
has an enigmatic role. The discourse on white is not simply a prescription of
an architectural practice. Its effects, like those of any theory, advertising
slogan, or quasi-religious doctrine, exceed its literal application. To speak of
its unique influence is to speak of much more than the actual use of white surfaces in Le Corbusier's buildings or any works of modern architecture. On
the contrary, it may have been insisted on, and used to construct the image of
modern architecture as white, precisely at the moment that the architecture

was no longer completely white. After all, even the practice of white had preceded its explicit theorization and codification. The early white designs were produced without the benefit of any legislation. The "Law of Ripolin" gave the white surfaces a special authority in the very moment that there were less of them. It invested them with authority over the colored surfaces that had just joined them but were yet to be acknowledged as such. The relationship between the theory and the practice was, as always, extremely convoluted and asymmetrical.

It is not by chance that Le Corbusier insists that white dislodge color after he starts dislodging white with color in his own designs. Making the theory of white precede and subordinate the theory of color has certain strategic consequences that cannot be underestimated. The impact of modern architecture depends a lot on whether its white surfaces appear against a background of color or the color appears against a background of white. To understand white in a certain way is to understand architecture in a certain way. Whiteness has to be given a particular charge by locking it into a relentless history that activates and legitimates dominant cultural phobias. Once supercharged against numerous perceived threats, it is able to structure the discourse without being theorized as such. Indeed, it is only able to become structural inasmuch as it is seen to precede or exceed theory. In other words, it has to be presented as that which requires no theory, that which is able to govern other practices, particularly those of color. Supposedly, white does not need to be disciplined by theory because it is itself a disciplinary mechanism. In the end, the theory of white is no more than the assertion that white is the transhistorical mechanism of truth. The unique role of *L'art décoratif d'aujourd'hui* is not to theorize white but to affirm that white is the possibility of all theory, an affirmation that must be seen to precede any color theory and yet only needs to be made when such a theory is already beginning to emerge. In the end, Le Corbusier will actually write more about color than he does about whiteness but what he writes presupposes his assertions about whiteness. Color is understood in terms of the white surfaces it appears to displace.

To speak a little more precisely of the timing then, *L'art décoratif d'aujourd'hui,* like the other three books, was constructed out of articles that had already been published in *L'Esprit Nouveau*. While its first call for a "crusade for whitewash" had appeared on a page of issue 19 in December 1923, the key chapter on "A Coat of Whitewash: The Law of Ripolin," which follows and answers that call, had symptomatically never been published before: 1925 is its date of publication and its theme. Nothing in the book's attack on the decorative atmosphere supporting that year's exposition prepares the reader for the color scheme of the L'Esprit Nouveau Pavilion that appeared within the exposition. In fact, the chapter on whitewash symptomatically concludes with an image of the Ozenfant atelier, the first project to be colored. But the colors are kept out of the picture. The black and white image of the interior (the book's only image of Le Corbusier and Pierre Jeanneret's work until Le Corbusier adds a series of images of the Pavilion to the preface of the 1959 edition) directs itself away from any of the major colored surfaces and washes out those colored surfaces that remain in its field of view—the window sills, stair, railings, screens, and so on. Even the dark floor finds most of its surface transformed by the light that pours in through the studio windows (the mullions of which have all been painted white on the inside except for the three opening panels that are dark like all the mullions on the outside). The floor is obviously not painted white like the walls and ceiling and yet it ends up exhibiting a brighter white than them. Color is bracketed out to produce the effect of a white space, a space bounded by whiteness.

Furthermore, the image of this space appears immediately opposite the claim that such a whiteness reveals and classifies the color of whatever is placed within it—like the purist painting by Ozenfant that appears on one wall in the photograph, the table and chairs, the people that use them, and so on. Even the viewer of the image, the reader of *L'art décoratif d'aujourd'hui,* is presumably framed by its whiteness, or, more precisely, by the complicated relationship between that whiteness and the whiteness of the page on which it appears—like that between the small area of white in the Ozenfant painting and the white walls of his atelier. The viewer is exposed by the absence of color in what is being viewed. The particular image being used preserves the sense that the painting is colored while the building is not.

The effect is quite unlike other images of the same building. A photograph of the gallery space next to the main entrance, which was published in 1925 in influential magazines like *L'architecture vivante* and *Oesterreichs Bau— und Werkunst,* demonstrates the affinity between the coloration of the paintings and the building. It shows the spiral stair through which the visitor passes in order to move from the white exterior to the white studio space on the top floor. Although the staircase is also white, it is not hermetically sealed off from the colored spaces. On the contrary, Le Corbusier goes out of his way to open it up to them. The visitor twists up through the colored gallery, forced to look down into the space that is not being physically entered. Furthermore, the journey is not simply from white to white. It begins in the ultramarine entrance lobby and ends with the terra-umbra library suspended within the studio space. The relationship between white and color is convoluted. The white may be dominant but it can never be separated from the colors. Still, the image of the gallery that captures this entanglement was abruptly withdrawn from circulation in favor of the canonic photographs of

the all-white interior and the all-white exterior. These images, which re-appear countless times in the ever-accumulating literature about modern ar-chitecture, sustain a white reading by bracketing color out. They liberate the euphoria about white that underpins the historiography, even encouraging it to occasionally erupt on the surface of the discourse.[13] The single image of the studio that Le Corbusier chooses to illustrate the "Law of Ripolin" in *L'art décoratif d'aujourd'hui* conceals what the whiteness it presents is sup-posed to reveal, effacing the fact that Le Corbusier insists that buildings can only scrutinize the color of any object they frame by being completely white at the very moment that he has already started to apply color to his own buildings.

The only clue about this gap between the theory and the practice is provided by two passing comments embedded earlier in the text. Having invited the eye to "rebel" against "the distracting din of colors and ornaments" in the seventh chapter, the following chapter on "The Lesson of the Machine," which was first published in the twenty-fifth issue of *L'Esprit Nouveau* of July 1924, nevertheless notes "the astonishing taste shown in the colors used by engineers to finish off their products."[14] Later, it describes how their pol-ished machines are "adorned by color, with grey, with vermillion, with green, with blue. Grey on the complex castings, bright colors on the pure geometry of the sections."[15] The beauty of such a scheme supposedly dismisses all "pre-machine" art. The removal of everything superfluous is aligned with a system-atic application of color. Color is seen to emphasize, rather than mask, the pure geometries of both the machine and the new forms it makes available. If modern architecture is the child of the machine age, it would seem to make sense that it is colored like a machine, and Le Corbusier's color scheme does resemble that of the engineers. But this possibility seems to be outlawed by the "Law of Ripolin" that soon follows. While the passage on colored machines precedes the discourse on white, it is not turned into a theory of architecture. The positive use of color is suspended in favor of a polemical rejection of all uses of it. When Le Corbusier repeatedly argues that architects need to learn from engineers but then transcend them, it would seem that part of what must be transcended is their use of color, no matter how rational and tasteful. Just as the architect is not simply an engineer, the building is not simply a machine. The apparent discrepancy between white theory and colored practice remains unaccounted for.

Unsurprisingly, it still remains unaccounted for in the accumulated historiography—despite the detailed attention that some scholars have paid to Le Corbusier's use of color in recent years.[16] All of the monumental histories of modern architecture pass over colored paint. Take Leonardo Benevolo's two volume *Storia dell'architettura moderna* (History of modern architecture) of 1960, for example. The text, which emphatically privileges Le Corbusier over the other architects, is one of the few to at least partially theorize the role of the white wall as such. When describing Le Corbusier's Villa Stein at Garches, for example, it refers to the way the white plaster interacts with the black window frames to "form an abstract composition emphasizing their geometrical values."[17] Likewise, it associates Gropius's use of white plaster on the Bauhaus building at Dessau to "stress the geometrical relations, by

7.6
Le Corbusier, Ozenfant atelier (1924), as illustrated in L'art décoratif d'aujourd'hui, *1925.*

7.7
Gallery of Ozenfant atelier, as published in Oesterreichs Bau- und Werkunst, *1925. Getty Research Center, Resource Collections.*

temporarily renouncing the typical physical determination of the various materials" with Brunelleschi's use of the same finish for the same reason.[18] Indeed, the text identifies modern architecture so closely with this abstracting property of the white surface that any compromise of that surface is portrayed as a degeneration of that architecture:

A constant characteristic was for example the use of smooth, white walls; this expedient served to reduce the wall to the simple function of a geometrical field, on which the proportional relations of the constructional elements could be made to stand out, so that the plaster was always smooth and uniform. Imitators accepted this suggestion, but were concerned not to let the wall lose its physical consistency, treating it in such a way that it retained a perceptible texture.[19]

To give the surface of the white wall a texture, and thereby restore its physical presence, is, for Benevolo, to "distort," "water-down," and "dilute" modern architecture. The limits of his radical privileging of abstraction from materiality and texture only become evident when the text compares the Swiss Pavilion of 1932, where "for the first time Le Corbusier rejected the expedient of uniform white plaster, and had every surface characterized by the materials used," to the Salvation Army building of the following year, which continued to use the white wall.[20] While the Swiss Pavilion is seen to envision the trend that would later dominate architectural practice, it is a practice the text never fully embraces. Benevolo holds onto the white wall in its absence. Even with the Salvation Army building, he clings to that wall by ignoring the striking color scheme of the entrance kiosk, the top floors of the facade and the interiors—which Le Corbusier intensifies in the 1951 renovation that Benevolo also illustrates, running it right across the main facade where the sheer glass wall used to be in a series of bright yellow, red, blue, gray and black bands.[21] In the interior, almost every surface is charged with a different color. Even in the original scheme, there is more color than white in the building. While the bulk of the main facade was all glass, the face of the top two floors was colored and the side wall was a big colored sign. Indeed, as Brian Brace Taylor points out, the renovation rendered the white even brighter than it had been before.[22] The whiteness of parts of the building that Benevolo refers to are actually the product of the bold color scheme that he does not address.

It is not that the text simply ignores color altogether. At one point, it patiently contrasts the way Gropius and Le Corbusier cover every wall with uniform white plaster to J. P. P. Oud's addition of different colors to certain surfaces, describing which color was applied where in great detail. The white walls turn out to be punctuated by red, blue, yellow, and gray details. After describing these details in the Kiefhoek housing of 1925, Benevolo argues that Oud "used the most threadbare resources of modern architecture to give dignity, by pure virtue of interplay of shape and color, to very poor material."[23] It would seem that color is able to participate in both the geometric and political order that the text privileges. It would seem that the white cannot be separated from a lively color scheme. Yet the rest of the text works extremely hard to produce an ideal image of modern architecture as smooth and white, a labor that requires a systematic color blindness.

This self-imposed blindness is shared by almost all of the dominant historiographies, most of which have even managed to ignore the white surfaces of the buildings that they are discussing. Again, it is not that they are unable to talk about color. Indeed, it seems that none of them are able to talk about De Stijl without describing its use of primary colors. The color of one or another of Le Corbusier's buildings may be referred to in passing but not the role of that color as such, let alone its relationship to the colored paint splashed over all the other projects. Color is detached from the master narrative—as if it would disrupt the narrative and subvert its capacity to master the modernity of architecture. Giedion, for example, only refers to the experimentation with polychrome in a caption to a photograph of Pessac that he publishes in *Space, Time and Architecture* and saves a passing reference to the colored walls of the L'Esprit Nouveau Pavilion for a small essay on furniture.[24] In 1965, Pevsner even rejected the topic "The Role of Color in the Aesthetics of Modern Architecture" as a "suitable subject for a Ph.D." at the Courtauld Institute of Art.[25] These gestures have been faithfully reproduced by the succeeding generations. The self-appointed custodians rigidly discipline themselves and others against the threat of colored paint.

7.8
J. P. P. Oud, Kiefhoek Housing, Rotterdam, 1925. As published in Die Form, *1930.*

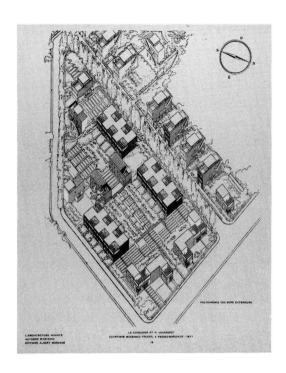

7.9
*Le Corbusier, Pessac
housing scheme, hand-
colored image from*
L'architecture vivante,
1927.

The primacy of color for Le Corbusier is obvious. Not only are so many of
his architectural drawings colored but many of his black ink or pencil
sketches are annotated with color references. He even attempted to resist the
color blindness of black and white photography by publishing hand-colored
images of Pessac, Villa La Roche-Jeanneret, Villa Jeanneret-Raaf, the small
artist's house at Boulogne, and Villa Cook, in a 1927 issue of *L'Architecture
Vivante* and later did the same thing with the Pavilion de nouveau temps and
some of his city plans. With the arrival of cheaper color printing, his *Oeuvre
complète* started to use color and the last posthumous volume uses many
color illustrations to, as his publisher puts it, honor his understanding of
"polychrome as an essential expressive element of his architecture."[26] It is not
simply a question of the color of his buildings. One of the subtexts of his
writing is its obsessive attention to color details. Not by chance does he seemingly go out of his way to point out that the fence that was originally put up
by the authorities to conceal the L'Esprit Nouveau pavilion was green.[27] Likewise, when he publishes his lectures, he often tells the reader the color of
each of the lines that he drew for the audience.[28] Symptomatically, the notes
from which the lectures are made have these colors pre-marked. Eventually,
this will be formalized when the "mental architecture" of the "Ascoral Grid"
for C.I.A.M. is color coded and Le Corbusier speaks of the advantages of using color as a model of communication, because "the eye is guided by color

signals to certain points of interest," while acknowledging the prohibitive expense of color reproduction.[29] It is not that color is an abstract code. Particular concepts are associated with particular colors. When describing the use of one color rather than another while drawing during a lecture, Le Corbusier points out that "it is useless to try to make colors say the contrary of what one means."[30] Indeed, throughout his career, conceptual drawings are almost always colored. Color is a conceptual issue long before it is theorized as such. It is a mechanism of classification, a way of thinking rather than a way of marking particular thoughts. In his "If I had to Teach you Architecture" of 1938, he advises students: "*Here is a golden rule:* use colored pencils. With color, you accentuate, you classify, you clarify, you disentangle. With black pencil you get stuck in the mud and you're lost. Always say to yourself: Drawings must be easy to read. Color will come to the rescue."[31] Likewise, in 1956, he describes the process of design as beginning with the selection of colored pencils, arguing that "color is the key of the process."[32] In the end, color is much more than a means of communicating architectural ideas. It is part of the technical means of producing architecture and part of its fundamental condition. For Le Corbusier, architecture is literally shaped by the colors it emerges out of. The question of color is the question of architecture itself. Before anything else, the architect must be a color expert.

In 1931 Le Corbusier attempted to demonstrate that expertise by producing a color chart for Salubra, a Swiss wallpaper company, which he updated in 1959. Designers and their clients were encouraged to use the chart to select matching wallpapers from the special edition that carried his name. For over thirty years, architectural magazines carried advertisements showing diverse interiors dressed by this wallpaper. The architect's signature could be applied to a space that he had not designed through the simple choice of particular colors, just as it could through the purchase of his furniture. By marketing the skin of buildings, Le Corbusier returned to the world of interior decoration from which he had so dramatically staged his departure twenty years earlier. His original campaign against the applied surface of wallpaper was continued by taking over that very surface. The colored surface is not simply stripped off the wall and abandoned. Rather, the architect enters the surface and attempts to control it, turning it into an agent of modernization by disciplining it against its own excesses, steering it away from the ancient but omni-present dangers of ornament. Le Corbusier appropriates the very technology of decoration to depower decoration. The surface of modern architecture appears to be transformed, setting up a curious relationship between white and colored walls, one that needs to be explored in some detail here because the unique enigmas of the white wall are at once exposed and deepened by it.

These enigmas are already in place in *Le voyage d'Orient,* the first book that Le Corbusier wrote, even though it was not submitted for publication until two weeks before his death in 1965. The book is a record of the five-month tour he took with his Swiss friend Auguste Klipstein between 1910 and 1911. It is the logbook of a tourist, describing the various images presented to a traveling eye. What is so striking is that Le Corbusier relentlessly reports the color of all the surfaces he sees. It is as if the specificity of each point on the itinerary is marked by its particular colors. Even the sketches he did at the time are carefully annotated with the matching colors, aligning themselves with the set of watercolors he also prepared. Indeed, the book refers to itself several times as if it is a colored painting.[33]

The implication of the travelogue is not that generic forms are coded with regional color schemes. The colors are seen to be an integral part of what they mark. At the very beginning of the text, the strength of the folk art that is as yet uncontaminated by the "sway of fashion" is identified with its ability to bond color and form: "In our travels we passed through countries where the artist peasant matches with authority the color to the line and the line to the form." Everywhere, different colors. Everywhere, color reigns. What rules is sensuality: "The color, it too is not descriptive but evocative—always symbolic. It is the ends and not the means. It exists for the caress and for the intoxication of the eye." The endpoint of art is blinding sensation. Its force is an erotic charge that engulfs the eye, blurring the line between vision and sensation, mind and body. To look and to think become physical acts. Such acts are not simply carried out by a stable subject. Rather, the limits of that subject are challenged by them. Color overwhelms and unhinges the person that looks at them. Indeed, Le Corbusier's whole journey becomes one of "unrestrained debauchery" merely by virtue of its relentless search for the authentic folk-object.[34]

It is, of course, common to identify color with sensuality. What is uncommon here is that sensuality is not presented as that which must be transcended but as the very possibility of transcendence. It becomes the foundation, the "healthy base," of the modern abstract eye that appears to supplant it:

The art of the peasant is a striking creation of aesthetic sensuality. If art elevates itself above the sciences, it is precisely because, in opposition to them, it stimulates sensuality and awakens profound echoes in the physical being. It gives to the body—to the animal—its fair share, and then upon this healthy base, conducive to the expansion of joy, it knows how to erect the most noble of pillars.

Thus this traditional art, like a lingering warm caress, embraces the entire land, covering it with the same flowers that unite or mingle races, climates, and places. It has spread out without constraint, with the spiritness of a beautiful animal. The forms are voluminous and swollen with vitality, the line continually unites and mingles native scenes, or offers, right alongside and on the same object, the magic of geometry: an astonishing union of fundamental instincts and of those susceptible to more abstract speculations.[35]

More than an object to be caressed, the artwork is itself a caress, a "warm caress" that exceeds any attempt to control it. The detached modern eye is a product of the traditional sensuality that it appears to leave behind and is constantly dislodged by that sensuality, confused whenever it looks back, set adrift in the very moment that it tries to master materiality. *Le voyage d'Orient* offers a sensuous account of the would-be architect endlessly drifting through colored spaces in a state of "fever," "intoxication," or "dream." The tour through the East is from color to color, with the traveler being physically led by the colors, dragged through the spaces they define as if in a kind of trance. From the decorative pattern on a utilitarian folk vase to the "explosion" of color in the "insane" and purposeless excesses of a street festival, where "the eye becomes confused, a little perturbed by the kaleidoscopic cinema where dance the most dizzying combinations of colors,"[36] the traveler is repeatedly dislodged by what he sees. Le Corbusier's celebration of actually being drunk or feverish in certain places becomes emblematic of the whole tour.

This trance-like state is intensified by the sun's movements, which change the quality of every space, mobilizing every surface, modifying every color. The text is obsessed with light and its effect on color. The light is itself a physical presence, able to "invade," "pierce," or "annihilate" spaces and the distinctions between them through its quasi-erotic charge. It is a kind of body, such that the traveler can find himself nestled "under the warm belly of the white sky" and buildings can "receive its warm caress."[37] The encounter between building and light, which will obsess Le Corbusier throughout his career, is always sexual. To occupy a space is to be caressed by surfaces that are able to caress because they have themselves been caressed by the light. The building actively positions itself to receive such caresses and pass them on. The experience of architecture becomes that of a ménage à trois in which the most active partners (and the most ambivalent in terms of gender) are the building and the light. The "masterly play of forms and light" is erotic. Yet it is only "masterly" inasmuch as its excesses are controlled, regulated by an architect so that the observer of a building can preserve a stable identity. The architect shelters the occupant of a building psychologically from the ambivalence of the physical shelter itself.

Although white paint is a key agent of this stabilizing mastery, it also participates in the sexual economy that it supposedly regulates. *Le voyage d'Orient*'s privilege of the sensuous encounter with surfaces is not simply abandoned when *L'art décoratif d'aujourd'hui* censors color along with all other forms of sensuous decoration in favor of a regime of white. Not by chance does the latter book end by describing the long journey as "decisive" because it "finally shattered" the "respect for decoration" fostered by the architect's training.[38] Indeed the book's whole argument is embedded within the early travelogue. *Le voyage d'Orient* already makes the call for "purification" in the face of the "infectious germ" of gold-colored bric-a-brac that will become the battle-cry of the 1920s.[39] And white plays a unique role within the text's blurry dream. The haze of color is always punctuated by white surfaces. This is already evident in the first description of the sensuous encounter with an authentic folk-object:

You recognize these joys: to feel the generous belly of a vase, to caress its slender neck, and then to explore the subtleties of its contours. To thrust your hands into the deepest part of your pockets and, with your eyes half-closed, to give way slowly to the intoxication of the fantastic glazes, the burst of yellows, the velvet tone of the blues; to be involved in the animated fight between brutal black and victorious white elements.[40]

It is the victory of the white that somehow releases the sensuous colors that will close down the very eyes that look at them in favor of an intimate embrace. It is white that maintains the fragile economy in which visuality is blurred with sensuality. It is white that allows the eyes to flutter, half closed, half open. Indeed, the rest of the text is obsessed with whiteness. It speaks of the whiteness of the ship on which the tourists traveled, the white stucco of peasant houses, the white mosques, the white sand, the white reflections on the water, the white sky, the white oarsman's cap, the white paving stones, the white curbstone of a well, the white hall of a monastery, the white marble bust, the white table, the white minarets, the white fabrics, the white room, the white carriages, the white trellis, the white coat of the toll taker, the white glass, the white wooden benches, the white turbans, the white mist, the white poppies, the white morning light, the white stars, the white sun, the white cap of the oarsman, the white lighthouse, and so on. This ubiquitous whiteness, which is variously described as "brilliant," "bare," "raw," "naive," "impassive," "icy," "blinding," "shining," and "majestic," is a crucial part of the dreamy journey. Indeed, it sometimes acts as a figure for the dreamlike nature of the journey, as when Le Corbusier describes his ship passing through a fog in which the sky cannot be distinguished from the sea: "like a white ghost, our boat floats in an elusive element."[41] It is the white that enables the passage through the blur.

Yet the white is not simply detached from the haze through which it negotiates. Even white buildings in the blazing sun are credited with an "icy mystery" that is related to the "mysterious relationships of form and color" that Le Corbusier finds in the white monasteries on top of Mount Athos.[42] Whiteness cannot be detached from the sensuous colors it appears to reveal. The "whitewashed room" of the particular monastery where he stayed, for example, is intensified by the rug "blooming with colors" on which he slept.[43] Indeed, the very intensity of the white blurs the distinction between it and the sensuality of the colors that offset it. It is here, at Athos, that the text speaks of the way "the glaring presence of a white sun confuses one's sense of color."[44] And it is precisely on this mountain, this "tremendous pyramid crowned with white marble," that he clarifies his search for the "millennial form" to be found all over the world (in "geometric combinations, the square the circle, and proportions in simple and distinctive ratios") with his most extreme fantasy about color: "To go even further, I imagine color in bands of yellows, reds, blues, violets, and greens, with sharp boundaries but otherwise like a rainbow of lines going from the vertical to the horizontal without the bisecting slope. Let rhythm alone arrange this pure graphic expression!"[45] White is the setting for color. Several times, the text literally speaks of white spaces as the "necessary" environment for colored artworks.[46] The euphoric discussion of whiteness leads into a detailed account of the specific colors of specific paintings.

In fact, the text never talks of white without talking of color. In a mosque, for example, the architectonic effect of its white garment is assisted by a strategic use of color: "All these things are clothed in a majestic coat of whitewash. The forms stand out clearly; the impeccable construction displays all its boldness. At times a high stylobate of delightful ceramic produces a blue vibration."[47] The sensuous vibration of the color clarifies the white surface whose limit it marks. Likewise, when talking of the white stuccoed houses of Rumanian peasants, Le Corbusier approves of the blue and yellow adorning the base, corners, windows, and pediments of the buildings: "thus the primitive man wraps himself in bright colors and creates beauty all around him."[48] The text repeatedly points to such accents of color, which both intensify the white and are intensified by it.

Furthermore, the white surface enters a dynamic relationship with the colors beyond the building. The "white blots" of the mosques at Stamboul, for example, serve to "brighten" the "carpet of violet and dark green" produced by the wooden houses of the city below that are covered with greenery.[49] And again, when talking of peasant houses throughout Serbia, Bulgaria, Constantinople, and Athos, Le Corbusier notes that: "Each spring, the house that one loves receives its new coat: sparkling white, it smiles the whole summer through foliage and flowers that owe to it their dazzle. . . . The rooms are whitewashed, and the white is so beautiful that I was very impressed. Already last year I had become enthused over the decorative power that people and things take on when seen against the white of peasant rooms."[50] The white at once brightens the colors that appear against it and renders them decorative. In turn, such colors are able to brighten the whiteness of a building. Indeed, this effect renders the white itself decorative. The green shadow cast by the plants on a white trellis onto a peasant house in Turkey, the flowerbeds, the multicolored clothes of the inhabitants, and the red and green lacquered doors, for example, "contrast and harmonize" with the white surfaces of that house to such an extent that "the three great whitewashed walls, which are repainted each spring, make a screen as decorative as the background of Persian ceramics."[51] The white wall becomes embroiled in the vibrations of color and starts to emit its own.

Even when Le Corbusier fantasizes about purifying what he sees so that it matches the image he carries in his mind, by whitewashing everything, he keeps some color. At one point, for example, he dreams of transforming the chaos of Stamboul into a unified "white city" by using the white mosques that rise above the jumble of colors of the houses below them as a model. But the fantasy of eliminating certain colors would be incomplete without the preservation of certain others:

I want Stamboul to sit upon her Golden Horn all white, as raw as chalk, and I want light to screech on the surface of domes which swell the heap of milky cubes, and minarets should thrust upward, and the sky must be blue. Then we would be free of this depraved yellow, this cursed gold. Under the bright light, I want a city all white, but the green cypresses must be there to punctuate it. And the blue of the sea shall reflect the sky.[52]

White would not be white without green and blue. Indeed, white is able to take on color. It ends up exhibiting the very colors it appears to have triumphed over. A crucial part of the traveler's delirium are forms that drift in and out of whiteness. This hypnotic effect can be seen in a description of the view from the bridge between Pera and Stamboul early in the morning. At first, "torn, whitish patches of fog float across a background of opaque grey," removing the distinction between water and sky and obscuring any view of the two cities from the "dizzy" spectator. The disorientation increases as the "thick gauzes of mist whiten, tear, become as white as snow." But then the white veil gives way to a colored sky that at once exposes and recolors the cities. The whiteness of those cities then returns only to be colored again. The surfaces of the buildings oscillate between white and color for a while until finally the white triumphs:

Steadily the clouds pressed on. There was no end to them. They rolled along with the boats, making the background appear sinister. The sun was worn out. Validé appeared still black, and nothing could be seen of Pera. In the meantime, high above the sky was turning pink. As hundreds of boats were passing by, I saw this unforgettable site: Suleyman, a delicate pink emerging from the dark draperies. For an instant it was deep blue against the pink clouds, but immediately after it turned alabaster white cold as granite. It kept appearing and re-appearing, while the entire atmosphere sparkled with pink. The sea was asserting itself. Colors were appearing, but still very pale. . . . Finally, the red disk of the sun asserted itself. It hurled terrible darts, it pierced the clouds, it triumphed. The mosques blanched, and Stamboul appeared. . . . When the last vaporous layers were lifted, I thought I had been dreaming.[53]

The ability of the white surface to take on the color of the atmosphere in which it is suspended becomes the basis of the ecstatic description of the Parthenon that concludes the text. When viewed from a ship, the building first appears as "bronze" when it "reflects" the red landscape in the bright sun. With the arrival of a storm, its color changes: "the hill becoming suddenly white and the temple sparkling like a diadem."[54] Later, this emergent "white cube" becomes a "yellow cube." Finally, it even turns "black." The supposedly naked building that is able to oscillate with color in this way "induces a caress" of its surface that turns out to be "as polished as a mirror."[55] The enchanted traveler caresses the surface whose display of color has caressed him from a distance. Whiteness is not detached from the sensuality of color, the "necessary sensuality," as the text puts it earlier, which "intoxicates and eludes reason" and "is a source of latent joy and a harness of living strength" because it is the very foundation of the reason whose grasp it eludes.[56] On the contrary, the white surface is the possibility of the most explosive sensuality. The whole book builds up to its final cathartic account of the polychrome possibilities of the parthenon's ostensibly monochromatic surface: "Never in my life have I experienced the subtleties of such monochromy. The body, the

7.10
Le Corbusier, sketch of Acropolis, 1911.

mind, the heart gasp, suddenly overpowered."[57] The delirium of color described throughout the text culminates in the orgasmic delirium of white.

This delirium is suppressed by *L'art décoratif d'aujourd'hui*'s seemingly puritanical call for white to eliminate sensuality. The sensuality of white itself seems to be effaced from Le Corbusier's architectural theory until he starts to account for his own use of color in *Almanach d'architecture moderne,* which symptomatically publishes the sections of the travelogue on the white mosques and the Parthenon. It would seem that it takes color to bring out the sensuality of white.

This sensuality can already be found buried within *Vers une architecture,* in which the Parthenon is so famously presented as the paradigm of rational standardization alongside an emphatic Loosian rejection of the sensuality of color: "Decoration is of a sensorial and elementary order, as is color, and suited to simple races, peasants and savages."[58] *Le voyage d'Orient*'s observation that the fluctuations in the light of the acropolis charge the naked surfaces of the buildings erected upon it with ever changing colors, in a way that overwhelms the spectator, goes unremarked. And this suppression of the sensuality of color seems to prop up the assertion made during the following chapter's account of a Byzantine church that: "there is only one color, white; always powerful since it is positive."[59] While Le Corbusier does not yet call for a white architecture, the image of modern architecture as naked, and the association between nakedness and whiteness, is already launched. And this image was to enjoy unparalleled currency.

But one of the neglected subtexts of *Vers une architecture* is that the whiteness it refers to and tacitly promotes does not simply mark the loss of sensuality. On the contrary, the erotic charge of the quasi-naked body of the building is quite explicit. In the last chapter before the book exhibits Le Corbusier's white projects, the Parthenon returns in order to set up the infamous declaration that "Architecture is the skilful, accurate and magnificent play of masses seen in light."[60] But now the building is presented as a model of the union of the senses and the mind: "Here the purest witness to the physiology of sensation, and to the mathematical speculation attached to it, is fixed and determined: we are riveted by our senses; we are ravished in our minds; we touch the axis of harmony."[61] The very union between the sensuous and the supersensual is something that is "touched" rather than simply "witnessed." Or rather, to witness is to touch, to touch is to witness.[62] The sensuousness of the Parthenon's plain surfaces, now credited with the effect of "naked polished steel,"[63] returns. When these surfaces are associated with the smooth, white, plastered walls of modern architecture, then that very smoothness, that very whiteness, becomes sensual. As does the light that activates such surfaces. When the previous chapter analyses one of the white mosques celebrated by *Le voyage d'Orient*, the play between "a great white marble space filled with light," a similar one in "half-light," smaller spaces in "subdued light" and even smaller ones in "shade," is described as "a sensorial rhythm" that "captures" and "enthralls" the visitor.[64] The sensuality of whiteness is restored in the very moment that it is credited with providing access to the supersensual.

The white surface does not simply regulate the delirium of color by excluding it. Rather, it absorbs that delirium in a way that makes available something supposedly beyond it, but not simply detached from it. The white wall is able to participate fully in the sensuous play between the colored walls that join it while keeping some kind of distance from them. If the seemingly abstract realm of "mathematical speculation" and "proportion" that the architect seeks emerges out of the sensual realm that it appears to leave behind, white surfaces facilitate this emergence by bridging both domains, binding the abstraction of form to the sensuality of color. The white wall fuses fine lines to erotic charges.

Beyond the Cream Jug

The basis for this unique bond was already laid in the 1920 essay with which Le Corbusier and Ozenfant introduced the concept of "Purism." The essay insists that form should subordinate color but warns that color is able to disorganize form because its sensuous quality "strikes the eye" before the mental quality of form.[65] Color is the supplementary layer that is uniquely able to subvert the structure meant to govern it. It can reconstruct form by disrupting the relationship between the surface of the painting and the volumes that the surface attempts to articulate. Color dislodges volume by dislodging the surface plane: "In the expression of volume, color is a perilous agent; often it destroys or disorganizes volume because the intrinsic properties of color are very different, some being radiant and pushing forward, others receding, still others being massive and staying in the real plane of the canvas, etc."[66] To counter this peril, the text attempts to classify color into the "major" ("constructive" "strong," "stable") colors that hold the surface plane, the "dynamic" ("disturbing," "animated," "agitated") colors that mobilize and disrupt the plane, and the "transitional" colors that are not involved in "construction" at all. Le Corbusier and Ozenfant choose to "discipline" themselves by working only with the first set of colors that reinforce the surface's capacity to construct volume: ocher yellows, reds, earth tones, white, black, ultramarine blue, and some of their derivatives. The sensuality of color is controlled by excluding all potentially disruptive elements and thereby "confining color to its hierarchical place."[67] Even then, the approved colors are seen to derive their "constructive" quality from mental associations rather than sensory effects. The qualities of color that immediately excite the senses are distinguished from those that are derived from memory. Memory is able to move surfaces forward or backward. Color reconstructs space:

Moreover, given the play of memory, acquired in looking at nature, logical and organic habits are created in us which confer on each object a qualifying, and hence constructive color; thus blue cannot be used to create a volume that should "come forward," because our eye, accustomed to seeing blue in depths (sky, sea), in backgrounds and in distant objects (horizons), does not permit with impunity the reversing of these conditions. Hence a plane that comes forward could never be blue; it could be green (grass), brown (earth).[68]

The spatial effect of color is psychological. More precisely, the "intrinsic property" of a color that moves or stabilizes a surface plane has actually been invested into that color by an association between its sensory qualities and a particular set of memories. Color is positioned at the critical intersection between the sensory and the mental. When Le Corbusier and Ozenfant argue that color should be "disciplined," they are attempting to limit the range of acceptable associations and thereby control the interaction between the body and the mind. They position themselves as border guards, patrolling the no-man's land around which the whole economy is organized. Certain colors are allowed to enter the privileged territory and work for form, but only after their credentials have been carefully checked. Even after they have been admitted, their movements are very restricted and closely monitored.

While this disciplinary argument is not applied to architecture itself, it is understood as an architectural argument. The first thing the essay says after raising the issue of color is that "painting is a question of architecture."[69] Those painters who misuse color are said to lack an "architectural aesthetic" because the color dictates the form. The subordination of color through purist rigor is even described as "the architectural achievement."[70] The colors that Le Corbusier and Ozenfant chose are the "essentially constructive" ones, the particular sensory stimuli that reinforce the mental qualities of the formal construction that will be experienced immediately afterwards. These colors are not applied to architecture at the time because color in painting is understood as assisting the two dimensional surface to produce the effect of volume. Such assistance is not needed in architecture if it is understood as volume itself. When Le Corbusier eventually starts to apply the same colors to architecture some four years later, it is an admission that architecture is no less a construction of surface than painting. The white surface is no longer understood as a mechanism for suppressing the sensuality of a building. Its own sensuality, and the role of that sensuality in the production of the effect of form is finally, albeit tacitly, acknowledged. White is finally seen to participate in the quasi-erotic play of color rather than simply expose that play to disciplinary action.

This unique relationship between whiteness and color starts to become evident in an essay on the modern house entitled "Notes à la suite" that Le Corbusier published in the February 1926 issue of *Cahiers d'art*. The substantial essay is illustrated with a survey of all the early projects in which Le Corbusier had already deployed color (except Pessac), which concludes with a hand-colored image of the Ternisien house at Boulogne-sur-Seine of 1926. The all-white Villa Besnus is, of course, absent. The text focuses on the sensuous quality of walls, embracing it but arguing for its precise control to avoid the "quality of seduction." Arguing that the specific details of each design (in terms of orientation, dimension, and window shape) produce different degrees of brilliance [*éclats divers*] in the walls, Le Corbusier announces that these details can be modified, or even transcended, by the careful use of color. The color of the various surfaces has its own geometry, one that is actually more precise than that of physical location: "Let us appreciate then that these walls of white plaster could on occasion speak a language more incisive than that formulated by their geometric measure." The text then rehearses the small argument about color and light intensity with which *Almanach d'architecture moderne* had pointed to the limitations of all-white buildings and finally acknowledged Le Corbusier's use of color. Color has its logic, an architectural logic that needs to be deployed and respected: "Our senses once again could be shaken by the red, irritated by the yellow, calmed by the blue, etc. How to distribute these colors that are the carriers of specific, precise effects? There are optical experiences, there is an optics of colors: red should be in plain light (to give it red value); blue lives well in the shadowy light (and is a better blue), etc."[71] The essay goes on to develop this argument. The "modern plan" of the house calls for polychrome reinforcement.

All the values of modern architecture, the much-advertised senses of proportion, geometry, purification, and classification that were previously associated with its whiteness, are now seen to be "given" by the color of its walls. Asking what it is to paint a wall red in a milieu of white, or to intersect an earth-colored wall at right angles to a white one, Le Corbusier answers: "To tell the truth, my house does not seem white unless I have disposed the active forces of colors and values in the appropriate places." Whiteness is an effect of color. But not just any color. It is the control of color, the strategic location of particular colors on particular surfaces, that produces the effect of white. Far from compromising white, the very sense of a white wall is a fragile effect of calibrated planes of color, an effect that is lost if more than one color appears on a single surface. When the essay later opposes the use of frescoes on the walls, insisting that "we love our wall *white;* and blank; or free; pure," the much-desired blankness of the white wall is actually produced by the sense that other walls are filled up by a color. Indeed, the essay concludes that: "The white, which makes you think clearly, is supported by the tonic forces of color."[72] White is propped up on color rather than weakened by it. Color is the support, the structure even, of modern space.

This argument was further developed a year later in the short text that Le Corbusier writes to accompany the hand-colored images of Pessac published in the 1927 issue of *L'Architecture vivante.* The text begins its brief account of the project's color scheme by reporting that "an illustrious aesthete, upon his return from Pessac, stated: 'A house is white'" and it goes on to describe several of the colors deployed there before announcing: "We have given the standard for appreciation: white facades."[73] White is no longer the house's color. Rather, it is the means for appreciating the color of the house. It is the standard against which color is to be read. More precisely, it is the standard against which the space produced by those colors can be read. Color is seen to transform the very condition of a space. The quasi-architectural argument of the "Purism" essay is finally applied to architecture. Blue, for example, is said to make a building "fly into the distance" while green makes it "mingle with the forest and the gardens' leaves." Furthermore, the strategic application of color can "camouflage" the mass of a building and the junction between such colors "provokes a suppression of volume (weight) and amplifies the unfolding of surfaces (extension)."[74] The play of color transforms fixed volumes into mobile surfaces that stimulate the viewer, defining a new kind of space by suspending discrete surfaces. Color is not simply applied to

7.11
Le Corbusier, Pessac housing estate, opening day 1926.

space. Color constructs space. As the text puts it: "Color could bring us [*apporter*] space. Consider color as the bearer [*apporteuse*] of space."[75] Three years after he started to use color, Le Corbusier had finally elaborated the quite radical theory of polychrome architecture first hinted at a year earlier in *Almanach d'architecture moderne*.

At the end of the following year, the Italian architect Piero Bottoni writes a letter to Le Corbusier asking for comments on his own polychrome vision of the city. Le Corbusier's reply argues that the creation of the modern plan through the disappearance of supporting walls demands research into polychrome. When the wall takes on a new role, producing space rather than holding it up, the color of its surface becomes critical to that production. Arguing that the colors in the reproduction of the Pessac development in *L'Architecture vivante* are "so horrifically fake (especially the green)" that they should not be taken seriously, Le Corbusier describes his attempt to reconstruct space with color: "instead of accepting the white uniformity of all these houses, one could indeed feel obliged to call upon color in order to modify these spaces . . . so as to pursue the effects of the layout *through color*." White is insufficient. Color takes over the dominant architectural role through its capacity to "fix solid points," "distance" others from the horizon, make others "disappear" into the landscape or behind the building's surface, and "intervene into the very affirmation of these houses' volume." The housing project turns into a "pure envelope" that has been "carved out" with color. Indeed, the color is the envelope. The logic of load and support has been dissolved into that of the paper-thin surface. The "weight" and "density" of volumes is literally "destroyed" by being "camouflaged." As a result, "space was gained." The ancient use of polychrome is finally restored by modern architecture. Colors are once again understood "as physical functions, as creators [*créatrices*] of space."[76]

Inasmuch as white is the standard for appreciating color, it is the means for appreciating the fundamental structure of architecture. It registers the structuring of space by color but does so precisely by not having the same structuring capacity. The white wall does not adjust space. While Le Corbusier describes the use of white to eliminate "accidents which occurred due to the complexity of the plan,"[77] removing the sensation of a particular volume by coating all of its surfaces in white, white does not inflect the surface it is applied to in quite the same way as the other colors. More precisely, it is able to transform volumes into surfaces but does not move those surfaces. If two adjacent surfaces are white they become one surface. Each disappears into the other without moving forward or backward. The neutrality of white is understood as a neutrality from space itself. Still, it is an active neutrality inasmuch as space would not be evident, or even possible, without it. White becomes, as it were, the space of space, the building site in which the architect labors with color. It allows the sensuality of color and the forms that emerge out of it to be experienced by acting as the intermediary between them, participating fully in both domains. Its capacity to expose the sensuality of color to either pleasure or discipline derives from its own sensuality.

This sensuality becomes evident in the moment that *Almanach d'architecture moderne* calls a stop to the regime of white walls in favor of polychrome. The very ability of color to organize space inasmuch as it is able to "inflect" walls, "lead the eye through complicated spaces," and "stretch the impression of space by far," intensifies the effect of the white surfaces that do not do this: "The 'whitewash' sparkles because of a section of wall that is dark (scorched or natural shadowy earth), of this other wall that is warm (ocher), of this wall which flees (blues, etc.)."[78] The white only begins to sparkle, to exude its own sensuality, in the face of the overwhelming sensuality of the colors that surround it.

While embracing this sensuality, Le Corbusier still insists that it needs to be controlled. The text boasts the quasi-scientific rationality of the color scheme used in the L'Esprit Nouveau pavilion, appealing to a "physics of color" and a "physiology of sensations" while insisting that "we have conducted research in polychrome."[79] The space-producing power of color is said to derive from psycho-physiological reactions that can be studied in a systematic way. The apparently subjective responses to color have supposedly been tied back into some sense of regulated bodily functions. Far from admitting the irrationality of color into architecture, color is proposed as the very agent of rationality. As the *L'architecture vivante* text insists: "This polychrome is absolutely new. It is fundamentally rational. It brings elements that are physiologically extremely potent to the architectural symphony."[80] Le Corbusier's polychrome is "new" because it is "rational." Polychrome is the ancient condition of architecture that has been newly ordered, modernized.

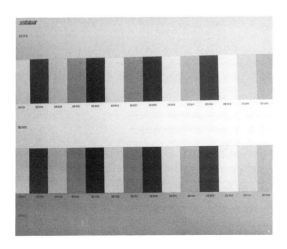

7.12
Le Corbusier, Salubra Color Keyboard, 1932.

7.13
Publicity image for Le Corbusier's Color Keyboards, as published in Domus, *1931.*

The exemplification of this pseudoscientific ordering of color would seem to be the "Color Keyboards" that Le Corbusier prepared for the Salubra wallpaper company where color is organized into a limited set of forty-three possibilities. And yet it is precisely here that he appears to open up the question of color, and therefore the whole question of architecture that is now seen to be based upon it, to individual subjective responses: "Each one of us, according to our own psychology, is governed by one or several dominant colors. Each person is drawn towards this or that harmony, according to the needs of their innermost nature. It thus became a matter or putting each person in a state of self-recognition through the recognition of their own colors." The rationalization of standardized physiological responses seems to give way to a realm of idiosyncratic psychological reaction beyond any standardization. But Le Corbusier quickly offers his own psychology as a transcultural and transhistorical model of psychological health. The architect offers himself as the standard type. This modest gesture enables the range of colors to be standardized and within that range only the colors that reside in the "terrain" of architecture are made available. Individual psychologies are free to roam but only within a particular field of colors that is seen to be uniquely bonded to architecture: "In order to establish this selection, I have remained in the sole terrain of architecture, after having made sure that my personal taste conformed to the constant predilection of the healthy man who, since the beginning of the world, regardless of race and of culture, has called upon polychrome to express his joy for life."[81]

Each of the forty-three colors is said to be an "eminently architectural" shade. They are grouped into eleven different sets of fourteen shades that form a "keyboard" with a particular "atmosphere." Cardboard masks are provided that act as viewing mechanisms that enable two or three colors within each set to be isolated for comparison. Combinations of colors are to be chosen from within a particular atmosphere. Before being applied to a particular surface, each color is seen to contribute to a particular kind of architectural quality, as is registered in the names given to the atmospheres: "space," "sky," "velvet," "masonry," "sand," "scenery," and so on. Any combination of these colors is already an architectural construction. The space within which the individual psychology can roam is understood to be the space of architecture itself. To choose colors is already to design.

This theory is expanded in detail in "Polychrome Architecturale," an unpublished manuscript of 1931 that was intended to explain the thinking behind the Color Keyboards. The text, which is Le Corbusier's most definitive statement on the architectural role of color, again argues that individual taste for color derives from the idiosyncracies of the unconscious. Indeed, "colors are like psychologies."[82] People are supposed to discover themselves in the colors they choose. At the same time, there are generic reactions based on the specific properties of colors that affect the perception of space in particular ways or produce "deep" physiological reactions like excitement or calm. The polychrome architect has to negotiate between the idiosyncracies of the unconscious and the universals of physiology. The "laws" of architecture supposedly dictate the use of certain "eminently architectural" colors rather than "nonarchitectural" ones. And again, these turn out to be the colors that Le Corbusier is attracted to: "my personal taste rallied itself to the constant and analogous manifestations of the healthy and the strong man."[83] The laws of architecture are somehow embedded in the unconscious of the architect, allowing him to become a figure for that which underpins all culture throughout history. The spatial effects of color are credited to civilization. These effects are "constant," even "eternal," inasmuch as the colors are bound to the natural forces of fire and earth that are used to produce them which all cultures share.[84] People are bound together through space and time by the generic operations of color.

This universalized spatial logic of color dictates a certain architectural protocol. While polychrome is "natural" for "smooth surfaces," it "kills" volumes. The two-dimensional surface is polychromed while the three-dimensional figure is monochrome.[85] Color is only to be used unnaturally when there is a defect in the forms to which it is applied. Polychrome can be used to kill unwanted volumes through "camouflage" like that used by animals or military equipment, to relieve "suffocation" by opening up volumes, to make the geometry of a space "elusive," to take away the solidity of wall, to make walls recede; and so on. In the end, the role of color is to "create space." Fixed material spaces are challenged by "interposing a certain atmosphere," a vaporous atmosphere that has no problem overwhelming physical forms.[86]

Everything is to do with the eye. Color reconfigures space by reconfiguring what meets the eye. The architect's client is even described as a "spectator" whose eye is the agent of his or her unconscious: "the eye must be akin to a skilful instrument at the service of a profound instinct." The "danger" of decorative patterns is at once psychological and physical. When forever confronted by their aggressive intricacies, "the retina may be overly stimulated and swiftly tired out, the mind as well." The role of the architect is to control the movements of the eye through the judicious application of color. Even the form of a closed room becomes "evasive" when the eye is encouraged to "skip" from surface to surface by the color scheme. Architecture is not form as such. Rather, it is defined as "the *wall* upon which the eye rests." Architecture is the surface illuminated by color in a way that attracts and moves the eye. The architect designs a path for the eye.[87]

As in *L'art décoratif d'aujourd'hui*, this control of the eye is seen as the basis of a system of classification. While the white wall enforced by the "Law of Ripolin" classifies whatever forms or colors are placed in front of the building, the colored wall is the classification of the building itself. The white wall assigns each surface a particular color. The "Polychrome Architecturale" manuscript moves smoothly from a section called "Color Modifies Space" to one called "Color Classifies Objects." Color gets rid of unwanted forms and classifies those that remain by arranging them in space, bringing some forward and moving others back. Polychrome is "the means of establishing order" because it "consists of creating a classification, of establishing a hierarchy, of rendering elusive the annoying but inevitable flaws or complications."[88] Surfaces are calibrated by being repositioned, and this repositioning can expose and interact with the idiosyncrasies of someone's unconscious precisely because it is effected by the generic quality of color that everyone shares. While the classifications are generic, the responses to them are idiosyncratic. Color monitors the endless exchanges between the universal and the individual. When architectural polychromy is called on to restore order to the walls of the home that are "no longer in plain, white lime (alas!), but are covered with wallpaper of all color and prints," as Le Corbusier puts it in a 1951 text, it is a matter of "summoning the psycho-physiological powers of color: reorganizing their enormous powers in the domain of classification as well as in the realm of sensation, of emotion."[89] Four years later, the point is emphasized even more strongly. The radical modernization of architecture demands the bridge between abstract order and sensory stimulation that is provided by color:

Polychromy, in particular, has come into being through modern techniques: steel, glass and reinforced concrete have led to the 'plan libre', which solicits and demands the introduction of color to serve as a classification, a codification as well as a psycho-physiological excitant.

Deep Skin

Side by side with modern techniques, polychromy has appeared once again in our times. In my opinion, it should be the task of the architect, since it cannot be disassociated from the conception of a building. And now a new danger appears, a new gap in the profession that is totally unprepared to employ color.[90]

The order provided by the supposedly nonsensuous white wall is succeeded by the sensuous order of color. Between the 1920 theory of color in Purist painting, which is tacitly associated with white architecture, and the 1931 theory of polychrome architecture there is a move from the need to classify color in order to preserve a sense of space to the use of color to classify space. The colors that were first chosen for their capacity to reinforce a structure are now understood to have the capacity to destroy it. In a later text, for example, Le Corbusier contrasts the use of the painter's mural, in which more than one color is applied to a single surface, as a form of "dynamite" that can "blow up the walls that stand in our way," to the architect's polychrome scheme.[91] The painter destroys while the architect classifies:

Architectural polychromy doesn't kill the walls, but it can move them back and classify them in order of importance. Here a skillful architect has wholesome and powerful resources to draw on. Polychromy belongs to the great living architecture of all times and of tomorrow. Wall-paper has enabled us to see the matter clearly, to repudiate deceitful trick effects and open all doors to great bursts of color, dispenser of space and classifier of essential things and accessory things. Color is as powerful an instrument of architecture as the plan and section are. Better still: color is the very element [élèment même] of the plan and section.[92]

Color is not a supplement to the drawings and buildings to which it appears to be added. Far from an accessory, it is the instrument for determining what is an accessory. It is an instrument of classification that orchestrates all the elements of architecture into structural hierarchies. Indeed, it is the very structure of architecture, the element out of which the organization of the building emerges. The abstract lines with which the limits of a particular building are precisely defined actually emerge out of the sensuous atmosphere of color long before color is added to any of the surfaces those lines might describe. Color produces the building it appears to be added to, actively rearranging every surface except for those that remain coated in white.

Le Corbusier's theory becomes increasingly radical. When he first describes the colors of Pessac in 1927, color follows in the footsteps of form. It is added to pre-existing structures to edit the space: "We have also applied an entirely new conception of polychromy, with a distinctly architectural aim in view: to model space by means of the physical properties of color, to emphasize certain masses in the housing development, and to tone down certain others—in a word, to compose with color as we did with forms."[93] Color becomes part of the strategic repertoire of the architect, supplementing and modifying the traditional labor in plan and section. After 1931, even that labor is dependant on color. The forms to which color is applied are themselves built out of color. The architect only ever labors in color. The already radical proposition of 1927 that "color could bring us space. Consider color as the bearer of Space" is radicalized even further into "color is the very element of the plan and section." Space emerges out of the colors that seem to be added to it. Color becomes responsible for the architectural condition it appears to merely adjust. It would seem that nothing could be more important than color.

As always, Le Corbusier insists that his work is at once modern and consistent with ancient tradition, of its time and yet timeless. He repeatedly appeals to the transhistorical importance of color. Polychrome is depicted as at once the oldest tradition of architecture and its most up-to-date manifestation. When the 1937 *Des Canons, des munitions? Merci! Des logis . . . s.v.p.* describes the color scheme of the Pavilion des temps nouveaux from the same year, it announces that: "Colors burst forth spontaneously during creative periods. The academic style works in grayness. All color is intrinsic to the human sensibility. It represents an immense architectural potency which, after the century of academicism that we have crossed, we have forgotten how to use."[94] Unsurprisingly, Le Corbusier plays down the moment in which he banned this millennial force from architecture, promoting the image of a lifelong struggle to identify the fundamental condition of color, as can be seen in his 1932 letter to Vladimir Nekrassov:

Color has a biological and sentimental function that is indispensable to human nature. Man cannot live without color. . . . I have always considered polychrome to be of the utmost importance and for years I attempted to discover the natural uses of color. These uses are physical and emotional. . . . An architect may thus work with color as he works with proportions, or rather (if you will), as he would work with the geometric relations between surfaces or volumes.[95]

Color can only be made into a modern architectural tool when its "natural" conditions can be discovered and those conditions are understood to be at once physiological and psychological. The labor to classify color so that it can in turn classify spaces is also an attempt to classify psychologies. The "Polychrome architecturale" manuscript argues that everyone is classified by their unconscious responses to color: "an individual is organized according to a personal equation which classifies him, enslaves him, binds him to inevitable choices."[96] The classification of space that follows the fixed laws of architecture allows the classification of that which has no known law, the depths of the psyche. This psychology of color is equally, if not only, that of the architect. If Le Corbusier bases his selection of "eternal" colors on his own reactions to them, his supposedly self-disciplined labor of organizing and controlling color is necessarily underpinned by uncontrollable fantasies that he constantly voices but is not necessarily able to address. This conflation of discipline and desire even seems to come to the surface in a parenthetical passage within a 1951 letter to some architects in Barcelona that describes his addition of a polychrome layer to his first Unité housing block:

(A note to the reader: in order to paint the Unité d'habitation in Marseille, it was necessary to give four thousand different orders so that each painter would go to the right place with their pot of color. This may seem astonishing; it is a fact: only the strictest rigor may lay down the problems of polychrome. I would go further and say that to create architectural polychrome, be it interior or exterior, the architect must practically go into a trance . . . but here I would be called a madman!)[97]

The feverish trance in which the architect moved through the myriad colors of the East returns over the drawing board. Once again, color dislodges the subject in the very moment in which it is supposedly being controlled. The strictest rigor emerges out of a delirious space of fantasy. Control is the ever fragile product of the uncontrollable. The designer is unable to bracket out his own desires in the name of the immutable laws of color. After all, the question of color is nothing more than the question of desire. As Le Corbusier put it three years earlier in his retrospective *New World of Space:* "One has the right to be lifted up by an irrepressible desire to bring whatever one is manipulating to the highest brilliance, whether it be colors on canvas, buildings or cities."[98] The architect, like the occupant, is driven to color by unstoppable yet unspeakable forces. It is no surprise that when the "Polychrome architecturale" manuscript identifies color as the mark of the unconscious, it goes on to describe the colors that have haunted the author's own work:

"Color is intimately bound to our being; each one of us perhaps has their color; even if we ignore it, our instincts do not. Astrology claims to explain these issues of uncontrollable determinations. . . . As for myself, in my twenty years of work, in which color took up half the day, I seemed to live under the command of blue: blue echoing with green. Yet for some time now, red seems to become more and more insistent, more abundant, colonizing: blue, still, but red conquered."[99] But what about the white that so dominates Le Corbusier's architecture? Is it likewise driven by irrepressible desire? Or does it mark the limited extent to which the architect is able to suppress desire, keeping color momentarily in check in the name of psychological and architectonic order?

New World of Space explicitly opposes the naturalness of color to the artificiality of white. It again describes the Color Keyboards as "a simple instrument which makes it possible for everyone to find the color harmony natural to him lodged in the bottom of his psycho-physiology" but now the comment is added that "raw white seemed to us too far away from natural visual sensation."[100] White is unnatural then. If the white wall was introduced to recover the eye that has been destroyed by the excesses of the decorative arts and is itself understood as a superhuman prosthetic eye, that eye turns out to be too artificial, too superhuman. It extends the body too far. Yet the text later approvingly cites the "Law of Ripolin" at length. The reign of whitewash does not simply end with the arrival of color. Polychrome is not opposed to the white. White's distance from "natural visual sensation" is made acceptable by being counter-balanced by color. The artificiality of white is made tolerable by natural colors. When *L'art décoratif d'aujourd'hui* promotes white by arguing that it is the mark of civilization, civilization is explicitly portrayed as the transcendence of nature. The white wall transcends the bodily world, the world of physical desire. White is detached from the uncontrollable realm of the unconscious to become the very figure of control.

But clearly the line between white and color, between the control and the release of desire, is endlessly convoluted. In the Salubra system, for example, white is one of the colors to be judged and the mechanism of that judgment. It slips around between the inside and the outside of the system with precisely the kind of mobility that is being denied to the other forty-two colors. In theory it does not have an "architectural nuance" like all the others. Rather, it is the color of the mechanism of judgment, the frame by which different combinations of color can be placed alongside each other. The background strips that frame and divide the two matching sets of shades which form the keyboard of each atmosphere are almost always white when there is no white in the keyboard itself. Furthermore, the viewing mechanism that isolates colors for comparison is itself white. White is the frame for revealing the different spatial possibilities and the individual psychological reactions to those possibilities. Le Corbusier is only able to authorize his personal choices as universal choices by identifying with the universal, prespatial condition of white. The play of color is made possible by asserting that white does not play. After all, there is only one shade of white in the Color Keyboards while every other color has many shades. Even gray, the other supposedly "neutral" color, has four shades. White is frozen, held in one place. The very fact that a particular white has been chosen is glossed over. The endless variations of white, which have to be understood as psychological variations, are bracketed out. Psychology is bracketed out for a moment so that the psychodrama of color can be registered. But what of the psychodrama of white itself? What pathology has to assert that white precedes all pathologies? Exactly what fantasies prop up the white wall? What are these structural desires that the polychrome skin brings to the surface rather than covers over?

It would be sorry to see ourselves capsizing in the fashion of the simple if the simple is not more than a fashion.

—Le Corbusier, 1926.

Machine-Age Wallpaper

The theory of polychrome architecture, like the theory of white, did not come out of nowhere. A series of events pulled certain lines of argument to the surface that had long been stitched into the discourse. These old threads were tied into new knots, new formulations for new practices. Although the knots were strong and had a major impact on architectural practice, they could be easily be undone by simply pulling lightly on any one of the threads. Shortly after the theory of polychrome was formulated, it was discretely undone by the very discourse that it had influenced and slipped back into the fabric of the discourse. It became more or less invisible to everyday transactions despite its unique impact on those very transactions. Even the traces of that impact quickly became obscured. The discourse was able to act as if modern architecture was not colored. But the conceptual knot did not simply disappear. A closer inspection of the discourse reveals the points at which its lines of argument were permanently stretched. The theory of color continues to orchestrate dimensions of the discourse that routinely overlook it. Even the briefest exploration of the conceptual milieu within which the theory of polychrome architecture was produced brings some of the hidden agendas of that theory back to the surface—agendas that continue to orchestrate contemporary debates even though they are unable to be recognized as such within those debates. The theory of color, like the theory of white, initiated a series of subterranean effects that can only be discerned by patiently locating the often twisted trajectories of the lines of argument that installed it.

To understand the strategic effects of the vestigial traces of white within the polychrome scheme of one of Le Corbusier's projects, for example, is not simply a question of monitoring the evolution of his conversion to polychrome architecture by analyzing each successive building design, identifying exactly which color went on which surface. Rather, it is a matter of looking at the successive stories he and his colleagues told about that conversion, identifying the particular arguments they drew upon and how those arguments have been reconfigured. These stories, which attempt to account for the color that is effaced by the black and white reproduction of modern architecture, are routinely moved to the background of the discourse around that architecture—a gesture that becomes increasingly symptomatic as the stories continue to be produced long after the discourse has managed to overlook the strategic role of color. Indeed, their production and level of detail escalates the more their subject is overlooked. It is not by chance that Le Corbusier's most comprehensive account of polychrome is produced on the threshold of the effacement of color by the emerging historiography. While it can be argued that the suppression of color was critical to that historiography's assumption of dominance, the suppression still seems too emphatic. Why would acknowledging the pivotal role of a coat of paint be so threatening?

To locate the conceptual framework within which the theory of the polychromed surface is produced may be to locate the nexus of a discomforting,
if not embarrassing, set of undercurrents.

Recounting White Cells

Le Corbusier's apparent switch from white to color began with his collaboration with the painter Fernand Léger. When he says that he turned to color because "raw white seemed to us too far away from natural visual sensation,"
the "us" is himself and Léger. The polychrome of the L'Esprit Nouveau pavilion cannot be separated from that of the murals that Léger hung within it
that were in turn a development of Léger and Robert Delaunay's attempt to
isolate color from form and produce environments out of the interplay between such fields of color. Le Corbusier's polychrome is as much indebted to
those earlier experiments as it is to his collaborative work on color with
Ozenfant. At the same time, Léger did not call for a polychrome architecture
as such before getting together with the architect. The theoretical defense of
such an architecture emerged somewhat slowly from the ongoing debate between them.

Léger made his first call for the creation of a polychrome architecture at the
conclusion of a July 1924 essay on "Le Spectacle" for *Bulletin de l'Effort
Moderne*,[1] which he continued later that year in "Architecture Polychrome," a
short essay for *L'architecture vivante*, which argues that color "must be used

8.1
*Fernand Léger, in the
illustration for his "New
York vu par Léger"
article in* Cahiers d'art,
1931.

with rigorous discernment to become a 'natural function of architecture'."[2] Supposedly, "surface color" can facilitate the production of a "calm" atmosphere which focuses the eye on whatever enters a space: "In this new environment a man can be seen, for the eye is not distracted by dispersed qualities. Everything is arranged. Against these big calm areas the human face assumes its proper status. A nose, eye, foot, hand or jacket button will become a precise reality."[3] This argument was elaborated right up until Léger's death in 1955 in over a dozen retrospective essays. Each one renegotiates the relationship between white and color. In seeing polychrome as a sharpening of the eye, Léger describes the colored environment in the same terms that Le Corbusier describes the white environment. Color satisfies the goals of white. Indeed, colored surfaces are portrayed as a necessary development of the white wall rather than its outright rejection. "The New Realism Goes On" of 1937, for example, argues that a new and better way of life is "made possible by Le Corbusier's two great gifts to us: the white wall and light" and insists that: "Let us learn to make use of all this, to cherish it, and let us see to it that, *here too,* we take no backward steps by putting up the hangings, the wall-papers, and the gewgaws of the year 1900."[4] The white wall is a crucial advance that must be defended against the retrograde contaminations of ornament. Likewise, "Un nouvel espace en architecture" (A new space in architecture) of 1949 argues that the role of the 1925 exposition within which the pavilion was presented was "to make the white wall appear with all the consequences it involved: a new, habitable rectangle or a false start."[5] White was at once exhibited and tested. Having accepted this new reality ("The white wall was there, present. Why not?") the essay challenges it ("What was going to happen on this white wall?") and ends up calling for it to be colored. The white surface is a necessary step that must be transcended. Before architecture could advance, the wall had to be turned into an "experimental field" by being stripped of degenerate ornament but the white wall that resulted goes too far and too easily regresses with the addition of decorative attachments. Color needs to be inserted somewhere between the excessive minimalism of the blank wall and the excesses of decoration. For Léger, color is a form of decoration. Colored surfaces vaccinate the building with a controlled dose of decoration against the decorative impulse that whiteness inadvertently fosters by provoking the generic horror of the vacumn: "The modern architect, he too, *has gone too far,* in his magnificent attempts to cleanse through emptiness," succumbing to "the intoxification of emptiness," as "Le mur, l'architecte, le peintre" (The wall, the architect, the painter) of 1933 puts it.[6] Emptiness has to be filled with a certain amount of color. Modern space must be colored space.

Each of Léger's essays likewise embraces the white wall only to condemn it. The celebration of whiteness is always followed by its rejection. The white surface gets rid of the horror of the nineteenth century only to become the horror of the twentieth century. As "Peinture Murale" (Mural painting) of 1952, puts it: "The walls emerged, bare, white, to the satisfaction of the public and of the enthusiastic producers. However, it was very quickly demonstrated that most of the people who were going to live in these places found white walls difficult to accept."[7] Being at once too little and too much, the white wall stifles life. The much advertised openness of modern buildings becomes a kind of closure, a "dead end" as "Modern Architecture and Color" of 1946 puts it. When all the oppressive layers of wallpaper had finally been stripped off every surface, "the white wall suddenly looked quite naked. An obstacle, a dead-end."[8] The means of attaining a new life become a new form of death. With each successive essay, Léger zooms ever further in on the deadly properties of this wall, its unique capacity to restrict the very life it supposedly liberates. By the time his 1950 "Peinture Murale et Peinture de Chevalet" (Mural painting and easel painting) describes the collaboration with Le Corbusier, white architecture is simply uninhabitable: "Now we have moved toward a complete clean-up of architecture, and we find ourselves confronting a blank, bare wall. But such a wall is like a waiting room. Most people cannot live surrounded by white walls."[9] The modern architect's polemical blankness has to be filled in before it destroys the people trapped inside it.

Far from assisting the modern search for a fluid space that collapses the traditional boundaries between inside and outside, the white wall renders those boundaries ever more solid. It produces a kind of claustrophobic space because the inhabitant is disoriented within it. Not knowing where you are, and therefore how to get out, becomes the most secure closure of all. The white wall prevents a stable sense of location, a sense of space. It dissolves the forms it is meant to present. To be faced by white walls is to be lost. As "Le mur, l'architecte, le peintre" puts it: "no more volume, no more form; an impalpability of air, of slick, brilliant new surfaces where nothing can be hidden any longer. Even shadows don't dare to enter; they can't find their places any more. . . . The average man is lost in front of a large dead surface."[10] Nothing is hidden and yet everything is lost. "Nouvel conceptiones d'espace" of 1952 elaborates the point by insisting that: "A blank white wall is perfect for a painter. . . . But walls were not made only for painters. Too many people found themselves out of their element, lost in the face of such a radical transformation of their visual habits."[11] While everything is visible in the modern building, vision itself is no longer able to operate. The white surface dislodges the eye in a way that disorients the person that tries to look at it. It re-configures the very space it is supposed to unify, reconstituting a whole other nightmarish environment.

Léger goes as far as describing this daunting psychological space as a prison. Unsurprisingly, his discourse in favor of a polychrome architecture is one of liberation. More interestingly, he argues that the white wall's imprisonment through disorientation is made possible by the confinement of color to mobile objects like dresses, hats, and make-up. The freeing of the wall has to be matched by a freeing of color from the objects to which it is "fast bound." Color has to be released from mobile objects so that it can mobilize stationary walls and thereby release the inhabitants of modern architecture. As "On Monumentality and Color," puts it: "The wall had first to be freed to become an experimental field. Then color had to be got out, extricated, and isolated from the objects in which it had been kept prisoner. . . . Color was the new object, color set free. . . . The feeling of a jail, of a bounded, limited space, is going to change into a boundless 'colored space.'"[12] White is of value to Léger only inasmuch as it can receive color. He even proposes to the organizers of the 1937 Paris exhibition that all the facades in Paris be stripped and painted white so that multicolored lights could be projected onto them from airplanes and the Eiffel Tower. Within the white spaces of modern architecture the painter likewise projects color onto the surfaces. The painter is the enemy of the "dead surface," rendering a space habitable by editing out defective elements.[13] Color is the agent of this spatial surgery because it is able to adjust the weight and volume of a building,[14] or move the walls it is applied to, even allowing the walls from one building to enter the space of another.[15] Color is structural. It can be either "supportive" or "destructive" of the wall.[16] The role of the painter is to "unleash" color where it is needed to eliminate unwanted architectural elements, strategically deploying colors that are able to "visually destroy" walls.[17]

This sets up a tension between the painter and the architect. At the time of his first collaborations with Le Corbusier, Léger accepts the subordinate role, modifying some of the architect's ready-made surfaces by supplementing them with murals,[18] but eventually he rejects such a role and steps up his criticism of the white wall. Yet even when he describes the subordinate concern with surface, this concern is understood to be one of life and death, the live surface versus the dead surface. The supplement of color provided by the painter destroys dead tissue to preserve life. It is a kind of surgery that operates on the surface rather than cutting through it. It puts some color, some life into the pale skin of the new-born modern architecture. More precisely, it is a strange intersection of the art of the surgeon and that of the mortician, using a layer of makeup to restore the sense of life to the deadly white wall.

This whole account of the capacity for colored paint to strengthen, modify, or destroy architectural form had, of course, been taken directly from the discourse of the De Stijl group, which had itself been influenced by Léger's earlier work. From the moment of its formation, the group renegotiated the relationship between painting and architecture. Indeed, this was arguably their central obsession. In the very first issue of the magazine *De Stijl* in 1917, the painter Bart Van der Leck, who had already collaborated with the preeminent Dutch architect Hendrik Berlage, calls for such a collaboration between the two disciplines, based on their shared commitment to the "plane surface":

Painting has developed independently during the course of time, separately from architecture, and through experiment and the destruction of the old and the natural, it has come to develop its own particular character, both formally and spiritually. It always requires the plane surface, however, and it will always remain its ultimate wish to make direct use of the necessary practical plane created by architecture. More than that, in its extension from the individual to the universal it will claim from the building, as its rightful domain, the whole of the color concept and that part of the form concept appropriate to painting. If architects are looking for a painter who can supply the desired image, the modern painter is no less seeking an architect who can offer the appropriate conditions for the joint achievement of a true unity of plastic expression.[19]

While the painter and the architect are destined to meet on the surface they share, the meeting necessarily takes the form of a confrontation because of their different attitudes toward that surface. It is not that the architect provides the space and the painter provides the colored emphasis of that space. It is the color that provides the space. The "flatness" of architecture is seen as "space-restricting" while the modern painter's reduction of "corporeality to flatness" is seen to produce "spatial relationship." Space is produced by the painter's "destruction" of the material forms that are produced by the architect, who is only able to think in terms of "construction." The painter works color onto the surface in a way that changes the status of that surface, displacing the logic of "load and support," opening up space rather than closing it down. The architect has to be restrained in order that the architecture can be set free: "We ask of the architect 'self restraint' because he has so much in his hands that does not really belong to architecture and which, in its extension, must be understood completely differently from the way the architect understands it."[20] In a sense, the history of the De Stijl group is the history of its changing relationship to this fundamental desire to overtake architecture with color.

8.2
*Piet Mondrian, project
for the salon of Ida
Bienert at Dresden, 1926,
as published in* L'Art
international
d'aujourd'hui, *1928.*

For some time, Piet Mondrian, who likewise understood his "neoplastic" paintings as mechanisms for producing space, argued that such paintings were not yet ready to engage with architecture in this struggle for space. Having contrasted the plastic freedoms of painting to the closed forms of architecture in the first issue of *De Stijl,* he uses the third issue to argue that neoplasticism will need to be "interdependent" with architecture but that it is not yet ready for this "complete unification."[21] It is not until 1922 that he starts to engage with the issue of architecture directly, arguing that painting and architecture have been purified enough to stage a new alliance and personally taking on the design of a number of colored interiors.[22] Yet from the beginning he had described the mechanism that made such an alliance possible more precisely than those of his colleagues who constantly struggled to achieve it.

In Mondrian's view, Neoplasticism "creates space" by reducing space to its "essential" condition: "a composition of planes which give the illusion of lying on one plane."[23] Each plane is given a single color, and color itself is reduced to the primary colors, which are "supplemented" by the "noncolors" white, black, and gray. Inasmuch as a composition of such planes is the fundamental mechanism of space, painting "expresses space *on a flat surface.*"[24]

In so doing, it rejects the world of everyday appearance. The appearance of natural form and color becomes but a "cloak." All concrete form needs to be "dissolved into color" and this color is seen to "arise" from the intersection of light and the material of a surface. Space becomes the product of the interaction of light and colored surfaces. Having dissolved concrete form with color, a new architecture of overlapping planes emerges, an architecture of pure surface in which surfaces are understood to constitute rather than cloak reality. In a reversal of the usual way of thinking, the surface becomes the agent of truth while three-dimensional form becomes a mask. The traditional economy of vision is twisted on itself: "Thus he shows himself to be truly modern man, who sees the outward as inward and penetrates the inward through the outward."[25] The opposition between a surface detail and a deep meaning is folded on itself and endlessly refolded until it disappears.

It is this transformation of the status of the surface that provided the strategy for those who attempted to color architecture. When Van Doesburg's important lecture of 1922 entitled "Der Wille zum Stil" (The will to style) announces that "In modern architecture the problem of color and space is the most important, indeed it is the most difficult problem of our age," it is not by chance that the announcement is preceded by the claim that in modern painting "form is deliberately altered and subordinated to the surface composition. . . . the surface of the picture, which up till now had always been treated in a negative way, obtains its real significance."[26] It is the perfection of the dissolution of form by surface that makes possible the new alliance between painting and architecture. It is not simply a question of giving new priority to the already existing surfaces of architecture. The lecture emphatically opposes elevating those surfaces into two-dimensional facades, insisting that the interior should determine the shape of the exterior. It is a matter of diplomatically combining the architect's ability to give a "proper proportional division of the total space" and the painter's ability to "strengthen" rather than "destroy" that architecture through the precise use of color. Likewise, van Doesburg's 1923 essay "De beteekenis van de kleur in binnen–en buitenarchitectuur" (The significance of color for interior and exterior architecture) argues that to simply decorate the planes of a building with color is to "camouflage" and "ultimately destroy" the architecture instead of "strengthening" it. Color has to be treated as a construction material to be deployed like any other. It is intrinsic to a building rather than added to it: "Color renders *visible* the spatial effect for which the architect strives. It is in this way that color makes architecture *complete* and becomes intrinsic to it. Until now color remained an element of secondary importance."[27] But while color is no longer secondary, it must not dominate as the dominance of painting over architecture leads to the "destruction" of architecture. The collaboration is supposedly between mutually reinforcing equals.

In practice, however, it was precisely Van Doesburg's ongoing emphasis on color's ability to destroy an architectural scheme that had led to the collapse of his collaboration with J. P. P. Oud the year before and the architect's abrupt departure from the De Stijl circle. Van Doesburg argues that the painter's newly refined surface should lead the way for architectural practice. Indeed, that surface is already understood as architecture. While the De Stijl painters had for some years accepted a subordinate position to the architects in their various collaborations, they ended up resenting it and eventually attempted to subordinate architecture. More precisely, they attempted to reconstruct architecture as the product of the refined surface. In 1928, Van Doesburg concludes his review of De Stijl's attempt to establish "the plastic use of color in space" by saying: "*In the final analysis it is only the exterior surface which defines architecture,* since man does not live within a construction but within an *atmosphere* which has been established by the exterior surface."[28] Architecture is only ever a surface effect.

This set of arguments about the way colored surfaces define space was enormously influential on Le Corbusier. The capacity of color to either reinforce or destroy material forms through the production of a particular atmosphere became a major part of his position. Yet he symptomatically attacks the De Stijl discourse in the very moment of appropriating so much of it. Indeed, the very first time he accepts the idea of a polychrome architecture is in a short in-

terview with Léger in the December 1923 issue of *L'Esprit Nouveau* about
the exhibition of De Stijl work at the Rosenberg Gallery in Paris, whose opening they had just attended. While enthusing over the possibilities of a polychrome architecture, they criticize the specific use of color in the exhibition.
Repeatedly insisting that the De Stijl group is indebted to Léger, Le Corbusier
opposes its use of polychrome on the exterior of buildings but approves of
the way it has been applied to interiors, "which while not completely novel,
nevertheless deserves the greatest attention."[29] Polychrome is credited with
transforming the status of the interior. By relocating the surfaces to which
they are applied (making one "static" while another "recedes") colors have
become "the elements of architecture."[30] Within minutes of the De Stijl exhibition, half of whose exhibits were collaborative works by Van Doesburg and
the young architect Cornelius van Eesteren, Le Corbusier was changing his
white architecture into a polychrome architecture and entering into a De Stijl
type collaboration with Léger, not only applying color to his projects but, as
Bruno Reichlin demonstrates, modifying his designs from prismatic forms to

orchestrated intersections of floating planes.[31] While the purist colors he deploys are radically different from those of De Stijl, having precisely the "natural" associations that the De Stijl artists wanted to avoid by using bright primary colors, the thinking behind their application was almost the same. Furthermore, the very qualities that Le Corbusier originally condemned in their use of external polychromy ("has the effect of camouflaging; it destroys, disarticulates, divides and is opposed to unity") quickly became a crucial part of his own discourse about the architectural use of color. Eventually, he would even adopt their primary colors.

Of course, this does not mean leaving white behind. On the contrary, white played a crucial role in De Stijl's architecture of color. Van Doesburg repeatedly referred to its spiritual quality relative to the other colors.[32] Already in 1915 he describes Mondrian's paintings as "colored architecture" and goes on to credit the whiteness of the surface on which they are produced with the exposure of any error: "The white canvas is almost solemn. Each superfluous line, each wrongly placed line, any color placed without veneration or care, can spoil everything—that is the spiritual."[33] In fact, it was Van der Leck who had introduced the use of a white ground within the painting. The white walls that formed the background of his paintings of 1912 gradually become abstracted into a white ground against which geometric figures appeared in 1913; by 1916 those figures were simply planes of primary colors. Mondrian quickly perfected this impression of colored planes floating above a white ground. For some years, the artists struggled to remove the simple opposition between colored figures and noncolored ground with strategies like interweaving the colors with the noncolors and using black lines to transform the white into a discrete surface like any other. It was not until 1918 that Mondrian was able to finally remove the sense of a white ground. But, even then, the paintings continued to be organized by the white surfaces within them. Although neither background nor foreground, white remained the dominant color.

Likewise, white played a key role in all the architectural projects on which the De Stijl artists collaborated. When describing the color scheme he prepared for a house designed by Jan Wils in 1917, van Doesburg claims to use white to "free" each of the colored surfaces he deployed. To free them, that is, from the material architectural forms: "All planes and panels freed by means of white. . . . Everything freed by means of white."[34] White liberates surface. The more the painters claimed the territory of architecture, the less they needed white to liberate color from the constraints of material form. With each successive year, white appears less and less as a ground against which colored surfaces float (belatedly following the evolution of neoplastic painting) as it starts to intermingle, overlap and intersect with those surfaces, but it continues to be understood as the surface that frees up all the others. Color's ability to actively "destructurize" architectural form turns on the apparently inactive white wall. The destructive force of color derives from what appears to be the most innocent of surfaces. In 1930 van Doesburg even manages to turn the modernity of white into a kind of manifesto:

"Brown," "Blue," and "White" correctly express the three phases of the development of humanity and of all its activities: science, art, religion, technology and architecture.

WHITE This is the spiritual color of our times, the clearness of which directs all our actions. It is neither grey nor ivory white, but pure white.

WHITE This is the color of modern times, the color which dissipates a whole era; our era is one of perfection, purity and certitude.

WHITE It includes everything.

We have superseded both the "brown" of decadence and classicism and the "blue" of divisionism, the cult of the blue sky, the gods with green beards and the spectrum.

White pure white.[35]

When the final issue of *De Stijl* was published in 1932 to commemorate van Doesburg's death, it is symptomatic that it included a 1930 text of his that again insists on the purity of white. The whiteness of the artist's studio, and even the artist, has the same role as the white within the painting or building: "Choose white, always much white and black, for the significance of color emanates only from the opposition of black and white. . . . The painter himself must be white, which is to say, without tragedy or sorrow. . . . The studio of the modern painter must reflect the ambience of mountains which are nine-thousand feet high and topped with an eternal cap of snow. There the cold kills the microbes."[36] Yet again, the polemic for polychrome is made possible by privileging whiteness. This privilege is a crucial part of the claim that space is the product of color, that architecture is only ever in the surface.

In admitting color, Le Corbusier was acknowledging this effect that he and Ozenfant were previously only able to credit to painting. It was immediately after the De Stijl exhibition of 1923, in which white was integrated into polychrome schemes without losing its central role, that Le Corbusier sent his letter to the contractor finishing the all-white studio for Ozenfant specifying the color scheme, turning the studio into his first experiment in polychrome architecture. But the building also acts as a manifesto for white architecture, illustrating the "Law of Ripolin" in *L'art décoratif d'aujourd'hui*. Indeed, what is so striking about the article in which Le Corbusier first accepts the idea of a polychrome architecture is that it is also the article in which he first calls for a white architecture. The interview with Léger about the polychrome in the De Stijl exhibition is preceded by a section in which Le Corbusier develops *Le voyage d'Orient*'s enthusiastic observations on the vernacular use of white into a prescription for contemporary architecture:

Whitewash has been associated with human habitation since the birth of mankind. Stones are burnt, crushed and thinned with water—and the walls take on the purest white, an extraordinarily beautiful white.

If the house is all white, the outline of things stands out from it without any possibility of mistake, their volume shows clearly; their color is distinct. The white of whitewash is absolute, everything stands out from it and is recorded absolutely, black on white; it is honest and dependable.

Put on it anything dishonest or in bad taste—everything hits you in the eye. It is rather like an X-ray of beauty. It is a court of assize in permanent session. It is the eye of truth.

Whitewash is extremely moral. Suppose there were a decree requiring all rooms in Paris (and the Salon d'Autonomne) to be given a coat of whitewash. I maintain that that would be a police task of real stature and a manifestation of high morality, the sign of a great people. Whitewash is the wealth of the poor and the rich—of everybody, just as bread, milk and water are the wealth of the slave and the king.[37]

Eventually, these lines (with minor modifications) become the center of the key chapter on the "Law of Ripolin" in *L'art décoratif d'aujourd'hui.* In a sense, the article is eventually split in two—the praise of white going to *L'art décoratif d'aujourd'hui* in 1925 and the praise of color going to the *Almanach d'architecture moderne* a year later. The turn to color, which did not become official until the *Almanach*, was actually accompanied by the turn to white. In fact, the manuscripts for the *Almanach*, which was originally going to be an issue of *L'Esprit Nouveau*, were already completed in 1925. The first acknowledgement of the Pavilion's color was prepared at the very same time as the first advertisements for white. The white and the color are bound together from the beginning. The logic of whitewash is intimately linked to that of polychromy. Just as *Le voyage d'Orient*'s celebration of color is organized by a fetishization of whiteness, *L'art décoratif d'aujourd'hui*'s call for white is organized by a surreptitious fixation on the color it appears to exclude. White participates fully in the claim that space is produced by sensuous surfaces. In the end, the white wall is not a wall. It is a surface that can only be recognized in its rhythmic play with other colored surfaces, a play that produces the effect of architecture. The theory of polychrome architecture ends up revealing much more about the white wall than it displaces. Symptomatically, the "Polychrome Architecturale" manuscript of 1931 recovers the play between white and color that had first been articulated in *Le voyage d'Orient:*

In every civilization, folklore or apogee and in every place on the earth, the same colors of *atmosphere* appear. . . . These colors are blue, in three or four values; red or pink; pale or bright green; earthy or ochre yellow. Most striking is the predominance of stark white which composes the very background of the atmosphere. In a stark white atmosphere, the colors mentioned above acquire an intense, inflected and precise significance: they are characters, they become characters. Automatically, a degree of lyricism clings to such a significance, like the flight from a strictly useful milieu to a region which belongs to sentimental well being.

This investigation also reveals the characteristics of a society as it is manifested by colors: youthfulness, strength, physical action, vitality, optimism all revel in strongly characterized colors, they *ring* in a stark white atmosphere. The pleasures of the body harmonize with intellectual sensations in a symbolism with strong, sober and even summary roots: physiology and lyricism.[38]

White plays a central role in the examples of polychrome strategies with which the manuscript concludes. In each case, the capacity for color to "create space" by transforming the status of surfaces is produced by what the strategic play between white and "architectural" colors does to the eye. The text gives a detailed analysis of the color scheme of the Pessac houses, arguing that through the alternation of white exteriors with colored ones, "the eye is constantly tricked" and the sense of space doubles. The next example shows how to "steal space" in a small hall. The largest wall "will be painted in a luminous color, white; it is very visible" and a volume that protrudes into the space because of the necessities of the plan is isolated from that wall with color. Because it "catches the eye and distracts it from the essential and simple form that is to be highlighted," it must be painted in "a somber, elusive color which will radically contrast with the white that covers the envelope of the hall." As a result, "The eye will no longer be drawn to this disastrous protuberance, it will rest upon the white walls, their whiteness extending everywhere, into the furthest distance." Color is used to maintain the authority of white. Rather than white being the ideal background for looking at the colors, the colors direct the eye towards the white. Color binds the eye to the white wall. The next example shows that white participates in the "shattering" of volumes. The "base" of a small sitting room is white because almost all of its surfaces are painted white. While two facing walls in light pink and pale green render the seemingly closed form of the room "evasive," this effect is compromised by an intruding chimney and some cabinets. The volumes that the architect wants are "unified" into a single mass by a dark color that transforms them into a piece of furniture detached from the white space. The unwanted elements, like the chimney duct, are painted white so that "it becomes linked to the white ceiling and indeed drowns in it, no longer existing for the eyes save in its cylindrical, pale luminosity and the purity of its half-tones." White paint can make architectural elements disappear. It participates fully in each of the "optical illusions" that Le Corbusier catalogs.[39]

More than just the base condition of modern architecture, the "stark white background," the white surface is an active mechanism for reorganizing space. But not so active in the end. It is precisely its calmness, as opposed to the brutality of other colors, that effects the reorganization: "Sensations of force and of violence attach themselves to red. White acts on the body like a sedative; red is a stimulant. One is repose, the other is action."[40] The frenetic reorganization of space with color turns around the calming effect of white. The often violent operations of polychrome are all carried out in the peaceful name of white, as becomes clear when the first volume of Le Corbusier's *Oeuvre complète* describes Villa La Roche: "In the interior, the first trial of polychromy, based on the specific reactions of the colors, introduced the possibility of architectural camouflage, i.e. the emphasizing of certain masses or, alternatively, their effacement. The interior of the house must be *white*, but *for the white to be appreciated a carefully devised multicolor scheme is also necessary*."[41] As was pointed out by Le Corbusier's "Notes à la suite" of 1926, the white wall needs the color in order to show off its whiteness. Indeed, it is only truly white in the company of color.

Even when Le Corbusier's clients called for a white building, that call was satisfied by the strategic application of color. Henry Church, for example, interrupted the painting of the pavilion at the Villa d'Avray in July 1928, criticizing the polychrome scheme and asking for the building to be "painted white inside and out." But Le Corbusier prevailed, insisting that the ground floor (which reused an existing building) be "painted dark green, which contrasts sharply with the brilliant white of the new construction." The brilliance of the white, and the modernity that this effect is supposed to mark, is a product of the color.

It is precisely to intensify the white that every project after Villa Besnus of 1922 is strongly colored. The all-white building gives way to color in the name of white. So much so that Le Corbusier has to announce that the famous pilgrimage chapel at Ronchamp of 1953, the building with which he most emphatically turned his back on the early phase of orthogonal "white" boxes, is an exception precisely because it is white: "All is white inside and outside."[42] And even this exception is not completely white. There are some colored surfaces within the chapel (red, purple), and the white is used to set up a certain color effect. A layer of white paint is applied to a thin layer of rough cement that has been sprayed onto the layer of recycled stone blocks that has itself been wrapped around the outside of an open concrete frame.

8.5

*Painter giving the all
important finishing
touches to the green and
white facade of the
pavilion of the Villa
d'Avray, 1929. Fondation
Le Corbusier.*

On the huge south wall there are not even the stone blocks, just a cement
wrapper. But the internally beveled surfaces of the windows that interrupt
this wrapper are also painted white to produce the illusion of an immense
solid wall that has been punctured by scattered openings. While Le Corbusier's drawings of the wall from the outside show these windows as dark
holes in a white surface, the drawings from the inside show the inner surfaces
of the windows, which catch the angled light of the sun, as white holes in a
dark surface. In one drawing, the whiteness of these surfaces is literally
painted onto a dark image of the wall and in the middle of each of these
bright flares of whiteness, the location of small colored pieces of glass to be
suspended in (as distinct from fill) the openings is identified. These locations
are actually marked with pencil on transparent tracing paper that is placed behind the window holes that have been cut out of the original opaque drawing, as if the drawing is meant to be held up to the light to test the effect of
the design. The floating inserts produce an endlessly changing play of color
on the white that is echoed on the outside by the colored enamel painting on
the large white processional door that pivots within the wall. Color is located
within the heart of the biggest white wall that Le Corbusier ever produced. It
occupies the core, seemingly impregnating the illusion of solidity that has
been produced by folding a thin white surface. The effect of the wall is dependent on the streaks of color that animate it. This play between white and

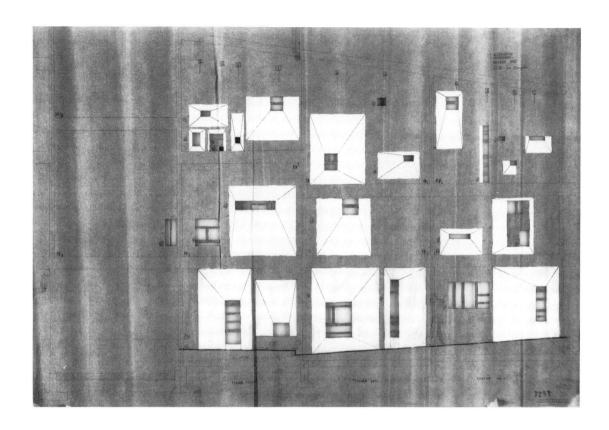

8.6

*Le Corbusier, drawing
with cut-outs of interior
of South Wall of the
pilgrimage Chapel at
Ronchamp, 1953.
Fondation Le Corbusier.*

color is then opposed to the unpainted gray concrete skin of the curving roof that is held up by the wall but polemically detached from it. The small gap between the top of the wall and the belly of the roof sets a complex polemic about white and color, the painted and the unpainted, the rough and the smooth, into motion. The building interrogates the unique status of white rather than simply exploits it, fusing the white surface to the colors that are seemingly applied to it. Far from returning to the all-white regime, the chapel is yet another essay on the hidden complicity between white and color.

From the beginning, the theory of the white wall and the theory of polychrome are intimately bound together. Neither can exist without the other. Not by chance does Léger argue in one essay that the role of the 1925 pavilion was to introduce the white wall and in another essay that its role was to introduce the colored wall.[43] They are both part of the reconceptualization of architecture as the effect of surface. Yet the white is given a unique privilege. It remains significant that Le Corbusier presents the respective theories as discrete moments, locating the theory of white before the theory of color. White is seen to precede, and yet depend on, the colors that are added to it. The logic of white is fulfilled rather than compromised by color. Its very whiteness is exposed by color. Color is the exposure of white. As such, it has to be avoided by the historiographical tradition that is so nervous about the underside of the image of white walls that it tacitly promotes.

Dressing up the Nomad

If color is the exposure of white, Le Corbusier's attempt to legalize but regulate polychrome necessarily exposes the Semperian sense of the structural role of the colored surface that is discretely buried within the white wall by the "Law of Ripolin." The discourse about clothing that underpins modern architecture necessarily becomes evident in its attempt to appropriate and discipline color. At first, Le Corbusier's theory of polychrome seems fundamentally incompatible with that of Semper. Although his definitive account of color in architecture—"Polychrome Architecturale"—argues that the use of color in "feminine dress," along with cosmetics, sports, and advertising, is the sign of a much needed renaissance of life in contemporary culture,[44] it explicitly rejects any association between polychrome architecture and the world of "clothes," "fashion," "fabrics," "wall hangings," and "tapestries." The manuscript begins by condemning the use of color to effect the "disappearance" of the wall. When color displaces architecture, "the wall becomes a hanging and the architect becomes a tapestry-maker." It is exactly this threat that calls for "dictatorial intervention" in the form of restricting the choice of available colors to "architectural" rather than "non-architectural" ones.[45] The colors that Le Corbusier dictates are meant to reinforce architecture rather than displace it. His whole polychrome system is set up in opposition to the wall hangings that Semper privileges. Architecture seems to be unambiguously distanced from the decorative world of fabrics. As the would-be dictator puts it: "I speak not of fabrics or of trinkets; I speak of architecture."[46] Later, he repeats the point by arguing that while the "strident" color shades produced by modern industry that "shake our nervous system with such violence, yet exhaust it so quickly" may be used in the manufacture of "clothes, materials, trinkets," he considers them "as non-architectural."[47] The decorative use of clothing is the antithesis of architecture. Referring back to the crusade launched by *L'art décoratif d'aujourd'hui,* he opposes the "cynical or innocent desire harbored by each man or woman to be decked out in princely ceremonial pomp."[48] The desire for ostentatious display is seen to take away the "architectural function" of the wall by transforming it into "the support for a mobile application of tapestries of fabric or paper."[49] The architectural function of the wall literally disappears as the fabrics draped over it usurp its role in defining space. The rejection of the Semperian logic seems explicit.

At the same time, in associating himself with the Salubra company, Le Corbusier appears to be embracing the very logic he is condemning. Colored wallpaper is nothing but the mobile application of a fabric to the wall. Le Corbusier is appropriating the technology that he had emphatically rejected for some time.[50] The advantage that he now appreciates in this technology is that it covers over any defect in the building's surface. It perfects the surface. With the old system of painting, "each flaw in the layout was crudely apparent, each flaw in the construction leapt out; moreover the inevitable fissures due to the cement compressing, expanding or receding ruthlessly pointed an accusatory finger at us."[51] Wallpaper seals up the cracks in the surface that call into question the machine-like smoothness of modern architecture. Indeed, wallpaper is "the first architectural application of a machine to the painting of a building."[52] Far from a painted surface simulating a machine finish, wallpaper is a machine finish available in a roll. It is painting taken to a new technological level. As the small text accompanying the Color Keyboards puts it, "Salubra is oil paint sold in rolls."[53]

What distinguishes architectural wallpaper from the simulated tapestry of anti-architectural wallpaper is the use of a single color: "Amidst the disarray and incoherence of wallpaper today, I have made a choice guided solely by architectural concerns. I do not believe in tapestry because with tapestry one can indiscriminately go Louis XIV, Turkish or Primavera, and cheat at every hour of the day. I believe in a wall that is animated by one color."[54] Monochrome wallpaper is understood as a form of resistance to the tradition of wall hanging that it appears to emulate. It keeps the spectator "within" architecture by resisting the seductions of fashionable surfaces: "These atmospheres, designed to prevent polychrome from lapsing into the domain of decoration along with fashionable materials or objects, have the mission of maintaining us within the event of architecture." Architecture is only to be found within the play between monochrome surfaces. To give a surface more than one color is to give it a pattern, a weave that destroys the building that props it up. But just like all the other loud rejections of fashion that punctuate the discourse of modern architecture in order to mask its own involvement in it, these rejections of the woven fabric are no more than the anxious attempt to mask an ongoing commitment to fabrics.

The text actually concludes by raising the possibility that Le Corbusier might enter the forbidden territory. The very strictness of his self-discipline against the seductions of decorative fabric supposedly allows him to risk employing some decorative patterns in addition to the plain colors: "Here one could leave architecture and embark upon tapestry, or the hullaballoo of billboards. . . . Just the once won't hurt! Everything is allowed to one who knows how to choose. . . . Having thus unlocked the door to the garden of

temptations, I could hold it ajar, and invite some elements of pure fantasy to enter, some particular cases of fragmentary camouflage." [55] Le Corbusier then describes his experiments with a number of patterns, including "stippling," "oblique streaks," and "diamond-shaped trellis" before announcing that he is keeping only two of them in their "calmest" combination—one trellis pattern in pale-green and a stipple pattern in eighteen different color combinations. He attempts to project the figure of stoic restraint in the face of intoxicating lures: "Its quite sensible and well-behaved for a boiling colorist! I hastily shut the door to the garden of temptations!" [56] But clearly the logic of the wall hanging is not left behind. The repeated rejections of the role of the "tapestry-maker" are made precisely because this is the role played by polychrome architecture. The very belief that the polychrome surface can dissolve or strengthen the building that holds it up credits the surface with the architectonic function outlined in Semper's account of wall hangings. Although Le Corbusier resists the use of more than one color on a single surface because of the destructive potential of such a weave, he embraces that very same potential when it is produced by the weave of color between surfaces. In the end, the use that he makes of color is not so detached from that used in fabrics and clothing. Not by chance does the original advertising image for the architect's colored wallpaper focus on the cut of his suit. The text even reads: "Le Corbusier, in the knowledge that the clothing [*Kleiden*] of walls is preferable to any sort of paint, decided on Salubra." Salubra advertised their wallpaper elsewhere by opposing an old interior with floral wallpaper matched to an old rumpled suit to a new interior lined with their paper matched to an image of a sharp new suit. The caption reads: "Clothing makes the people, wall clothing [*Wandkleider*] makes the space." [57]

The sense that colored surfaces produce rather than adorn space that is embraced by Le Corbusier reproduces Semper's basic argument. Indeed, some of his projects seem to take the form of polemical diagrams of the argument. In the Pavillion des Temps Nouveaux of 1937, for example, the structure is detached from the colored fabrics that it holds up. Canvas is literally suspended from a light prop as if in homage to Semper's image of the origin of architecture in nomadic wall hangings. The structure is not visible from the interior, only the fabrics. Furthermore, it is not the canvas screens that define the interior but the colors added to them. Even the floor is turned into a fabric by assuming a reflected color. Alongside a hand-colored reproduction of the interior in his *Des Canons, des munitions? Merci! Des logis . . . s.v.p* of the same year, Le Corbusier publishes a short text entitled "Polychromie = Joie," which describes the space "created" by the colors in a way that makes it clear that they have assumed the physical force usually associated with a building's structure:

Here . . . the poverty of credit: a temple of canvas sheet! One could only attempt to give it splendor through color: the purple rear facade exalted by the ceiling's golden color, the space created by the green wall and the blue wall and all of this supported by the dark gray color of the second lateral wall. Its humble gravel floor looked like a beautiful beach of ochre yellow.

8.8
Salubra advertisement,
Das Werk, *1932.*

8.9
*Le Corbusier, Pavilion de
temps nouveaux, 1937.
Fondation Le Corbusier.*

The choice of such violent, powerful and even crude colors represented a certain boldness, which has the effect of clubbing its visitor on the head, or triggering a sudden shock. One may even call it a certain spontaneous respect, a powerful atmosphere which silences the prattler.[58]

Le Corbusier even goes as far as describing the plans of C.I.A.M. cities displayed within the pavilion as resembling "Moroccan rugs." This figure of the tent, which had played such an important part in his discourse from the beginning and is explicitly associated with the image of the whitewashed wall in *Une maison—un palais* in 1928, emerges again with his very last project, the 1967 pavilion in Zurich for exhibiting some of his own work. The space is defined by a thin polychrome screen, with the structure again completely detached from it. To occupy the space is to occupy the screen, or, more precisely, to occupy the colors enamelled onto its surface. The structure provides physical shelter but does not define the space. The space is defined by a new kind of wallpaper. Indeed, in some of the color studies for the building, Le Corbusier seems to have literally developed the color scheme by gluing together small pieces of colored wallpaper onto yellow tracing paper to form

8.10
Page from Le Corbusier,
Une maison—une palais,
1928.

8.11
*Le Corbusier, Heide
Weber Pavilion, Zurich,
1965–67.*

the screen, while drawing the structure with colored pencil. The gap between the volumetric structure and the planar screen is emphasized. Even the glass panels are given a blue shading to preserve the sense of a continuous colored surface, a fabric.

This Semperian sense of a space produced by polychrome fabrics became completely literalized in the tapestries that Le Corbusier produced from 1936 onward, culminating in the huge wall hangings he did for Chandigarh between 1955 and 1956. In the sixth volume of his *Oeuvres complète,* he argues that the principle governing these tapestry designs is that they occupy the full wall surface rather than hang in the middle of the wall like paintings.[59] They become the wall rather than simply decorate it, a "woolen wall" as he puts it in a 1960 essay that was published in an issue of *Zodiac* that also carried advertisements for his wallpaper. The polychrome weave defines the space, its play of color taking over the architectonic function of the wall.

Tapestries "enter into the composition of modern architecture not as decoration but as a useful element."[60] Their functional role is the constitution of space. The advantage of the wall hanging is its mobility, its complete independence from the structure that holds it up. Le Corbusier speculates that "modern man is a nomad."[61] The tapestries he designs are "*Muralnomad*" that can be moved from room to room, building to building.[62] To a certain extent, they become the building. Modern nomads, like their primitive ancestors, carry their space with them. The home defined by the fabric is distinguished from the shelter it is suspended in. The fabric itself has an "architectural potential" that can be applied in any situation: "Our nomad moves because his family increases in number, or, on the contrary, because his children have married. Tapestry gives him the opportunity to possess a 'mural,' that is, a large painting of architectural potential. He unrolls the tapestry and spreads it on the wall such that it touches the ground. Is he moving? He will roll up his mural, tuck it under his arm and go down the stairs to install it in his shelter [*gîte*]."[63]

Modern "man" travels with his wall hangings, wrapping himself in color, just as Le Corbusier had himself traveled around the East with the carpet that he bought at Mount Athos, a multicolored fabric that he often slept in under the stars. Not by chance were the same kind of Bedouin carpets carefully placed on the floor of the L'Esprit Nouveau Pavilion. When Le Corbusier produced his own tapestries, it is as if the nomad's carpet ended up taking over the role of the wall that once was played by the polychrome surfaces of the pavilion

and the murals by Léger that were displayed upon them. The tapestry relocates the architectural play between colors from a play between surfaces to a play within one surface, blurring the distinction between colored murals and polychrome architecture that he had so repeatedly made. The multicolored weave of the mural joins the polychrome scheme in making space "palpitate," becoming "integral to the architecture" it might appear to merely decorate:

> Modern architectural polychrome, already exploited today, makes space palpitate. The "mural" may participate in this, destroying or highlighting a wall (a surface), or creating the occasion for grand speeches, but the mural will be integral to the architecture. The painter will thus have to love and know architecture and be like some sort of a plastician, one who is absolutely connected to, and fully participates in, volumes, lights, distances, spaces, proportions, materials. . . . Tapestry is an unexpected and legitimate form of the mural. Life within the home may extend the taste for painted works so that it encompasses mural composition. Modern society will organize its homes within buildings with common services. The occupant will no longer be a lord in his castle, he is henceforth a nomad: a tenant. Tapestry is a fresco that may be rolled up, carried under the arm and moved out with the tenant.[64]

The mobility of the textile takes over from the mural that mobilizes walls but remains fixed in one place. While the painted wall still makes sense in public spaces, it can no longer define the space of the home, a space that is once again worn by a mobile subject. In a late interview, Le Corbusier argues that to be "at home" today is not to occupy the "rental boxes" in which the modern nomad lives, no matter how palatial or well they are designed, but to experience the sensuous "intimacy" provided by the weave of the tapestries that are carried from box to box. The suspended tapestry recovers the role of defining space that it had in the Middle Ages and the Renaissance.[65] Le Corbusier ends up in an explicitly Semperian mode. Yet his tentlike projects simply emphasize a strategy that can be found throughout his work ever since the Dom-ino system polemically separated the physical structure from the suspended screens that define space. The ubiquitous white wall that was

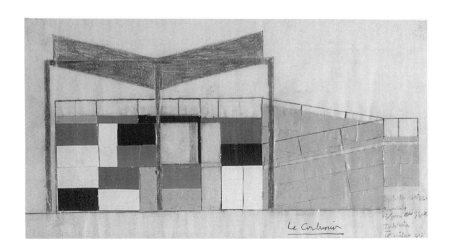

launched at that time is fully implicated in this strategy. It is itself a fabric, even if the sensuousness of its texture appears to have been minimized. The apparent move from white to polychrome is a move within the realm of clothing rather than a move toward clothing. It is not by chance that *Entretien avec les étudiants des écoles d'architecture* of 1943 explains his shift from white to polychromed architecture as a move from contemporary clothing designs for men toward those of women:

Nowadays people are unaware of the power of color as it was used in Doric or medieval times. They know nothing of the clarity or glitter of golds, or mirrors, or silk, or brocades or of Louis XIV and Louis XV felts. . . . That revolution of consciousness belatedly emerging now after having too long burdened society, will one day even affect our dress. Women have already taken the lead. Their styles and fashions are bold, sensitive, expressive. Just look at the young girls of 1942. Their hair styles reflect a healthy and optimistic outlook. They go forth crowned with gold or ebony. But in the reign of Louis XIV or during the Renaissance, you boys are the ones who would have been as radiant as archangels with hair like theirs, and strong as Mars and handsome as Apollo. But the women have stolen your thunder!

Our clothing is completely unadapted to our needs. We have also abandoned the use of color, one of the sure signs of life. Since 1910 I have believed in the refreshing, purifying quality of whitewash. Practice has convinced me that if you want to highlight the delicious brilliance of white, you must surround it with vibrant suggestions of color. Discerning in the use of reinforced concrete the possibilities of the "open plan," free of space-clogging walls, I turned to architectural polychromy to define space and to give it variety, for color responds to life's motions. The use of many colors causes life itself to flourish.[66]

The text passes seamlessly from a description of the role of color in clothing to the assertion that space is defined by colors rather than by walls. Indeed, walls tend to "clog" space rather than produce it. There is a marked tension between the material wall and the color spread across its surface. Surfaces sustain spaces that may be occupied by walls. Walls become occupants of architecture. Like people, they need to be at once disciplined and liberated. And women's clothing serves as the model of this simultaneous disciplining of form to the dictates of material function and liberation from the burdens of material life. There appears to have been a significant shift away from the privileging of men's clothing that accompanies the polemic of *Vers une architecture*. At the very moment in which that text had condemned color, the caption to an image of a car being compared to an image of the Parthenon announces: "It is a simpler matter to form a judgment on the clothes of a well-dressed man than on those of a well-dressed woman, since masculine costume is standardized. It is certain that Phidas was at the side of Ictinos and Kallicrates in building the Parthenon, and that he dominated them, since all temples of the time were of the same type, and the Parthenon surpasses them all beyond measure."[67] While suppressing the multicolored effects of the plain surface of the Parthenon that were celebrated in *Le voyage d'Orient*, the manifesto promotes men's clothing, just as *L'art décoratif d'aujourd'hui* will do when it promotes whiteness over color. Whitewash is understood as masculine clothing. The architect has reduced the English suit down to the white shirt upon which it is based. It comes as no surprise that Le Corbusier embraces women's clothing when he promotes polychrome architecture. This was already explicit during his 1929 lecture series in Argentina, which was published the following year as *Précisions sur un état présent de l'architecture et de l'urbanisme* (Precisions: on the present state of architecture and city planning). One of the lectures includes a lengthy passage on the superiority of contemporary women's dress to that of men:

Women have preceded us. They have carried out the reform of their clothing. They found themselves at a dead end: to follow fashion was to give up the advantages of modern techniques, of modern life. Renounce sports, and, an even more material problem, be unable to take on the jobs that have made women a fertile part of contemporary production and allowed them to *earn their living*. To follow fashion: they couldn't have anything to do with cars, they couldn't take the metro or a bus, nor move lively in an office or store. To carry out the daily *construction* of a "toilette," hairdo, boots, buttoning a dress, they would not have had time to sleep. So women cut their hair and their skirts and their sleeves. They went off bare-

headed, arms naked, legs free. And get dressed in five minutes. And they are beautiful: they lure us with the charm of their graces of which the designers have accepted taking advantage.

The courage, the liveliness, the spirit of invention with which women have operated the revolution in clothing are a miracle of modern times. Thank you![68]

Women's clothing acts as the new paradigm for the combination of functional efficiency and aesthetic charm required of modern architecture. The mobility of the modern woman requires a new form of dress. The inefficiencies and supplements imposed by fashion have been trimmed off. The realm of excess has been transformed into a realm of efficiency without sacrificing the "lure" of the woman. On the contrary, the lure has been intensified. The modern look "takes advantage" of the woman's body. Her clothing allows her to become active in the world while remaining the fixed object of man's attention. Of course, Le Corbusier has to pretend that fashion has played no role in the emergence of this new look that renders man's clothing out of date. The English suit is transformed from the paradigm of modernity to but a necessary step, one that must be transcended in favor of the functional styles developed for sports, work and women's clothing:

We men? A sad question! In dress clothes, we wear starched collars and resemble the generals of the Grand Armée. In street clothes, we are not at ease. We need to carry an arsenal of papers and small tools on us. The pocket, pockets, should be the keystone of modern clothing. Try to carry everything you need: you've destroyed the line of your costume; you are no longer "correct." One must choose between working and being elegant.

8.14
Illustration from Le Corbusier, Précisions sur un état présent de l'architecture et de l'urbanisme, *1930.*

The English suit we wear had nevertheless succeeded in something important. It had *neutralized* us. In town it is useful to have a neutral appearance. The important sign is no longer in the ostrich feathers of a hat, it is in the eyes. That's enough. . . . At Saint-Moritz on the snow, modern man is up-to-date. At Levallois-Perret, at the headquarters of the automobile industry, the mechanic is a forerunner. We office workers are beaten by a serious length by women.

Thus, the spirit of reform has only just appeared. It remains for it to influence all the acts of life.[69]

> The lecture (which Le Corbusier refers back to years later when describing the regrettable impossibility of buying undecorated pajamas)[70] goes on to illustrate the principles of modern furniture design with the storing of hats, shoes, dresses, and underwear in standardized cabinets that are "suited to what they are to contain," such that "every object is stored as in a jewel case" and "your clothing is spread out before your eyes."[71] The whole argument turns around clothes. This strategic emphasis on the outer layer that covers the body is yet again aligned with a privileging of surface. In an earlier passage on the "fundamental elements of the architectural sensation"— which begins by describing the architectural strategy of his Villa Stein at Garches of 1927 and culminates in one more reference to the "overwhelming power" of the Parthenon—Le Corbusier explicitly identifies architecture with the sensuous surface. The experience of space turns out to be no more than the experience of surfaces:

To evoke attention, to occupy space powerfully, a surface of perfect form was necessary first, followed by the exaltation of the flatness of that surface by the addition of a few projections or holes creating a back and forth movement. Then, by the opening of windows . . . an important play of secondary surfaces is begun, releasing rhythms, dimensions, tempos of architecture.

Rhythms, dimensions, tempos of architecture, inside the house and outside. A motive of professional loyalty obliges us to devote all our care to the interior of the house. One enters: one receives a shock, first sensation. Here we are impressed by one dimension of a room succeeding another dimension, by one form succeeding another. That is architecture!

And depending on the way you enter a room, that is to say depending on the place of the door in the wall of the room, the feeling will be different. That is architecture! But how do you receive an architectural sensation? By the effect of the relationships that you perceive. These relationships are provided by what? By the surfaces that you see and that you see because they are in *light*.[72]

> Even the functional role of spaces is a question of surface. As the text puts it: "For every function, an exactly proportioned surface."[73] The architectural logic of clothing is that of the strategically deployed surface. What women's

clothing offers is a new paradigm of this deployment. The seductions of color are seen to be completely compatible with the functional efficiency afforded by the modern cut. The architect is offered a wider range of techniques for producing the "sensation" of architecture. The neutrality of the white shirt can successfully be supplemented by the active play of color.

At first, this argument seems to move beyond the thinking of the architect's early books. Yet the shift is not as great as it might appear. In fact, Le Corbusier had identified women's clothing as a field of modern experimentation at the very beginning of his career. When *Vers une architecture* and *L'art décoratif d'aujourd'hui* suppress his own fascination with color, even to the extent of banning it in favor of white, they also suppress his fascination with women's clothing. Already in 1915, he had explicitly identified women's clothing with modernity. In one of his sketchbooks he writes about the new kinds of "magazines, boutiques, clothes, objects of pleasure" that are being produced and asserts: "Wait 10 years; modernity [will take over] everywhere: the Vieux Colombier, Perret's theater, etc. Women take to it. Women feel flattered in that framework."[74] On the back of the text, he draws the clothing of four women, comparing the line of the dresses to the line of the body. Likewise, *Le voyage d'Orient* constantly pays detailed attention to the clothes worn in each region the tour passes through.[75] So many of Le Corbusier's architectural sketchbooks through the years are filled with studies of women and their clothing, most of which are either done in color or annotated with the respective colors. Modern efficiency is repeatedly aligned with sensuality. Modernity is understood as a scene of seduction that "flatters" women by producing clothes that "lure us with the charm of their graces." The lessons to be learned from the past are lessons about seductive surfaces.

This obsession is just as much a part of the promotion of white architecture as it is of polychrome. The praise of the vernacular whitewashed wall is almost always accompanied by a discussion of the multicolored clothing that appears in front of it. *Le voyage d'Orient* repeatedly dwells on the color schemes of the peasant costumes that decorate the white wall so intensely that they render the wall itself decorative:

The women are most beautiful; the men clean-looking. They dress themselves with art: flashing silks, notched and multicolored leather, white short-sleeved shirts with black embroidery work; the nervous legs and small bare feet of such a fine brown skin; the women move with a swinging of hips which unfurls. Like the skirt of a dancing girl, the thousand folds in the short dresses where the silk flowers ignite under a sun of golden fire. This costume delighted us; the people contrasted and harmonized with the enormous white walls and with the flowerbeds of courtyards which make here and there a strangely successful complement to the distinguished appearance of the streets.[76]

8.15
*Page from Le Corbusier,
sketchbook A2, 1915.
Fondation Le Corbusier.*

The unique status of white depends on particular fantasies of colored clothing. When *Précisions* revives Le Corbusier's early use of women's clothing as
a model for modern architecture, it is clear that the white surface that had
previously been identified with men's clothing is not abandoned. On the contrary, the "vibrant suggestions of color" are necessary to "highlight the delicious brilliance of white," as Le Corbusier's later account of the advantages
of contemporary women's clothing puts it.[77] The white garment remains a crucial part of the polychrome outfit. The sensuality of color brings out the "delicious" sensuality of white. It exposes the very qualities of men's clothing that
the ostensible neutrality of that clothing supposedly stands against. Men's
clothing is seen to exhibit supposedly feminine attributes. Indeed, its basic operation is seen to depend on those attributes. The switch from men's to wom-
en's outfits is not as straightforward as it appears. The white wall, in its very
whiteness, becomes a seductive object. Its supposed neutrality becomes an
irresistible lure.

Le Corbusier's argument is not so idiosyncratic. On the contrary, it is drawn out of a very particular discourse that had been evolving for some time. To say the least, the same link between dress and color is articulated by his collaborators. Ozenfant, with whom he determined the colors of Purist painting, was always involved in the fashion trade and used it as a model for color. And Léger, with whom he displaced those colors from paintings to buildings, designed costumes for plays and films to match many of his stage sets and repeatedly related his use of color to dress designs.

For Ozenfant (whose fashion advertisements would end up alongside Le Corbusier's discussion of colored architecture in the early issues of *Cahiers d'art*), the taste for certain colors is marked by the taste for certain clothes, as became clear in a series of essays on polychrome architecture that he published in *Architectural Review*.[78] Furthermore, the "expert selections" of colors in dress making have contributed to the modern eye's increased sensitivity to color, a sensitivity that makes any inexactitude in the application of color "compromise the whole architecture of a building."[79] Dress design has forced a greater level of precision onto the architect who must now deploy color as an intrinsic condition of form. At the same time, the colors used for certain kinds of clothing are not appropriate for buildings. In the essay entitled "Color Solidity," Ozenfant discourages the use of "fragile" colors, like pink and rose, that are commonly used for hats and expensive dresses because they are quickly discarded. A building requires a sense of permanence, a sense of solidity that is produced by the colors rather than the structure that they are added to.[80]

The essay goes on to insist that this architectonic use of color turns around the application of white: "WHITE—From an aesthetic point of view it might almost be said that there cannot be too much white in a room; there cannot be too much silence to hear the music of the colors. This is in contrast to other colors which must be administered in exact quantities."[81] But the white surface is not simply the backdrop, the neutral skin of the mannequin upon which the precisely tailored colored outfit is to be hung. When Ozenfant had earlier identified the modern sensitivity to color with clothing, the white wall around which all such color schemes have to be organized was, of course, understood as a white shirt—one whose whiteness is brightened by the garments around it, just as the color of those garments is intensified by the light it reflects: "The whites sing gaily, because they generously reflect practically all the light; and these whites appear all the brighter when their surroundings are darker: and the somber colors, by contrast, become beautiful and telling.

London requires linen collars. The old London architects provided whites. Why have they been totally abandoned?"[82] A year later, Ozenfant picks up on this seemingly passing comment to reaffirm that the white has to be purified to expose the fine cut of the outfit. Polychrome architecture is once again presented as a form of hygiene that is based upon a clean white:

I once asked that London should be provided with white collars: the dinner jacket is smart and distinguished, not by mere convention, but precisely because of its strong contrasts of dark and white:

It must be realized, however, that where the facade painters in the old days had the courage to use bold tones and whites, those of today, convinced that they are following them, imitate dirty tones and foul whites, and think it is smart. But, is there anything more depressing and ill-bred than a dirty collar or one that appears so? And a nice white collar lends dignity to a well cut coat, even a threadbare one. Well, London's coat is well cut, but old, so let's wash its underwear.[83]

To clean all the white garments is to reveal the unique space produced by the clothing that is the city. Ozenfant plots the spread of white surfaces from the facade of his own building to its neighborhood and then throughout London, ironically describing the clean white as having "contaminated" the dirty city. But his essay emphatically rejects the idea that "It's white, so it's modern."[84] Rather, it calls for a carefully controlled relationship between white and color. The white enables the colors of the outfit to be recalibrated, as demonstrated by a number of black and white photographs to which white and color have been polemically added. It is not the white or the color that is modern but the particular relationship between them. Each of the essays in the series describes this interaction in great detail.

A similar concern for the play between white shirts and colored clothing can be found throughout Léger's essays. He repeatedly describes metropolitan street life, detailing what people are wearing. More precisely, he focuses on window dressing and the clothing displayed by it. In 1923 he argues that "the astonishing art of window display" is a model for modern art.[85] The prototypical artwork is the "majestically dressed" store window, preferably one whose innovative lines are matched by the clothes it advertises. In the following year, for example, a display of seventeen waistcoats surrounded by cufflinks and neckties acts as the paradigm. Likewise, when Léger takes the argument further in 1928, by arguing that the street should be considered as one of the fine arts rather than simply the model for them, he points to the evolution of women's fashions: "From the day when a woman's head was considered an oval object to be emphasized, hair has disappeared and more care than ever is taken with make-up, the eye, the mouth . . . and, naturally, the store mannequin has followed the trend."[86] The mannequins in the window register the heart beat of the modern city, faithfully reflecting the shifting criteria of display. Store windows display display itself, at once leading and following the precise adjustments in the way people present themselves. In Léger's view, modern art needs to base itself on the "spectacle" of everyday metropolitan life, a spectacle exemplified in the display of clothing. As he insists in 1924, it is not that art should simply follow fashion, but that it should share fashion's creative impulse, its endless attempt to modernize itself in the face of the brutally modern age of mechanization:

There must be invention at any cost. Adapting to fashion is inferior and very far from dealing with the problem to be solved. . . . Present day life never adapts; it creates unceasingly, every morning, good or bad, but it invents. . . . Commercial endeavors are so competitive that a procession of models at a good couturier's equals and even surpasses a number of average stage shows in entertainment value. . . . This frenzy, this craving for distraction at any price, must arise from a need for reaction against the harshness and demands of modern life.[87]

UN PERSONNAGE

Dessin de LÉGER

8.16
Fernand Léger, costume design for the ballet "Le création du monde," as illustrated in L'Esprit nouveau *no 18, 1923.*

A crucial detail of such shifts in fashion is color. Indeed, Léger's whole discourse on color is organized around descriptions of particular clothing styles. Colored clothing is the model for colored spaces. "Couleur dans le monde" (Color in the world) of 1938, for example, insists that "man dresses himself in colors. His action is not merely decorative: it is also psychological . . . it becomes a social and human need," before going on to describe the colored clothing of the middle ages.[88] When Léger started to collaborate with Le Corbusier in 1923, he was already focusing on the play between men's and women's styles: "A contemporary fashionable party contrasts the men's severe, crisp black clothes with the prettier and more delicately colored dresses of the women. An epoch of contrasts. An eighteenth-century party was simply tone on tone, all the clothes were similar."[89] In fact, he had made the same point in a 1914 essay that uses the peasant's "taste for violent contrasts in his costume" as a model for the transformation of clothing that is occurring within the city. The evolution of this contrast is compared to the lack of evolution in the color schemes of bourgeois interiors.[90] The contrast between the black and white of the man's suit, and between that suit and the colors of a women's outfit, is used as a model for bringing surfaces to life. Dead surfaces "acquire movement" by being coated with color and this revitalization of the surface is already described as "construction through color."[91] Colored clothing acts as the model for constructing space. Or, rather, it is the construction of space. Léger is not simply making an analogy between the colors of clothing and the coloration of space. Rather, he is describing the space produced by that clothing. The architecture is in the color.

Indeed, for Léger, color itself is a form of dress. As his "On Monumentality and Color" puts it, color "dresses" everyday routine.[92] In the end, architecture is but the dress of everyday life. The colors of a space are worn by its occupant rather than by the structure of the building to which it is applied. Even clothes are seen to "wear" their color. While color once came into the home on the "dresses, hats, make-up" that "had the task of wearing color,"[93] it now constitutes that home. Color is architecture because it is clothing.

Léger's fascination with clothes always leads into a polemic for colored architecture. His original call to "orchestrate" the visual world of the modern city by creating a polychromed architecture "from scratch" in 1924, for example, immediately follows an account of a woman's concern with a coordinated physical appearance. Yet again, the provincial use of clothes acts the model for metropolitan order:

From our need to arrange the room we live in, to the discreet arrangement of a lock of hair under a hat, the desire for harmony penetrates everywhere. Don't think, for example, that taste in clothes concerns young people alone. Go into the shop of a little dressmaker in the provinces. Have the patience to watch all through a fitting that a local businesswoman is having. To get the effect she wants, she will be more meticulous, more exacting than the most elegant Parisian. This stout, fifty-year old lady, she too wants to achieve a harmony that is appropriate for her age, her environment, and her means. She too organizes her spectacle so that it will make its effect where she thinks necessary; she hesitates between the blue belt and the red one, indicates her choice, and accordingly worries about 'the Beautiful.'[94]

This precisely orchestrated spectacle of dress sets up the call for an architecture "dressed up in multicolor."[95] When architecture wears the dress of color, it is able to assume a "social function" through color's "psychological value," one that is, in the end, a "moral value." The morality of modern architecture hangs on its clothing. But the model here is the color coordinated woman's outfit rather than the austere man's suit. The somber outfit built up around the white shirt is no longer the guarantee of moral responsibility. On the contrary, it becomes a figure of moral negligence.

At one point, Léger even argues that the color of spaces sometimes makes up for deficiencies in men's dress. When his 1924 essay on "L'Esthétique de la machine" praises the coloring of machines (as Le Corbusier does in July of the same year), for being "polychromed mechanical architecture," it suggests that: "All these colored objects compensate for the loss of color that can be observed in modern dress. The old, very colorful fashions have disappeared; contemporary clothing is gray and black. The machine is dressed up and has become a spectacle and a compensation."[96] Machines become architecture by dressing up, entering the kaleidoscopic spectacle of everyday life and taking the place of worn-out clothing. Likewise, buildings become architecture by dressing up. If they do not, their capacity to define space is vulnerable to being taken over by those clothes that do. The essay symptomatically concludes by arguing that "a sixteen-year-old with fiery red hair, a new canvas coat, orange pants, and a hand splattered with Prussian blue . . . clothes of a modern worker, blazing with color" managed to destroy one of his own exhibitions simply by entering the space of the gallery, dissolving both its "vast surfaces, dismal and gray" and the paintings attached to them, such that "nothing remained on the walls than vaporous shadows in old frames."[97] Just as colored spaces can compensate for colorless clothes, colored clothing can compensate for colorless spaces. When Léger's 1931 essay on New York for *Cahiers d'Art* complains that the city is colorful by night but colorless by day, it goes as far as calling for a "dictator of color" that would impose colored outfits according to strict regimes that would produce a color-coordinated city: "clothing manufacturers could be compelled to put out a group of green dresses and green suits."[98] There is a continuous exchange between the two forms of clothing, those held up by the body and those held up by the structure of a building. A well-dressed building is even able to raise the standards of dress

8.17
*Le Corbusier in Moscow,
October 1928.*

of those who enter it. Yet another of Léger's essays, "Color in Architecture" of 1948 argues that one of the effects of the polychrome factory is that the workers end up "better dressed."[99] Architecture challenges dress and dress challenges architecture. The truly coordinated outfit is the one that matches the surfaces of the garment to the surfaces of the buildings. It comes as no surprise that the essay's account of the collaboration with Le Corbusier begins with the architect's clothes:

I met Le Corbusier about 1921 or 1922, I believe in a rather odd way. At the time I lived in Montparnasse, and I used to go occasionally to the terrace of the rotunda with friends and models of the Quarter. One day one of them said to me: "Just wait, you are going to see an odd specimen. He goes bicycling in a derby hat."

A few minutes later I saw coming along, very stiff, completely in silhouette, an extraordinary mobile object under the derby hat, with spectacles and in a dark suit. It was the outfit of a clergyman and of an Englishman on a week end. He advanced quietly, scrupulously obeying the laws of perspective. The picturesque personage, indifferent to the curiosity he awakened, was none other than the architect Le Corbusier.[100]

This decisive outfit, a calculated ensemble that the architect carefully presents to the world in numerous images that often juxtapose it with his designs, is immediately associated with the "nudity" of the white wall that needs to be dressed in color:

Suddenly it "appeared"; and it was a revelation, a bath of nudism. Le Corbusier made us a present of the white wall. We needed it. A completely white wall is a beautiful thing. Architecture set out once more again from zero. . . . Cult of the void. Voluptuousness of the absolute. . . . At the same time, once intoxicated with the white wall we thought we ought to pay a little attention to it after all. It was at this moment that architects began to look at it from the point of view of color, from the painter's viewpoint. Color was going to be an intimate part of the wall which had just been discovered.[101]

To change out of the white is to change clothes, to take off the man's suit and put on a woman's outfit, to shed the pious image of the clergyman, no matter how "picturesque," "beautiful," "intoxicating," or even "voluptuous," it might seem, and put on a colorful dress. The eccentric charm of the English gentleman needs to be displaced by the polychrome Parisienne. The static form of the suit needs to be replaced by the mobility of fashionable dress. Women's clothing is a different kind of clothing and a different way of wearing and changing clothes. Polychrome architecture is not simply a matter of replacing one outfit with another but of replacing one attitude toward outfits with another. The desire for universal standards needs to accommodate the relentless urge to modernize exemplified by fashion. In turning to the economy of women's clothing, the architect of polychrome must negotiate an ever more treacherous slippage between modern and mode. Although abandoning the suit might open architecture up to whole new set of pleasures, each of these pleasures is accompanied by new threats to the very identity of the architect. More precisely, the polychrome outfit exposes and exploits the fantasies that the white wall attempts to suppress by effacing its very status as an item of dress.

I believe in the skin *of things, as in that of women.*

—Le Corbusier, *Quand les cathédrales étaient blanches,* 1937.

Sexual Charges

Once changed, the polychrome outfit has to last for more than one season, even if that change, if not the specific details of the design, takes its cue from the world of women's fashion. Le Corbusier and Léger had been jolted into action by the De Stijl experiments that completely reconfigured architecture's outfit but did so in the name of a very limited set of strategies. Although van Doesburg and Mondrian violently disagreed about whether their works constituted the end point or just another phase in the reconfiguration of space, each of their designs was understood to have an extended life. The De Stijl environment is clearly meant to last much longer than any fashionable set of clothes. Having produced the canonic polychrome Schröder House in collaboration with Mrs. Truus Schröder in 1924, Gerrit Rietveld ended up making a Loosian distinction between the relatively constant design required of the fabrics that define the modern interior and the fluidity of "woman's clothes."[1] Architecture may be based on woman's dress and may even be understood as a form of dress, but it is a very particular kind of dress with a very particular relationship to fashion. Léger and Le Corbusier were caught between their attraction to the logic of fashion that exemplified modernity and a desire to exceed that logic in the name of the permanence of art. This ambivalent tension was underpinned by a very particular psychopathology, one whose organizing role in the discourse of modern architecture should not be underestimated.

9.1
Fernand Léger, drawing in Forms et vie, *1951.*

The terms of this structural psychodrama become explicit in 1951 with the publication of the second issue of the magazine *Forms et Vie*. Its cover, like that of the first issue, which had republished Léger's five year old essay "Modern Architecture and Color," was designed by Le Corbusier and exhibited his "modulor" system of proportions. Léger contributed a drawing of an idiosyncratic outfit over which he has written the following lines:

The accord between fashion and architecture is dated or ends in the eighteenth century. Today *la couture* strives for graceful and seductive lines, at the limit of the impossible these tenuous "tight-rope" outfits worn by mechanical models. But fortunately not all women are models.

I will mention here the story of the *petite Bretonne* that I met fifteen years ago. I think I was with le Corbusier, and when we reached some woods, our eyes suddenly fell upon a remarkable apparition in absolute contrast with our surroundings. Our *petite Bretonne* was beautiful, a very romantic age; a fiction come to life, a peasant fiction, artisan without a trace of architecture. Corbu agreed.[2]

In the same issue is an ink sketch of some dress designs by Le Corbusier, which are accompanied by an explanatory "Note." Just as he did so many times when promoting his architectural designs, Le Corbusier begins the note by insisting that the clothing designs displayed in the sketch by "four women and a leg" are not haute-couture creations that will be displaced by the fashions of next season. Rather, they are "permanent" forms. Yet interestingly, it is here, when addressing the question of dress, that he acknowledges that the line between the two is not so clear cut, something he was unable to do when talking about architecture: "This is a costume for the woman of today, it is not an haute-couture creation. It is therefore permanent rather than transient, a distinction which is not absolute but simply delineates two perfectly acceptable stages in a woman's dress."[3] Some fluidity between high fashion and art is finally acknowledged. They become stages in the same continuum rather than separate worlds, one honorable and the other not. Nevertheless, the architect-couturier places himself on the side of permanent forms that have been crystallized out of everyday type outfits. Predictably, he goes on to emphasize that he is offering "comfortable wear" for "a mobile and transitory group of people" that can accommodate all their different activities and sitting positions. Clothing is to be organized around the new functions of modern life made available by abandoning old-fashion etiquette.

But clearly it is not just a question of function. The text zooms in on legs and feet. On the one hand, the "daintily crafted sandals" worn by the models sup-

Modèle déposé

9.2
Le Corbusier, dress designs, Forms et vie, *1951.*

posedly have a "useful" low heel for walking that can alleviate corns while, on the other hand, they expose the feet to the "same degree of attention that is generally bestowed upon fingernails. Eyes would thus be drawn agreeably both to the coral on the ground and the coral at the tips of the fingers."[4] Nylons are banned because they are "attractive" but "inconvenient" and the boot worn by the leg that seems to be amputated by the frame of the drawing is designed for the "cold and damp" but also for its "contrast" with "feminine slenderness." As always, Le Corbusier oscillates between functional and aesthetic criteria. But here the aesthetic is unambiguously to do with a certain ideal of the erotically charged woman's body. Or, more precisely, the body that is erotically charged by being sometimes concealed, sometimes revealed, through the strategic use of fabrics:

This costume is tailored for a living being with a bony build, useful muscles and curves, flesh and slenderness, all essential feminine characteristics which Monsieur has taken into consideration. For while he may be an architect and a painter, he is not blind and knows how to appreciate what is always pleasurable to see, and what is sometimes interesting to conceal, thus letting circumstances be opportunities or pretexts for the joys of discovery.[5]

Having said this, the architect concludes by again insisting that the designs are not haute couture. His account is defensively framed, protected on all sides, by the rejection of fashion. A letter offering his designs to *Harper's Bazaar* insists yet again that each dress is not haute couture but "a lady's costume that is useful for today (and which does not sacrifice the potential feminine charms of its wearer)."[6] The dresses are meant to negotiate between modern functional mobility and a certain image of beauty. Having pointed out that he has secured the copyright on their label and description and put his literary agent in charge of managing their sale, Le Corbusier concludes by insisting on the combination of the functional and the aesthetic, the mobile, and the seductive: "I would like to make a fortune in dollars in the U.S., but I would be even happier to see this costume worn, to have it tailored in all kinds of qualities and fabrics, thus allowing the woman of today to move with more freedom and to display a grace that is an extension of bodily grace (when grace indeed exists)."[7] The dresses grant the woman a freedom to move but only within the strict confines of an ostensibly male gaze. The loose surfaces of the dress are closely scrutinized for erotically charged traces of the movements of the body that they conceal.

The Semperian impulse in Le Corbusier's work comes full circle with these dress designs. He belatedly joins the brigade of modern architects that design dresses and draw their architectural philosophy from the world of dress reform. As with all the others, Le Corbusier's dresses are meant to participate in the thinking that organizes his architecture. Indeed, they were published in a special issue of *Forme et Vie* dedicated to the question of "Evolution du Costume en rapport avec l'Architecture." Yet again, architecture is explicitly aligned with dress design. The issue opens with an advertisement for fashions by Balmain and has an editorial by L. Bruder that argues that "dress is architecture expressed in terms of the human body, under the protean form of material." The harmony between the "cubist bachelor girl and a modern block of flats," whereby "buildings become cubic, women rectangular," sustains a millennial "bond" between dress and architecture: "dressmakers' scissors and architects' equations always end by meeting in a certain way across their epoch . . . an architectural system will always call for the costume it deserves and vice-versa."[8] For Bruder, this millennial "dialogue" leads to an association between Le Corbusier's buildings and Poiret's dresses, between, as he puts it, "reinforced concrete" and "nylon." Le Corbusier's own dress designs are seen to present his architectural thinking even more clearly. Indeed, they are architectural statements.

When Le Corbusier insists that the fabric of his dresses plays a "decisive" role, it is understood to be as decisive as that played by the fabric of his buildings. He looks for "fluid materials that never wrinkle and yet fall well!" Such fabrics can range from "plain" to "extravagantly colorful" and thereby provide "an endless gamut of textile and decorative innovations." As in his architecture, "a combination of the plain and the colorful can be worn by the same person."[9] The move from men's to women's clothing, from the plain white surface to the polychrome outfit, is reproduced within women's clothing. The plain is accentuated by the colorful and the colorful by the plain. The logic organizing men's clothing is incorporated rather than left behind. Men's clothing opens itself to the color of woman's clothing, which in turn incorporates the more stable type-form of men's. A kind of compromise be-

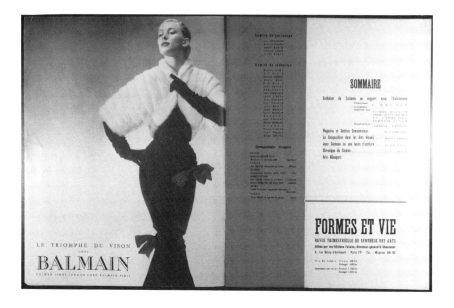

9.3
Frontispiece, Forms et vie, *1951.*

9.4
Illustration accompanying L. Bruder's editorial, Forms et vie, *1951.*

Veüe et perspective de l'Orangerie et du Château de Versailles du coste du Jardin

tween the two forms of clothing is reached and launched as a paradigm for a truly modern architecture.

Still, the logic governing both forms of clothing remains that of the gaze directed at the women's body, or rather, the body (whether of a man or a woman) understood as feminine. After all, Léger has no hesitation in describing the "intoxicating" "voluptuousness" of the white wall that is always associated with the man's suit. While Le Corbusier is much more hesitant to acknowledge the sensuous charge of the white wall, his turn to woman's clothing starts to expose exactly what is involved in his infatuation with that wall. If color is, as he insists, a question of psychology, then the ongoing psychopathology that props up his white wall comes to the surface when he engages with women's dress design. Rather than reconfigure the basic operation of his architecture, the polychrome surface exposes and exploits the extraordinary investment that has been made in the white wall.

In the theory of polychrome architecture, the application of a thin coat of color is understood to transform the building into a psychological space. The very sensuality it introduces triggers mental responses. Surface acquires depth

274

through psychological responses to it. As Léger's "Le mur, l'architecte, le peintre," puts it, "Color is not merely a simple, skin-deep satisfaction. I reject that; it is vital. . . . It is a psychological concern rather than a matter of plastic satisfaction."[10] The sensuous skin offers access to the unconscious. Because the white wall is actually used to admit and even promote the very colors it once appeared to so vigilantly exclude, it facilitates the return of the psyche, a return that seemingly transforms the basic condition of space. Static forms become mobilized by desire: "The white wall accepted its partial destruction through applications of color . . . the permanent, habitable rectangle of four white walls became an elastic rectangle. I say elastic because each color applied, even when shaded, has a mobile effect. Visual distance becomes relative. . . . Psychological action has been set in motion by itself."[11] With the arrival of polychrome, modern architecture appears to be overrun with the very desire that it had so rigidly opposed. More precisely, its own desire to control desire becomes manifest. After all, when the white surface liberates color, it does so only to control it. A crucial part of the reconstitution of space by surface is the call for discipline, precision, and order. Color is the agent of that control and part of what must be controlled. For Mondrian, for example, it is the "dominance" of color in nature that must be overcome. Color must be "governed" and can be so "only through the exact expression of equilibrated color relationships."[12] Symptomatically, it is this call for discipline that leads into the discussion of color as architecture. The desire to unify painting and architecture is, after all, a desire for control. The claim that architecture is in the surface leads to the frantic attempt to control color, to figure out how to build stable structures out of its complex sensual interactions. If architecture is in the surface, the architect has to actively discipline the surface, taming its wildest possibilities in the name of order.

This obsessive disciplinary fixation on the surface was already evident in Le Corbusier and Ozenfant's attempt to control color by dividing it into three classifications in their "Purism" essay of 1920 and then "discipline" themselves by choosing only the "constructive" colors. When those colors were later used to construct architecture on more than one surface, in a kind of delamination of purist painting, this desire for discipline was stepped up as the perceived risks became even greater. "Polychrome Architecturale" describes itself as a "dictatorial intervention" that "confines" each color to a certain value by invoking the "law of light" that defines architecture. It sets itself against the "perversion of minds" that results from overdecorated and colored interiors in which "one's mind was molded to new pleasures."[13] The mental disorders provoked by the uncontrolled use of color in the pursuit of pleasure can only be countered by the authoritarian figure of the architect wielding a color chart as a disciplinary instrument.

T A K E   9

Likewise, when Léger argues that color should be released from the dresses, hats, and make-up on which it has been held prisoner, it is only so that architecture "could command it unreservedly."[14] Architecture is an effect of color and yet it is used to control color. Part of the color world is controlled in a way that allows that part to control the rest of that world. But inasmuch as some dimension of color constitutes the very mechanism of control, color always threatens to subvert the attempt to control it. Architecture is a disciplinary effect that is always vulnerable to internal breakdown. In one essay, Léger calls for an ongoing regime of surveillance to keep color in check: "Color, being a new powerful reality, ought to be kept 'under surveillance' whenever it comes in contact with architecture."[15] The architect-painter is positioned as a surveillance device, scrutinizing the surfaces of buildings to make sure everything is in order. The remnants of the white wall embody this surveillance function, standing in for the designer, even affirming that the building is indeed "architecture."

If it is closely monitored in this way, color can supposedly become the faithful agent of the very control to which it has been subjected. In a public dialogue with Léger and Aragon on the status of painting, in which Léger speaks yet again of Le Corbusier's "gift" of the white wall, Le Corbusier describes the relationship between the painter and the architect in a way that makes it clear that the polychrome of the architect, in which each surface is given a single color, is—no matter how "sensational," "soft," or "violent"— explicitly a form of control: "I have seen that tumults can be disciplined by color, lyrical space can be realized, classifications realized, dimensions enlarged and the feeling for architecture made to burst forth in joy."[16] Joy is the product of constraint. Color has to be subordinated to the "mathematical" logic of architecture "whose controls are proportion."[17] After being disciplined, it, too, becomes a disciplinary technique. Indeed, it is this sense of discipline that supposedly triggers the unique pleasure of modern architecture. Color is transformed from an uncontrolled sensual pleasure that overwhelms the spectator into an agent of the pleasures of order, the pleasures of containment. Not the physical containment of those that occupy modern architecture but the containment of their psyche. The murals of the painter, on the other hand, which subdivide a surface into different colors, can "with one stroke open all the doors to the depths of a dream, just where actual depths did not exist."[18] Polychrome controls by maintaining the integrity of each surface that it might move while the mural opens up the space defined by the surface to a limitless psychological depth. Polychrome constrains the space of fantasy, severely limiting the psychological space it opens up. Architecture is understood as a precisely defined yet fragile psychological space.

Inasmuch as the architectural effect of surface is psychological, the architect needs to operate with, if not control, desire. It is not just a matter of classifying and thereby disciplining colors. It is also a matter of disciplining desire for color. As Léger puts it: "We must start to organize and classify the demand for color."[19] White is the possibility of such a classification inasmuch as it is presented as the only color that precedes desire. It is carefully positioned before the psychological territory that polychromy cautiously admits. Le Corbusier does not identify it with nature, the source of psychological associations. Its only affinity is with the sun, that part of the natural world that makes nature visible. In the three-way tryst between light, surface, and psyche that produces the architectural experience, the white surface leans away from the psyche and the body to bond with the light. The unique artificiality of white even takes it out of the realm of time and space. The white surface is meant to be pre-bodily, pre-psychological, pre-temporal, and pre-spatial. Inasmuch as it can fuse with pure light, it is able to isolate itself from the bodily world of nature and the psycho-physiological responses to that world and thereby act as the measure of both.

Of course, Le Corbusier has to suppress his own delirious response to white to position white as the test of desire. His "Polychrome Architecturale," which symptomatically associates the misuse of color with "those who do not resist dangerous caresses," insists that the white wall provides no stimulation. Indeed, it is the withdrawal of stimulation: "White acts on the body like a sedative; red is a stimulant. One is repose, the other is action."[20] The white surface is supposedly isolated from the fantasies produced by the colors whose sensuous operation it facilitates. The desire for white is a desire for the control of desire. But, like all obsessively puritanical rejections of sexuality, it is itself sexual.

While Le Corbusier repeatedly associates the white wall with "chastity," "purity," "virginity," and "decency,"[21] this association is almost always accompanied by explicit sexual fantasies. His "discovery" of architecture in the *Le voyage d'Orient,* for example, is accompanied by endless speculation on the sexual desires of the women in the dresses that are juxtaposed with the white walled architecture that he repeatedly describes. In a sense, what he discovers is this juxtaposition. His attention to certain architectural conditions is underwritten by an erotic charge. When he talks of the "burning pavements" of Bucharest, for example, he disappears into his obsession with the erotic entanglement of bodies, dresses and buildings:

Forcefully, they tell of the supremacy of the flesh, and a certain implacable sensuality is forced upon them. Bucharest is full of Paris; but there is so much more here. The women are beautiful to behold, beautifully coiffured even in the harsh light and all decked out in exquisite dresses. To us they are not like strangers whose costumes alone would create a barrier. During the long promenade along the via Victorii, upon their return from the races, they would recline gracefully in the carriages, in their Parisian dresses made of sumptuous but sober fabrics, their big hats, black, gray, or blue with enormous floppy feathers, or tiny toques placed over overgrown hair, and their eye makeup and lipstick always of a muted color, as aristocratic in appearance as the beautiful bodies beneath the caress of the fabrics—all these things urged us to notice and to admire them—and with the same sentiment we recalled seductive visions of fashionable Paris. One senses that, inevitably, everything here encourages the cult of the woman, and it seems that because of her beauty, she alone is the great goddess of the city.[22]

The tourist describes himself as "dazzled," and "tortured" by these "splendid women" who are compared to flowers. In fact, he makes the same comparison whenever he describes himself as "seduced" by a particular combination of dress and body.[23] The book is repeatedly punctuated by such seduction fantasies, whose preconditions are described in some detail. Le Corbusier does not hesitate, for example, to describe the beauty of young women that is lost when they grow older while discussing the details of their dress.[24] A very particular image of outward innocence and inward desire is systematically built up. And it is this obsessive gaze that is directed at architecture. Architecture is evaluated in exactly the same terms. At one point, Le Corbusier literally identifies "healthy, normal sensuality" with cleanliness, flowers, colored clothes, and whitewashed walls.[25] Indeed, flowers, colored dress, sensuality, and white walls form a knot that is retied many times throughout the book. The scene of the whitewash is not so chaste.

When speaking of "returning home after seeing the triumphal joy of white mosques," Le Corbusier describes the veiled women of Turkey in great detail and how the structure of their dress arouses an uncontrollable desire in him. He speculates that they are actually "coquettes underneath" their garments and are ingenious in revealing their individual beauty "in attires that show no difference of cut, style, without embroidery or any combinations that could have displayed a personal fancy. How do they manage it? Simply because they have the will to appear pretty, and thereby they perform their first womanly duty."[26] Sexuality is credited to the woman being observed rather than to the seemingly stereotypical desires of the observer. When likening the young girls and women in a Viennese street festival to flowers, for example, Le Corbusier speculates that they are "somewhat depraved, perhaps a little inflamed by their desires."[27] The would-be architect constantly imagines that the objects of his interest are as interested in him as he is in them and this fantasized exchange of desirous looks underpins the play between white and color that constitutes the architecture discovered on the tour.

278

It is not by chance that the most intense fantasy about color in the book comes amid the whitewashed monasteries on Mount Athos where women are excluded: "Not a single woman is to be seen; thus everything is missing here in the East where, if only for the sight of her, woman is the primordial ingredient."[28] In the absence of his object of desire, Le Corbusier stares at the white walls and has technicolor dreams. The plain surface is as sexually charged as the colored one, if not more so. The same fantasies can be found, although more discretely buried, in *L'art décoratif d'aujourd'hui*. Indeed, the very first time that the text refers to white walls and Ripolin is when its attack on the "abominable little perversion" for decoration is framed as a defence of the "purity" of the look of the decorated flower girl, the very look that had so obsessed him during the tour of the East:

Take some plain calico and soak it in color; the printing machine will instantly cover it in the most fashionable patterns (for example, copies of Spanish mantillas, Bulgarian embroidery, Persian silks, etc.) and without much expense one can double the sale price. I quite agree that it can be as charming, as gay, and as shop-girl as you could want, and I would want that to continue. What would spring be without it! But this surface elaboration, if extended without discernment over absolutely everything, becomes repugnant and scandalous; it smells of pretence, and the healthy gaiety of the shop-girl in her flower-patterned cretonne dress, becomes rank corruption when surrounded by Renaissance stoves, Turkish smoking tables, Japanese umbrellas . . . the pretty little shepherdess shop-girl in her flowery cretonne dress, as fresh as spring, seems, in a bazaar such as this, like a sickening apparition from the showcases of the costume department in the ethnographic museum.

Not only is this accumulation of false richness unsavory, but above all and before all, this taste for decorating everything around one is a false taste, an abominable little perversion. I reverse the painting; the shepherdess shop-girl is in a pretty room, bright and clear, white walls, a good chair—wickerwork or Thonet; table from the *Bazaar de l'Hotel de Ville* (in the manner of Louis XIII, a very beautiful table) painted with ripolin. A good well-polished lamp, some crockery of white porcelain; and on the table three tulips in a vase can be seen lending a lordly presence. It is healthy, clean, decent.[29]

The colors and decorative patterns that the text attacks remain acceptable on a woman. The role of masculine white surfaces, whether of the walls, the table, or the crockery, is to expose her charms all the better, charms that are yet again marked by the presence of flowers on the dress and in the vase. Everything is controlled. The feminine vice of decoration is controlled so that a certain image of femininity is sustained. And when the colors on the dress become the model for some of the surfaces of the room, with the arrival of polychrome, they remain complicitous in this all too familiar logic of patriarchal control. The shift from the subordinate peasant girl to the modern woman is not as great as it might seem. The liberation of color is not so liberating in the end.

AUX TROIS QUARTIERS - Paris

GRAND CHOIX DE
COSTUMES DE BAINS
MARQUES "JANTZEN"
ET "ATLANTIC"

MAILLOT en jersey laine... | MAILLOT en jersey laine... | CANADIEN en jersey laine... | MAILLOT pour bains de... | MAILLOT en très beau tricot... | CANADIEN en tricot de... | COSTUME DE BAIN en...

9.5

"Flowers, sun, joy. Who is going to wear these beautiful bathing costumes created by our big stores? And how soon." Illustration from Le Corbusier, La Ville Radieuse, *1935.*

Indeed, the whole attempt to control color in the early 1920s is explicitly understood as the control of the feminine. When the concluding part of Mondrian's extended essay on "Neoplasticism in Painting," which is published in the first issues of *De Stijl,* describes that form of painting as the collapse of the simple opposition between the outwardness of the feminine and the inwardness of the masculine, attained by purifying both, the threat posed to both is the feminine. The male element has to be "free" from the feminine and the feminine has to be controlled through a "culture of outwardness" that is understood as the meticulous control of the external surface: "*the controlling and tensing of the capricious, the determining of the fluid and vague.*" [30] Likewise, when van Doesburg calls for color to transform architecture in the following issue of *De Stijl,* it is understood as a call for a "masculine architecture" that can overcome the "weak, feminine architecture of the past." [31] An architecture emerging out of colored planes has to be distinguished from a decorated, and hence feminine, architecture. Van Doesburg and van Estereen's "Vers une construction collective" (Towards a collective construction) insists that the fixed "laws" that they deploy are opposed "to animal spontaneity (lyricism), to the domination of nature, to artistic *coiffure* and *cuisine.*" [32] De Stijl repeatedly defines itself in opposition to the stereotypically feminine.

While women's clothing might act as the paradigm of polychrome architecture, such an architecture is clearly organized around the control of the feminine. The discourse of liberation through color is from the beginning one of discipline and control. Theories of polychrome are theories of surveillance. The feminine is at once the model for the controlled surface and the model of that which must be controlled. And this is not simply an abstract philosophical argument. Mondrian's *Le Néo-Plasticisme* of 1920 provides the literal corollary when it asserts that "The female and the material govern life and society and hamper the male tool of spiritual expression. A futurist manifesto's proclamation of hate of the female is perfectly valid. The Woman in Man is the direct cause of the domination of tragedy in art."[33] The threat posed is not women as such, but the feminine qualities identified with them that can be found within the man. In an ancient move, the disciplining of the feminine is understood as self-discipline. The control of the surface is understood as the preservation of masculinity. In the oldest of ironies, the image of masculine inwardness can only be sustained by mastering the stereotypically feminine art of the surface.

To understand the convoluted logic organizing the discourse around polychrome architecture, it is necessary to follow arguments like Mondrian's much more closely. After all, he too is acutely sensitive to the world of fashion and describes his art in terms of women's dress. Like Léger, he uses metropolitan street life as the model. In fact, the whole disruption of the traditional opposition between inside and outside that he seeks takes its key from fashion. While Van Doesburg spent two weeks with him in February of 1920 collaborating on the second De Stijl manifesto, Mondrian also started writing "De groote boulevards" (The great boulevards), a short essay that explores the relationship between images and truth by studying the multiple images displayed by the modern city. The architecture of the street acts as a retrograde backdrop to the relentless mobility of heterogeneous images that end up fusing into a single image that has a capacity to capture the truth of the city, making it a model for art. The thread that runs through the essay, holding it together, is fashion. The essay turns on the ability of the fashionable look of the Parisienne to locate the inward in the outward, the truth in rather than behind the surface:

Parisiennes: refined sensuality. Internalized outwardness. Tensed naturalness. Was Margaret like that? Yet Margaret went to heaven. But was it through her outwardness? . . . Parisian: fashion transforms the boulevard from year to year. Every age has its expression. . . . Displays change more rapidly than shops, and I see architecture lagging behind. . . . Even immobility is relative. Everything on the boulevard moves. . . . Together these parts form a unity of broken images, automatically perceived. A Parisienne. . . . *Plastically* seen, everything fuses into a single image of color and form . . . A Parisienne. The outward is ahead of the inward on the boulevard. But not everywhere. Nevertheless the one is the other. . . . There is one fashion at a time. Parisiennes—one is like another in face and dress. An unconscious chastity: With

color, the face is covered. Did Margaret do this? . . . What is here on display is more universally wanted. Everything here is *real:* art often is not.[34]

Mondrian pays attention to the way dress changed after the war, such that
even undertakers "are demanding a costume more in keeping with the
times."[35] Everyone's outer surface is modernized to produce discrete events
within the kaleidoscopic movements of daily street-life. Later the same year,
Mondrian wrote another essay on the way the street collapses the distinction
between inward and outward, focusing on the display of color. By the time he
turned from painting to architecture, such observations had become the basis
of his prescription for architecture. His 1925 essay for *L'Architecture Vivante*
entitled "L'Architecture future néoplasticienne" (The neo-plastic architecture
of the future), for example, argues that architecture needs to become a "multi-
plicity of planes" rather than a group of volumes, while avoiding "facade-
architecture" in which volumes are simply concealed by planes. The multiplic-
ity of planes, like those presented by the city, is meant to fuse into a single
plastic image. Each such plane is to be defined by its color, one that is consti-
tutive of it rather than added to it.[36] Mondrian emphatically rejects the use of
color in architecture as an "accessory." The fundamental condition of a space
is produced by the mental fusing together of all the floating planes of color.
Likewise, his 1927 "De woning–de straat–de stad" (Home-street-city), which
is illustrated with the polychrome interior of his own studio, points to the
metropolitan street as the appropriate image for the revision of architecture.
Again, the model for the way the planar quality of "smooth and bright" architectural surfaces detaches itself from nature and thereby attains depth
within the surface itself, is fashion: "To denaturalize is to deepen. Denaturalization takes place consciously or unconsciously. The progress of fashion exemplifies the latter. Aren't our clothes becoming purer in form, even opposed
to natural forms? Doesn't the use of cosmetics show a dislike of the natural
appearance of skin?"[37] Mondrian, like Léger, bases his account of polychrome architecture on a certain understanding of the fashionable use of
clothes. Eventually, this understanding was turned into a kind of manifesto.
Toward the end of 1929 he concluded an article in a Swiss newspaper entitled "Die rein abstrakte kunst" (Pure abstract art) by insisting on the deep
truth of the surface manifestations of fashion:

Life as a whole moves toward the collective. Our cultural life proves this in its fashions, cosmetics, and many other outward expressions of social life where individuality is increasingly
lost in the whole.

Pure abstract art has grown directly from the culture and refinement of mundane life; from
culture—imperfect as it may be. It does not come directly from isolated philosophical or religious thinking of feeling. Fashion has a deep meaning: fashion is cultural expression. Although

it may be an exteriorization, like the various forms of art, it nevertheless shows inner content.

It is now commonly accepted that the content of our age is expressed by its outwardness . . . The "outward" is of the greatest importance in art, just as it is in life.[38]

The seemingly superficial play of fashion is accorded the greatest depth. Its surfaces offer the only access to the interior. Or, rather, they are the interior. The ever so thin surface is ever so deep. Fashion purifies everyday life, gathering all the heterogeneous operations into a single highly charged image. This transformation of three dimensional material life into a calibrated two dimensional surface is the model of art. Indeed, it is art. The very purity of abstract art, even its very abstractness, derives from the surfaces of fashionable clothes. It is clothing that launches the transcendence of the bodily world. In the following year, Mondrian joins a number of leading writers and artists commentating on fashion and argues that fashion needs to detach itself from the forms of the bodies that it clothes:

Fashion is not only the faithful mirror of a period, it is one of the most direct plastic expressions of human culture.

In fashion, however, just as in free art, we see a tendency to return to natural appearances. Nothing is more inhuman than regression. In order not to fall back merely into a new expression of the past, it is therefore most important for fashion to create an appearance expressing "man-nature" in equivalence . . . to oppose the undulating lines and soft forms of the body with tautened lines and unified planes so as to create more equilibrated relationships.[39]

Far from taking one closer to the body, clothing is the mechanism for detachment from the body. The role of fashion in Mondrian's thinking, which begins with the obsessive gaze at the Parisienne, is somehow desexualized. The desire to control the feminine is a desire to detach oneself from the feminine domain of the body—whether it be that of a woman or a man—the desire to escape the dictates of mother nature, the generic desire to escape desire. The fashions on a women's body exemplify denaturalization understood as a form of control. The Parisienne is not introduced as a figure of sensuality, but as a figure of the calculated abstraction from sensuality. Mondrian, as it were, heads towards the stereotypical domain of the sensual in order to transcend it, a double-gesture that becomes explicit when he identifies jazz as the closest parallel to neoplastic art that can be found in the city. Jazz appropriates the "open rhythm that pervades the great city" and thereby allows culture to "assimilate the machine properly to its own rhythm." Its potential is to cross and convolute the divide between sensuality and spirituality by locating the spiritual within the sensual. But it remains isolated from general cultural practice, restricted to bars in which the extreme capacity to "annihilate" form that it shares with Neo-plastic painting is unable to develop fully:

> No link with the old remains, for in the bar only the Charleston is seen and heard. The structure, the lighting, the advertisements—even in their disequilibrium—serve to complete the jazz rhythm. All ugliness is transcended by jazz and by light. Even sensuality is transcended.

> Free of limiting form, sensuality *opens*. So does spirituality. The two opposites have the same action in their different spheres. Sensuality deepened to the extreme is spirituality and conscious spirituality is expressed sensually. In the bar sensuality is not sufficiently deepened: it is refined but not spiritualized. . . .

> The dancers with made-up faces move and come to rest. No room for particular emotion. The makeup and clothes are culture too; but the bar reflects our culture's lack of deep inwardness. . . . Jazz is an "attraction." And so jazz is now in the bar.[40]

Mondrian works hard to desexualize the attraction of the deep surface, insisting that "Dance is not for the sake of woman."[41] In an interview from the year before, he rejects the attempt to ban the Charleston from Holland because of its "sensuality," arguing that "the dancers are always so far from each other, and have to work so strenuously, there is no time for amorous thought." Far from an orgiastic display, "with the Negroes, a Josephine Baker, for instance, it is an innate, brilliantly controlled style."[42] The spectacle of the frenetic movement of fashionably calibrated surfaces fuses into a single image of control, the control of sensuality. The relation between the dancers, and between Mondrian and the dancers, is desexualized in the very moment that the sensuous surface is offered as the means for transcending sensuality. Mondrian at once embraces the charge of the surface and keeps his distance from it. This doubled maneuver organizes all his accounts of his work. At one point, he even prepares some notes for an interview which carefully insist on the "sensual," as distinct from "sensuous," nature of his art works, unless the sensuous is understood as a "deeper grade" of the sensual.[43] Mondrian does not avoid the dangers of the surface by avoiding the surface itself. On the contrary, he avoids them by going deeper into it. Abstraction emerges out of the sensuality it seems to leave behind.[44] The fastidiously prepared surface of his work is seen to effect this delicate maneuver that is constantly threatened by the very sensuality that it deploys.

Likewise, the spectacle of polychrome architecture is drawn out of the fashionable surfaces of women's clothing but only after those surfaces have been detached from the bodies that prop them up. Spectacle is distinguished from seduction. When Léger and Le Corbusier follow Mondrian and van Doesburg in moving color from dresses to buildings, and even thinking of buildings as dresses, it is not to give the building the sensuality traditionally credited to the woman, despite their use of "natural" colors at the beginning. On the contrary, it is to redeploy, control, and ultimately bracket that sensuality out. Colored buildings are just as puritanical as all white ones. Polychrome architecture is organized by a certain fear of the very scene of seduction on which it is based. Its carefully modulated play between white and color marks a unique psychopathology, the subterranean operations of which are not only evident throughout the discourse of so called modern architecture but also throughout the millennial discourse of architecture to which it constantly appeals for authority. Indeed, it is arguably the psychopathology that props up the very concept of "architecture." The thin layer of paint on the outer surface articulates the discourse's deepest fears and desires. More precisely, it articulates its fear of desire, the overwhelming of architecture's defined order by uncontrollable rhythms and unpredictable flows.

Tormented by Skin

This entanglement of color, clothing, and sexuality is most emphatically marked in *Quand les cathédrales étaient blanches* (When the cathedrals were white), the book that documents Le Corbusier's three-month lecture tour through the United States in 1935 at the invitation of the Museum of Modern Art. In a sense, it is the companion book to *Le voyage d'Orient*. Its tour of the emerging modern world acts as the counterpart of the tour of the disappearing ancient world twenty-five years earlier. Ostensibly a book about reconfiguring urban architecture, the text is actually organized around a particular argument about color. It identifies the modernity of the States with the cleanliness and purity of its whiteness, a modernity that Europe has supposedly not experienced since its cathedrals were new. In the words of a medieval monk that Le Corbusier uses as an epigraph, "the whole world, in a common accord, had shaken off the rags of its past in order to put on a white robe of churches." The white garment purifies an age, cleaning away the detritus of the past to open up a new future. When the cathedrals are "called up as witnesses on the side of modern times" by the book, it is their whiteness that testifies to the emergence of a new age: "the cathedrals were white, completely white, dazzling and young—and not black, dirty, old. The whole period was fresh and young. . . . And today, yes! today also is young, fresh, new. Today also the world is beginning again." Whiteness is at once ancient and modern. While it faithfully repeats an ancient ritual of cleansing, the ritual has always signaled a new start.[45]

Having argued that cleanliness is a "national virtue" in America—as confirmed, for example, by the fact that "the immaculate personnel, in shirt

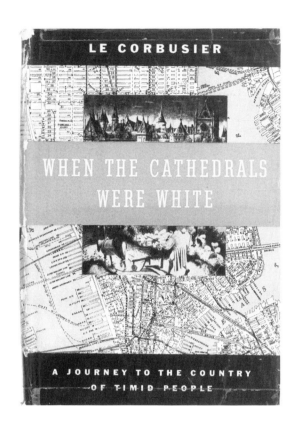

9.6
Cover of Le Corbusier,
When the Cathedrals
Were White.

sleeves, is shining white"[46]—Le Corbusier reconstructs the observations made in *Le voyage d'Orient* that organizes *L'art décoratif d'aujourd'hui*'s call for a white architecture:

People who wash their shirts, paint their houses, clean the glass in their windows, have an ethic different from those who cultivate dust and filth. . . . A true culture manifests itself in fresh color, white linen and clean art. Among the Cyclades of Greece, in the islands where a volcanic topography has prevented the introduction of the wheel—cart, bicycle, car— where transportation is possible only by mule-back; where consequently customs have remained millenary; where you still seem to recognize Agamemnon or Ulysses in the villages, the tradition of a living culture demands that, each Saturday, the joints of the stones forming the steps of the house and those of the flagstones in front of the house, be painted with bright whitewash—a radiant filigree. Thus in the Islands each Sunday begins in cleanliness and whiteness; life is magnified by this testimony: be clean.[47]

As in *Le voyage d'Orient*, such a regime of white is accentuated rather than contaminated by the presence of color. American towns, for example, are admired inasmuch as they are "painted with white and with intense colors."[48] While organizing itself around the image of a white building, the book is actually a manifesto for color. And, once again, the model for color is the lively color of women's clothing versus the somber black of men's clothing. Le Corbusier turns an account of the clothes worn on his cruise ship as it travels to America into a paradigm for the development of the machine age and, in so doing, makes his most extreme statements about the importance of clothing. The seemingly superficial layer of garments is bound into both the general ethical and institutional structure of a culture and the unique psyche of the person that wears them:

On board I asked the purser for dinner clothes with some color: the stewards dressed in vermillion are in keeping with the pomp of the ship; at dinner the rest of us are like people at a country funeral; the beautiful women seem like flowers in the splendors of their gowns. It is a curious end-result of civilization that men, who used to wear ostrich plumes on their heads, rose, white, and royal blue, a vesture of brocades or shimmering silk, should no longer know how to do anything but thrust their hands into the pockets of black trousers. Ten years ago Maurice de Waleffe felt this decadence; but his crusade broke its nose on silk stocking and shoes with incongruous buckles. The question has to be reconsidered and the transformation of masculine costume is necessary. It is as difficult as changing the ethics and the institutional state of a society. Costume is the expression of a civilization. Costume reveals the most fundamental feelings; through it we show our dignity, our distinction, our frivolity, or our basic ambitions. Though standardized, masculine dress does not escape individual decision. But it is no longer suitable. From what persists, we have proof that the machine age revolution has not reached maturity.[49]

The problem with America is the problem with the man's suit. America is far too obsessed with black. The colors that should express the liveliness of the machine age are blotted out by black surfaces. Although America is "animated by an architectural spirit which is manifest in everything, skyscrapers, machines, objects, bars, clothes,"[50] that spirit is repressed. Unable to handle its modernity, the country shrouds itself in a "funerary spirit." The skyscrapers like the Empire State Building that exemplify the greatest achievements of modern technique are condemned for being clad in black marble. The book is not so much a promotion of white walls as it is a demotion of black ones.

Clothing is the paradigm because it is the surface layer that "reveals the most fundamental feelings." As always, everything is a question of surface. Clean surfaces, like those of American cars—"gleaming, impeccable, without a spot of oil or grease, without even a fingerprint on the shining varnish"[51]—are opposed to those that have been blackened by the accumulation of dirt. Color is, as it were, the underside of the surface, waiting to come out at the dawn of each new age. When noting that removing the black patina from an old painting produces a "fanfare of color" by revealing colorful clothing, hangings, and marble, the text announces "Color? It is the blood circulating vigorously in the body. Color? It is the very sign of life. . . . Through the centuries painting incarnates diverse moments in time, turned into clean and brilliant colors."[52] Color is the life suppressed by the deadly black. To clean is to color. And color is linked to clothing. At one point, Le Corbusier even identifies the loss of the ancient polychrome, and eventually the collapse of Greek culture, with a change in clothing styles from the short tunics, which accommodated the mobility of physical labor, to the toga, which favored intellectual discourse.[53] The shift from body to mind results in a loss of color. Modern women's dress recovers a balance between the physical mobility, aesthetic charm, and intellectual strength required of the modern woman.

It is not just women's clothing that acts as the paradigm of this argument about surface. It is also women's bodies. From his very first essays, Le Corbusier identifies clothing with skin. In "Architecture d'époque machiniste," published in *Journal de psychologie normale et pathologique* in January of 1926, for example, he argues that "in general, the attention is fixed on the skin or the dress of things. In particular on the skin or dress of the house."[54] After detailing the way in which this outer layer can be reduced down to its simplest condition, the text concludes by warning that: "It would be sorry to see ourselves capsizing in the fashion of the simple if the simple is not more than a fashion."[55] The dress must be thinned down to the point where it is indistinguishable from the skin of the building's body. Within the fashion for simplicity is that which supposedly exceeds fashion. Effacing the distinction between skin and dress is the key to resisting the degenerate forces of the economy of fashion that is necessarily being engaged with at some level. The smooth surface that is at once skin and dress conjures up the image of a body, a woman's body, that is never seen as such. Early on in *Quand les cathédrales étaient blanches,* Le Corbusier interrupts its discussion of the misguided restoration of the surface of an old church to suddenly announce: "I believe in the *skin* of things, as in that of women."[56] This seemingly abrupt declaration does not arrive without warning. The book's introduction actually begins with a story of a confusion between propriety and seduction on liberation day in Paris. Although war torn Europe was unable to clean its surfaces— "no wax for the floors, no paint for rooms and houses, no soap to wash with"—its women improvised to make their own surfaces attractive, only to be rejected by the American soldiers:

The women of the suburb, like those in all of Paris, had dressed in their prettiest in anticipation of the liberation. They were adorned with smiles and joy. The women of Paris had been extraordinary: without dressmaking materials, without means of maintaining their customary elegance, they managed the trick of being desirable; without hats, they had invented ways of turning their hair into gold, bronze, or ebony helmets, a warlike coiffure which had made

them luminous and magnificent. Feminine centaurs on bicycles cutting through the fog of
Paris in the springtime or in the dog days, legs, hair, faces, breasts whipped by the wind, indifferent but disturbing, they passed under the noses of the sinister-purposed, drearily colored
"green mustard" soldiers. . . .

They climbed up the American tanks; they kissed the Americans, leaving lipstick on dusty
cheeks; they sat down beside the crews and drivers. Alas, they were taken for whores![57]

If everything turns on the coding of the surface and that surface is explicitly
understood as feminine, it is the puritanical reaction of American men to that
surface that turns out to be the main focus of the book. The obsessively clean
surfaces of the United States manage to repress the sensuality of modernity,
an explosive sensuality that the country at once makes possible and conceals.
Shiny black marble exemplifies a cleanliness that should expose the joyous
colors that embody modern life but has in fact incorporated the blackness of
dirt into its very fabric.

Throughout his tour, Le Corbusier finds himself caught between a euphoric
celebration of the modernized body of American architecture and the sadness
that motivates its coverup. The tour is exemplified by his search for naked
women: "On Broadway, divided by feelings of melancholy and lively gaiety, I
wander along in a hopeless search for an intelligent burlesque show in which
the nude white bodies of beautiful women will spring up in witty flashes under the paradisiac illumination of the spotlights."[58] While *L'art décoratif
d'aujourd'hui* had already insisted that nudity in the music hall meets "legitimate needs—purgative needs," the burlesque show comes to the surface at
four different points within *Quand les cathédrales étaient blanches*, each
time without warning. The architect complains that while the "intense powerful color" of the pulsating billboards on Broadway "excited us and gave us
pleasure," the "objects of enjoyment" behind them were "often mediocre."
And later in the book, it becomes clear that the "nude white bodies" he seeks
are attractive only inasmuch as they assume color:

Color enters in violently whenever money is involved. To call, you cry out; to cry effectively
in the uproar of the crowd, you use signs colored red, yellow, green, and blue. Magic incanta-
tion on Broadway. In the burlesques women with dazzling skin have golden locks, like metal
chiseled by a goldsmith, with the vividness of something cut by a chisel. Incisive casques (not
vaporous!), clean, curly, dense, lively, full in style. Along with that the woman is a healthy,
beautiful animal.[59]

The "dazzling" skin of the body for which the architect hunts, as if on a sa-
fari, is made more alluring by being framed in gold. But still this color does
not compete with that of the bright lights outside. As the book later points
out, the funereal spirit even invades the burlesque:

In the entrances of skyscrapers, in the halls of skyscrapers, in the lobbies of moving-picture palaces and theaters, a funereal spirit reigns, a solemnity which has not yet succeeded in coming alive.

Outside, in the street, along Broadway, on the other hand, the night streams with mobile lights. Inside, the burlesque shows, movies, revues, are never joyous, but rather tragic or desperately sentimental.[60]

The whole text seems to be organized around the figure of the architect looking at the "healthy" bodies of women. When he lectures at Vassar College, for example, he acknowledges the intelligence of the students, but only after admiring their physical condition: "They are in overalls or in bathing suits. I enjoy looking at these beautiful bodies, made healthy and trim by physical training."[61] Each woman is scrutinized as she enters the text. Yet the book exhibits more than a stereotypical obsession with women's bodies. Le Corbusier's gaze is also directed toward men. In fact, it is precisely during an erotically charged meal with some engineers that he formulates the central thesis of the book:

Opposite me are three men who are certainly engineers. Every five minutes one speaks. Silence and mastication. The three men have handsome heads, characteristic of their country: balanced, strong, energetic. . . . Those men won me with their handsome faces. . . . Several days previously some New York engineers had given a lunch for me at their club. Observations of the same sort. Considering their look, I notice once more the presence of the sexual question. Their eyes are striking.[62]

In the middle of expressing his attraction to these engineers, Le Corbusier theorizes that they are sexually frustrated. The thousand-foot skyscrapers they produce are seen to emerge from an inferiority complex endemic to American culture: "Relations of men and women. Engineers at work, 'hard labor' in the business community, the urban crime of frightfully extended city regions. Life injured every day by the unbalance of machine age times. I begin to put my reflections together: the core of the family is affected. Americans who live in cities often say: 'We are victims of an inferiority complex'. . . . Thus those thousand-foot skyscrapers."[63] Hence the subtitle of the book: *Voyage au pays des timides* (Journey to the land of the timid people). Le Corbusier's mealtime theory is that the nervous American male is unable to experience pleasure. Immediately after speaking of the healthy naked women of the burlesque, he points to the "sadness of strong-armed, full-hearted young men. Their spirits have not set out in search of the inner joys." The men are physically as developed as the women but psychologically they are adolescents that are far too "tormented" to take pleasure in life. Unlike French university students who engage sensuously with the world by living "in the promiscuity of alleys and dark stairways," American students are isolated in idyllic campuses which detach them from their own sensuality. Inevitably they end up liking the paintings of Caravaggio, whose studio was symptomatically painted black rather than white, and who exhibited "under well-bred external features, a complex disturbance and the anxieties of sexual life." Underneath all the clean surfaces of bodies and buildings dwells a cauldron of sexual frustration. Unable to confront that nexus of desire, Americans have "plunged into a hazardous puritanism."[64] Their obsessive hygiene attempts to clear away dirty thoughts. Buildings become manifestos of moral hygiene. Sexuality is taken out of its physical location and ghettoized in a tormented psyche.

Despite his seemingly puritanical call for clean surfaces, Le Corbusier opposes such sexual repression, condemning the division of physical labor and sexuality that organizes most of American culture. What he likes about Broadway is that it conflates utility and sexuality. It is like the "general store" in a new colony "where you can find whatever is useful: nails, string, shirts, and somewhat gaudy ties, shoes, and in this case, in place of finding them in red light districts, pretty girls in burlesque shows. Eating places along the way: supplies and passions, suspenders and girls, useful things and sexual excitement."[65] American architecture, on the other hand, supplies the utilitarian body, the pumped up atheleticism of the skyscraper, but constrains that body within a black suit rather than find the appropriate cut, fabric, and fit for its new forms of mobility. The skyscraper is hardly able do its exercises, let alone enter some kind of intimate relationship with its neighbors or occupants.

Le Corbusier's perception of the pent-up sexuality of the engineers turns into a complete theory of the American psyche, which in turn becomes the basis for reorganizing the American city. Despite its apparent obsession with women's bodies, the book is based on a homoerotic encounter. Its account of the meal with the engineers is reminiscent of a 1925 essay in which Léger describes a dance hall in which the men are just as concerned with their appearance as the women. The look they cultivate is that of the white shirt rather than the color of the women's outfits, but both stand out against the white walls of the dance-hall itself, an environment in which "nothing is hidden" and anybody who enters becomes "the target of every eye."[66] Like Le Corbusier, Léger focuses on the eyes of the men, who often dance with each other. He describes the dances in detail while insisting that they are asexual:

The men's dances are the most curious. Head against head, they dance stiffly, holding each other at the sides, their hands flat, their necks glued to their bodies. . . . The dances are frank and lively, augmented with perfectly suited imaginative frills. The couples touch each other very little. Whether slow or fast, they dance lightly, without any sexuality. The American dances and fashionable aberrations have had very little effect on them.[67]

The white shirt and the white wall are aligned with asexual contact between men. Not only between the dancers but also between Léger and the dancers. Le Corbusier's argument is organized around the same move. The body of the skyscraper that he is trying to release is that of a man but it is understood as feminine inasmuch as it is a body and the model for its release is women's clothing.

More precisely, the construction of the sexually inhibited man is accompanied by the construction of the dominant woman. Le Corbusier quotes an editor of "one of the smartest fashionable magazines" in America as saying: "The men are tired of everything, the women are tired of the men. . . . The women live with themselves; the men are in the city; the women seek entertainers or amuse themselves in the company of other women. American women are dominators and dominate."[68] He accepts and elaborates the comments. The organization of the city is to blame. Its division into a business center and distant suburbs harasses the male commuter: "the husband is intimidated, thwarted. The wife dominates . . . for the man, the woman is like a dream difficult to take hold of. He showers her with attentions—money, jewels, furnishings, comfort, luxury, vacations. . . . He is in a sort of perpetual arrears."[69] The mismatch between the spatial division of the city and the reality of the modern economy produces a dream world in which the woman rules by virtue of being an unreachable fantasy. More than just a reflection of a degenerate psyche, architecture is seen to be responsible for that psyche—a gendered pathology that so strikes Le Corbusier that it resurfaces in the very last text that he wrote in July 1965:

The page is going to turn over, a great page in human history, the history of the life of men before the machine, the life that the latter has shattered, ground up, pulverized. Example in the USA. In New York 15 million inhabitants, the horror of an affluent society without aim or reason. . . . USA: the women, psychoanalysis everywhere, the act without resonance, without goal.[70]

Quand les cathédrales étaient blanches is itself a kind of psychoanalysis. It presents its reconfiguration of the city as a form of therapy. Like an earnest therapist, it pays attention to dreams. Le Corbusier, like Léger, looks at the mannequins in the window displays to locate these fantasies:

The wax manikins in the windows of the smart dress shops on Fifth Avenue make women masters, with conquering smiles. Square shoulders, incisive features, sharp coiffure—red hair and green dress, metallic blonde hair and ultramarine blue dress, black hair and red dress.

The Greek coiffure, the Doric and Ionic of Asia Minor, predominates. The face, with its strong features, stands out. The casque is gold, platinum, auburn, sandy, even white.

The manikins in the windows have the heads of Delphic goddesses. Green, lamp-black, red hair. Antique-like heads, here one as if from a tragedy, there one like a Caryatid, Athenas from the Acropolis Museum. Polychromy. When polychromy appears it means that life is breaking out.

Next door I note the funereal entrances of the Empire State Building.[71]

> The black surfaces of the buildings are paralleled by the polychrome outfits of dominant women. But Le Corbusier hastens to insist that the dominant woman is just a dream, an ideal image constructed by the ruses of dress as a kind of fetish, a colorful image that is driven by the same pathology that takes all the color out of buildings:

This magnificent and dominating type of woman does not exist in the USA. It is an ideal. Do the women instinctively feel, through the creative conceptions of dress designers, that they will shine like goddesses? I sense that men, held at a certain distance by the hard labor of their normal life, would thus satisfy the obscure need of their spirits for adoration. . . . Shall I be plunging into the ridiculous if I make the supposition that the people are creating feminine fetishes? For ordinary purposes and for daily use, the little blonds of the movies. To finish off, the vamp—an American invention.[72]

> Supposedly, this image contradicts the reality that the majority of American women remain as "slaves" in the suburbs, as one of Le Corbusier's sketchbooks argues.[73] It is an unrealized metropolitan image. And yet Le Corbusier immediately acknowledges that he has met some women of this type in New York City and later in the book he abruptly announces that "Women are Amazons,"[74] repeating the description he had given of the students at Vassar who embody the trajectory of the modern woman. The assertive woman clad in polychrome is an ideal but one that is actually starting to be realized. It is the modernity of this image that attracts the architect, not its political implications. Indeed, it is those implications that guide his attempt to moderate the image. His 1947 book on the *UN Headquarters* refers again to the dresses in the window, suggesting that they remain too "provocative" while other dresses displayed in Manhattan store windows are already realizing the ideal of modern dress for a modern life: "Amid work and amid rest the institutions of bodily culture are constantly present: running tracks, basketball, tennis courts, swimming pools, walks, sunlight. Some day, dress too will change and adapt itself to modern activities; the precursory signs appear everywhere. Fifth Avenue, New York has show windows that are as yet but provocative, but in Madison Avenue 'real' modern clothing can already be seen."[75]

The whole discourse about sexual anxiety turns around the question of dress. It is not by chance that its account of the dominant woman pictured in the store windows and encountered in exclusive cocktail parties on top of skyscrapers is repeatedly punctuated by a story about a costume ball in New York. Noting the capacity for costumes to "satisfy the ambitions which struggle against the realities of everyday life,"[76] he complains about the fact that everyone else at the ball wears too much color. It is as if they are overcompensating for their inability to take pleasure in their daily lives. The architect describes the color construction of his own outfit in great detail, before insisting that "to achieve effects of color in costume many neutral tones are needed, and judicious accents of color."[77] The model for psychological well-being is some kind of "color balance" between neutral tones and diverse colors. White, of course, plays an important role in Le Corbusier's outfit. Without it, who knows what fantasies might be liberated.

In the end, the book's attempt to reorganize the American city turns on revising the outfits worn by skyscrapers. The body of the American building, like that of its citizens, is highly developed, to the point of being "athletic," but its surface clothing represses that development. Le Corbusier complains that most skyscrapers have been "fitted out with architecture" from the wrong time.[78] Most still wear the fancy dress of Beaux-Arts classicism, a feminine dress that turns a building into "a coquettish plume rising straight up from the street."[79] And those that have taken this old outfit off have done so only to replace it with a somber black attire rather than draw on the new image of feminine strength. Modern times require modern clothes. At one point, Le Corbusier condemns a French professor for trying to promote the Beaux-Arts in America by saying: "You do not walk into a battlefield or into one of the vast workshops of the world in dress clothes and patent leather shoes, mouthing discourses."[80] The difference is all in the surface. France is able to assist in developing the correct form of dress because its expertise in the surface matches America's expertise with the body. When Le Corbusier contrasts his experiences of New York and Paris he points to the surface: "I notice that it is the finish of the houses and the details which have an architectural purpose (very much on the surface moreover) which make up an important part of the good breeding of the Paris street."[81] There is a need for a "solid handshake" between the American body and the French eye for surface in the same way that there is a need for a handshake between the bodily world of the engineer and the intellectual world of the architect.

The whole text is literally framed between America and France, between the body and the eye that looks at it. It centers on the voyage between the two that Le Corbusier took in the "magnificent" ocean liner *Normandie.* Not by chance is his call for women's clothing rather than men's made on the ship, surrounded by its white walls, the very walls with which *L'art décoratif d'aujourd'hui* illustrates the "Law of Ripolin." The architect uses the ship to import an architectural outfit that will allow Americans to engage with the sensuality of their mechanized culture, an engagement the whole culture is designed to resist. In fact, the only example of such an intersection between sensuality and the machine that Le Corbusier, like Mondrian, finds in the United States is "Negro music":

The melody of the soul joined with the rhythm of the machine. . . . Psycho-physiologically it is so powerful, so irresistible that it has torn us form the passivity of listening and has made us dance or gesticulate, participate . . . the Negro orchestra is impeccable, flawless, regular, playing ceaselessly in an ascending rhythm: the trumpet is piercing, strident, screaming over the stamping of feet. It is the equivalent of a beautiful turbine running in the midst of conversations. Hot jazz.[82]

Le Corbusier's account of jazz is highly sexualized. Its not just that jazz is understood as sexual but the way it is experienced subverts the architecture designed to suppress sexuality. Through records and the radio, the black male is able to break the "implacable color line," entering homes and exciting women. Through his music, "the whole fashionable world of balls and drawing rooms—from the working girl to the millionaire's daughter—is delighted."[83] Modern technology allows the "immense and splendid body of black music" to stimulate a repressed culture and such a breakdown of the excessive puritanism of America is presented as a model for a new architecture: "Jazz, like the skyscrapers, is an *event* and not a deliberately conceived creation. They represent the forces of today. The jazz is more advanced than the architecture. If architecture were at the point reached by jazz, it would be an incredible spectacle."[84] An architecture that releases the sensual potential of the machine age would, like jazz, contain the pre-machine past as well as the present, putting "dynamism into the whole body" by putting people in touch with the irreducibly sensual origins of humanity.

The skyscraper, like jazz, is seen to be at once modern and the product of primeval forces. Le Corbusier's account of the implicit violence of jazz parallels his account of the violence of skyscrapers. The skyscraper is afraid to expose its savage origins. Ironically, it is precisely by putting on a black skin that it represses its sensuality. Le Corbusier's call to revive the white skin of the cathedrals is underpinned by a mythology of the noble savage, which in turn is paralleled by his repeatedly expressed desire for colored women. The lure of white skin is inseparable from the lure of black skin. The nomadic figure whose act of dressing acts as the paradigm for the white wall in *L'art décoratif d'aujourd'hui* is unmistakably colored—sometimes African, sometimes

Arabian, but always colored. Le Corbusier and Ozenfant's *La Peinture moderne* likewise concludes its discussion of the way that art transforms the naked body by finding the evidence of the transhistorical and transcultural value of abstract geometry in the pattern of a Zulu woman's clothing, as distinct from the flowery patterns on the dress of a Rumanian woman.[85] As was already clear in *Le voyage d'Orient,* the architect's desire for such white peasant women is exceeded by that for colored women. This fetishized figure is even more explicit in Ozenfant's *Art* of 1928, which likewise speaks of the "hypnotic potency of jazz"[86] and whose frontispiece is an image of two naked adolescent African girls. Symptomatically, the first image in the text is that of an "up-to-date" Zulu chief wearing a suit while leading a "tribal dance" of semi-naked warriors.[87] The "primitive" man civilized by a suit, which acts as the paradigm of modern architecture in *L'art décoratif d'aujourd'hui,* is always linked to the erotic image of the colored girl. Indeed, this desire is just as marked by the figure of the colored man as it is by the colored woman. Not by chance is the image of the Ozenfant studio that the book uses to illustrate the "Law of Ripolin" accompanied by an image of three African men ("Sultan Mahembe and his two sons") against a white sky. The empty white interior of the modern building is seemingly filled by the three black men that occupy the adjacent frame. The caption reads "Three black

9.7

Comparison of Rumanian and Zulu clothing from Ozenfant and Jeanneret (Le Corbusier), Le peinture moderne, *1925.*

9.8
*"Sultan Mahembe and his
two sons." Illustration
from* L'art décoratif
d'aujourd'hui, *originally
taken from* L'Illustré.

9.9
*Illustration from Amédée
Ozenfant,* Art, *1928.*

9.10
*Illustration from Amédée
Ozenfant,* Art, *1928.*

heads against a white background, fit to govern, to dominate . . . an open
door through which we can see true grandeur."[88] The white wall is, as always,
configured as the site of a fluid exchange between nobility and sexuality. Or,
more precisely, as the articulation of nobility as the control of an ever present
sexuality.

Of course, this image of control is infinitely suspect. Ozenfant's text is repeatedly punctuated by unexplained images of African life. Although the images
are not addressed as such, they are explicitly staged within a scene of colonization. The opening image of naked girls, along with another such image
and, symptomatically, one of "negro" architecture, were taken from André
Gide's "Voyage au Congo" that had been published in *Nouvelle Revue Fran-
çaise.* The gesture of colonization, which is, as always, just as sexual as it is
economic, is exemplified by another image of naked girls whose caption
reads "Negress seeing herself for the first time in a good mirror." The colo-
nial gaze presents itself as the delivery of clear vision, one that is tacitly associated with a subsequent, and civilizing, gesture of clothing. In many of the
images, the issue is one of clothing, or its absence. The chapter on the "Discipline of the Arts of Sight," for example, literally compares an image of the
hats worn by two besuited white city dwellers to an image of "sacred dance
masks" worn by two African men. Supposedly, these masks are already beginning to absorb the forms of modern European dress, forms that participate in
the universal "language" of "permanent art." Indeed, "Fetish-worshipping
Negroes" are seen to be "less primitive" inasmuch as they respond to such
forms.[89] The image of primitive truth that is used as the paradigm of modern
art is actually that of the subordinated other. It is not by chance that Ozenfant, who elsewhere insists on the superiority of white as the measure of
color, illustrates the book's short discussion of nineteenth-century scientific
"optimism," as embodied in Darwin's theory of evolution, with an image of
"African pygmies" climbing a tree followed by one of Darwin holding a mon-

key. The very first image of the tribal leader in a suit is similarly followed by one of a monkey in a zoo. Likewise, *L'art décoratif d'aujourd'hui* uses an image of two monkeys playing the guitar to conclude its discussion of folk-art, while using one of "Nimba, Negro god" to begin its discussion of the need to "respect" permanent works of art, as distinct from the transient forms of decoration, from older, if not extinct, cultures. In the end, it is not black culture that is the model, but the transcendence of black by white.

This helps to explain why the chapter that precedes the announcement of the "Law of Ripolin" is abruptly interrupted by an isolated image of a boxing match between a black man in white shorts and a white man in black shorts. Of course, the black man is being struck and the referee is white and wears white. The image returns as *Quand les cathédrales étaient blanches* concludes its extended call to strip off the repressive black skin of the modern skyscraper by saying: "A victorious boxer offers a most discouraging and pitiable spectacle: swollen face, disheveled hair. Tomorrow, washed and rested, he is *the champion!* The machine is champion and the new times are here." [90] Architecture comes to terms with its modernity precisely in the moment that it understands its deep affinity with "savage" people. Having completed the machine's violent reorganization of space, a clean white skin is meant to absorb the sexual force of the black body and discipline the eye. It comes as no surprise that Le Corbusier turns to black culture to reinforce the white wall by pointing to the way in which the sexuality of jazz reconfigures space.

Untitled illustration from
L'art décoratif
d'aujourd'hui.

The same argument already appears in Le Corbusier's 1932 sketchbook when
it describes a record of "negro jazz" being played by some French women in
a hotel on the Mediterranean Island of Formentera against the background
of a "pretty whitewashed wall":

A few young French-women have chosen the records. And they chatter: the music amuses
them. It's even more serious: they flirt with it. Is it decent to flirt? Oh, disguised in the de-
luxe hotel and in the virginity of Easter? The products of the first machine age have reached
their sexuality. It is a song of hidden, prohibited, forbidden sex. It's the world's great tor-
ment. Sexuality has been tamed (2000 years of christianity, priests and pastors): civilization.
One is right back at the starting point; nature pleads together with the negro, implores, begs,
desires, aspires: man, woman. . . . As long as mechanized civilization doesn't find a new moral
to put men on their feet again and men and women together the way they should be, the
black's song will unnerve us. Oh sociologists of minimum housing, why don't you study the
stages of the minimum heart.[91]

Although Le Corbusier's much beloved white wall acts as the site of this "musical copulation," in the end the scene makes him "sweat." Likewise, in
Quand les cathédrales étaient blanches, he ends up preferring the "controlled
sensuality" that defines the "architecture" of French dance hall music, which
his wife is able to bring into their apartment with the record player, to the
jazz of the dance halls in Harlem. His book seeks some kind of compromise
between the sensuality of the modern world made possible by American technology and the control exercised by French reason, a compromise that is fig-
ured in the "balance" between the white of the man's shirt and the

polychrome of the woman's outfit. Both the white and the polychrome are seen to open up sexuality and act as its nervous control. The minutely calibrated surface of the modern building at once marks and effaces an erotic charge. The white wall is as involved in this ambivalent gesture as the polychrome. Both are premised on the control of sexuality rather than its celebration or repression. In the end, Le Corbusier shares Mondrian's belief that the controlled surface is the one that controls the sensuous so that mental order is able to emerge out of it. The so-called abstraction of modern architecture is to be found within the very sensuality of its surfaces. The architect's capacity to control the sensuous play between colors literally extracts a new space out of the sensual world which in turn is used to hold sexuality in check. The psychosexual charge of the white wall is, to say the very least, as ambivalent is it is suspect.

If one has loved the surface of things for a long time, one will finally look for something more. This "more,"
however, is already present in the surface one wants to go beyond.

    —Citation from M. Seuphor in Mondrian's notebooks

TAKE

10

Whiteout

The psychosexual charge of the white wall can be found throughout the diverse polemics of modern architecture, even if it rarely becomes as explicit as it does in some of Le Corbusier's writing. Indeed, one of the unique roles of his numerous texts was to provide some kind of guarantee to the architecture, a rhetorical seal of legitimation that insulated certain practices from further scrutiny. Of those practices, it was the white wall that was able to proceed with the least questioning. In a strange way, Le Corbusier's evolving but insistent polemic about color contributed to the strategic silence around that wall, a silence that would eventually envelop that very polemic and the colored walls it promotes. As the outer layer of paint became increasingly codified, it ceased to be a point of discussion and the extraordinary investments that had been made in it seemingly moved into the background. But they continue to organize many of the everyday operations of architectural discourse. The discourse is driven by what it will not discuss. The psychodrama is still being played out.

The curious way in which the white wall vacates the theoretical discourse in the very moment that it becomes ubiquitous in practice can be seen by returning to where we began, the infamous Weissenhofsiedlung, which was constructed in 1927 as part of the "Die Wohnung" (The dwelling) exhibition organized by the Deutsche Werkbund. It marks the first moment of solidarity between the protagonists of modern architecture, the moment in which six-

10.1
Weissenhofsiedlung at night, as published in Bau und Wohnung, *1927.*

teen architects and numerous interior designers from different countries collaborated on a single advertising image—the moment, that is, that the very idea of "modern architecture" as a single trajectory could be established. The exhibition, which was assembled on a hill overlooking Stuttgart with the uncannily prophetic name of Weissenhof (white court), facilitated the reduction of the diverse tendencies and contradictions of the avant-garde into a recognizable "look" that turns around the white wall. It was precisely the stability and marketability of this look that led Muthesius to condemn the Weissenhofsiedlung for packaging a fashion that would eventually be discarded like any other, and Giedion to insist that it was not a fashion and would not be turned over in favor of a new style. The exhibition projected the internal argument about fashion that had occupied the Werkbund from the beginning outside the traditional limits of professional architectural discourse and onto an international stage. Arousing considerable controversy and debate, out of which much of the dominant historiographical tradition gradually emerged, the exhibition was critical in determining the fate of the white wall. In an intriguing twist, the debate around the Weissenhofsiedlung played a crucial role in both the dissemination of the white wall throughout the international domain of architectural practice and the generic silence that surrounds that wall—a silence that is usually only broken to announce, in passing, that the wall is itself "silent."

Color-Blindness

Two months before the exhibition opened, its director, Mies van de Rohe, wrote to a number of the architects and asked them "to choose the lightest shade of color possible" to preserve a sense of "unity." During a meeting in Stuttgart a few days later (attended by J. P. P. Oud, Le Corbusier, Adolf Schneck, Adolf Rading, Mart Stam, and Josef Frank) the architects agreed that "off-white" would be used for all exterior surfaces except for discrete parts that could be painted in different colors.[1] This level of agreement about white was unprecedented. There had, of course, been a long history of high design buildings that gradually codified the vernacular practice of white walls, running through the works of Voysey, Mackintosh, Wagner, Loos, and so on—a history that Le Corbusier's first villas simply capitalized on. But these were somewhat scattered incidents. White had been used to unify a number of large developments, whether speculative—like Tony Garnier's Cité Industrialle of 1904 to 1917, which envisions the modern city as a coordinated ensemble of buildings in the spirit of the Mediterranean, and Victor Bourgeois's Cité Moderne of 1922 to 1925—or built—like Muthesius's housing scheme at Hellerau of 1910, Oud's Witte Dorp (white village) at Oud-

Mathenesse of 1922 and Gropius's Bauhaus complex at Dessau of 1925 and 1926. But the Weissenhofsiedlung was the first time that this code was seemingly accepted by a very diverse range of architects. The success of the exhibition turned on this sense of unity within diversity. The collection of buildings could only be used as the definitive sign of the arrival of a new architecture if a wide range of architects from different countries could be seen to be independently operating in the same manner, expressing "one spirit" as Oud puts it.[2] Of course, the defenders of the exhibition repeatedly declared that this was exactly what had happened.[3] The seamless white skin that cloaked the buildings, along with the flat-roof that was the only other stipulation by the organizers, was the key to this image.

For the white to become the unambiguous sign of modernity, it had to be detached from its precedents. It is significant that Loos and Muthesius, who had imported the white wall from England along with their suits (insisting that it was the appropriate form of resistance to fashion), were not involved. While Loos had effected the transition from the whitewash on the pitched roofed country houses of Voysey and Mackintosh to the whitewash on the cubic forms of modern architecture, he was removed from the list of participants by Mies. It is not surprising that Muthesius, who had put the whitewash onto his own English-styled country houses and pitched roofed siedlungen, dismisses the exhibition by denouncing the cubic forms as but a fashion statement. The success of the exhibition hung on the strength of the perceived bond between the white wall and the flat roof.

In fact, there was a lot of color in the exhibition. Only about a third of the houses were completely off-white. Most of the rest were various light shades in the spirit of Mies's initial request (Behren's apartment block in light ocher, Mies's in pink, Hilberseimer's in light gray, Bourgeois' in light red ocher, and so on). But those of Bruno Taut, Mart Stam, and Le Corbusier (in partner-

10.2
Bruno Taut's Weissenhofsiedlung house, as published in Die Form, *1927.*

10.3
Le Corbusier and Pierre Jeanneret's Weissenhofsiedlung houses, as published in Die Form, *1927.*

ship with Pierre Jeanneret) were heavily colored. Taut's house deployed bright shades of yellow, deep blue, red, green, and black. Stam's row of three houses were lavender blue on the front with dark porches and yellow on the sides and the back. Le Corbusier's smaller "citrohan" house was pink, while his double-house was a white volume suspended on dark blue-gray pilotis and a burnt sienna retaining wall that reemerges in the roof terrace alongside green, blue-brown, yellow, and blue-gray surfaces, with gray around the servant rooms below and pale green around the staircases attached to the back. The interiors employed white, dark grey, yellow, burnt sienna, dark brown, and light blue.[4] These "orgies of color," as the press put it, were repeatedly attacked during the heated controversy about the exhibition. Because the controversy was dominated by Le Corbusier's houses and what he said about them (particularly his claim that the house is a "dwelling-machine"), it is not surprising that the issue of color turned on the relative merits of his and Taut's color schemes.

Karl Konrad Düssel's report for *Deutsche Kunst und Dekoration* is typical. After a short introductory section, it describes the respective colors of the buildings as combining to form a single "organic image":

The house by Le Corbusier, whose simple, powerful and clearly defined building-mass rests on slender iron columns, is pleasantly set apart from the pale green of the rest of the block by its white surfaces, overlapped by the gray cube of Hilberseimer's house. The houses of Poelzig, Döcker, M. Taut and Frank follow, which with their pale gray, pale yellow and white surfaces stand together handsomely, while the curve of Scharoun's house, with its somewhat mechanical form, provides the finish. Over this entire row of houses, which is a single unified, lucid, organic image, the massive block of Mies van der Rohe rises, yellow-brown, formally very impressive with its black frames of broad window bands and the roof-garden's T-shapes in cement. On the whole an image of singular beauty.[5]

The text immediately launches a long discussion of Le Corbusier's houses that starts with the "pink" of one and the "light green and white" of the other and moves into the details of his planning and philosophy of housing. The majority of the article is devoted to this discussion before it finally returns to the color of Taut's house and then allocates one or two quick sentences about the designs of each of the other architects. Having earlier been described as part of the unified image offered by the siedlung, Taut's colors are now attacked: "Bruno Taut, however, rages all too violently with colors in his small house, where they clash harshly in the small rooms."[6] The whole article is framed by the difference between Le Corbusier and Taut's colors. While other writers rejected all the colors in the exhibition, associating Le Corbusier's seemingly painterly concern with color with his disregard of functional issues, many contrast the "crassness" of Taut's scheme to the relative "subtlety" of Le Corbusier's.[7] Taut's colors were repeatedly condemned as "brutal," "screaming," and so on, in the press while also being criticized by most of his colleagues.[8]

Taut's interest in color was well known. He had long been an activist for colored architecture. Already in 1905 his journal argues that he will "unify" his painterly concern with color and his architectural abilities to produce "spatial composition with color, colored architecture."[9] In the following year, he used his very first commission for a church renovation to produce a multicolored interior. Indeed, he rethinks architecture in terms of painting to such an extent that he describes his multicolored housing estate at Falkenburg in 1912 to 1914 as a "picture" that has been "enlivened by an extremely vivacious and, at times, intensive application of color."[10] Its pink, olive-green, golden brown, and blue surfaces aroused considerable opposition, to which he replied that it was simply recovering the ancient tradition of polychromy. The manifesto for this recovery was the highly publicized glass house that he constructed with Franz Hoffmann for the 1914 Werkbund congress at Cologne, which embodied Paul Sheerburt's idealistic accounts of an architecture of pure color. Its spaces were conceived as color chambers in which the visitor would be suspended in the colored light streaming through the stained glass walls. To progress through the space was to progress through different colors. While the focus of attention at the congress was the intense struggle over the issue of standardization versus artistic freedom, by 1919 Taut was able to get all the architects from each of the bickering groups within the Werkbund to countersign his "Aufruf zum Farbigen Bauen" (Call for colorful building). In fact, the only issue they were ever able to unilaterally agree on was color:

We do not want to build any more joyless houses, or see them built. . . . Color is not expensive like molded decorations and sculptures, but color means a joyful existence. As it can be provided with limited resources, we should, in the present time of need, particularly urge its use on all buildings which must now be constructed.[11]

Taut managed to persuade both the individualistic artists and the designers searching for type solutions to standard problems of the most esoteric, if not romantic, vision of color. He envisioned color as a universal force that would enliven all cultural life. It was in the same year that he published *Die Stadtkrone* (The city crown), his expressionist fantasy about an ideal city washed in color: "Then color blossoms forth once more, the colorful architecture today craved by only the few. The range of pure unbroken colors again falls over our houses and delivers them from their dead-on-gray. And a love of brightness awakens; the architect no longer avoids the bright and shiny."[12] Having been laid over old spaces, color becomes the new space, the new city: "The glowing light of purity and transcendence shimmers over the carnival of unrefracted, radiant colors. The city spreads out like a sea of color, as proof of the happiness in the new life."[13] This seemingly mystical faith in color is, for Taut, tied into the search for rational solutions. His housing schemes were models of low-cost efficiency and their intense coloration was presented as a crucial part of that efficiency. The expressionist and functionalist fantasies were linked by the layers of color they share. Indeed, the functionalist schemes were a development of the expressionist ones rather than a break from them. When Taut became the city architect of Magdeburg in 1921, he described his attempt to cover the whole city in a polychrome skin in terms of rational choices, insisting, for example, that he takes detailed account of the specific lighting conditions in each location and chooses each color to "underline the spatial character of the development."[14] Likewise, he describes the layout of his 1930 housing estate at Zehlendorf as "supported and emphasized" by colors that can even "permit the spatial layout to be expanded in certain directions and contracted in other directions."[15] After detailing the specific effects of color, in terms of controlled rhythms of "passivity" and "activity," he argues that "these distinctions are supplemented by the architectural grouping of the forms."[16] If color supplemented and corrected the physical organization of the early schemes, it is now understood as the basis of that organization. Color is transformed into a basic element of rational city planning. Indeed, its role is predominantly physical. When describing the Zehlendorf development a year later, Taut explicitly argues that "it is just as impossible to exclude color from the process of construction as it would be to exclude the bricks of a wall or the iron and concrete of a structural skeleton, the use of color must be just as logical and consistent as the use of any other building material."[17]

But while calling for a rational use of color, Taut did not have a specific theory of color as such. In fact, he argues in a 1925 lecture on "Wiedergeburt der Farbe" (The rebirth of color) that there can be no such general theory due to the complex interaction of all the factors involved in the perception of a specific color in a specific place at a specific time of the day: "this chain of factors is not taken into account by any theory and is so endless that no law you could set up would ever do it justice." Color cannot simply be controlled. It is a form of play, but a serious one: "my hypothesis is that this spirit of fun—which color as a property of light definitely contributes to—that this spirit of fun has a cleansing and basically a more serious effect than even the most ostensibly serious things can ever have." Color is, in the end, more a moral and ethical issue than an aesthetic one.[18]

In the same year as the Weissenhofsiedlung, Taut published *Ein Wohnhaus* (A dwelling-house), which is devoted to the design of his own house at Dahlewitz.[19] It is one of the most detailed analyses of a building produced by an architect. The frontispiece is a color image of one of the multicolored interior spaces and inside the book the colors used throughout the house are systematically detailed and discussed. The back of the book even has a fold-out color chart in which each shade that has been used in the design is given a letter that corresponds to the letters on each of the numerous drawings. Every surface, including those of plumbing and fittings, is color-coded. At the same time, the book goes to great lengths to detail the functional improvements of the house, focusing on each of its energy saving features with numerous analytical drawings and photographs of the house in operation. Again, the precision of the color scheme is aligned with all the programmatic rigor typically attributed to modern architecture.

Still, Taut's use of color was strongly opposed in the name of function. Although he campaigned long and hard for the modern city as a polychrome artifact, catalyzing the colored city movement that was very successful in transforming the color of many cities, that movement was soon challenged by a growing countermovement that argued that the modern city should be white, a movement within which the evolving interpretation of the Weissenhofsiedlung played an important role. In 1930, even the Werkbund journal *Die Form*, which had frequently addressed the question of color, published an article by J. E. Hamman entitled "Weiss, alles weiss" (White, everything white), which announces that white walls are necessary because they expose any error and control any space. Furthermore, everything is being painted white because white establishes the sense of the present. White is the modern state of mind. It is both a color and a concept. White "has been newly invented as a concept, newly given life, and perceived as organically necessary to our new world-image [*Weltbild*]."[20] It is both a visual sign of modernity and an organizing principle of modern life. Something to be seen and a way of seeing.

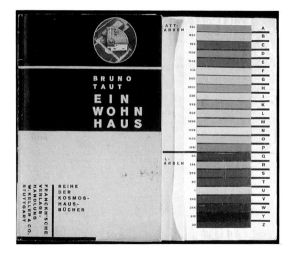

10.4
Bruno Taut, Ein Wohnhaus, *1927. Getty Research Center, Resource Collections.*

This white, however, is more than just the color white and the wall that is painted with it. It, the color white, the "tone" white, has become an important cultural factor today, a new expression of value and of the times. It is, seen colorfully, a characteristic of our understanding of the times, and a component of the entire modern world view of today. Seen in this way, white today, pure white, is judged to be a key formative value of its time. White—decisively positive in its impression and effect—not even considered a color earlier and not included in the color circle, gives our times their totally determined and clear colorful note.[21]

For Hamman, white is an attitude long before it is an applied surface. Indeed, the painter's frame has been "traded in" for that of the photographer. The whitewashed wall is displaced by the cinema screen. While "everything stands and moves in front of white, the white walls of the room," as exemplified for Hamman in Gropius's Bauhaus complex, that whiteness actually dissolves the room. The interior has "the effect of being exploded even at the level of pure impression, through white as a wall color. . . . Because of white, the room seems as though it recedes into infinity just as the faculties of modern man want to conquer and storm into the distance through varied activities."[22] White reconfigures architecture to meet the new relationship to the world.

A year later, Taut conceded this shift to white in an article entitled "Die Fabre" (Color) in an issue of *Die Farbige Stadt* (The colored city), the house journal of the organization that had put together more than 100 exhibitions, numerous lecture series, and publications, in addition to getting over a million buildings polychromed between 1925 and 1929:

The marked emphasis on function in architecture, the preference for smooth, simple and purely constructional forms, the flat roof and other similar features produced a situation in which color was considered as part of romanticism. White became the order of the day, white as colorlessness "per se," or expressed in another way, white as the fullness of color per se; white as the harbinger of absolutely functional architecture. What small amounts of color remained had to be subservient to the domination of white.[23]

Taut argues that the regime of white was just an understandable overreaction to the "total victory" of color ten years earlier, a reaction that must be "overcome." He goes on to point out all the problems with white. Far from a clean white shirt, the white wall is uniquely vulnerable to degeneration: "Of all colors white is the first to get dirty; dust and soot do not combine with white as they do with other colors to soften the original shade or even perhaps to deepen it; white simply turns into a dirt-ingrained, dead grey. Or alternatively—and this is even worse—a white house after a certain time looks as if it is wearing a dirty white shirt."[24] Even before it gets dirty, white looks "dismal" from a distance because of the effect of light intensity in the German climate, such that "the same pure white which in Mediterranean countries produces such perfect harmony should in our latitudes fail completely." [25] The functional role of white is transformed, if not dissipated by the local conditions. When Taut inserted his colored building into the white environment of the Weissenhofsiedlung four years earlier, he seemingly was voicing a note of protest to the association between white and function within the very exhibition that would end up monumentalizing that association. While every color scheme that he composed, beginning with very his first commission, had aroused considerable controversy, if not rejection, the emphatic rejection of his house at Weissenhof was the turning point in his campaign for color. At the same time, it must be noted that many of the critics of the exhibition used his numerous housing schemes as a model for the kind of functionalist rigor that the exhibition boasted of but did not achieve. The critics simply peeled the colored paint off his buildings in order to praise them. While Le Corbusier's color scheme is not subjected to the same level of attack, his houses are repeatedly condemned for their functional inadequacy and moral depravity (because of the absence of divisions between bedroom, toilet and living space)—so much so that he was quick to publish an essay in their defense. [26]

Taut shared Le Corbusier's feeling that architecture must satisfy and yet exceed functional demands, [27] and that color is a crucial part of both the satisfying and the exceeding. Of course, Le Corbusier could see no affinity between his color scheme and Taut's, reportedly taunting to his colleagues that Taut must be "color blind." [28] While Taut argued that no systematic theory of color is possible, Le Corbusier was dedicated to formulating such a theory as a fundamental part of the elaboration of modern architecture and his own houses at Weissenhof exhibit his highly codified Purist palette. Although he picked up Taut's expressionistic association of color with joy, his attempt to apply a systematized set of colors was intended as a polemical form of resistance to the kind of colors that Taut employed and the way that they were applied. This form of resistance is organized around the role of white. To specify the color scheme, Le Corbusier sent a piece of wallpaper from his Paris studio to his assistant Alfred Roth, who was supervising the construction in Stuttgart. On the back, the color samples were pasted around, alongside and over the largest sample, which is the white. The dominant role of the white in the samples matches its role in the building. The largest surfaces are the white ones of the main volume of the double house. The other colors above, below, behind, and inside that volume, including the pink of the smaller house, subordinate themselves to the white. In *Zwei Wohnhäuser von Le Corbusier und Pierre Jeanneret,* a book about the two houses that was published shortly after the exhibition opened, Roth explains the organizing role of white:

Le Corbusier generally never places color on color, color all around, above, below, etc., but rather always places color beside white. He uses white as the opposite of color. In this way he abandons indeterminate, cramped brightness for a totally defined colorfulness.

White expresses a certain incorporeality. The use of white is therefore decisive for the bodily appearance of a space. Concrete bodies decrease the space more or less depending on their color value. Against white, one can exactly establish the intensity of clashing colors, white determines the tone in the first place. Because of this it is possible to take up any given colors and make them harmonize.[29]

This sets up a whole protocol for the use of white. The text goes on to argue that white should be used on unlit interior walls, the ceiling because of its "disembodied nature" and walls lit from one side by raking light. The Weissenhof houses are as much a manifesto to the systematic use of white as the control of color. In contrast, Taut's house employed little or no white. But he was not simply opposed to white. Indeed, he defended his color scheme by saying that it was meant to be read against the white background provided by the other buildings and thereby would assume some kind of relationship with Le Corbusier's coloration.[30] It is precisely his argument that all color schemes are site-specific, and therefore untheorizable, that leads him to set up the colors of his building in contrast to the other buildings. Indeed, white had played an important role in his understanding of the functional character of color ever since his very first commission in 1906, which set the white gallery of a church against light blue walls, red-brown ceiling, green pews, and an orange-red choir.[31] This strategic role was already clarified by Adolf Behne's 1913 description of the Falkenburg housing, in which the color scheme that Taut uses to break the standardization imposed by modern industrial techniques is seen to be organized around the "brilliant white" that "heightens" the impact of each color:

The colors . . . are, besides a basic white, mainly a light red, a dull olive green, a strong blue and a bright yellow-brown. They are distributed such that when one enters the court one faces a brilliant white house across the way, the two houses at either corner on the avenue are light red and olive green. Between these poles the rows of semi-detached dwellings recede into the distance. . . . The colors of the walls are heightened wonderfully by a brilliant white on window-frames, sashes and shutters, cornices, verandas and wooden balcony railings, while the doors and trellises are most often a dark color. White appears again on the chimneys and arbors.[32]

White is the key to Taut's color scheme. Not only does it appear inside the color chart of *Ein Wohnhaus* but it plays a crucial role in the application of all the other colors. Not by chance do the colors produced inside the dome of the 1914 glass house begin with deep blue at the bottom and culminate in what he calls a "brilliant creamy white."[33] Likewise, the entrance door punched into the large curved black facade of his own house is white and the passage through the colors inside the house culminates in the two large white walls at the rear of the house. These two walls literally enclose all the play of color that goes on behind them. The house is a kind of intricate color mechanism that props up two white planes. As with Le Corbusier, color is intensified rather than opposed by white, and the play of colors always gives way to white in the end, regardless of how many surfaces are actually white. In 1916, Taut had even shared Le Corbusier's perception of the way that white mosques harmonize with the multicolored buildings around them.[34] His Weissenhof house likewise plays off the white of the other buildings, thereby emulating, as Karin Kirsh argues, his 1919 observation about Lithuanian villages that "there is nothing more delicious than glowing, colored houses in the snow."[35] Taut protects the white his critics accuse him of affronting. Still, the expression "orgies of color," with which he originally described the effect of polychromed vernacular buildings against a white background, is eventually turned against him.

Taut's orgy is condemned in the same terms as Le Corbusier's sexualization of the domestic interior. The critics repeatedly condemn the "promiscuity" of Le Corbusier's planning and tacitly identify this with his use of color. In *Das Werk*, a magazine that used color plates in each issue and regularly published articles about color in the city, Hans Schmidt portrays Le Corbusier's two houses as artist's studios in which "the bed stands ready for models and lady friends, with bath and bidet conveniently at hand" and then immediately notes that the colors are "muddy, almost dirty—overtones of black pudding and graphite." But the link between color and sexuality remains tacit. It is as if the sexual fantasies underpinning Le Corbusier's seemingly more discrete use of color are pushed to the background by the large white surfaces he presents, and the fantasies behind the white completely disappear in the face of the excessive sensuality of Taut's bold colors. Schmidt's text begins by talking about the overall prospect of the Weissenhofsiedlung, with the "delicate tonation of the buildings in pale-green, pale-yellow, pale-pink" that "look very nice on the green of the lawns and garden lots," but hastens to add: "with the exception of the streetcar colors of Bruno Taut of course."[36] Taut's house seems to overwhelm the wide range of colors in the exhibition and protect the white walls from scrutiny.

After all, the debate about color was not simply between color and its absence. It was a debate within color, or, more precisely, between different proportions of white and color. The Werkbund always intended to raise the issue at the exhibition. The very first agreement between them and the city govern ment in June 1925 includes "Color in construction and in the home" as one of the eight categories to be exhibited,[37] and much of the *Die Wohnung* exhibition hall was devoted to color. The organizers of the Weissenhofsiedlung also presented arguments about the relationship between white and color. In *Innenräume: Herausgeben vom Deutschen Werkbund* (Interiors: edited by the German Werkbund), the official catalog of the siedlung's interiors and furnishings, Willi Baumeister published an essay entitled "Farben im Raum" (Colors in space), which argues that the modern architect's primary concern to "dissolve individual compartments in favor of a continuous feeling of space" necessarily yields coloration. The colors that are deployed to produce the effect of space include those that are applied to a material and those of the material itself. While color "makes visible and tangible" the "constructive" condition of each architectural element, it can "kill off the material" that it is added to by transforming the material into "surfaces." The surface, rather than the material, constructs the space. White acts the default setting. Certain spaces (bedrooms, bathrooms, kitchens, and stairs) and certain surfaces (window walls) are to be "left as architecture in white."[38] It is against the "stasis" of this white background that particular combinations of colors are able to dissolve traditional spatial divisions in favor of a flowing sense of activity and rest.

Likewise, Richard Lisker, who did the interior design of one of Mies' apartments at the exhibition, contributed an essay to the catalog entitled "Über Tapete und Stoff in Der Wohnung" (Concerning wallpaper and fabric in the dwelling) that addresses the effect of the "rediscovery" of the white wall on the interior.[39] The new architecture is seen to have finally emerged out of the Jugendstil experiments when it coats its surfaces with white:

Wall and fabric colors were brought together in convincing relation, used as a medium of expression and subdivision of the room and in this way the white wall was rediscovered, which coordinates everything. In the white painted room the clarity of spatial sensation and disposition was surest and most convincing, all the details of the form and color of the furnishings could be developed undisturbed in front of this background and the minor disadvantage of glare and the disappearance of darker tonal values was tolerated. In this a form was discovered (rediscovered) which was completely convincing in its simplicity and which could be seen as one of the essential formulas for wall treatment in "closed" spaces.[40]

The white space turns out to be a space filled with color. It is not just the furnishings that are colored. The new reign of the white wall is seen to accept the presence of colored walls as long as they are monotone and not too strong. Indeed, different walls can be painted different colors as long as it is done in a way that preserves the "sense of space." Lisker portrays the evolution from the ornamentalism of Jugendstil to the stripped down forms of modern architecture as an evolution in color coordination rather than an evolution away from color. The coloration of the original experiments survives but in a different form. Color becomes an ever more faithful agent of the definition of space rather than its dissolution. Consequently, the Weissenhofsiedlung presented a wide range of combinations of white and color from which to choose.

Outmoded Suits

The choice of color was understood at the time as a choice of appropriate clothing. Like Le Corbusier, Taut repeatedly identifies color with dress. Colored building is colored dress. His "Farbenwirkungen aus Meiner Praxis" (Color effects from my practice) of 1919, for example, praises the colorful clothing of the orient, contrasting it with the funereal black of the West and offering it as a model for contemporary architectural practice: "In Siam one celebrates the dead in a true sense through a festival of the most luxuriant colors. And there one even lives colorfully. Every day of the week has its own brightly colored garment. Should we wait until the creators of fashion convert to color, even if it means unilaterally wanting to have an effect on culture through colored houses, before the colored outfit is even there yet?"[41] By modeling buildings after oriental dress, the architect moves ahead of the fashion designer, producing spaces that will match the new forms of clothing that will inevitably arrive. Likewise, Taut's book *Die Neue Wohnung: Die Frau als Schöpferin* (The new dwelling—woman as creator) of 1924, which symptomatically begins by citing Semper, goes on to explicitly relate the color of buildings to the color of clothes by appealing to the East:

The delicacy and restraint of the color, and the way the delicate colors blend into the large but gentle light-reflecting surfaces, is entirely in keeping with the costume of the individual Japanese. Just as he lays cushions in glowing colors on the floor, he himself wears garments of colored silk. This individual in his own room is supremely himself, and he underlines this through the plainness of the forms and colors of the room, and through the prominence afforded to his own costume.

It might be asked, in this connection, whether we can make the same use of color for ourselves. The first requirement would be the colorful costume; but, as this cannot be introduced overnight, and would therefore look like fancy dress, we should conclude, by analogy from the Japanese model, that our largely colorless clothing should go with colorful walls. And it is a fact that a person dressed in gray or black has more physical presence in front of a red background than in front of a gray one.[42]

While there was no single theory of color throughout Taut's career, if not an active resistance to such a theory, his campaign was always based on a sense of the development of clothing. This sense was brought to bear at the Weissenhofsiedlung. In *Bau und Wohnung* (Building and dwelling), the official catalog of the exhibition, Taut concludes his contribution by citing a section of his *Ein Wohnhaus* from the same year that deals with clothing: "The house must fit the occupant like a good suit; it must clothe him. The main aesthetic principle is this; the look of the rooms without people in them is irrelevant; what counts is how the people looked in them."[43] It is not just that the house is to be conceived in relationship to the person's clothing. The house is itself a form of clothing. The relationship between the color scheme of the house and the person is the relationship between two kind of outfits.

In fact, the modern outfit is more of a dress than a suit. In the same year, Taut published *Bauen der Neue Wohnbau* (Building the new dwelling), which argues that men's clothing is completely outdated: "with its insistence on the silly vest and the lined coat, its ridiculous tie pin, its extravagant overuse of fabric and buttons, its completely unhygienic and awkward solutions (athletic clothing excepted to some degree)."[44] At the same time, the text approves of women's clothing, which has changes that "are rapid and moody, but they are fluid and as a result have reached a sufferably good, simple form today."[45] Taut even publishes a drawing of the millennial evolution of women's dress to show that its modern forms recover the simplicity of those of ancient Egypt and Greece while noting that the "striving toward absolute precision" in modern dress is shared by contemporary architects as well as those of ancient Egypt and Greece. But he quickly insists that while he opposes the stasis of men's clothing he is not approving of the rapid changes of women's dress as such.[46] Modern architectural dress must change through progressive rationalization while avoiding the fluctuations of fashion. Taut's rejection of the generic "white shirt" in the "Die Fabre" essay concludes by insisting that the colors it calls for must avoid the "elegance and smartness which is suited only to the fashionable young lady of some boulevard."[47]

10.5
Illustration from Bruno Taut, Bauen der Neue Wohnbau, *1927. Getty Research Center, Resource Collections.*

Likewise, the identification of architecture and clothing in *Ein Wohnhaus* is accompanied by a rejection of fashion. While "the dwelling is closer to the individual than his own shirt," people employ architecture as "a collective product, of ready-made fashion" rather than the unique clothing of an individual. Even then, the "ready-made dwelling" is unable to keep up with the rapid changes in the "fashion in ready-made clothing." The "unwieldy" quality of architecture's material apparatus and complex organization prevent it from assuming the fluidity of forms of dress, even though its producers deliberately play on this quality to activate "the superfluous wishes of the consuming public."[48] Architecture ends up caught somewhere between the artificial demands of fashion and the realistic demands of modern functional life. The modern dress successfully negotiates the tension between them, satisfying generic functional demands without sacrificing the idiosyncratic look.

While the logic of clothing also organizes Le Corbusier's thinking about architecture, he attempts to detach the look of the garment from its fit, as can be seen in the reported conversation during a preliminary organizational meeting on the Weissenhofsiedlung held at Stuttgart with Mies and Stam:

"Architecture is a suit which has to fit," said someone.

"No" retorted Le Corbusier. "Architecture is more than a suit. The value of architecture does not depend on material and body size. Of course, both are elements in it: the technique and the spatial program. But the essence of architecture is the expression that can be achieved through it, the design."[49]

For Le Corbusier, it is not the fit that counts but the space defined by the shape of clothing. The body is just the prop for a work of art. And as an art, architecture is more of a dress than a suit. In fact, it is precisely when describing the interiors of his Wiessenhof houses that Le Corbusier forges the claim that women's dress is the model for a modern architecture, making the association between modernity, dress, and furniture that he will elaborate a year later in his Argentina lectures. His own contribution to the *Innenräume* catalog uses contemporary women's clothing as the paradigm for modern design:

And the chairs? I have this to say: the laws of traditional etiquette have succumbed to the advance of the machine (automobile, bicycle, subway, sport, office, etc). The way women dress today is abundant proof of this. The chairs that we have inherited from our ancestors were sat upon only in certain circumstances and in "polite" poses governed by etiquette. Etiquette went hand in hand with fashion, and with social relations. We have left all that behind us long ago, and yet we continue to sit very uncomfortably and disagreeably in our own houses. At the office, and especially at the club, or on the decks of ocean-liners, we have allowed ourselves *new habits of sitting*. . . . To satisfy reason is to make the lady of the house happy.[50]

10.6
Advertisement for
Mercedez Benz model 8/
38, using
Weissenhofseidlung
double-house by Le
Corbusier and Pierre
Jeanneret, 1927.
Mercedez-Benz AG,
Historisches Archiv.

More than a man's suit, the building is a women's dress. The logic of the dress underpins its white and colored surfaces. It is not simply that Le Corbusier's dress reads against the white walls that he provides in the same way that Taut's garment reads against the white of the other buildings. White is a crucial part of the outfit. The two Weissenhof houses are two different garments propped up on the side of a hill, each with its own look. Two models by the same couturier. This sense of stylish dress was literally picked up by Mercedez Benz, which launched an advertising campaign that associated the look of their latest cars with that of fashionably dressed models and some of the Weissenhof buildings. The white dress that is juxtaposed with the surfaces of Le Corbusier's double-house to advertise the model 3/38 sports car brings the fundamental logic of that architecture to the surface.[51] Yet clearly it is a fashion image. Le Corbusier's building is understood as a fashion statement, despite his insistent protestations to the contrary. The old etiquette that resisted the mobility of the modern nomad, and thereby blocked the modernization of architecture, went, as he puts it, "hand in hand with fashion." The free plan and the free facade that he offers are supposedly free precisely because they have eluded the grip of fashion. Not by chance does his and Jeanneret's "Five Points of a New Architecture," which was originally presented in *Bau und Wohnung* to explain the thinking behind their Weissenhof houses, emphatically reject fashion. The two houses came with somewhat nervously repeated guarantees attached.

In fact, all the architects offered such a guarantee by rejecting fashion. Just as Mies' speech at the opening dismissed fashion, insisting that the architecture on display was not a "modish phenomenon" but an international movement,[52] Oud concludes his review of the exhibition by asserting that: "What is present here in the germ of an idea is above style-searching and no longer may be destroyed."[53] As always, the architectural logic of clothing had to be detached from that of fashion. But the colors that were identified with women's dress proved more difficult to detach than the white walls. The layer of color makes the logic of clothing unavoidable while the white wall is able to conceal its own status as a garment to such an extent that it is even able to act as a figure for the absence of clothing. The white surface became so transparent that a recent history of modern architecture is able to say of August Perret's influential Garage at 51 Rue de Ponthieu, Paris of 1905, that its concrete is "completely exposed (though, admittedly, protected by white paint)."[54] White is seen to facilitate rather than interfere with total exposure. White is no longer seen as such.

Unsurprisingly, black and white photography played a major role in consolidating the white image. In the photographic reproduction of the Weissenhofsiedlung, the colors are bleached out. Mies's pink is turned into white and Le Corbusier's pink and pale green likewise disappears. But the effacement of color also required a complex and sustained discourse that was able to efface the logic of clothing on which the polychrome and the white were based. After all, it is not that the photographic reproduction removed evidence that was unmistakable in the exhibition itself. One of the major critics of the exhibition, Rudolf Pfister, who devoted thirty-nine pages of the February 1928 issue of *Der Baumeister* to vehemently condemning the siedlung and extensively citing other people's criticisms, was already able to identify the "lack" of color as one of the signs of the "new style" of architecture.[55] As Richard Pommer and Christian Otto point out, some of the on-site commentators perceived the exhibition as intensely colorful while others perceived it as completely white, the contradictory opinions even appearing in the same journal.[56] Furthermore, the significance attributed to whatever colors were seen varied enormously. While Adolf Behne had earlier identified the privileging of white over color with racism,[57] the biggest opponents of the exhibition attempted to mock its whiteness by identifying it with Arab culture. Color was, from the beginning, an open field of interpretation. A discursive labor was needed to spin the exhibition toward white and gradually remove the need to interpret that white.

The most obvious evidence of this labor is the production of the proto-histories of modern architecture that appeared simultaneously with the exhibition. Indeed, the apparent solidarity between the architects launched a small publication industry that attempted to define and market the basis of that solidarity. As Reyner Banham puts it:

That maturity [of the new architecture] was confirmed at Weissenhof when the buildings were seen, and seen to be internationally unanimous in style, and with its international maturity the style became explicable, to some extent, in verbal terms, with the result that Weissenhof triggered off a spate of books by German authors that aim to deal encyclopedically with the materials, the history or the aesthetics of the new style.[58]

The exhibition was accompanied by a book by Walter Behrendt (the editor of the Werkbund's journal *Die Form*) that was optimistically entitled *Der Sieg des Neuen Baustils* (The victory of the new building style). Significantly, the black and white image of the siedlung on its cover (the same one used as the frontispiece of *Bau und Wohnung*) is one that does register the fact that the buildings had different colors and a section of the text is devoted to the

10.7
*Cover of Walter
Behrendt,* Der Sieg des
Neuen Baustils, *1927.*

question of color. Color, in Behrendt's view, will increasingly take over the role of the ornamental details that modern architecture necessarily abandons to embrace the machine. Furthermore, this reconfiguration of the surface is functional: "It is an essential moment of the new interpretation of form that a certain colorfulness is appropriate to it. . . . The new architecture needs color, needs it as a means of design, in order to articulate the plain surfaces of its walls, and it needs it further in a *functional* sense, in that it uses color-values, to express, with the gradation of these values, the potential relations of the spatial organism."[59] Once again, color is conceived of as a structural element.

In the same year, Gustave Platz's influential *Der Baukunst der Neuesten Zeit* (The latest building art), which is illustrated by a number of colored plates, argues that color is important in modern building because it "influences perception." The book appeals to ancient and Eastern uses of polychromy, arguing that the "sense of color's worth for the cityscape" has unfortunately been lost along with the rest of the logic of the building arts. The color of the city "organism" needs to be unified. Indeed, color is the "highest law" of the city. It is the colors that "maintain a closed impression of space." Space is to be defined by color. Certain colors "create a territory of their own."[60] This definition of space may require the collaboration of the painter and the architect, with the painter often taking the stronger role. Their decisions will be subjective. When Platz goes on to detail the strength of different types of coloration in the work of different architects, he insists, like Taut, that the intuition and experience involved in choosing the correct color cannot be reduced to a color theory. Although color is responsible for the effect of space, it cannot be codified.

These accounts of the structural role of color are aligned with a rejection of fashion. Indeed, Behrendt establishes the role of his book as the identification of the "intellectual atmosphere" that distinguishes the new style from that of a fashion. The book supposedly goes behind the aesthetic surface to demonstrate that the new architecture emerges from something more than the desire for a fashionable look:

With the attempts at a renewal of architecture we are not dealing with a capricious fashion in art [*Kunstmode*] or with any kind of new ism, but rather with an intellectual movement with which we must concern ourselves . . . it is not enough to simply value its intentions, even valuing its previous accomplishments from a purely aesthetic view point. In order to grasp its essence one has to dig deeper to seek out the intellectual atmosphere from which this movement grew up.[61]

Likewise, Platz carefully distinguishes the style of contemporary architecture from fashion. His account of style begins by saying that the style of an epoch is manifested in its "dwelling, clothing, custom, visual arts, music or literature."[62] It is not by chance that dwelling is immediately followed by clothing. Having cited Semper on the relationship between the work and the material fabric, Riegl's elaboration of Semper, and Behren's response, the text goes on to bind architecture to clothing: "New forms grow for our time, the house and garment of the new humanity grows out of chaotic fermentation in a process of formation in whose decisive moments we are now living and whose outcome will be the new style."[63] But what unites architecture and clothing is immediately disassociated from the forces of fashion so obviously at work in clothes. Style is distinguished from fashion as the channel of a large river is distinguished from its multiple tributaries. Its relentless development in one direction resists the "moody escapades" and "extravagances" of fashion that are appropriate to the "decorator" or "exhibition architect." At the same time, fashion is not simply rejected:

Even fashion has its metaphysical underpinnings, just as it has its material background. Mass production and the hunger for goods are merely the instigators of fashion; its actual executioner is the by now familiar aspect of [cultural] weariness, the quick boredom attendant on the inevitable repetition, the demand for new impressions and effects.

The changes of fashion are determined by the tempo of life of a given time.... Without a doubt fashion alternates today faster than ever. Precisely in our times, the saying is especially valid that nothing stays the same except change.[64]

While the modern architect has to resist the rhythms of fashion, ensuring that "the new bears the sign of necessity on its brow," those rhythms articulate the very modernity that architecture must capture. The channel of the river cannot simply be detached from its seemingly gratuitous tributaries.

A similar argument can be found in Behne's *Neues Wohnen—Neues Bauen* (New dwelling—new building), which was published in the same year. Again, the book is organized a thinly veiled clothing analogy. Its first image compares suits of armor to the modern machinery that architecture is emulating and later it literally compares clothing styles with architectural forms. This sense of architecture as clothing is again distinguished from the sense of architectural fashions, and yet Behne, like Muthesius when reviewing the Weissenhofsiedlung, is acutely aware of the enigmas of such a distinction. When the book begins by addressing fashion it seems clear that the new architecture is emphatically opposed to fashion: "This direction may only claim necessity, liveliness, capacity for development, and thus permanence, for only those new forms which are the logical result and emanation of a new mode

10.8
Illustration from Adolf Behne, Neues Wohnen—Neues Bauen, *1927. Getty Research Center, Resource Collections.*

of life, whereas the 'new forms' thought up in the design studio remain transient matters of fashion—even when they have been thought up with wit, taste and talent." But Behne immediately notes in parenthesis that this distinction is a difficult one to make: "it is not always easy even for the practiced observer to differentiate 'new fashion' from 'new work'." The difficulty arises because such fashionable tendencies are seen to continue the thinking behind the Jugendstil practices of the young Peter Behrens and Henry van de Velde, architects whose work eventually developed into and pioneered modern forms. After tracing this development, Behne concludes: "Above all we have to be fair and admit that even the best representatives of the new work had their beginnings in another camp, that is, that even the best in fashion has developed into work. You cannot blame them for their origin, indeed, it would be strange if it were any other way."[65] The modern form of resistance to fashion emerges out of the very world of fashion.

A year after the exhibition, Behne published *Eine Stunde Architektur* (An hour of architecture), which has a photograph of the roofdeck of Le Corbusier's Weissenhof double-house on the cover onto which a lady's dress hat has symptomatically been montaged. The relationship between clothing and architecture is repeatedly raised by the book. The frontispiece is a sequence of images running from an African mask to a helmet of a suit of armor to a Prussian helmet of the first world war to the bald held of Paul Scheerbart. Later the image of a woman in an ornate dress from 1883 is associated with a cluttered Berlin apartment and contrasted with a drawing of a man in a white tennis outfit that is associated with the stark white interior of Hannes Meyer's Co-op Zimmer of 1926. The corresponding text argues that old forms correspond to old needs and therefore no longer satisfy contemporary demands. New forms, like those of the white interior, even go beyond contemporary needs, projecting us into the future. Throughout the text, images of the old are contrasted with images of the new, with projects by Bruno Taut, Mart Stam, Hannes Meyer, Karl Schneider, Le Corbusier, and the Weissenhofsiedlung itself, exemplifying the new. The floor plan of Taut's own house at Dahlewitz, for example, is contrasted to that of a sixteenth-century house. Contemporary forms supposedly emerge from contemporary functions. Behne everywhere insists on the priority of function. Alongside an image of Le Corbusier's double-house at Weissenhof, he asks "How does this principle of the 100% performance in housing look like?" and accepts Le Corbusier's definition of the house as a dwelling-machine. The machine is the "prototype" for a new architecture. But a warning is immediately issued. Machine-like forms will be just as much fashions as those they replace. The white surface can easily establish a fashion rather than resist it: "The reference would be misunderstood though when one would take the machine as a stylis-

10.9
*Illustration from Adolf
Behne,* Eine Stunde
Architektur, *1928.*

10.10
*Illustration from Heinz
and Bodo Rasch,* Wie
Bauen?, *1928.*

tic concept and when one would believe that the house, the dwelling, the furniture, should look smooth, cold, polished and white in a falsely understood constructivism. This would only mean that one would arrive at a new derivation of Jugendstil, a new taste, a new fashion."[66] To avoid the relentless slippage between function and fashion, Behne insists that satisfying contemporary functional demands is insufficient. New forms need to generate new functions. When the text earlier compares an image of a woman in old-fashioned house-dress reclining seductively in a rococo chair with an image of a woman in a modern dress sitting upright reading in a contemporary chair designed by the architects Heinz and Bodo Rasch, for example, the new chair is meant to produce a new way of sitting. Like modern clothing, it keeps its distance from the world of fashion to which it is inevitably related. The white tennis outfit embodies this distance. In fact, Behne had used the same drawing in a 1925 issue of *Wasmuth's Monatshefte für Baukunst* where he associates it with some smooth white bowls and jugs in an essay that identifies decoration with "angst-psychosis." Again, the argument is illustrated with comparisons between clothing and architecture. A year later, the essay was republished in the third issue of the magazine *ABC* (the first issue of which had published Lissitsky's claim that white is the color of hygiene and space). And not by chance does Behne's drawing of the modern tennis player appear there alongside an essay by Lebeau attacking fashion but embracing clothing.

A similar logic can be found in Heinz and Bodo Rasch's own *Wie Bauen?* (How shall we build?) of 1928, a largely technical book that examines the materials and construction technologies of modern architecture in great detail. Clothing and fashion provide the framework. An early section of the text, entitled "The Intentions of Design Succumb to Fashion," is illustrated by an image contrasting old and new clothing styles which is placed opposite an image that contrasts old and new building styles. Architectural transforma-

tions are identified with transformations in clothing. The modern dress is associated with the sleek lines of the Berliner Tageblatt building designed by Mendelssohn and Neutra the year before. And the fashionable status of both is not simply dismissed. Contemporary forms are no less bound to the logic of fashion than those of Jugendstil:

And so as the times change, houses and neighborhoods become unmodern, are abandoned by the inhabitants and thus freed up for those of lesser means, like the kind of mistress' worn-out dress that the serving-maid inherits.... A sure sign of fashion is that people are quickly sick of it. Thus all historical forms of building succeed each other at a rapid pace.... Intentions of forms are subject to fashion, Jugendstil and Cubism too. Forms derived from organic and mechanical functions only appear to be a revolutionary step; in truth they are just a change of scenery [*changement des decorations*] Fashions change quickly.... The dwelling-place must, therefore, take changes into account and, for this reason, be variable.[67]

A few pages later, the Weissenhofsiedlung is introduced as the sign of the future. The book is everywhere influenced by the exhibition (for which the Rasch brothers had done interiors for Mies and Behrens). Its cover is made up of images of Gropius and Oud's houses under construction while the interior shows the whole siedlung and virtually all of the individual buildings both finished and under construction. The question of the finish is repeatedly raised by these images but is not addressed in the text other than by way of its discussion of the particular technologies that make a smooth surface possible. The Weissenhofsiedlung is placed in the context of clothing but its specific clothing is not addressed. Color is no longer part of the argument.

While color, clothing, and fashion were originally bound so tightly together, the question of color very quickly fades away from the discourse. Eventually, the clothing analogy would also be edited out, leaving only the obligatory attack on fashion, which is repeated like some kind of religious mantra by successive generations of architects and writers.[68] This trend first becomes visible in the shorter texts, even the briefest of which contain the obligatory dismissal of fashion. Shortly after the exhibition opened, Ludwig Hilberseimer publishes his "Internationale neue Baukunst" that was commissioned by the Werkbund and appeared as a special issue of *Modern Bauform* before being published as a book a year later. It opens with an image of the Weissenhofsiedlung under which the introductory text rejects fashion: "It is not an affair of fashion as is so often assumed, but rather an elementary expression of a new way of thinking about architecture."[69] It is a picture book with a telegraphic text, in the tradition of Gropius's *Internationale Architecture* of 1925 (whose second revised edition also appeared in 1927), which presents the reader with a succession of images of buildings from around the world, a panorama that consolidates the aesthetic formula the fashionable status of which is being so emphatically dismissed, but its disinterest in color indicates the direction that the more substantial texts would take. In 1929, even Taut's own *Modern Architecture,* within which images of the Weissenhof buildings again play an important role, does not address color. The clothing argument remains but in a very watered down version alongside the generic attack on fashion.

One of the last texts to maintain the bond between color, clothing, and fashion is Shelden Cheney's substantial, but often overlooked, *The New World Architecture* of 1930, which attempted to provide the first "bird's eye" history of architecture "from the modern point of view." Having introduced the idea of a new architecture, the first chapter immediately turns to the Weissenhofsiedlung, which is presented as the "most concentrated group, the outstanding object-lesson" within the German context that is supposedly leading the world in the production of innovative architecture.[70] Images of the exhibition, "wherein all the buildings breathe a strange geometric unity," keep turning up in the book. By the end, most of the houses have been shown. In fact, the book is dominated by a succession of images of white buildings by Baillie Scott, Voysey, Le Corbusier, Gropius, Oud, Schindler, Mallet-Stevens, and so on, into which the Weissenhof buildings are grafted. At one point, this whiteness is explicitly defended. The "hospital-like" starkness of white walls is supposedly made attractive by the best architects because they operate as artists: "Frankly, many of the earliest Functional houses had that bareness, that overemphasized whiteness. But no, even in the hands of Le Corbusier or Gropius or Oud (because they are artists) there is already an overvalue, a thing added beyond mere practicality."[71] Such architects manipulate plain surfaces until they achieve a "decorative effect" that replaces that of the ornament and color that has been removed. The white wall takes over the role of those elements whose removal it advertises. Yet again, this transformation of the surface is understood in terms of clothing. Late nineteenth- and early twentieth-century eclecticism is seen to have concentrated on the outer layer, "dressing" the building in a "decorative coat." Likewise, the practitioners of Art Nouveau and the Viennese Secessionists (with the exception of Josef Hoffmann) are only concerned with "the flaunting of a more attractive decorative garment."[72] This degenerate concern for decorative dress is exemplified by the confusion between fashion design and architecture at the 1925 exposition in Paris. Cheney condemns the "seductively millinered building . . . 'stunts' of fashion experts, window dressers, and stage costumers who imagined that they were for the moment architects."[73] Contemporary work by Parisian architects is likewise described as being dominated by "its own effective if somewhat dressmaker-y accent."[74] Dressmakers act like architects and architects act like dressmakers. Opposing such "modish European wall-dressing," the book concludes that the best architects, like Wright, Hoffmann and Le Corbusier, "are the ones who never forgot usefulness in their hurry for a new sort of 'look'; they accepted as fundamental that function would determine form. . . . They knew better than try to 'dress' buildings with easily arranged clothes."[75]

It would seem that modern architecture abandons all the layers of clothing. Throughout the text, the new architecture is portrayed as being "stripped" down to the "naked body" of the building to match the "modern clean athletic body" of its inhabitants. But yet again this does not simply include the removal of all clothing. The best buildings are the ones that "frankly stated in their outer garb the sort of bodies confined within."[76] Frank Lloyd Wright's Prairie Houses, for example, are praised for "creating a different outer garment, quite unlike the old . . . the most striking, the most brilliant outward, architectural investitures known to these times."[77] The new architecture is a new form of clothing, such that at the very end of the book, the age of mobility facilitated by the machine can be symbolized by "the woman of today, wearing scarce a third of the clothes that her grandmother carried around."[78] The look of modern architecture turns out to be that of the trimmed down modern dress. And just as the new building is not naked, it is not white either. Cheney's concern for clothing is paralleled by a concern for color. Immediately after defending the decorative effect of artistically arranged white walls, he admits that the Weissenhofsiedlung has a little too much "hospital-like monotony and regimentation about it," too much "sickroom bareness."[79] He ends up calling for color to restore the values lost in the ruthless elimination of everything that is superfluous to function. Color supposedly restores humanity to modern architecture: "Color makes the house human and intimate for us. And it is in the realm of color, of consciously designed color backgrounds to living, that the next great advance is likely to come."[80] The fabrics stitched together to make the modern dress of a building must be colored. Cheney's proto-history consolidates the longstanding bond between color and clothing.

Yet by the time of Pevsner's enormously influential *Pioneers of the Modern Movement* six years later, the interrelated questions of color and clothing had gone away. The famous text systematically avoids color. It even overlooks the whiteness of the walls that it promotes, while referring to the whiteness of the precursors to modern architecture a couple of times. At one point, it includes "whiteness" in the list of features of C.F.A. Voysey's furniture that are "of particular importance for the coming Modern Movement," and a few pages later it describes the "whiteness of the walls" of Voysey's houses. Likewise, when referring to the upper floors of Louis Sullivan's Carson Pirie Scott department store, it argues that an image of the "horizontal windows with the unbroken white bands which separate them horizontally would no doubt be misdated by nearly everybody."[81] But the text does not address the whiteness of modern architecture. Whiteness is tacitly understood as one of the key traits of that architecture, such that its presence can be used to identify precursors, but is never discussed as such. Even when comparing the surfaces of Loos's buildings to those of the 1920s the book does not point to the whiteness that is one of the most obvious features that makes that comparison possible.

A year later, Behrendt is able to publish his *Modern Building* without promoting color. The color argument that he had put forward to defend the Weissenhofsiedlung has been watered down to a brief reference to Oud's understanding of the "functional means of color."[82] Indeed, the text retells a story that opposes the play of colors of Henry van de Velde's own house, which "matched the mistress's dress," to the superior "white enamel" that was restricted to the nursery and bathroom.[83] The white wall is tacitly accorded its unique status and the clothing argument gives way to that of hygiene. Later, the white is explicitly theorized in terms of dematerialization:

The loosening of the building bulk and the dynamic grouping of the masses afford by means of the resulting shadows all the molding desirable, and lead to a plain treatment of the facades which are consequently designed for graphic rather than plastic effects. This explains the preference for smooth, white-colored plaster for covering the outer walls; it is favored because it emphasizes the intended effect by strengthening the black–white appearance. And this kind of surface treatment, showing no longer any joints, also helps to express the tendency toward dematerializing of the walls, the lightness of its mass and weight, and to articulate its new character as a mere skin, which it achieved with the adoption of modern skeleton construction.[84]

The white wall conveys the new status of the surface to which it is applied, the skin rather than the clothing of a modern body. While the status of this skin will preoccupy Giedion's *Space, Time and Architecture,* first delivered as a series of lectures in 1938 and 1939, the book has no difficulty overlooking the whiteness of that surface, let alone all the other colors that accompany it. Likewise, the successive generations of canonic historians have had no difficulty overlooking the question of color. Between the Weissenhofsiedlung and Pevsner's monumental history, the heated debate about color has been displaced by a strategic silence. Color has become a specialized subject for occasional scholarly analysis. If modern architects worked so hard to make color an integral component of their architecture, the discourse has successfully transformed it into a supplement that can be discarded. If anything, the ostensible revival of color by so-called postmodern architecture intensified the white image of modern architecture and confirmed the transformation of color into a gratuitous ornament.

This effacement of the color of the surfaces of modern architecture by the very texts that are manufacturing and distributing the idea of such an architecture is much more than a simple blindness to color. It is a very particular institutional effect that took some time to put in place. If the success of the Weissenhofsiedlung turned on bonding the white wall to cubic forms, a battalion of critics and historians immediately leapt into action to defend that bond against any threat. This coordinated effort of embattled historians paralleled the establishment of the C.I.A.M. organization shortly after the exhibition to keep all the architects in line. Not by chance was the organization under the earnest secretaryship of Giedion.[85] The historians and architects presented a unified front, systematically shaping each other's productions, easing color into the background in order to promote the image of the white wall. It is not just that the historiographers effaced the color of the buildings. The very success of their efforts would only be marked by the rapid disappearance of white as an issue in the discourse. If, as so many commentators argue, "the Weissenhofsiedlung became the first international manifestation of the white, prismatic, flat-roofed mode of building which was to be identified in 1932 as the International Style,"[86] that moment of canonization in 1932 is the moment that white itself slips into the background, the moment that white can become the default condition of the discourse that never needs to be addressed as such.

Naturalizing White

The twists in this curious process can be traced by following the thinking of Henry-Russell Hitchcock who, with Philip Johnson and Alfred Barr, effected the canonization of the style. Hitchcock, who was deeply influenced by Platz's book and of course visited the Weissenhofsiedlung,[87] is very sensitive to the question of color. After all, the only way to get rid of the question is not to ignore it but to talk about it in a certain way that allows everybody else to ignore it. Even though the infamous *The International Style* book (which succeeded the original catalog that was entitled *Modern Architecture: International Exhibition*) reduces the complexity of each project that it displays down to a single image taken from the angle that best fits its aesthetic formula, the text does not simply allow the photographs to bleach the color out of the architecture. The majority of the images are accompanied by a caption that details the various colors of the buildings. Nevertheless, the collective effect of those captions is to privilege white. The image of Le Corbusier's

Villa at Garches, for example, is accompanied by: "The prevailing color is cream-white. At the back of the terraces one wall is grey and one green to emphasize the planes."[88] The Villa Savoye, which receives more pages than any other building in the book, is accounted for by: "The white second story appears weightless on its round posts. Its severe symmetry is a foil to the brilliant study in abstract form, unrestricted by structure, of the blue and rose windshelter above."[89] The polychromy is at once acknowledged and effaced in favor of white (it must be remembered that the facade—perhaps the most famous facade of the twentieth century—which was completed only two years earlier, seems to have originally been composed of a pale green second floor floating under the curving Rose windshelter and over a dark green ground floor).[90] This subtle maneuver is duplicated in the text:

Also in the use of color the general rule is restraint. In the earliest days of the contemporary style white stucco was ubiquitous. Little thought was given to color at a time when architects were preoccupied with more essential matters. Then followed a period when the use of color began to receive considerable attention. In Holland and Germany small areas of bright elementary colors were used; in France, large areas of more neutral color. The two practices were in large part due to the influence of two different schools of painting, as represented on the one hand by Mondrian and on the other by Ozenfant. In both cases colors were artificially applied and the majority of wall surfaces remained white.[91]

White is seen to survive the onslaught of color. It is precisely at this point that the text refers to the image of Le Corbusier's houses at Weissenhof, whose caption reads: "Projecting rear wings distinguished by being painted pale green."[92] The pink of the smaller citrohan type house in the foreground disappears and the polychrome scheme of the other house is reduced down to one inflection of the dominant white. Indeed, the text proceeds by announcing that the advertising value of color has to give way to the integrity of white:

At present applied color is used less. The color of natural surfacing materials and the natural metal color of detail is definitely preferred. Where the metal is painted, a dark neutral tone minimizes the apparent weight of the window frame. In surfaces of stucco, white or off-white, even where it is obtained with paint, is felt to constitute the natural color. The earlier use of bright color had value in attracting attention to the new style, but it could not long remain pleasing. It ceased to startle and began to bore; its mechanical sharpness and freshness become rapidly tawdry. If architecture is not to resemble billboards, color should be both technically and psychologically permanent.[93]

White is transformed into a "natural" color of a material, an extraordinary move that is slipped in as if nothing has happened. A moralistic tone of truth to materials is credited to white in the very moment that it successfully masks the material that it is added to. The integrity of modern architecture is guaranteed by a dissimulating coat of white paint. While Hitchcock and Johnson pay attention to the color of most buildings, they systematically transform them into white with color accents, condemning the use of "different colors on different walls" because it destroys the effect of volume. The new space of modern architecture coincides with the transformation of white from an artificial mask into a natural material. Once naturalized, it needs no comment. It is no longer even a move by the architect. It is simply the color of the building material that provides a certain kind of surface, a "smooth texture" that is in some way threatened by any color that might be applied to it.

This displacement from polychrome to white with color accents was set up by Hitchcock's first history of modern architecture, *Modern Architecture: Romanticism and Reintegration,* which was published two years after the Weissenhofsiedlung. Although the text does not address white directly, it does address color. Having privileged Le Corbusier over all the other architects, it documents his use of color. Hitchcock points to the polychrome of the Pessac housing scheme, which "applied to exteriors the principle hitherto used only in interiors, of painting different walls different colors," the "blue and ocher walls, now unfortunately in need of painting" of the studio houses for Miestschaninoff and Lipchitz, the "dark red-brown coloring" of the 1926 studio house, and so on. But clearly his preference is for the "exquisite egg-shell color" of Maison Cook and he soon shows some resistance to the strong coloration of the other projects, arguing that in the Weissenhof houses, "the use of color is far more subtle and effective than at Pessac." The exhibition houses emerge as some kind of aesthetic model, even if they failed "sociologically." André Lurçat, for example, is seen to produce better housing projects

and even have a better sense of the future of the new architecture than Le Corbusier but his composition, particularly his use of color, is "not quite acceptable aesthetically in the way of the audacities of Le Corbusier."[94]

In the end though, Hitchcock's attitude to Le Corbusier's color scheme is ambiguous. He is acutely aware of the strategic importance of the exhibition in which those colors were presented, arguing that "the publications which the constructions at the Stuttgart Weissenhofsiedlung engendered—cement hardly drying in Germany before buildings there are published in illustrations and text—presented to the world more completely than any previous books both the accomplishments and the dangers of the manner of the New Pioneers."[95] But it would seem that one of those dangers is the color of Le Corbusier's buildings. Having approved of their subtlety relative to Pessac, Hitchcock does not describe the colors in any detail. Indeed, he soon passes them over, offering instead the color scheme of Oud's street of houses in the Hoek van Holland that had been designed in 1924 and completed in 1927 as the appropriate role model. Describing them as "the finest monument of the new style," he argues that: "The use of color is delicate and discrete. The yellow brick basement, the dark grey band beside the blue door, the black iron work with only a touch of red on the lighting fixtures, provide against the reduced white of the plaster exactly the proper amount of contrast and variety."[96] The play of discrete color accents against a white background, as distinct from the "brilliant" colors of Oud's superintendent's house and Café de Unié that are discussed earlier in the text, becomes the paradigm for modern architecture. While acknowledging at one point that color has "vast untouched possibilities,"[97] the book settles for a quiet formula. A year earlier, in

10.11
J. P. P. Oud. Hoek van Holland 1926–27, as published by Henry-Russell Hitchcock in J. P. P. Oud, 1931.

10.12
The painters starting to apply the canonic color scheme to Oud's row of houses at Hoek van Holland, having already completed the white coat on the left-hand end of the row. Nederlands Architectuurinstituut.

his essay on Oud, Hitchcock began the description of the coloration of Hoek van Holland by saying "at last he is content to let color speak discretely, as in all good architecture," [98] a sentiment he would repeat in his 1931 book on Oud. [99] This "serene" coloration is again praised in *Modern Architecture: International Exhibition*, the original catalog of the 1932 exhibition, which goes as far as saying that it is with the project that "at last the world could see that a new style existed." [100] The surface of modern architecture must be discrete. Its very discretion marks the breakthrough into a new form of building.

This image of a predominantly white building with subordinate color accents was to act as an unspoken paradigm throughout the discourse. Out of the wide range of color possibilities presented by the Weissenhofsiedlung, it was the one that gradually became the accepted norm. The gesture by which Hitchcock moves polychrome into the background was endlessly reproduced by his successors even if they did not share his readings of particular projects. Color faded out of sight and out of mind. Indeed, subsequent housing projects and individual buildings were increasingly likely to be white, with the whiteness being associated with functional efficiency. Although Hitchcock was not very impressed by Oud's Weissenhof houses, most of the critics were. Oud, who was symptomatically the very first architect invited to take part in the exhibition, was seen to have produced dwellings that function better than Le Corbusier's. His internal planning was singled out for praise by those who condemned the supposed functionalism of the rest of the exhibition. Le Corbusier's display of color was tacitly associated with his insensitivity to functional operations in favor of exterior display while Oud's white row of housing units was seen as more modern in look and function. The exterior display of white became identified with a concern for internal order. The colored walls at Weissenhof were moved into the background to launch the white image of modern architecture, an image that would become so dominant that eventually it was all to easy to overlook. As Pommer and Otto put it:

With the growing emphasis on *Sachlichkeit* later in the decade, white increasingly came to predominate in the work of the leaders of the Modern Movement. White or near-white carried the connotations of hygiene and hospitals, of ships and the Mediterranean vernacular (perhaps, too, of ancient temples) but above all of a tabula rasa reshaped only by pure form, space, structure, and function. Gropius was a leader of this trend. . . . In its color as in its site plan, therefore, Weissenhof represented a last moment before rationalist orthodoxy eliminated the early diversity of the new architecture.[101]

In 1929, even van Doesburg produced his manifesto for white as the color of modernity and in the following year he built an all white studio house for himself and his wife to a design that he had first sketched out in 1927 immediately after visiting the Weissenhofsiedlung. Only the three doors are colored (red, blue, and yellow) in an echo of Oud and Gropius's formula. The surfaces of modern architecture were all but codified.

Nudism Dress

This increasing dominance of white did not simply mean the loss of the theories behind polychrome architecture. While figures like Gropius and Oud may have assumed the symbolic leadership in the use of white, the tacit theory behind their white surfaces was still that of the structural role of the surface originally put forward by Semper's theory of colored paint. After all, Gropius, who remained dedicated to the understanding of architecture as clothing throughout his career, was equally committed to the structural role of color. Likewise, Oud, who continued to campaign on behalf of color, was committed to a theory of clothing. Gropius had been one of the signatures on Taut's "Call for Colorful Building" in 1919, and in the same year his "Sparsame Hausrat" (Thrifty household goods) concludes its own call for color by associating buildings, furniture and clothing, arguing that they should all be colored:

The common people want color. The more their class pride develops, the more will they scorn the imitation of the rich bourgeois, and will devise their own style for their own sort of life. This instinct among the common people will be the foundation for the new art. Where today traditional art is still alive among the people—in the Orient, in Russia, still here in part in southern Germany—then there, on house and costume, glows color. Especially today, as a joyful protest against the external austerity and poverty which fate has forced upon us, we should muster the courage to brighten up the grayness of our shabby surroundings—houses, furniture, clothes—with cheerful colors. The happy result would be a great impact achieved with the slenderest of means.[102]

Just as the analogy between architecture and clothing continued to organize Gropius' writing till the end of his career, so too did his commitment to color. At the 8th C.I.A.M. congress in 1951, for example, he argues that the "psychological effect" of an enclosed space can only be transformed by the "surface illusions" of color. The "psychology of space" is revealed by the way certain colors make a wall recede while others make it advance.[103] When making the same point in a 1969 interview just before his death, he goes on to say of these surface illusions that "here architecture really starts, beyond all its technical problems."[104] For Gropius, as for the others, architecture emerges out of color rather than simply being decorated by it. Color is the beginning of architecture, rather than the end. Even the Bauhaus buildings at Dessau had multicolored interiors.[105] Although Gropius's Weissenhof houses seemed polemically white, and he did end up as the unofficial role model for the use of white, the whiteness was propped up on a color theory embedded in a psychology of surface. The only traces of that theory are the gray, red, yellow, blue, and violet accents he employed throughout his work, but they remained central to the conception of the buildings in which they appear to

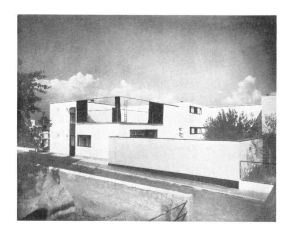

10.15
One of Walter Gropius's two Weissenhofsiedlung houses, as published in Die Form, *1927.*

10.16
J. P. P. Oud, Strand Boulevard Housing Scheme, 1917. Model published by Oud in Mein Weg in 'de Stijl.'

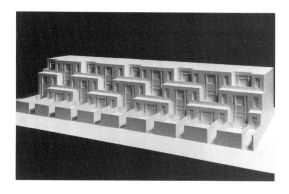

play such a small role. Even the prefabricated Weissenhof house had a red door, a pale blue door, an orange pergola, a few gray panels, and some yellow ones.

Likewise, Oud was not so discrete about color. While his "strand-boulevard" housing scheme that was published in the first issue of *De Stijl* in 1917, and discussed there by van Doesburg, was polemically white, he immediately started collaborating with van Doesburg to produce brightly colored spaces. After they broke up in 1921, Oud went on to employ less bold color schemes but did not simply replace color with white. In fact, white was a big part of van Doesburg's color schemes. The problem between them was not the color per se but the relationship between the color and the architectural elements. The scheme they broke on was predominantly white on which planes of color floated. Van Doesburg related those planes through an abstract compositional order that bore little relationship to the building. After they broke up, Oud simply went on to tie those planes to the building elements. Van Doesburg later wrote to him saying that he was now using the very kind of scheme they had separated over. In fact, for Oud, it was precisely van Doesburg's "pictorial" use of white rather than color on doors (so that they would inevitably get dirty with use) that symbolized the painterly attitude that he was no longer willing to collaborate with.[106] He remained committed to color. In his important essay "Over de toekomstige bouwkunst en hare architectonische mogelijkheden" (On the building art of the future and its architectonic possibilities) of 1921 he predicted an escalation of the use of color as the technology of the surface has been modernized as much as the structure:

As the last power factor in this new, revolutionary process, color must be taken into account. In present-day architecture the color element must, as a matter of course, be largely a matter of indifference. With new processes, however, for the smoothing and coloring of roughcast concrete, new possibilities occur for the greater and more deliberate use of color in building. Thus with these new processes, it is possible for the whole aspect of architecture to be changed.[107]

Not by chance did Behrendt talk about Oud when talking about the use of color in *Der Sieg des Neuen Baustils*. In 1925 Oud had concluded a list of manifesto-like points about the new architecture with a compromising position on color: "I just adore the resurrection of color in architecture, although I do agree with those who claim that too much color is not colorful, but garish."[108] In 1922, he published an article on Taut that criticized the destructive effects of his seemingly uncontrolled use of color.[109] By the time of Weissenhof, Oud had been using white with accents for some years. He launched the color scheme in the Oud-Mathenese housing of 1922 (with its transitional combination of white walls and pitched roofs) and developed it in the Hoek van Holland housing that Hitchcock so admired and the Kiefhoek housing of

(AFB. 9)   (AFB. 10)

AFB. 9. HEERENKLEEDING. ONOPZETTELIJK GEWORDEN SCHOONHEID. EVENALS BIJ AFB. 7 EN 8, HET
SCHOONHEIDSACCENT VERLEGD NAAR STRAKKEN VORM EN STRAKKE LIJN. VORMOVEREENKOMST MET
AFB. 7 EN 8 VERTOONEND. AFD. 10. GEBRUIKSVOORWERPEN. ZIE OPMERKINGEN ACHTER AFB. 7, 8 EN 9.

in eersten aanleg in zich en kunnen als aanknoopingspunten tot den uiterlijken ver-
schijningsvorm der nieuwe kunst beschouwd worden.

Door hun gemis aan versiering, hun strakken vorm en vlakke kleur, door de
betrekkelijke volkomenheid van hun materiaal en zuivere verhoudingen — voor een
belangrijk deel gevolg der nieuwe (machinale) productiewijze — werken zij indirect
bevruchtend op de bouwkunst in haar tegenwoordigen vorm, en doen daarin een —
ook door meer directe oorzaken geïnspireerden — drang naar abstractie ontstaan,
die zich voorloopig als vergeestelijking van traditioneel vormwezen, niet als mani-
festatie van nieuw levensgevoel openbaart.

Dat deze drang naar abstractie nog negatief is, d.w.z. gevolg meer van levens-

(AFB. 11.) VOORBEELD VAN ARCHITECTUUR VAN ZUIVERE VERHOUDING, LANGS TECHNISCHEN
WEG ONTSTAAN EN EENHEID VORMEND MET DE DAARIN AANWEZIGE INSTALLATIES.

10.17
*J. P. P. Oud, page from
"Over de toekomstige
bouwkunst en hare
architectonische
mogelijkheden,"*
Bouwkundig Weekblad,
*1921. Getty Research
Center, Resource
Collections.*

153

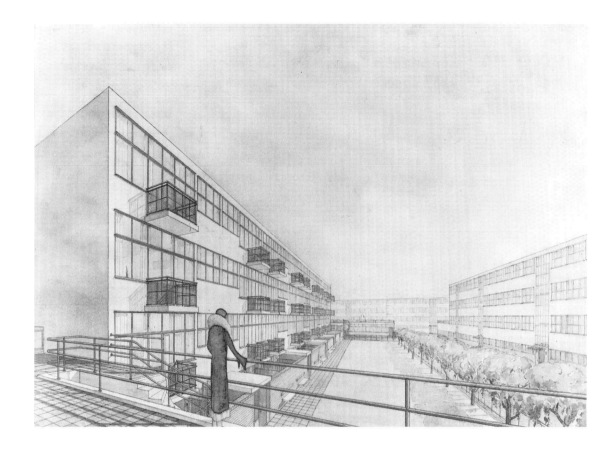

10.19
J. P. P. Oud, housing
scheme for Blijdorp,
Rotterdam, 1931.
Nederlands
Architectuurinstituut.

the De Stijl use of color. Indeed the very label "De Stijl" comes from Berlage's
Gedanken über Stil in der Baukunst (Thoughts on style in the building-arts)
of 1905, which in turn takes it from the treatise of Semper that it follows in
detail. The De Stijl group was indebted to Berlage, even though almost all of
its members eventually turned around to launch some kind of oedipal critique of him. Their liberation of the wall surface was absolutely dependant
on his liberation of the wall. Berlage had argued that the wall had to be transformed into a pure surface plane, understood as the dominant "space-
determining" element. He expressed reservations about Semper's emphasis on
the surface mask and attempted to turn the wall itself into a woven brick fabric, effacing Semper's distinction between the structural prop and the fabric
suspended from it. In extraordinarily influential projects, like the Amsterdam
Stock Exchange of 1896 to 1903, the wall emerged as a seamless surface, a
relatively thin membrane that defines both the inside and the outside surface
of each space, a solid fabric extending over the full dimension of the building
that may be perforated but never broken. The wall is folded around the corners to produce a single envelope and the visible metal structure that supports the glass roof of the building extends out of the wall and is itself

painted at the point where it emerges. The structure is portrayed as a delamination of the wall surface, the stubby columns seemingly produced by removing bricks. The fabric like patterns in the coloration of the brick merge with the patterns produced by removing small groups of brick and peeling back layers of brick. The surface assumes a visible thickness but creates an impression of thinness inasmuch as that thickness is understood to be structural. The self-supporting surface rises up, like some kind of magic carpet, to define the space. In Berlage's colored perspectives of his projects, this sense of a space produced by a continuous wrapping of woven materials, from floor to wall to ceiling and back, is explicit. The brickwork, tiles, and carpets become exchangeable, as if each space could happily be turned over on its side.

Arguing against any split between body and clothing, Berlage insisted that architects have to study the skeleton first in order to merge the fabric of the wall into it whereas Semper had argued that the structural prop had to be studied first in order to better hang the fabric of the wall from it:

Natural, comprehensible things should once again be made, i.e. a thing without the clothing which hides the body. But furthermore: we architects must first study the skeleton as do the painters and sculptors, in order to be able to give the figure its correct form thereafter. For the clothing of every natural creature is to some degree an exact reflection of the inner structure, which, insofar as it represents to us the perfect construction and can ultimately be called a building, in which the logical principle of construction predominates, and in which the actual cloaking part does not sit around it like a hull opposed to this construction, is not like a suit, but rather is fully integrated with the inner construction. . . . Thus for the moment the study of the skeleton, i.e. the sober construction in all bluntness, in order to come back to the full body, but this without confusion with clothing.[118]

While Berlage goes on to speak of stripping architecture down to the "stark naked" body, he is not rejecting clothing as such. As he had already made clear in his 1894 essay "Bouwkunst en Impressionisme" (Architecture and impressionism), the "great wall surface" is understood as an "interwoven" form of "costume" that is punctuated by a few isolated ornamental details.[119] Rather than cover up a hidden body, this costume is able to convey identity. *Gedanken über Stil in der Baukunst* argues that certain forms of clothing are able to articulate natural order: "And thus it follows that style-conscious clothing, the national costume, indeed even the military uniform, correspond to nature once again, precisely because they once again make manifest a beauty of a higher order."[120] If contemporary clothes are to be abandoned in favor of "natural clothing," like that of an animal, the problem is not simply the dissimulation of the body. Rather, the problem is the substitution of fashionably mobile surfaces for the stability of material order. Attacking the dissimulations of architectural surfaces in terms of the dissimulations of a nineteenth-century suit, Berlage argues that "Architecture was someone dressed according to bad fashion. . . . the clothing of fashion shall be torn asunder, and the unconcealed figure, that is, healthful nature, shall come forth." [121] Like Semper he opposes fashion, choosing as the epigraph for his *Grundlagen und Entwicklung der Architektur* (The principles and development of architecture) of 1908 Sheraton's claim (in "The Cabinet Maker") that "Time alters fashions . . . but that which is founded on geometry and real science will remain unalterable." [122] He seeks a form of clothing that articulates and is inseparable from the structure.

This logic was already evident in his travel diaries from 1880, which defend national costume, with its "strong" sense of clothing, against contemporary dress, which is far too "drab." Berlage condemns "that boring mixture chosen by the nineteenth century to cover itself with; that is still tolerable when well-made and on a good figure, neither of which is the case for the majority of the population, especially in our country, in the latter case; such clothing, looked at more closely, becomes ridiculous." [123] He opposes the loss of color in clothing just as he later opposes white walls: "the cold indifference closes in on you, is not your first reaction at sight of the white naked walls to button up your coat and turn up your collar?" [124] White played an important role in his woven spaces, particularly between 1901 and 1919 during his somewhat tense collaboration with a color consultant, Bart van der Leck, who was at that very time responsible for transforming the status of white in painting. The small white counterpoints on the interiors and exteriors of the earlier projects started to assume a larger role, a development that even becomes programmatic within the St. Hubertus hunting lodge, the color scheme of which was developed between 1917 and 1918. The narrative sequence of spaces that symbolizes the story of St. Hubertus is supported by an evolution in the status of white. The white grid painted onto the underside of the wood frame on the ceiling of the entrance hall, and echoed in the tiles below, progressively evolves (in a play between white stone, white glazing on tiles, and white paint) to the final room where even the steel beams that were black in the earlier rooms are painted white. From but one of the many colors being used, if not a minor one, it ends up as a major color, dominating the last room and therefore being associated with the security and calm that the room is meant to symbolize. But the only all-white space is the kitchen. The logic of hygiene is kept separate from that of clothing. In Berlage's work, the cool artificiality of whitewash is opposed to the warmth of the brick that he almost invariably used because it articulates its status as structure and cladding. The clothing of the building is understood in terms of the clothing of the body. In the good building, they become indistinguishable, just as the body becomes indistinguishable from what clothes it. At the same time, Ber-

10.20

*Jan Duiker and Bernard
Bijvoet, Open Air School,
Amsterdam, 1927–28.*

10.21

*Jan Duiker and Bernard
Bijvoet, laundry for the
Diamond Workers Fund,
Diemen, 1924. As
published in* Cahiers
d'art, *1926.*

lage emphatically opposed the idea of a single architectural style, understood
as a single clothing style. His "Bouwkunst en Impressionisme" essay rejects
the idea of a "uniform apparel for the entire world" in favor of national and
individual style.[125] He praises uniforms but disapproves of uniform dress.

While Berlage emphatically resisted the dissimulations of a surface mask and
saw the white wall in the same terms, his followers embraced the surface, conceived of architecture in terms of the nineteenth–century suit that he criticized and fell in love with the white wall. Indeed, the white surface was seen
to satisfy his call for appropriate clothing. While becoming the basis for the
appeal to a generic style that he had opposed, it was conceived in his terms.
His direct influence extended well beyond the De Stijl group to include the
whole *Nieuwe Bouwen* (New Building) tradition of Dutch functionalism that
Oud (and later Rietveld and van Eesteren) had joined. His translation of
Semper's argument was retranslated such that he unwittingly became a means
of access to the very dimensions of that argument that he was critical of. This
is even evident when the wall surface appears to be completely exploded to reveal a structural organization, as in the remarkable Open Air School in Amsterdam of 1927 to 1928 by Jan Duiker and Bernard Bijvoet. Within the sea
of glass, the white surfaces covering the slim parapets and the structural
frame are conceived in terms of Berlage's call for a form of clothing that expressed a stripping away of excess layers to expose the fabric of the space.

Duiker and Bijvoet had begun this process of stripping in their 1924 laundry at Diemen for the Diamond Workers Fund (a client that was passed on to them by Berlage). It was the first building in which they used sheer white surfaces adjacent to equally continuous glass ribbons that were punctuated only by thin blue mullions (the load being carried by a concrete frame that is concealed by the white painted infill). This hygienic look, which echoed the cleansing operations going on inside the building, received much attention. The original rendering of the unbroken white surfaces was immediately published (along with the plans and sections) in a 1924 issue of *L'architecture vivante* and the resulting effect of the completed building appeared in a 1926 issue of *Cahiers d'art*. As Duiker and Bijvoet's work progressed, the structure separated itself from the floating white surfaces but it too was coated with white. The increasingly lean structural frame was always clothed in a lightweight white garment. By 1925, even the ever thinner window mullions were often painted white.

When the De 8 group in Amsterdam and the Opbouw group in Rotterdam of the early 1920s eventually joined forces, Duiker published a series of articles on architecture and clothing in their new magazine *De 8 en Opbouw* (which would actually do a special issue on fashion in 1935). The essays make the by then standard set of associations between architecture and clothing and insist that architecture should base itself on the rational dress evident in the streets and in sports activities. But then the clothing argument is taken to its limit. In an essay entitled "Hoe is het met onze kleeding?" (What about our clothes?), Duiker appeals to principles of hygiene to oppose the excessive way that people are "dressing their home and themselves." Supposedly, the first

10.22
*Jan Duiker and Bernard
Bijvoet, Zonnestraal
Sanatorium, Hilversem,
1925–1928. As published
in J. B. Loghems,*
bouwen, bauen, bâtir,
building: holland, *1932.*

genuine change in men's clothing occurred with the development of a "reasonable functioning underwear." The way that the use of lightweight fabrics that can breathe has gradually influenced the construction of the entire outfit is seen to be "quite analogous with the aims of the new functionalism in architecture."[126] Duiker goes even further in an essay on whether a "bare and undressed" watertower in the landscape should "get dressed up" or not. He argues that while the contemporary suit, with its "tall hat, black coat, white shirt, black tie, white cuffs," is rational, it will eventually be rendered irrational by "nudism dress."[127] The extreme rationalization of dress becomes a model for "architectural nakedness." Seemingly undressed industrial structures are seen in terms of a new kind of dress. What Duiker calls "nudism dress" is the form of clothing that represents the stripping off of old clothes to reveal the new body of the building, a system of representation that marks the absence of representation.

The white wall that wraps itself around a lightweight structural frame, as in Duiker and Bijvoet's innovative Zonnestraal Sanatorium for tuberculosis patients of the Diamond Worker's Fund, is a health garment, a therapeutic outfit. The white clothing of the complex (whose main building was designed in 1925 and completed in 1928) joins those of the doctors and the patients in reinforcing the philosophy of sun, air, light, and exercise that Duiker promoted in his many essays. The all-encompassing white surface (with only minor color accents provided by the green on the metalwork leading to the patient's terraces and the red of the canvas sunshades) is a mechanism for purifying the body, whether it be that of the building or its occupants. This role becomes clear in the influential manifesto for functionalist architecture *bouwen, bauen, bâtir, building: holland* that was published by the architect J. B. Loghems in 1932. The book, which begins with a collage centered on the white walls of Oud's Kiefhoek housing, documents the international work by Le Corbusier and all the others but devotes the most pages to the Zonnestraal sanatorium. Having earlier cited Van Doesburg and Van Eesteren's 1924 call for the use of color to "organically" define space, it attempts to explain the white as a system of purification:

the white plaster work, enameling or tiling of nearly every new building is not a mask for constructional or technical imperfections; they are the interpretation of the desire for fineness and purity of expression, whereas tension and rigidness is also expressed best by a smooth finish.

the whiteness is also to be explained as a means of reducing, at least for the eye and feeling, the remaining heaviness which is still preserved by the structural form, to the utmost. probably a purer technique will still be able to accelerate the appearance of buildings, so that the still strongly pronounced white can be done away with for a part.

the degree of purity by which the building harmonizes and contrasts with the surroundings, the radiating exterior appearance of the building, and the interior radiating from the building, will in the future determine its value.[128]

Even while declaring that white is not a mask, the announcement that its future removal is possible confirms that it is still a form of clothing, the "nudism dress" that Duiker describes. There is a relationship between the purifying outfit and the naked body. One produces the other. Immediately after introducing the idea of nudism dress in *De 8 en Opbouw* (the hardline functionalist journal that nevertheless carried advertisements for Le Corbusier's colored wallpaper), Duiker says:

The new clothes will have to be rational in the first place. This can only be done if general physical culture and other 'Aufschung-revival' of sports and hygenics, physical and mental, favorably developed in the last few years, will make all people look the way nature meant them to. . . . The next generation will require from the architectural nakedness that the designer takes seriously the most logical, cosmic, and economical construction and does not cover up this monstrosity.

Rational dress and the rationalized body cannot be separated. Each enables the other. The white garment perfects the body that might eventually discard it. It is the clothing that facilitates nakedness. Loghems and Duiker (arguably the most extreme functionalists of the *Nieuwe Bouwen* movement) point to, and celebrate, the enigmatic status of the white wall that is evident throughout its use in modern architecture. The expression "nudism dress" is perhaps the most precise description of this enigma.[129] Despite the fact that Duiker, like most of his Dutch colleagues, went on to criticize Berlage's attitude towards modern style, he had taken Berlage's basic argument about stripped down clothing, the clothing of nakedness, to its extreme.

In the end, Berlage was a major influence on modern architects. As such he had been symbolically invited to attend the first C.I.A.M. meeting in 1928—even though he did not recognize or affirm its project. The new regime of the surface that was launched at Weissenhof and quickly monumentalized remains as bound to his transmission of Semper's arguments about the structural role of surface as it does to the similar gestures of Louis Sullivan and Otto Wagner. The success of the white wall depended on a very particular discourse about surface, which has obvious precedents in mid nineteenth-century debates, even if the means by which the white wall was stitched into the discourse of the avant-garde are multiple and almost always circuitous. Yet again it must be noted that Semper's argument about the surface is inscribed throughout the discourse around modern architecture, even if its understanding of architecture as clothing has been gradually erased.

Returning to the Surface

It is not by chance that the article for *Het Bouwbedrijf* in which van Doesburg analyses the Weissenhofsiedlung is the one in which he comes up with his most decisive theory of the architecture of the surface. When talking about the emergence of "unjointed materials, which by their purity, simplicity and their *Gespanntheit* [surface tension] are in keeping with the modern mentality," he insists that "only the *ultimate surface* is decisive in architecture . . . only the surface is important for people. Man does not live within the construction, within the architectural skeleton, but only touches architecture essentially through its ultimate surface." He associates this surface with people's "features, posture, gait, clothing" and condemns previous forms of architecture for having "violated" the "purity of the surface." This privileging of surface is accompanied by the typical criticism of Le Corbusier's houses at the exhibition. The contributions by Mies, Stam, and Gropius are approved of while Le Corbusier's effort is seen to be "geared to an aesthetic (albeit purist-picturesque) effect." Its "depressing" interiors are "sculptures in color, having a very surprising visual effect, which are however, only in exceptional cases serviceable as living space."[130] Le Corbusier's particular concern with "outward appearance" is contrasted with the primacy of surface, the surface as the functional element of architecture. His polychrome is seen to be detached from functional efficiency and the rationality of construction. In a thoroughly Semperian gesture, van Doesburg identifies the functional dominance of surface with a perfection of the structure that it masks.

While the emerging historiography uniformly opposes fashion, it sustains this particular logic of surface, one that ends up underpinning, if not orchestrating, the canonic histories of Pevsner and Giedion. The logic is preserved by Hitchcock in the very moment that he gently eases color out of the picture. Indeed, *The International Style* turns on a theory of surface. It begins by portraying the nineteenth-century precursors of modern architecture as working on "the new art of proportioning plane surfaces." The traditional conception of architecture as solid masses starts to give way to the sense of an architecture defined by suspended surfaces. The building's mass is supposedly transformed into volume when architects like Wagner "developed the plane surfaces of his architecture for their own sake" and van de Velde experimented with "continuity of surface." Their lightening of the building's mass is then taken over by Wright's conception of architecture "in terms of planes existing freely in three dimensions," which in turn stimulated De Stijl's experimental dissolution of solidity in favor of free floating surfaces. Architects like Oud "came to realize the aesthetic potentialities of planes in three dimensions." Space became the product of planes. All subsequent modern architecture is seen to be "directly influenced" by these experiments. Modern architecture is the new architecture of the surface, the surface liberated from structural mass.[131]

Having offered this historical overview, Hitchcock goes on to define the three "principles" of this architecture. The first is "architecture as volume," which turns out to be no more than the call for "unbroken" surfaces. Any breaks in the building's surface, as for windows, have to be consistent with each other because "the more consistently a surface is arranged, the more conspicuous will be its character as a surface." The surface must present itself as a surface. The design goal of the modern architect is "the smooth continuous surface." Soon, the text actually starts referring to the principle of volume as "the principle of surface." After that principle has been introduced, another chapter is devoted to the material of the surface before the second principle, "regularity," is offered. But here again, the issue is how the consistency of the surface needs to be developed into the regularity of proportion. Likewise, the final principle, "The Avoidance of Applied Decoration," is devoted to the effects of ornamentation on surface. Nothing should be allowed to "break the wall surface unnecessarily."[132] The very solidity of ornament is seen to transfer itself to the surface it is attached to and thereby compromise the modern effect of volume. One by one, all the distinguishing principles of modern architecture are identified as mechanisms for sustaining and controlling the surface.

Hitchcock's promotion of white walls over colored ones is intimately tied into this overriding "principle of surface." Symptomatically, it is only when the principle has finally been developed into that of the removal of ornament that the discussion of color occurs. The complex maneuvering with color presupposes the decisive role of surface. Color is understood as a form of ornament that needs to be controlled. The withdrawal of polychrome from modern architecture in favor of white is presented as a withdrawal of the risks of ornament. What forces the complex negotiation over color is that, unlike other forms of ornament, polychrome does not threaten the integrity of the surface as such. Rather, it interferes with the precious identity between surface and volume: "It emphasizes strongly the effect of surface, but it breaks up the unity of volume."[133] Color does simply break individual surfaces. Rather it breaks surfaces apart, collapsing the delicate illusion of space. The white paint supposedly restores the cohesiveness of the surface, the integrity of the fragile but all important envelope that is presented to the eye. It is a seal, holding the very effect of architecture together.

The same economy of surface can be found in Hitchcock's earlier *Modern Architecture: Romanticism and Reintegration* when it rejects fashionable surfaces like those of Mallet-Stevens's "mode-modernity."[134] The theory that modern architecture emerges from the displacement of mass by surface is already in place and architects are again portrayed as rejecting ornament because it breaks the integrity of the surface. The modern architect struggles to attain a surface the very smoothness of which points to the structural role of the surface itself: "Instead of diversity and richness of surface texture, they strive for monotony and even poverty, in order that the idea of the surface as the geometrical boundary of the volume may most clearly be stressed."[135] The plainer the surface, the more its importance is revealed. Ornament is not scraped off to expose an inner truth. On the contrary, the scraping exposes the truth of the outer layer. The most sophisticated architects are seen to be those that highlight the surface as such. Even the moments when the surface is broken become the moments where the very continuity and dominance of the surface is established. The location of the ribbon windows in Le Corbusier's studio for Ozenfant, for example, is praised for "emphasizing the fact that an architecture of surfaces could have plasticity of volume."[136] The best modern architecture not only achieves the effect of volume through the play of surfaces but it displays its very capacity to do that. The technological expertise of the modern architect is seen to lie in the technology of the surface. Hitchcock questions the assumption that modern architecture emerges out of modern building technologies, arguing that people do not really understand the construction of a building. Rather, they interpret the building according to whatever they expect the structure to be. If people do have "faith" in the reality of new technologies that modern architects refer to, then masonry construction is just as appropriate as plaster surfaced ferro-concrete. What counts is the surface that governs the psychological response to a building.[137] To control the material condition of the surface is to control the psychological responses to the building:

The question of surfaces might appear to be subsidiary to what has already been said. But it is peculiarly central since the new aesthetic is concerned primarily with the surfaces of volumes. . . . Surface treatment remains certainly that which more than anything else requires the attention of technical experimenters, and in which the use of traditional materials is most obviously precarious psychologically.[138]

Hitchcock appreciates color only inasmuch as it contributes to the dominance of surface. In an article published later in the same year, he analyzes Le Corbusier's villa at Garches ("the most important executed work by Le Corbusier"), in terms of the ability of its surfaces to defy any sense of depth, mass or gravity,[139] before going on to approve of the way the "delicate, restrained use of polychromy helps to achieve this effect."[140] The "limpid effect of suspension" initiated by the "monochrome" white wall of the front facade is propped up by the light coloration of the subordinate planes. Color is at most a servant to the white wall, one that must be constantly disciplined lest it renders the surface decorative rather than structural.

Hitchcock's position is extreme, and the infamous 1932 *The International Style* exhibition based around that position is routinely condemned for being just that, the exhibition of a style packaged for international distribution. While Hitchcock's first book on modern architecture warns against the inevitable tendency to confuse a new fashion with absolute truth,[141] he ends up being condemned for exactly that, promoting a new fashion. His fixation on the surface is all too easily identified with the salesman's concern for the superficial marks of style, presenting only the surface of a much more complicated phenomenon to an undiscriminating market. Yet the architects and historiographers of modern architecture use the same theory of the structural role of surface. Hitchcock is no more extreme than writers like van Doesburg. While the centrality of surface in the writings of Wagner, Loos, Muthesius, Gropius, Le Corbusier, Taut, Giedion, and Pevsner has been pointed to here, the list can be expanded almost indefinitely. Modern architecture is simply unthinkable outside it. In fact, the same privileging of the surface can easily be found within the writings of the self-appointed security guards who continue to earnestly patrol the discourse and adamantly denounce such a privilege. As always, those who claim to subordinate surface want that subordination to be registered in the very surface being subordinated. They cultivate an economy of surface in the very gesture of denouncing such an economy. The "simplicity," "plainness," "neutrality," and so on, that are so routinely and casually associated with the functional, technical, political, and moral integrity of modern architecture are but a surface effect that can only be produced by an elaborate artifice and maintained by a supportive discourse.

To focus on the surface is not, by definition, to simplify the complex discourse around modern architecture. On the contrary, much of the complexity of that discourse derives from its privileging of the surface. What is critical in Hitchcock's maneuvers is not simply their role in disseminating the overdetermined image of white walls. Rather, they exemplify the operations of the wider discourse. Although he aggressively promotes the understanding of architecture as a surface effect, the perception of architecture as clothing that made that understanding possible is symptomatically withdrawn. The silence about color that the text carefully negotiates is, in the end, a silence about dress. Clothing does not figure in Hitchcock's reading while color is carefully phased out. With the success of white in practice, white gradually fades away from the historiography. Hitchcock continues to touch color but ever more lightly. While he refers to Le Corbusier's "natural" use of white in his 1948 *Painting Towards Architecture,* which explores the relationship between twentieth century painting and architecture,[142] he no longer mentions it in his 1957 survey *Architecture: Nineteenth and Twentieth Centuries.* All that remains is one small reference to Oud's "restriction of color to white-painted rendering with only small touches of the primaries on some of the minor elements of wood and metal."[143] Meanwhile, Pevsner and Giedion have produced their monumental histories in which neither color nor white make an appearance. They no longer have to make any delicate maneuvers around color. The argument about surface can be reproduced while overlooking the color of the surface.

Of course, Hitchcock's negotiation around the question of color merely facilitated the transformation that was occurring on many fronts and was not without its opponents. A year after the 1932 exhibition at the Museum of Modern Art consolidated the emerging reading of the Weissenhofsiedlung, Platz published *Wohnräume der Gegenwart* (Living spaces of today), which is illustrated with colored plates of interiors by all the major protagonists of modern architecture and explicitly attempts to block the rise of the white wall. It asks "what would space be without color?" and opposes the "striking predominance of white walls and rooms, practiced in the same way by puritans and fashionable architects, praised as the highest truth by theoreticians of a certain stripe."[144] Platz quotes Hamman's *Die Form* essay on the glories of white at length, before arguing that the worship of white is the inevitable but regrettable consequence of the worship of machines—a stance seen exemplified in Hamman's claim that a spray-machine is the best way to apply this "universal tone." Platz questions the value of white's capacity to dematerialize a building:

Even if it were true that white explodes the walls of the room, that the homeowner standing in front of white walls is "as if outdoors" or "appears to be hanging in space," even then one would be compelled to ask: is this goal worth striving for? . . . The design of the room, even when it is well proportioned, only gains life through color. White means nothing other than an indifferent, cool, variously even passive background. It goes well with furniture pieces but they tend to be isolated without creating a unity.[145]

At the same time, Platz acknowledges the merit of many of the arguments employed on behalf of white and distances himself from the "orgies" of color deployed by those who unilaterally oppose the regime of white—arguing that the "harshest contrasts" of colors employed at the Weissenhofsiedlung (presumably those of Taut whose polychromed cities he had praised in the earlier book), are equally involved in the misguided attempt to "explode" the room. The book attempts to negotiate some kind of compromise between white and color. Significantly, Platz is no longer talking about architecture as a form of clothing. On the contrary, space is now the neutral display case for clothes: "Since one can never predict what colors people will be bringing into the rooms with their clothes one would do well to create the most neutral background possible which will not be disturbing in any case." Gentle tones are needed to support the effect of the clothes. Platz's discussion of color eventually singles out Le Corbusier for special attention, noting that "even here white plays a decisive role" although it is always supplemented by color. Having established that Le Corbusier's avoidance of an all white space is exemplary, he is able to conclude the discussion by arguing that "unusual and strong colors" have to be avoided in the "normal" dwelling and that "pure white is exclusively chosen for workrooms for reasons of hygiene, of cleanliness, of indifferent (but not soporific) effect."[146] The explosive regime of white has to be tamed by controlled does of color.

It was in the same year that Léger gave his important address about the dangers of an all white environment to the 4th C.I.A.M. meeting, which was held on a symptomatically white walled ocean liner as it cruised between Marseilles and Athens:

You are deserting the cultivated minority of which you are sure in order to build for the "average" man, the man who has lived among his furniture, colors, his fully decorated walls and windows. This timid creature now finds himself against the starkness of your bare walls, enveloped in light, and moving among new and shiny surfaces, in an atmosphere where it is impossible to hide oneself and where one's head begins to spin.

The average man's values, which you are now destroying, must be replaced. Your average man lags behind and will not accept your bare walls.[147]

Having identified the psychopathology of white, Legér once again made a plea for an ongoing collaboration between painters and architects that would negotiate some kind of compromise between the increasingly generic white wall and the excessive application of color. As he sailed back from the same meeting, Le Corbusier likewise responds to a letter about the unique status of the Acropolis by insisting that the white walls of the mediterranean world are dependant on the simultaneous use of color. The ideal environment is a polychrome space dominated by white: "There was white everywhere. White, white because of the red, the blue, the yellow. . . . Polychrome (a white dominant) is the manifestation of vitality."[144] Like Legér, he ends up arguing for a symbiosis between white and color, as distinct from a white environment with color accents. But by 1933 this argument about the interdependency of white and color was already disappearing into the unconscious of the discourse around modern architecture. Color was erased to leave the white wall, a surface that is not addressed as such, one that became so ubiquitous that it

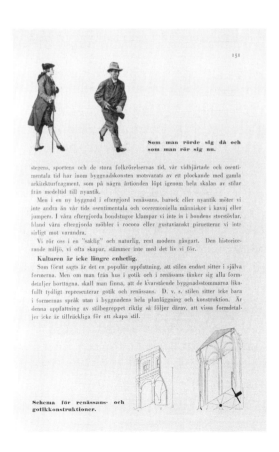

10.23
"This is how we used to move. This is how we move now." Page from Gunnar Asplund, Sven Markelius, et al., Acceptera, *1931.*

was hard to see, let alone reveal the extraordinary investments that had been made in it.

And as color was erased from the discourse, so too was the clothing logic that accounted for that color and gave the surface its structural role. For a few years after the Weissenhofsiedlung, the clothing argument that it had promoted circulated widely in architectural discourse. In 1931, *Acceptera*—,the Swedish manifesto for modern architecture produced by Gunnar Asplund, Sven Markelius, and their colleagues, for example, maintained the tradition established at Weissenhof by insisting that modern architecture needed to follow modern clothing. Having earlier contrasted an image of a Japanese woman in traditional dress to an image of one in modern dress that is then aligned with a futuristic architectural project, the book contrasts an image of a man in an old outfit to an image of one in a new suit and argues that the modern suit marks the new sense of mobility the modern building must cater for and participate in. It calls for a recovery of the harmony between architecture, dress, and way of life found in the past, poking fun at those that wear modern sweaters in buildings that have been newly constructed in Late Renaissance, Baroque, or Antique style and noting that people do not wear big farmer's boots in their fashionably old-styled farmhouses.[149] This argument about clothing was based on the 1928 lecture to the Finnish Association of Architects on "Rationalization Trends in Modern Housing Design" with which Markelius had introduced functionalism to Sweden after visiting Weissenhof at the end of a tour. The lecture contrasted the demand for "strict utility and comfort from everything relating to our clothing, luggage and personal effects" to the regressive impulse to treat the fittings of houses as a form of decoration and thereby turn architecture into a form of camouflage. The modern building should wear a discrete outfit. The ideal, as symbolized by the aeroplane and express train, is "modern comfort clothed in matter-of-fact form."[150]

The argument was rehearsed in almost every country, as in Duiker's 1932 articles for *De 8 en Opbouw*, the first issue of which symptomatically advertised upcoming lectures by Le Corbusier in Amsterdam and Rotterdam with a cartoon of the already famous architect's outfit. While Duiker was a precise but not elegant dresser,[151] Markelius picked up the image of the well-dressed architect from Le Corbusier and passed it on to Aalto and the others.[152] As Banham's *Theory and Design in the First Machine Age* argues of Le Corbusier: "even his personal appearance was the subject of comment, for he endeavored to present himself as an *homme-type* of the age, in the dark clothes, bowler hat, pipe and bow tie of an engineer."[153] Indeed, one of the few changes Banham makes from the doctoral thesis on which his book was based was to remove the corresponding footnote, which added: "This tendency to dress up as businessmen or engineer seems to have been general among progressive architects of the period, and Gropius's post-expressionist bow ties have been evaluated in the same way."[154] The look of the rationalized structure is aligned with the look of the engineer supposedly responsible for that rationalization.

But while the modern architect's concern for an appropriate outfit had been firmly established, the argument that modern architecture was itself such an outfit soon became increasingly rare. Like color, clothing disappears into the unconscious of the literature. Even on the rare occasion when it returns, its status has been fundamentally shifted. Indeed, it only returns to open up the gap between architecture and clothing even further. Perhaps the most obvious example of this is when it reappears in the opening lines of the first chapter of Bruno Zevi's *Verso un'architettura organica* (Toward an organic architecture) of 1945, whose first illustration is symptomatically a white-walled house by Voysey, the architect who did so much to popularize the white wall, and, by now it should go without saying, described his work in terms of dress. Zevi begins by announcing that:

> The classical example of the transformation of taste is the difference between the way we are dressed today and the fashions of past centuries. The owner of a limousine that looked like a stage-coach would be ashamed of it: on the other hand the owner of a new house with a Tudor or a Queen Anne facade is still only too often very satisfied with his acquisition. Our houses, no less than our clothes or our means of transport, ought to be different from those of our ancestors, to be more convenient and simpler.[155]

Architect Le Corbusier, Parijs, spreekt 11 en 13 Januari a.s. te Rotterdam voor het genootschap Nederland-Frankrijk, afdeeling Rotterdam. 12 Januari voor Civiel en Bouwkundig Studentengenootschap „Praktische Studie" van de Technische Hoogeschool te Delft.

In verband hiermede organiseert de Rotterdamsche Kunstkring van 8—15 Januari een tentoonstelling van fotos naar zijn werk, Witte de Withstraat 35, Rotterdam.

15 JANUARI ORGANISEERT „DE 8" EEN LEZING MET LICHTBEELDEN TE AMSTERDAM VAN LE CORBUSIER.

ONDERWERP: „ARCHITECTURE ET URBANISME." (NADER BERICHT IN DE DAGBLADEN).

10.24
Announcement of lectures by Le Corbusier in the first issue of De 8 en Opbouw, 1932.

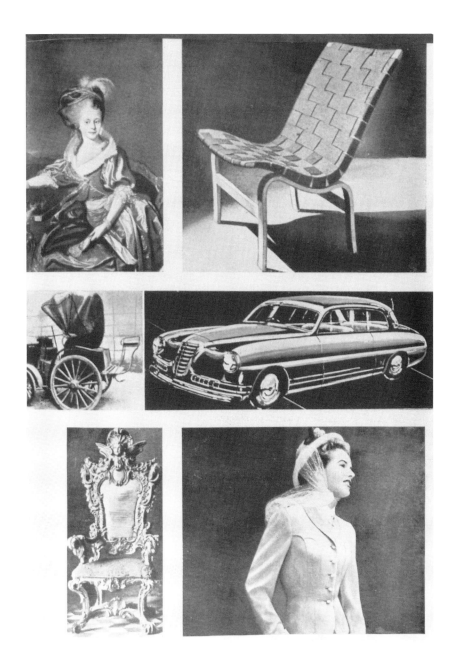

10.25
*Illustration from Bruno
Zevi,* Storia
dell'architettura
moderna, *1950.*

Such a change of taste is seen to fuse with a change of technology to produce the preconditions for modern architecture. Zevi repeats the argument with some modifications five years later in the opening lines of his definitive *Storia dell'architettura moderna* (History of modern architecture) where he adds the lines: "And don't you see that if a rococo armchair emphasizes well a lady dressed up in the luxurious costume of the epoch, today the same armchair aesthetically suffocates a lady dressed up in a modern dress? Don't you understand that to accentuate the sober linearity of contemporary dress a modern Swedish or Finnish chair would be best?"[156] The point is illustrated with matching images of old and new chairs, cars and dresses (echoing Behne's similar illustration in *Eine Stunde Architektur* of 1928). The argument that was formulated in Otto Wagner's reading of Semper, distributed by Loos and rehearsed by so many of the protagonists in the production of modern architecture, reappears almost twenty years after it had disappeared in the very moment of its success. But, like so many of the secondary promotional texts (but so few of the authorized histories) Zevi sees it as but a useful way to introduce the modernity of modern architecture, what he calls a "classical example" as distinct from an organizing principle. It is a user-friendly image rather than a historical or conceptual condition. By the fifth edition of 1975, the illustrations are removed, along with the reference to Swedish or Finnish chairs. It would seem that the text has succumbed to the very shifts in taste that it is addressing. The chairs, cars, and dresses have moved on while the exemplary status of clothing remains. But dresses do not form part of the history, despite the fact that the text immediately locates the origin of the architecture in the work of William Morris, Voysey, Mackintosh, van de Velde, Berlage, and so on. All the dress designers are turned into architects and dress itself is left far behind. Or so it would seem.

In fact, the clothing logic remains buried within the theory of surface that is sustained by Zevi, as it is by most of the discourse. Modern architecture is again presented as an art of pure surface, a purified surface that exhibits a structural order. Once again, the inner truth is seen to lie in the outer layer. Far from disappearing, the discussion of clothing has been seamlessly displaced into a discussion of architecture. Modern architecture is understood as a form of clothing even if it is no longer described as such.

After-all

It must be remembered that this generic logic of surface, like all logics of clothing, is orchestrated by an all-too familiar pathology. By patiently teasing the texts of the historiography, the psychosexual baggage that engendered this logic can be exposed. Even though the white wall was rendered invisible in the moment of its triumph, it retains within its very thinness all the intense charge that the various polemics for polychrome architecture attempted to re-distribute and control. To use the crudest possible terms, the theory of the structural role of surface that underwrites the discussion remains highly charged in terms of race, gender and sexual orientation. The white wall is far from innocent. When the image of the white building with a few color accents is extracted from the range of colors at Weissenhof and codified to the point of invisibility, that image is massively overdetermined. It carries an extraordinary range of investments, a whole complex of biases that dictate its strange status in the discourse. It is not by chance that Giedion (who became sufficiently close to Oud that they went on ski trips together) writes to Oud after the exhibition to tell him that his row of houses satisfies his "desire" like a "real woman":

You are in fact the only architect who can formulate types and yet who has behind him the practical experience in mass housing that the others simply lack. How many dwellings have you built? Two thousand? One feels behind every detail the reflection on experience—as the burnt child does—which leads to synthesis rather than routine. Dear Oud, one senses the human being, and today we again have a desire for that, as we do for a real woman. Are we philistines? Oh no. Biologists, that's what we are.[157]

The white building with a little color is first and foremost an object of desire. As we have already seen, the nature of this desire will later surface and orchestrate Giedion's historiography but only when it is ostensibility disassociated from the white surface. The machinations of desire are seemingly withdrawn in the very moment of white's triumph, only to return in a displaced form. Yet again, the pleasure of white cannot be acknowledged as a pleasure. The relentlessly puritanical tone of the emerging historiography that tries to overlook the surfaces of modern architecture to protect them is but an ongoing disavowal of its own attraction to those very surfaces.

This disavowal, which structures so much of the discourse around modern architecture, became institutionalized when the discussion about the relative merits of Le Corbusier and Taut's use of color gave way to a whiter option and the logic of clothing that underpins their respective attitudes to color, and articulates their overdetermined fantasies, seemingly fades away. But these fantasies can still be found throughout the discourse. The psychosexual charge that was invested into the surface by figures like Loos, Le Corbusier, and Giedion exploits a millennial set of biases that work their way through the discourse of less well known figures and assumes less obvious forms while underwriting the discourse's operations at every level. When Cheney's protohistory *The New World of Architecture,* to take but one last example, tries to clarify his basic argument that everything is in the surface and yet the surface must be completely subordinate to the structure—so that the surface itself becomes structural rather than decorative—it is not by chance that he too invokes the image of a man looking at a woman's body:

In contrived as in natural (or cultivated) beauty, one may mark two general sorts: an inner, fundamental, characteristic sort, and an outer shallower, sensuous sort. In the example of natural beauty that is most with us, that of woman, we are accustomed to say that surface prettiness is bootless without soul shining through (though we do indeed value "just" surface loveliness, grace, and style, more than we usually confess); and that is a warrant that there is such a thing as spiritual beauty, expressing itself under a woman's prettiness. . . . In the realm of art one soon becomes confused if one does not make a similar distinction between a surface sensuous appeal and a deeper characteristic one.[158]

The desiring gaze again acts as the model for the design and experience of architecture. When the text repeatedly opposes surface to structure, the potential for architectural surfaces to mislead the viewer is symptomatically identified with femininity: "Let us beware of the too effeminate thing, the assumed prettiness, the sensuous loveliness without innate architectural virtue."[159] The results of the confusion between architecture and "fashion experts, window dressers, and stage costumers," between the structured surface and the unstructured one, are described as "but oh! so feminine."[160] The dilemma produced by the slippage between modern architecture and clothing is first and foremost one of sexual identity. This was already clear in Cheney's *A Primer of Modern Art* of 1924, whose chapter on architecture sketches out the argument of the later book. It attacks neoclassical architecture as "merely imitative developments, marked by differing modes of prettifying their models by varying types of refinement in the decorative elements. The same old girls, getting pretty seedy looking if one inquired beyond the surface, dolled up in changing fashions of clothing."[161] Unsurprisingly, Cheney goes on to fantasize about the removal of such clothing: "Don't be fooled by the Greek fronts and Beaux-arts flourishes. Look the other way and you may surprise beauty naked and unashamed."[162] But the voyeuristic fantasy has to remain a fantasy, one stirred by the very clothing that is to be removed. The outer layer has to faithfully convey the form that it covers. While the surface of architecture is the clothing of a woman's body, it must be organized by the body beneath it in a nonfeminine, which is to say nondissimulating way. The architect has to vigilantly control the surface to contain the feminine. And the historian has to watch over the architect's shoulder, keeping everything in check. Both insistently proclaim the glories of structure to cover up the fact that, as Cheney admits, the discourse values surface loveliness more than it can usually confess.

It is not a question of the idiosyncratic and suspect desires of particular architects and historians. Rather, it is a question of the institutionalized logic that they simply reinforce and exploit. Indeed, it is the very ordinariness of such statements that marks their force. It is the taken for granted status of these structural biases that is aligned with the white wall. They are its props. The wall can only be taken for granted when these biases are operational. To not overlook the white wall, to interrogate it, to see how it was constructed as a dress, to see modern architecture as an ongoing performance, a play of fragile but charged surfaces, is necessarily to expose the biases that haunt the discourse. The dress is always suspended in a psychosexual economy. To see the dress as a dress is already to expose the institutional apparatus, if not interfere with it.

Yet again, the problem is not the feminine per se, but the feminine within the masculine, the femininity of the architect as fashion designer and the femininity of the spectator who falls for the dissimulating clothes such an architect produces—as becomes astonishing clear when Zevi ends up promoting modern architecture by literally identifying the symmetry of the classical architecture that it displaces with homosexuality.[163] If modern architecture is a form of dress, it has to be controlled by heroic figures, architects and historians whose masculinity and heterosexuality is established by their very ability to control the surface. The story of modern architecture is an old one. The public image of masculine control is produced by the private mastery of the stereotypically feminine art of the surface. A sophisticated use of the representational system of the surface is used to announce the absence of representation.

In the same way, the image of the white skin requires the appropriating control of colored skin. Although the discourse declares that modern architecture takes its shape from the "savage" forms of modern technology and thereby echoes the simple shelters and tents of indigenous cultures, these sources must be covered over by the architectural garment. As with the body, the garment must communicate a sense of what is behind it while keeping it at a distance. The other is praised, but praised as other, as separate. Again the deepest threat is the thought of the other within, the blackness or color within the supposedly white. The modern architect is meant to be unambiguously white. If the white clothing of the building, or, more precisely, the fantasy of such a form of clothing, is meant to act as a "mirror," as Le Corbusier puts it, it is meant to return an image of white skin to the nervous eye of the architect. It makes distinctions, draws lines, classifies, making certain things stand out as other, rendering them as other, so that they can be patronized or removed. The surface has to be controlled so that it can become an agent of control. The fabric has to be selected and cut with the greatest care lest all the nightmares return to the surface, transforming the white garment with colored trim into a halloween costume—or, even worse, lest the white wall is itself perceived as such a costume.

The only way the discourse can control the dresslike condition of modern architecture is to deny that it is a dress, let alone a garment suspended within the unreliable world of fashion rather than the supposedly reliable world of modern technology and functional rationalization. More precisely, it is to deny that modern technology is the technology of the surface, that all modern architectural forms are but new forms of clothing, understood as prosthetic extensions of the physically and culturally fragile body. Yet the very repetition of such denials that punctuates, if not perforates, the discourse serves only to remind us that the overdetermined arguments about clothing that launched so much of the discourse did not go away. On the contrary, they had been invested in the white wall that seems to be so emphatically detached from them, covertly establishing the structural role of the surface and thereby legitimizing numerous architectural practices while relieving them of detailed critical or historiographic scrutiny. No matter how many surfaces of particular buildings are white, and how many appear to faithfully exhibit the materials of construction, the fragile coat of white that dissimulates its material prop continues to act as the device for exposing which materials are covered and which are not. The dissimulations of white continue to underwrite architectural discourse's institutionalized opposition to dissimulation. White remains the default setting. Its enigmas still haunt the debate, twisting every seemingly straightforward move. The extraordinary psychosexual investments that have been made in it still return in unusual ways in unusual places. In the end, this extended essay has but lightly scratched the seemingly innocuous yet pathologically charged surface of this all too chic coat of paint, this slippery "nudism-dress" that we still find ourselves wearing so often.

Notes

Introduction

1

Le Corbusier, *L'art décoratif d'aujourd'hui* (Paris: Éditions G. Grès et Cie, 1925), 193. Translated by James Dunnet as *The Decorative Art of Today* (Cambridge: MIT Press, 1987), 192.

2

William J. R. Curtis, "Le Corbusier: Nature and Tradition," in *Le Corbusier: Architect of the Century*, ed. Michael Raeburn and Victoria Wilson (London: Arts Council, 1987), 13–23, 20.

3

Kenneth Frampton, "The Other Le Corbusier: Primitive Form and the Linear City 1929–52," in *Le Corbusier: Architect of the Century*, 29–34, 29.

4

Nikolaus Pevsner, "Time and Le Corbusier," *Architectural Review*, 125, no. 746 (March 1959): 159–165, 160.

5

Stephen Gardiner, *Le Corbusier* (New York: Viking Press, 1974), 40.

6

"The aim of the authors in this series is to encourage us to look at the objects of everyday life with fresh and critical eyes. Thus while increasing our own daily pleasure we also become better able to create surroundings which will give us permanent pleasure. To achieve this in the furnishing and the equipment of our homes, we must buy with discrimination and so prove to the designers who set the machines to work, that we are no longer bound by habit or indifference to accept whatever is offered." Lionel Brett, *The Things We See: Houses* (West Drayton: Penguin Books, 1947), back cover text.

7

Ibid., 34–36.

8

Ibid., 37.

9

J. M. Richards, *An Introduction to Modern Architecture* (Harmondsworth: Penguin Books, 1940), 50. The wording was slightly changed in the 1953 edition.

10

Ibid., 10.

11

Ibid., 16.

12

Ibid., 19.

13

F. R. S. Yorke, *The Modern House* (London: Architectural Press, 1934), 18.

14

Ibid., 25.

15

Ibid., 47.

16

Reyner Banham, "The Last Formgiver," *Architectural Review* (August 1966): 97–108, 98. "For thirty years he discovered, codified, exploited, demonstrated—even invented—and gave authority to more forms than any other architect around." Ibid.

17

Reyner Banham, *Age of the Masters: A Personal View of Modern Architecture* (New York: Harper and Row, 1962), 39. It is precisely the limits of the white image of modern architecture that forms the basis of Banham's historiography. In the same year, his *Guide to Modern Architecture* notes that in the 1950s Edward Stone "clearly senses that the pure white image of a new architecture that he revealed to Americans in the design of the Museum of Modern Art has become a threat, a whited sepulchre in which modern architecture could die. . . . Many critics and architects in the 1950s went round, like Stone, announcing with gloomy good cheer that modern architecture was dead, and drawing the wrong conclusions. All that had happened, in fact, was that modern architecture had ceased to be a stylistic teenager, and its practitioners were no longer compelled to wear the uniform of their peer-group for fear of expulsion from the gang, demotion from christian-name status at C.I.A.M. Any discussion of modern architecture must concern itself largely with this period of almost paranoid teenage conformity, when walls were white, windows large, roofs flat, *or else*, just as any biography of someone in his twenties will be somewhat preoccupied with his teens. But the teen-age uniform of modern architecture, the so called International Style, or White architecture, nowhere exhausts the possibility inherent in its heredity and formation." Reyner Banham, *Guide to Modern Architecture* (London: The Architectural Press, 1962), 18.

18

Reyner Banham, *Theory and Design in the First Machine Age* (Cambridge: MIT Press, 1960), 218, 248.

T A K E   1

The Emperor's New Paint

1

Le Corbusier, *L'art décoratif d'aujourd'hui* (Paris: Éditions G. Grès et Cie, 1925), 193. Translated by James Dunnet as *The Decorative Art of Today* (Cambridge: MIT Press, 1987), xix.

2

Ibid., 188.

3

Ibid., 192.

4

For the references to the "Law of Ripolin" in recent scholarship, see Lion Murand and Patrick Zylberman's entry "Decor (1925): Il s'agit d'une epaisseur de blanc" in *Le Corbusier, une encyclopedie*, ed. Jacques Lucan (Paris: Centre Georges Pompidou, 1987), 116–118; and Bruno Reichlin, "La 'petite maison' à Corseaux. Une analyse structurale," in *Le Corbusier a Geneve 1922–1932: Projets et Realisations*, ed. Isabelle Charollais and Andre Ducret (Lausanne: Payot, 1987), 119–134.

5

Georges Vigarello, *Concepts of Cleanliness: Changing Attitudes in France since the Middle Ages*, translated by Jean Birrell (Cambridge: Cambridge University Press, 1988), 227.

6

"Clothes retained, at whatever cost, their ability to differentiate. A certain sort of white was distinctive, confirmation that the concept of cleanliness, gradually elaborated by means of this architecture of linen, was social. . . . To mention linen, then, and associate it with whiteness, was to associate it with a certain condition. . . . The effect of washing and the effect of the material were the same. Together, they exuded a cleanliness which was not accessible to all." Ibid., 72.

7

Ibid., 136.

8

Ibid., 70.

9

"The shirt had broken through the surface of the clothes, enabling the physical body to be imagined, indirectly but clearly. It supposed a sensibility no longer confined to what was visible. Changing linen was also cleaning the skin, even if the skin itself was not touched by a cleansing hand." Ibid., 60.

10

Ibid., 231.

11

Le Corbusier, *The Decorative Art of Today*, 189.

12

Ibid., 189 [translation slightly modified].

13

Ibid., 190.

14

Le Corbusier, letter to William Ritter from Pisa, 1911, in Giuliano Gresleri, *Le Corbusier Viaggio in Orient* (Venice: Marsilio Editori, 1984), 401.

15

Le Corbusier, *The Decorative Art of Today*, xix.

16

Ibid., 207.

17

Adolf Loos, "Damenmode," *Neue Freie Presse* (August 21, 1898). Translated as "Ladies Fashion" by Jane O. Newman and John H. Smith in Adolf Loos, *Spoken into the Void: Collected Essays 1897–1900* (Cambridge: MIT Press, 982), 99–103, 102. "The lower the cultural level of people, the more extravagant it is with its ornament, its decoration. . . . To seek beauty only in form and not in ornament is the goal toward which all humanity is striving." Adolf Loos, "Das Luxusfuhrwerk," *Neue Freie Presse* (July 3, 1898). Translated as "The Luxury Vehicle" by Jane O. Newman and John H. Smith in Adolf Loos, *Spoken into the Void: Collected Essays 1897–1900*, 39–43, 40.

18

"Decoration: baubles, charming entertainment for a savage. . . . It seems justified to affirm: *the more cultivated a people becomes, the more decoration disappears.* (Surely it was Loos who put it so neatly.)" Le Corbusier, *The Decorative Art of Today*, 85. "Elsewhere, around 1912, Loos wrote that sensational article, *Ornament and Crime.*" Ibid., 134.

19

See Beatriz Colomina, "*L'Esprit Nouveau*, Architecture and *Publicité*," *Architectureproduction* (New York: Princeton Architectural Press, 1988), 77. Stanislaus von Moos, "Le Corbusier and Loos," *Assemblage* 4 (1987): 25–38.

20

Adolf Loos, "Ornament und Verbrechen," lecture of 1908. Translated as "Ornament and Crime" by Wilfred Wang in *The Architecture of Adolf Loos* (London: The Arts Council, 1985), 100–103, 100.

21

Adolf Loos, "Architektur," *Der Sturm* (December 15, 1910). Translated as "Architecture" by Wilfred Wang in *The Architecture of Adolf Loos*, 104–109, 104.

22

von Moos, "Le Corbusier and Loos," 31.

23

Adolf Loos, "Das Prinzip der Bekleidung," *Neue Freie Presse*, September 4, 1898, translated as "The Principle of Cladding" by Jane O. Newman and John H. Smith in Adolf Loos, *Spoken into the Void: Collected Essays 1897–1900*, 66–69, 67. *Bekleidung* is being rendered here as "dressing" following Mallgrave and Herrmann's translation rather than Newman and Smith's translation as "cladding." For the respective notes on this issue, see Gottfried Semper, *The Four Elements of Architecture and Other Writings*, translated by Harry Francis Mallgrave and Wolfgang Herrmann (Cambridge: Cambridge University Press, 1989), 293 and Adolf Loos, *Spoken into the Void*, 139.

24

Loos, "The Principle of Cladding," 67.

25

Gottfried Semper, *Vorläufige Bemerkungen über bemalte Architektur und Plastik bei den Alten* (Altona: Johann Friedrich Hammerich, 1834). Translated as "Preliminary Remarks on Polychrome Architecture and Sculpture in Antiquity," in Harry Francis Mallgrave and Wolfgang Herrmann, *The Four Elements of Architecture and Other Writings*, 45–73, 52.

26

Gottfried Semper, *Der Stil in den technischen und tektonischen Künsten, oder Praktische Aesthetik* (Frankfurt: Verlag für Kunst und Wissenschaft, 1860). Translated as "Style in the Technical and Tectonic Arts or Practical Aesthetics," in Harry Francis Mallgrave and Wolfgang Herrmann, *The Four Elements of Architecture and Other Writings*, 181–263, 254.

27

Gottfried Semper, *Die vier Elemente der Baukunst* (Braunschweig: Friedrich Vieweg und Sohn, 1851). Translated as "The Four Elements of Architecture," in Harry Francis Mallgrave and Wolfgang Herrmann, *The Four Elements of Architecture and Other Writings*, 74–129, 104.

28

"It is well known that even now tribes in an early stage of their development apply their budding artistic instinct to the braiding and weaving of mats and covers (even when they still go around completely naked)." Ibid., 103. "The art of dressing the body's nakedness (if we do not count the ornamental painting of one's own skin discussed above) is probably a later invention than the use of coverings for encampments and spatial enclosures." Gottfried Semper, "Style in the Technical and Tectonic Arts or Practical Aesthetics (1860)," 254.

29

Ibid., 257.

30

The artist must not "violate the material to meet halfway an artistic intent that demands the impossible from the material." Ibid., 189.

31

"Masking does not help, however, when *behind* the mask the thing is false or the mask is no good. In order that the material, the indispensable (in the usual sense of the expression) be completely denied in the artistic creation, its complete mastery is the imperative precondition. Only by complete technical perfection, by judicious and proper treatment of the material according to its properties, and by taking these properties into consideration while creating form can the material be forgotten." Ibid., 257.

32

"But have you ever noticed the strange correspondence between the exterior dress of people and the exterior of buildings? Is the tasselled robe not appropriate to the Gothic style and the wig to the Baroque? But do our contemporary houses correspond with our clothes?" Adolf Loos, "Architecture (1910)," 107.

33

Loos, "The Principle of Cladding (1898)," 66.

34

Gottfried Semper, *Der Stil in den technischen und tektonischen Künsten, oder Praktische Aesthetik*, vol. 1, 445. Cited in Henry Francis Mallgrave, "Gottfried Semper: Architecture and the Primitive Hut," *Reflections* 3, no. 1 (Fall 1985): 60–71, 65.

35

Semper, "Preliminary Remarks on Polychrome Architecture and Sculpture in Antiquity (1834)," 56.

36

Ibid., 59.

37

Le Corbusier, *The Decorative Art of Today*, 188. "The time is past when we . . . can lounge on ottomans and divans among orchids in the scented atmosphere of a seraglio and behave like so many ornamental animals or humming-birds in impeccable evening dress, pinned through the trunk like a collection of butterflies to the swathes of gold, lacquer or brocade on our wall-panelling and hangings." Ibid., 192.

38

Le Corbusier, *Vers une architecture* (Paris: Éditions Crès, 1923), 110. Translated by Frederick Etchells as *Towards a New Architecture* (London: John Rodker, 1931), 138.

39

"The study of folklore gives us no magic formulas for the resolution of the problems of contemporary architecture. It lovingly teaches the profound, natural needs of man as they are revealed to us in solutions that have stood the test of time. Folklore shows us 'man naked,' dressing himself, surrounding himself with tools and objects, with rooms and a house, reasonably satisfying his minimum requirements and coming to terms with the surplus to permit him the enjoyment of his great material and spiritual well-being." Le Corbusier, *Entretien avec les étudiants des écoles d'architecture* (Paris: Donoel, 1943). Translated by Pierre Chase as *Le Corbusier Talks to Students* (New York: Orion Press, 1961), 60.

40

Le Corbusier, *Towards a New Architecture*, 143 [translation slightly modified].

41

Le Corbusier, *The Decorative Art of Today*, 6. When this chapter was originally published in *L'Esprit Nouveau* no. 19 of December 1923, it was illustrated with a photograph of the current President of the Republic in a less modern outfit.

42

Clothing sometimes occupies both the beginning and the middle of the list: "Our modern life, when we are active and about (leaving out the moments when we fly to gruel and aspirin) has created its own objects: its costume, its fountain pen, its eversharp pencil, its typewriter, its telephone, its admirable office furniture, its plate-glass and its 'Innovation' trunks, the safety razor and the briar pipe, the bowler hat and the limousine, the steamship and the airplane." Le Corbusier, *Towards a New Architecture*, 95.

43
"Let us imagine a true museum, one that contained everything, one that could present a complete picture after the passage of time, after the destruction by time . . . let us put together a museum of our own day with objects of our own day; to begin: A plain jacket, a bowler hat, a well made shoe. An electric light bulb with bayonet fixing; a radiator, a table cloth of fine white linen . . . " Le Corbusier, *The Decorative Art of Today*, 16.

44
Ibid., 54.

45
"At this point it looked as if decorative art would founder among the young ladies, had not the exponents of the *decorative ensemble* wished to show, in making their name and establishing their profession, that male abilities were indispensable in this field: considerations of *ensemble*, organization, sense of unity, balance, proportion, harmony." Ibid., 134

46
Ibid., 72.

47
Ibid., 69.

48
Ibid., 22.

49
Ibid., 170.

50
Gratuitous decoration not only covers over flaws in the structure of the object, it also covers over flaws in the structure of contemporary life: "Then *background noise* to fill in the holes, the emptiness. Musical noise, embroidered noise or batiked noise." Ibid., 30.

51
"Architecture has another meaning and other ends to pursue than showing construction and responding to needs," Le Corbusier, *Towards a New Architecture*, 110. The Parthenon, for example, is seen as the climax of the gradual passage "from construction to Architecture." Ibid., 139.

52
Kenneth Frampton, *Modern Architecture: A Critical History* (London: Thames and Hudson, 1985), 248.

53
John Winter, "Le Corbusier's Technological Dilemma," in *The Open Hand: Essays on Le Corbusier*, ed. Russell Walden (Cambridge: MIT Press, 1977), 322–349, 326.

54
"The human-limb object is a docile servant. A good servant is discreet and self-effacing in order to leave his master free." Le Corbusier, *The Decorative Art of Today*, 79. "Rather, it is a question of being dressed *in a way that one stands out the least*." Adolf Loos. "Die Herrenmode," *Neue Freie Presse* (May 22, 1898). Translated by Jane O. Newman and John H. Smith as "Men's Fashion," in Adolf Loos, *Spoken into the Void: Collected Essays 1897–1900*, 10–14, 11.

55
Le Corbusier, *The Decorative Art of Today*, 114.

56
Ibid., 76.

57
Ibid., 77.

58
Ibid., 163. "Feeling dominates. Feeling is never extinguished by reason. Reason gives feeling the purified means it needs to express itself." Ibid., 168.

59
"Thus, from this perspective, too, art appears isolated and shunted off to a field especially marked out for it. The opposite was true in antiquity; then this field was also part of the same domain where philosophy held sway. Philosophy was, as it were, an artist itself and a guide to the other arts." Gottfried Semper, "Style in the Technical and Tectonic Arts or Practical Aesthetics (1860)," 194.

60
"What is the purpose of this constant separation and differentiation that characterizes our present theory of art? Would it not be better and more useful to stress the ascending and descending integration of a work into its surroundings and with its accessories, rather than always to distinguish and divide? . . . must we again rob it of its necessary accessories?" Gottfried Semper, "The Four Elements of Architecture (1851)," 89.

61
Ibid., 102.

62
Semper, "Style in the Technical and Tectonic Arts or Practical Aesthetics (1860)," 183. Semper is referring to the title "Household of Art" that von Rumohr's uses for his Introduction in *Italienishce Forschungen*, vol. 1, Berlin, 1827. See editorial note to Semper, *The Four Elements of Architecture and Other Writings*, 304.

63
"Before this separation our grandmothers were indeed not members of the academy of fine arts or album collectors or an audience for aesthetic lecturers, but they knew what to do when it came to designing an embroidery. There's the rub!" Gottfried Semper, "Style in the Technical and Tectonic Arts or Practical Aesthetics (1860)," 234.

64

Ibid., 184.

65

"It remains certain *that the origin of building coincides with the beginning of textiles.*" Ibid., 254.

66

Ibid., 255.

67

Semper, "Preliminary Remarks on Polychrome Architecture and Sculpture in Antiquity (1834)," 55.

68

"It ranks among the earliest of all inventions because the instinct for pleasure, as it were, inspired man. Delight in color was developed earlier than delight in form." Semper, "Style in the Technical and Tectonic Arts or Practical Aesthetics (1860)," 234.

69

Semper, "Preliminary Remarks on Polychrome Architecture and Sculpture in Antiquity (1834)," 61.

70

"To complete the image of an oriental residence one has to imagine the costly furnishings of gold-plated couches and chairs, divans, candelabras, all kinds of vases, carpets, and the fragrance of incense." Gottfried Semper, chapter 10 of *Vergleichende Baulehre* (1850) (Comparative building theory), Manuscript 58 fols. 94–120 in the Semper-Archiv. Translated as "Structural Elements of Assyrian-Chaldean Architecture" in Wolfgang Herrmann, *Gottfried Semper: In Search of Architecture* (Cambridge: MIT Press, 1984), 204–218, 216. Semper cites Bruno Kaiser on speculative aesthetics: "If form, color, and quantity can only be properly appreciated after they have been sublimated in a test tube of categories, if the sensual no longer makes sense, if the body (as in this aesthetics) must first commit suicide to reveal its treasures—does this not deprive art of the basis for its independent existence?," Semper, "Style in the Technical and Tectonic Arts or Practical Aesthetics (1860)," 194.

71

On the play between the visual and the tactile in Adolf Loos, see Beatriz Colomina, "Intimacy and Spectacle: The Interiors of Adolf Loos," *AA Files 19* (Spring 1990): 5–15.

72

Le Corbusier, *The Decorative Art of Today*, 76 [translation slightly modified].

73

"The work of art, the 'living double' of a being, whether still present, or departed, or unknown; that faithful mirror of an individual passion." Ibid., 118. As opposed to decorative art, "in which particular is absorbed in the general." Ibid., 121.

74

Ibid., 137.

75

Le Corbusier, *Towards a New Architecture*, 19.

76

Ibid., 15 [translation modified].

77

Le Corbusier, *The Decorative Art of Today*, 125.

78

Ibid., 77.

79

Ibid., 118.

80

Le Corbusier, *Quand les cathédrales étaient blanches: Voyage au pays des timides* (Paris: Plon, 1937), translated by Francis E. Hyslop as *When the Cathedrals Were White* (New York: Reynal and Hitchcock, 1947), 202.

81

The argument is repeated in *The Decorative Art of Today:* "The railway brought him wagon-loads full of delicate porcelain covered with roses as fine as the flowers themselves, with seashells, and leafy tendrils of the brightest gold. The peasant on the Danube was immediately dazzled, quite overcome, and lost faith in his folk culture: he let it drop like a load of bricks, wherever the railways reached— throughout the world. . . . Later, the cinema would finish off the work of the railways. The peasant on the Danube has chosen. Folk culture no longer exists, only ornament on mass-produced junk. Everywhere!" Le Corbusier, *The Decorative Art of Today*, 57.

Le Corbusier, *Le Voyage d'Orient* (Paris: Éditions Force Vives, 1966). Translated by Ivan Žaknić as *Journey to the East* (Cambridge: MIT Press, 1987), 59.

83

Le Corbusier, *The Decorative Art of Today*, 189.

84

Ibid., 112.

85

Ibid., 190.

86

Beatriz Colomina, *Privacy and Publicity: Modern Architecture as Mass Media* (Cambridge: MIT Press, 1994).

87

Le Corbusier, "Où en est l'architecture?" *L'architecture vivante* (1927): 7–11, 11.

88

"What is architecture? Where is architecture? In palaces bedecked with sculptures and paintings: such is the doctrine they have been taught. . . . At the summit of 'Polytechnique,' the most renowned of schools in the country, the mind has not emitted a wave that may illuminate the country. Zero! . . . Where is architecture? If the doctrine is: to order, group, bind, organize according to a lofty intention, to endow works with the technique, unity, polish and grace that nature everywhere manifests in its creations. Nature's creations: geology; organic life; seed, root, trunk, branches, leaves, flowers and fruits; chemical and physical phenomena, purely technical phenomena led through the purest of paths to their coordinated, harmonious expression,—from that point on, the polytechnician is a demiurge." Le Corbusier, *Croisade, ou le crépuscule des académies* (Paris: Crès, 1933), 20.

89

Le Corbusier, *When the Cathedrals Were White*, 118.

T A K E   2

The Fashion Police

1

Le Corbusier, *L'art décoratif d'aujourd'hui* (Paris: Éditions G. Grès et Cie, 1925). Translated by James Dunnett as *The Decorative Art of Today* (Cambridge: MIT Press, 1987), 206.

2

Le Corbusier, *Le voyage d'Orient* (Paris: Éditions Forces Vives, 1966). Translated by Ivan Žaknić as *Journey to the East* (Cambridge: MIT Press, 1987), 100.

3

Le Corbusier, *The Decorative Art of Today*, 118.

4

Le Corbusier, *Vers une architecture* (Paris: Éditions Crès, 1923). Translated by Frederick Etchells as *Towards a New Architecture* (London: John Rodker, 1931), 94, 25.

5

Ibid., 17.

6

Ibid., 286.

7

Le Corbusier and Amedée Ozenfant, "Purism," *L'Esprit Nouveau* (Paris) 4, 1920. Translated by Robert L. Herbert in *Modern Artists on Art: Ten Unabridged Essays*, ed. Robert L. Herbert (Englewood Cliffs: New Jersey, 1964) 58–73, 73.

8

Le Corbusier and Pierre Jeanneret, "Fünf Punkte zu einer neuen Architektur," *Die Form* 2 (1927): 272–274. Translated as "Five Points of a New Architecture," in *Architecture and Design: 1890–1939*, ed. Tim Benton and Charlotte Benton (New York: The Whitney Library of Design, 1975), 153–155, 153.

9

Le Corbusier, *Oeuvre complète 1910–29* (Zurich: Girsberger, 1929), 11 [translation slightly modified].

10

Ibid.

11

Sigfried Giedion, *Space, Time and Architecture: The Growth of a New Tradition* (Cambridge: Harvard University Press, 1941), 115.

12

Sigfried Giedion, *Bauen in Frankreich. Eisen. Eisenbeton.* (Berlin: Klinkhardt and Biermann Verlag, 1928), 5.

13

Ibid., 5, 106.

14

Richard Becherer, "Monumentality and the Rue Mallet-Stevens," *Journal of the Society of Architectural Historians* 40, no. 1 (March 1981): 44–55. A recent example, which confirms Becherer's claim, even employing Giedion's original term "elegant," can be found in Tafuri and Dal Co's survey: "The elegant and refined works of Mallet-Stevens, beginning with the De Noailles villa of 1923 in Hyères, were yet another product of an intimate converse with the Cubist vanguard that nonetheless kept its eye on the latest modes and fashions." Manfredo Tafuri and Francesco Dal Co, *Modern Architecture* (New York: Rizzoli, 1986), 233.

15

Giedion, *Bauen in Frankreich. Eisen. Eisenbeton.* 3.

16

"History can reveal to our period the forgotten elements of its being, just as our parents can recover for us those childhood and ancestral peculiarities which continue to determine our natures though they are not to be found in our memories. A connection with the past is a prerequisite for the appearance of a new and self-confident tradition." Giedion, *Space, Time and Architecture*, 30.

17

"We intend to see how our period has come to consciousness of itself in one field, architecture. . . . For a hundred years architecture lay smothered in a dead, eclectic atmosphere in spite of its continual attempts at escape. All that while, construction played the part of architecture's subconsciousness, contained things which it prophesied and half-revealed long before they could become realities." Ibid., 23.

18

Ibid., 175.

19

Ibid., 175, 184.

20

Ibid., 402.

21

Ibid.

22

Ibid, 15.

23
Sigfried Giedion, "Mode oder Zeiteinstellung," *Information* (Zurich) (1 June 1932): 8–11, 9.

24
Ibid., 8.

25
Ibid., 10.

26
Ibid.

27
Ibid., 11.

28
Sigfried Giedion, *Space, Time and Architecture*, 99.

29
"At the present time the problem of constancy is of special consequence, since the threads of the past and of tomorrow have been brought into disorder by an incessant demand for change for change's sake. We have become worshipers of the day-to-day. Life runs along like a television program: one show following relentlessly upon another, barely glancing at problems with never a notion of taking hold of them organically. This has led to an inner uncertainty, to extreme shortcomings in all essential phases of life: to what Heidegger calls 'a forgetfulness of being.' In this situation the question of what has been suppressed and driven back into the unconscious and of what must be restored if man is to regain his equipoise becomes a prime requirement for any integrated culture." Sigfried Giedion, *The Eternal Present: The Beginnings of Art* (Princeton: Princeton University Press, 1962), 7.

30
Ibid., xx.

31
Sigfried Giedion, *The Eternal Present: The Beginnings of Architecture* (Princeton: Princeton University Press, 1964), x.

32
"I was so fascinated by pre-history that I gave it a good many years of my life, because in pre-history you see mankind struggling against huge odds, making tools, and somehow finding (through the shamans or whatever it was) direct contact with the unknown forces. And we are somehow today in a similar position. We are also opposed by unknown forces which we have to conquer." Sigfried Giedion, "Time-scale in History and our Position Today," *Ekistics* 21, no. 123 (February 1966): 81–82, 82.

33
Sigfried Giedion, *Space, Time and Architecture* (1962 edition), liii.

34
Ibid., xliii.

35
Giedion, *Space, Time and Architecture* (1941 edition), 239.

36
Sigfried Giedion, "Ist das neue Bauen eine Mode?" *Basler Nachrichten* (Basel) (13 November 1927): 215–216. Giedion associates fashion with the cult of the individual that he had emphatically condemned in "Gegen Das Ich (1918)" [Against the Ego], one of his first articles, which calls for unification: "This has been the malady of the century: the Ego! We stand where it falls apart. We are at a point where desire wants to see form split into folds no longer but wrapped in a grand curve; where form does not remain solitary in space, aloof and separate from all others, but overwhelmed and swept away by the curve, into the great chain . . . The more impious times have grown, and the more lost in triviality, the more stress has been laid on this: show your Ego, develop your singularity . . . what distinguishes you from others is valuable, not what unites. We acknowledge this: what unites will turn into value!" Sigfried Giedion, "Gegen Das Ich," *Das Junge Deutschland* (Berlin) 8/9 (1918): 242–243, translated by Romana Schneider and Miriam Walther, in *Domus* 678 (December 1986): 20–24.

37
"The historian, the historian of architecture especially, must be in close contact with contemporary conceptions. . . . History is not simply the repository of unchanging facts, but a process, a pattern of living and changing attitudes and interpretations. As such, it is deeply a part of our own natures. To turn backward to a past age is not just to inspect it, to find a pattern which will be the same for all comers. The backward look transforms its object; every spectator at every period—at every moment indeed—inevitably transforms the past according to his own nature. . . . History cannot be touched without changing it . . . observation and what is observed form one complex situation—to observe something is to act upon and alter it." Giedion, *Space, Time and Architecture*, 5.

38
See Mark Wigley. "Theoretical Slippage: The Architecture of the Fetish," *The Princeton Architectural Journal* 4 (1992): 88–129.

39
Giedion, *Space, Time and Architecture*, 18.

40
"The furniture of the ruling taste, like the painting of the ruling taste, is an outgrowth of fashion. Every period shapes life to its own image and drapes it in forms peculiar to itself. By a historical necessity, each fashion—indeed every style—is bounded within its own limited time. But across and beyond this circumscribed period there enters another factor, of fluctuating intensity: This is the quantum of constituent elements, of fresh impulses generated within the period. In them lies the historical import of an era. They can wither from memory perhaps for centuries,

as did the antique heritage. But at a certain time they come up again in man's consciousness, reaffirm their reality, and form the solid ground for new departures. So, for instance, the Renaissance used Antiquity as its springboard, and so in recent decades, the study of primitive man furthered insight into repressed instincts." Sigfried Giedion, *Mechanization Takes Command* (New York: Norton, 1948), 389.

41
Ibid., 344.

42
"What is normally meant by *operative criticism* is an analysis of architecture (or of the arts in general) that, instead of an abstract survey, has as its objective the planning of a precise poetical tendency, anticipated in its structures and derived from historical analyses programmatically distorted and finalized . . . operative criticism *plans* past history by projecting it towards the future . . . this type of criticism, by anticipating the ways of action, forces history: forces past history because, by investing it with a strong ideological charge, it rejects the failures and dispersions throughout history, and forces the future because it is not satisfied with the simple registering of what is happening, but hankers after solutions and problems not yet shown (at least, not explicitly so)." Manfredo Tafuri, *Theories and Histories of Architecture*, translated by Giorgio Verrecchia (New York: Harper and Row, 1976), 141. Operative criticism gives history an "instrumental value": "a typical feature of operative criticism: its almost constant presentation of itself as a prescriptive code." Ibid., 144.

43
Ibid., 169. While opposing history and fashion in this way, the book later acknowledges that fashion has its own history: "The proliferation of studies on the semantics and semiology of architecture is due not only to a snobbish keeping up with the current linguistic *vogue*: every snobbism, anyway, derives its reasons from historical events, and the snobbisms of architectural culture do not escape this rule." Ibid., 174.

44
It is symptomatic that Tafuri does not acknowledge that Giedion spells out in detail the operative role of history. Giedion is made into an example of a phenomenon he had in fact theorized in detail and then, characteristically, has the operative role of his history of certain Italian developments analyzed rather than his claims about historiography. In an almost comic turn, Giedion is, in the end, incriminated for being exactly what he announces that he is from the beginning. The question that remains is not so much the role of operative criticism in the formation of modern architecture, but the role of its acknowledgment, and, it could be added, the role of its ostensible rejection today.

45
Ibid., 11.

46
Ibid., 7.

47
"And it is certainly not difficult to see, underneath an immediately fashionable phenomenon, made evasive by those who appropriated it for snobbish reasons, a frustrated revolt against a modern tradition which, often with sincere despair, one saw fail." Ibid., 50.

48
Ibid., 51.

49
When Tafuri condemns the "'fashionable' architect" Robert Venturi because his book "employs 'fashionable' analytical methods, turning them, without any mediation, into 'compositive' methods," for example, this practice is sharply distinguished from those of the historical avant-garde—particularly Le Corbusier, with whom Vincent Scully is seen to have mistakenly compared it. Ibid., 213.

50
A critical practice is understood to be one that removes fashionable masks without installing new ones. It must "unmask the current mythologies . . . without proposing new myths." Ibid., 201. For Tafuri, these masks are not simply ornamental covers which conceal some structural reality. Rather they actively resist that reality. He describes the way in which the architectural discipline resists the danger of its own exposure posed by semiotics, for example, precisely by appropriating semiotics, instrumentalizing it and thereby transforming it into a fashion. The ongoing "comfort" of the discipline is maintained by the mechanisms of fashion: "After all, what is comfortable in the present confused and contorted cultural situation is the possibility of continuous exchange between game and evasion, essential needs and fashionable phenomena, research and rhetorical toying with worn-out instruments, honest critical commitment and conscious skepticism *à la jongleur*. We were saying that this is a desperate but comfortable situation." Ibid., 211.

51
"'Operative criticism' accepts the current myths, enters into them, tries to create new ones, judges architectural production by the yardsticks of the objectives it itself has proposed and advanced. A criticism that pays attention to the relations between the single work and the system to which it belongs tends to throw light on and to unmask the current mythologies, invites a pitiless coherence. Even the extreme coherence of those who decide to remain (but consciously and critically) in the most absolute silence." Ibid., 201.

52
For Tafuri's eloquent revision of the status of history, which proposes a extreme self-critique to deal with the consequences of accepting the constructive—i.e. operative—nature of history, see particularly "Introduction: The Historical 'Project'," translated by Pellegrino d'Acierno and Robert Connolly, in *The Sphere and the Labyrinth: Avant-Gardes and Architecture from Piranesi to the 1970's* (Cambridge: MIT Press, 1987), 1–24. While stressing the need

to "weave together" multiple methodologies, the text still detaches itself, and the idea of history it promotes, from the complex effects of surface masks that the subsequent essays will go on to analyze in detail (particularly in the section on avant-garde theater costumes). Despite his refusal of a distinction between historiographical method and content, Tafuri never acknowledges his own use of masquerade, pushing certain surfaces forward for at once aggressive and defensive reasons rather than, as he symptomatically puts it, "penetrating" them. On the contrary, he attempts to fragment and redistribute the apparently unified fabric of history in order to resist its own deployment of dissimulating masks: "To look for fullness, an absolute coherence in the interaction of the techniques of domination, is thus to put a mask on history; or better, it is to accept the mask with which the past presents itself." Ibid., 7. And this understanding of a unified sense of history as but a mask is based on Georg Simmel's account of the mask of conformity in his classic essay on fashion. The essay literally turns from a discussion of Nietzsche to Simmel's essay to establish the impossibility of a single totalizing history. Ibid., 5. Once again, all of the sophistication of Tafuri's argument is marshalled against fashion. The image of a single fashionable outfit, a single look, is opposed to that of a multiple, discontinuous, embattled reading. The mask, whose enigmas he elsewhere celebrates, is abruptly simplified. For comprehensive and invaluable analyses of the strategic role of the surface as mask, see: Manfredo Tafuri, "*Cives esse non licere:* The Rome of Nicholas V and Leon Battista Alberti: Elements Towards a Historical Tradition," translated by Stephen Sartarelli, *Harvard Architectural Review* 6 (1987): 60–75; and Manfredo Tafuri, "The Subject and the Mask: An Introduction to Terragni," *Lotus International* 20 (September 1978): 5–29.

53

Nietzsche locates the authentic "historical sense" in the study of the turnover of misfitting garments: "The hybrid European—all in all, a tolerably ugly plebeian—simply needs a costume: he requires history as a storage room for costumes. To be sure, he soon notices that not one fits him very well; so he keeps changing. Let anyone look at the nineteenth century with an eye for these quick preferences and changes of the style masquerade; also for the moments of despair over the fact that 'nothing is becoming.' It is no use to parade as romantic or classical, Christian or Florentine, baroque or 'national,' *in moribus et artibus:* it 'does not look good'. But the 'spirit', especially the 'historical spirit', finds its advantage even in this despair: again and again a new piece of prehistory or a foreign country is tried on, put on, taken off, packed away, and above all *studied:* we are the first age that has truly studied 'costumes'—I mean those of moralities, articles of faith, tastes in the arts, and religions—prepared like no other age for a carnival in the grand style, for the laughter and high spirits of the most spiritual revelry, for the transcendental heights of the highest nonsense and Aristophanean derision of the world. Perhaps this is where we shall still discover the realm of our *invention,* that realm in which we, too, can

still be original, say, as parodists of world history and God's buffoons—perhaps, even if nothing else today has any future, our *laughter* may yet have a future." Friedrich Nietzsche, *Beyond Good and Evil* (1886), translated by Walter Kaufmann (New York: Vintage Books, 1966), section 223, 150. I would like to thank Bastiaan van der Leck for pointing this passage out to me.

54

Manfredo Tafuri, "There is no Criticism, only History," *Design Book Review,* no. 9 (Spring 1986): 8–11, 11. A few years later, in what can only be described as a fashionable art magazine, Tafuri again condemns fashion, dismissing talk of the crisis of modernism as "fashionable social chit-chat," and criticizing the once "fashionable" applications of structuralism and semiology to art before describing the "elaboration of what merely amounts to so many modes of European dress" by American architects in the 1970s as being like "that taste for the exotic that was so fashionable in eighteenth-century salons." Again, fashion is associated with anxiety and simplistically opposed to the qualities of "science" with which Tafuri always associates "good" history: "It's clear that fashion performs the function of reducing anxiety caused by the new. In fact, if we weren't accustomed to being saturated by artistic phenomena, we'd have no capacity for aesthetic understanding, or at least there would not be our widescale acceptance of modernity as a fact of mass culture. But this is a question of human behavior, and is not any basis for the existence of, say, fashion in scientific fields, since science is based on conditions that are independent of facts of daily human nature." Manfredo Tafuri, "Interview," *Flash Art International,* no. 145 (March/April 1989): 67–71, 68.

T A K E   3

Scratching the Surface

1

Adolf Loos, "Architektur," *Der Sturm* (December 15, 1910). Translated as "Architecture" by Wilfred Wang in Yehuda Safran and Wilfred Wang eds., *The Architecture of Adolf Loos* (London: Arts Council, 1987), 104–109, 107.

2

See Roula Geraniotis, "German Architectural Theory and Practice in Chicago: 1850–1900," *Winterthur Portfolio* 21, no. 4 (1986): 243–306.

3

For a revealing analysis of this weave, see Jennifer Bloomer, "D'Or," *Sexuality and Space,* ed. Beatriz Colomina (New York: Princeton Architectural Press, 1992), 163–184.

4

"It would be greatly for our aesthetic good, if we should refrain entirely from the use of ornament for a period of years, in order that our thought might concentrate acutely upon the production of buildings well formed and comely in the nude." Louis Sullivan, "Ornament in Architecture" (1892), in *Louis Sullivan: The Public Papers*, Robert Twombly ed. (Chicago: University of Chicago, 1988), 79–84, 80.

5

For a detailed analysis of these successive readings, see chapter three of Juan Pablo Bonta, *Architecture and Its Interpretation: A Study of Expressive Systems in Architecture* (London: Lund Humphries, 1979).

6

Ibid., 80.

7

Adolf Loos, "Ornament und Erziehung (1924)," in Adolf Loos, *Sämtliche Schriften* (Vienna: Verlag Herold, 1962), 391–398.

8

"May the material speak for itself and appear undraped, in that form and under those conditions that experience and science have tested and proven the most suitable. May brick appear as brick, wood as wood, iron as iron, each according to its own law of statics. This is the true simplicity based on which one can then devote oneself lovingly to the innocent needlepoint of decoration." Gottfried Semper, *Vorläufige Bemerkungen über bemalte Architektur und Plastik bei den Alten* (Altona, 1834). Cited in Fritz Neumeyer, *The Artless Word: Mies van der Rohe on the Building Art* (Cambridge: MIT Press, 1991), 365n8.

9

"Whereas Semper did suggest that material and technique play a role in the genesis of art forms, the Semperians jumped to the conclusion that all art forms were always the direct product of materials and techniques. 'Technique' quickly emerged as a popular buzzword; in common usage, it soon became interchangeable with 'art' itself and eventually began to replace it. . . . They were, of course, not acting in the spirit of Gottfried Semper, who would never have agreed to exchanging free and creative artistic impulse [*Kunstwollen*] for an essentially mechanical and materialist drive to imitate. Nevertheless their misinterpretation was taken to reflect the genuine thinking of the great artist and scholar." Alois Riegl, *Problems of Style: Foundations for a History of Ornament*, translated by Evelyn Kain (Princeton: Princeton University Press, 1992), 4. "Semper would surely have been the last person to discard thoughtlessly truly creative, artistic ideas in favor of the physical-materialist imitative impulse; it was his numerous followers who subsequently modified the theory into its crassly materialist form." Ibid., 19. "According to Semper . . . technology played its formative role at a more advanced stage of artistic development and not at the very inception of artistic activity. This is precisely my conviction." Ibid., 23.

10

"This is not the first time such a proposition has been made; Semper himself expressed it several times." Ibid., 31.

11

"It will become evident, namely, that the human desire to adorn the body is far more elementary than the desire to cover it with woven garments, and that the decorative motifs that satisfy the simple desire for adornment . . . surely existed before textiles were used for physical protection. . . . Surface decoration becomes that larger unit within which woven ornament is but a subset, equivalent to any other category of surface decoration. In general then, one of the main objectives of this book is to reduce the importance of textile decoration to the level it deserves." Ibid., 5.

12

Elsewhere, I have discussed the unique complications of this disciplinary tradition. See Mark Wigley, *The Architecture of Deconstruction: Derrida's Haunt* (Cambridge: MIT Press, 1993).

13

"The clearest case is architecture, next the crafts, particularly when they do not incorporate figurative motives: often architecture and these crafts reveal the basic laws of *Kunstwollen* with an almost mathematical clarity." Alois Riegl, *Die spätrömische Kunstindustrie nach den Funden Österreich-Ungarn* (Vienna: 1901). Translated by Rolf Winkes as *Late Roman Art Industry* (Rome: Giorgio Bretschneider, 1985), 15.

14

"It is true that the engineer is the hero of our age, and that it is to him that we owe our economic position and our international standing. . . . But it cannot be claimed that the creations of the engineers are in themselves already elements of an artistic style.

A certain modern school of aesthetic thought has promoted this misconception by wishing to derive artistic form from utilitarian function and technology. This view of art stems from the theories of Gottfried Semper, who defined the concept of style by demanding that the work of art should be the product first of its function and second of its materials and the tools and procedures involved. This theory comes from the middle of the last century, and should, like many others from this period, be seen as one of the dogmas of Positivism (Riegl).

Admittedly, when one recalls the 'artistic' goods produced by industry over the last decades, one can understand how Semper's view could have been seen as a new truth. . . .

The bad workmanship and cheap materials of these products were covered up by as rich a decoration as possible. . . . I am convinced that this shortcoming cannot be overcome by instructing the manufacturers to keep only to the most functional form. On the contrary, it seems to me much more important to try to understand the essential nature of art.

Art originates as the intuition of powerful individuals and is the free fulfillment of a psychological need. . . . Or, as the Viennese scholar Riegl has put it, 'Semper's mechanistic view of the nature of the work of art should be replaced by a teleological view in which the work of art is seen as the result of a specific and intentional artistic volition that prevails in the battle against functional purpose, raw materials, and technology.' These three last-named factors lose, thereby, the positive role ascribed to them by the so-called Semper theory, and take on instead an inhibiting, negative role: '. . . they constitute, as it were, the coefficient of friction within the overall product.'" Peter Behrens, "Art and Technology (1910)," translated by Iain Boyd Whyte, in Tilmann Buddensieg, *Industriekultur: Peter Behrens and the AEG, 1907–1914* (Cambridge: MIT Press, 1984), 213.

15

Even the subsequent, and apparently anti-Semperian claim that "architecture is the creation of volumes, and its task is not to clad but essentially to enclose space" (Ibid., 217), is Semperian, following Semper's basic argument that cladding is the production of space rather than an addition to it.

16

Walter Gropius, "Die Entwicklung moderner Industriebaukunst," *Jahrbuch des Deutschen Werkbundes*, 1913, 17–22. Translated as "The Development of Modern Industrial Architecture" in *Architecture and Design: 1890–1939*, ed. Tim Benton and Charlotte Benton (New York: Whitney Library of Design, 1975), 53–54.

17

Sigfried Giedion, *Space, Time and Architecture: The Growth of a New Tradition* (Cambridge: Harvard University Press, 1941), 402.

18

Sigfried Giedion, *The Eternal Present: The Beginnings of Art* (Princeton: Princeton University Press, 1962), 15. For the elaboration of this argument, see ibid., 40–42.

19

Sigfried Giedion, *The Eternal Present: The Beginnings of Architecture* (Princeton: Princeton University Press, 1964), 499.

20

Le Corbusier, *Vers une architecture* (Paris: Éditions Crès, 1923), 9. Translated by Frederick Etchells as *Towards a New Architecture* (London: John Rodker, 1931), 19.

21

See Harry Francis Mallgrave, "The Idea of Style: Gottfried Semper in London," unpublished doctoral dissertation, University of Pennsylvania, 1983.

22

For Giedion, 1910 is a key date: "a decisive year, marking the breakthrough of the movement." Giedion, *The Eternal Present: The Beginnings of Art*, 40. It is the year of the

"optical revolution," beyond which artworks are no longer "out of fashion." Ibid., xx. By identifying Semper with the period before 1910, Giedion systematically associates him with the pre-modern rule of fashion. It is significant that Semper plays almost no part in *Space, Time and Architecture*, which tries to detach modern architecture from the Arts and Crafts Movement.

23

Karl Ernst Osthaus. "Austellung wiener Künstler im Folkwang," in *Hagener Zeitung* (Hagen) (December 1, 1906). Cited in Werner J. Schweiger, *Wiener Werkstätte: Design in Vienna 1903–1932* (New York: Abbeville Press, 1984), 90. Osthaus became van de Velde's first biographer in 1920. On the dresses designed for his house, see Klaus-Jürgen Sembach. *Henry van de Velde* (New York: Rizzoli, 1989), 126.

24

"It is known that fashion loves to fall from one extreme to another and one could perhaps explain the psychological causes for this change in that certain organs that are activated in admiring form become weary in time and then make another place for this activity by directing themselves towards other forms." Hermann Muthesius, "Die Moderne Umbildung Unserer Ästhetischen Anschauungen (1902)," in *Kultur und Kunst,* 2d edition (Jena: Berlegt Bei Eugen Diederichs, 1909), 39–75, 39. The essay was originally published in *Deutsche Monatsschrift für das gesamte Leben der Gegenwart* 1.

25

Ibid., 64.

26

In the second edition of his *Stilarchitektur und Baukunst* of 1903, Muthesius added the following passage:

> Somewhere an idea is born that contains an entire program for the future, that is capable of deeply influencing and advancing culture. The multitude, if it notices it at all, laughs it away. Then there steps forward a single form, a formula, a superficiality. Immediately this is taken as essential, puffed up, cried out, and taken as the heart of the matter. The spirit is driven out and the letter deified. Thus it has generally been in religion and morals; in a lesser way the same has come to pass again, as the whiplash curve was taken for the new art and the Jugenstil was founded upon it. Under its dominance people of fashion rejoice, the philistine frets, and the friend of art sighs. For a moment the world opened itself to a welcome liberation; the style machine of the last twenty years had been driven to the absurd and the clockwork of stylistic imitation stood still. But this was true for only a moment. Immediately the opportunity closed upon itself as the whiplash curve and the little flower ornament emerged and worked with redoubled energy. Again there was a style, and now one that was indubitably the very latest. Perhaps it is just as well that the formalism of this whiplash line (for it had degenerated to such even in the hand of its inventor) was put into the mill of industrial fabrication in order to play a role in the fashion market. Thus the warning was given that it would

soon be brought to ruin. The more thoughtful were obliged to maintain their distance and thus perhaps to inch closer to the central question of the time.

Hermann Muthesius, *Stilarchitektur und Baukunst* (Mulheim an der Ruhr: K Schimmelpfeng, 1902/1903). Translated by Stanford Anderson as *Style-Architecture and Building-Art* (Santa Monica: Getty Center, 1994), 87.

27

"Incidently, however, a change was introduced: the demand for variety led by fashion steered toward imitation of other predominately later styles of baroque, of the French style of Ludwig, of the empire. Throughout all the changes in style, the industrial arts held true the basic principle of inciting the historical styles against utilitarian form. . . . If the eternal regurgitation of past forms was already in its own right a dubious activity, then it finally became positively degrading after fashion had chased the artists from one style to another. This aroused an aversion against historical style itself." Hermann Muthesius, "Weg und Ziel," in *Kunstgewerbe und Architektur* (Jena: Berlegt Bei Eugen Diederichs, 1907), 5. The essay was originally published in *Deutsche Kunst* 8 (1905).

28

Hermann Muthesius, "Kunst und Maschine," *Dekorative Kunst* 5 (1902): 141–147, 144.

29

Hermann Muthesius, "Architektur und Publikum," in *Transactions of the VII International Congress of Architects* (London: RIBA, 1906), 304–312, 307.

30

Hermann Muthesius, *Style-Architecture and Building-Art*, 78. The text goes on to argue that: "This type of modern style is, in almost all cases, only a debased edition of the earlier superficially employed historical styles, which it was supposed to displace. It absolutely remains in the realm of architecture–mongering imprisoned in a formal prejudice of which we rightly should have had enough. For the new cannot arise in such outward appearances; architecture, like every other expression, presumes a vital presence. We expect new ideas, not commonplaces clothed in new words." Ibid.

31

Hermann Muthesius, "Landhäuser der Architekten J. W. Bedford und S. D. Kitson in Leeds," *Dekorative Kunst* 6 (1903): 81–97, 82.

32

"Speculating business people think they have recognized a new specialty as being catchy, the Werkbund-specialty as they call it. In many cases it is clear that here the driving element is a purely external spirit of commercialism and not an inner conviction, one that sees a new fashion in the Werkbund-specialty and wants to enjoys its advantages." Hermann Muthesius, "Die Werkbundarbeit der Zukunft Vortrag auf der Werkbund-Tagung Köln 1914," in

Zwischen Kunst und Industrie der Deutsche Werkbund (Munich: Staatliches Museum für Angewandle Kunst, 1975), 85–96, 87.

33

Adolf Loos, "Damenmode," *Neue Freie Presse* (August 21, 1898). Translated as "Ladies Fashion" by Jane O. Newman and John H. Smith in Adolf Loos, *Spoken into the Void: Collected Essays 1897–1900* (Cambridge: MIT Press, 1982), 99–103, 99.

34

"In those days one decorated his home the way one outfits himself today. We buy our shoes from the shoemaker, coat, pants and waistcoat from the tailor, collars and cuffs from the shirtmaker, hats from the hatter, and walking sticks from the turner. None of them knows any of the others, and yet everything matches quite nicely." Adolf Loos, "Intériurs," *Neue Freie Presse* (June 5, 1898). Translated as "Interiors: A Prelude" by Jane O. Newman and John H. Smith in Adolf Loos, *Spoken into the Void: Collected Essays 1897–1900*, 19–21, 19.

35

Adolf Loos, "An Den Ulk (1910)," in Adolf Loos, *Sämtliche Schriften*, 238.

36

Adolf Loos, "Von einem armen, reichen Mann," *Neues Wiener Tagblatt*, April 26, 1900. Translated as "The Poor Little Rich Man (1900)," by Jane O. Newman and John H. Smith in Adolf Loos, *Spoken into the Void: Collected Essays 1897–1900*, 125–127.

37

Adolf Loos, "Ornament und Verbrechen," lecture of 1908. Translated as "Ornament and Crime" by Wilfred Wang in Yehuda Safran and Wilfred Wang, eds., *The Architecture of Adolf Loos* (London: The Arts Council, 1985), 100–103, 102.

38

Kenneth Frampton, *Modern Architecture: A Critical History* (London: Thames and Hudson, 1985), 81.

39

"Regardless whether it is a matter of architecture proper, of designing a piece of furniture, a metal utensil, a wallpaper, a dress: There are always the same conditions of creation from which the work comes." Leopold Kleiner, *Deutsche Kunst und Dekoration* 54 (1924): 161. Cited by Eduard Sekler, *Josef Hoffmann: The Architectural Work* (Princeton: Princeton University Press, 1985), 240.

40

Cited in Werner J. Schweiger, *Wiener Werkstätte: Design in Vienna 1903–1932* (New York: Abbeville Press, 1984), 211.

41

"At times he [Hoffmann] even used to appear personally in the sales-room of the textile department of the Wiener Werkstätte in order to suggest to customers, with the aid of improvised draping, which fabrics they ought to wear in what manner." Sekler, *Josef Hoffmann*, 221.

42

"Against the background of this reality, 'aesthetic sermons' by ideologists of the Wiener Werkstätte claiming that they were well on the way to creating an art that was true to design and materials for the enlightened human race of the twentieth century must have brought a smile to the face to realistic social reformers, let alone dyed-in-the-wool Marxists." Wolfgang Gerd Fischer, *Gustav Klimt and Emilie Flöge: An Artist and His Muse* (Woodstock, N.Y.: Overlook Press, 1992), 37.

43

Describing his visit to Hoffmann's Stoclet Palace, Poiret says "Hoffmann designed everything, including Madame's dresses and Monsieur's sticks and cravats. This substitution of the taste of the architect for the personality of the proprietors has always seemed to me a sort of slavery—a subjection that made me smile." Paul Poiret, *En habillant L'epoque*, translated by Stephen Haden Guest as *King of Fashion: The Autobiography of Paul Poiret* (Philadelphia: J. Lippincott, 1931), 159.

44

Isabelle Anscombe, *A Women's Touch: Women in Design from 1860 to the Present Day* (New York: Elizabeth Sifton Books, Viking, 1984), 115.

45

Sekler, *Josef Hoffmann*, 129.

46

Cited in Traude Hausen, *Wiener Werkstätte Mode: Stoffe— Schmuck—Accessories* (München: Christian Branstätter, 1984), 14.

47

Loos, "Ornament und Erziehung (1924)," 395

48

The newspaper reports that are the only surviving records of the lecture are cited Eduard Sekler, *Josef Hoffmann*, 190.

49

Cited from newspaper reports, in Schweiger, *Wiener Werkstätte*, 118.

50

Germain Boffrand, *Livre d'Architecture*, 1745. Cited in Peter Collins, *Changing Ideals in Modern Architecture: 1750–1950* (Montreal: McGill University Press, 1967), 266.

51

"While they had to go back to simplified forms and clear-cut lines to find a new starting-point, they were animated most by the desire to create a surface style. . . . No one . . . so charmingly feminized architecture; no one . . . so richly colored buildings without breaking up wall sense." Sheldon Cheney, *The New World Architecture* (London: Long-

mans Green, 1930), 25. Partially cited in Sekler, *Josef Hoffmann*, 517n65.

52

Adolf Loos, "Kulturentartung," essay dated 1908 and first published in Adolf Loos, *Trotzdem* (Innsbruck: 1931). Translated as "Cultural Degeneration" (1908) in *The Architecture of Adolf Loos*, ed. Yehuda Safran and Wilfred Wang, 98–99, 99. "Ten years ago these artists went in search of new conquests and tried to bring the tailoring trade under their control, after they had already brought down the craft of joinery. . . . They were dressed in frock coats of Scottish plaid and velvet lapels, a piece of cardboard stuck in their turned-down collars—trade-mark 'Ver Sacrum'—was covered with black silk and gave the illusion of a tie which had been wound around their necks three times. I managed to drive these gentlemen out of the tailors' and shoemakers' work-shops with a few forceful essays on the subject. . . . The master tailor, who had shown himself to be so accommodating to these cultural and artistic endeavors, was abandoned, and gentlemen took a subscription with a Viennese bespoke tailor." Ibid., 98.

53

Sigfried Giedion, "R. J. Neutra: European and American," in *Richard Neutra: Buildings and Projects*, Vol. 1 (1923–1950), ed. Willy Boesiger (Zurich: Verlag für Architektur, 1992), 8–10, 8.

54

Sigfried Giedion, "Zur situation deutscher architektur (Die kunstgewerbliche Infiltration)," *Der Cicerone* 18 (1926): 216–224. Translated by Tim Benton as "The State of German Architecture," in *Documents: A Collection of Some Material on the Modern Movement* ed. Tim Benton (Milton Keynes: Open University, 1975), 11–15, 12.

55

Ibid., 15.

56

Ibid., 13.

57

Ibid., 15.

58

Giedion, *Space, Time and Architecture*, 207.

59

Ibid., 209.

60

Giedion, *Space, Time and Architecture*, 5th ed., 1962, xxxii–liii.

61

Sigfried Giedion, "The Tragic Conflict (1936, 1955)," in Sigfried Giedion, *Architecture, You and Me* (Cambridge: Harvard University Press, 1958), 25–39.

62

"There are forces inherent in man, which come to the surface when one evokes them. The average man, with a century of falsified emotional education behind him, may not be won over suddenly by the contemporary symbol in painting and sculpture. But his inherent, though unconscious, feeling may slowly be awakened by the original expression of a new community life. This can be done within a framework of urban centers and in great spectacles capable of fascinating the people." Sigfried Giedion, "The Need for a New Monumentality (1944)," in *Architecture, You and Me*, 25–39, 38.

63

Giedion, *The Eternal Present: The Beginnings of Art*, 4.

64

Sigfried Giedion, *Walter Gropius: Work and Teamwork* (New York: Rheinhold Publishing, 1954), 36.

65

A notable exception is Leonie von Wilckens, "Künstlerkleid und Reformmode—Textilkunst in Nürnberg," in *Peter Behrens und Nürnberg*, exhibition catalog, Germanisches Nationalmuseum Nuremberg, ed. Peter-Klaus Schuster (Munich: Prestel, 1980).

66

Even Osthaus, who wrote the first biography on van de Velde in 1920, does not describe the dress designs, though some of them were done to match his own house, which features prominently in his book. A significant exception is Kenneth Frampton's *Modern Architecture: A Critical History*, which illustrates one of van de Velde's clothing designs modeled by Maria Van de Velde and refers to Loos's parody of such designs. Francesco Dal Co illustrates one of these dresses, along with a design by Behrens and another by Wimmer, but does not discuss them in the text, even though it does address the general question of fashion in some detail. Francesco Dal Co, *Figures of Architecture and Thought: German Architecture Culture 1880–1920* (New York: Rizzoli, 1990). Sekler's comprehensive book on "The Architectural Work" of Hoffmann does address his dress designs briefly. Coffee table books on Art Nouveau and ornamentation that are not directed toward an architectural audience, however, do not hesitate to illustrate and discuss the dress designs. The line between dress design and architecture is almost always preserved, even in the face of a practice whose declared purpose is to efface that line.

67

See Beatriz Colomina, "On Adolf Loos and Josef Hoffmann: Architecture in the Age of Mechanical Reproduction." *9H* 6 (1983), 52–58; and Beatriz Colomina, "The Split Wall: Domestic Voyeurism," in *Sexuality and Space*, ed. Beatriz Colomina (New York: Princeton Architectural Press, 1992), 73–130. Colomina's decisive reading of Loos's deployment of fashion as a mask is elaborated further in her *Privacy and Publicity: Modern Architecture as Mass Media* (Cambridge: MIT Press, 1994).

Redressing Architecture

1

Josef Hoffmann, "Das individuelle Kleid," *Die Waage* 15, no. 9 (1898) 251–252. Cited in Traude Hansen, *Wiener Werkstätte: Staffe-Smucke-Accessories* (Munich: Christian Branstätter, 1984), 13.

2

"We must be . . . modern, i.e., we must not refer back too much to old dead things. It is impossible to imagine the chauffeur of an auto in the Old Viennese costume of a coachman. . . . We must advance to a unified form. England . . . instinctively knows only the city cut, and avoids every attempt at country folk costume which often leads to costume ball-like aberrations of taste. . . . Respect for the frequent genius of the design of such folk costumes should force us not to masquerade frivolously in them." Josef Hoffmann, "Vorschläge zur Mode," *Neue Wiener Journal* (17 July 1936). Cited in Eduard Sekler, *Josef Hoffmann: The Architectural Work* (Princeton: Princeton University Press, 1985), 515n11.

3

Henry van de Velde, *Die Renaissance im modernen Kunstgewerbe* (Berlin, 1901), 47, 48, 81f; *Die drei Sünden wider die Schönheit* (Zurich, 1918), 26ff. Cited in Frank-Lothar Kroll, "Ornamental Theory and Practice in the Jugendstil," *Rassegna* 41 (1979): 58–65, 64.

4

Nikolaus Pevsner, *Pioneers of the Modern Movement: From William Morris to Walter Gropius* (London: Faber and Faber, 1936), 18.

5

In his reply to Muthesius, van de Velde says that the artist resists anyone who "attempts to drive him into a universally valid form, in which he sees only a mask." Henry van de Velde, "Counter-Propositions," translated in *Documents: A Collection of Some Material on the Modern Movement*, ed. Tim Benton (Milton Keynes: The Open University, 1975), 6.

6

"Since it was inconceivable to me that beauty could ever be in part the product of reason and in part of its opposite, I refused to allow the presence of any object in my own home which was not as basically honest, genuinely straightforward and altogether above suspicion in design as the character of the friends we received there. An interior which displays downright shams, capricious whimsicalities or wild formal travesties clearly exerts just as immoral an influence as a man who deliberately bases his life on a tissue of false pretenses. Designs are moral as long as they do not transgress the dictates of reason; they become immoral so soon as they show signs of being subordered by the lure of fantasy." Henry van de Velde, "Extracts From his Memoirs: 1891–1901," *Architectural Review* 112, no. 669 (September 1952): 143–155, 153.

7

Henry van de Velde, "Was Ich Will (1901)," in Henry van de Velde, *Zum neum stil* (Munich, 1955), 81. Cited in Christian Schädlich, "Van de Velde and the Construction of Rational Beauty," *Rassegna* 45 (1979): 38–49, 41.

8

Henry van de Velde, "Die Linie (1910)" in Henry van de Velde, *Zum neum stil,* 193. Cited in Schädlich, "Van de Velde and the Construction of Rational Beauty," 45.

9

"Just as evil is for ever seeking to corrupt virtue, so throughout the history of art some malignant cancer has ceaselessly striven to taint or deform man's purest ideals of beauty. The brief interlude of *art nouveau,* that ephemeral will o' the wisp which knew no law other than its own caprice, was succeeded, as I had foretold, by the hesitant beginnings of a new, disciplined and purposeful style, the style of our own age. . . . [which] will synchronize with the realization of a rationalized aesthetic, whereby beauty of form can be immunized against recurrent infections from the noisome parasite fantasy." Van de Velde, "Extracts From his Memoirs: 1891–1901," 155.

10

In fact, van de Velde argues that the reason his work would not become a vogue was that its lack of familiar ornament always aroused the same kind of antagonism as that directed towards his own house: "One can only suppose this excited the suspicion that the virus of some dangerously subversive tendency must lurk beneath my wholesale elimination of conventional ornament." Ibid., 154. As Christian Schädlich puts it: "It is necessary to bear in mind that Van de Velde's architectural production was only marginally influenced by the current denominated as Jugendstil . . . he kept a distance . . . both because it was a widely diffused movement, often influenced by fashion and by the orientations of the market, and because of the formal excesses to which it was subject during the phase around 1900 with the affirmation of the new ornamental art." Christian Schädlich, "Van de Velde and the Construction of Rational Beauty," 38.

11

Henry van de Velde, "Le nouveau: pourquoi toujours du nouveau? (1929)," in his *Pages de doctrine* (Brussels, 1942). Reprinted in Henry van de Velde, *Deblaiement d'Art* (Brussels: Editions des Archives d'Architecture Moderne, 1979), 72–107, 91.

12

Ibid., 80.

13

Eduard Sekler, *Josef Hoffmann,* 37.

14

Josef Hoffmann, "Simple Furniture," *Das Interieur* II (1901). Translated in Eduard Sekler, *Josef Hoffmann,* 483–485, 483. Compare the passage in Hoffmann's 1924 essay, "The School of the Architect," which argues that when art scholars out of touch with contemporary design recommend the purchase of old buildings and furnishings: "a modern gathering in tailcoat and uniform with ladies in modern dresses had to have a disturbing effect in such a room." Josef Hoffmann, "The School of the Architect," *Das Kunstblatt* (April 1924). Translated in Eduard Sekler, *Josef Hoffmann,* 493–495, 494. This essay also contains the Behrens-like argument: "We know today that, without using decorative forms, we can arrive at a new design that aims only for the causative. But we also know that the best calculated form of construction does not achieve a satisfying product, that in addition to a command of the technical requirements, one must have a cultivated taste, a feeling for relationships and the rhythm of the visual, as well as that secret sensitivity which only artistically oriented people possess, in order to bring satisfying results." Ibid., 494. It is precisely this sense that enables Le Corbusier to identify with Hoffmann: "And among the ordinary productions, often devoted to narrowly circumscribed utilitarian tasks, the works of Hoffmann left a deep impression because he, like myself, starts from the conviction that architectural work must possess a spiritual content, provided of course that it completely fulfills the demands of appropriateness . . . what remains is the 'indispensable superfluous,' *art* (a word today kicked around like a football.) *And in the history of contemporary architecture, on the way to a timely aesthetic, Professor Hoffmann holds one of the most brilliant places.*" Le Corbusier, "The Wiener Werkstätte (1929)" in *Die Wiener Werkstätte: 1903–1928,* translated in Eduard Sekler, *Josef Hoffmann,* 496.

15

"Is that again the disgusting mania of the *parvenu* to seem more than he is, or is it a resigned retreat after deep disappointment . . . seized by the giddiness of the masquerade with its spurious, false knickknacks, with its lack of style despite all the styles of all times and countries." Josef Hoffmann, "Simple Furniture (1901)," 483.

16

Ibid., 484.

17

Ibid.

18

Ibid., 483.

19

Jane Kallir, *Viennese Design and the Wiener Werkstätte* (New York: George Brazilier, 1986), 32.

20

Rob Mallet-Stevens, "La mode et le moderne," text dated February 23 1938, translated as "Modern Versus Modish" in *Rob Mallet-Stevens: Architecte,* Dominique Deshouliès and Hubert Jeanneau eds., (Brussells: Editions des Archives d'Architecture Moderne, 1980), 377. "Fashion dictates if the silhouettes of women's hats are pure fancy; the almost universal adoption of the soft hat for men is an aberration. This soft material, folded upwards to gather the rain and which loses its shape in the wind, is at the very least comic. Custom demands that man's suits have buttons at the cuff as a reminder of the rows of copper buttons sewn on the jackets of Zouave soldiers in order to prevent their blowing their noses on them! And what can be said about the two buttons nicely placed on the back of evening suits, which once served to raise the coat-tail in order to permit the wearer to rise a horse! Fashion." Ibid.

21
Adolf Loos, "Architektur," *Der Sturm* (December 15, 1910)." Translated as "Architecture" by Wilfred Wang in *The Architecture of Adolf Loos*, Yehuda Safran and Wilfred Wang eds. (London: The Arts Council, 1985), 104–109, 107.

22
Adolf Loos, "Damenmode," *Neue Freie Presse* (August 21, 1898). Translated as "Ladies Fashion" by Jane O. Newman and John H. Smith in *Spoken into the Void: Collected Essays 1897–1900* (Cambridge: MIT Press, 1982), 99–103, 100.

23
Elizabeth Wilson, "All the Rage," in Jane Gaines and Charlotte Herzog, *Fabrications: Costume and the Female Body* (New York: Routledge, 1990), 28–38, 29.

24
Loos cites himself in "Josef Veillich (1929)," Adolf Loos, *Sämtliche Schriften* (Vienna: Verlag Herold, 1962), 436–442, 437.

25
Adolf Loos, "Kultur," *März* (Munich), (October 1908), Translated as "Culture" in Safran and Wang, *The Architecture of Adolf Loos*, 97–99. He describes the influence of riding clothes on the evolution of "dress suit," and predicts the influence of workers clothes, arguing that the "man in overalls" from America "has conquered the world."

26
Adolf Loos, "Die Herrenmode," *Neue Freie Presse* (May 22, 1898). Translated by Jane O. Newman and John H. Smith as "Men's Fashion," in Adolf Loos, *Spoken into the Void: Collected Essays 1897–1900*, 10–14, 11.

27
Beatriz Colomina, "The Split Wall: Domestic Voyeurism," in *Sexuality and Space*, ed. Beatriz Colomina (New York: Princeton Architectural Press, 1992): 73–130, 93. "For Loos, the interior is Pre-Oedipal space, space before the analytical distancing which language entails, space as we feel it, as clothing; that is, as clothing before the existence of readymade clothes, when one had to first choose the fabric. . . . The spaces of Loos's interiors cover the occupants as clothes cover the body (each occasion has its appropriate 'fit'). . . . But space in Loos's architecture is not just felt. . . . The 'clothes' have become so removed from the body that they require structural support independent of it. They become a 'stage set.' The inhabitant is both 'covered' by the space and 'detached' from it." Ibid., 90.

28
Hermann Muthesius, *Das englische haus, entwicklung bedingungen, anlage, aufbau, einrichtung und innenraum* (Berlin: Wasmuth, 1904–1905). Translated by Janet Seligman as *The English House* (New York: Rizzoli, 1987), 10.

29
Le Corbusier, *Vers une architecture* (Paris: Éditions Crès, 1923), 115, 112. Translated by Frederick Etchells as *Towards a New Architecture* (London: John Rodker, 1931), 145, 143.

30
"To abuse or ridicule any nostalgia for ornamentation can only deter people from studying the modern style and from trying to appreciate it. . . . I need hardly add that I have tried not to mistake the modern for the beautiful, nor a fashion for that much profounder expression of a new period in the history of humanity which we call a style." Nikolaus Pevsner, *Industrial Art in England* (Cambridge: Cambridge University Press, 1957), 10. The book, which Pevsner prepared at the same time as his book on modern architecture, promotes the modern style (because ninety percent of British industrial art is "devoid of any aesthetic merit") but opposes the "modernistic fashion," understood as the "disease of modernism."

31
Pevsner, *Pioneers of the Modern Movement*, 206.

32
"The reasons for the fight were more against the person of Muthesius than the content of his thesis. He was an unpleasant man who used tricky methods to get into the lead. His mind was also much too rigid and 'unartistic.' I was the youngest Board member in the *Werkbund* and acted as *enfant terrible* to bring Muthesius's methods into the open. But you are quite right; when one looks at the substance of that fight, one wonders about the strange distribution of participants on both sides." Walter Gropius, "Letter to the Editor," written in reply to an article by Pevsner, *Architectural Review* 134 (July 1963): 6.

33
Walter Gropius, *The New Architecture and the Bauhaus*, translated by P. Morton Shand (London: Faber and Faber, 1935), 34.

34
Letter from Fritz Mackensen to Walter Gropius dated October 2, 1915, in Hans M. Wingler, *The Bauhaus: Weimer, Dessau, Berlin, Chicago* (Cambridge: MIT Press, 1969), 22.

35
Letter from Fritz Mackensen to Walter Gropius dated October 14, 1915. Ibid., 22.

36
See, for example, Walter Gropius, "Sociological Premises for the Minimum Dwelling of Urban Industrial Populations" (1929), in his *Scope of Total Architecture* (New York: Collier Books, 1955), 91–102. See also Walter Grop-

ius, "The Formal and Technical Problems of Modern Architecture and Planning (1934)," translated by P. Shand, *Journal of the Royal Institute of British Architects* (19 May 1934): 679–694, 694.

37

On women at the Bauhaus, see Magdalena Broste, *Bauhaus 1919–1933* (Berlin: Bauhaus-Archiv Museum für Gestaltung and Benedikt Taschen, 1990), 38–40. As Broste earlier points out, the number of women trained in the Prussian handicraft schools had increased from the moment that the government revised them all by adding workshops and appointing artists as teachers on Muthesius's advice. Ibid., 11. Note that this contrasts markedly with Anscombe's optimistic version: Isabelle Anscombe, *A Woman's Touch: Women in Design from 1860 to the Present Day* (New York: Viking Penguin, 1984), 131–144.

38

Magdalena Broste, *Bauhaus 1919–1933*, 74.

39

Dirk Scheper, "Die Bauhausbühne," in *Experiment Bauhaus* (Berlin: Bauhaus Archiv, 1988), 256. Cited in Broste, *Bauhaus 1919–1933*, 158.

40

Werner Graeff, "Bemerkungen eines Bauhäuslers," in Werner Graeff, *Ein Pionier der Zwanziger Jahre*, exhibition catalog, Skulpturenmuseum der Stadt Marl, 1979, 7. Cited in Magdalena Broste, *Bauhaus 1919–1933*, 57, 31.

41

Nikolaus Pevsner, "Gropius and van de Velde," *Architectural Review* 133, no. 793 (March 1963): 165–168, 168. Loos praises overalls again in "Antworten auf Fragen aus dem Publikum (1919)," in Loos, *Sämtliche Schriften*, 355–378, 365.

42

Herbert Bayer, "Homage to Gropius," in *Bauhaus and Bauhaus People* ed. Eckhard Neumann (New York: Van Nostrand Reinhold, 1993), 141. Compare to Hoffmann's dress: "Hoffmann always valued a good appearance, and the colors gray, black, and white were his preferred personal choice in dressing. As far as dressing for the evening was concerned, he was of the opinion that—in contrast to the many colors of women's fashions—man should wear only nonchromatic hues." Eduard Sekler, *Josef Hoffmann*, 235.

43

Walter Gropius, "Die Entwicklung moderner Industriebaukunst" *Jahrbuch des Deutschen Werkbundes*, 1913, 17–22. Translated as "The Development of Modern Industrial Architecture" in *Architecture and Design: 1890–1939*, ed. Tim Benton and Charlotte Benton (New York: Whitney Library of Design, 1975), 53–54, 53. "Occasionally an architect was called in to add irrelevant decoration to the naked form of the utilitarian building. Points of conflict were concealed on the exterior, and because one was ashamed of it, the true character of the building was hidden behind a sen-

timental mask taken from an earlier age according to the whim of the owner . . . ornamental decoration is only a final touch." Walter Gropius, "Industriebau," catalog to travelling exhibition of Deutsches Museum für Kunst in Handel und Gewerbe, 1911 translated by Iain Boyd Whyte as "Industrial Buildings" in Tilmann Buddensieg, *Industriekultur: Peter Behrens and the AEG, 1907–1914* (Cambridge: MIT Press, 1984), 247–248, 247.

44

Walter Gropius, *The New Architecture and the Bauhaus*, 23.

45

Walter Gropius, *Scope of Total Architecture*, 12.

46

"Were mechanization an end in itself it would be an unmitigated calamity, robbing life of half its fullness and variety by stunting men and women into sub-human, robot-like automatons. (Here we touch the deeper causality of the dogged resistance of the old civilization of handicrafts to the new world-order of the machine.)" Walter Gropius, *The New Architecture and the Bauhaus*, 33.

47

Walter Gropius, "Eight Steps Toward a Solid Architecture," *Architectural Forum* (February 1954): 173–182, 182.

48

Ibid., 174.

49

Ibid, 174, 178.

50

Walter Gropius, "Ornament and Modern Architecture," *American Architect and Architecture* (January 1938): 21–22, 22.

51

Walter Gropius, "Wohnhaus-Industrie," in *Ein Versuchshaus des Bauhauses in Weimer* ed. Adolf Meyer (Munich: Albert Langen Verlag, 1924). Translated as "Housing Industry," in Walter Gropius, *Scope of Total Architecture*, 128–135, 128.

52

Walter Gropius, *Bauhaus Dessau, Grunsätze der Bauhausproduktion* (Dessau: Bauhaus, 1926). Translated as "Bauhaus Dessau—Principles of Bauhaus Production (1926)," in *Architecture and Design: 1890–1939*, ed. Tim Benton and Charlotte Benton, 148–149, 148.

53

Walter Gropius, *Bauhausbücher* 12, *Bauhausbauten Dessau* (Munich: 1930), 99–121.

54

Walter Gropius, "The Development of Modern Industrial Architecture (1913)," 54.

55

Ibid.

56

Walter Gropius, "Is There a Science of Design?" in *Scope of Total Architecture,* 35. The article originally appeared as "Design Topics" in *Magazine of Art* (December 1947, 299–304, 301), in which the line reads: "This is an important fact to know for fashion design." Gropius removed the newspaper's fashion tip, however, for the revised article's publication in the well-known collection of essays.

57

Walter Gropius, "Housing Industry (1924)," 134.

58

Walter Gropius, *Bauhausbücher 7, Neue Arbeiten der Bauhauswerkstätten* (Munich: 1925), 7.

59

"*The provision of housing for people is concerned with mass needs.* It would no longer occur to 90 per cent of the population today to have their shoes specially made to measure. Instead, they buy *standard products* off-the-peg, which, thanks to much improved production methods, satisfy the requirements of most individuals. Similarly, in the future the individual will be able to order a house *from stocks* which suits his needs. . . . Standardization of parts places no restrictions on the individual design. Their recurrence in differently shaped buildings will have an orderly and soothing effect as does the uniformity of our clothes." Walter Gropius, "Wie Bauen Wirbilligere, Bessere, Schönere Wohnungen?" *Die Form,* (1927): 275–277. Translated as "How can we build cheaper, better, more attractive houses?" in *Architecture and Design: 1890–1939,* ed. Tim Benton and Charlotte Benton, 195–196, 195.

60

Walter Gropius, *The New Architecture and the Bauhaus,* 40.

61

Walter Gropius, "Programm zur Gründung einer Allgemeinen Hausbaugesellschaft aug künsterisch einheitlicher Grundlage," manuscript of 1910, translated as "Program for the Establishment of a Company for the Provision of Housing on Aesthetically Consistent Principles," *The Architectural Review* (July 1961): 49–51, 49.

62

Walter Gropius, "The Inner Compass," a lecture of May 1958 published in Walter Gropius, *Apollo in the Democracy: The Cultural Obligations of the Architect* (New York: McGraw Hill, 1968), 14.

63

Walter Gropius, *Scope of a Total Architecture,* 11.

64

Walter Gropius, *The New Architecture and the Bauhaus,* 91. An example of such an accusation is made by Ernst Kallai: "Bauhaus style: one word for everything. Wertheim sets up a new department for modern-style furniture and appliances, an arts-and-crafts salon with functionally trimmed high-fashioned trash. . . . A fashion magazine in Vienna recommends that ladies' underwear no longer be decorated with little flowers, but with more contemporary Bauhaus-style geometrical designs. Such embarrassing and amusing misuses in the fashion hustle of our wonderful modern age cannot be prevented . . . exchanging the historical robe for a sort of pseudo-technological raciness . . . a taste-oriented arbitrariness decked out in new clothes." Ernst Kallai, "Ten Years of Bauhaus (1930)," in *Architecture and Design: 1890–1939,* ed. Tim Benton and Charlotte Benton, 172–175, 172.

65

Walter Gropius, *The New Architecture and the Bauhaus,* 23. Note that Gropius had published this claim a year earlier. Walter Gropius, "The Formal and Technical Problems of Modern Architecture and Planning (1934)," 679.

66

Reyner Banham, *Theory and Design in the First Machine Age* (Cambridge: MIT Press, 1960), 79.

67

Letter from Carl Benscheidt to Walter Gropius, dated March 20, 1911. Cited in Reyner Banham, *A Concrete Atlantis: U.S. Industrial Building and European Modern Architecture* (Cambridge: MIT Press, 1986), 187.

68

Klaus Herdeg, *The Decorated Diagram: Harvard Architecture and the Failure of the Bauhaus Legacy* (Cambridge: MIT Press, 1983), 12. On the back of the book, Colin Rowe offers the following: "The persistence of the mystique of Walter Gropius is very hard to understand. For, as both architect and educator, Gropius was surely inept . . . it was supposed that Gropius was a supreme Moses-figure, preparing and illuminating *the way;* but, then, when *the way* turned out to be little more than relentless *kitsch* catastrophe, the mystique survived and it continues to plague architectural education to this day. For the confusions of so-called Post Modernism are not only a reaction to Gropius but also an explicit product of that abysmal failure to recognize the complex nature of architectural discourse, which Klaus Herdeg here alleges was the ultimate result of the Harvard 'establishment' sponsored by Gropius."

69

Herdeg's argument that the works of the Gropius school "devalue what were the once rigorous standards of architecture" (ibid., 2), for example, depends on being able to successfully contrast Le Corbusier's "ironic" use of the "false-front" to that of Gropius's school and of Main Street USA (the paradigm for postmodernists).

70

"The same person who transacts his shrewdly calculated business affairs in the most modern up-to-date office, actually inhabits a dwelling which is its very antithesis in its old-fashionedness, despite the installation of electric light, wireless, etc. The man who travels abroad in his car, with which he is familiar to the minutest detail, prefers to stay at an inn with tiny diamond-paned windows and, if possible, with a steep, thatched roof—an inn frequented once upon a time by be-wigged, long coated gentlemen and ladies in hoops. What would he say, were a crinolined lady with powdered locks to settle herself in the driver's seat of his car? What would he say were whole compartments in express trains to be occupied by these ladies and gentlemen? According to his present views on architecture he should by rights say nothing, for he prefers crinolines and wigs in house and home." Bruno Taut, *Modern Architecture* (London: The Studio Limited, 1929), 2.

71
Ibid., 3.

72
"For those who are only capable of visualizing the surface of architecture—the facade, so to speak—all remains facade. This term has become the figurative expression for the veiling of makeshifts and doubtful moral characteristics, in respect of individuals, firms, and political parties. The expression 'facade' has already been adopted in Germany in the sense of disguise, a mask, intended to conceal personality, as if to say, the wolf in sheep's clothing." Ibid., 8.

73
Ibid., 140.

74
Ibid., 139.

75
Ibid., 169.

76
Theo van Doesburg, "Vernieuwingspogingen der architectuur in Duitschland en Oostenrijk," *Het Bouwbedrijf* 2, no. 5 (May 1925): 197–200. Translated as "The Ambiguous Mentality: Factory and Home" by Charlotte I. Loeb and Arthur L. Loeb in *Theo van Doesburg: On European Architecture* (Berlin: Birkhäuser Verlag, 1990), 57–63, 62.

77
Elsewhere, van Doesburg identifies Semper, along with Viollet-le-Duc, as "the starting point of what is being completed in our time, or more correctly: what is still in the process of being completed, an elementary architecture, *of an inner purity and with an outer surface of equal merit.*" Theo van Doesburg, "Architectuurvernieuwingen in het buitenland,"*Het Bouwbedrijf,* 4, no. 15 (July 1927): 352–355. Translated as "Swiss ABC for a Logical Building Method" by Charlotte I. Loeb and Arthur L. Loeb in *Theo van Doesburg: On European Architecture,* 154–158, 157.

78
Theo van Doesburg, "Architectuurvernieuwingen in het buitenland," *Het Bouwbedrijf,* 3, no. 5 (May 1926): 191–194. Translated as "Defending the Spirit of Space: Against a Dogmatic Functionalism," by Charlotte I. Loeb and Arthur L. Loeb in *Theo van Doesburg: On European Architecture,* 88–95, 88.

79
Theo van Doesburg, "Architectuurvernieuwingen in het buitenland," *Het Bouwbedrijf* 3, no. 10 (September 1926): 346–349. Translated as "Misunderstanding Cubist Principles in Czechoslovakia and Elsewhere (1926)," by Charlotte I. Loeb and Arthur L. Loeb in *Theo van Doesburg: On European Architecture,* 110–117, 113. "By applying cubist forms the Czech architects simply replaced Wiener-Werkstätte-*Ornamentik,* which had oppressed them for years, by cubist ornamentation." Ibid., 115.

80
Ibid., 113.

81
Margaret Olin, "Self-Representation: Resemblance and Convention in Two Nineteenth Century Theories of Architecture and the Decorative Arts," *Zeitschrift für kunstgeshte* 49, no. 3 (1986) 397.

82
Theo van Doesburg, "Swiss ABC for a Logical Building Method (1927)," 157.

83
Theo van Doesburg, "De architectuurtentoonstelling 'Die Wohnung'," *Het Bouwbedrijf* 4, no. 24 (November 1927): 556–559. Translated as "Stuttgart-Weissenhof 1927: *Die Wohnung* (1927)," by Charlotte I. Loeb and Arthur L. Loeb in *Theo van Doesburg: On European Architecture,* 164–173, 167.

84
Sigfried Giedion, *The Eternal Present: The Beginnings of Art* (Princeton: Princeton University Press, 1962), xix–x.

85
I would like to thank Mark Jarzombek for pointing this out to me.

86
Heinrich Wölfflin. *Prolegomena to a Psychology of Architecture* (1886), translated by Harry Francis Mallgrave and Eleftherios Ikonomou, in *Emphathy, Form and Space: Problems in German Aesthetics 1873–1893,* (Santa Monica: Getty Center for the History of Art and the Humanities, 1994), 149–192, 182.

87
Ibid., 183.

88
"Modern artists have shown that mere fragments lifted from the life of a period can reveal its habits and feelings . . . the furniture of daily life, the unnoticed articles that result from mass production—spoons, bottles, glasses, all the things we look at hourly without seeing—have become part of our lives without our knowing it." Sigfried Giedion, *Space, Time and Architecture: The Growth of a New Tradition* (Cambridge: Harvard University Press, 1941), 4. "The most important developments are the changes that have come about in daily life." Ibid., 8.

89

Ibid., 462.

90

Ibid., 315.

91

Sigfried Giedion, *The Eternal Present: The Beginnings of Architecture* (Princeton: Princeton University Press, 1964), 522.

92

"The dimension of depth . . . is suppressed, whenever possible, by ancient art . . . the visual arts to be responsible for representation of objects as individual material phenomenon not in space (hereafter meaning always deep space), but on the plane . . . not the optical plane, imagined by our eye at a distance from the objects, but the tactile plane suggested by the sense of touch. . . . From the optical point of view, this is the plane which the eye perceives when it comes so close to the surface of an object, that all the silhouettes and, in particular, all shadows which otherwise could disclose an alteration in depth, disappear." Alois Riegl, *Die spätrömische Kunstindustrie nach den Funden Österreich-Ungarn* (Vienna: 1901). Translated by Rolf Winkes as *Late Roman Art Industry*, (Rome: Giorgio Bretschneider, 1985), 24.

93

Ibid., 525.

94

Giedion, *Space, Time and Architecture*, li.

95

Ibid., xxxix.

96

Le Corbusier, *Towards a New Architecture*, 37.

97

Giedion, T*he Eternal Present: The Beginnings of Architecture*, 507.

98

Ibid., 48.

99

Ibid., 94.

100

Ibid., 161.

101

Le Corbusier, *L'art décoratif de'aujourd'hui* (Paris: Éditions G. Grès et Cie, 1925). Translated by James Dunnet as *The Decorative Art of Today* (Cambridge: MIT Press, 1987), 135.

102

William Morris, "The Lesser Arts of Life (1877)," in *Architecture, Industry and Wealth: Collected Papers by William Morris* (London: Longmans, Green, 1902), 73. First published in *The Architect* 8 (December 1877).

103

Ibid., 6.

104

Ibid., 99.

105

Le Corbusier, *La Ville Radieuse* (Boulogne: Éditions de l'Architecture d'Aujourd'hui, 1935), translated by Pamela Knight et al. as *The Radiant City* (New York: Orion Press, 1967), 107, 8.

106

Sigfried Giedion, *The Eternal Present: The Beginnings of Art*, 41.

107

"Everything must take place upon the plane surface: space is excluded. This explains how Worringer, almost in the same way as Riegl, sees ornamentation as the purest and most lucid expression of artistic volition." Ibid., 42.

108

Marcel Breuer, "Where do we Stand? *Architectural Review*, vol. LXXVIII (April 1935).

109

"But only in the last fifty years have women acquired the right to develop themselves physically. It is an analogous process: as to the rider of the thirteenth century, the concession will be made to the twentieth-century female bicyclist to wear pants and clothing that leaves her feet free. And with this, the first step is taken toward the social sanctioning of women's work . . . we are approaching a new and greater time. No longer by an appeal to sensuality, but rather by economic independence earned through work will the woman bring about her equal status with the man. The woman's value or lack of value will no longer fall or rise according to the fluctuation of sensuality." Adolf Loos, "Ladies' Fashion (1898)," 102.

110

Geoffrey Boumphrey, "Facade and Function," *Architectural Review*, vol. LXXVII (1935): 125–128. In the previous issue, Boumphrey had collaged the image of a man in a modern suit into the same Louis XV interior before focusing on the question of women's outfits.

111

Citation from 1929 interview with Henry Ford on frontispiece of Sigfried Giedion, *Befreites Wohnen* (Zurich: Orell Fübli, 1929). Cited by Stanislaus von Moos, "Giedion e il suo tempo," *Rassegna* 25, 1979, 6–17, 7.

112

Giedion, *Space, Time and Architecture*, 236.

The Antifashion Fashion

1

For a survey of this development, see Stella Newton, *Health, Art and Reason: Dress Reformers of the Nineteenth Century* (London: John Murray, 1974).

2

See Elaine Shefer, "Pre-Raphaelite Clothing and the New Woman," *The Journal of Pre-Raphaelite Studies* 6, no. 1 (November 1985): 55–82.

3

Van de Velde's sensitivity to the standardization of English clothes is evident in his description of the art critic Meier-Graefe, who promoted him in his first major exhibition in Paris: "He wore his clothes with a nicely calculated air of negligence suggestive of the type of young English diplomat who allows himself certain minor individual liberties in an otherwise severely orthodox attire" Henry van de Velde, "Henry van de Velde: Extracts form his Memoirs, 1891–1901," *Architectural Review* 112, no. 669 (September 1952): 148–55, 151.

4

Henry van de Velde, *Die künstlerische Hebung der Frauentracht* (Krefeld: Druck und Verlag Kramer & Baum, 1900), 13.

5

Ibid., 9.

6

Ibid., 10.

7

Ibid., 11.

8

Cited in Othmar Birkner, "The New Life-Style," in *The Werkbund: History and Ideology, 1907–1933* ed. Lucius Burckhardt (New York: Barron's, 1980), 52–54, 53.

9

Maria van de Velde, *Album moderner, nach Künstlerentwürfen ausgeführter Damenkleider* (Düsseldorf: Verlag Friedrich Wolfrum, 1900). After a short account on the campaign against fashion, the book presents three colored sketches of dress designs by Mohrbutter, twelve photos of designs by Henry van de Velde, three photos of designs by Margerethe von Braychitsch, and seven double-page colored drawings of ornamental panels for van de Velde dresses. On the exhibition's "attack" on fashion in favor of "logic," see also idem, "Sonderausstellung moderner Damenkostüme," *Dekorative Kunst* 4, no. 1 (1901).

10

Henry van de Velde, "Was Ich will," *Die Zeit* (March 1901); cited in Howard Dearstyne, *Inside the Bauhaus* (New York: Rizzoli, 1986), 35.

11

Henry van de Velde, *Die künstlerische Hebung der Frauentracht*, 13.

12

Ibid.

13

Ibid., 22.

14

E. W. Godwin, *Dress and its Relation to Health and Climate*, pamphlet 1184, 1; cited in Stella Newton, *Health, Art and Reason*, 89.

15

Henry van de Velde, "Die neue Kunst-Prinzip in der modern Frauen-Kleidung," *Deutsche Kunst und Dekoration* 10 (1902): 363–371.

16

Gottfried Semper, *Wissenschaft, Industrie und Kunst* (Braunschweig: Friedrich Vieweg und Sohn, 1852). Translated by Harry Francis Mallgrave and Wolfgang Hermann as "Science, Industry and Art" in Gottfried Semper, *The Four Elements of Architecture and Other Writings* (Cambridge: Cambridge University Press, 1989), 130–67, 137.

17

William Morris, "The Lesser Arts of Life," *The Architect* (8 December 1877). Reprinted in *Architecture, Industry and Wealth: Collected Papers by William Morris* (London: Longmans, Green, 1902), 37–79, 73.

18

Ibid.

19

"With my practical experience in designing patterns for fabrics, I had grown to regard all decorative design as part of a true artist's ambition, and I declared that until our craft again employed itself in devising beautiful forms, taste in furniture, in costume, and even in architecture would remain as bad as, or grow worse than it had been for the last fifty years. . . . Nor did we pause till Rossetti enlarged upon the devising of ladies dresses and the improvement of man's costume, determining to follow the example of early artists not in one branch of taste only but in all." William H. Hunt, *Pre-Raphaelitism and the Pre-Raphaelite Brotherhood* (London, 1905), 110, 151; cited in Elaine Shefer, "Pre-Raphaelite Clothing and the New Woman," 56.

20

Paul Schultze-Naumburg, *Die Kultur des weiblichen Körpers als Grundlage der Frauenkleidung* (Leipzig, 1903).

21

On the nationalistic use of dress reform, see Othmar Birkner, "The New Life-Style."

22

See Joachim Petsch, "The Deutsche Werkbund from 1907 to 1933 and the Movements for the 'Reform of Life and Culture,'" in *The Werkbund,* ed. Lucius Burckhardt 85–93.

23

Anna Muthesius, *Das Eigenkleid der Frau* (Krefeld, 1903).

24

See Leonie von Wilckens, "Künstlerkleid und Reformkleid: Textilkunst in Nürnberg," in *Peter Behrens und Nürnberg* (Munich: Germanisches Nationalmuseum, 1980), 198–203.

25

"Just like every new art direction begins with external decoration, the new clothing movement begins by slapping a new ornament on the old dress. Just remember the first exhibition at Krefeld. Thus it is most delightful that, as the current exhibition shows, one has now penetrated to the essence of the thing. This essence is seen correctly in the construction, in the color, in the property of the fabric and in the individual fit on the wearer." Anna Muthesius, "Die Ausstellung künstlerischer Frauen-Kleider im Waren-Haus Wertheim-Berlin," *Deutsche Kunst und Dekoration* 14 (1904): 441–43, 442. For Muthesius's dress designs, see Alfred Mohrbutter, *Das Kleid der Frau* (Darmstadt-Leipzig: Alexander Koch Verlag, ca 1904), 7, 46, 47.

26

Eckart Muthesius, "Muthesius," in *Hermann Muthesius, 1861–1927* (London: Architectural Association, 1979), 3–5, 4.

27

"From painting, his influence extended to room furnishings to clothing fashion, to all the decorative arts, period. . . . His fantastic women's costumes had such an impact that for a long time a whole community of women dressed themselves Pre-Raphaelitely, a fashion that in part still has after–effects in England today. . . . And, finally, he was the main motivator for that rebirth of industrial art with which England in its time pointed out the way into a new art land for the world and that would later lead to this drastic shift in the middle of which presently we find ourselves." Hermann Muthesius, "Dante Gabriel Rossetti," *Kunst und Kunsthandwerk* 4 (1901): 373–89, 388.

28

Hermann Muthesius, "Kultur und Kunst" (1904), in Hermann Muthesius, *Kultur und Kunst* (Leipzig: Jean, 1909), 1–38. The essay originally appeared in *Deutsche Monatsschrift für des gesamte Leben de Gegenwart* 3 (1904): 72.

29

Hermann Muthesius, "Die moderne Umbildung unserer äesthetischen Anschauungen" (1902), in Muthesius, *Kultur und Kunst,* 39–75, 42. The essay originally appeared in *Deutsche Monatsschrift für des gesamte Leben der Gegenwart* 1 (1902): 686.

30

Ibid., 61.

31

Hermann Muthesius, *Stilarchitektur und Baukunst* (Mülheim an der Ruhr: K. Schimmelpfeng, 1902/1903). Translated by Stanford Anderson, *Style-Architecture and Building-Art* (Santa Monica: Getty Center, 1994), 80. After describing the failure of contemporary architecture, and looking to the "general tectonic realm" of bridges, steamships, railway cars and bicycles for a model, Muthesius finds the paradigm in clothing:

> In such new creations we find the signs indicating our aesthetic progress. This can *henceforth* be sought only in the tendency toward the matter-of-fact [*Sachlichen*], in the elimination of every merely applied decorative form, and in shaping each form according to demands set by purpose. Other signs, such as our clothing, confirm this. Men's clothing in the second half of the eighteenth century (at least for the nobleman) retained the richest forms, bearing embroidered decorations that were made from costly, easily damaged materials. In the nineteenth century there was continuous simplification, leading up to today's unornamented dress and topcoat. Today's clothing is the same for all the classes of society: its singular characteristic is that it defines in every respect the middle-class ideal, whereas in the eighteenth century the particular customs, way of life, and clothing of the highest class set the standard. *Even the king appears today, when not in uniform, as a simple burgher; there truly is no other form of clothing available to him—he is obliged to dress the same as his chancery clerk.* Only in the military uniform has a remnant of the old, embellishing culture been retained; one can observe, however, that its days are also numbered now that the image of the lusterless and colorless military dress of the future, abstracted from soldier's uniforms, appears on the horizon.

Ibid., 79 [the passages in italic were added to the second edition of 1903].

32

Hermann Muthesius, "Kultur und Kunst (1904)," 35.

33

Reyner Banham, *Theory and Design in the First Machine Age* (Cambridge: MIT Press, 1960), 71.

34

Hermann Muthesius, "Wo stehen Wir?" *Jahrbuch des Deutschen Werkbundes* (Leipzig: Jean, 1912), 60–64. Translated as "Where Do We Stand? (1911)" in *Architecture and Design, 1890–1939: An International Anthology of Original Articles* ed. Tim Benton and Charlotte Benton (New York: Whitney Library of Design, 1975), 48–51, 48.

35

Ibid., 51.

36

Ibid., 50. The essay argues that "form stands higher than function, material and technology" and that an educated people should "experience as urgent a need for form as for clean clothes," but complains that even the "man who goes to the best tailors" in Germany, unlike the English, still doesn't bother to go to an architect when building a house. It insists that the nation will attain the required level of good taste "only when every member of the population instinctively clothes his basic needs with the best forms available." Ibid., 48, 51.

37
Hermann Muthesius, "Kultur und Kunst (1904)," 35; idem, "Stilarchitektur und Baukunst," 157.

38
Gottfried Semper, "Science, Industry and Art (1852)," 137.

39
Ibid., 146.

40
Ibid., 150.

41
Ibid., 141.

42
Gottfried Semper, *Der Stil in den technischen und tektonischen Künsten, oder Praktische Aesthetik* (Frankfurt: Verlag für Kunst und Wissenschaft, 1860). Translated by Harry Francis Mallgrave and Wolfgang Herrmann as "Style in the Technical and Tectonic Arts or Practical Aesthetics," in Semper, *The Four Elements of Architecture and Other Writings*, 181–263, 188.

43
"If the shop owner has special capacities then he becomes the leader of public taste. Often he lacks the courage to energetically put himself on the line for a product. Instead of a planned lasting work, it often comes down to temporary attempts and experiments. Then the shop owner remains the servant of the public and fashion. Work from the Werkbund, however, means in every case overcoming a fashion through quality" "Denkschrift über die Organisation und die Arbeit des DWB, ausgearbeitet von der Geschäftsstelle, genehmigt vom Viererausschus, undatiert [Ende 1907]" (Memorandum about the organization and the work of the DWB, prepared by the administrative office, approved by the committee of four, undated (at the end of 1907)), in *Der Deutsche Werkbund: Sein erstes Jahrzehnt* (Berlin, 1982), 144–50, 144.

44
Karl Ruplin, "Handwerk, höhere Schulen und Werkbund," *Die Form* 6, no. 8 (1931): 281–84; cited in Joan Campbell, *The German Werkbund: The Politics of Reform in the Applied Arts* (Princeton: Princeton University Press, 1978), 218.

45
Hermann Muthesius, "Die Bedeutung des Kunstgewerbes. Eröffnungsrede zu den Vorlesungen über modernes Kunstgewerbe an der Handelschochschule in Berlin," *Dekorative Kunst*, vol 10, 1907, 177. Translated as "The Meaning of

the Arts and Crafts" in *Architecture and Design, 1890–1939*, ed. Tim Benton and Charlotte Benton, 38–40, 39.

46
"We have today a style of the whiplash forms with which many German adherents in the arts and crafts, notwithstanding that it arose with van de Velde and arrived through him from Belgium. Yet what is still more significant is that fashion seized the whiplash line as the characteristic of the new style, that it had so long awaited. Thereupon industry acted immediately to commercialize this new style. The principle of the whiplash line appeared so easy and simple; at last one had something tangible to utilize, something with which to manufacture. In no time the world had the Jugendstil." Muthesius, *Style-Architecture and Building-Art*, 86.

47
"Nevertheless it would be dangerous to assume that merely satisfying purpose is itself sufficient. 'Reform clothing,' in whatever form it is recommended, affects us emotionally like a caricature. Today's simple clothing is also not without its unnecessary elements." Ibid., 80.

48
"In principle, however, I am not far from believing that a truly well designed dress would clothe every woman. If its beauty is based on its construction and ornamentation then it cannot lose by virtue of the fact that Frau A wears it instead of Frau B. And what does fashion do otherwise than to invent dresses coats and hats which are intended for all bodies and all heads? Why should this circumstance, which does not in the slightest weaken the reputation of fashion, mark our interpretation of clothing as an unfruitful one, when our creations are based on organic principles of logical construction, whereas fashion acts only according to its fantasy?" Henry van de Velde, *Die künstlerische Hebung der Frauentracht*, 31.

49
Peter Jesson, "Die Deutsche Werkbund-Ausstellung Köln 1914," *Jahrbuch des Deutschen Werkbundes* (1915): 2; cited Campbell, *The German Werkbund: The Politics of Reform in the Applied Arts*, 87.

50
"Architecture and fashion have in common that they already existed as fields when the social scientific and technical changes of the last century began. Therefore, for a long time, they have totally lost a relationship to life. Thus it is so difficult for both to find a way to a healthy, unproblematic, unliterary, and unartistic way of working. And yet a step toward this has already been made." Roger Ginsburger, "Bemerkungen eines Architekten zur Mode," *Die Form* 16 (15th August 1930): 424–35, 424.

51
Lilly Reich, "Modefragen," *Die Form* 5 (1922): 7.

52

The only monograph on Reich's work is Sonja Güntha, *Lilly Reich 1885–1947: Innenarchitektin, Designerin, Ausstellungsgestalterin* (Stuttgart: Deutsche Verlags-Anstalt, 1988), 83–88, 84.

53

"It can be argued that he never found a later collaborator who rounded out his own formative talents as effectively as she did. Yet during the years of their closeness his natural proclivity toward elegance and subtlety of style was sharpened, and in his work of the Weissenhof period and thereafter, a demonstrable authority over architectural fundamentals was amplified by increasing attention to the appointments of his interiors." Franz Schultz, *Mies van der Rohe: A Critical Biography* (Chicago: University of Chicago, 1985), 139.

54

Lilly Reich, "Modefragen (1922)," 86

T A K E 6

White Lies

1

"Only recently have artists become aware of their true task. They have recognized that if they only represent beauty in paintings and monumental statues they are neglecting large areas as varied and fertile as life itself. . . . They have proceeded in the same way, without knowing it, as primitive man who first, after he had taken care of his nutrition, thinks to build himself a roof in order to win a wife, then to decorate himself and finally to protect himself from wind and weather through clothing. The modern rebirth of applied art has busied itself first with architecture, then with furniture and everything that goes along with it, objects of use and decoration, and is now going *over to* its last conquest, clothing." Henry van de Velde, *Die künstlerische Hebung der Frauentracht* (Krefeld: Druck und Verlag Kramer & Baum, 1900), 6.

2

Ibid., 15.

3

Henry van de Velde, "Die neue Kunst-Prinzip in der modern Frauen-Kleidung," *Deutsche Kunst und Dekoration* 10 (1902): 366.

4

"All objects can and must be considered as food for our nervous consumptions. . . . A suit of clothes that we order from the tailor to fit our requirements and measurements exactly, and which we control during production by repeated fittings, thus becomes, in a physiological sense, our own suit of clothes. The increase of nervous comfort and effective co-ordination caused by well-fitting clothes and shoes is measurable and beyond doubt. Men and women engaged in sports are distinctly aware of the fuller control over their bodily properties when dressed to suit their particular sport. The articles of clothing they wear are thus owned by them in a deeper sense than merely because they bought them in the sporting-goods store and paid cash." Richard Neutra, *Survival Through Design* (Oxford: Oxford University Press, 1954), 263.

5

"I should first indicate what has stayed with me most, it was his faith in, and almost cult of, 'lastingness', as compared with passing fashion. He was reaching out for some contact with history, to produce this 'lastingness' despite the fashions of the day. They were to him as obnoxious as were the fashions of the parvenu, the upstart, who demanded a cultural adherence from his architect, who, in turn, had dispossessed the craftsman." Richard Neutra, review of L. Müntz and G. Künstler, *Adolf Loos: Pioneer of Modern Architecture, Architectural Forum* 125, no. 1 (July–August 1966): 88–89, 89.

6

Sigfried Giedion, *Space, Time and Architecture: The Growth of a New Tradition* (Cambridge: Harvard University Press, 1941), 301. Likewise, van de Velde argues that his own house "fitted like a glove our personal ideal of the life we wished to live." Henry van de Velde, "Henry van de Velde: Extracts form his Memoirs, 1891–1901," *Architectural Review* 112, no. 669 (September 1952): 148–55.

7

Sigfried Giedion, *Mechanization Takes Command* (London: Oxford University Press, 1948), 674. Later, the variety of bathroom fittings based on the adaption of standard units is compared to the way one hat with different trimmings can be adapted "to various tastes and ages" with a matching illustration. Ibid., 690.

8

Ibid., 376.

9

See Leonie von Wilckens, "Künstlerkleid und Reformkleid: Textilkunst in Nürnberg," in *Peter Behrens und Nürnberg* (Munich: Germanisches Nationalmuseum, 1980), 198–203, 201.

10

Anne Hollander, *Seeing Through Clothes* (New York: Penguin Books, 1978), 365. "Nothing, therefore, could better exemplify the intensity of the mid-nineteenth century's fervor for social reform than its attack on the concept of fashion itself and . . . the inevitable result was the creation of new fashions." Stella Newton, *Health, Art and Reason: Dress Reformers of the Nineteenth Century* (London: John Murray, 1974), 2.

11

Elizabeth Wilson, *Adorned in Dreams: Fashion and Modernity* (Berkeley: University of California Press, 1985), 213.

12

Hollander, *Seeing Through Clothes,* 357, 360.

13

Ibid., 364.

14

Le Corbusier, *Précisions sur un état de l'architecture et de urbanisme* (Paris: Crès, 1930). Translated by Edith Schreiber Aujame as *Precisions: On the Present State of Architecture and City Planning* (Cambridge: MIT Press, 1991), 106.

15

Reyner Banham, for example, while describing "White Architecture" as the "teen-age uniform of modern architecture" that was eventually outgrown, refers to Le Corbusier's houses of the twenties as "such radical good-fits on their inhabitants that it is almost impossible for later, more tradition-bound tenants to live in them." Reyner Banham, *Age of the Masters: A Personal View of Modern Architecture* (New York: Harper and Row, 1962), 19.

16

For a reading of the fundamental differences between Loos's Villa Steiner and Hoffmann's Stoclet Palace, see Beatriz Colomina, "On Adolf Loos and Josef Hoffmann: Architecture in the Age of Mechanical Reproduction," *9H,* no.6 (1983): 52–58.

17

Nikolaus Pevsner, *Pioneers of the Modern Movement from William Morris to Walter Gropius* (Harmondsworth: Penguin Books, 1936), 192.

18

In the second edition, the line is changed to read: "who, without being informed, would not date this house about 1924–30, or even later?" Nikolaus Pevsner, *Pioneers of Modern Design: From William Morris to Walter Gropius* (New York: Museum of Modern Art, 1949). In the final version of the text, the line reads: "Here for the first time the layman would find it hard to decide whether this might be 1930." Nikolaus Pevsner, *The Sources of Modern Architecture and Design* (London: Thames and Hudson, 1968), 169.

19

Nikolaus Pevsner, *Pioneers of Modern Design,* 1st ed., 191. In the revised second edition, the two passages are conflated to read: "in the Steiner house in Vienna, he achieved the style of 1930 completely and without any limitation." Nikolaus Pevsner, *Pioneers of Modern Design: From William Morris to Walter Gropius* (Harmondsworth: Penguin Books, 1960), 200.

20

Buildings like Wagner's "Postal Savings Bank are not prophetic of the twentieth century: they belong to it, that is, they contributed to its creation, out of the new materials and their authentically integrated use, out of the anti-historicism of Art Nouveau and out of William Morris'

faith in serving people's needs. The buildings designed in the same years by Josef Hoffmann and Adolf Loos must be looked at in the same way." Ibid.

21

"Otto Wagner's Post Office in Vienna, of 1904–06, should be contrasted with Horta's Maison du Peuple. The linearity is now taut and hard, and the individual elements, despite the curve of the ceiling, are essentially rectangular and seek a machined, not an organic, character. The design has been swept clean of movement, of overt continuities, and of what the period itself would have called 'decoration'. . . . Loos' own design of the period carries further the tripped, linear, taut, and planar character." Vincent Scully, *Modern Architecture* (New York: George Braziller, 1961), 24. Likewise, after discussing Mackintosh, and before discussing the Palais Stoclet and Villa Steiner, Curtis argues, "If we follow Wagner from his late nineteenth century designs to the Vienna Post Office Savings Bank of 1904–06, we enter an entirely different world from that of Art Nouveau, a world in which a nuts-and-bolts rationality and a stable and dignified order have replaced the dynamic tendrils and curvaceous effects." William Curtis, *Modern Architecture Since 1900* (Oxford: Phaidon Press, 1987), 33. Symptomatically, the old curves are but an "effect" while the new straight lines are an "order."

22

Muthesius credits the collaboration of Mackintosh and McDonald with instigating the transformation by which "the interior attains the status of a work of art" while "the sole purpose of the exterior of which is to enclose the rooms . . . without laying any particular claim to an artistic appearance itself." Hermann Muthesius, *The English House,* translated by Janet Seligman (New York: Rizzoli, 1987), 51–52. But, while promoting their work, he makes a Loosian call for restraint from the extremes of art: "Even a book in an unsuitable binding would disturb the atmosphere simply by lying on the table, indeed, the man or woman of today—especially the man in his unadorned working attire—treads like a stranger in this fairy-tale world. There is for the time being no possibility of our aesthetic cultivation playing so large a part in our lives that rooms like this could become general. But they are milestones placed by a genius far ahead of us to mark the way to excellence for mankind in the future." Ibid., 52.

23

Cited in Benedetto Gravagnuolo, *Adolf Loos* (New York: Rizzoli, 1982), 131.

24

Otto Wagner, "Inaugural Address to the Academy of Fine Arts" (1894), translated by Harry Francis Mallgrave, in Otto Wagner, *Modern Architecture* (Santa Monica: Getty Center for the History of Art and the Humanities, 1988), 159–63, 159.

25

Otto Wagner, *Modern Architecture,* 78.

26
Ibid., 77.

27
Ibid., 118.

28
Ibid., 76.

29
Harry Francis Mallgrave, Introduction to Wagner, *Modern Architecture*, 1–51, 45.

30
Otto Wagner, *Modern Architecture*, 68. "Art, if she would arouse the interest of and give satisfaction to the average man, must seize on every opportunity that gives promise of producing a favorable impression. Industry, trade, fashion, taste, comfort, luxury, all provide media for artistic impression, and must all be availed of to attract the attention of the average man toward Art, so that he may be disposed to bestow favorable judgement upon works of art." Otto Wagner, "The Development of a Great City," *Architectural Record*, (May 1912): 485–500, 490.

31
Otto Wagner, *Modern Architecture*, 76.

32
"With regard to the furnishing of our rooms, artists today have already succeeded in influencing the public, at least to the extent of strengthening the idea that THE APPEARANCE AND OCCUPATION OF THE INHABITANT WOULD HARMONIZE WITH THE APPEARANCE OF THE ROOM. . . . The room that we inhabit should be as simple as our clothing. This does not mean that the room cannot be richly and elegantly furnished or that works of art may not adorn it. But richness and elegance cannot be expressed by forms that are incongruous with our demands for comfort and with our present feeling for form and color." Ibid., 118.

33
Ibid., 120.

34
Adolf Loos. "Die Herrenmode," *Neue Freie Presse* (May 22, 1898). Translated by Jane O. Newman and John H. Smith as "Men's Fashion," in Adolf Loos, *Spoken into the Void: Collected Essays 1897–1900* (Cambridge: MIT Press, 1982), 10–14, 11.

35
Adolf Loos, "Antworten auf Fragen aus dem Publikum," *Neues 8 Uhr-Blatt*, June 21–October 18, 1919. Reprinted in Adolf Loos, *Sämtliche Schriften* (Vienna: Verlag Herold, 1962), 355–78, 370.

36
Ibid.

37
See Beatriz Colomina, "On Adolf Loos and Josef Hoffmann," and idem, "The Split Wall: Domestic Voyeurism," in *Sexuality and Space*, ed. Beatriz Colomina, (New York: Princeton Architectural Press, 1992) 73–130.

38
Beatriz Colomina, "On Adolf Loos and Josef Hoffmann," 53.

39
Adolf Loos, "Men's Fashion," 12.

40
Adolf Loos, "Die Herrenhütte," *Neue Freie Presse* (July 24, 1898). Translated by Jane O. Newman and John H. Smith as "Men's Hats" in Adolf Loos, *Spoken into the Void: Collected Essays 1897–1900*, 50–53, 53.

41
"Reproductions of earlier styles can satisfy only the parvenu. The ordinary citizen of today, like the worker, must be proud and fully aware of his own worth and not seek to compete with other social stations which have accomplished their cultural task and are justified in looking back on an artistically splendid heritage." Josef Hoffmann, "The Work Program of the Wiener Werkstätte (1903)," in *Josef Hoffmann: Architect and Designer, 1870–1956*, exhibition catalogue (London: Fisher Fine Art, 1977), 7–10, 9.

42
Eduard Sekler, *Josef Hoffmann: The Architectural Work* (Princeton: Princeton University Press, 1985), 165.

43
"The 1924 top hat is definitely possible, and if I could have worn it twenty years ago and still wear it today, everything would be fine. And because I can actually wear it, this top hat is fully justified in production terms, or more generally speaking, in commercial terms. But these are just fashions, which soon change. But if it so happens that a desk loses its aesthetic value for me after ten years, that I find it impossible, get rid of it and buy myself a new one, then that is a gigantic waste in commercial terms. . . . Someone who has a lot of clothes takes good care that they do not go out of fashion. Someone who has only one suit has no need to be cautious. On the contrary. Through constant use, he wears out his suit in a very short time, and in so doing forces the tailor to keep inventing new styles. . . . Fashion is something ephemeral only because we do not make things last. As soon as we have objects that last a long time and stay beautiful, fashion ceases. We should measure beauty in terms of time." Adolf Loos, "Regarding Economy," article compiled by Bohuslav Markalous from various conversations with Adolf Loos, translated by Francis R. James, in *Raumplan versus Plan Libre*, ed. Max Risselada (Delft: Delft University Press, 1988), 131–141, 137.

44

Neutra, *Survival Through Design,* 122. "I decided at this early age that frills and fashions were splendid for the ladies' apparel branch but bewildering to the person scraping together his savings, straining all his credit to build and to expose his life to a building for decades to come. . . . While architecture once used to be related to eternity, now it is subject to the latest copy of the fashion journal." Richard Neutra, "Human Setting in an Industrial Civilization: Recollection and Outlook," *Zodiac* 2 (1957): 69–75, 71.

45

Adolf Loos, "Ornament und Erziehung," *Wohnungskultur,* no. 2/3, 1924. Reprinted in Adolf Loos, *Sämtliche Schriften,* 391–398, 395.

46

Although Hoffmann's article makes the very claim that Loos was most opposed to, that the "artist" needs to take responsibility for "the wallpaper, the ceiling painting, as well as furniture and utensils," it nevertheless appears to be the model for Loos's famous essay of 1910 in the way it praises the "brilliantly white walls" of the Mediterranean vernacular "folk art" set against the "blue sky" and the need "forcefully" to resist their contamination by restricting polychromy to the interior and stopping the intrusion of "architectural fakes," the "forced-on architecture" resulting from "decorating over the bad skeleton of a building with ridiculous ornaments of cast cement produced in the factory." Josef Hoffmann, "Architectural Matters From the Island of Capri," *Der Architekt* III (1897) translated in Sekler, *Josef Hoffmann,* 479.

47

"Slowly but surely, however, it was discovered with dismay that in fact even the king lives quite simply. The retreat was abrupt. Simplicity was the last word, even in ballrooms. In other countries, the march of fashion is once again beginning to advance, while we are just preparing to retreat. There is no escape from it, no matter how much—alas, very, very much!—our craftsmen would like. Taste and the desire for variety always go hand in hand. Today we wear narrow pants, tomorrow wide ones, the day after tomorrow, it's back to the narrow style again. Every tailor knows this. Yet, you will say, but we could spare ourselves the next wave of wide pants. Oh no! We need them so that we will be glad to get back to narrow ones again. We need a period of simple ballrooms in order to prepare ourselves for the return of the elaborate ballroom. If our craftsmen want to get over the period of simplicity more quickly, there is only one way: to accept it." Adolf Loos, "Die Intérieurs in der Rotunde," *Neue Freie Presse* (June 12, 1898). Translated by Jane O. Newman and John H. Smith as "Interiors in the Rotunda," in Adolf Loos, *Spoken into the Void: Collected Essays 1897–1900 Spoken into the Void,* 22–27, 25.

48

"Reform-clothing supported itself, however, only on the principles of health; its representatives thoroughly neglected consideration of beauty—a proof of how unfamiliar they were with female psychology. In order to be successful, it should have opposed fashion with another fashion and should have claimed that that was a new fashion; for example, the 'German fashion' as opposed to the French." Henry van de Velde, *Die künstlerische Hebung der Frauentracht,* 15.

49

Hermann Muthesius, "Die Wekbundarbeit der Zukunft Vortrag auf der Werkbund-Tagung Köln 1914," in *Zwischer Kunst und Industrie der Deutsche Werkbund* (Munich: Staatliches Museum für Angewandle Kunst, 1975), 87.

50

This essay begins by noting the general disenchantment with the reform dress promoted by the Werkbund and the architects and artists responsible for it: "The German reform dress was said to be insufferable; to let it be revived now was out of the question. It was said that we Germans are not even capable of accomplishing anything in matters of fashion, that taste in women's clothing was a privilege of Paris. Furthermore, it was believed that, in the face of the circumstance that the German Werkbund had accepted this [reform] movement, architects and interior designers should not design clothing because the artistic or individual-dress [*eigenkleid*], which had been attempted ten years ago, had gone down hill." Hermann Muthesius, "Der Krieg und die deutsche Modeindustrie," *Die Woche,* 17, 1915, 363–365, 363. Muthesius agrees that fashion should no longer be in the hands of architects but argues that the issue is not what kind of design to produce but how to produce and market it, which was, after all, the original goal of the Werkbund: "If Germany wants to secure its market it will have to develop a way into international fashion. And, with that, reflections on reform and individual-dress fall away. The Werkbund's interest in the reform movement was an organizational one because it was concerned with mutual discussion between the different sales people and industrialists participating in the fashion industry and stimulated the formation of working committees. Furthermore, the Werkbund appointed artists to the fashion industry who, because of their field of interest, appeared capable of advising the industry in matters of taste." Ibid., 364. The essay concludes that "the position of Germany will become so uplifted through this war that it will be able to complete its assumption of the lead in architecture and the industrial arts in the future. We hope that in the fashion movement we become, if not leading, at least self-sufficient colleagues. All questions of taste ultimately flow from the same source and whoever governs the great main field will also carry the marginal areas. The first attempt to make ourselves independent of Paris in ladies' fashion has succeeded. It must now be raised to a national support so that our women and our business people do not leave it at this first attempt." Ibid., 365.

51

Hermann Muthesius, *Stilarchitektur und Baukunst* (Mülheim an der Ruhr: Verlag von K. Schimmelpfeng, 1902). Translated by Stanford Anderson as *Style-Architecture and Building-Art* (Santa Monica: Getty Center, 1994), 80. This identification between the unornamented aesthetic of the machine and modern clothes can also be found in a key essay of the same year: "A small taste of this truth is given us already by our ladies' fashion. It is within the realm of possibility that one day every man will find our factory products beautiful" Hermann Muthesius, "Kunst und Machine," *Dekorative Kunst*, vol. 5, 1902, 141–47, 143.

52

Hermann Muthesius, "Kunst und Modeströmungen," *Wasmuths Monatshefte für Baukunst*, 11, 1927, 496–98, 497.

53

"Thus fashion is not solely a product of a particular commercial system of working, but at the same time a mirror-image of the perceptions of the age. The changing movements in visual art have in common with fashion that they also represent the time's perceptions. It departs insofar as the acknowledgment has not progressed so far as to see something eternally changing in the occurrences of the age. On the contrary: each new mode of expression takes care to be set forth as the now finally achieved solution to the artistic problem." Ibid.

54

Ibid., 498.

55

Hermann Muthesius, "Die neue Bauweise," *Die Baugilde* 9, (1927). Reprinted in Julius Poesner, *Anfänge des Funktionalismus: von Arts und Crafts Deutscher Werkbund* (Frankfurt: Verlag Ullstein, 1964) 176–77.

56

Sigfried Giedion, "Ist das neue Bauen eine Mode?" *Basler Nachrichten* (13 November 1927): 215–16, 216.

57

Sigfried Giedion, "Mode oder Zeiteinstellung?" *Information* (June 1932): 8–11, 8.

58

"For us, history is not an instance of botany for preserving heroic feelings, not a hotbed for 'neutral' portrayals. For us, history constitutes a guideline. For us, history is living just as long as it remains productive, as long as it explains our past-existence and gives us support and an overview of our ego and our generation. This is also the meaning of the attitude of the times. Whoever has a critical look at the elements of our time will not be led astray by an externally transposed tempo. . . . A *sameness* of method is discernible in the great variety of fields of knowledge." Ibid., 10.

59

See Nancy J. Troy, *Modernism and the Decorative Arts in France: Art Nouveau to Le Corbusier* (New Haven: Yale University Press, 1991).

60

Charles-Edouard Jeanneret, *Étude sur le mouvement d'art décoratif en Allemagne* (1912) (New York: Da Capo Press, 1968), 54.

61

Nancy Troy, *Modernism and the Decorative Arts in France*, 120.

62

"I got to know the Wiener Werkstätte (actually the work of Professor Hoffmann) from art magazines when I was still a young fellow attending the school of my native city; that was in the years 1903–1906. The works of Hoffmann were for me the most luminous expression of the architectural development. . . . In 1907 (I was 19 years old), on returning from my first art journey in Italy, I went to Vienna, and I was very proud to be received and encouraged by Professor Hoffmann. Afterward I went to Paris where the 'constructors' (architect Perret) attracted me. Since then I have not been able to follow the development of the Wiener Werkstätte. But I always experienced a true artistic pleasure when I saw here and there the architectural work of Professor Hoffmann. . . . Today, when the new generations, without looking back (and without saying 'thank you') appropriate the fruits of the labor of the steadfast seekers, today when the situation is comparatively clear, and the obstacles have been removed and the *great directives* are given, today it is only just—and what a pleasant task—to express our gratitude to men like Professor Hoffmann and to enterprises that were as daring as the Wiener Werkstätte." Le Corbusier, "Die Wiener Werkstätte 1903–1928" (Vienna, 1929), translated in Eduard Sekler, *Josef Hoffmann,* 496.

63

"In Berlin and Vienna I went to all the exhibitions of the decorative arts. It was then that I made the acquaintance of the chiefs of the Schools, such as Hoffmann, the creator and director of the Wiener Werkstätte, Karl Witzman, M. Muthesius, Wimmer, Bruno Paul, and Klimpt. . . . In Berlin I met a whole swarm of architects who were seeking for the New, and sometimes found it. . . . I spent whole days in visiting modern interiors, built and arranged with such a wealth of new ideas that I had seen nothing like them at home. . . . I dreamed of creating in France a movement of ideas that should be capable of propagating a new fashion in decoration and furnishing." Paul Poiret, *King of Fashion: The Autobiography of Paul Poiret,* translated by Stephen Haden Guest (Philadelphia: J. Lippincott, 1931), 159.

64

Le Corbusier and Amédée Ozenfant, "Purism," *L'Esprit Nouveau* (Paris) 4, 1920 translated by by Robert L. Herbert. In *Modern Artists on Art: Ten Unabridged Essays*, ed. Robert L. Herbert (Englewood Cliffs: New Jersey, 1964) 58–73, 73.

65

Amédée Ozenfant, "'Je voudrais être le Stravinsky de la peinture': Un entretien d'André Parinaud," *Arts* (October 1962): 11; cited in Susan Ball, *Ozenfant and Purism: The Evolution of a Style 1915–1930* (Ann Arbor: UMI Research Press, 1981), 30.

66

Amédée Ozenfant, *Mémoires, 1886–1962* (Paris: Seghers, 1968), 93; partially cited in Susan Ball, *Ozenfant and Purism*, 31.

67

Ibid.

68

William Morris, "The Lesser Arts of Life," *The Architect* (8 December 1877). Reprinted in *Architecture, Industry and Wealth: Collected Papers by William Morris* (London: Longmans, Green, 1902), 37–79, 75.

69

The report was published in the *Bulletin du Comité Central Technique des Arts Appliqués et des Comités Régionaux*, as a supplement to *L'Arts Francais*, in four parts between 1918 and 1919.

70

Charles-Edouard Jeanneret, "Rapport de la sous-commision de l'enseignement, présenté au conseil de direction," *Bulletin du Comité Central Technique des Arts Appliqués et des Comités Régionaux* 25 (1919): 2.

71

Ibid.

72

Eduard Sekler, *Josef Hoffmann*, 113, 511n30.

73

Le Corbusier and Pierre Jeanneret, "Fünf Punkte zu einer neuen Architektur," *Die Form* 2 (1927): 272–274. Translated as "Five Points of a New Architecture," in *Architecture and Design: 1890–1939*, ed. Tim Benton and Charlotte Benton (New York: Whitney Library of Design, 1975), 153–155, 153.

74

Le Corbusier, *Oeuvre complète, 1910–29* (Zurich: Éditions Girsberger, 1929), 23.

T A K E   7

Deep Skin

1

Le Corbusier, *L'art décoratif d'aujourd'hui* (Paris: Éditions G. Grès et Cie, 1923). Translated by James Dunnet as *The Decorative Art of Today* (Cambridge: MIT Press, 1987), 135.

2

Ibid., 190.

3

Mary Sekler, *The Early Drawings of Charles-Eduard Jeanneret (Le Corbusier)*, Ph.D. dissertation from Harvard University, 1973 (New York: Garland Publishing, 1977).

4

Le Corbusier, *Oeuvre complète 1910–29* (Zurich: Girsberger, 1929), 48.

5

Le Corbusier, *L'atelier de la recherche patiente* (Paris: Vincent Fréal, 1960). Translated by James Palmes as *Creation is a Patient Search* (New York: Praeger, 1960), 60.

6

"Interview with Le Corbusier," *Modulus* (1979), 65–75, 66. "My first construction was on the road to Vaucresson, for a man who told me: 'I read one of your articles and I like it a lot. We would like to build a house, a little house here in Vaucresson. We don't have any money, very little.' I said, 'All right, I'll do it for you,' and we did it. It was terribly difficult to deliver the modern architectural aesthetic, and this house was the reason for the difficulty." Ibid., 68.

7

Banham, for example, refers to the house at Vaucresson in passing as "his first Modern house," only to later describe the Ozenfant atelier as "the first building of Le Corbusier's second career as an architect." Reyner Banham, *Theory and Design in the First Machine Age* (London: The Architectural Press, 1960), 220, 237. Likewise, Hitchcock's *Modern Architecture* of 1928 treats the villa at Vaucresson as "the first building executed in the new manner" but argues that it is less successful than the unbuilt projects (because of the overcomplication of the front facade and symmetry of the rear, along with supposedly unresolved proportions) and proclaims the L'Esprit Nouveau Pavilion as "his first true manifesto in executed building." Henry-Russell Hitchcock, *Modern Architecture: Romanticism and Reintegration* (New York: Payson and Clark, 1929), 166. The majority of the histories simply omit the villa altogether. The only detailed account is offered in Tim Benton, *The Villas of Le Corbusier 1920–1930* (New Haven: Yale University Press, 1987), 23–29.

8

Arthur Rüegg is careful to note that the Villa Besnus is the only one for which no evidence of color has turned up yet. Arthur Rüegg, "La couleur fille de la lumière," in *Le Corbusier et la couleur*, ed. Claude Prelorenzo (Paris: Fondation Le Corbusier, 1992), 35–48. In this regard, one should also note that a section of the text that Badovici provides to account for his publication of the Villa Besnus, a project by Loos and one by Van Eestereen, reads: "The only corrective that they employ is color. Like the artists of antiquity, young architects have realized the resource that one can get from the orders of luminosity that descend over all things." Jean Badovici, *L'architecture vivante* (1923), 36.

9

Le Corbusier, letter to Pierre Vié, dated 11 June 1924, Fondation Le Corbusier, Paris.

10

Le Corbusier, *Oeuvre complète, 1910–29* (Zurich: Girsberger, 1929), 60.

11

Le Corbusier, *Almanach d'architecture moderne* (Paris: Le Éditions Crès et C, 1926)

12

Ibid., 146.

13

A good example of this euphoria can be found in a recent essay by Vincent Scully: "The interior of his Ozenfant house literally explodes into space; all the old details of the great European tradition, which had qualified edges and modified changes of plane, are burned away in the whiteness of the light. All planes are as thin as paper, all frames are as taut as lines. High up in space, one plane curves alone, modeling the white light." Vincent Scully, "Le Corbusier, 1922–1965," in *Le Corbusier*, ed. H. Allen Brooks (Princeton: Princeton University, 1987) 47–55, 48.

14

Le Corbusier, *L'art décoratif d'aujourd'hui* (Paris: Éditions G. Crès et Cie, 1925), 193. Translated by James Dunnet as *The Decorative Art of Today* (Cambridge: MIT Press, 1987), 84, 107.

15

Ibid., 112.

16

See particularly: Martina Colli, "Le Corbusier e il colore: i *Claviers* Salubra, " *Storia dell'arte,* 43, 1981, 271–293; Martina Colli, "Vers une polychromie architecturale," entry in *Le Corbusier: une encyclopidie,* ed. Jacques Lucan (Paris: Centre Georges Pompidou, 1987), 104–110; Arthur Rüegg, "Le Corbusiers Polychromie Architecturale und seine Farbenklaviaturen 1931 und 1959," in *Le Corbusier Synthèse des Arts: Aspekte des Spätwerkes 1945–1965*, ed. Andreas Vowinckel and Thomas Kesseler (Berlin: Ernst and Sohn, 1986) 34–52; and the collection, *Le Corbusier et la couleur* (Paris: Fondation Le Corbusier, 1992).

17

Leonardo Benevelo, *History of Modern Architecture,* trans. H. J. Landry (Cambridge: MIT Press, 1971), 446.

18

Ibid., 426.

19

Ibid., 548.

20

Ibid., 530.

21

"The color samples established in the spring are erroneous. The Salvation Army colors, which are beautiful, ought to be reproduced in their exact tonality; that is to say: dark red, dark blue, and a yellow which is composed of yellow ochre and not of chromium. The facade will sing, with the large entrance portal, and will produce a superb impression." Le Corbusier, Letter to Wycliffe Booth. Cited in Brian Brace Taylor, *Le Corbusier: The City of Refuge, Paris 1929/33* (Chicago: University of Chicago Press, 1987), 121.

22

"However, once again, his previously specified recommendation as to the precise tint to be given to the three primary colors, blue, red, and yellow, were not respected. The sunscreen, which Le Corbusier had said should be left in its natural concrete state, was painted a brilliant white; so too, were the masonry portions of the two upper stories, which (in the author's estimation) had never had such a glaring, whitewashed intensity." Ibid., 123.

23

Leonardo Benevelo, *History of Modern Architecture,* 461.

24

Sigfried Giedion, "Furniture Design and the Common Object," in *Le Corbusier: Architect Painter Writer* ed. Stano Papadaki (New York: Macmillan, 1948), 39–42, 39. The essay is a reworking of a section of *Mechanization Takes Command,* which likewise mentions in passing that the walls of the pavilion were colored.

25

Letter from Pevsner to Professor G. Zarnecki dated 24th November 1965. The Getty Center for the History of Art and The Humanities, special collections, Santa Monica.

26

"In this last volume of the Oeuvres Complètes, Artemis Architectural Publishers have kindly permitted me to use a large number of illustrations in color, and this is particularly gratifying to me. The use of color helps to enrich and clarify our understanding of Le Corbusier's great achievement, for he regarded polychromy as an essential expressive element of his architecture." W. Boesiger. Introduction to *Le Corbusier, Oeuvres complètes, Vol. 8 1965–69* (Zurich: Les Editions d'Architecture, 1970), 7.

27

Le Corbusier, *The Decorative Art of Today,* xv.

28

"I take great pleasure in making large, ten-foot, colored frescoes which become the striking stenographic means, enlivened by red, green, brown, yellow, black or blue, for expressing my *Radiant City* thesis or my ideas about the reorganization of daily life." Le Corbusier, *Quand les cathédrales étaient blanches* (Paris: Plan, 1937). Translated by Francis E. Hyslop as *When the Cathedrals Were White* (New York: Reynal and Hitchcock, 1947), 137.

29
Le Corbusier, "Description of the CIAM Grid, Bergamo 1949," in *C.I.A.M. 8 The Heart of the City: Towards the Humanization of Urban Life* (New York: Pellegrini and Cudhy, 1952), 171–176, 174.

30
Le Corbusier, "Convocation Address," translated by Richard Amdt in *Four Great Makers of Modern Architecture* ed. Richard Miller (New York: Columbia University, 1963), 164–167, 166. "Here I'm sketching the engineers, here the architects, here physical laws, here man and his environment, nature and the cosmos. And here I shall put in red the tasks of the engineer and in blue that of the architect, the engineer in red because this symbolizes action and the power of natural forces, and in blue the architect because here we have a game of the mind." Ibid., 167.

31
Le Corbusier, "If I had to Teach you Architecture," *Focus* 1 (1938). Republished in *The Rationalists: Theory and Design in the Modern Movement*, ed. Dennis Sharp (London: Architectural Press, 1978), 78–83.

32
Le Corbusier, preface to *Le Corbusier: textes et dessins pour Ronchamp* (Paris: Minuit, 1956).

33
When talking of the section on the Parthenon: "I shall give this entire account an ocher cast," Le Corbusier, *Le voyage d'Orient* (Paris: Fondation Le Corbusier, 1966). Translated by Ivan Žaknić as *Journey to the East* (Cambridge: MIT Press, 1987), 207. "Using the free language of the Sunday painter, let me tell you in three lines, Madam, with colors and daubs about the soul of the city." Ibid., 55.

34
Ibid., 15.

35
Ibid., 15.

36
Ibid., 26.

37
Ibid., 189, 158.

38
Le Corbusier, *The Decorative Art of Today*, 207.

39
Le Corbusier, *Journey to the East*, 171.

40
Ibid., 14.

41
Ibid., 35.

42
Ibid., 193.

43
Ibid., 185.

44
Ibid., 185.

45
Ibid., 183, 177, 176.

46
Several times he describes white as an appropriate frame for colored paintings: whether it be the walls of the Toledo: "White, raw, impassive, they are the necessary and majestic environment for such glowing painting," Ibid., 52; or the empty white hall of the refectory of the monastery at Iviron: "It was whitewashed, and the ground was partly paved. The tables consisted of enormous thick slabs of white marble. Every step echoed with solemnity in a hall so empty and white that the black monks moved about it not like volumes but more like spots or holes. High up on the wall terminating in an apse was a large icon framed in black . . . I think that a painting presented in this manner is very convincing." Ibid., 201.

47
Ibid., 100.

48
Ibid., 164.

49
Ibid., 154.

50
Ibid., 60.

51
Ibid., 23.

52
Ibid., 85.

53
Ibid., 146.

54
Ibid., 212.

55
Ibid., 291.

56
Ibid., 162.

57
Ibid., 212.

58
Le Corbusier, *Vers une architecture* (Paris: Éditions Crès, 1923), 112. Translated by Frederick Etchells as *Towards an Architecture* (London: John Rodker, 1931), 143.

59
Ibid., 161.

60
Ibid., 218.

61
Ibid., 220. Le Corbusier returns to the sensuous effect of the seemingly abstract proportions of the Parthenon at the beginning of *Le Modulor II:* "Effect of a work of art (architecture, statue or painting) on its surroundings: waves, outcries, turmoil (the Parthenon on the Acropolis at Athens), lines spurring, radiating out as if produced by an explosion: the surroundings, both immediate and more distant, as stirred and shaken, dominated or caressed by it." Le Corbusier, *Le Modulor II* (Cambridge: Harvard University Press, 1954), 26

62
"I was twenty-three when, after five months on the road, I reached Athens and the Parthenon. The pediment was still up, but the whole length of the temple had fallen. . . . With respectful, restless, wondering hands, over many weeks I touched these stones. . . . Touch is a second kind of sight. Sculpture or architecture, when their forms are inherently successful, can be caressed; in fact, our hands are impelled towards them." Le Corbusier, *Entretien avec les étudiants des écoles d'architecture* (Paris: Donoel, 1943). Translated by Pierre Chase as *Le Corbusier Talks to Students* (New York: The Orion Press, 1961), 59.

63
Le Corbusier, *Towards an Architecture,* 217.

64
Ibid., 182.

65
"When one says painting, inevitably he says color. But color has properties of shock (sensory order) which strike the eye before form (which is a creation already cerebral in part)." Le Corbusier and Ozenfant, "Purism (1920)," in Robert L. Herbert ed. *Modern Artists on Art: Ten Unabridged Essays* (Englewoods Cliffs: Prentice-Hall, 1964), 58–73, 70.

66
Ibid.

67
Ibid., 71.

68
Ibid., 72.

69
Ibid., 70.

70
Ibid., 71.

71
Le Corbusier, "Notes à la suite," *Cahiers d'art,* 2 (February 1926), 46–52, 48.

72
Ibid., 49, 51, 52.

73
Le Corbusier, "Pessac," *L'Architecture vivante,* 1927, 29–30, 29.

74
Ibid., 30.

75
Ibid.

76
Le Corbusier, Letter to Piero Bottoni dated 15 January 1928, in *Le Corbusier: "Urbanismo"* (Milan: Gabriele Mazzotta, 1983), 26.

77
Ibid.

78
Le Corbusier, *Almanach d'architecture moderne,* 146.

79
Ibid.

80
Le Corbusier, "Pessac (1927)," 30.

81
Le Corbusier, "Color Keyboards," text accompanying Salubra color charts, 1932.

82
Le Corbusier, "Polychrome Architecturale (1931)," unpublished manuscript, Fondation Le Corbusier, Paris, B1–18, 9.

83
Ibid., 7.

84
"To call them eternal is even more defensible considering that these few constant colors are the products of a primitive industry born in the most cursory of civilizations, and which sustained itself throughout all (civilizations); the raw materials of this distant industry exist in every corner of the globe; earth and fire, and mortar to pulverize, preceded all conscious notions of chemistry." Ibid., 6.

85
"what is sculpted would thus be in monochrome, what is smooth would be in polychrome." Ibid., 6.

86
Ibid., 10.

87
Ibid., 24, 20, 5.

88
Ibid., 13, 17.

89
"Abstract art begins at architectural polychrome. Modern architectural polychrome could not have been imagined with the 'free plan' brought about by steel or reinforced concrete. The 'free plan' merely came to impose itself as a technical response to the innumerable demands of our modern clientele: today's home, the office, the factory, the public edifice, etc. . . . as well as: the automobile, the airplane, the steamship. Architectural polychrome was born

out of the organization of these infinitely complex constructed biologies. Summoning the psycho-physiological powers of color: reorganizing their enormous powers in the domain of classification as well as in the realm of sensation, of emotion." Le Corbusier, text dated Cap Martin, 1st December 1951, in Jean Petit, *Le Corbusier Lui-même* (Geneva: Editions Rousseau, 1970), 169.

90

Le Corbusier, preface to Paul Damaz, *Art in European Architecture* (New York: Rheinhold Publishing, 1956), dated May 9, 1955, vii–xii, ix.

91

"We'll get the painters in *to blow up the walls that stand in our way.* Architectural polychromy seizes the entire wall and qualifies it with the powerful throb of the blood, or the freshness of the prairie, or the glow of the sun, or the depth of sea and sky. Think of the forces available! This is *dynamics,* or I might just as well say *dynamite,* having let my painter into the house." Le Corbusier, "Peinture, sculpture et architecture rationaliste," in Francois de Franclieu, *Le Corbusier-Savina, Sculptures et Dessins* (Paris: Fondation Le Corbusier, 1984), 18.

92

Ibid., 20.

93

Cited Maurice Besset, *Le Corbusier: To Live with the Light* (New York: Skira/Rizzoli, 1987), 96.

94

Le Corbusier, *Des Canons, des munitions? Merci! Des logis . . . s.v.p.* (Paris, 1937), 22.

95

Le Corbusier, letter to Vladimer Nekrassov dated December 20, 1932. In *Le Corbusier: Le passé à réaction poétique* (Paris: Caisse nationale des Monuments historiques et des Sites, 1988), 74–76, 74.

96

Le Corbusier, "Polychrome architecturale (1931)," 21.

97

Le Corbusier. Letter to architects of Barcelona, dated 8 October 1962. In Jean Petit, *Le Corbusier Lui-même,* 130–131, 131. "color is the sign of life, color bears life. The world that opens up before us today becomes polychrome, has become polychrome. Open your eyes and look at the diverse colors of automobiles which were black not so long ago. Open your eyes and look at the shops on the street. I began to use architectural polychrome when, short of funds to complete the Unité d'habitation the boulevard Michelet in Marseille, I picked out pots of vivid colors and sent the workers off to each of the seven hundred loggieas east, south and west of the building, in order to paint the walls and ceilings of the loggias in a polychrome which provoked emotions, caused shocks, called upon the curiosity of the spectator and brought and uncontested joy into this house." Ibid., 130. See also Le Corbusier, *The Marseille Block* (London: Harvill Press, 1953).

98

Le Corbusier, *New World of Space* (New York: Reynal and Hitchcock, 1948), 11.

99

Le Corbusier, "Polychrome architecturale (1931)," 21.

100

Le Corbusier, *New World of Space,* 14, 18.

T A K E   8

Machine-Age Wallpaper

1

"Let's tackle the problem in all its scope. Let's organize the exterior spectacle. This is nothing more or less than creating 'polychromed architecture' from scratch." Fernand Léger, "Le Spectacle," *Bulletin de L'Effort Moderne,* no. 7–9 (1924). Translated by Alexandra Anderson as "The Spectacle: Light, Color, Moving Image, Object-Spectacle," in *Functions of Painting,* ed. Edward Fry (New York: Viking Press, 1973) 35–47, 46

2

Fernand Léger, "Architecture polychrome," *L'Architecture vivante,* vol 2 no. 4 (1924): 21–22. Translated by Charlotte Green as "Polychromatic Architecture," in *Léger and Purist Paris* (London: Tate Gallery, 1970), 95–96, 95.

3

Ibid., 96.

4

Fernand Léger, "The New Realism Goes On," translated by Samuel Putnam in *Art Front,* vol. 3 no. 1 (1937): 7–8. Republished in *Functions of Painting,* ed. Edward Fry, 114–118, 116.

5

Fernand Léger, "Un nouvel espace en architecture," *Art d'Aujourd'hui,* 3 (1949): 19. Translated as "A New Space in Architecture," in *Functions of Painting,* ed. Edward Fry, 157–160, 157.

6

Fernand Léger, "Le mur, l'architecte, le peintre," unpublished lecture in Zurich of May 1933. Translated as "The Wall, the Architect, the Painter," in *Functions of Painting,* ed. Edward Fry, 91–99, 94.

7

Fernand Léger, "Peinture Murale," *Derrière la Miroir* (1952). Translated as "Mural Painting," in *Functions of Painting,* ed. Edward Fry, 178–180, 178.

8

Fernand Léger, "Modern Architecture and Color," in Charmion von Weigard and Fritz Glarner, *American Abstract Artists* (New York: Ram Press, 1946): 31–38. Republished in *Functions of Painting,* ed. Edward Fry, 149–154, 150.

9
Fernand Léger, "Peinture Murale et Peinture de chevalet," unpublished text of 1950. Translated in "Mural Painting and Easel Painting," in *Functions of Painting*, ed. Edward Fry, 160–164, 161.

10
Léger, "The Wall, the Architect, the Painter (1933)," 94–95.

11
Fernand Léger, "Nouvel conceptiones d'Espace," *XXe-siècle*, 1952. Translated as "New Conceptions of Space," in *Functions of Painting*, ed. Edward Fry, 181–182, 181.

12
Fernand Léger, "On Monumentality and Color (1943)," in Sigfried Giedion. *Architecture You and Me: The Diary of a Development* (Cambridge: Harvard University Press, 1958), 40–47, 41.

13
"My architect friends, we should be able to get together about this wall. You want to forget that painters are put into this world in order to destroy dead surfaces, to make them livable, to spare us from overly extreme architectural positions." Fernand Léger, "The Wall, the Architect, the Painter (1933)," 96. "An architectural structure is composed of live surfaces and dead surfaces. The dead surfaces are reserves of repose; they will not be touched. The live surfaces are organized for form, for the painter and the sculptor." Fernand Léger, "Couleur dans le monde," in *L'Homme, la Technique, la Nature*, ed. Jean Cassou (Paris: Riecher, 1938): 105–120. Translated as "Color in the World (1938)," in *Functions of Painting*, ed. Edward Fry, 118–131, 122.

14
"The exterior volume of an architecture, its sensitive weight, its distance can be reduced or increases as a result of all the colors adopted." Fernand Léger, "On Monumentality and Color (1943)," 41.

15
"A wall can be made to advance or recede, to become visually mobile. All this with color." Léger, "Color in the World (1938)," 123. "Through the open window, the wall across the street, violently colored, comes into your house. Enormous letters, figures twelve feet high, are hurled into the apartment. Color takes over. It is going to dominate everyday life. One will have to adjust to it." Ibid., 120.

16
"Freedom in the arrangement of lines, forms, and colors allows a resolution of the architectural problem of supportive or destructive colors. A Melodious arrangement 'supports the wall,' a contrasted arrangement destroys the wall. There are modern architectural imperatives." Fernand Léger, "The Problem of Freedom in Art," unpublished text of 1950. Translated in *Functions of Painting*, ed. Edward Fry, 165–166, 165.

17
"pure color, dynamically laid on, may visually destroy a wall." Fernand Léger, "The New Realism Goes On (1937)," 117.

18
"I oppose flat surfaces to volumes that play against them. I have collaborated in doing some architectural designs, and have then contented myself with being decorative, *since the volumes were provided by the architecture and the people moving around.* I sacrificed volume to surface, the painter to the architect, by being merely the illuminator of dead surfaces. In works of this kind, it is not a question of hypnotizing through color but of refining the surfaces . . . *illuminating the walls. . . . Ornamental art,* dependent on architecture, its value rigorously relative (almost traditional), accommodating itself to the necessities of place, respecting live surfaces and acting only to destroy dead surfaces. (A materialization in abstract, flat, colored surfaces, with the volumes supplied by the architectural and sculptural masses)." Fernand Léger, "L'Esthétique de la machine: l'ordere géometrique et le urai," *Propos d'artistes* (1925): 98–106. Translated as "The Machine Aesthetic: Geometric Order and Truth (1925)," in *Functions of Painting*, ed. Edward Fry, 62–66, 63.

19
Bart van der Leck, "De Plaats van het moderne schilderen," *De Stijl*, vol. 1, no. 1 (1917). Translated by R. R. Symonds as "The Place of Modern Painting in Architecture (1917)," in Hans L. C. Jaffé, *De Stijl*, (London: Thames and Hudson, 1970), 93–95, 93.

20
Ibid., 94.

21
Piet Mondrian, "De Nieuwe Beelding in de Schiblerkunst: De Nieuwe Beelding als abstract—reële schilderkunst; Beeldingsmiddel en composite," *De Stijl*, vol. 1, no. 3 (1918): 29–31. Translated by R. R. Symonds as "Neoplasticism in Painting: The New Plastic as 'Abstract-Real Painting': The Plastic Means and Composition, [part I]" in Jaffé, *De Stijl*, 52–55, 55.

22
"The new aesthetic for architecture is that of the new painting. A purer architecture is now in a position to achieve the same consequences that painting, purified through Futurism and Cubism, realized in Neoplasticism. Thanks to the unity of the new aesthetic, architecture and painting can merge into a single art and can resolve into each other." Piet Mondrian, "Moet de Schilderkunst minderwaaardig zijn aan de bouwkunst?" *De Stijl*, vol. 6, no. 5 (1923): 62–64. Translated by R. R. Symonds as "Is Painting Secondary to Architecture?," in Jaffé, *De Stijl*, 183–184, 184.

23

Piet Mondrian, "Neoplasticism in Painting: The New Plastic as 'Abstract-Real Painting': The Plastic Means and Composition [part II]," *De Stijl*, vol. 1 no. 4 (1918). Translated by R. R. Symonds, in Jaffé, *De Stijl*, 56–60, 57.

24

Ibid., 57.

25

Piet Mondrian, "De Nieuwe Beelding in de Schilderkunst: Van het natuurlijke tot het abstracte, d. i. van het onbepaalde tot het bepaalde." *De Stijl* vol. 1, no. 9 (1918): 88–91. Translated by R. R. Symonds as "Neoplasticism in Painting: From the Natural to the Abstract: From the Indeterminate to the Determinate [part II]," in Jaffé, *De Stijl*, 70–78, 71.

26

Theo van Doesburg, "Der Wille zum Stil: Neugestaltung von Leben, Kunst und Technik," *De Stijl*, vol. 5, no. 2–3. Translated by R. R. Symonds as, "The Will to Style: The Reconstruction of Life, Art and Technology" in Jaffé, *De Stijl*, 148–163, 161, 154.

27

Theo van Doesburg, "De beteekenis van der kleur in binnen- en buitenarchitectuur," *Bouwkundig Weekblad*, XLIV no. 21 (1923): 325–34. Translated as "The Significance of Color for Interior and Exterior Architecture (1923)" in Joost Baljeu, *Theo van Doesburg* (New York: Macmillan, 1974), 137–140, 137.

28

Theo van Doesburg, "Farben im Raum und Zeit," *De Stijl* 8 (1928): 26–36. Translated as "Space—Time and Color," in Baljeu. *Theo van Doesburg*, 175–180, 180.

29

Le Corbusier, "Salon d'automne (1923)," *L'Esprit Nouveau* 19 (December 1923).

30

Ibid.

31

Bruno Reichlin, "Le Corbusier vs De Stijl," in *De Stijl et l'architecture en France*, ed. Yve-Alain Bois and Bruno Reichlin (Bruxelles: Pierre Madaga, 1985), 91–108.

32

See, for example, van Doesburg's account of the evolution of a stained-glass window design: "I had stretched it on the wall in black and white in three parts above each other; only white planes (I had not yet put in the colors), separated by black lines. . . . Monday I put in the colors, but felt that the sacredness of the black and white drawing had got lost." Letter from van Doesburg to A. Kok dated May 9, 1917, cited in Carol Blotkamp, "Theo van Doesburg," in Carel Blotkamp et al. eds., *De Stijl: The Formative Years 1917–1922* translated by Charlotte I, Loeb and Arthur L. Loeb (Cambridge: MIT Press, 1986), 3–37, see p. 14.

33

Theo van Doesburg, "Fragments Concerning Mondrian," *Eenheid*, 283 (1915). Translated in Baljeu, *Theo van Doesburg*, 105–108, 108.

34

Letter from van Doesburg to Antony Kok dated September 9, 1917. Cited in Sjarel Ex and Els Hoeck, "Jan Wils," in Carel Blotkamp et al. eds., *De Stijl: The Formative Years 1917–1922* (Cambridge: MIT, 1986), 187–203, 189.

35

Theo van Doesburg, "Vers la peinture blanche," *Art concret*, vol. 1, no. 1 (1930): 11–12. Translated as "Towards White Painting" in Baljeu, *Theo van Doesburg*, 183.

36

Theo van Doesburg, "Élémentarisme (les éléments de la nouvelle peinture)," *De Stijl*, Van Doesburg issue (1932): 17–19. Translated as "Elementarism (the Elements of the New Painting)," in Baljeu, *Theo van Doesburg*, 184–185.

37

Le Corbusier, "Salon d'automne (1923)."

38

Le Corbusier, "Polychrome Architecturale (1931)," unpublished manuscript, Fondation Le Corbusier, Paris, B1–18, 5.

39

Ibid., 15, 17, 14.

40

Ibid., 14.

41

Le Corbusier, *Oeuvre complète 1910–29* (Zurich: Girsberger, 1929), 60 [italics in original].

42

Le Corbusier, *Le Corbusier: textes et dessins pour Ronchamp* (Paris: Minuit, 1956), 12. For details of the exchanges between Le Corbusier and Henry Church over color, see Tim Benton, *The Villas of Le Corbusier 1920–1930* (New Haven: Yale University, 1987), 104–127; Bruno Reichlin, "The Pavilion Church," in *In the Footsteps of Le Corbusier*, ed. Carlo Palazzolo and Riccardo Vio (New York: Rizzoli, 1991): 59–72.

43

While "A New Space in Architecture (1949)" argues that the goal of the 1925 Exposition was "to make the white wall appear," "Color in Architecture" of the year before argues that "At the Exposition of 1925 we proposed to the public the colored wall." Fernand Léger, "Color in Architecture," in Stano Papadaki ed., *Le Corbusier: Architect, Painter, Writer,* (New York: Macmillan, 1948), 78–80, 79.

44

"Each renaissance of vitality corresponds to a direct intervention of color. [We may see this in advertising, in cities,

outside cities, in the country, in car advertisement, in feminine dress and cosmetics, in sports, on the beach, etc.]:
Color expresses life." Le Corbusier, "Polychrome Architecturale (1931)," 22.

45
"Such a misfortune is always possible, and when it occurs,
the wall becomes a hanging and the architect becomes a
tapestry-maker. I am opposed to such a debasement.
This calls for a dictatorial intervention: eliminating those
colors that may be *called non-architectural*; even better,
seeking out, choosing colors that may be qualified as *eminently architectural*." Ibid., 1.

46
Ibid., 5.

47
Ibid., 8.

48
Ibid, 10.

49
Ibid.

50
"Until now I have always been resistant to wallpaper; I discerned in customary decors a latent obsession with disconcerting patterns; I sniffed out the architectural cheating
enabled by impertinently busy designs; the mediocre quality of both the idea and the execution was antithetical to
all that I had hoped for in terms of a new architecture.
Wallpaper seemed to bear the same crimes as the first wave
of mechanization, junk, pomp, bluff, deceit." Ibid., 17.

51
Ibid., 24.

52
Ibid.

53
Le Corbusier, "Color Keyboards (1932)." "Instead of covering walls and ceilings with 'three coats of oils'—necessarily applied amidst the hazards and hindrance arising from
other work—we can now utilize this 'machine-prepared-
painting'; and we apply it at the very last moment of finishing. Salubra is prepared on a hygienic and durable
ground which is strong and supple. It is made of fine colors,
the purity of which has been chemically tested. It is
both fadeless and washable.
The architect is always more or less at the mercy of indifferent workmanship in the matter of painting. The use of
Salubra gives him peace of mind; for its proportions of oil
and color are always accurate. Its consistent quality of
tone and material is guaranteed." Ibid.

54
Le Corbusier, "Polychrome Architecturale (1931)," 28.

55
Ibid., 26, 27.

56
Ibid.

57
Advertising brochure for Salubra, published in Werner
Oechslin, editorial, *Daidalos* 52 (1994), 24–25.

58
Le Corbusier, *Des Canons, des munitions? Merci! Des
logis . . . s.v.p.* (Paris, 1937), 22.

59
"At Aubusson, tapestry owes its renaissance to a decision
based upon a principle; to cease treating tapestry like a
kind of painting suspended in the middle of a wall and
framed with garlands. On the contrary, the aim was to
make the tapestry touch the ground, to make it as tall as a
person (at least 2.20m high) and to give it the breadth of a
normal wall." Le Corbusier, "à propos de la tapisserie," in
Le Corbusier, oeuvres complètes, vol. 6, *1952–1957* (Zurich: Editions Girsberger, 1958), 132.

60
Le Corbusier "Tapisseries Muralnomad," *Zodiac* 7 (1960):
57–65, 57.

61
Le Corbusier. "à propos de la tapisserie," 132.

62
"An interest in Art has become a widespread phenomenon,
and one that is new (books, prints, photographs, apparatus
for luminous projections, etc.). We cannot have murals
painted on the walls of our apartment. On the other hand,
the woolen wall that is tapestry may be taken off the wall,
rolled up, tucked under one's arm and hung elsewhere.
Thus I have named my tapestries "Muralnomad." Tapestries in the home respond to a legitimate poetic desire. Its
texture, its material, the sensibility gone into its making,
all introduce a veritable radiance into the apartment: colors, lines, and occasionally, evocation." Le Corbusier, "Tapisseries Muralnomad (1960)," 57.

63
Le Corbusier, "à propos de la tapisserie," 132.

64
Le Corbusier, Letter to the architects of Barcelona, dated 8
October 1962, in *Le Corbusier Lui-même,* ed. Jean Petit
(Geneva: Editions Rousseau, 1970), 130–131, 131.

65
"As for the *mural*—to which I now return—I believe it to
replace the *decorative*, it is reserved for train stations and
town halls. Mural painting is a discourse with powerful
words, it should be located where one may hear it, where
it should be heard. The mural is out of proportion in a
home. It has to be replaced by something else. We are nomads. Modern life has reduced us to a nomadic state. If
only for this reason, the mural does not have a place in the
home. The modern home defines itself through *units of
conforming size*: we are in 'rental boxes,' in the rental
mode, in absolute palaces—true—but we are nevertheless

not 'at home.' We may be the owners of our lodgings, surely, but the owner may oblige the renter to put everything back in order when he leaves the premises. The mural is thus displaced. But tapestry exists. Tapestry which, in the Middle Ages and during the Renaissance was legitimated by the need to cover vast panels of walls, large surfaces of cold stones, and which enabled the division of spaces into smaller, more intimate rooms. Tapestry is reborn . . . Tapestry is a mural painting which an individual may roll up and take with him. It caters to the demands of our nomadic life. I like to see tapestry in an individual's home. Its texture, its material gives it an intimate character." "Entretien avec Le Corbusier," in Georges Charbonnier, *Le monologue du peinture* (Paris, René Julliard, 1960), 99–107, 104.

66
Le Corbusier, *Entretien avec les étudiants des écoles d'architecture* (Paris: Donoel, 1943). Translated by Pierre Chase as *Le Corbusier Talks to Students* (New York: The Orion Press, 1961), 68.

67
Le Corbusier, *Vers une architecture* (Paris: Éditions Crès, 1923), 110. Translated by Frederick Etchells as *Towards a New Architecture* (London: John Rodker, 1931), 145.

68
Le Corbusier, *Précisions sur un état présent de l'architecture et de l'urbanisme* (Paris: Crès, 1930). Translated by Edith Schreiber Aujame as *Precisions: On the Present State of Architecture and City Planning* (Cambridge: MIT Press, 1991), 106. "Modern woman has cut her hair. Our eyes have learned the form of her legs. The corset is out. 'Etiquette' is out. Etiquette was born at the court. Only certain persons had the right to sit, and only in a certain way. . . . Well, today, all that bores us. . . . And the house has been emptied of its furniture." Ibid., 118.

69
Ibid., 107.

70
"With Corbu at a shirtmakers where he wishes to buy pajamas: 'I would like pajamas that are dark, in a strong single shade, without lapels, without edges lined with white stitching.' We don't have that, Sir. We only have ones with the stitching. Le Corbusier protests: 'You shirtmakers haven't managed to invent pajamas that are becoming and that don't make one feel perpetually as though one were in a bedroom on stage!'
—Sir, we've always made them this way . . .
We leave and go to a more distinguished shirtmaker located on the avenue de l'Opera. Sir, we always make them this way. . . . We go to the boulevard Saint-Michel. —Sir, we always make them this way . . . Corbu says: 'I wrote somewhere, in 1927 or so: as long as the costume cannot be transformed, the revolution will never be repeated." Le Corbusier in *Le Corbusier Parle* ed. Jean Petit (Paris: Les éditions Force Vives, 1967), 53.

71
Le Corbusier, *Precisions*, 115.

72
Ibid., 72.

73
Ibid., 42.

74
Le Corbusier, sketchbook A2, p. 97, in *Le Corbusier Sketchbooks*, vol. 1, *1914–1948*, translated by Agnes Serenyi (London: Thames and Hudson, Fondation Le Corbusier, 1981), 8.

75
To give but one of so many examples: "A suburban train beings us slowly toward Budapest. It is full of peasants in their Sunday finery. Handsome men, young and excitable, are dressed in shiny black close-fitting garments. They wear three or four roses in their lapels or on their hats. The woman are dark-skinned and energetic, as if made out of some tough substance. Their costume is low keyed. Decorative panels are painted against the black of their aprons . . ." Le Corbusier, *Le voyage d'Orient* (Paris: Fondation Le Corbusier, 1966). Translated by Ivan Žaknić as *Journey to the East* (Cambridge: MIT Press, 1987), 39.

76
Ibid., 23.

77
Le Corbusier, *Le Corbusier Talks to Students*, 68.

78
"The gentle English range of colors is little known to the stranger; though it is quite well known in the costumier's shops that the English choose soft colorings." Amédée Ozenfant, "Color and the English Tradition," *Architectural Review* 81 (1937): 41–44, 41.

79
"But, as regards color, our modern eye is very precise and exacting. . . . The tremendous progress of color printing, of posters, the high level of fabric dyeing, the expert selections of dress-making, have made the modern eye extremely sensitive; our eyes are perhaps even more sensitive to color than those of the ancients. As a result, the least departure from the exactness of a color is notice and can compromise the whole architecture of a building." Amédée Ozenfant, "Color and Method," *Architectural Review* 81 (1937): 89–92, 92.

80
"An architect, at any rate, will admit without hesitation that while certain ultra-fragile harmonies, obtained by the use of fragile pigments like pink or rose, can be used in hats or expensive dresses (which have only to exert a limited effect for the duration of a ceremony) there are some shades that are not a suitable choice for walls or furnishing: architecture, even when it aims at charm, must maintain dignity, and suggest the security which comes from lasting things." Amédée Ozenfant, "Color Solidity," *Architectural Review,* vol. 81 (May 1937), 243–246, 243.

81

Ibid., 246.

82

Amédée Ozenfant, "Color and Method," 90.

83

Amédée Ozenfant, "Color in the Town," *Architectural Review*, vol. 82 (July 1937), 41–44, 43.

84

"We have already stated our liking for white. But it must be understood that we will not commit the errors of those architects who are justly charmed with the white islands of Greece and who would, ridiculously enough, make a Greek (or a Frenchwoman) of London. Every locality has its own particular requirements . . . often—too often—the modern architect solves the problem of town color with artless simplicity. He builds in any material, and then applies to the facades a whitish pseudo stone facing; and the trick is done. 'Its white, so its modern'—not quite good enough." Ibid., 41.

85

Fernand Léger, "Kurzgefasste Auseinandersetzung uber das Aktuell kunsterische Sein," *Das Kunstblatt*, 7 (1923): 1–4. Translated as "Notes on Contemporary Plastic Life," in *Functions of Painting*, ed. Edward Fry, 24–27, 25.

86

Fernand Léger, "La Rue: objets, spectacles," *Cahiers de la République des Lettres, des Sciences et des Arts*, 12 (1928): 102–104. Translated as "The Street: Objects, Spectacles," in *Functions of Painting*, ed. Edward Fry, 78–80, 78.

87

Fernand Léger, "The Spectacle: Light, Color, Moving Image, Object-Spectacle (1924)," 37.

88

Fernand Léger, "Color in the World (1938)," 119.

89

Fernand Léger, "Notes on the Mechanical Element," unpublished text of 1923. Translated in *Functions of Painting*, ed. Edward Fry, 28–30, 30.

90

"The old-fashioned costume of the towns has had to evolve with everything else. The black suit, which contrasts with the bright feminine outfits at fashionable gatherings, is a clear manifestation of an evolution in taste. Black and white resound and clash, and the visual effect of present-day fashionable parties is the exact opposite of the effect that similar social gatherings in the eighteenth century, for example, would have produced. The dress of that period was all in the same tones, the whole aspect was more decorative, less strongly contrasted, and more uniform. Evolution notwithstanding, the average bourgeois has retained his ideas of tone on tone, the decorative concept. The red parlor, the yellow bedroom." Fernand Léger, "Les Révélations picturales actuelles," *Soirées de Paris*, 25 (1914):

349–56. Translated as "Contemporary Achievements in Painting," in *Functions of Painting*, ed. Edward Fry, 11–19, 13.

91

Ibid., 16.

92

Fernand Léger, "On Monumentality and Color (1943)," 45.

93

"Until the pictorial realization by the painters of the last fifty years, color or tone were fast bound to an object, to a representative form. A dress, a human being, a flower, a landscape, had the task of wearing color." Ibid., 41.

94

Léger, "The Spectacle: Light, Color, Moving Image, Object Spectacle (1924)," 45.

95

Ibid., 47.

96

Fernand Léger, "L'Esthétique de la machine: l'objet fabriqué, l'artisan et l'artiste," *Der Quershnitt*, 3 (1923): 122–129. Translated as "The Machine Aesthetic: the Manufactured Object, the Artisan, and the Artist," in *Functions of Painting*, ed. Edward Fry, 52–61, 55.

97

Ibid., 61.

98

Fernand Léger, "New York vu par Fernand Léger," *Cahiers d'Art*, 9/10 (1931): 437–39. Translated as "New York (1931)," in *Functions of Painting*, ed. Edward Fry, 84–90, 87.

99

"In the new factory—without any hint having been made to them, without any instruction—it was seen that at the end of a certain time, they were more tidy, gayer, better taken care of, better dressed. It was simply the light and color—this new truth—which had brought about the change." Fernand Léger, "Color in Architecture (1948)," 80.

100

Ibid., 78.

101

Ibid.

T A K E   9

Sexual Charges

1

"Typical everyday materials such as linen, duck, cotton and wool fabrics—tweed, gabardine and similar cloths—

will always last longer than designs that are constantly changing, and which will continue to do so because the combination of threads is so much less convincing. In the case of fabrics for women's clothes, other arguments apply that do not concern us here." Gerrit Th. Rietveld, "Interiors (1948)" in *Gerrit Th. Rietveld: The Complete Works, 1888–1964*, ed. Marijke Küper and Ida van Zijl. (Utrecht: Centraal Museum Utrecht, 1992), 40–47, 46.

2
Fernand Léger, *Forms et Vie* 2 (1951).

3
Le Corbusier, "Note," *Forms et Vie* 2 (1951): 11.

4
Ibid.

5
Ibid.

6
Le Corbusier, letter to "Harper's Bazaar" dated February 25, 1952 in *Le Corbusier: Le passé à réaction poétique* (Paris: Caisse nationale des Monuments historiques et des Sites, 1988), 474.

7
Ibid.

8
L. Bruder, "Evolution of Dress in Keeping with Architecture," *Forms et Vie* 2 (1951): 7–10, 7.

9
Le Corbusier, "Note (1951)," 11.

10
Fernand Léger, "Le mur, l'architecte, le peintre," unpublished lecture in Zurich of May 1933. Translated as "The Wall, the Architect, the Painter (1933)," in Fernand Léger, *Functions of Painting*, ed. Edward Fry (New York: Viking Press, 1973), 91–99, 99.

11
Fernand Léger, "Un nouvel espace en architecture," *Art d'Aujourd'hui*, 3 (1949): 19. Translated as "A New Space in Architecture (1949)," in *Functions of Painting*, ed. Edward Fry, 157–159, 158.

12
Piet Mondrian, "Die Nieuwe Beelding in de Schilderkunst: De Nieuwe Beelding als abstracte–reële schilderkunst; Beeldingsmiddel en composite," *De Stijl*, vol.1 no. 3 (1917): 88–91. Translated by R. R. Symonds as "Neoplasticism in Painting: The New Plastic as 'Abstract-Real Painting': the Plastic Means and Composition [part I]," in Hans L. C. Jaffé, *De Stijl* (London: Thames and Hudson, 1970), 54–56, 56

13
Le Corbusier, "Polychrome Architecturale (1931)," unpublished manuscript, Fondation Le Corbusier, Paris, B1–18, 1, 10.

14
"Before the developments in painting of the last fifty years, a color and tone were bound completely to an object, to a representational form. A dress, a figure, a flower, a landscape was obliged to be of a certain color. Then—so that architecture could command it unreservedly, so that the wall could become a new field for experience—it became necessary to extricate and isolate color from the objects that held it prisoner." Fernand Léger, "Modern Architecture and Color," in Charmion von Wiegand and Fritz Glarner, *American Abstract Artists* (New York: Ram Press, 1946): 31–38. Republished in *Functions of Painting*, ed. Edward Fry, 149–154, 150.

15
Fernand Léger, "The New Realism," lecture delivered at the Museum of Modern Art, translated by Harold Rosenberg, *Art Front*, vol. 2 no. 8 (1935). Republished in *Functions in Painting*, 109–113, 113.

16
"Léger spoke of the formidable dynamic of color. It is through polychromy that the sensational play, the colored epic, soft, violent, can be introduced into a house. For a long time I have been studying the perfection of the magnificent resources of polychromy; and using just those organic necessities of the modern plan, I have seen that tumults can be disciplined by color, lyrical space can be created, classifications realized, dimensions enlarged and the feeling for architecture made to burst forth in joy." Le Corbusier, "Discussion with Léger and Aragon on 'Painting and Realism'," translated by M. J., *Transition* 25 (Fall 1936): 109–118, 116.

17
"I believe that painting and statuary will be incorporated in architecture for the reason that architecture is beginning over again at zero to reorganize everything from the skeleton through to the flesh. Animating this skeleton, architecture, which has edified an authentic symphony through light and the manner in which this light clarifies walls, whose lyricism is made of intensely real psychophysiological events, this architecture, which is a mathematical work—and here mathematics is mentioned for beauty and not as a school task—whose controls are proportion; the human ladder is ready to accept fine speeches, in places of complete agreement. We will take pleasure in calling in the painter or sculptor. . . . I love walls, beautiful in their proportion, and I am apprehensive at turning them over to unprepared minds. For if a wall is spoiled if it is soiled, if we kill the wholesome clear speech of architecture by the introduction of an inappropriate style of painting or statuary, if we are not in the spirit, but against the spirit—it will mean just so many disappointing crimes." Ibid., 115.

18
"This is not yet painting. There is no need for it. This is architectural polychromy. I can, when walls overwhelm me by their presence, dynamite them with an appropriate color. But I can also, if the place is suitable, have recourse

to a painter, ask him to inscribe his plastic thought in the spot, and with one stroke open all the doors to the depths of a dream, just there where actual depths did not exist. Here, then, is an extremely favorable opportunity to collaborate with the painter. It would be camouflage in the service of thought." Ibid., 116.

19
Fernand Léger, "A New Space in Architecture (1949)," 159.

20
Le Corbusier, "Polychrome Architecturale (1931)," 21, 14.

21
As, for example, when Le Corbusier describes vernacular houses of Spain in 1931: "whitewash and still perfect maintenance of an architecture which = a state of mind the road has not disturbed. . . . The houses in the midst of the Fields are *chaste*." Le Corbusier, sketchbook A, p. 97, in *Le Corbusier Sketchbooks*, vol. 1, *1914–1948*, translated by Acnes Serenyi (London: Thames and Hudson, Fondation Le Corbusier, 1981), 414.

22
Le Corbusier, *Le voyage d'Orient* (Paris: Fondation Le Corbusier, 1966). Translated by Ivan Žaknić as *Journey to the East* (Cambridge: MIT Press, 1987), 54.

23
"You are utterly seduced by a young Persian girl dressed in scarlet beneath a golden canopy in an Isfahan garden with tulips and hyacinths everywhere." Ibid., 140.

24
"Tall men with turbans and variegated skirts; women covered by indigo-blue veils bordered with material the color of wine dregs. The young girls are very beautiful, much more so than their swiftly faded elder sisters. They all wear culotte skirts, the very stylish culotte skirts, simple and finely modeled." Ibid., 66.

25
"When the blood is young and the mind is healthy, normal sensuality asserts itself. Men work less and search for well-being. They take care of their dwellings with a solicitude that, to us would appear exaggerated. They want them to be clean, gay, and comfortable: they adorn them with flowers. They dress in embroidered clothing whose flamboyant colors tell of their joy of life. And each spring, the house that one loves receives its new coat: sparkling white, it smiles the whole summer through foliage and flowers that owe to it their dazzle." Ibid., 60.

26
"And the ladies, my dear Klip, are charming in their mysterious black veils, their disquieting anonymity of identical silks, their hidden treasures all alike. Now it seems to me they are ravishing despite and also because of that second skirt flung over their heads, that makes an impenetrable veil. You will find real coquettes underneath. I bet you, you old bony fakir, that almost all of them are young, adorable, with ivory cheeks a little full and with the innocent

eyes of gazelles—delicious! After all, these veils conceal a penetrable mystery. It seems to me that there are thousands of them who wish to display their beauty, and devilish as they are, they know how to get around all the codes. They have a touch of genius: slaves of a despotic custom—maybe a wise one—which we have declared ugly and humiliating: they accomplish the miracle of revealing their individualities in attires that show no difference of cut, style, without embroidery or any combinations that could have displayed a personal fancy. How do they manage it? Simply because they have the will to appear pretty, and thereby they perform their first womanly duty." Ibid., 129. After finally one such woman talks to him briefly, Le Corbusier adds: "As for me, I was as much delighted as disturbed! It would be superfluous for me to tell you that she was young and exquisite and that during our entire conversation I admired her through her veil." Ibid., 130. On Le Corbusier's fetishization of Arab women, see Zeynep Çelik, "Le Corbusier, Orientalism, Colonialism," *Assemblage*, 17 (1992): 59–77; and Beatriz Colomina, "War on Architecture; E. 1027," *Assemblage* 20 (1993): 28–29.

27
"Everything is smothered in flowers, and under these ephemeral bouquets, other ephemeral bouquets—as a poet would say, other flowers—young girls, beautiful women, smiling, somewhat depraved, perhaps a little inflamed by their desires. Gentlemen in black play second fiddle in this orchestra of colors, serving inevitably as the subjects for intrigues that culminate in roses tossed and lilies proffered cynically." Le Corbusier, *Journey to the East*, 25.

28
Ibid., 206.

29
Le Corbusier, *L'art décoratif d'aujourd'hui* (Paris: Éditions G. Grès et Cie, 1925), 193. Translated by James Dunnet as *The Decorative Art of Today* (Cambridge: MIT Press, 1987), 89.

30
"The purified female element is the *interiorized* female element, but remains *female*: never—in time—does it become male. It is only stripped of its most outward character; or rather, the most outward female is crystallized to a *more pure* female. The purified male element is the male element free from the dominant influence of outwardness—of the female element. . . . *Interiorization* of the female is made perceptible by intensifying naturalistic color and increasing the tension of form *to the extreme. It is, therefore, the controlling and tensing of the capricious, the determining of the fluid and vague*," Piet Mondrian, "De Nieuwe Beelding in de Schilderkunst: Natuur en Geest als vrouwelijk en mannelijk element," *De Stijl*, vol. 1, no. 12 (1917). Translated by R. R. Symonds as "Neo-Plasticism in Painting: Conclusion: Nature and Spirit as Male and Female Elements" in Hans L. C. Jaffé, *De Stijl*, 88–93, 89.

31

Theo van Doesburg, "Aanteekeningen over monumentale kunst," *De Stijl*, vol, 2, no. 1 (1919). Translated by R. R. Symonds as "Notes on Monumental Art with Reference to Two Fragments of a Building," in Hans L. C. Jaffé, *De Stijl*, 99–103, 100.

32

Theo van Doesburg and Cornelius van Eesteren, "Vers une construction collective," *De Stijl*, vol. 6 no. 6/7 (1924). Translated by R. R. Symonds as "Towards a Collective Construction," in Hans L. C. Jaffé, *De Stijl*, 190–191, 191

33

Piet Mondrian, *Le Néo-Plasticisme* (Paris: Éditions de L'effort moderne, 1920), cited in Herbert Henkels, *Mondrian: From Figuration to Abstraction*, translated by Ruth Koenig (London: Thames and Hudson, 1987), 30.

34

Piet Mondrian, "De groote boulevards," *De nieuwe Amsterdammer*, (1920). Translated as "Les Grands Boulevards," in *The New Art—The New Life: The Collected Writings of Piet Mondrian*, ed. Harry Holtzman and Martin S. James (Boston: G. K. Hall, 1986), 126–128, 126.

35

Ibid., 128.

36

Piet Mondrian, "L'Architecture future néoplasticienne," *L'Architecture vivante*, vol. 3 no. 9 (1925): 11–13. Translated as "The Neo-Plastic Architecture of the Future," in *The New Art—The New Life: The Collected Writings of Piet Mondrian*, ed. Harry Holtzman and Martin S. James, 196–197, 197.

37

Piet Mondrian, "Neo-plasticisme: De woning—de straat—de stad," *i 10*, vol. 1 no. 1 (1927): 12–18. Translated as "Home—Street—City," in *The New Art—The New Life: The Collected Writings of Piet Mondrian*, ed. Harry Holtzman and Martin S. James 205–212, 211.

38

Piet Mondrian, "Die rein abstrakte kunst; L'Art abstrait pur," *Neue Zürcher Zeitung*, no. 2060 (1929). Translated as "Pure Abstract Art," in *The New Art—The New Life: The Collected Writings of Piet Mondrian*, ed. Harry Holtzman and Martin S. James, 223–225, 225.

39

Piet Mondrian, "A Note on Fashion (1930)," translated in *The New Art—The New Life: The Collected Writings of Piet Mondrian*, ed. Harry Holtzman and Martin S. James, 226.

40

Piet Mondrian, "De jazz en de Neo-plastiek," *i 10*, vol. 1 no. 12 (1927): 421–427. Translated as "Jazz and Neo-Plastic" in *The New Art—The New Life: The Collected Writings of Piet Mondrian*, ed. Harry Holtzman and Martin S. James, 217–221, 221.

41

Ibid.

42

Cited by Harry Holtzman and Martin S. James in *The New Art—The New Life: The Collected Writings of Piet Mondrian*, 217. For the full text of the interviews, see "At Piet Mondrian's: Three Interviews with the Artist," translated by Ruth Koenig, in Herbert Henkels, *Mondrian: From Figuration to Abstraction* (London: Thames and Hudson, 1987), 24–32.

43

"M. says his art is sensual. He said, [in answer to the writer's comment that she saw it as *sensuous*] 'when sensuous means a deeper grade of the sensual, then the definition sensuous will be just what I mean to say. But will it be directly understood in this case that sensuous remains unified with sensuality?' The word sensual embraces the whole human sense-faculty and art is produced by this whole." Piet Mondrian, "Notes for an Interview (ca. 1941)," unpublished text translated in *The New Art—The New Life: The Collected Writings of Piet Mondrian*, ed. Harry Holtzman and Martin S. James, 336–337, 336.

44

"Every art must be expression of our whole being and can be approached only with our whole being. But the kind of expression depends on the grade of profoundness that sensuality has. This fact explains the culture of art toward pure abstraction. For true abstraction is not rejection or the elimination of parts of the whole of reality but the intensification of it.
The culture of art is a continuous effort toward greater profoundness.
M. says, not on philosophical grounds but based on pure plastic and technical experience, that it cannot be emphasized enough that abstraction is not rejection but intensification." Ibid.

45

Le Corbusier, *Quand les cathédrales étaient blanches. Voyage au pays de timides* (Paris: Plon, 1937). Translated by Francis E. Hyslop as *When the Cathedrals Were White* (New York: Reynal and Hitchcock, 1947), 29, xiii, xxi.

46

Ibid., 46.

47

Ibid.

48

Ibid., xiii.

49

Ibid., 108.

50

Ibid.

51

Ibid., 168.

52
Ibid., 129.

53
Le Corbusier argues that you can divide all the works of art in the Athens museum "at the precise point at which the Greeks abandoned the short tunic, falling halfway down the thigh, which allowed them to hunt, fight and run, in favor of the toga whose folds flattered the gestures of discourses, hagglings and palavers in the colonnades of the agoras—the exact moment that they began to talk, to 'talk well'—which followed the time when they acted. The polychroming of sculpture comes to an end at this time." Ibid., 131.

54
"Architecture d'époque machiniste," *Journal de psychologie normale et pathologique* (January 15–March 15, 1926): 303–350, 334.

55
Ibid., 348.

56
Le Corbusier, *When the Cathedrals Were White*, 14.

57
Ibid., xii.

58
Ibid., 102.

59
Ibid., 110.

60
Ibid., 156.

61
Ibid., 136.

62
Ibid., 105.

63
Ibid.

64
Ibid., 110, 135, 145, 125.

65
Ibid., 108.

66
"Most of the men one meets there are young; they have the look of well-groomed workmen. A white shirt, without a stiff collar, cuts off the mask at shoulder height. That gives the effect of a medallion. Only there have I observed men's profiles; the girls, too, are accentuated because of the severity of their flattened hair and made-up eyes. When they are dancing, they are clearly outlined against the bare-white background. . . . They [the men] prize their elegance, they care for it, they shiver in the winter, but their style is to wear neither a vest nor an overcoat. They have their style

and their tastes, they carefully choose their shoes and caps; their hairstyle is as studied as any woman's." Fernand Léger, "Popular Dance Halls (1925)," in *Functions of Painting*, ed. Edward Fry, 74–77, 74.

67
Ibid., 76.

68
Le Corbusier, *When the Cathedrals Were White*, 149.

69
Ibid., 154.

70
Le Corbusier, "Rien n'est transmissible que la pensée," (Nothing is transmissible but thought), dated July 1965, in *Le Corbusier: Oeuvre complètes, 1965–69*, ed. Willy Boesiger (Zurich: Les editions d'Architecture, 1970), 168–177, 174.

71
Le Corbusier, *When the Cathedrals Were White*, 165.

72
Ibid., 165.

73
Le Corbusier, sketchbook E20, in *Le Corbusier Sketchbook*, vol. 2, *1914–1948*, translated by Acnes Serenyi (London: Thames and Hudson, Fondation Le Corbusier, 1981), 452.

74
Ibid., 213.

75
Le Corbusier, *UN Headquarters* (New York: Rheinhold, 1947), 32.

76
Le Corbusier, *When the Cathedrals Were White*, 151.

77
"Not being a handsome fellow, I keep my anatomy out of sight. In spite of some protests, I insist on white and blue striped convict's trousers and an Indian army Guard's vermillion coat (he would have loved to see me in a high-ranking officer's coat!); I find an enormous gold epaulette which I fasten on the left side. No military cap, sir, a white, pointed clown's hat, please. For color balance, I put on a dark blue sash as a shoulder-belt, cut by a gold band. There are no pockets in my convict's trousers: bills go into my socks, my pipe and tobacco pouch into my belt. To finish off, three differently shaped spots of white on my cheeks and forehead, to perplex the curious." Ibid., 151.

78
Ibid., 55. "The USA is young, very young, at the age of Olympic champion: with a handsome shock of hair on an athletic body." Ibid., 214. "The body of the USA—which I have often drawn: enormous hands, titanic shoulders, feet like bridge foundations—appalls them." Ibid., 148.

79

Ibid., 71.

80

Ibid., 77.

81

Ibid., 112.

82

Ibid., 158.

83

Ibid.

84

Ibid.

85

Amédée Ozenfant and Charles-Eduard Jeanneret, *La pein-ture moderne* (Paris: Les Éditions G. Crès & C, 1925), 48. The chapter was originally published as "Nature et cré-ation," *L'Esprit Nouveau* 19 (December 1923).

86

Amédée Ozenfant, *Art* (Paris: Editions Budry, 1928), trans-lated by John Rodker as *Foundations of Modern Art* (New York: Dover Publications, 1931), 169.

87

Ibid., 3.

88

Le Corbusier, *The Decorative Art of Today*, 190.

89

"Less primitive races, which are exceptionally sensitive to the direct influence of form, have not feared, in their recent masks, to welcome elements of European origin, such as saucepans or top-hats. They use them in manufacturing the head-dresses of the participants in the religious festivit-ies, or in the masks for sacred dances. Rich with the experi-ence of an age-long selective tradition, they feel or they know, that form and color and the symphony evoked by them provoke certain definite reactions in men, and that every form and color is linked with a specific emotion. A language that is felt (not symbolical), and which is that of all great universal and permanent art.
The universality of Great Art is possible, for all men have common factors, physical and moral. The Negroes were able to realize that the top-hat owed the nobility of its ap-pearance, not to the use which convention had dictated for it among Europeans, but to the specific appearance of the cylinder with its dominant verticals and its specifically seri-ous color, black." Amédée Ozenfant, *Foundations of Mod-ern Art*, 240.

90

Le Corbusier, *When the Cathedrals Were White*, 216.

91

Le Corbusier, sketchbook B7, in *Le Corbusier Sketchbook,* vol. 1, *1914–1948,* translated by Acnes Serenyi (London: Thames and Hudson, Fondation Le Corbusier, 1981), 617.

TAKE 10

Whiteout

1

Richard Pommer and Christian Otto, *Weissenhof 1927 and the Modern Movement in Architecture* (Chicago: Uni-versity of Chicago, 1991), 59.

2

"It is striking to find out from this drawing [an axonomet-ric of the whole Weissenhofsiedlung] that there already exists within the work of such an international group of ar-chitects such a striking unity of conception that in the grand view of a single scheme one could say it expressed one spirit. And this had occurred despite the fact that the chief architect does not want to regulate his colleagues any further then to specify the parcelling of the land for the res-idences and to indicate the building heights." J. P. P. Oud, "International Architecture: Werkbund Exhibition, 'The Dwelling,' July-September 1927, Stuttgart," *i 10* 6 (1927) 204–205, translated by Suzanne Frank, *Oppositions* 7 (Winter 1976): 78–79, 79. Oud goes on to clarify the sig-nificance of this unified spirit in terms of the question that ignited the 1914 controversy within the Werkbund:
"Those who think that the new architecture is on the wrong track because it does not recognize the individual sensibility of the artist who prefers to live his life to the full, rather than worry about the morality of his commis-sions, here would perhaps detect something new that only in past times seemed possible: unity. Unity is generally much more important than being different, however good it may be to be different. In the architecture of the period directly preceding ours, the architecture was unimportant since the individual thought himself to be of more signifi-cance than his commission: in the modern period, architec-ture will blossom again since the architect is willing to make himself subordinate to his commission." Ibid.

3

"Even though it is not what those responsible for the proj-ect had in mind it must be said that what strikes one most in the whole exhibition is the superficial form impact. No one had expected to find that it was already possible today to get together more than a dozen architects from all parts of Europe to work together on a project, to give them com-plete freedom in the handling of all the exterior details (apart from the design of the roof) and still not detract from the unity of the general appearance. . . . That an indi-vidualist form should have been followed so swiftly by an entirely non-personal form is something that grows out of the whole structure of the age we live in." Walter Riezler, "Die Wohnung," *Die Form* 2, no. 9 (Sept. 1927): 258–266, 259.

4

For a detailed record of the exact location of these colors, see Karin Kirsch, *The Weissenhofsiedlung: Experimental Housing Building for the Deutscher Werkbund, Stuttgart, 1927,* translated by David Britt (New York: Rizzoli Inter-national, 1989), 116. The account of the color at Weissen-hof offered here draws on the research of Kirsch along with that of Pommer and Otto in *Weissenhof 1927 and the Modern Movement in Architecture*. Pommer and Otto, in turn, draw on Andreas Menrad, "Die Weissenhofsiedlung- farbig: Quellen, Befunde und die Revision eines Klischees," *Deutsche Kunst und Denkmalpflege* 34, no. 1 (1986), 95–108.

5
Karl Konrad Düssel, "Die Stuttgarter Weissenhof-Siedlung," *Deutsche Kunst und Dekoration* 61 (October 1927): 91–98, 92.

6
Ibid., 96.

7
Edgar Wedepohl, for example, describes Le Corbusier's use of color in some detail, arguing that his external application levitates the architecture: "Through this coloration of the lower section, the impression is created that the houses are held floating in the air, just as if held by a thin anchorline." Edgar Wedepohl, "Die Weissenhofsiedlung der Werkbundausstellung," *Wasmuth's Monatshefte für Baukunst* 11 (1927): 391–402, 396. Wedepohl goes on to lightly suggest that different balance of incoming light and color tone could have been used on the interior but then rejects Taut's colors outright: "Bruno Taut's crass color scheme . . . screams uninhibitedly out across the landscape and makes apparent, especially alongside the subtle coloration of Le Corbusier's buildings, that the weaker the color sense the more intense the color values and contrasts. The interiors are colored on the same principle. The only people who could live in such rooms would be those with blunted visual nerves, who need the strongest possible visual stimuli: the equivalent in chromatic terms of the hard of hearing." Ibid., 400. The latter quote is cited by Karin Kirsch, *The Weissenhofsiedlung*, 137.

8
"Bruno Taut could not be dissuaded from having his houses painted inside and out with the most vulgar colors he could find . . . he shrank from no coarseness of color-schemes in order to attract attention (a blonde oak writing desk in front of an ultramarine blue wall is the most modest example. But: in the extensive writings about Weissenhof, precisely his house is silently ignored. Indeed the only positive thing one could say about House Nr. 19 is that it is unified in itself, insofar as its plan and elevation, its internal and external design and its color-scheme are all equally banal and bad. We know very well that Taut has accomplishments to his name which have absolutely nothing to do with his Stuttgart project." Rudolf Pfister, "Stuttgarter Werkbundausstellung, 'Die Wohnung'," *Der Baumeister* 26, no. 2 (February 1928): 33–72, 66. "Its a pity that the walls of Bruno Taut's house, by its bright colors (Prussian blue and stone red), destroy the harmony of the whole in an interferring (*hinderlijk*) way." R.L.A. Schoemaker, "Tentoonstelling 'De Woning' Te Stuttgart," *Het Bouwbedrijf*, 4, no. 20 (September 1927): 423–429, 425.

9
Cited by Ian Whyte, *Bruno Taut and the Architecture of Activism* (Cambridge: Cambridge University Press, 1982), 20.

10
Ibid., 31.

11
Bruno Taut, "Aufruf zum Farbigen Bauen!," *Das hofe Ufer*, I, no. 12 (November 1919), 272.

12
Bruno Taut, *Die Stadtkrone* (Jena: 1919), 63. Cited by *Architecture and Design: 1890–1939* ed. Tim Benton and Charlotte Benton (New York: Whitney Library of Design, 1975), 83.

13
Ibid., 70.

14
Bruno Taut, letter to Municipal inspectors of the District Zehlendorf, dated April 14, 1930. Cited by Franziska Bollery and Kristiana Harmann, "The Chromatic Controversy: Contemporary Views of the Twenties," in *Color in Townscape*, ed. Martina Düttmann et. al., translated by John William Gabriel (San Francisco: W. H. Freeman, 1981): 18–28, 24.

15
Bruno Taut, "Betr. Zehlendorf, Bauteil V," dated 14th April 1930, in *Die Bauwerke und Kunstdenkmäler von Berlin*, ed. Helge Pitz and Winfried Behne (Berlin: Gebr. Mann Verlag, 1980): 146–149, 147.

16
Ibid., 149.

17
Bruno Taut, "Die Fabre," *Die Farbige Stadt* 6, no. 3. (20 June 1931): 29–30, reprinted and translated in *Die Bauwerke und Kunstdenkmäler von Berlin*, ed. Helge Pitz and Winfried Behne 151–156, 154.

18
Bruno Taut, "Wiedergeburt der Farbe" in *Farbe am Hause: Der Erste Deutsche Farbenfag*, (Berlin: Bauwelt Verlag, 1925), 12–21. A partial translation appears in *Color in Townscape*, ed. Martina Düttman, et. al., 12–15, 13.

19
Bruno Taut, *Ein Wohnhaus* (Stuttgart: Franckh'sche Verlagshandlung W. Keller, 1927).

20
J. E. Hamman, "Weiss, alles weiss," *Die Form* 5, no. 5 (March 1930): 121–123, 121.

21
Ibid.

22
Ibid, 122.

23

Bruno Taut, "Die Fabre," 151.

24

Ibid.

25

Ibid., 152. "Apart from the need for relatively frequent renewal, white has another important characteristic feature in the optical field: a white housewall when situated immediately next to a yellow wall is of course brighter in its light intensity. Nevertheless when seen at a distance the white will appear darker than the yellow beside it. Due to the lack of brightness beside the yellow it will give an impression of a dismal grey even if the coat of paint is brand new, i.e. even if there is still no dirt on it. It must be a property of our climate, the nature of its sunlight, the high incidence of dull days and rain etc." Ibid.

26

Le Corbusier, "Wie wohnt man in meinen Suttgarter Häusern?," *Das Neue Frankfurt* 2 (January 1928).

27

"To see architecture only in beautifully designed fulfillment of goals, in the decorative clothing of that which is simply necessary, that is, to see its role as a kind of craft, is indeed an all too demeaning interpretation of its significance . . . it emerges as a play of fantasy which has only a loose relationship to these goals." Bruno Taut, "Architektur," *Das Hohe Ufer* 1, no. 5 (May 1919): 125–126, 125.

28

"One day when I was walking through the Weissenhofsiedlung with Le Corbusier, he started back at the sight of the house and said: 'My God, Taut is color-blind!'" Werner Graeff, "Hinter den Kulissen der Weissenhofsiedlung." cited by Karin Kirsch, *The Weissenhofsiedlung*, 137.

29

Alfred Roth, *Zwei Wohnhäuser von Le Corbusier und Pierre Jeanneret* (Stuttgart: Akad. Verlag Dr. Fr. Wedekind, 1928), 38.

30

"I made careful enquiries as to the colors of the neighboring houses, and heard that, beside white, Le Corbusier is using a pink; on looking at the site, and from the photographs I had taken, I came to the conclusion that in relation to the large expanses of white in the neighborhood this small building in the specified color scheme would be exactly right." Bruno Taut, Letter to Mies van de Rohe, July 22, 1927. Cited by Karin Kirsh, *The Weissenhofsiedlung*, 139.

31

Manfred Speidel, "Color and Light: On Bruno Taut's Oeuvre as a Painter," *Daidalos* no. 45 (15 September 1992): 117–135, 127.

32

Adolf Behne, "Die Bedeutung der Farbe in Falkenbeg," *Die Gardenstadt* 7 (December 1913): 249. Cited in Franziska Bollery and Kristiana Harmann, "The Chromatic Controversy: Contemporary Views of the Twenties," 20.

33

Bruno Taut, "Farbenwirkungen aus meiner Praxis," *Das Hohe Ufer* 1, no. 11 (November 1919): 263–266, 266.

34

"The mosques and the multi-colored turmoil—form a total unity." Bruno Taut, "Reiseeindrücke aus Konstantinopel," *Das Kunstgewerbeblatt* 28, no. 3 (December 1916): 50. Cited, Iain Boyd Whyte, *Bruno Taut and the Architecture of Activism*, 78.

35

Bruno Taut, "Eindrücke aus Kowno," *Sozialistische Monatshefte* 24, (1918): 897–901, 899. Cited in Karin Kirsh, *The Weissenhofsiedlung*, 138.

36

Hans Schmidt, "Die Wohnungausstellung Stuttgart, 1927," *Das Werk* 14 (1927): 259–277, 263, 261.

37

Provisional plan for the execution of the Werkbund exhibition, Stuttgart 1926, signed by Peter Bruckman and the Mayor of Stuttgart. Cited in Karin Kirsh, *The Weissenhofsiedlung*, 17.

38

Willi Baumeister, "Farben im Raum," in *Innenräume: Herausgegeben vom Deutschen Werkbund* (Stuttgart: Akad. Verlag Dr. Fr, Wedekind, 1928), 135.

39

"In the last twenty years one can observe an increasing refusal of ornament. Patterned wallpaper had to give way—not for reasons of cost, to the monotone wall treatment. Finally, we ended up with white walls. The rigor of this development indicates that it has to do with a thorough change in the attitude towards basic architectonic/artistic principles." Richard Lisker, "Über Tapete und Stoff in Der Wohnung," in *Innenräume: Herausgegeben vom Deutschen Werkbund*, 138–141, 138.

40

Ibid., 139.

41

Bruno Taut, "Farbenwirkungen aus Meiner Praxis," *Das Hohe Ufer* 1, no. 11 (November 1919): 263–266, 263.

42

Bruno Taut, *Die Neue Wohnung: Die Frau als Schöpferin* (Leipzig: Bei Klinkhardt and Biermann, 1924), 29–30. Cited in Karin Kirsh, *The Weissenhofsiedlung*, 139.

43

Bruno Taut, "Wunsch und Erfülung," *Bau und Wohnung* (Stuttgart: F. Wedekind, 1927), 135, taken from Bruno Taut, *Ein Wohnhaus*.

44

Bruno Taut, *Bauen der Neue Wohnbau* (Leipzig: Architektenvereinigung "Der Ring," 1927), 14.

45

"Not only do old laws and rights drag on like an eternal illness, but so do equally false forms once they've been made to a binding norm too early. An example of this is men's clothing, made to a binding norm in England, after nearly a century essentially unchanged (regardless of whether pants are tight one time and loose another), still holding fast to its original mistake, but they are fluid and as a result have reached a sufferably good, simple form today." Ibid.

46

"This comparison between the quickly-changing women's fashion and these times is not intended as a comment on the new architecture, despite the strange points of comparison found in the striving toward absolute precision which is just as characteristic for the architects of the present-day as for the Egyptians and the Greeks." Ibid.

47

Bruno Taut, "Die Fabre (1931)," 155.

48

Bruno Taut, *Ein Wohnhaus*, 4.

49

Heinz Rasch, "Wege der neue Architektur," *Stuttgarter Neues Tagblatt* (26 November 1926). Cited in Karin Kirsh, *The Weissenhofsiedlung,* 103.

50

Le Corbusier, "Die Innenausstattung unserer Häuser auf dem Weissenhof," in *Innenräume: Herausgegeben vom Deutschen Werkbund,* 122–125, 124.

51

I would like to thank Beatriz Colomina for drawing my attention to this image.

52

Karin Kirsh, *The Weissenhofsiedlung,* 22.

53

J. P. P. Oud, "International Architecture: Werkbund Exhibition, 'The Dwelling,' July-September 1927, Stuttgart." 79.

54

William Curtis, *Modern Architecture since 1900* (New Jersey: Prentice-Hall, 1982), 42.

55

Rudolf Pfister, "Stuttgarter Werkbundausstellung 'Die wohnung,'" 42.

56

Richard Pommer and Christian Otto, *Weissenhof 1927,* 79.

57

In 1919 Behne complains that uneducated people like grey and white but not strong colors: "colorlessness is the mark of education, white like the European's skin! Civilized people of our climes look down on chromatic art and chromatic architecture as they look down on colored human bodies—with a kind of horrified shudder. And where does this fear of color come from? Your philistine senses in color the presence of something immediate, unclothed." Adolf Behne, *Wiederkehr der Kunst* (Berlin, 1919). Cited in Franziska Bollery and Kristiana Harmann, "The Chromatic Controversy: Contemporary Views of the Twenties," 21.

58

Reyner Banham, *Theory and Design in the First Machine Age* (London: The Architectural Press, 1960), 288.

59

Walter Behrendt, *Der Sieg des Neuen Baustils* (Stuttgart: Akadem Verlag dr. fr. Wedekind and Co., 1927), 45.

60

Gustave Adolf Platz, *Der Baukunst der Neuesten Zeit* (Berlin: Im Propylä -Verlag, 1927), 157, 158.

61

Walter Behrendt, *Der Sieg des Neuen Baustils,* 15.

62

Gustave Adolf Platz, *Der Baukunst der Neuesten Zeit,* 89.

63

Ibid., 91.

64

Ibid., 92.

65

Adolf Behne, *Neues Wohnen—Neues Bauen* (Leipzig: Heffe and Becker Verlag, 1927), 14, 16.

66

Adolf Behne, *Eine Stunde Architektur* (Stuttgart: Akademischer Verlag Dr. Fritz Wedekind, 1928), 55.

67

Heinz Rasch and Bodo Rasch, *Wie Bauen?* (Stuttgart: Akademischer Verlag, Dr Fritz Wedekind, 1928), 16.

68

Eliel Saarinen's discourse is typical: "Again, when it was said that 'form must follow function'—which also is perfectly correct and fundamental—then 'functionalistic' style forms were readily used, no matter whether the function was there or not. . . . For sure, architectural problems have been handled much in the same spirit as if the question had been about ladies spring hats or fur coat trimming. Style in architecture must not be understood as a fashion of the day, but as an expression of the age. Even if many style-varieties might appear, mirroring the shiftings of life, nevertheless these varieties must be based on such fundamental form-characteristics as are ultimately going to shape the coming style of that respective culture in the making." Eliel Saarinen, *The City: its Growth, its Decay, its Future* (New York: Reinhold, 1943), 161.

69

Ludwig Hilberseimer, "Internationale Neue Baukunst," *Modern Bauform* 26, no. 9 (1927): 325–364, 326.

70

Shelden Cheney, *The New World Architecture* (New York: Tudor Publishing, 1930), 27.

71

Ibid., 258.

72

Ibid., 195.

73

Ibid., 208.

74

Ibid., 364.

75

Ibid., 208, 377.

76

Ibid., 146.

77

Ibid., 201.

78

Ibid., 395.

79

Ibid., 260.

80

Ibid., 288.

81

Nikolaus Pevsner, *Pioneers of Modern Architecture: From William Morris to Walter Gropius* (London: Faber and Faber, 1936), 152, 157, 186.

82

Walter Curt Behrendt, *Modern Building: Its Nature, Problems, and Forms* (New York: Harcourt Brace and Company, 1937), 153.

83

"This fatal failure to reconcile theory and practice, which does not in any way diminish the aesthetic originality of the new forms created in the course of the movement, is forcibly illustrated in a fine episode told by Gotthard Jedlicka in his book on Toulouse-Lautrec. In 1894, van de Velde built himself a small house in Uccle near Brussels. Down to the last detail it was intended to demonstrate his own ideas. to it, one day, came Toulouse-Lautrec and Joyant his friend and biographer. The guests, after having inspected the house, were charmed with their impressions. Nothing had been left to chance: the library was really a place to study in, the nursery, painted in white, was joyous. The hostess' gown harmonized beautifully with the dining room and the colored glasses on the table. The colors of the plates, even of the food in the dishes were but single parts of an ensemble. The tendency towards har-

mony, as Joyant diffidently remarked was rather too distinctly felt. They were perplexed with the play of *valeurs* covering the table top; lit up by the sun, the grating of the windows cast its shadow on the floor; the light, falling through the stained-glass window panes, split the room in layers of various colors. Yellow eggs and red beans were served on china, tinted in green and violet. Joyant, a gourmet, later remarked cynically that it all seemed to have been done at the expense of the cooking. The guests said farewells. On the way home, their opinions, as they reflected on their impressions, underwent a change. "Well," said Toulouse-Lautrec at last "the only successes are the bathroom, the nursery, painted with white enamel, and the W.C." In that story, all is told." Ibid., 89.

84

Ibid., 150. Behrendt goes on to limit the clothing analogy to the question of form rather than surface, appealing to the relative standardization of clothing shapes (as distinct from fabrics) across classes as a model for the standardization of simple furniture designs: "In the pure form of use, the objects are freed from the implication of being an index of social status. Look at clothing, for example: in the change of social structure we have abandoned particular costumes representing different ranks. The banker's secretary wears an evening gown of quite the same pattern as his wife, except that hers is of silk, while that of the secretary is only of rayon. The banker's wife wears with her evening gown a necklace of pearls, and so does his secretary, though hers is of Tecla pearls (and frequently that of the banker's wife, too, because the genuine ones are kept in the bank vault for safety). And so as to furniture, it has practically become uniform for the various classes differing only in quality of material and execution. Such sociological facts account for the approval of the pure form characteristic of the taste of the age. This approval manifests itself in our decided admiration for the forms produced by modern technique; it is reflected in the entire outward appearance of both sexes, through the innumerable fluctuations of fashion particularly in dress, with its tendency to conform in pattern to the natural movements of the body." Ibid., 195

85

For the complex relationship between the Weissenhofsiedlung and the CIAM meetings, see Giorgio Ciucci, "The Invention of the Modern Movement," *Oppositions* 24 (Spring 1981): 68–91.

86

Kenneth Frampton, *Modern Architecture: A Critical History* (London: Thames and Hudson, 1985), 163. Cf. "Yet a year later the French and German schools, Cubist and abstract, had fused into a single style. For a stirring moment at the Weissenhof exhibition of 1927, they stood before the world united in forms and intentions; the show houses designed by Gropius, Oud, Mies, Le Corbusier and others were so much of one mind that Alfred H. Barr coined the term *International Style* to describe it." Reyner Banham, *Guide to Modern Architecture* (London: Architectural

Press, 1962), 35. "Yet there is no gainsaying the historic impact of the exhibition. The twenty-one separate structures comprising sixty dwellings proved to be astonishingly unified in their clean, unarticulated, shimmering white rectilinear facades, flat roofs, and ship's-railing balconies. The various strains of architectural theorizing had apparently merged into the reality of a single International Style—the name by which modern architecture as a whole later came to be known. Here, at Weissenhof, was the fullest communal realization of the new art of building in concert with progressive politics, the closest thing to the brave new world which modernism had dreamed of since the war." Franz Schulze, *Mies van der Rohe: A Critical Biography* (Chicago: University of Chicago Press, 1985), 135.

87
Terence Riley, *The International Style: Exhibition 15 and the Museum of Modern Art* (New York: Rizzoli, 1992), 202n9.

88
Henry-Russell Hitchcock, *The International Style* (New York: Norton, 1932), 118.

89
Ibid., 119.

90
On the remaining evidence of the original colors, see Tim Benton, "Villa Savoye and the Architects' Practice," in *Le Corbusier*, ed. H. Allen Brooks (Princeton: Princeton University, 1987), 83–105, 92.

91
Henry-Russell Hitchcock, *The International Style,* 75.

92
Ibid., 144.

93
Ibid., 75.

94
Henry-Russell Hitchcock, *Modern Architecture: Romanticism and Reintegration* (New York: Payson and Clarke, 1929), 169, 172.

95
Ibid., 195.

96
Ibid., 181. In fact, the color scheme involved blue metalwork on the dividing walls and balconies, yellow around the streetlamps that were held up by red fittings on black columns, and a grey band running around the base of all the walls.

97
Ibid., 215.

98
Henry Russell Hitchcock, "The Architectural Work of J. P. P. Oud, " *The Arts* 13 (February 28, 1928): 97–103, 102.

99
Henry-Russell Hitchcock, *J. P. P. Oud* (Paris: Les éditions Cahiers d'Art, 1930), 4.

100
Henry-Russell Hitchcock and Philip Johnson, *Modern Architecture: International Exhibition* (New York: Museum of Modern Art Press, 1932), 95. Oud's 1922 housing estate at Oud-Mathenesse, with its "smooth, white, amply fenestrated walls above bases of yellowish brick and beneath roofs of red tiles," is seen to "make evident that a new style has come into being" and is "an achievement of primary importance." Ibid., 94.

101
Richard Pommer and Christian Otto, *Weissenhof 1927,* 80.

102
Walter Gropius, "Sparsamer Hausrat," *Das hohe Ufer* 1, no.7 (July 1919): 180. Cited in Iain Boyd Whyte, *Bruno Taut and the Architecture of Activism,* 166.

103
Walter Gropius, "The Human Scale," in *CIAM 8, The Heart of the City: Towards the Humanization of Urban Life,* ed. Sert. J. L. et al. (New York: Pellegrini and Cudahy, 1952), 54.

104
"As an example: this room [gesturing to his compact office] has certain actual dimensions, but I could give them different illusions. If I paint this ceiling matte black, it comes down to us; if it is glossy it goes away. If that wall is in canary yellow, it approaches; if it is dark blue, it retreats. The knowledge of optical illusions is most important for the artist and for the designer. Here architecture really starts, beyond all its technical problems." Walter Gropius, "Conversation with Walter Gropius," in *Walter Gropius: Das Spätwerk* (Darmstadt: Bauhaus-Arhiv, 1969): 14–18, 14.

105
The original design for the main building had a detailed color scheme of which only parts were completed and later elaborated. Dearstyne describes the role of the Wall-Painting Laboratory run by Hinnerk Scheper: "Gropius's great new Bauhaus building and the four nearby masters' houses were to be painted. The job, logically enough, was turned over to the *Wandmalerei.* The stucco exteriors of these buildings were not the subject of any unusual psychological or aesthetic experimentation. Following the mode which prevailed in the modern architecture of that day, they were painted almost entirely in the flat white. Gropius and Scheper preferred to preserve the boxlike character of the structures by painting their walls a uniform color. The interior of the Bauhaus building was likewise done largely in blank white, though some unobtrusive departures from the prevailing monotone were permitted in the public areas—entrance hall, auditorium, and cafeteria. The color treatment of the interiors of the master's houses was left to

the discretion of the occupants; here some color experimentation was attempted by Breur and Moholy-Nagy, assisted by the students of the wall-painting workshop." Howard Dearstyne, Inside the Bauhaus (New York: Rizzoli, 1986), 148.

106
"While I was collaborating with van Doesburg, a conflict was getting increasingly serious between us, because his views sprang from an uncontrolled pictorial urge whereas I recognized that the brakes imposed on creation by the collectivity are one of the bases of new architecture. For example, van Doesburg for some of my workers' houses designed white doors, although practice had taught me that I can never produce a work of lasting value if I fail to take into account in the project life as it is normally lived. A building must be able even to tolerate dirty hands if it is to have collective value." J. P. P. Oud, Mein weg in "de Stijl" (Den Haag-Rotterdam, 1960). Cited in Sergio Polano, "Notes on Oud: Re-reading the Documents," Lotus International 16 (September 1977): 42–49, 48.

107
J. P. P. Oud, "Over de toekomstige bouwkunst en hare architectonische mogelijkheden," Bouwkundig Weekblad 24 (11 June 1921): 147–160. Partially translated by as "Architecture and the Future," The Studio 46 (1933): 403–406, 453.

108
J. J. P. Oud, "Ja und Nein: Bekentnisse eines Architekton," Bouwkundig Weekblad, 35 (29 August 1925): 431–432, 432.

109
J. P. P. Oud, "Uitweiding bij eenige afbeeldingen," Bouwkundig Weekblad (1922): 428–424.

110
J. P. P. Oud, letter to Wedepohl, undated September-October 1927, cited in Karin Kirsh, The Weissenhofsiedlung, 86.

111
See letter from Paul Meller to Oud, 21 July 1927, in Richard Pommer and Christian Otto, Wiessenhof 1927, 244 note 16.

112
J. P. P. Oud, "Over de toekomstige bouwkunst en hare architectonische mogelijkheden," 152.

113
J. P. P. Oud, "Oriëntatie," De Stijl 3, no. 2, 12–15, 14. Partially cited in H. L. C. Jaffé, De Stijl 1917–1931: The Dutch Contribution to Modern Art (Cambridge: Belknap Press, 1986), 65.

114
Ibid., 13.

115
Ibid., 14

116
J. P. P Oud, "Architectonische Beschouwing Bij Bijage III," De Stijl 3, no. 3, 26. Cited in H. L. C. Jaffé, De Stijl 1917–1931, 64.

117
J. P. P. Oud, "Over de toekomstige bouwkunst en hare architectonische mogelijkheden," 153.

118
Hendrik Berlage, Gedanken über Stil in der Baukunst (Leipzig: Julius Zeitler Verlag, 1905), 23.

119
"There, looming in greyish red, stands the great wall surface, darker towards the top, its sharp simple contours cut out against the sky; a beautiful, naturally interwoven, thousand-colored yet tranquil background for the gaudy bustle of the street; stained with dark areas, a few only marked by richly plastic mouldings, distinguished ornament against the otherwise sober costume." Hendrik Berlage, "Bouwkunst en Impressionisme," Architectura 2 (2 June 1894): 93–95, (9 June): 98–100, (16 June): 105–106, (23 June): 109–110. translated in Style, Standard and Signature in Dutch Architecture of the Nineteenth and Twentieth Centuries ed. Bernard Colenbrander (Rotterdam: Netherlands Architecture Instittue, 1993), 341–343, 342.

120
Ibid., 36.

121
Hendrik Berlage, Gedanken über Stil in der Baukunst, 24.

122
Hendrik Berlage, Grundlagen und Entwicklung der Architekture (Berlin, 1908), 1. [English in original]

123
Hendrik Berlage, Portfolio III, (November 1880), 28–30. Cited in Pieter Singelenberg, H.P. Berlage: Idea and Style, the Quest for Modern Architecture (Utrecht: Haentjens Dekker and Gumbert, 1972), 31.

124
Hendrik Berlage, Portfolio III (November 1880), 49–50. Cited in Pieter Singelenberg, H. P. Berlage, 33.

125
Society is in the process of change, and so it is urgently asking for new raiment, because the old is worn out, through and through. There is no point in trying to patch it, because it would soon be obvious that what seemed new would have to be hidden away. So the new apparel is the new style which has to be made. It must be sought with all the seriousness we possess, and when we utter 'Eureka', the discovery must be welcomed with unprecedented rejoicing.
Good heavens, no. I did not want to get into that hobby-horse of 19th and 20th century architectural style!
On the contrary, I think we are farther away from that fantasy of the future than ever: serious visionaries have certainly not seen it yet. Those dreamers of style think and speak so narrow-mindedly, so disapprovingly, so very bigotedly about a style

which will reflect our modern life—that modern life which is so varied and eventful that one wonders who will be the maker of the uniform apparel for the entire world.

Which nation will be so powerful that the whole world will don that clothing as being fashionable? . . .

No! as the great social idea gains ground, we see each nation of any significance and conscious of its own strength, its own identity, also supporting its own art, and only looking and learning from others, not following neighboring influences slavishly.

And that is not only a national, but also an individual characteristic.

Hendrik Berlage, "Bouwkunst en Impressionisme (1894)," 341.

126
J. Duiker, "Hoe is het met onze kleeding," *de 8 en Opbouw* 1 no. 16 (5 August 1932): 166. Translated as "What about our clothes?", in *J. Duiker, 1890–1935* ed. B. Bijvoet (Amsterdam: Ir. E. J. Jelles and Ir. C. Alberts, 1975), 145.

127
"our ideas about clothes are founded on a certain rationality. . . . Sometimes our clothes are not at all ridiculous, they may even be frighteningly rational. . . . Would it be possible in the future that man takes off his eternal fancy dress and accepts as an expression of higher culture a 'nudism dress' of higher level? . . . I note a clearly visible rationality in progress in the direction of nudism. . . . It is possible that our grandchildren will wear nudism dress or something akin because other clothes are no longer rational or superfluous or a hindrance . . . if this is true then our grandchildren will also have seen that architectural nakedness is equally rational." J. Duiker, "Naar aanleiding van een ingezonden artikel van Henri E. van den Pauwert over een waterton," *de 8 en Opbouw* 1, no. 7, (1 April 1932): 88–92. translated in *J. Duiker, 1890–1935*, ed. B. Bijvoet, 142.

128
J. B. Loghems, *bowen, bauen, bâtir, building: holland* (Amsterdam: Kosmos, 1932), 62.

129
J. Duiker, "Naar aanleiding van een ingezonden artikel van Henri E. van den Pawwert over een waterton," 142.

130
Theo van Doesburg, "De architectuurtentoonstelling 'Die Wohnung' te Stuttgart," *Het Bouwbedrijf*, vol. 4, no. 24 (1927): 556–59. Translated as "Stuttgart-Wiessenhof 1927: Die Wohnung," in Theo van Doesburg, *On European Architecture: Complete Essays from Het Bouwbedrijf 1924–1931*, translated by Charlotte I. Loeb and Arthur L. Loeb (Basel: Birkhäuser Verlag, 1986), 164–173, 167, 170.

131
Henry-Russell Hitchcock and Philip Johnson, *The International Style*, 23, 24, 25, 30.

132
Ibid., 46, 52, 47, 73.

133
Ibid., 76.

134
Henry-Russell Hitchcock, *Modern Architecture: Romanticism and Reintegration*, 169.

135
Ibid., 160.

136
Ibid., 166.

137
"In architecture, the new, when solidly based on new methods of construction, can at first only be appreciated by those who understand that construction either discursively or intuitively. Ferro-concrete building cannot be appreciated by the naive who analyze it consciously or unconsciously in terms of masonry or wood. Comprehension must for the majority of people become automatic, since few take architecture seriously enough to give much effort to its appreciation. It establishes itself slowly as the result apparently of what amounts to an act of faith. . . . The faith in a new method of construction once established becomes so inherent in observers that it is not easily or rapidly changed. Indeed, to change it too frequently would have the very opposite effect to that desired by those who urge it. For appreciation of architecture as the aesthetic expression of structure would generally cease if new methods were perpetually substituted for those in use before the belief in those became inherent and unconscious. . . . Once the new aesthetic was sufficiently established there would be no possibility of ambiguity in the interpretation of traditional materials or traditional methods of construction, provided they were selected and used completely in accordance with the new aesthetic . . . there is no assurance that in certain fields of architecture, such as domestic building, plaster surfaced ferro-concrete is superior to construction largely of some sort of masonry. Once the traditional interpretation of brick and stone is forgotten there may well be a considerable return to their use where they are technically and economically satisfactory." Ibid., 211.

138
Ibid., 214.

139
"Studied thus as a surface, without depth or mass or sense of gravitation, this facade is nevertheless not flat nor overbalanced. For the windows allow the eye to penetrate beyond the wall surface at the same time that their glass panes mask the continuity of the plane, and the open construction of the balconies and the canopy provide the relief of subsidiary and contrasting planes without suggesting mass or inducing the gravitation empathy which would inhibit the peculiar Alpine exhilaration the architect desired to produce." Henry-Russell Hitchcock, "Houses by Two Moderns," *The Arts* (New York) 16 (1929): 33–40, 35.

140

"Moreover, while the front is monochrome, here those planes which are at the back of the terrace are almond green, while the planes at right angles are white or grey. This delicate, restrained polychromy helps to restrain any tendency on the part of the observer to judge the three dimensional relations in terms of mass. Even more than on the front it is necessary that gravitational empathy should not destroy the limpid effect of suspension in the air which the cantilevered construction makes possible." Ibid.

141

"Furthermore this may certainly be psychologically supported in general terms. The need for the new is recurrent but not continuous except as a matter of mode. A part, at least, of the satisfaction of accepting the new is the idea that it shall be as permanent as what preceded. There is an illusion closely connected with each innovation that because that innovation appears temporarily more valid than whatever it is replacing its validity is actually more absolute." Henry-Russell Hitchcock, *Modern Architecture: Romanticism and Reintegration*, 211.

142

"The smooth, flat, rendered surfaces of his [Le Corbusier's] buildings had the immateriality of the colored shapes in post-cubist painting. And soon the darker colors of his pictures of the mid-'20s were introduced in addition to pastel tones in order to contrast certain wall surfaces more boldly with the off-white tone which he considered the natural color of the actual stucco." Henry-Russell Hitchcock, *Painting Toward Architecture* (New York: Duell, Sloan and Pearce, 1948), 28.

143

The book refers to Le Corbusier's polychromy without referring to the white wall: "Different colors were often used on different walls to emphasize them as individual planes, particularly interiors . . . the use of different colors and of curves produced, particularly at the Savoye house, a lyricism closely related to that of Purist paintings of the early twenties." Henry-Russell Hitchcock, *Architecture: Nineteenth and Twentieth Centuries* (Harmondsworth: 1958), 371. In Oud's Hoek of Holland project "all overt emulation of contemporary painting disappeared except for the restriction of color to white-painted rendering with only small touches of the primaries on some of the minor elements of wood and metal." Ibid., 378.

144

Gustav Platz, *Wohnräume der Gegenwart* (Berlin: Im Propyläen-Verlag, 1933), 179.

145

Ibid., 181.

146

Ibid., 184, 185.

147

Fernand Léger, "Discorso agli architetti," *Casabella* 207 (1955): 69–70, 69.

148

Le Corbusier, "La Grece," in Jean Petit, *Le Corbusier Parle* (Paris: Les éditions force vives, 1967), 80–85, 84.

149

Gunter Asplund, Sven Markelius, et. al., *Acceptera—* (Stockhom: Tiden, 1931), 150.

150

Sven Markelius, "Rationalization Trends in Modern Housing Design," lecture delivered to a meeting of the Finnish Association of Architects in Turku on April 28, 1928. Cited in Göran Schildt, *Alvar Aalto: The Decisive Years* (New York: Rizzoli, 1986), 205.

151

"Jan Duiker was definitely not an elegantly dressed man although he wore tailor made suits. I can remember how my mother and he one day bought some pieces of fabric (undoutedly for a very cheap price) from which three suits were fabricated. The design of the fabric was different, but the difference of color was remarkably small. The gray one was slightly lighter than the other one. They were nice and solid suits." Arthur Hofmans, *Herinneringen aan Jan Duiker* (Lelystad: Meditekst, 1990), 39.

152

"When Viola [Markelius's wife] first met Aalto, he seemed 'like a little country lad' to her. Bjertnaes, too [Aalto's assistant] . . . spoke of the 'baggy knees of his unironed trousers.' Two years later we see Aalto in a photograph of the nearly completed Agricultural Cooperative Building, dressed as elegantly as Markelius had been for many years: black tie, English trench coat, beret, razor-sharp trouser seams and well-polished shoes. Le Corbusier had taught his colleagues that this was what an architect should look like: neither a Bohemian artist nor a gentleman of leisure, but more like an engineer." Göran Schildt, *Alvar Aalto: The Decisive Years*, 52.

153

Reyner Banham, *Theories and Design in the First Machine Age*, 247.

154

Reyner Banham, *The Theory of Modern Architecture 1907–1927*, unpublished doctoral thesis presented to The Courtauld Institute (June 1958), 428.

155

Bruno Zevi, *Verso un'architettura organica* (Milan: Einaudi, 1945). Translated by Bruno Zevi as *Towards an Organic Architecture* (London: Faber and Faber, 1945), 23. For Voysey's attitude toward dress, see, for example, C.F.A. Voysey, *Individuality* (London: Chapman and Hill, 1915).

156

Bruno Zevi, *Storia dell'architettura moderna* (Rome: Giulio Einaudi editore, 1950), 20.

157
Sigfried Giedion, Letter to J. P. P. Oud, October 1927. Cited in Richard Pommer and Christian Otto in *Weissenhof 1927* 122.

158
Shelden Cheney, *The New World of Architecture*, 174.

159
Ibid., 211.

160
Ibid., 208.

161
Shelden Cheney, *A Primer of Modern Art* (New York: Boni and Liveright, 1924), 314.

162
Ibid.

163
"Symmetry = a spasmodic need for security, fear of flexibility, indetermination, relativity, and growth—in short, fear of living. The schizophrenic cannot bear the temporal aspect of living. To keep his anguish under control, he requires, immobility. Symmetry = passivity, or, in Freudian terms, homosexuality. This is explained by psychoanalysts. *Homo*logous parts instead of *hetero*nymous parts. It is the infantile fear of the father—the academy, in this case, is a father figure, protective of the cowardly child—who will castrate you if you attack a heteronymous figure, the woman, the mother. As soon as one becomes passive and accepts symmetry, the anguish seems to subside, because the father no longer threatens, he possesses." Bruno Zevi, *The Modern Language of Architecture* (Seattle: University of Washington Press, 1978), 17.

Illustration Credits

Index